DISCOVERING DOOYEWEERD

PAIDEIA PRESS

 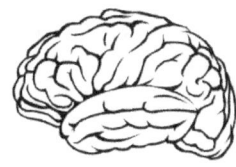  

DISCOVERING DOOYEWEERD

D.F.M. STRAUSS

GENERAL EDITOR

   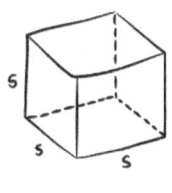

$V = s^3$

www.paideiapress.ca

Discovering Dooyeweerd
D. F. M. Strauss, General Editor
A publication of Paideia Press
3248 Twenty First St., Jordan Station, Ontario, Canada L0R 1S0.

© 2023 by Paideia Press. All rights reserved.

All rights reserved. Except for brief quotations in critical publications or reviews, no part of this book may be reproduced in any manner without prior written permission from Paideia Press at the address above.

Copy-editor: Harry Van Dyke

Cover Art and Book Design by Steven R. Martins

ISBN 978-0-88815-322-7

Printed in the United States of America

Table of Contents

Foreword	XI
Introduction *by Danie F. M. Strauss*	1
1. The Idea of a Christian Philosophy *by Roy Clouser*	27
2. The Ground-Motive of Greek Culture *by Herman Dooyeweerd*	49
3. Dooyeweerd on The Medieval Ground-Motive of Nature and Grace *by Herman Dooyeweerd*	55
4. The Rise of the Ground-Motive of Nature and Freedom *by Herman Dooyeweerd*	61
5. The Internal Tension Present in the Ground-Motive of Nature and Freedom *by Herman Dooyeweerd*	67
6. The Significance of Dooyeweerd's Philosophy for Understanding the Foundational Role of Worldview *by Michael W. Goheen*	73
7. Dooyeweerd and Radical Orthodoxy *by Danie F. M. Strauss*	79
8. Dooyeweerd and Theology *by Willem J. Ouweneel*	97
9. Reformed Scholasticism and Reformational Thinking *by Joseph Boot*	105
10. The Church, Society, and the Kingdom *by Willem J. Ouweneel*	121

11. Realism and Nominalism – Part 1   131
by Danie F. M. Strauss

12. Realism and Nominalism – Part 2   141
by Danie F. M. Strauss

13. The Distinction between Structure and Direction   147
by Danie F. M. Strauss

14. Dooyeweerd's Perspective on Early Greek Philosophy   153
by Danie F. M. Strauss

15. The Scope of Sphere Sovereignty   165
by Danie F. M. Strauss

16. Dooyeweerd's Philosophy of Time   171
by Danie F. M. Strauss

17. Philosophical Reflection on Physical Entities   179
by Danie F. M. Strauss

18. Dooyeweerd: Enriching Our Understanding of Number and Space   191
by Danie F. M. Strauss

19. Modal Universality   199
by Danie F. M. Strauss

20. Philosophical Roots of Psychology   207
by Willem J. Ouweneel

21. Galileo and Einstein   215
by Danie F. M. Strauss

22. Modes of Explanation making Identity Understandable   221
by Danie F. M. Strauss

23. Understanding Enkapsis as Contrasted with the Chemical Bond   229
by Martin A. Rice, Jr.

TABLE OF CONTENTS

24. Antimony and Contradiction 235
    by Danie F. M. Strauss

25. Different Kinds of Criticism 243
    by Danie F. M. Strauss

26. The Significance of Dooyeweerd's Work for the
    Natural Sciences 259
    by Richard Gunton

27. What Happened to "Evolution"? 273
    by Danie F. M. Strauss

28. Of History and the Science of History 283
    by Harry Van Dyke

29. Constitutive and Regulative Historical Principles 299
    by Danie F. M. Strauss

30. The Significance of Dooyeweerd's Philosophy for
    Understanding the Complexity of Technology 307
    by Maarten J. Verkerk

31. The Significance of Dooyeweerd's Philosophy for
    Understanding Human Responsibility in Technology 317
    by Maarten J. Verkerk

32. Understanding One's Own Professional Practice:
    The Triple I Model 325
    by Maarten J. Verkerk

33. Basic Aesthetics, as Dooyeweerd Could Have Written It 335
    by Calvin Seerveld

34. Is Language Uniquely Human? 345
    by Danie F. M. Strauss

35. The Prevalent Technicism in Society 351
    by Egbert Schuurman

36. Popular Sovereignty ... 357
   by Danie F. M. Strauss

37. The Intriguing Nature of Firms and/or Markets and/or Workers ... 363
   by Frederick C.v.N. Fourie

38. Developments within Roman Law ... 373
   by Danie F. M. Strauss

39. Dooyeweerd's Critical-Empirical Theory of Law ... 377
   by Alan Cameron

40. The Relationship between Dooyeweerd's Systematic Philosophy and his Theory of the Basic Concepts of the Science of Law ... 387
   by Alan Cameron

41. Civil Private Law ... 397
   by Herman Dooyeweerd

42. Theory of an International Legal Order ... 401
   by Romel Regalado Bagares

43. Are Norms and Principles Ethical or Moral in Nature? ... 409
   by Danie F. M. Strauss

44. What Is Inherent in Normativity? ... 417
   by Danie F. M. Strauss

45. Compound Basic Concepts ... 431
   by Danie F. M. Strauss

46. Traditional Societies ... 443
   by Danie F. M. Strauss

47. Differentiation and Integration ... 449
   by Danie F. M. Strauss

TABLE OF CONTENTS

48. Dooyeweerd on Romanticism   453
by Herman Dooyeweerd

49. Classifying Social Forms of Life   459
by Danie F. M. Strauss

50. Context Is Everything, or Is It?   471
by Albert Weideman

51. The Meaning of Technology   477
by Egbert Schuurman

52. Human Freedom and Political Order   483
by James W. Skillen

53. The Good of Politics: Dooyeweerd's Contribution   489
by James W. Skillen

54. Political Idolatry: Assessing the Ideologies of Our Day   495
by David T. Koyzis

55. Dooyeweerd and Vollenhoven: What They Share, How They Differ, and How They Complement One Another   501
by Jeremy Ive

56. Everyday Life with Dooyeweerd   513
by Andrew Basden

57. Understanding and Practicing Research with Dooyeweerd's Help   523
by Andrew Basden

58. Adam and Biology   539
by Willem J. Ouweneel

59. Dooyeweerd's Approach to Philosophical Anthropology   549
by Gerrit Glas

60. What Could Dooyeweerd Teach Us About
the Study of the Brain?   563
by Gerrit Glas

61. Health Care from a Dooyeweerdian Perspective:
A Normative Practices Approach   577
by Gerrit Glas

Bibliography   591

Subject Index   627

Glossary   635

FOREWORD

DURING THE EARLY Spring of 2021 John Hultink of Paideia Press approached me with the suggestion to write a book entitled, *Discovering Dooyeweerd*. I immediately contacted Willem J. Ouweneel and proposed to him and Mr. Hultink that I would prefer to make it a joint effort involving reformational scholars from a variety of scientific fields and practices. Willem supported the idea wholeheartedly, and in addition to contributing four chapters, served as *Consulting Editor*. All original chapters passed the test of peer reviewing. (Some seven chapters are extracts from Dooyeweerd's published works.)[1]

The aim of this work is to provide an orientation in the philosophy of Dooyeweerd. Our target readers are intelligent scholars (including academics), followers of his philosophy, laymen from all walks of life, and also people fascinated by a theory of reality (an ontology) and those who may want to explore the way in which it brings to expression the basic tenets of the Christian life and worldview by articulating its implications for a non-reductionist ontology.

1. It is constituted by chapters that *explain or explore* Dooyeweerd's unique and novel insights.
2. The chapters are relatively independent units but may still refer to other chapters or the Introduction.
3. The work is guided by a design embedded in the systematic structure of Dooyeweerd's philosophy.

---

1. For a critical appraisal of Dooyeweerd's theory of the *Gegenstand* relation and an inter-modal meaning-synthesis, see D. F. M. Strauss, "The antinomies entailed in Dooyeweerd's epistemological view of a Gegenstand," *Journal for Christian Scholarship* 55 (2019): 169-185.

Dooyeweerd anticipated two key insights from the philosophy of science of the previous century, namely that all theoretical thinking is (a) rooted in an ultimate commitment, and (b) that it is guided by a "paradigm," a theoretical framework.

Dooyeweerd distinguished between a central ground-motive and a basic transcendental Idea (see the chapter on Ultimate Commitments and the opening chapter of Roy Clouser). Dooyeweerd employs the term *transcendental* in a twofold sense: (i) to refer to the *conditions* (based in the creation order) that make possible what we can experience; and (ii) to refer to the *direction* in which the potential of this order could be opened up, disclosed or deepened.

(a) Dooyeweerd identified four basic religious ground-motives at work in the history of the "Avondland," the *West*, namely the form-matter motive, the biblical motive of creation, fall and redemption, the medieval motive of nature and grace and the modern Humanistic motive of nature and freedom. The present work contains five chapters on these ground-motives, extracted mainly from Dooyeweerd's own work, *Roots of Western Culture* (2012).

(b) The transcendental ground-Idea of a thinker articulates perennial philosophical issues, namely: unity and diversity, discreteness and continuity, infinity, the whole-parts relation, individuality and universality, constancy and change, differentiation and integration, contradiction and antinomy, to mention a few problems.

(c) The history of philosophy harbours distortions of the cosmic diversity in various kinds of absolutizing some *thing* or one or another aspect or trait in reality. Consider *ismic* orientations such as individualism, atomism, universalism, holism, rationalism, irrationalism, realism, nominalism, as well as monistic isms spread over all the modal aspects: arithmeticism (everything is number) geometricism (space metaphysics), a mechanistic orientation, physicalism (materialism), diverse biological isms [(mechanistic and physicalistic) evolutionism, (neo-)vitalism, ID (Intelligent Design), holism, organismic biology, pan-psychism, emergence evolutionism], psychologism, logicism, historicism, the linguistic turn of the 20th century (everything is interpretation), the reification of social relations (social system theory), economism (capitalism and socialism), aestheticism, legalism, moralism and pietism (reifying certitudinal piety.

We now briefly look at the way in which our preceding remarks serve as an orientation for the structure of the *Discovering Dooyeweerd* book.

The reader is advised to read the Introduction first.

It should be noted in the first place that each chapter of this book, with a few exceptions, could be considered as a unit on its own. This entails that it contains multiple complementary points of entry to an understanding of Dooyeweerd's philosophy. A mere view of the table of contents of the book will provide the prospective reader with an insight into those chapters which are closely connected but yet independent parts of the book. This is an important philosophical distinction, namely that between uniqueness and coherence exemplified in the work as a whole.

SECTION 1
Ultimate commitments and ground-motives

SECTION 2
The indispensable role of the
modal aspects in understanding creation

Subsection 2A: The role of the first four aspects

Subsection 2B: Philosophical orientations
in the post-physical aspects

SECTION 3
Culture, Economy, and Society

SECTION 4
Diverse themes

The whole is followed by an Index of Subjects and a Glossary.

Spring 2023

Danie F. M. Strauss, editor, and
Willem Ouweneel, consulting editor

INTRODUCTION
by the Editor

HERMAN DOOYEWEERD (1894–1977) was born in Amsterdam. He established the *Philosophy of the Cosmonomic Idea*, a philosophy which explicitly gives an account of the laws holding for the cosmos. Professor Dooyeweerd taught the *Encyclopedia of the Science of Law* (philosophy of law) at the *Free University* of Amsterdam from 1926 until 1965.

- 1912–1917: University: Attended the Free University of Amsterdam.
- 1917: Ph.D. dissertation: *De Ministerraad in het Nederlandsche Staatsrecht* [The Cabinet in Dutch Constitutional Law].
- 1918: Work in tax office, Harlingen, Friesland.
- 1918: Legal advisor for municipal government in Leiden.
- 1919–22: Employee at the Health Office, Department. of Labour, The Hague, examining draft legislation.
- 1922 approx: First conception of the idea of law-spheres (modal aspects) originates.
- 1922–26: Work at the Kuyper Institute, The Hague; a time of intense study and writing, during which the idea of law-spheres received its first theoretical articulation.
- 1926: Appointed professor in the Faculty of Law at the *Vrije Universiteit* (Free University), Amsterdam (retired in 1965).

Dooyeweerd never wanted to exclude any intellectual tradition from the *thought-community* of the West. Therefore, the originality of his philosophical endeavors developed in confrontation with Western philosophy and by learning from multiple philosophical schools of thought. Yet his distinctive new insights transcend what is found in the history of Western philosophy.

The Greek-Medieval Legacy

Dooyeweerd realized that Greek antiquity was in the grip of what he designated, following Aristotle, as the motive of *matter* and *form*. Initially one or another fluid element dominated thought but eventually the motive of form, measure and harmony assumed the guiding role in Greek culture. During the medieval period the attempt was made to obtain a *synthesis* between Greek philosophy and biblical Christianity, the latter being in the grip of the basic ground-motive of creation, fall and redemption. This attempted synthesis resulted in the *nature-grace* motive. The state was supposed to bring humans to their highest temporal fulfilment, *goodness*, while the church as supra-natural institute of grace had to take them to *eternal bliss*.

The Tension in post-Renaissance Humanism

Then, during the Renaissance (fourteenth-fifteenth centuries) and the Enlightenment (eighteenth century), modern Humanism transformed the former three into a new motive, that of *nature* (with its natural science ideal) and *freedom* (with its ideal of a free and autonomous personality). In his work on the social contract Rousseau claimed that freedom is obedience to a law which we have prescribed to ourselves.

The Legacy of Reformational Philosophy

The reformational line continued via Willem Groen van Prinsterer (1801–1876) and Abraham Kuyper (1837–1920). These thinkers in particular paved the way for the contribution of Herman

INTRODUCTION

Dooyeweerd (1894–1977) who, alongside his brother-in-law, D. H. Th. Vollenhoven (1892–1978), developed a philosophical understanding of reality directed and informed by the biblical distinction between Creator and creation—an approach liberating philosophy from the antinomic impasse of reductionist *isms* (to which we shall return throughout this work). The humanistic science-ideal commenced by advancing the idea that the autonomous person could control all of reality with the aid of the necessity of cause and effect. However, if all of reality is subjected to the universal force of causality, human freedom is sacrificed, because then the human person is reduced to an atom among atoms, a cause among causes, and an effect among effects, fully causally determined with no freedom.

Before we proceed with our intended Introduction of Dooyeweerd's philosophy, commencing with the distinction between *aspects* and *things* or *individuality structures*, let us look at Dooyeweerd's philosophy through the eyes of various scholars (coming from different backgrounds).

(i) ". . . the most original philosopher Holland has produced, even Spinoza not excepted" – Professor G. E. Langemeijer (former Attorney General of the Dutch Appeal Court and a former Chairman of the Royal Dutch Academy of Sciences – he is not a Christian (1965).

(ii) ". . . the most profound, innovative, and penetrating philosopher since Kant" – Giorgio Delvecchio, a well-known Italian neo-Kantian philosopher (1965).

(iii) "Herman Dooyeweerd is undoubtedly the most formidable Dutch philosopher of the 20th century.... As a humanist I have always looked at 'my own tradition' in search of similar examples. They simply don't exist" – Dr. P. B. Cliteur (President of the Humanist League in The Netherlands and Professor of Philosophy at the Technical University of Delft (1994).

(iv) An internationally well-known Dutch philosopher, C. A. van Peursen (who practically throughout his life was a critical conversation-partner who differed radically from Dooyeweerd and who influenced many philosophers worldwide), remarked toward the end of his life that many books written within the domain of philosophy of science should not have been written had the authors familiarized themselves with Dooyeweerd's insights (1995).

(v) "After a lifetime pilgrimage across the philosophical desert of scholastic, Hegelian and many other schools, I finally crossed the Jordan into the first truly Christian philosophy in the history of philosophy, the only truly systematic and professional philosophy that has challenged the scholastic synthesis since the time of Justin Martyr." Thus wrote Professor Adolfo García de la Sienra, a well-known national researcher at Mexican National University, currently at the Centre for Research and Teaching of Economics, Mexico City.

Entities Functioning Within the Various Aspects of Reality

Dooyeweerd once remarked that his theory of modal aspects is the best-known part of his philosophy but at the same time also the least understood part. Let us now briefly look at the many perspectives which provide access to the analysis of a *social object*. We shall first look at a lounge chair and then turn our attention to a well-known societal entity, the state. In each instance we note which scholarly discipline concerns itself with this distinctive perspective.

INTRODUCTION

A Chair is not merely a "Physical Object"
In our brief discussion of the way in which a chair functions in the various aspects of reality, the reader will, after a moment's thought, be able to discern these aspects themselves.

- the most basic aspect is number (quantity, more or less)
- followed by space (continuous extension)
- movement (uniform, rectilinear flow)
- the physical aspect (energy-operation)
- The first question is: Does a chair have a function in the arithmetical aspect? Certainly, because it is *one* and may have *four* legs. This numerical aspect underlies the interest of arithmetic. A chair is *big* or *small* (spatial aspect: mathematical theory of space); it could be a rocking chair or simply continue its movement around the sun (kinematic aspect: kinematics); it is strong or weak (physico-chemical aspect).

Notice that in these four aspects a chair functions as a *subject*. In the more complex aspects, a chair functions as an *object*. Consider:

- A chair can be useful in human life (as biotical *object*: since the chair itself is not alive—biology studies it as part of the *bio-milieu* of living entities).
- It may be comfortable (sensitive-psychic aspect: psychology).
- A person can conceive it (analytical aspect: logic).
- It is culturally shaped (historical aspect: historical science, which is interested in the historical development of various chair styles).
- It has a name (a verbal sign, semiotic aspect: general semiotics and linguistics).

- Chairs are used in the interaction among people (social aspect: sociology).
- A chair has a price (economic aspect: economics).
- It is beautiful or ugly (aesthetic aspect: aesthetics).
- It belongs to someone who has a subjective right (pleasure and dispositional competence) to it (jural aspect: the science of law).
- It is someone's beloved chair (ethical aspect: ethics).
- A chair worthy of the name is trustworthy—everybody trusts that the chair will bear the person sitting in it (faith aspect: perspective of theology as a science).

The Uniqueness and Interrelatedness of Modal Aspects

Dooyeweerd characterized aspects in terms of their uniqueness (sphere sovereignty) and interconnections (sphere-universality). Although the core meaning of an aspect exceeds our conceptual understanding, it could be approximated by specifying a *word* that captures our immediate, intuitive insight.

Dooyeweerd mentions the attempt made by Russell to *define* the number 2. Russell defines number with the aid of his supposedly purely logical concept of *class*. The logical concept, he claims, enables the reduction of mathematics to logic. For example, the number "2" is "defined" in the following way: "1 + 1 is the number of a class w which is the logical sum of two classes u and v which have no common terms and have each only one term"[1]. The outcome of Russell's attempt is simply that his "definition" ended in a *circular argumentation*: he used the number 2 ("two classes u and v") in order to define it (in logic this is known as a *petitio principii* and in popular parlance a "catch 22").

---

1. B. Russell, *The Principles of Mathematics* (Cambridge: Cambridge University Press, 1903), 119; see H. Dooyeweerd, *A New Critique of Theoretical Thought*, vol. 2, Collected Works of Herman Dooyeweerd, Series A, General Editor D. F. M. Strauss (Lewiston, NY: Edwin Mellen, 1997), 82.

INTRODUCTION

It is a mere *tautology*—2 is 2!

Defining Law?

The alternative option is also problematic. The Dutch legal scholar Leo Polak attempted to define "law" as follows: "retribution is an objective, trans-egoistic, harmonization of interests." The term "objective" here has the meaning of not being limited to any particular person, i.e., it is employed in the sense of what is *universal*. Does it say anything distinctive about the jural? Not at all, because every aspect of reality participates in this feature of *universality*. The term "trans-egoistic" derives its meaning from *moral love*, which demands that a person ought not to be self-centred. Therefore, this element of the given definition also does not at all touch on the jural meaning of *retribution*. "Harmonization" represents the meaning of the aesthetic aspect and therefore fails equally to capture the core meaning of the jural. Finally, the term "interests" is multivocal—people may have economic interests, aesthetic interests, legal interests, and so on, hence "interests" cannot reveal the unique or core meaning of the jural because it can take on many different qualifications. What Polak did was to use *non-jural* terms in his attempted definition of the jural, which resulted in a formulation totally bypassing the core meaning of the jural. Dooyeweerd, in his (as yet still unpublished *Encyclopedia of the Science of Law*), justifiably concludes: "The result is a general concept fully lacking any delimitation. It could just as well be seen as a moral rule regarding the distribution of alms."[2] Clearly, the meaning nucleus of an aspect is not only unique and irreducible, but also *indefinable*.

Modal Analogies: *Retrocipations* and *Anticipations*

Another way to explain this state of affairs is to point out that the uniqueness of an aspect only comes to expression in its *coherence* with other aspects. This insight concerns "moments of coherence,"

---

2. H. Dooyeweerd, *Encyclopedia of the Science of Law*, vol. 3, 10-11.

also designated by Dooyeweerd as *modal analogies*. An analogy could be backward-pointing or forward-pointing, it could be a *retrocipation* or an *anticipation*. Whenever two entities or aspects are similar in that respect in which they differ, we meet an *analogy*.

Example: The Corona-19 Pandemic and "Social Distancing"

During the Corona-19 pandemic one of the public-health rules was specified as *social distancing*. Consider the following case. The President and his bodyguard are close to each other in a *spatial* sense, but far apart in terms of the respective *positions* they occupy within society. The similarity here is "distance"—but in this similarity the difference is shown: spatial distance is "close-by" whereas social distance is "far-apart." The phrase *social distance* therefore reveals an analogy of space within the structure of the social aspect. Obviously, the guideline should not be "social distancing" but simply (keep your) *distance* or *physical distance*.

Unity and Diversity

Analogies between different aspects embody the philosophical problem of *uniqueness* and *coherence* (unity and diversity). One facet of this foundational philosophical problem is given in the unavoidability of employing *analogical terms*, that is, in the use of terms reflecting the interconnection between different aspects. This follows from the fact that different modal aspects are interrelated in such a way that each of them, within its own structure, reflects the modal meaning of others. We have just now argued that "social distance" instantiates a spatial analogy within the structure of the social aspect. Physical extension or distance, alternatively, shows a likeness with spatial extension or distance. However, in this moment of similarity, namely extension, the modal difference is simultaneously expressed—spatial extension is continuous in the sense that it allows for an infinite divisibility, whereas physical space or extension is not continuous (since it is determined by the quantum-structure of energy) and is therefore not infinitely divisible (already in 1925, the mathematician David Hilbert has mentioned these differences).³

Sensitive space, for example the sensitivity for distinct sensations on the human skin, may be experienced as continuous in spite of the fact that the stimuli are physically distinct, discontinuous.⁴

Living entities are subject to the biotic time order of birth, growth (differentiation and integration), maturation, ageing and dying. Within the social aspect we find a retrocipatory analogy in *social* differentiation and *social* integration.

In another example, Dooyeweerd stresses what he calls "the undeniable coherence of meaning between the analogical and the non-analogical use of the term *economy*," and he then points out that "the fundamental meaning-moment that every economical analogy refers to is that of frugality, the avoidance of superfluous or excessive ways of reaching our aim."⁵ On the previous page Dooyeweerd refers to logic which recognizes an anticipatory analogy in its "principle of *logical economy*."

Still another example of an anticipatory analogy is present in *credit*, because credit embodies economic *trust* which in turn highlights the core meaning of the faith aspect.

Implicit in the preceding examples is an element of normativity, because both what is *excessive* and what *cannot be trusted* are instances of *antinormativity*. They evince what normative contrariness are all about because contraries like economic/uneconomic and logical/illogical presuppose a normative standard or principle with a universal scope.

---

3. See D. Hilbert, "Über das Unendliche," *Mathematische Annalen* 95, (1925): 164.
4. See A. Gosztonyi, *Der Raum; Geschichte seiner Probleme in Philosophie und Wissenschaften*, vol. 1 (Freiburg: Alber, 1976), 13.
5. Dooyeweerd, *New Critique*, 2:67.

There are modal norms or principles found within each post-sensitive aspect and they underlie normative contraries such as historical/unhistorical; clear/confused; polite/impolite; aesthetic/unaesthetic (beautiful/ugly); legal/illegal; moral/immoral (love and hate); and certainty/being-in-doubt. The principles on the law-side (norming-side) of these aspects are correlated with human subjects at their factual side and they apply equally to subject functions and subject–object relations.

Laws of nature, by contrast, are correlated with entities such as material things, and plants and animals according to their physical subject functions. The law of gravity is valid for every physical entity and the same holds for the law of energy-conservation. Keep in mind that human beings also function within the pre-logical aspects of reality. Only within the realm of normativity can one discern examples of *illogical concept formation*. Consider one mentioned by Immanuel Kant: a *square circle*. This example is actually derived from Immanuel Kant (1783:341) (1724–1804).[6]

One can say that confusing two spatial figures violates the demands for identifying and distinguishing properly—a square is a square (logically correct identification) and a square is not a non-square (such as a circle—logically correct distinguishing). Such an illogical concept disobeys the logical principles of identity and non-contradiction.

Before we go on to discuss norms or principles briefly, it may be helpful at this point to study a few diagrams:

---

6. See his *Prolegomena zu einer jeden künftigen Metaphysik die als Wissenschaft wird auftreten können* (Hamburg: Felix Meiner, [1783] 1969), 341; §52b.

INTRODUCTION

DIAGRAM 1

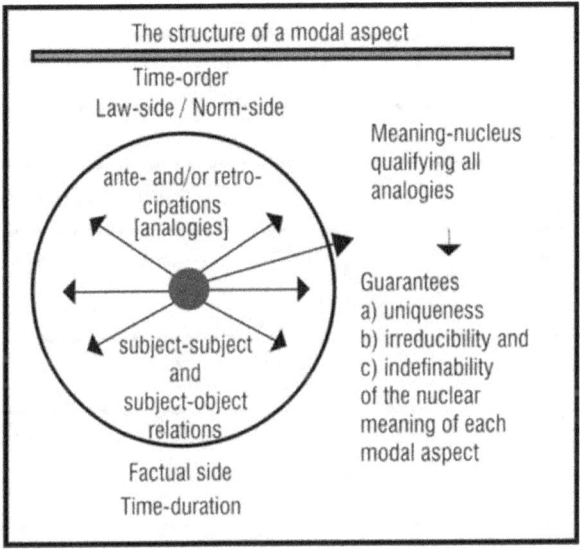

DIAGRAM 2

Aspects	Retrocipations and Anticipations
Faith aspect	Jural/legal certainty trust)
Ethical aspect	Jural/legal morality (fault, good faith, etc.)
Jural aspect	[Meaning-nucleus: retribution]
Aesthetic aspect	Jural/legal harmony
Economic aspect	Jural/legal economy (avoiding excess)
Social aspect	Jural/legal interaction
Lingual aspect	Jural/legal signification and interpretation
Cultural-historical aspect	Jural power / Legal competence

Logical-analytical aspect	Jural lawfulness and unlawfulness (consistency)
Sensory aspect	Jural/legal sensitivity (intention, will)
Biotical aspect	Jural/legal life
Physical aspect	Jural/legal dynamics (causality)
Kinematic aspect	Jural/legal constancy/movement (transfer, conveyance)
Spatial aspect	Jural/legal sphere, jurisdiction, ambit
Arithmetical aspect	Jural/legal order (unity & multiplicity)

Norms or Principles
(See also the chapter, "What is inherent in Normativity?")
Defining a norm or principle involves a complex analysis in which one has to employ terms derived from multiple aspects. Since a principle serves as a point of departure, i.e., as a starting-point for human action, it is *distinct* from other principles (echoing something of the meaning of the numerical aspect: a *multiplicity* of principles). Its scope is universal (everywhere) and enduring (constant)—spatial and kinematic terms. Yet it needs the intervention of a human subject to be made valid, to be given a positive shape and form.

Short of a reasoned account of the nature of a norm or a principle, it should be kept in mind that every modal analogy on the law side of the normative aspects opens up a way to come to a theoretical articulation of a distinct modal principle (norm). Our example of the anticipation of the logical aspect to the economic aspect underlies the principle of *thought-economy*. Likewise, the logical principles of identity and non-contradiction depend upon

DIAGRAM 3

The Various Aspects and Entities within Creation

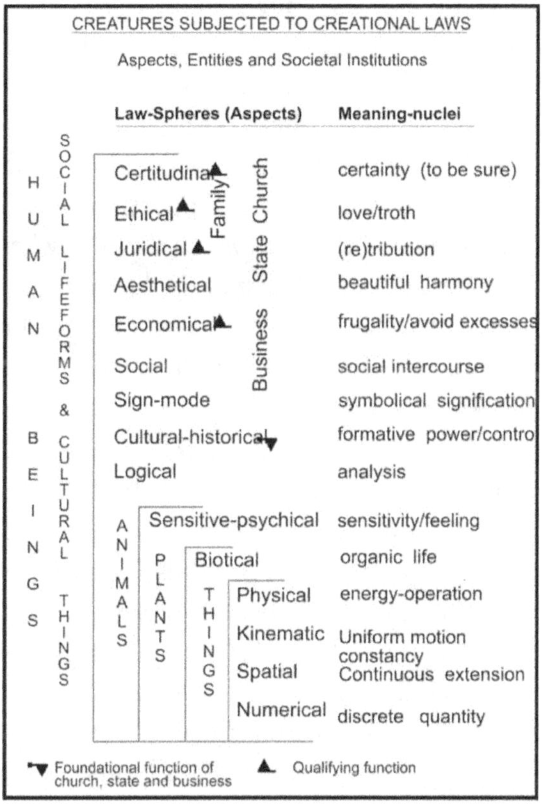

```
CREATURES SUBJECTED TO CREATIONAL LAWS
Aspects, Entities and Societal Institutions
```

Law-Spheres (Aspects)	Meaning-nuclei
Certitudinal	certainty (to be sure)
Ethical — Family	love/troth
Juridical — State Church	(re)tribution
Aesthetical	beautiful harmony
Economical — Business	frugality/avoid excesses
Social	social intercourse
Sign-mode	symbolical signification
Cultural-historical	formative power/control
Logical	analysis
Sensitive-psychical	sensitivity/feeling
Biotical	organic life
Physical	energy-operation
Kinematic	Uniform motion constancy
Spatial	Continuous extension
Numerical	discrete quantity

(Left margin groupings: HUMAN BEINGS / SOCIAL LIFEFORMS & CULTURAL THINGS; ANIMALS / PLANTS / THINGS)

▼ Foundational function of church, state and business   ▲ Qualifying function

the numerical analogies on the norm-side of the logical-analytical aspect.

Modal Laws and Type Laws

Yet we have to keep in mind that there are two distinct kinds of laws: (i) "laws for aspects" (universal modal laws), and (ii) "laws for entities." We may call (i) *modal laws* and (ii) *type laws*.

Re (i): When we direct our theoretical attention toward the modal aspects or functions of reality—such as the spatial aspect, the physical facet, or the social function—we are no longer involved in the classification of entities according to the kinds or types to which they belong and are therefore also not interested in the "kind laws" or "type laws" for entities. The mere distinction between economic and un-economic, for example, is not specified in any typical way. Both a state and a business can waste their money (and thus act un-economically) and both are called to function under the guidance of economic considerations of frugality. But it is only possible to phrase these perspectives when the economic aspect is understood in its *modal universality*, i.e., when the typical nature of the business and the state is disregarded. Modal laws hold universally without any specification: universities, businesses, states, families and sport clubs all have to observe the general meaning of economic norms.

Re (ii): The law holding for a specific kind or type of entity still has its own universality, but this universality is specified. The law for being a state is universal in the sense that it holds for all states. But because not everything is a state, this "type law" is specified—it only applies to states. Likewise, businesses and states belong to different kinds of societal entities, and this typical difference is seen in the typical differences between the function of a state and the function of a business within the economic aspect—business economy differs from state economy (a business cannot "tax" its clients, but the state can tax its citizens). In general, one can say that modal laws encompass all possible entities, whereas typical laws (type laws) only hold for a limited class of entities.

What is Time?
(also look at the chapter on Dooyeweerd's view of Time)
Dooyeweerd has developed a unique understanding of time. He realized that all definitions of time actually terminate in defining certain *aspects* of time. The most prominent physicists of the past century contemplated views on units of measurement while using terms derived from the first four aspects distinguished by

INTRODUCTION

Dooyeweerd. This Diagram is also inserted in the Chapter on Dooyeweerd's view of time.

	Lorenzen	Heisenberg (a)	Heisenberg (b)	Heisenberg (c)	Heisenberg (d)	Weinert
Physical	charge	quantum of action			energy	temperature
Kinematical	duration	c (velocity of light)	time	velocity	velocity	second
Space	length		length	length	length	meter
Number	mass		mass	mass		kilogram

Within each post-physical aspect time expresses itself in conformity with the character of the aspect concerned. We mention a few examples. The biotic time phases of birth, growth, maturation, ageing and dying are non-homogenous because they are accelerating constantly. In emotional time five minutes could be like one hour and *vice versa*. Economic time is the proverbial "time is money." Jural time could even be *retroactive*.

In order to obtain a meaningful overview on Dooyeweerd's philosophical orientation, attention should also be given to the various cosmic dimensions distinguished by him.

Dimensions of Reality

First of all he distinguishes between God and creation, with God's law as the creaturely intransgressible boundary. Any philosophy choosing as its starting-point something within creation is designated as *immanence philosophy* by Dooyeweerd. Transcendence philosophy acknowledges the creatureliness of reality within which the following four dimensions are identified:

a) The central religious dimension.
b) The dimension of cosmic time.

c) The dimension of modal aspects.

d) The dimension of entities (individuality structures)

Religion

The word "religion" may be used in two different but related senses:

(1) it may refer to the radical, central and integral depth dimension of creation, touching the *heart* of being human and therefore giving direction to all the issues of life proceeding from this core dimension;

(2) it may designate one amongst the many articulations of life, familiar to us in faith and confessional activities found alongside all the other differentiated issues of life.⁷

In English, the word *religion* is normally used to designate only the faith function of reality and activities qualified by it, so-called "religious endeavours." The important distinction is therefore between the aspectual sense of faith in its life-encompassing radical and integral sense, where *radical* means *touching the root of* human *existence*, and *integral* means embracing *all of life*.

We now turn to a brief characterization of the multiple isms present in the various academic disciplines, the natural sciences and the humanities.

ISMIC Orientations in Scholarship

Perhaps the genius of Dooyeweerd's philosophy is given in the way in which he had an antenna for the most basic traits of reality. *Diversity* is one such a trait for which every possible philosophical orientation has to account. But this problem entails its correlate as well, namely *unity*. Is there a *unity* in the *diversity* and if so, how can we get a grip on this combined problem of *unity* and *diversity*? One attractive but misleading option is to try to explain the diversity which we experience in terms of one privileged mode of

---

7. See Proverbs 4:23.

explanation, oftentimes accompanied by the reductionistic slogan: "nothing but."

The "nothing but" Fallacy and Materialism

Monistic *ismic* orientations reify or absolutize one privileged aspect and then claim that whatever there is, is *nothing but* the over-emphasized mode of existence. Even non-Christian scholars sometimes object to such *reductionistic* orientations. Attempts to reduce what is irreducible proceed by saying "space is *nothing but* a collection of points"; "life is *nothing but* a complex interaction of atoms, molecules and macromolecules"; "love is *nothing but* feeling," and so on. Or consider how Roy Clouser explains a materialist orientation. For such a person "reality is ultimately physical, so that everything is either matter or dependent upon matter." Clouser also mentions the philosopher Paul Ziff, who once remarked that he is not certain why he is a materialist: "It's not because of the arguments. I guess I'd just have to say that reality looks irresistibly physical to me."[8]

These remarks are similar to what Sorokin said: "Hence the general tendency of the sensate mentality to regard the world—even man, his culture, and consciousness itself—materialistically, mechanistically, behavioristically. Man becomes, in sensate scientific definitions, a 'complex of electrons and protons,' an animal organism, a reflex mechanism, a variety of stimulus-response relationships, or a psychoanalytical 'bag' filled with physiological libido. 'Consciousness' is declared to be an inaccurate and subjective term for physiological reflexes and overt actions of a certain kind."[9]

The field for monistic *isms* is as wide as creation itself, explaining why somewhere in the history of the West every aspect of reality was deified. We pursue a few steps in this direction.

---

8. R. Clouser, *The Myth of Religious Neutrality; An Essay on the Hidden Role of Religious Belief in Theories* (Notre Dame, IN: University of Notre Dame Press, 2005), 38.
9. P. Sorokin, *Crisis of our Age* (New York: E.P. Dutton & Co., 1941), 93–94.

Greek Philosophy: Exploring the First Modes of Explanation

Greek philosophy commenced with the Pythagorean slogan, "Everything is number." As C. B. Boyer explains in his *A History of Mathematics*:

> "It had been a fundamental tenet of Pythagoreanism that the essence of all things in geometry as well as in the practical and theoretical affairs of man are explainable in terms of *arithmos,* or intrinsic properties of whole numbers or their ratios."[10]

No sooner was this arithmeticism confronted with irrational numbers—such as the square root of two ($\sqrt{2}$), i.e., numbers that cannot be represented as the ratio of integers, or π —which gave birth to the first foundational crisis of mathematics. In the school of Parmenides static space became the new basic denominator, reaching its extreme in Zeno's paradoxes (Achilles and the tortoise; the flying arrow, the bisecting paradox) which are directed against the reality of *number* and *movement.*

It is worth noting here that the tension between an overestimation of number and space is alive in all the special sciences, for all the disciplines without exception had and still have to deal with the tension between individualism (atomism) and universalism (holism). According to Jellinek, for example, his discipline, *Allgemeine Staatslehre* (General Theory of the State), is indeed dominated by two opposing *worldviews*, namely an *individualistic-atomistic* and a *collectivistic-universalistic* one.

Next, Heraclitus got involved in the kinematic and physical aspects while wrestling with the problem of *constancy* (the kinematic) and *change* (the physical). After some pan-mechanistic tendencies pan-vitalism claimed that "everything is alive."

Another problem derived from the same two aspects is given

---

10. C. B. Boyer, *A History of Mathematics* (London: John Wiley & Sons, 1968), 79-80.

in the distinction between *universality* and what is *individual*. It forms the crux of the controversy between *realism* and *nominalism*, also known as the *universalia* controversy (see the chapters dedicated to the realism-nominalism controversy).

The *universalia* Controversy of the Medieval Era

The term *universality* has at least two important meaning-nuances: (i) modal universality (see the chapter dedicated to *modal universality*) and (ii) typical universality. Both are instances of *ontic* universality, i.e., of universality "out there," not a product of human thought. Both forms of universality condition the nature of concept-formation. A proper understanding of universality should acknowledge the universality of God's law, the lawfulness (law-conformity) of creatures subject to God's law and the universality of features or traits united in (non-theoretical and theoretical) concepts.

The realistic tradition wrestled with these forms of universality by distinguishing between the ideas in God's "Mind" (*ante rem* – the Platonic position), the ideas in existing things (*in re* – the Aristotelian legacy) and as human concepts (*post rem*). With his theory of ideas Plato stumbled upon God's law as *order for* creatures and Aristotle recognized the lawfulness or law-conformity of creatures. He once remarked that when "this" house passes away *houseness* endures: "the being of house is not generated, but only the being of this house."[11] When it is said that *this* house is *a* house, the *universal* side and *individual* side of a house are captured.

Rationalism restricts knowledge to conceptual knowledge, i.e., to what is *universal*. In an exchange between Dooyeweerd and Van Til in the *album amicorum* that bears the title *Jerusalem and*

---

11. Aristotle, *Metaphysics* 1039b23-25, in *The Basic Works of Aristotle*, ed. Richard McKeon, intro. C.D.C. Reeve (New York: The Modern Library, 2001).

Athens,[12] Dooyeweerd defined rationalism as an absolutization of "conceptual knowledge." Irrationalism only acknowledges what is unique and individual.

Nominalism: Rationalistic and Irrationalistic
(*see the Chapters on realism and nominalism*)
Against this background we can now assess the *hybrid* nature of nominalism. Nominalism rejects every form of universality outside the human mind and therefore rejects both God's order for and the correlated orderliness of reality, typical of irrationalism. For nominalism our concepts are merely mental substitutes (*nomina*) for the multiplicity of individual entities outside the human mind. Descartes (1596–1650) categorically states: "number and all universals are only modes of thought."[13]

Rationalism results from a deification of universal features, that is, it absolutizes conceptual knowledge. Irrationalism, on the other hand, deifies what is unique, individual, unrepeatable and contingent, thus restricting knowledge to the approximating understanding of concepts stretched beyond the limits of their natural application (i.e., concept-transcending knowledge or idea-knowledge). The implication is that nominalism comprises both these elements: in respect of the typical structure of entities, nominalism does not accept any conditioning order (universal structures or laws) for—or any orderliness (universal structuredness) of—such entities. Every entity is strictly individual. In terms of the distinction between rationalism and irrationalism, nominalism therefore represents an irrationalistic view of the nature

---

12. E. R. Geehan, ed., *Jerusalem and Athens: Critical Discussions on the Philosophy and Apologetics of Cornelius Van Til* (Phillipsburg, NJ: Presbyterian and Reformed Publishing Co., 1971).
13. R. Descartes, *The Principles of Philosophy*, in *A Discourse on Method, Meditations and Principles*, trans. John Veitch (London: Everyman's Library. [1644] 1965), Part I, LVII, 187.

of entities, since every individual entity is completely stripped of its universal orderliness (law-conformity) and conditioning order, and at the same time it represents a rationalistic view of the universal concepts within the human mind (in *mente humana*). This characteristic applies to both moderate nominalism, *viz.*, conceptualism (Locke, Occam, Leibniz and others), and to extreme nominalism, which rejects all general and abstract ideas and only accepts general names (Berkeley and Brentano).

As promised, we conclude this *Introduction* by looking at the functioning of the *state* in the various aspects of reality.

The State

The fact that natural and social entities (as well as all events or processes) within reality in principle function in all the various distinguishable aspects can also be observed in the case of the state.

The state is a social entity comprising a *multiplicity* of individuals (designated as citizens). As such the state therefore definitely has a function within the quantitative aspect (or: modus) of reality. We are familiar with the term *modus* due to expressions such as "modus operandi" and "modus vivendi"—in both cases indicating a way of going about things. In the case of our example: when we say that the state functions within the numerical aspect of reality, we are highlighting one of its modes of being (modes of existence). But there are more of them—the existence of the state is not exhausted by its arithmetical functioning.

We have already referred to its function within the spatial aspect—consider the *territory* of a state. On the basis of this locality a state, in a specific (as we shall see: in a public legal) way, not only embraces the relatively situated nature of its citizens, but the citizens are also dependent upon their connection to the state in spite of their relative *movement* (a term stemming from the kinematic aspect of *uniform motion*).

Through its juridical organization the "sword power," the state is capable of using the required force whenever it is necessary—in the service of restoring law and order when certain legal interests are encroached upon (think of actions of the police or the defense forces). The term *force* stems from the physical aspect of energy-operation and it elucidates the function of the state within this aspect. Also think about *law-enforcement*.

As a public legal institution the state binds together the lives of its citizens in a specific way—in the sense that a certain portion of one's life-time actually "belongs" to the state (insofar as one has to work for that part of one's income destined for tax-paying), and also in the sense that the state can maintain its territorial integrity against possible threats from outside only if citizens are integrated within the defense forces—even running the risk of being killed in military action. Clearly, life and death play their own peculiar role within the state as an institution—and it undeniably testifies to the fact that the state does function within the *biotic* aspect of reality as well.

The nation residing in a state (transcending diverse ethnic communities without eliminating their right to exist) operates on the basis of a national consciousness and an emotional *sense* of belonging. Although it does not apply to all citizens, a worthwhile state should succeed in making its citizens *feel* at home. These phenomena clearly cannot be divorced from the sensitive-psychic function of the state.

Furthermore, once we realize that citizens ought to feel at home within the state, they can also positively identify with it (compare the role of ID documents)—the political contents of what sociologists would call the "we" and the "they." We are Americans and "they" could be from any other nationality (Australian, Canadian, German, Namibian, and so on). The core meaning of the *logical-analytical* aspect is captured in the reciprocity of identification and distinguishing—whoever identifies something is at once involved in distinguishing it from something else. Therefore, the national identity of the citizens of the state testifies to the fact that this identity cannot be understood apart from the function of the state within the logical-analytical aspect. When we take into account the argumentative possibilities entailed by functioning within the logical-analytical aspect of reality, we will soon discover that the nature of *public opinion* operative within any particular state in a broader sense manifests the function of the state in the aspect in question.

The *historical* aspect of reality concerns formations of power since it brings to expression the basic trait of culture: the uniquely human calling to subdue the earth and to disclose the potential of creation in a process of cultural development. Such a process takes place hand-in-hand with an on-going development of human society in which—through increasing differentiation and integration of particular societal zones (spheres)—distinct societal collectivities, such as the state, eventually emerge. It is only on the basis of its "sword power" that the state can function as a public legal institution, because maintaining a public legal order requires the monopoly of the "sword power" on the territory of the state. Later, we shall argue that this function of the state within the historical aspect of reality actually constitutes one of its two outstanding (or characterizing) functions—the other one being the jural aspect. Of course, the function of the state in the historical aspect is also clearly evidenced in the actual history of every distinct state.

That the state has a function within the *sign-mode* of reality is obvious from its national symbols (anthem, flag, etc.) and from its official language(s).

Similarly, the state functions within the *social* aspect of reality, since by binding together its citizens within a public legal institution it thus determines a specific kind of social interaction taking place within it. Participating in a general election, acquiring an

ID, observing traffic rules on the road, respecting the rights of fellow citizens—all these and many more forms of social interaction exemplify the function of the state within the social aspect of inter-human interaction.

Raising taxes not only affects the financial position of the citizen but also enables the state to fulfill its legal obligations in governing and administering a country—bringing to light a facet of the *economic* function of the state.

Although a state is not an artwork, it typically belongs to the task of a government to *harmonize* clashing legal interests.

But establishing balance and harmony amongst the multiplicity of legal interests within a differentiated society is always guided by the *jural* function of the state. The idea of public justice is impossible without the function of the state within the jural aspect of reality.

The state also requires an *ethical* integrity amongst its citizens, for without this loyalty the body politic will fall apart. It is therefore appropriate that the extreme of disobedience to this loyalty is punishable if a citizen is found guilty of high treason.

The nation that resides in a state must also share in its vision, in its convictions regarding establishing a just public legal order, giving each citizen his or her due. It is only on this basis that the highly responsible task of governing a country could be entrust-ed to those in office. Terms like trust, certainty, and faith are simply synonymous. The certitudinal or fiduciary aspect of reality—the *faith* aspect—is therefore not foreign to the existence of the state. Just like all the other mentioned aspects it intrinsically co-conditions the existence of every state and at once explains why no single state can exist without also functioning within the faith aspect of reality.

We conclude with a diagram of the spheres of law in a differentiated society distinguished by Dooyeweerd.

INTRODUCTION

Spheres of Law

Public law, civil private law and non-civil private law

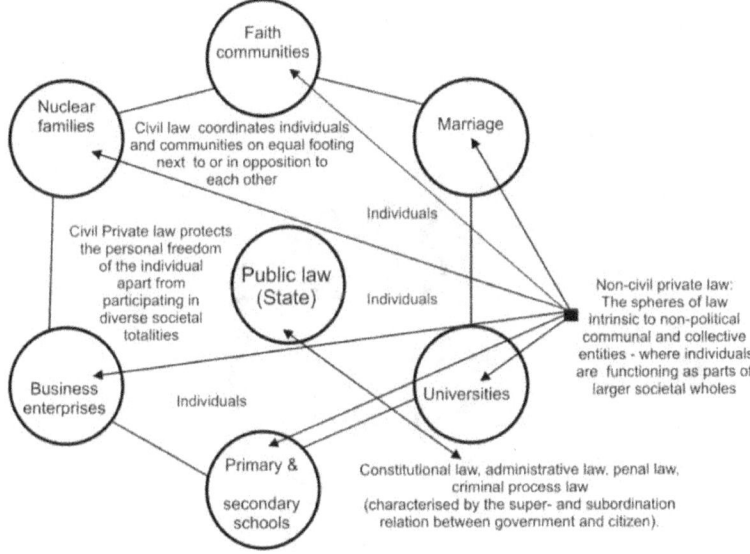

1
THE IDEA OF A CHRISTIAN PHILOSOPHY

by Roy Clouser

THE VAST MAJORITY OF Christian thinkers through the ages have denied that a distinctly Christian philosophy is possible. As one of them once put it: There is no more a Christian philosophy than there is a Christian mathematics or a Christian biology.[1] But there is a tradition of Christian thinkers who came to the opposite conclusion. I'm referring to the Dutch Calvinist line of thought that began in the 19th century with Willem Groen van Prinsterer (aristocrat and historian, 1801–1876), and has since included such gifted thinkers as Abraham Kuyper (1837–1920), Dirk Vollenhoven (1892–1978), and Herman Dooyeweerd (1894–1977).

So what is it, exactly, that most Christians have thought impossible that these men held to be a legitimate and needed Christian enterprise? And what reasons could they have had for disagreeing with such a long-standing position of so many fellow-Christians?

Warning: Before I begin to explain what philosophy is, and why there can be and needs to be a Christian one, you need to know that just because it's Christian and you are a Christian doesn't mean it will sound familiar or comfortable to you. Christian theology can do that, and it should. But a Christian philosophy will not. If you stick with it, however, you will come to see the point of contact between Christianity and the enterprise of philosophy.

---

1. F. Copleston, *A History of Philosophy* (Westminster, MD: Newman Press, 1960), 2:557.

And you will see how and why Christianity calls for a distinctive strategy for constructing philosophical theories.

What is Philosophy?

Philosophy consists mainly of two types of theories: a theory of reality, and a theory of knowledge. The technical name for a theory of reality is "ontology," while the technical name for a theory of knowledge is "epistemology." (Ontology is also sometimes called "metaphysics.") Saying that these are "theories" means two things. First, they are educated guesses (hypotheses) that we make to explain things, and second that they are highly abstract guesses that require highly abstract reasoning and argument to attack or defend them.[2]

What is traditionally sought by an ontology is to specify the *ultimate nature of reality*. Think of it this way: we have disciplines that study many different aspects of the world around us: math, physics, biology, psychology, logic, sociology, economics, ethics, for example. So if each of those disciplines makes theories about a distinct aspect of reality, then ontology wants to know what they are all aspects _of_. What is the nature of the reality that is common to them all? Similarly, we have knowledge of different kinds: mathematical, physical, biological, logical, economical, and so on. But epistemology wants to know what is the nature of knowledge that is common to all the particular kinds of it. It wants to discover the conditions under which identifying that nature can show us when we can (or cannot) be certain of a belief, and how to answer the question, What is truth?

At this point you may feel like asking, Why do we need such

---

2. The works devoted to the philosophy of some field of study such as philosophy of science, philosophy of law, philosophy of history, philosophy of religion, etc., differ from non-philosophical works in those fields by first advocating a theory of reality or knowledge, and then applying it to problems in that special field.

theories? Isn't it difficult enough to form theories within specific aspects of reality and knowledge? Why do we also need to have theories that supply an overview of how all the aspects relate to one another?

The answer is that any theory constructed *within* a particular subject matter always assumes some view as to how its subject matter relates to all the other subject matters. In other words, work in a particular field presupposes—even if unconsciously—some view of how it relates to what is outside its field, which amounts to some sort of overview about the nature of reality and/or knowledge. The Dutch Calvinist tradition said that because such philosophical overviews are unavoidable, therefore we, as Christians, need to make a concerted effort to be sure those overviews are guided by our belief in God. In that way we may be able to transfer that guidance from the overview to our ontology and epistemology, and from our ontology and epistemology to the theories we make or accept within the various natural and social sciences.

This is an important point about which there has been significant misunderstanding, so it bears repeating: a Christian philosophy is needed in order to give Christians a God-guided overview for the nature of reality and knowledge, the benefit of which is to guide the making and evaluating of theories in the natural and social sciences. I mean subjects such as math, geometry, kinetics, physics, biology, psychology, logic, history, linguistics, sociology, economics, aesthetics, jurisprudence, and ethics. Dooyeweerd himself put the point this way:

> All Christians who in their scientific work are ashamed of the Name of Christ Jesus, because they desire honor among people, will be totally useless *in the mighty struggle to recapture science, one of the great powers of Western culture, for the Kingdom of God.* This struggle is not hopeless, however, so long as it is waged in the full armor of faith in

Him who has said "All authority in heaven and on earth has been given to Me," and again, "Take heart! I have overcome the world."³

What Philosophy Is Not

This means, among other things, that we should not expect a Christian philosophy to yield new knowledge of God beyond what is revealed in God's word. It will not replace or enlarge theology, and it is not the same as theology. Theology formulates into doctrines the truths revealed in Scripture, and it proposes views as to how those doctrines are to be related to one another. Philosophy does neither of those things.

Nor will philosophy replace pastoral counselling. It will not, for example, comfort a grieving widow, or aid a person who has just lost his or her job. It is not the same as apologetics; it does not attempt to prove the truth of the Christian Faith nor does it seek to convert unbelievers.⁴ As a side-effect it has, at times, helped clear up misunderstandings about certain doctrines of the Faith, but even then, that is not its main purpose. Its main purpose remains *to guide Christians who are engaged in making and evaluating theories in the sciences, by giving them a God-guided overview on the nature of reality and knowledge, the benefits of which can then be transmitted to their work within the fields of the specific sciences.*

Nor is it the case that the hypotheses of a Christian philosophy will automatically be true, or closer to the truth, for being Christian. A Christian philosophy is still a set of *theories;* it therefore

---

3. H. Dooyeweerd, *Christian Philosophy and the Meaning of History*, Series B, vol. 13, Collected works of Herman Dooyeweerd, General Editor, D. F. M.Strauss (Grand Rapids, MI: Paideia Press, 2013), 104 (ital. added).
4. Cornelius Van Til once phrased his objection to Dooyeweerd's work to me this way: "That's no way to present the gospel to unbelievers." Although that's not what a Christian philosophy is trying to do, Christian philosophy can have some apologetic value. It can help to expose misunderstandings of Christianity and to rebut criticisms, for example.

remains human guesswork. This is why Dooyeweerd once said to me: "All my theories may need to be changed or abandoned." Above all, it does not mean that a Christian philosophy will take its hypotheses from Scripture or theology. It's this assumption that has led to the view that there can be a Christian view of, say, justice or ethics but not of physics or chemistry. The Scriptures do contain specific teachings that bear on justice and on ethics (though they don't come within miles of supplying a *theory* of either), while they don't say anything whatever about metal stress or chemical valency.

So, in what sense can an ontology or epistemology be Christian? The answer is actually simple: there is one sort of error that has infected just about every ontology and epistemology ever made, and which should be ruled out from the start for a Christian because it is incompatible with the belief that God is the creator of everything "visible or invisible" (Col. 1). The sense in which an ontology or epistemology can be Christian, is that all its hypotheses (guesses) *must be consistent with the doctrine of creation as Colossians 1 states it.*

So why have most Christian thinkers come to the conclusion that there can be no such thing as a God-guided theory of reality or knowledge? To answer this, we must think briefly about the beginnings of philosophical thought, that is, about the ancient pagan and naturalist Greek thinkers who began the task of making theories instead of myths (around 650 BC). Early on, they recognized that getting a theory of reality needed to begin with identifying the divine reality. The divine, they said, is whatever is the self-existent reality that all else depends on.[5] Since they were

---

5. This was Anaximander's definition; see Werner Jaeger, *The Theology of the Early Greek Philosophers* (Oxford: Clarendon Press, 1947), 27–35; see also Aristotle, *Physics* 203b and *Metaphysics* 1064b, 28–38, in *The Basic Works of Aristotle*, ed. Richard McKeon, intro. C.D.C. Reeve (New York: The Modern Library, 2001). That *something* must be self-existent is obvious.

all without access to the Scriptures, they ransacked the cosmos for the divine reality and came up with a series of proposals as to what that might be. One of them proposed that the self-existent reality is earth, another that it's air, another that it's fire, and another said it's water. Around 440 BC, Leucippus of Miletus proposed the theory that the stuff the cosmos is made of is tiny invisible and indivisible self-existent particles he called "atoms." And he suggested that it's how the atoms combine that determines whether they form earth, air, fire, or water.

During this same era another line of thinkers stressed that merely accounting for the material everything is made of is not sufficient to explain the nature of the world we experience. Our world isn't merely a random pile of stuff but an *ordered* cosmos. Whatever stuff it's made of has to be given order, organization, and definiteness. So, a theory of reality has to include the nature of the self-existent source of the order of the world, as well as of the nature of the stuff that gets ordered. The Pythagoreans, for example, said that numbers were the stuff that gets ordered and that mathematical laws provided the order of everything.[6] The two

---

Consider the sum total of reality. This totality must be self-existent either in part or as a whole *because there is nothing else for it to depend upon*. Hinduism and Buddhism say it is the whole that is the self-existent (divine) reality. Judaism, Christianity, and Islam say it is one part that is self-existent: God.

6. There can be no doubt that the Pythagoreans regarded numbers as the divine (self-existent) reality. Here is their prayer to the number 10: "Bless us, divine number, thou that generatest gods and men! O holy, holy tetraktys, thou that containest the root and source of eternally flowing creation! For divine number begins with the profound, the pure unity until it comes to the holy four; then it begets the mother of all, the all-encompassing, the all-bounding, the first born, the never swerving, never tiring holy ten, the keyholder of all." Quoted in T. Danzig, *Number: The Language of Science* (Garden City, NY: Doubleday-Anchor, 1954), 42.

THE IDEA OF A CHRISTIAN PHILOSOPHY

most influential thinkers of this era were Plato and his student Aristotle. Plato also held that it is mathematical laws that order the cosmos, whereas Aristotle held that the nature of the cosmic order is characterized by the axioms of logic.[7] Both of them defended the theory that the world we inhabit is made out of stuff they called "matter," and that it is given its shape and order by what they called rational "Forms."[8]

The Response to Philosophy in Western Christianity

What we first need to notice about these theories, is that they are all pagan or naturalist. They all picked out something *in the creation* as their candidate(s) for the self-existent (divine) reality because they knew nothing of the transcendent Creator revealed in Scripture. So, if we represent the divine by a solid line and the dependent cosmos by a dotted line, then schematically what they proposed can be illustrated by the following diagram:

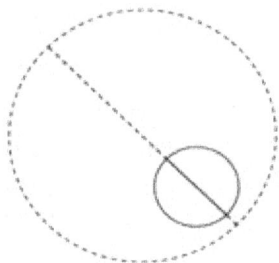

---

7. *Metaphysics* 1064a. Most philosophers since Plato and Aristotle have taken both the mathematical and the logical laws together to comprise what they call the *rational* order of reality.
8. Aristotle came to prefer the term "secondary substances" rather than "forms" for the rational order that organizes matter into knowable objects, and that is the term used by most philosophers since. It connotes the permanent, abiding identity of a thing that remains the same throughout all the changes the thing undergoes.

Within the dotted circle there is a solid circle (the divine), indicating that the divine is to be found within the cosmos. The solid circle is divided because there are two divine realities, Form and Matter. It is the interaction of the two divine realities that generates everything else, all of which consists of dependent things that come into being and pass away.[9]

In Plato's theory, the realm of self-existent Forms included more than just the laws of math and logic. It also included what came to be called "Perfections." This meant that every quality or type of thing we experience on earth is an imperfect copy of its perfect instance in the realm of divine Forms. For example, in our world there are only imperfect instances of green, or square, justice, or a horse. But in the realm of divine Forms, there is the perfect green, the perfect square, perfect justice, and the perfect form for a horse.

Early Christian thinkers of course rejected the idea that anything in the cosmos is the divine creator of the rest of it. Nevertheless, many of them were impressed with Plato's (and later Aristotle's) theories. And some of them—notably St Augustine—thought Plato had actually figured out the biblical idea of God when he (Plato) said that the highest Form is "the God and Father of all things." The theory of Perfections, said Augustine, is the truth.[10] Plato simply didn't know that all the individual perfections are to be found unified in the One True God. This theory was developed by Augustine and others who followed him into a theology that defined God—the God of the Bible—as "the being with all (and only) perfections." It said that every characteristic of God exists

---

9. This interpretation of the schematic drawing is not intended to characterize all ancient philosophy, and still less all philosophy since then. Some ontologies had only one divinity, for example, and others have endorsed many different kinds of candidates for divinity.
10. Augustine, *The City of God*, trans. William Babcock (Hyde Park, NY: New City Press, 2012), viii, 6.

in Him in the highest possible ("maximal") way. In Him there is maximal goodness, justice, love, power, knowledge, and whatever other perfections there may be whether we know of them or not. The fact that creatures have imperfect copies of such qualities, is due to God's imparting His qualities to them in a less-than-maximal mode. So this theology defined God as the being with all and only Perfections, and a perfection as the maximal mode of any property that makes something better to have it than to lack it.[11]

In this way, early Christian thought retained the idea that some created entities in the cosmos may be more real than the rest of creation. For surely whenever a creature possesses (even imperfectly) a quality that is a maximal perfection in God, that creature possesses a quality that is uncreated and self-existent. And any quality that is self-existent is more real than any other quality that is not self-existent. The fact that creatures exist and have that quality is a fact created by God; and the fact that the quality imparted is in an imperfect mode is also determined by God. But since it is the *same quality* in both God and the creature, the quality cannot be uncreated in God but created in the creature. (It is an axiom of logic that the same thing cannot be both created and uncreated at the same time in the same sense.) As Aquinas later explained it, the modes in which the quality is possessed by creatures vary and are less than perfect, but the quality we're talking about (the "*res significata*") is the same.[12] Even in less-than-perfect-modes, then,

---

11. The definition is A. Plantinga's; see his *God, Freedom, and Evil* (New York: Harper & Row, 1967), 98. Augustine insisted that all the perfections are identical with God's being, so God does not merely *possess* them, He *is* the unity of them. Anselm and Aquinas followed him on this point. They called this the doctrine of God's *simplicity*.

    So far as I know, no one has ever answered the question: Why does there have to be a maximal instance of any perfection? Why can't they be like the natural number series which has no last number?

12. This is a key point in Aquinas' theory of proper proportionality, which he

the qualities of creatures that are also attributes of God are uncreated, and thus more real in creatures than their qualities that are not attributes of God.

This means that love, beauty, goodness, and justice, wisdom, and so on—in addition to the laws of math & logic—were not created by God. They just *are* God. And the key point here for philosophy is that when these same qualities occur in creatures in a lesser degree, they are still more real than the rest of creation because the properties of the rest of creation are not uncreated. For example, spatial properties, physical properties, properties of change (motion), biotic properties (healthy, sick, growing), sensory qualities (red, smooth, sweet), and so on, are not perfections.

This is why it seemed to Augustine (and to Anselm and Aquinas after him) that the strategy for explaining the natures of creatures could be the same for Christians as it had been for the pagan and naturalist thinkers before them, namely: some part(s) of the cosmos are more real than the others, and the less real (non-divine) parts are explained by showing how they depend upon the more real parts.[13]

---

offered to explain how religious language is possible (*Summa Theologia*, I, 13, 15 & 16; *C.G.*, I, 33 & 34, and *De Pot.*, 7, 7). For an excellent exposition of that theory, see J. F. Ross, "Analogy as a Rule of Meaning in Religious Language," *International Philosophical Quarterly*, I/3 (Sept. 1971): 468–504.

13. In fact, this strategy for explanation opened the way for more than just the attributes of God to have greater reality than other qualities when they occurred in creatures. This is because God could make some other kinds of properties and laws more real than the rest without their having to be true of Himself at all. So not only were there in creation self-existent Perfections that creatures share with God, but He could make, say, physical properties to be more real than some other kinds of properties. In that case, if a Christian wanted to keep some version of the Form/Matter ontology, he could propose that God had made the physical properties of creatures to be more

THE IDEA OF A CHRISTIAN PHILOSOPHY

The key idea to Christianizing this strategy is this: all the rest of creation may be explained as dependent on some one or two kinds of entities in creation, *so long as we add that those entities, in turn, depend on God.* Moreover, this strategy for explanation seemed to be not only suggested by, but supported by, the most fundamental Christian doctrine of all: the doctrine of God in which God is understood as the being with all and only Perfections.

This strategy allowed Christian thinkers to adapt virtually any theory to belief in God. For example, Epicurus was a materialist. He held that reality is comprised of infinite (and self-existent) space in which an infinite number of (self-existent) atoms go through every possible combination over an infinite length of time. A Christian could now adapt that theory simply by regarding space and matter as more real than any other aspects of creation but denying that space and atoms are self-existent, adding that they in turn depend on God. He or she could then go on to explain everything else as combinations of atoms. (There are Christian philosophers today who advocate something very close to this position!)

It is this idea about how to do philosophy that has led almost every Christian thinker in the western church to say there's no such thing as a distinctly Christian philosophy. It's because it is always possible to alter any theory that regards its ultimate explainers as the divine realities, by adding the claim that they are not divine because they, in turn, depend on God. *This is precisely why most Christians in philosophy still reject the idea that a distinctly Christian philosophy is even possible, let alone needed. And it is why they reject in advance Dooyeweerd's work of constructing a Christian ontology.*

So, what's wrong with this prevailing idea? It doesn't deify anything in creation, and it seems to accommodate virtually any

---

real than, say, biotic and sensory properties, so those could be explained as dependent on (caused by) the physical.

theory anyone could possibly come up with. It allows any theory of reality or knowledge to have belief in God pinned onto the end of it. Instead of calling for a distinct program of explanation for Christians, it generates a philosophical agenda that was once described to me as "the peaceful view of Aquinas."[14]

The Reformational Objection

Our first objection to this strategy strikes at the heart of it, namely, the claim that something in creation can be what everything else in creation depends on. We say that giving any created reality that status is ruled out by Scripture, so that merely adding that "it in turn depends on God" does not neutralize its anti-Christian character. This is because the New Testament says that everything in creation depends directly on the Divine nature of Jesus Christ alone:

> For by him were all things created that are in the heavens and on the earth, the visible and the invisible… all things have been created through him and for him, and by him all things hang together (Col. 1:16–17) (my translation).

Two quick comments on this text: First: the scope of its claim is everything "visible and invisible," and it's a truism that everything without exception is either visible or it's not. Second, there is not the slightest hint that Paul means to leave open the possibility that anything else could share this status with Christ. In short, there is no created reality that mediates God's creative and sustaining power to the rest of creation. This is because it is Christ in his Divine nature who alone sustains every creature in existence. He alone hangs all things together: not purely physical matter, or rational forms plus matter, or sensory data plus logic, nor any other member of the long list of candidates for this status that has been

---

14. These are the words of Ernan McMullen in a letter to me. Professor McMullen was a great admirer of St Thomas.

THE IDEA OF A CHRISTIAN PHILOSOPHY

proposed in the history of western philosophy.

This is not, however, a stand-alone point. It is coupled with a doctrine of God that rejects the definition that God is the being with all and only Perfections. Again, please notice that the scope of what Paul says in Colossians is "all things . . . visible and invisible." Taken at face value, this would require that the attributes of God are also created (they depend on God). They are not self-existent Platonic perfections. God has, on this view, created so that there is such a thing as goodness, justice, power, etc., and has taken them into Himself. In fact, Proverbs 8 explicitly asserts this of God's wisdom. So why not understand the other attributes that comprise God's nature the same way?

This is, in fact, the position taken by the Cappadocian Fathers of the Eastern Orthodox Church, and they did so before Augustine proposed reading Plato's theory into the New Testament. They were: St Basil, bishop of Caesarea, his brother St Gregory of Nyssa, and his brother-in-law, St Gregory Nazianzus, as well as Basil's sister St Macrina. Their theology of God distinguished between God's originating being, which they called God's "essence," and God's manifestations to humans, which they called God's "energies." God's essence, they said, is altogether unknowable; His energies are His actions and relations to humans by which He makes Himself known.

Please notice that saying God created wisdom, goodness, knowledge, and power does not mean there ever was a time He didn't have them. That's because God created time also.[15] This means that the creation of time, as well as each of the attributes of God's nature, was independent of time. That is why there never was and never will be a time when God has any nature other than the nature He reveals in Scripture. But that nature is, nevertheless,

---

15. Heb. 1:2 says that God "created the ages of time," while other texts assert that God's plan—and therefore God himself—is "before time": I Cor. 2:6-8, II Tim. 1:9, Titus 1:2, and Jude 25.

one He created (it depends on Him for its existence) and took into himself eternally.[16] Basil summed up this position in one pithy remark: "If there are perfections, God created them."

This doctrine of God was re-discovered in the Western Church by Martin Luther and John Calvin in the 16th century,[17] and was re-affirmed by Swiss theologian Karl Barth in the 20th century. Let's start with Luther:

> . . . God does not manifest himself except through his works [*energies*] and the Word, because the meaning of these is understood . . . Whatever else belongs to the Divinity cannot be grasped and understood such as being outside time.[18]

> Now God in his own nature and majesty is to be left alone; in this regard we have nothing to do with him, nor does he wish us to deal with him. We have to do with him as clothed by his Word, by which he presents himself to us.[19]

---

16. The 14th-century Orthodox theologian, St Gregory Palamas, put the point this way: "[God's] energies do not comprise the being of God; it is he who gives them their existence . . . God by a superabundance of goodness towards us [although] transcendent over all things, incomprehensible and inexpressible, *consents to become* particible *to our intelligence . . . [and] in his voluntary condescension imposes on himself a really diversified mode of existence*" (ital. added). Quoted in John Meyendorff, *A Study of Gregory Palamas* (London: Faith Press, 1964), 226.
17. This doctrine was not, however, supported in the mainstream of subsequent Protestant theology, which lapsed back into the doctrine of Augustine, Anselm, and Aquinas. That is why I call this doctrine of God the "Orthodox/ Reformational" view.
18. "Lectures on Genesis," in J. Pelican, ed, *Luther's Works* (St Louis: Concordia Publishing House, 1958), I:11.
19. J. Dillenberger, *Martin Luther* (Garden City, NY: Anchor Books, 1961), 191.

Calvin is just as clear:

> ...in the enumeration of his perfections, [God] is revealed not as he is in himself, but in relation to us...Every perfection [ascribed] to God may be contemplated in creation; and, hence, such as we feel him to be when experience is our guide, such he declares himself to be in his word.[20]

> The Lord is manifested by his perfections . . . Hence . . . in seeking God, the most direct path . . . is not to attempt with presumptuous curiosity to pry into his essence . . . but to contemplate him in his works [*energies*], by which he draws near, becomes familiar, and in a manner communicates himself to us.[21]

Here is the way Karl Barth (1886–1968) put the same position:

> ... the object of divine action in the Incarnation is man. God's free decision is and remains a gracious decision; God becomes man, the word becomes flesh. The Incarnation Means . . . a real and complete descent of God, *God actually became what we are*, in order actually to exist with us . . . for us . . . and so actually, in our place, in our situation and position to be the new man. It is not in His eternal majesty —in which he is and remains hidden from us—but as this new man, and therefore the word in the flesh, that God's Son is God's revelation to us and our reconciliation with God. *Just for that reason faith cannot look past His humanity . . . the cradle . . . the cross . . . in order to see Him in His Divinity.* Faith in the eternal word of the Father is faith in Jesus of Nazareth or it is not the Christian faith.[22]

I call this the "Incarnational model" for understanding God's attributes: Just as in the Incarnation God took into Himself the

---

20. J. Calvin, *Institutes of The Christian Religion*, 1.x.2.
21. Calvin, *Institutes*, 1.v.9.
22. K. Barth, *Credo* (London: Hodder & Stoughton, 1936), 66 (ital. added).

entire (created) person of Jesus Christ, so too that is the way in which God eternally acquired the (created) attributes that comprise His revealed nature. It is why Calvin speaks of "the nature in which [God] is *pleased to manifest himself*,"[23] rather than speaking of an uncreated nature He cannot help but have. The schematic representing this idea looks like this:

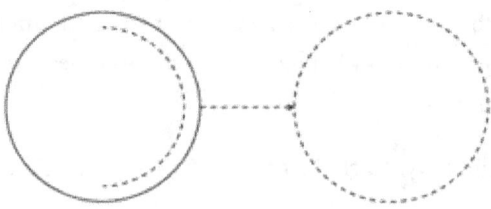

How Does This Difference Impact Theories?

If there is no created reality that is basic to the existence of all other created things—no "substance" in the universe whether created by God or not—that fact alone sets a distinctive agenda for theory-making that had never been tried until Dooyeweerd's theory of reality. All ontologies up until his had attempted to find *within creation* the kind of entities that are either all there is or are what the rest of creation depends on. And this was so whether or not they also attempted to baptize their proposals by saying that those entities, in turn, depend on God.

By contrast, Dooyeweerd's theory begins by regarding *every* kind of property and all the laws in the cosmos as directly created and sustained by God, the laws of rationality included. None are more real than any others, because all depend entirely and directly

---

23. Calvin, *Institutes*, 3.ii.6.

on God. What gives to things and to their properties the orderliness they exhibit, are the laws God has built into creation. And what sustains both the laws and the things that exist and function under those laws, is the power of God. Moreover, that Divine power—says Colossians 1—is mediated to creation *only* by the Divine Son of God, Jesus Christ. This is why Orthodox theologian Gregory Palamas said:

> Christians cannot admit any intermediate substance between Creator and creatures, nor any mediating hypostasis.[24]

In philosophy, the term for arguments that try to show something in creation is the explanation of all the rest of creation are called "reduction" arguments.[25] The term is intended to convey that things of a particular nature (mathematical, physical, sensory, logical, etc.), either (a) are all there is, or (b) are what produce everything else. So the Christian agenda for theories of reality or knowledge—the agenda that takes Colossians 1 seriously—can be said to be that of constructing theories that are entirely "non-reductionist."[26]

One of the consequences of such an ontology is that while it gives an account of the distinctive natures of types of created things – everything from atoms and animals to family, state, and church – it does not offer any such proposal about the nature of creation as a whole (the view I said earlier is the "traditional" idea

---

24. Quoted by John Meyendorff, *A Study of Gregory Palamas* (Faith Press, 1964), 130.
25. This means that a Christian view will deny that any one entire kind of properties-and-laws is the cause of another. This is to be understood globally, however, not locally. Heating a copper wire causes it to glow green, for example; but hot copper wires are not the reason there are such things as green glows in the cosmos.
26. For some of the more frequently employed senses of reduction, see the Appendix below.

of ontology). That is because, from this viewpoint, creation as a whole cannot be characterized by any one or two of its aspects (kinds of properties and laws). It is not more basically physical, or physical/mathematical, or sensory, or sensory/logical, etc. *That is because the most basic nature of the universe is only to depend on God.* In that case, an ontology will be confined to giving an account of the natures of the types of creatures found in the created universe: things, events, states-of-affairs, persons, relations, social organizations, etc.

That is what Herman Dooyeweerd did. He constructed a theory of reality that offers an account of the diverse natures of types of creatures without resorting either to the hypothesis that all creatures are really of the same kind, or the hypothesis that all the rest of creation is produced by created entities of one (or two) particular kind(s). Instead, he took all the aspects exhibited by creatures to our everyday experience to have been real from the beginning of creation, and all things to have (some) properties of every aspectual kind.[27] He then distinguished the laws that hold among the properties of each aspect (aspectual universality) from the type laws[28] that hold across aspects and make possible the combinations of properties that typify classes of individuals (laws for individual entities). His theory also recognizes the way a par-

---

27. S. Hawking and L. Krauss have suggested that for quite a while after the Big Bang there were no laws whatever other than universal gravitation. Apparently, they don't realize that if there were no logical laws by which that era of the universe was governed, it could not now be logically distinguished from anything else by us. Similarly, if no mathematical laws applied to that era, nothing about it could now be so much as counted, let alone calculated.

28. Dooyeweerd's own term for these laws was "individuality structures." But that term seemed to connote individual things rather than the laws which made each type of them possible. So I have proposed the expression "type laws."

ticular aspect can more centrally qualify (characterize) the nature of a thing, and it shows how our intuitive grasp of those natures can be confirmed (or not) by the way the laws of the qualifying aspect govern the internal organization of things of a particular type when each is considered as a whole. Thus his theory recognizes (at least) three sorts of laws:

1. Laws that hold among the properties of a particular aspect;
2. Laws that hold across aspects to make possible specific types of individuals;
3. Causal Laws which are themselves multi-aspectual events and, like individual things, have varying qualifying functions.

In this way, Dooyeweerd provided fellow-Christians with a theory of reality by which they can carry its non-reductionist agenda into theories in each of the scientific disciplines.

APPENDIX
Some of the more frequently employed senses of reduction

A. Hard Reduction

1. **Eliminative Reduction.** The nature of reality is exclusively that of aspect X, so that all things have only properties of kind X and are governed only by laws of kind X. This is not defended by claiming that the terms used for non-X properties are equivalent in meaning to X terms, or that the seemingly non-X properties are in fact identical with X properties. Instead, the entire experience of non-X things and/or properties is dismissed as totally illusory, on the ground that it is able to be ignored in favor of speaking of, and dealing with, reality only in the terms of the science of X. (Paul Churchland has used this method for defending materialism.)

2. **Meaning Replacement.** The nature of reality is exclusively that of aspect X so that all things have only properties of kind X and are governed only by laws of kind X. This is defended by arguing that all the *terms* supposed to have non-X meaning can be replaced by X-terms without loss of meaning, while not all X-terms can be replaced by non-X terms without loss of meaning. (Berkeley, Hume, and Ayer used this strategy to defend phenomenalism.)

3. **Factual Identity.** The nature of reality is exclusively that of aspect X, so that all things have properties of only aspect X and are governed only by the laws of aspect X. This is defended by arguing that although the meaning of non-X terms *cannot* be replaced with only X-terms without loss of meaning, such terms may *reference* only X-things all the same. The selection of the kind(s) of terms that correspond both extensionally and intentionally to the nature of reality is then defended on the basis of explanatory superiori-

ty: the argument tries to show that for anything whatever, the only or best explanation is always one whose primitive terms and laws are of the X kind. (The Australian philosopher J. J. C. Smart (1920–2012) defended materialism this way.) More recent theories try to regard non-X properties as identical with *functions* that are purely X, rather than with specific things or events that appear to be non-X.

B. Soft Reduction

1. **Causal Dependency.** The nature of reality is basically that of aspect X (or of aspects X and Y). It is the X-ness of things that makes possible and actual the other kinds of properties and laws that are true of reality as experienced pre-theoretically. So while non-X properties are real, and can be proper objects of scientific investigation, there is a one-way causal dependency between non-X aspects and aspect X. The non-X aspect could not exist without X, while X can exist without any others. (Aristotle and Descartes both defended theories in which certain aspects were the nature of "substance," and properties of all other kinds were "accidental" or dependent on substances.)

2. **Epiphenomenalism.** This version is much like causal dependency, except that the non-X aspects are thought to be much less real – similarly to the way a mirror image is less real than its object. They exist, but they do not have their own laws, nor do they exert causal effects. Thus they are not proper objects of scientific investigation. All genuine explanations must therefore be given in terms of only X properties and laws. (Huxley and Skinner argued that states of consciousness are epiphenomena that depend upon bodily processes or behavior.)

These strategies are not mutually exclusive and can be combined in various ways within the same theory of reality.

2

The Ground-Motive of Greek Culture[1]

ALTHOUGH IT WAS the famous Greek philosopher Aristotle who first coined the term "form-matter," the "form-matter" ground-motive controlled Greek thought and civilization from the beginning of the Greek city-states. It originated in the unreconciled conflict within Greek religious consciousness between the ground-motive of the ancient nature religions and the ground-motive of the then more recent culture religion—the religion of the Olympian deities.

The Matter Motive

Outside of their primeval Greek core, the nature religions contained much that was pre-Greek and even of foreign origin. These religions differed greatly in local ritual and in specific faith content. Reconstructing all the early forms of nature religions is largely guesswork for lack of information, but it is clear that from at least the beginning of the so-called historical age (the age documented by written records), the communal ground-motive of these religions sustained a great influence on Greek culture.

What was at stake in this ground-motive was the deification

---

1. Extracts from H. Dooyeweerd, *Roots of Western Culture, Pagan, Secular and Christian Options*, Collected Works of Herman Dooyeweerd, Series B, vol. 15, General Editor D. F. M. Strauss (Grand Rapids, MI: Paideia Press, 2012), 15–19.

of a formless, cyclical stream of life. Out of this stream emerged the individual forms of plant, animal, and human being, which then matured, perished, and came to life again. Because the life stream ceaselessly repeated its cycle and returned to itself, whatever had individual form was doomed to disappear. The worship of the tribe and its ancestors was thoroughly interwoven with this religious conception. Closely related to this belief was its view of time: time was not linear, as in Newton's modern conception of an ongoing continuum, but cyclical.

Mysterious forces were at work in this life stream. They did not run their course according to a traceable, rational order, but according to *Anangkē* (blind, incalculable fate). Everything that had a life of its own was subjected to it. The divine was thus not a concrete form or personality. On the contrary, the nature gods were always fluid and invisible. The material names used to indicate them were just as undefined as the shapeless divinities themselves. Instead of a unified deity, a countless multiplicity of divine powers, bound up with a great variety of natural phenomena, were embodied in many fluid and variable conceptions of deities. The state of constant variation applied not only to the "lesser" gods (the so-called demons: shapeless, psychical powers) and to the "heroes" (worshipped in connection with the deification of life in tribe and family), but with equal force to the "great" gods such as Gaia (mother earth), Uranus (god of the skies), Demeter (goddess of grain and growth) and Dionysus (god of wine).

In this context it is understandable that the rise of relatively durable, individual forms in nature was considered an injustice. According to the mysterious saying of the Ionian philosopher of nature, Anaximander (sixth century BC), these individual forms would "suffer retribution in the course of time." With a genuinely Greek variant on Mephistopheles' saying in Goethe's *Faust*, one could express this thought as follows: "*Denn alles, was entsteht, / Ist wert, dass es zugrunde geht*" (For all that comes to be / Deserves to perish wretchedly).[2]

On the other hand, it is also understandable that in this nature religion one's faith in the continuity of a divine stream of life provided a certain comfort with respect to the inevitable destruction of all definite, visibly shaped and formed individual life. "Mother earth" sustained this religion; out of it the stream of life began its cycle.

The Form Motive

The newer culture religion, on the other hand, was a religion of form, measure, and harmony. It became the official religion of the Greek city-state, which established Mount Olympus as one of history's first national religious centers. The Olympian gods left "mother earth" and her cycle of life behind. They were immortal, radiant gods of form: invisible, personal, and idealized cultural forces. Mount Olympus was their home. Eventually the culture religion found its highest Greek expression in the Delphic god Apollo, the lawgiver. Apollo, god of light and lord of the arts, was indeed the supreme Greek culture god.

This new religion, which received its most splendid embodiment in the heroic poetry of Homer, tried to incorporate the older religion in its own ground-motive of form, measure, and harmony. It was particularly concerned to curb the wild and impassioned worship of Dionysus, the god of wine, with the normative principle of form that characterized Apollo worship. In the city of Delphi, Apollo (culture) and Dionysus (nature) became brothers. Dionysus lost his wildness and took on a more serious role as the "keeper of the souls."

Early in this period of transition the ancient Greek "seers" and poet-theologians (Hesiod and Homer) sought to convince

---

2. *Goethe's Faust*, trans. and intro. Walter Kaufmann, bilingual ed. (Garden City, NY: Doubleday & Company, 1961), lines 1339–1340.

the people that the Olympians themselves had evolved out of the formless gods of nature. Hesiod's teaching concerning the genealogy of the gods, which deeply influenced subsequent Greek philosophical thought, gave the ground-motive of the older nature religions a general, abstract formulation: the basic principle of all that comes into being is *chaos* and *formlessness*.

But the inner connection between the culture religion and the older nature religions is most evident in the peculiar part played by *Moira*. Originally, *Moira* was nothing other than the old *Anangke* of the nature religions: inexorable fate revealing itself in the cycle of life. But later it was adapted somewhat to the form motive of the culture religion. Moira is related to *meros*, a word that means "part" or "share." Among the Olympian gods *Moira* became the fate that assigned to each of the three most important deities a "share" or realm: the heavens to Zeus, the sea to Poseidon, and the underworld to Hades (Pluto). This already implied something of design instead of blind fate. *Moira* actually became a principle of order. Its order, however, did not originate with the Olympian gods but with an older, impersonal, and formless divine power. Thus *Moira* still revealed its original dark and sinister self when it decreed the fate of death upon mortals. Even Zeus, lord of Olympus, father of gods and human beings, was powerless before *Moira* (although sometimes Homer designated Zeus as the dispenser of fate). *Moira*, the fate that held death for all the individual forms of life, was incalculable, blind, but nonetheless irresistible.

At this point, where both religions united in the theme of *Moira*, the culture religion revealed an indissoluble, dialectical coherence with the religions of nature. The religion of culture is inexplicable without the background of the nature religions. With intrinsic necessity, the ground-motive of the culture religion called forth its counterpart. *Moira* was the expression of the irreconcilable conflict between both religions. In the religious consciousness of the Greeks this conflict was the unsolved puzzle standing at

THE GROUND-MOTIVE OF GREEK CULTURE

the center of both tragedy and philosophy. Likewise, the religions of nature continued to be the threatening antipode to the Greek cultural and political ideal.

We have seen that the new culture religion of Olympus and the poetic teachings regarding the origin of the gods sought to reconcile the antithetical motives of the older religions of nature and the newer religion of culture. These attempts failed for at least three reasons, the first of which is decisive.

1. The newer culture religion neglected the most profound questions of life and death. The Olympian gods protected humans only as long as they were healthy and vigorously alive. But as soon as dark *Anangke* or *Moira*, before whom even the great Zeus was impotent, willed the fate of a mortal's death, the gods retreated. Death is a thing that comes to all alike. Not even the gods can fend it away from a person they love, when once the destructive doom [*Moira*] of levelling death has fastened upon him.[3]

2. The Olympian culture religion, given mythological form by Homer, came into conflict with the moral standards of the Greeks. Even though the Olympian gods sanctioned and protected Greek morality, the Olympians themselves lived beyond good and evil. They fornicated and thieved. Homer glorified deception as long as it expressed the grand manner of the gods.

3. The whole splendid array of deities was far too removed from ordinary people. The Homeric world of the gods suited Greek civilization only during its feudal era, when the relation between Zeus and the others served as a perfect analogy to that of a lord and his powerful vassals. But

---

3. Homer, *The Odyssey of Homer*, trans. and intro. Richmond Lattimore (New York: Harper & Row, 1965), 3:236–238.

after feudalism had run its course, the divine world lost all contact with the cross section of the people. Thereafter it found support only in the historically formative Greek *polis*, the bearer of culture. The critical years of transition between Mycenian feudalism and the Persian wars marked a religious crisis. The Greek city-states withstood the ordeal brilliantly. Nilsson, the well-known scholar of Greek religion, characterized this crisis as a conflict between an ecstatic (mythical) movement and a legalistic movement.[4] The first revived and reformed the old suppressed religions, and the second, finding its typical representative in the poet-theologian Hesiod, stood on the side of the Olympian culture religion.

In light of these circumstances, it is understandable that the Greeks observed the ancient rites of nature religions in private but worshipped the Olympians as the official gods of the state in public. This also explains why the deeper religious drives of the people became oriented to "mystery worship," for in this worship the questions of life and death were central. Hence it is not surprising that the culture religion in its Homeric form began to lose its strength already in the sixth century B.C. Criticism against it grew more and more outspoken in intellectual circles, and the Sophists, the Greek "enlightenment" thinkers of the fifth century, enjoyed relative popularity, although there was a reaction against them in the legal trials dealing with "atheism."

---

4. Most likely, Dooyeweerd is referring to chapter 6 ("Legalism and Mysticism") of Martin P. Nilsson's classic book *A History of Greek Religion*, 2nd ed., trans. F. J. Fielden (New York: W. W. Norton & Company, 1964). The book first appeared in 1925.

3

Dooyeweerd on The Medieval Ground-Motive of Nature and Grace[1]

We have demonstrated in an earlier context how the matter motive served as the spiritual motive power in the older religions of nature. The religions deified the eternal flux of life as it originated from "mother earth." This stream of life was impersonal and without any form. Whatever was born from it in an individual form and shape was doomed to decline, in order to allow the cyclic movement of birth, maturation, passing away, and rebirth to continue in the whole of "nature" without interruption. This autonomous process of near-mechanical births is not governed by any rational calculable order, since it is controlled by blind fate, by the dreadful *Anangkē*.

As we have seen, the form motive, by contrast, finds its origin in the younger culture religion of the Greeks, which deified the cultural powers of Greek society. Since this motive oriented itself to the cultural aspect of temporal reality (which is characterized by the shaping of a given material according to a free rational design), these deities became the gods of form, measure, and harmony.

---

1. Passages selected from H. Dooyeweerd, *Roots of Western Culture, Pagan, Secular and Christian Options*, Collected Works of Herman Dooyeweerd, Series B, vol. 15, General Editor D. F. M. Strauss (Grand Rapids, MI: Paideia Press, 2012), 111–120.

They left "mother earth" from whose womb the eternally flowing stream of life originates. They acquired their seat on the mountain of Olympus where they were raised to become radiant form gods with a super-sensory (invisible) form and shape, elevated above the fate of mortals, free from all influences of the earthly matter principle. But then, as mere culture gods, they did not have any power over the fate of mortals. The matter motive of the older religion of life remains the opposing power directed against the form motive.

The ground-motive which governed the entire Greek world of ideas thus exhibited two faces which, as it were, looked at each other with hostility. The *matter motive* had its foundation in the deification and absolutization of organic development (the biotic aspect of life of created reality); the *form motive*, by contrast, had its foundation in a deification of the *cultural aspect* of created reality, in a deification of human culture.

. . .

In the Hellenistic period it was not difficult to combine the Greek ground-motive with the dualistic ground-motives of the near-eastern religions with which the Greeks had already made acquaintance. The ground-motive of the Persian Zoroastrian religion consisted of a battle between a divine principle of light and an evil principle of darkness. Thus one could easily identify the Greek form motive with the Zoroastrian motive of light and the Greek matter motive with the evil principle of darkness.

The Temptation of Dualism
. . .Under the influence of the Greek and near-eastern dualism, the unbreakable unity of the ground-motive of the Divine Word-revelation, that of creation, fall, and redemption through Christ Jesus and the communion of the Holy Spirit, was broken apart. A schism was introduced between creation and redemption, between the God of the Old Testament and the God of the New

Testament. In the spirit of Greek philosophy, the speculative theoretical knowledge of God, the *gnosis*, was elevated above the faith of the Christian congregation. . . .

Particularly through maintaining the unbreakable unity of the Old and the New Testament, the Christian church during this period managed under God's guidance to conquer the religious dualism accompanying this gnosticism in its attempt to create a split between creation and redemption. Yet, we shall see how the Greek ground-motive in a hidden way continued to exert its influence within Christian thinking.

. . . The Greek church fathers in particular conceived of creation as being the result of the divine activity of giving form to matter. Therefore, since they could not consider matter itself to be divine, they did not want to fully acknowledge that the Word, through which all things were created and which became flesh in Jesus Christ, is synonymous with God. Accordingly, they degraded the Word (the *Logos*) to a "demigod" who, as "mediator" of creation, stood between God and creature. In this context, the speculative theoretical knowledge of God, elaborated in a philosophical theology, was positioned above the faith of the church community. . . . Even after the Christian church established the doctrine of the Trinity the influence of the Greek religious ground motive continued in the thought of the church fathers.

Augustine

. . . However, they failed to see that because of its radical character the ground-motive of the Christian religion demands an inner reformation of one's scientific view of the world-order and of temporal life. Instead of *reformation* they sought *accommodation*; they sought to adapt pagan thought to the divine Word revelation.

This adaptation laid the basis for *scholasticism*. Scholasticism seeks a *synthesis* between Greek thought and the Christian religion. It was thought that such a synthesis could be successfully achieved if philosophy, with its Greek basis, were to be made subservient to Christian theology.

... As for Augustine, he merely replaced this Greek notion of "philosophical theology" with Christian theology, as the scientific theory concerning Christian doctrines. ... Similarly, he conceived of the relation between the "soul" and the "body" within the framework of the Greek ground-motive. For him the soul was an immortal substance characterized by the faculty of theoretical thought. The body was but a "material vehicle" of the rational soul. The divine revelation of the religious root-unity of human existence was thus again undermined by Greek dualism.

The Roman Catholic Ground-Motive

The effort to bridge the foundations of the Christian religion and Greek thought had to lead over time to the further attempt to find a deeper reconciliation between their respective religious ground-motives. During the Middle Ages, when the church of Rome gradually gained control over all of temporal society, this attempted religious synthesis produced a new dialectical ground-motive in the development of western culture: the well-known motive of "nature and grace" (nature and supernature).

... Thomas Aquinas, for example, viewed "nature" as the independent "stepping-stone to grace," the substructure of a Christian superstructure. He construed the mutual relation between these antithetical motives in Greek fashion, understanding it as a relation between "matter" and "form." He believed that nature is but material for a higher form of perfection infused into it by grace. In other words, the Redeemer works in the manner of a sculptor who shapes his material into a new form.

... However, neither the matter *principle* (the principle of endless becoming and decay) nor the pure *principle* of form (the principle of perfection) were created. Thomas held that they are the two metaphysical principles of all perishable existence. As to their origin, Thomas was silent.

Thomas also maintained that the principle of matter was the principle of imperfection, arguing that what "comes into being" is still imperfect. But how it is possible that a principle of imperfection finds its origin in God? Conversely, he continually called the "thinking soul," the "rational form" of human nature, "divine." He never referred to matter as divine. Clearly, the Greek form-matter motive led to a dualism in Thomas's conception of the creation, a dualism reinforced by the contrast between nature and supernature. Unintentionally, Thomas allowed the Greek form-matter motive to overpower the creation motive of the Christian religion. Although he did acknowledge God as the "first cause" and the "ultimate goal" of nature, he divided the creation order into a natural and supranatural realm. And his view of the "natural order" stemmed from Aristotle.

. . . Thomas employed the Aristotelian idea of God in his "natural theology." This idea was the product not of purely intellectual reasoning but of the religious ground-motive of Greek thought. The various "proofs" for the existence of God, which Thomas developed in Aristotle's footsteps, stand or fall with one's acceptance of both the form-matter ground-motive and the religious priority Aristotle attached to the form motive of Greek culture religion. For Aristotle, God was pure form that stood completely apart from matter. This divine form was "pure thought" itself. Aristotle did not grant matter, the principle of the eternal stream of life, a divine status, for to him matter represented the principle of imperfection.[2]

---

2. Dooyeweerd analyzes this development further in *Roots of Western Culture*, 120–147.

4

The Rise of the Ground-Motive of Nature and Freedom[1]

ROOTED IN THE ground-motive of nature and grace, ecclesiastically unified culture began to disintegrate. In short, numerous indications pointed clearly to the dawning of a new age.

In this critical period a movement arose within late-medieval scholasticism that fractured the church's artificial synthesis between the Greek view of nature and the Christian religion. This proved to be of decisive significance for the modern period. Denying any point of contact between nature and grace, this movement exposed the deep rift between the Christian religion and the Greek view of nature. Western culture seemed presented with two options: it could either pursue the "natural" direction which ultimately would lead to a complete emancipation of a person from the faith of the church, or return to the pure ground-motive of Scripture, namely, creation, fall, and redemption through Jesus Christ. The Renaissance movement, the early forerunner of humanism, followed the first path; with varying consistency, the Reformation followed the second.

The Renaissance was basically concerned with a "rebirth" of humankind in an exclusively natural sense. The "new age" that

---

1. Extracts from H. Dooyeweerd, *Roots of Western Culture, Pagan, Secular and Christian Options*, Collected Works of Herman Dooyeweerd, Series B, vol. 15, General Editor D. F. M. Strauss (Grand Rapids, MI: Paideia Press, 2012), 149-152.

dawned required a "new people" who would take their fate into their own hands and would no longer be faithfully devoted to the authorities. This is the ideal of the *risorgimento*, the ideal of rebirth in the sense of the Renaissance. Rebirth was to occur through a revitalized participation in Greco-Roman culture, freed from the damage it had incurred in its accommodation to Christianity. But the Renaissance did not return to the original Greek religious ground-motive. The deepest religious root of the Renaissance movement was the humanistic religion of human personality in its freedom (from every faith that claims allegiance) and in its autonomy (that is, the pretension that human personality is a law unto itself).

From the beginning the Renaissance revealed the inevitable conflicts between the Christian religion and the natural religion of human personality. For instance, the Italian Niccolo Machiavelli [1469-1527] was a fierce adversary of Christianity. The Christian message that one should love one's enemy contradicted human virtu, human initiative and heroism. Virtu expressed the ideal of the heroic Renaissance person who could make Fortuna, blind fortune, serve his or her own ends.

However, humanism did not reveal itself in its first representatives in terms of these anti-Christian tendencies. Men like Erasmus [1466-1536], Rodolphus Agricola [1443 or 1444-1485], and Hugo Grotius [1583-1645] represented a "biblical humanism"; along with their admiration for the Greek and Roman classics they also pleaded for a free study and exegesis of Scripture. They certainly did not attack the abiding doctrines of the Christian faith. To all appearances their sharp criticism of medieval scholasticism was intended as a return to the simple teachings of the gospel, and they greatly admired the church fathers, many of whom, after all, had also been steeped in classical culture.

But a more careful examination reveals that the real spiritual force behind "biblical humanism" was not the ground-motive of

THE GROUND-MOTIVE OF NATURE AND FREEDOM

the Christian religion. The biblical humanists viewed the Christian religion more as a moral code than as the revealed path of salvation for a human race lost in sin and spiritual death. Already among them the dignity of human personality stood at the center of religious attention. When Erasmus, who remained a Roman Catholic, defended the moral freedom of the human will against Luther, his civilized and dispassionate argument must have compared favorably with Luther's heated prose which expressed the basic convictions of the latter's faith. But Erasmus lacked the profound Christian earnestness that moved the German Reformer. Humanism began to reveal its true intentions even before its emancipation from the authority of Scripture was complete.

The new motive of freedom was inseparably linked to a new view of nature. As we saw earlier, in the Greek view of human nature the mysterious matter motive with its stress on inexorable fate had been the continuous and tragic counter-force to the optimistic form motive which emphasized the good and the beautiful in the cosmos. Likewise, the scriptural view of reality, which contained the teaching of a radical fall, cut off any superficial optimism about nature at the root. But humanism approached nature from a completely different frame of mind. Already the early Renaissance detached its conception of nature from both the Greek idea of fate and the Christian doctrine of radical depravity. Proudly conscious of its autonomy and freedom, modern humankind saw "nature" as an expansive arena for the explorations of its free personality, as a field of infinite possibilities in which the sovereignty of human personality must be revealed by a complete mastery of the phenomena of nature.

Copernicus's discovery of the earth's dual motion – around its own axis and around the sun – revolutionized the traditional Aristotelian and Ptolemaic picture of the world, which viewed the earth as the fixed center of the universe. Unjustifiably, the church continued to defend the old conception for many years, considering the centrality of the world in the history of salvation indispensable to the faith. In view of this, humanism proclaimed the Copernican world view as a new kind of gospel, turning against the authority of the church and scholasticism with revolutionary passion. When Galileo and Newton later laid the foundations for mathematical physics, thereby demonstrating that one could indeed control nature by discovering the fixed laws to which moving things are subject, humanism, driven by its religious personality ideal, embraced the new scientific method and elevated it to a science ideal that should be accepted as the directive in every area of science; an ideal that pretended to disclose the true coherence of the whole of reality.

The religious motive of the absolute freedom and autonomy of human personality did not permit scientific thought to proceed from a given creation order. The creation motive of the Christian religion gave way to faith in the creative power of scientific thought which seeks its ground of certainty only within itself. With this change, the idea of the autonomy of science was given a completely different meaning from that of Thomistic scholasticism. Although Thomas Aquinas had also taught that natural reason is autonomous with respect to the Christian faith and divine revelation, his position was wholly embedded in the Roman Catholic ground-motive of nature and grace. Nature was merely the preamble to grace, and natural reason itself was brought to a higher stage of perfection by the supernatural gift of grace. As long as reason operates in a purely scientific manner, it can never lead to conclusions in the area of natural knowledge that conflict with the supranatural means of revelation. If seeming conflicts do arise, they are attributed to logical errors of thought, as Thomas promptly points out. Wherever Thomas followed Aristotle's Greek view of nature, his idea of the autonomy of natural reason continually led him to adapt Aristotelian theory to Roman Catholic doctrine.

But the humanistic approach was very different. Humanism was controlled not by the Roman Catholic ground-motive of nature and grace but by the modern motive of nature and freedom. Faith in the absolute autonomy of free personality could not tolerate a distinction between natural and supranatural truths. It could not endorse the Roman Catholic adaptation of autonomously discovered natural truths to the authoritatively binding teachings of the church.

By the same token, humanism also broke with the Greek view that the order of reality is anchored in an invisible world of forms. The humanistic science ideal could not possibly subscribe to the Greek "forms" which for Aristotle constituted the essence of perishable things. The Greek form-matter motive communicated nothing to a modern person. For in that motive, the contemplative reflection of a "beautiful world of forms" which brings measure and harmony to chaotic "matter" was but idle speculation. After all, the driving force of modern humankind's scientific research was the ideal of complete mastery of nature by means of which the autonomous freedom of human personality – that is, its independence from supranatural powers – could be revealed.

It would soon be clear, however, that the new nature motive stood in religious conflict with the humanistic freedom motive, a conflict similar to the tension within the Greek motive of form and matter and the Roman Catholic motive of nature and grace.

5

The Internal Tension Present in the Ground-Motive of Nature and Freedom[1]

Dialectical Tensions

THE RELIGIOUS ground-motive of humanism is just as internally divided as the Greek and Roman Catholic ground-motives were. It too bears a so-called dialectical character; that is, it consists of two religious motives which are in inner conflict with each other and which alternately drive the stance and world view of humanism from one pole to the other.

In essence, the nature motive of modern humanism is a motive of control. The control motive is intensely and religiously tied to the new freedom motive which originated in the humanistic religion of personality, the cult of autonomous humankind which desires to make itself absolutely independent of every authority and of every "supranatural power" in order to take its fate into its own hands. Like Copernicus, who brought about a revolution in the traditional picture of the universe with the earth at its center, so humanism brought about a revolution in the religious valuation of human personality. In the humanistic conception, this personality is the measure of all things, including religion. As the great philosopher Immanuel Kant declared near the end of the

---

1. Extracts from H. Dooyeweerd, *Roots of Western Culture, Pagan, Secular and Christian Options*, Collected Works of Herman Dooyeweerd, Series B, vol. 15, General Editor D. F. M. Strauss (Grand Rapids, MI: Paideia Press, 2012), 152-156.

eighteenth century (in the preface to the first edition of his *Critique of Pure Reason*):

> Our age is, in a special degree, the age of criticism, and to criticism everything must submit. Religion through its sanctity, and law-giving through its majesty, may seek to exempt themselves from it. But they then awaken the just suspicion, and cannot claim the sincere respect which reason accords only to that which has been able to sustain the test of free and open examination.[2]

When the motive of control arose out of the new religion of personality (with its motive of freedom), the conflict between "nature" and "freedom" soon began to reveal itself. For the control motive of autonomous humanity aims at subjecting "nature" and all of its unlimited possibilities to humankind by means of the new method of mathematical science. Nowhere in reality does it tolerate the validity of limits to the operation of the natural-scientific method. The motive of control thus expressed itself in the new science ideal which sought to grasp all of reality in a closed chain of cause and effect, a chain determined by the universal laws of mechanical motion. It will not accept the validity of anything as "truly real" if it does not fit into this chain of mechanical cause and effect. The firm ground of theoretical inquiry lies neither in a divine creation order nor in a realm of the eternal forms of being, as the Greek philosophers thought. The humanistic freedom motive sanctioned no other basis for theoretical thought than mathematical natural-scientific thinking itself. There was a profound conviction that the certainty of mathematics lay within mathematics itself with its exact methods of proof. Autonomous humankind trusts the certainty of its thought and depends on it.

But it was precisely when the new science ideal was taken seriously that a problem presented itself. It became apparent that when science determined all of reality as an uninterrupted chain

---

2. I. Kant, *Critique of Pure Reason*, trans. Norman Kemp Smith (New York: St. Martin's Press, 1965), 9.

of cause and effect, there would no longer be room anywhere in that reality for human freedom. Human willing, thinking, and acting required the same mechanical explanation as did the motions of a machine. For if the human person itself belongs to nature, then it cannot possibly be free and autonomous. "Nature" and "freedom," science ideal and personality ideal, turned out to oppose each other as declared enemies. A genuinely inner reconciliation between these antagonistic motives was impossible, since both were religious and thus absolute. Although the freedom motive had evoked the new motive of nature, each motive excluded the other. Humanism had no choice but to assign religious priority or primacy to one or the other.

Humanism's self-conscious point of departure during the first period of its development (dating from the sixteenth to the seventeenth and the greater part of the eighteenth centuries) was the primacy of the new science ideal. Humanism believed that science would make modern humankind truly free and would raise it above the dogmatic prejudices of church doctrine. Science would bring true enlightenment that could oust pagan barbarism and the dark realm of medieval superstition. True freedom was sought where the foundation of modern science had been found – in autonomous, lucid, and distinguishing thought.

. . .

But again, it was here that obstacles arose. Did not the new science ideal require that thinking itself be explained in terms of the mechanism of the soul's motions? Indeed – at least if this science ideal with its new nature motive would be consistently applied. But already here some humanistic thinkers raised objections. The motive of freedom required that at least mathematical thought, the core and center of free personality, be exempt from natural-scientific explanation.

Descartes and Hobbes

Along these lines the founder of humanistic philosophy, the famous Frenchman René Descartes [1596–1650], drew a firm line between the bodily or material world and the human soul. Descartes limited "nature" to the material world. In this world the new science ideal reigned supreme; here it could explain all phenomena mechanistically. But the "human soul" was considered independent of the "natural body" as a substance or as a self-sufficient entity which depends on nothing outside of itself for its existence.

. . .

Thus, in conformity with the dualistic motive of nature and freedom, Descartes split human existence into two rigorously separated parts: the material body and the thinking soul. The ultimate ground of scientific certitude and, for that matter, of moral freedom, lay in consciousness, in the "I think."

But Descartes did not succeed in consistently maintaining this strict division between material reality and the thinking soul. Under the leadership of the famous Englishman Thomas Hobbes [1588-1679], another stream of humanistic thought directed itself against Descartes's dualistic view of reality which limited the nature motive in favor of the freedom motive.

. . .

But in contrast to Descartes, Hobbes did not call a halt to the application of the new science ideal to what was believed to be the seat of human freedom, namely, autonomous thought and free will. Well versed in the new natural-scientific method of the great Italian scientist Galileo, with whom he had made personal contact during his travels, Hobbes aimed at applying Galileo's method consistently, utilizing it in the areas of morality, law, political life, and even the motions of the human soul.

. . .

THE INTERNAL TENSION IN NATURE AND FREEDOM

In Hobbes's opinion this exact method provided the key to explaining all of reality. For this reason he could not acknowledge a boundary between "body" and "soul." He reduced everything – including mathematical thinking – to the motions of material things. . . . Scientific integrity demanded that mathematical concepts themselves be understood as products of the mechanical motions of the soul, motions caused by the impressions of bodies in one's psychical life. Clearly, then, the nature motive was dominant in Hobbes. And yet his vision that only the new science would chart the way toward human freedom testified to his solidarity with Descartes.

. . .

Before the humanistic concept of natural laws could arise, it was necessary that the modern view of nature be discovered; "nature" needed liberation from both the Greek idea of fate and the Christian idea of the fall into sin. "Nature" had to be deprived of its "soul" before it could be subjected to human control.

We see, then, that humanism entangled itself in the dialectic of its own ground-motive already at its first stormy appearance. Nature and freedom soon began to reveal their inherent conflict as religious motives. The first philosophical conflict between Descartes and Hobbes pointed towards the further development of this dialectic. At this stage, however, humanism still had the vitality of its youth. It was aware that the future of the West lay in its hands. Gradually, both Roman Catholicism and the Reformation were forced onto the defensive, surrendering more and more of western culture to humanism. The sun of humanism was rising, and an optimistic faith in humanity's creative power inspired its leading figures.

Humanism has human-ized the Christian ground-motive of creation, fall, and redemption within its own ground-motive. Hence humanism is not a paganism; it passed through Christianity which it changed into a religion of human personality. Soon it also assimilated the ground-motives of Greek culture and Roman Catholicism.

6

The Significance of Dooyeweerd's Philosophy for Understanding the Foundational Role of Worldview

by Michael W. Goheen

The Urgency of Christian Scholarship

THERE IS A spiritual battle in the powerful cultural arena of scholarship. Years ago, as I took a university post to teach worldview, I was moved by Herman Dooyeweerd's essay *The Secularization of Science*. He describes secular science as one of the dominant religious and formative powers of Western culture: "science, secularized and isolated, has become a satanic power, an idol which dominates all of culture" with the capability to "wither the seed of the gospel." The spirit of secularization must be exposed as idolatrous, and the messianic pretensions of science unmasked for the good of humanity. I resonated then and still do with his clarion call to join the Christian academic "vocation to war against the spirit of apostasy."[1]

To engage secular science with the gospel, Dooyeweerd believes, we need a systematic philosophy shaped by biblical faith to function as a comprehensive framework to serve all academic disciplines. If this is to be achieved the central core of the Christian faith must be elaborated in a biblical worldview as a foundation for philosophy.

---

1. H. Dooyeweerd, *The Secularization of Science* (Jordan Station, ON: Paideia Press, 2020), 1-3. Science here refers to all academic disciplines.

Worldview in the Neocalvinist Tradition

Dooyeweerd's philosophical project is part of the bigger story of Dutch neocalvinism. Neocalvinism is not simply the recovery of 16th century Calvinist theology but emerged in the context of the growing hegemony of Enlightenment humanism in European life.[2] The Enlightenment marks the conversion of a whole civilisation to a new faith. This secular humanist faith reached its pinnacle during the late 19th century subjugating the public life of Europe to its control. Christ and his church were relegated to the private realm and stripped of cultural power. Neocalvinism arose in response to this reduction of and threat to the Christian faith.

Thus, neocalvinism from its outset was moulded by the conviction that every aspect of cultural life must be brought under the Lordship of Christ. The gospel is not a message of individual salvation but of the comprehensive restoration of God's rule. The church is not a private religious community but the new humanity who exercises cultural power through ordinary Christians in their vocations.

The only defence against the formidable Enlightenment tide was to recover a robust understanding of the Christian faith capable of matching modernism's scope and power, capable of equipping Christians for faithful involvement in the public square. Kuyper seized the term 'worldview' from German philosophy for this task.

The core of the Christian faith is the comprehensive restoration of the good creation from the creation-wide effects of sin through Jesus Christ and by the Spirit. What is striking about this definition is the comprehensive scope of each key term: the *whole of reality* is God's creation, is distorted by sin, and is being restored

---

2. I speak simply of "humanism" meaning "secular humanism" in its various forms such as liberalism or socialism. Abraham Kuyper used the term "modernism" to refer to the liberal form of humanism dominant in nineteenth century Netherlands.

to its original goodness. To engage any part of culture one must take account of the created design, the distorting impact of sin, and the possibility of renewal even in the present. This all-encompassing worldview offers an alternative to reigning humanism as a basis for cultural involvement. Dooyeweerd embraced this confessional tradition and worked out its insights for scholarship.

Elaborating a Biblical Worldview

The essential core of the Christian faith must be elaborated to provide a foundation for scholarship. This core can be summarized as "creation, fall, and redemption through Jesus Christ in the communion of the Holy Spirit."[3] This is not first doctrine or worldview but a spiritual power renewing the core of our being. Yet to be serviceable for Christian philosophy its content must be elaborated in a worldview.

In *creation* God creates and orders his world by his law-word so it is like a symphony manifesting a diversity of sounds and a coherent harmony. He creates humanity in his image as religious beings to respond obediently to the all-embracing reign of his law. He mandates his human creatures to disclose the potential he has enclosed in the creation to form a civilisation in service of love for God and humanity. The human heart is the unifying religious centre out of which flows cultural formation. Humanity is created as a spiritual community animated by a religious spirit that shapes the whole culture as its central power. In the beginning this was God's Spirit.

In the wake of human *sin*, relationships to God, humanity, and the world are ruptured. Fallen humanity remains religious but now misdirects life toward idolatry. God's law continues to order the creation and cultural development remains, but now human society is animated and distorted by a different spirit – the spirit

---

3. H. Dooyeweerd, *Roots of Western Culture: Pagan, Secular, and Christian Options* (Toronto: Wedge Publishing, 1979), 28.

of apostasy. Nevertheless, in the story of *redemption* God comes in Jesus Christ, who dies, rises again, and gives his Spirit to redirect the human heart back to God. God's work of restoration embraces his entire creation and the entirety of human life. Until God completes his restoration when Christ returns there remains a battle for the whole creation between the spiritual power of two kingdoms: God and Satan. The church is the new humankind who shares in God's kingdom, who is animated again by his Spirit, who offers total allegiance to Christ, and who align themselves with God in this spiritual battle.

Thus, there remains an unrelenting struggle between the kingdoms of God and of darkness for all human culture. At the same time God continues to uphold his creation order and humanity as his image-bearers and culture-makers, thereby curbing the full destructive effects of sin. This common grace, rooted in the work of Jesus Christ (Col 1:15-20), allows for much good, truth, and justice to shine in the world.

This biblical worldview embraces the entirety of the world. It functions as a solid foundation for cultural engagement and equips God's people for their task by providing a lens to view public life. All cultural products and institutions manifest something of the creational *structure* of God's enduring law as well as the *misdirection* of sin and cultural idolatry. In his work of redemption God's renewing power is *redirecting* it all back to God and its original design. Every part of human culture thus displays both God's creational structure and sinful misdirection, inviting obedient action toward its redirection.

Biblical Worldview for Christian Scholarship

This elaboration of the Christian faith guides Dooyeweerd as he erects a structure of Christian scholarship with the following characteristics. First, Christian scholarship needs a systematic philosophy[4] guided by biblical faith that serves as a comprehensive theoretical framework capable of providing rich resources for Christian scholarship within the various scientific disciplines. He rejects the label 'Calvinist' and instead describes his philosophy as 'Christian' because it is based on the gospel which all Christians share.

Second, Christian scholarship is thus internally shaped by Scripture without falling into the prevalent dangers of biblicism or dualism. Biblicism rightly wants the Bible to function internally within scholarship but makes simplistic hermeneutical moves that do not respect the proper nature of Scripture. Dualism allows secular scholarship to flourish as it reduces the comprehensive authority of Scripture to a spiritual or theological sphere alongside other disciplines. Contrary to both, this approach allows for the inner renewal of the disciplines by the gospel in harmony with Scripture's true nature.

Third, this approach creates the possibility for critical dialogue across philosophical traditions. Christians must be engaged in the shared task of scholarship if the gospel is to have its renewing effect. An elaboration of a comprehensive philosophy internally integrated with the Christian faith equips academics to sustain rigorous communication with those from other religious orientations. In an encounter with non-Christian scholarship this comprehensive vision provides resources for identifying and critiquing other religious visions at work as well as appreciating and embracing their insights. There will be an antithetical encounter with faith commitments at a religious depth level but also an affirmation of valid insights contained in their accounts of the creation order. The task of Christian scholarship thus recognizes all creational insights, liberates them from their idolatrous framework, and relocates them within a theoretical structure shaped by Scripture.

---

4. This is Dooyeweerd's primary contribution, to be elaborated in the rest of this volume.

Conclusion

We cannot "battle this spirit in our own power" but only "in the power of the Holy Spirit" rooted in "a life of prayer."[5] The battle will not be won by worldview or Christian scholarship alone. Yet, rooted in prayer, faithful scholarship may be an important weapon in the hands of the Spirit for the cosmic battle that wages for every inch of human life.

---

5. Dooyeweerd, *Secularization of Science*, 3.

7

Dooyeweerd and Radical Orthodoxy

by Danie F. M. Strauss

A KEY CONCEPT IN THE Christology of Milbank is *methexis* (participation/sharing). It derives from Plato's theory of ideas where it is employed alongside the notions of *parousia* (presence) and *koinonia* (communion) as applied to the *eidè*, which have an existence in themselves. Milbank explains that the central theological framework of radical orthodoxy is found in the notion of "participation" as "developed by Plato and reworked by Christianity."[1]

In his work on *Radical Orthodoxy*, Smith (2004) introduces this movement as "post-secular". This qualification reveals crucial shared concerns operative in the circles of *Radical Orthodoxy* (RO) as well as within *Reformational Philosophy* (RP). One of these concerns is their rejection of the dogma of the *autonomy of reason*.

Transcending the "Modern Bastard Dualisms of Faith and Reason, Grace and Nature"

Milbank[2] investigates the theological critique of Hamann, Jacobi, Wizenmann and Herder – "of philosophy construed as the autonomy of reason". In the *Introduction to Radical Orthodoxy*, Milbank

---

1. J. Milbank, C. Pickstock & G. Ward, eds., *Radical Orthodoxy* (New York: Routledge, 2006), 3.
2. J. Milbank, "The theological critique of philosophy in Hamann and Jacobi," in *Radical orthodoxy*, eds. J. Milbank, C. Pickstock & G. Ward (New York: Routledge, 2006), 22.

et al.[3] explains that the essays compiled in this volume attempt "to reclaim the world by situating its concerns and activities within a theological framework". Speaking theologically should display "a theological *difference*" while mingling "exegesis, cultural reflection and philosophy in a complex but coherently executed collage." Therefore, they distance themselves from the inclination of Barthianism which assumes "a positive autonomy for theology, which rendered philosophical concerns a matter of indifference." They remark that *nouvelle théologie* is exceeded by radical orthodoxy that "wishes to reach further [by] recovering and extending a fully Christianised ontology and practical philosophy consonant with authentic Christian doctrine."

The term 'orthodox' is understood "in the most straightforward sense of commitment to creedal Christianity and the exemplarity of its patristic matrix." The term 'radical' indicates a "return to patristic and medieval roots, and especially to the Augustinian vision of all knowledge as divine illumination, [thus transcending] the modern bastard dualisms of faith and reason, grace and nature." While realising that the tradition should be reconsidered, this orientation intends to deploy its vision by systematically engaging in a critique of "modern society, culture, politics, art, science and philosophy."[4]

This shows that *Radical Orthodoxy* advocates an integral (in the sense of all-encompassing) view of creation which rejects the idea that any sphere or realm of creation may be withdrawn from the *gift* which creation is. In this view, Christian theology does not surrender to an "alien Hellenistic theme" because it does realize that "for Greek philosophy there was an uncreated material residue that was not created, and so not a gift, and which therefore limited the sway of *methexis*."[5] Does an integral view of creation

---

3. Milbank et al., *Radical Orthodoxy*, 1.
4. Milbank et al., *Radical Orthodoxy*, 2.
5. J. Milbank, *Being Reconciled, Ontology and Pardon (Radical Orthodoxy)*.

challenge the distinction between philosophy and theology?

Milbank complains that it was Duns Scotus who *for the first time* established a radical separation of philosophy from theology by declaring that it was possible to consider being in abstraction from the question of whether one is considering created or creating being. Eventually this generated the notion of an ontology and an epistemology unconstrained by, and transcendentally prior to, theology.[6]

This conviction already reveals a key element of the way in which Milbank understands theology.

Philosophy and Theology

In his *Foreword* to Smith's work on *Radical Orthodoxy*,[7] Milbank elaborates on his understanding of philosophy and theology. He understands philosophy as "the coordination of all merely natural enquiries."[8] He also states that "being" is the "'object' of philosophy."[9] In addition, he mentions that he finds "Kuyper's understanding of theology . . . bizarre and inadequate". In the context of the "best Catholic tradition," theology for *Radical Orthodoxy* cannot be a "specialism" as for "Kuyper and Dooyeweerd." He adds the following significant remark:

> If it were, it would be idolatrous, for theology concerns not one area, not one ontic item among others, but esse as such, the ground of all beings, and all in relation to this ground and source. It follows (and this is one point that Smith fails to grasp) that if the

(London: Routledge, 2003), xi.
6. Milbank et al., *Radical Orthodoxy*, 23.
7. J. K. A. Smith, *Introducing Radical Orthodoxy, Mapping a Post-secular Theology* (Grand Rapids, MI: Baker Academic, 2004).
8. J. Milbank, "Foreword," in *Introducing Radical Orthodoxy, Mapping a Post-secular Theology* by J.K.A. Smith (Grand Rapids, MI: Baker Academic, 2004), 37.
9. Milbank et al., *Radical Orthodoxy*, 37, note 49.

Christian contribution to, say, economics, is always a theological contribution, then this is precisely because even the articulation of faith has, in part, to do with the economic realm and the difference faith makes to our consideration of this realm (think of many of the sayings of Jesus). One does not here need overcomplex divisions among types of theology. For Catholic tradition, every Christian is a theologian, because faith is always somewhat reflective, albeit in the mode of symbol, ritual, and narrative.[10]

In passing we may note that in his work on the subject philosophy of the science of faith, Troost explains the critical position assumed by reformational philosophy in respect of Kuyper's view of theology.[11]

Theology is "the Queen of the Sciences"

In his *Theology and Social Theory*, Milbank remarks that the first eleven chapters of this work are preludes to the assertion that sociology is "a social science". For the "inhabitants of the *altera civitas*, on pilgrimage through this temporary world" theology is "the queen of the sciences."[12]

We have noted that according to Milbank, theology concerns not one area, not one ontic item among others, but *esse* as such, the ground of all beings, and all in relation to this ground and source. In an equally serious tone Dooyeweerd warns that dogmatic theology is a very dangerous science!

Milbank believes that theology will have to provide its own particular, and historically specific faith.[13] It is striking to note that, although the subject "Encyclopedia of Theology" is taught at

10. Milbank, "Foreword," *Introducing radical orthodoxy*, 14.
11. See A. Troost, *Vakfilosofie van de geloofswetenschap, prolegomena van de theologie*, (Budel: Damon, 2004), 384, 386 ff.
12. J. Milbank, *Theology and Social Theory. Beyond Secular Reason* (Oxford: Blackwell, 2006), 382.
13. Milbank, *Theology and Social Theory*, 382.

Faculties of Theology, this discipline does not classify itself as one of the theological subdisciplines! Thus, it acknowledges that the task of defining theology is not theological in nature.

Gratia natura non tollit, sed perficit

According to Milbank, theology saves reason and *fulfils* and *preserves* philosophy, whereas philosophy, left to itself, brings itself, as Heidegger noted, "to its own end."[14]

The first problem is that *both* philosophy and theology are defined as directed at "being". Then it is claimed that philosophy, on its own, inherently leads to aporetic and nihilistic conclusions. This means that, if theology does not perform a saving role, at once *preserving* and *fulfilling* philosophy, philosophy will bring itself to its own end. In fact, this position derives from the classical dualistic view of Thomas Aquinas regarding the relationship between *nature* and *grace*.

This entire mode of thinking goes back to the well-known (nature-grace) statement of Thomas Aquinas captured in the phrase: *gratia naturam non tollit, sed perficit* ("grace does not eliminate nature, but perfects it").[15] "Preserve" is the equivalent of "does not eliminate" whereas *sed perficit* is equivalent to *fulfilling*. Note the similarities between this view of philosophy and what Milbank mentions in the attempt of the *nouvelle théologique* to arrive at a synthesis "between theology and philosophy (understood as the coordination of all merely natural enquiries)."[16] The "merely natural enquiries" remind us of the above-mentioned "philosophy left to itself" and the qualification that "reason *cannot* ground the

---

14. J. Milbank, C. Pickstock & G. Ward, eds., *Radical Orthodoxy* (New York: Routledge, 2006), 37, note 49.
15. See E. Von Hippel, *Geschichte der Staatsphilosophie, Vol. I.* (Meisenheim am Glan: Verlag Anton Hain, 1955), 309.
16. Milbank, "Foreword," *Introducing Radical Orthodoxy*, 13.

attempted purely rational disclosure of being."[17]

Instead of contemplating the distinction between Christian and non-Christian philosophy, Milbank opts for a "theological salvation" of philosophy, which entails that the only way in which philosophy can be Christian would be to "surrender" itself to theology!

Compare Milbank's position with Dooyeweerd's explanation of *Reformed Scholasticism*:

> Reformed Scholasticism always binds the natural light of reason to the light of Scripture. In so doing, moreover, it falls into the same misconception regarding the relationship of theology and philosophy that I pointed out earlier in connection with the great church father [Augustine]. Theology is supposed to take the non-Reformed philosophy of the schools under its wing, in order to accommodate it to orthodox Reformed doctrine and to keep its latent dangerous tendencies under control. It will be very suspicious of a Reformed philosophy that does not bind itself to theology, for it is theology, as the "queen of the sciences" (*regina scientiarum*) [according to *Reformed Scholasticism*], that is supposed to come up with the Scriptural principles to which the other sciences must conform.[18]

Apart from the obvious differences between *Reformed Scholasticism* and *Radical Orthodoxy*, the above quotation highlights remarkable similarities. As long as theology is appreciated as the "queen of the sciences," its scientific character is at least acknowledged. But then the conviction that for the "Catholic tradition, every Christian is a theologian, because faith is always somewhat

---

17. Milbank et al., *Radical Orthodoxy*, 47.
18. H. Dooyeweerd, *In the Twilight of Western Thought. Studies in the Pretended Autonomy of Philosophical Thought*, Collected Works of Herman Dooyeweerd, Series B, vol. 4, General Editor D. F. M. Strauss (Grand Rapids, MI: Paideia Press, 2012), 38.

reflective, albeit in the mode of symbol, ritual, and narrative"[19] becomes highly problematic.

Faith and Theology

The crucial question is whether "faith" could be equated with "theology"? Because having faith entails that we are sure of what we hope for and certain of what we do not see (Heb. 11:1), one cannot replace or identify faith with the calling of being a theologian. Christian faith always incorporates *analysis* (identification and distinguishing) without which "the mode of symbol, ritual, and narrative" cannot function. This remark also applies to *creedal* or *confessional* issues, for an element of reflection or thinking will always be found in *identifying* what is considered to be the appropriate faith *distinctions*. Likewise, in our everyday (non-scientific) experience, anyone involved in legal, economic or cultural practices must also proceed on the basis of *identifying* relevant legal, economic or cultural *distinctions*. But no everyday jural practice, economic endeavour or cultural activity could be transformed into a scholarly discipline, such as the science of law or the science of economics. But if being a Christian cannot be identified with being a theologian solely because "faith is always somewhat reflective" then we first have to *"reflect somewhat"* on the meaning of faith.

The Meaning of Faith

As explained in the Introduction, the theory of modal aspects for the meaning of faith has been subjected to a thorough analysis by the *Philosophy of the Cosmonomic Idea*. These aspects are not only unique, but are also fitted in an inter-modal coherence, exhibiting the scope of the principles of sphere-sovereignty and sphere-universality. According to this theory, every modal (functional) aspect has backward-pointing and forward-pointing analogies reflecting the inter-modal coherence present between them.

---

19. Milbank, "Foreword," *Introducing Radical Orthodoxy*, 14.

An *analogy* entails not only similarities and differences, but also differences evinced in the similarities and vice versa. Consider physical space and mathematical space – which are both *extended*. But whereas mathematical space is both *continuous* and *infinitely divisible*, physical space is *neither* continuous nor infinitely divisible.

In the Introduction these *moments of coherence* are also explained as retrocipatory and anticipatory analogies (retrocipations and anticipations). Identifying a sphere or realm is, therefore, not a "cordoning-off of certain domains – for example the economic" – as Milbank alleges in reaction to Kuyper's idea of sphere-sovereignty.[20] The idea of *enkapsis* embodies an account of the intertwinement of (natural and social) entities, whereas the principle of sphere-universality illustrates the coherence between the various aspects.

For example, *certitudinal integrity* reflects an ethical (retrocipatory) analogy within the faith or fiduciary aspect, whereas *certitudinal vitality*, *sensitivity* and *frugality* reflect biotic, sensitive-psychic and economic analogies within the modal structure of the faith aspect. Anticipatory analogies, pointing from pre-fiduciary aspects towards the certitudinal mode, are, for example, *credit* (economic trust), representing an anticipation from the economic aspect to the faith aspect; an axiom in mathematics (logical certainty – an anticipation from the logical-analytical mode to the certitudinal aspect), and *bona fides* (jural certainty – an anticipation from the legal aspect to the faith aspect).

Perhaps the most basic feature of the ontic dimension of modal aspects is that all concrete (natural and social) entities and processes in principle function within all aspects. This feature is decisive for a proper understanding of the distinctive characteristic of scientific thinking.

Where Derrida affirms that faith is *absolutely universal*, he uses

---

20. Milbank, "Foreword," *Introducing Radical Orthodoxy*, 13.

credit (*economic trust*), a fiduciary anticipation within the economic aspect, as his example.[21]

What Is Theology? Not a Theological Question

The sociologist Peter Berger, briefly discussed by Milbank in his work *Theology and Social Theory*, provides an account approximating the theory of modal aspects and the notion of modal abstraction:

> The sociologist finds his subject matter present in all human activities, but not all aspects of those activities constitute this subject matter. Social interaction is not some specialized sector of what men do with each other. It is rather a certain aspect of all these doings. Another way of putting this is by saying that the sociologist carries a special sort of abstraction.[22]

This argument also requires a reference to two other theologians, namely Popma and Kuitert. Popma comes from the tradition of Reformational Philosophy and Kuitert from a broader Dutch background. Kuitert poses the question: What are the criteria for the discipline of theology in order to be accepted as a science? Then he becomes more specific by stating that, considering the field of investigation of theology leads to the question, from which angle of approach does it approach reality? ["welke is de invalshoek waaronder zij de werkelijkheid benadert?"[23]]

Popma dedicated a monograph to the question what theology is. He opposes the idea that every Christian should be a scholar. Moreover, he is correct in realizing that theology has to orient it-

---

21. J. Derrida, *Deconstruction in a Nutshell, A Conversation with Derrida*, ed. John D. Caputo (New York: Fordham University Press, 1997), 22.
22. P.L. Berger, *Invitation to sociology, a humanistic perspective* (Harmondsworth: Penguin Books, 1982), 39-40.
23. H.M. Kuitert, *Filosofie van de theologie* (Leiden: Marthinus Nijhof, 1988), 18-19.

self to the aspect of faith and "that the question regarding the place of theology is itself not theological in nature."[24] But he is mistaken in his view that the certitudinal aspect as such constitutes the field of investigation of theology.[25]

The crucial point to observe is that the modal structure of an aspect does not as such form the field of investigation of any special science, as it merely provides the various academic disciplines (special sciences) with their distinct angle of approach to all of reality. Therefore, Popma is mistaken in holding that an aspect as such forms the field of investigation of a special science.[26]

Compare the above-mentioned views with Dooyeweerd's perspective on the modal structure of an aspect and the phenomena actually functioning within that structure:

> Every scientific discipline does this when it seeks to investigate empirical reality from a specific point of view. But in this investigation it does not focus its theoretical attention upon the modal structure of such an aspect itself; rather, it focuses on the coherence of the actual phenomena which function within that structure. Where they are grasped only in certain specific, abstract aspects, these phenomena no longer come into view in their integral reality but only in terms of specific modal functions.[27]

Once the special scientific nature of theology is acknowledged without "dividing" reality, it follows that one must always bear in mind that there is a difference between the task of *defining* theology and those who are involved in *doing* theology. When a special scientist identifies a modal aspect as its point of entry (to the *whole*

---

24. K.J. Popma, *De plaats der theologie*. (Franeker: T. Wever, 1946), 12.
25. Popma, *De plaats der theologie*, 13.
26. Popma, *De plaats der theologie*, 13.
27. H. Dooyeweerd, *Christian Philosophy and the Meaning of History*, Series B, vol. 13, Collected Works of Herman Dooyeweerd, General Editor D. F. M.Strauss (Grand Rapids, MI: Paideia Press, 2013), 11.

of reality!), such a scholar must distinguish it from other modal points of entry, which requires a (philosophical) totality view of reality.

Misunderstanding Spheres

Milbank rejects the idea of distinct "spheres":

> RO [*Radical Orthodoxy*] would not subscribe to the rather ahistoricist and static division of human life into distinct 'spheres'. For RO, they are more shifting and contingent, and the question of their validity and their boundaries is more uncertain.[28]

This remark requires a reference both to an article entitled "The best known but least understood part of Dooyeweerd's philosophy"[29] and to the nature of, and criteria for the recognition of a modal aspect.[30]

Milbank's remark that "RO would not subscribe to the rather ahistoricist and static division of human life into distinct 'spheres'" raises several questions. First, the term "ahistoricist" is misplaced – Milbank should have said *a-historical*. Secondly, the suggestion that modal aspects "divide" human life in distinctive *spheres* merely shows that Milbank does not comprehend the meaning of a *modal aspect* and modal abstraction as distinctive features of scholarly thinking. Modal aspects concern the *how*, not the concrete *what* of things. Every aspect is, therefore, a *modus quo*, a *way of existence*, indicating that as *modes of existence* the various aspects do not "divide" anything. The notion of modal aspects merely underscores the *many-sidedness* of human life by identifying and

---

28. Milbank, "Foreword," *Introducing Radical Orthodoxy*, 13.
29. D. F. M. Strauss, "The Best-known but Least Understood part of Dooyeweerd's Philosophy," *Journal for Christian Scholarship* 42, No. 1 & 2 (2006): 61-80.
30. See D. F. M. Strauss, *Philosophy: Discipline of the Disciplines* (Grand Rapids, MI: Paideia Press, 2009), 77-79, where 10 criteria are stipulated.

distinguishing the multiple modes in which human beings (and everything else within the universe) function. (See the chapter on modal universality.)

Clearly, identifying any aspect by distinguishing it from the other aspects of reality does not "divide" "human life" in any way – it solely focuses on an irreducible dimension of human existence and experience, namely the dimension of *modal aspects*. All the aspects of reality form the constant framework within which we experience and know the world.

Are the Aspects *A-historical* and *Static*?

Milbank's objection that the notion of modal law spheres reflects something *a-historical* and *static* reveals another shortcoming in his approach, namely the absence of a meaningful account of the relationship between *constancy* and *change* (see the chapter on identity). In this instance, the basic distinctions flowing from a non-reductionist ontology are required. An integral part of such an ontology is found in Dooyeweerd's theory of modal aspects (briefly explained in the *Introduction*). It opens up the way to investigate within which aspect of reality certain terms "reside", have their "modal seat" or "unique meaning." That the numerical aspect concerns discrete quantity, i.e., our awareness of the *one* and the *many*, entails that these terms have their modal seat within the *arithmetical* aspect. Similarly, the phrase *continuous dimensional extension* (entailing infinite divisibility, connectedness, coherence and, therefore, also the whole-parts relation) reflects the core meaning of the aspect of space. The term *constancy* captures the *kinematic* meaning of *uniform rectilinear motion*.

When theologians and philosophers struggle with the problem of relativity, they easily forget that every emphasis on *change* is always accompanied by an underlying element of *constancy*. Consider the well-known statement: things are *constantly changing*.

Traditionally, the substance concept incorporated the intimate connection between constancy and change. In the second edition of his *Critique of pure reason*, Kant states: "amidst all changes within the world substance persists, only its properties change."[31] Kant also refers to the *law of the continuity of all change* ("das Gesetz der Kontinuität aller Veränderung").[32]

The Impasse of Historicism

However, when historicism emphasizes change at the cost of constancy, it generates an antinomy, which is clear in the following contradictory implications. If everything *is* history (historical change), then there is nothing left that can *have* a history. Only what itself *is* not history can *have* a history. The only option left to the idea of "everything is history" is the equally problematic and self-contradictory construction of "a history of a history."

The objection raised by Milbank against the idea of law-spheres also claims that this idea entails a "static division of human life into distinct 'spheres'. For RO, they are more shifting and contingent, and the question of their validity and their boundaries is more uncertain."[33] As pointed out earlier, the modal spheres do not *divide* reality in any way, since they form an *ontic condition* for the functioning of (natural and social) entities. Their ontic universality provides the constant (not *static*) framework necessary for those specific kinds of entities subject to their peculiar type laws. Since the meaning of modal aspects may be deepened or disclosed, they are not *static*. For example, when the primitive meaning of number, manifest in the order of numerical succession, i.e., one, another one, yet another and so on indefinitely, endlessly, is deepened by the meaning of space where the whole-parts relation is

---

31. I. Kant, *Kritik der reinen Vernunft*, 2nd ed. (Hamburg: Felix Meiner, [1787] 1956), 227.
32. Kant, *Kritik der reinen Vernunft*, 254.
33. Milbank, "Foreword," *Introducing Radical Orthodoxy*, 13.

original, then we may exceed the primitive meaning of infinity (as endlessness) by introducing the deepened idea of infinite totalities, that is, the idea of the at once infinite (traditionally designated as the actual infinite). This shows that, although the modal aspects are constant modes of being, their meaning may be deepened or disclosed as they participate in the dynamics of the disclosure process. Within living entities, macromolecular chemical constituents, investigated by organic chemistry, display a deepened, biotically directed functioning, an opened up functioning in principle studied by biochemistry (in practice, biochemistry partially conquered the field of investigation of organic chemistry).

When the structure of the logical-analytical mode is opened up, we first encounter the analytical mastery of a given knowledge-material (field of investigation). Now the anticipation to the economic aspect could be opened up – in the principle of *thought-economy*. These examples suffice to illustrate the *dynamics* intrinsic to the inter-modal coherence between the various aspects of reality.

The upshot of these considerations is that modal abstraction implies that all the academic disciplines that observe reality in its totality from the perspective of one or another modal aspect always operate on the basis of a philosophical orientation. This amounts to the fact that theoretical thinking requires an idea of the *cohering diversity of aspects* (and entities) within reality. This entails the necessity and inevitability of a theoretical total view of the universe. But, since a special science is delimited by the angle of approach of one modal aspect only, it stands to reason that such a totality view of reality exceeds every special science, even though concrete reality in its fullness features within the purview of a special science. A special science is not restricted merely to a "part sliced off from reality," because every academic discipline observes the entire universe, albeit from a modally distinct perspective.

Since God transcends creation, it is not meaningful to advance the idea that God is the "study-object" of theology. Therefore, Ouweneel is justified in his acknowledgement of the certitudinal or pistical point of view explored by theology: "I have argued extensively that theology is the special science that investigates empirical reality from the pistical viewpoint."[34]

Interestingly, Milbank[35] does not hesitate to speak of the "economic realm." Of course, the way in which we account for the various modal aspects of reality is subject to continuous reconsideration, but alterations in our understanding do not imply that the given modal aspects of reality in an ontic sense are not *constant*. The connections between various aspects are equally striking, even though the (retrocipatory and anticipatory) analogies between them may be accounted for in different ways. Remember what we have said about *credit* as *economic trust*. Derrida articulates the coherence between the economic aspect and the faith aspect of reality, notwithstanding the fact that he does not know the theory of modal aspects. He emphasizes that "faith is absolutely universal."[36] When he elaborates on his claim, by referring to credit as *economic trust*, he not only distinguishes between the economic sphere and the certitudinal sphere (faith), but also clearly states that the faith entailed in *economic trust* should not be reduced or defined by religion as such.

> There is no society without faith, without trust in the other. Even if I abuse this, if I lie or if I commit perjury, if I am violent because of this faith, even on the economic level, there is no society without this faith, this minimal act of faith. What one calls credit in capitalism, in economics, has to do with faith, and the economists know

---

34. W. J. Ouweneel, *What then is Theology?* (Grand Rapids, MI: Paideia Press, 2014), 107.
35. J. Milbank, "Foreword," *Introducing Radical Orthodoxy*, 14.
36. J. Derrida, *Deconstruction in a Nutshell, A Conversation with Derrida*, ed. John D. Caputo (New York: Fordham University Press, 1997), 22.

that. But this faith is not and should not be reduced or defined by religion as such.[37]

In other words, Derrida discerns the undeniable state of affairs that on the "economic level" of a society *credit* embodies *economic trust*. Likewise, when the jural aspect is deepened *legal-ethical* principles come into play. They are also designated as principles of *jural morality*, such as the principle of *fault*, in both its forms, *intent* and *negligence* (*dolus* and *culpa*), *equity*, *bona fides* and so on.

Of course, the faith aspect also entails retrocipatory analogies, such as certitudinal integrity (moral retrocipation), certitudinal fairness (jural analogy), certitudinal harmony (aesthetic analogy), and certitudinal identification and distinguishing (logical-analytical retrocipation).

The latter analogy reveals that faith entails an element of reflection, a point made by Milbank in an earlier quote: "For Catholic tradition, every Christian is a theologian, because faith is always *somewhat* reflective, albeit in the mode of symbol, ritual, and narrative."[38]

Having transformed every Christian into a theologian, it is a matter of consistency to defend the view that any Christian contribution to something like economics has to be *theological* in nature: "... the Christian contribution to, say, economics, is always a theological contribution."[39]

From the perspective of modal abstraction we have noted that a special science does not "divide" reality into segmented parts, because the various aspects of reality merely serve as spectacles through which the totality of reality is viewed and investigated. An analysis of the structure of the aspects themselves belongs to philosophy and the latter also has the task to give an account of the

---

37. Derrida, *Deconstruction in a Nutshell*, 23.
38. Milbank, "Foreword," *Introducing Radical Orthodoxy*, 14.
39. Milbank, "Foreword," *Introducing Radical Orthodoxy*, 14.

foundations of the various special sciences and to investigate the question what a special science is. Philosophy and theology ought to proceed from the same *root-commitment* (the biblical basic motive of creation, fall and redemption), for both a Christian philosophy and a Christian theology to be possible at all. Nonetheless, the theoretical view of reality underlying all scholarly endeavours remains *philosophical* in nature.

8
Dooyeweerd and Theology
by Willem J. Ouweneel

IN CONTRAST WITH THE apostles, staff members at theological faculties practice theology as a *science*, a theoretical enterprise—a very special science indeed, yet a science like so many others. Usually they do "Christian" theology. This is not only a theology that studies Christian doctrine, but also a Christian way of doing theology, just as, in my view, there is a Christian as well as a non-Christian (or even anti-Christian) way of doing *any* science. Such statements presuppose a certain philosophy of science. Is theology "science," and if so, what does this involve? How can one distinguish between scientific and non-scientific, or even *un*scientific, theology? What makes theology an *academic*, a *scientific*, a *theoretical* enterprise, as opposed to our practical reading and handling the Bible (no matter how thorough)?

In answering such questions, Herman Dooyeweerd has been of tremendous help. He wrote in his *In the Twilight of Western Thought*: "[I]f the possibility of a Christian philosophy is denied, one should also deny the possibility of a Christian theology in the sense of a science of the biblical doctrine... Luther called natural reason a harlot which is blind, deaf, and dumb with respect to the truths revealed in the Word of God. But, if this prostitute can become a saint by its subjection to the Word of God, it is hardly to be understood why this wonder would only occur within the sphere of theological dogmatics. Why may not philosophical thought as well be ruled by the central motive of Holy Scripture?"

Not only did Dooyeweerd ask this question but he answered it by laying the foundations for a philosophy rooted in the divine revelation. Until today, however, unfortunately only a small group of orthodox theologians seem to have some idea of what such a philosophy might involve, and what its possible meaning might be for Christian theology.

Theology and Philosophy

If theology and philosophy as disciplines are carefully distinguished, I see three possible relationships between the two:

(a) *Theology and ("neutral") philosophy must be distinguished but kept together* (a view beginning with Thomas Aquinas). This implies a *profane* philosophy, supposed to lead up to *sacred* theology. However, *both* philosophy and theology are occupied with divine revelation (in nature and Scripture), and both work by the light of human reason (preferentially guided by the Holy Spirit). Moreover, philosophy is a "totality science," whereas theology, as we will see, is "only" one of the many special sciences. Moreover, philosophy should be congenial with theology such that it is never neutral but should be founded in the same "religious ground-motive" (a typically Dooyeweerdian term) as theology.

(b) *Theology and ("neutral") philosophy must be separated* (a view beginning with William of Ockham). In its most extreme form, this means that, henceforth, theology has nothing to do with human reason anymore, not even with common sense—allegedly, it is only occupied with the mysterious, "the absurd"—whereas philosophy, including all the special sciences, has nothing to do with divine revelation; it can work with natural reason alone. However, as a science, theology is a thoroughly rational (not rationalist!) enterprise. Moreover, in my opinion, a Bible believing Christian can only consider a *Christian* philosophy.

(c) *A Christian philosophy underlying a Christian theology.* This option involves the notion of a theology that is "only" one of many special sciences, founded in Christian philosophy (like all of them, *ideally*, of course). In my view, the two are closely linked: theology, as a special science, has its own preceding theoretical questions (e.g., "what is science?"), which by definition are of a philosophical nature. And a Christian philosophy is rooted in (pre-theoretical) biblical ideas that have been thoroughly investigated in theology. The former does not make theology "philosophy," though, just as the latter does not make (Christian) philosophy "theology."

Necessity of Philosophical Premises for Theology

Academic theology without proper philosophical prolegomena either lands in the arms of ancient scholasticism, that is, the half-pagan philosophy of the Middle Ages and of early Protestantism. Or it lands in one of the modern or postmodern humanistic schools: (neo)positivism, existentialism, analytical philosophy, postmodernism, etc. Or it lands in biblicistic fundamentalism, itself a queer mixture of scholasticism and (neo)positivism. For all these three categories, unfortunately, many present-day examples could be mentioned.

Many theologians seem to have great difficulty discerning these things at all. Great twentieth-century theologians, such as Heinrich Ott and Otto Weber, still spoke of theology and philosophy in terms of the relationship between revelation and reason—obviously a false contrast. And Gerhard Ebeling said that "the orientation upon Jesus Christ" and the notion of sin are foreign to philosophy. Apparently, he referred to *secular* philosophy only, without thinking of the possibility of a *Christian* philosophy. Of course, Christian philosophy does give a place to sin, to redemption, to Christ. And it can do so without ever becoming "theology." This is because theology does not have a monopoly of talking about God and the Bible. Christian philosophy, as well as every Christian "special philosophy" underlying one of the various special sciences, does talk about God and the Bible as well.

This certainly does not mean that humanistic philosophy is useless to Christian theology. First, every scientific enterprise, no matter how much grounded in an apostate ultimate commitment, contains important truth elements. The "perspicuity," the "intrusiveness," of the truth shines even through the darkest philosophies. However, such truth elements are no excuse for also adopting the humanistic framework in which they are contained. Only a Christian philosophy can help us to safely "filter" the truth elements from the rest of such philosophies.

Secondly, theology is always done in dialogue and interaction with the culture to which it belongs, and thus also with the philosophical schools of its time. In that respect, the specific form of a certain philosophy or theology always has a limited significance, bound to the time in which it is designed. Philosophy and theology only keep their relevance if they are capable of answering, not only the questions of the time in which they were designed but, also the questions of later times. A Christian philosophy that is not relevant for a certain time period, including the latter's secular philosophies, is useless.

The Modal Aspect of Faith

In the view of theologians working within the framework of radical Christian philosophy (in the sense of Dooyeweerd and congenial thinkers), theology is "just" one of many special sciences. These are sciences that look at cosmic reality from one specific modal "angle": arithmetics from the arithmetical angle, biology from the biotic angle, linguistics from the lingual angle, ethics from the moral angle, to mention just a few examples.

It is very imprecise to say that special sciences study various "parts" or "domains" of cosmic reality. It is the opposite: *all* special sciences study the *totality* of cosmic reality—not distinctive "parts" or "domains"—*but each of them does so from one specific modal viewpoint.* Therefore, I would never say that "the Bible" is the study object of theology. Theologians study *the totality of cosmic reality*, but *only* from the pistical perspective, just like other sciences study that same cosmic reality from the energetic, or the psychical, or the social, or the aesthetic perspective, etc.

The most fundamental misunderstandings concerning the pistical modality are the following:

(1) The pistical aspect of the *immanent*-functional reality is confused with faith in its *transcendent*-religious meaning. It is neither the believing faith of the heart (*fides qua creditur*), nor the whole of all the things believed (*fides quae creditur*). The "pistical" lies in an altogether different dimension, so to say: it refers to a "side," a *mode*, an "aspect" of cosmic reality, just like the spatial, the physical, the biotic, the logical, the social, the aesthetic, and the ethical sides, or modes, or aspects.

A few practical examples may help. There are logical things (e.g., scientific handbooks), lingual things (e.g., traffic signs), social things (e.g., park benches), economic things (e.g., bank notes), aesthetic things (e.g., paintings), ethical things (e.g., birthday gifts). In a similar sense there are also pistical things, for instance church buildings, pulpits, baptismal fonts, synagogues, mosques, temples, altars, and even all ideological communities, such as a synagogal or church denomination, but also a political party or a humanist union. All these things function in *all* modal aspects, but they are specifically qualified (typified, characterized) by one of these aspects.

(2) Concrete entities, such as this or that belief or creed, are confused with the modal *aspects* in which these entities function. Remember, creeds have a "thing-like" character, which means that they function in all modal aspects, whereas the pistical *aspect* is only one of these.

(3) A philosophical notion like the pistical aspect is confused with concrete Scriptural statements, in this case rather the lack of them, so that people argue, "Scripture does not know of a pistical

aspect." My reply is that the Bible does not contain or teach any philosophical notions at all. The notion of the pistical aspect is fruit of Christian philosophical reflection.

(4) The pistical modality is confused with some general "belief" that all humans allegedly have in common, or some "faith capacity," or "faith possibility" that all humans are supposed to possess. This again is a confusion between the modal and the entitary dimension of cosmic reality.

Paradigms and Ground-Motives

The *history* of theology involves the succession of the various theological movements throughout church history, and the sometimes drastic way in which one school made place for a subsequent one. Philosopher of science Thomas S. Kuhn has forever thoroughly influenced the discussion about this phenomenon of various "theologies" (and "philosophies," for that matter) by introducing the term *paradigm*. In his view, the choice of scientific theories is ultimately determined not (only) by rational, but (also) by psychical, social, economic, cultural, political and religious factors. Kuhn explained why he rejected the standard view of some continual, gradual progress in science. He pointed to long periods of "normal science" in the history of the various special sciences, which alternate with short periods of scientific revolutions. During periods of "normal science," scientific investigation takes place entirely within the framework of a so-called paradigm. This is a model of problem solving, with which a scientist approaches a certain field of study. It is also a *disciplinary matrix* in the sense of a theoretical thought framework with which a scientist approaches his science.

One fundamental starting point for some analysis of the philosophical paradigm concept is the insight that beliefs are never exclusively the subjective choice of an individual. For the far greater part, they are the—what we call—inter-subjective choice of a *community*. Not only the Christian faith but also the apostate faith of secular thinking is almost always the faith of a certain community. This also holds for a scientific community, which in a period of "normal science" works within a certain paradigm. It is a (written or unwritten) confession that keeps a church denomination together, it is an (unwritten) paradigm that keeps a scientific community together.

Kuhn was not the first to launch the idea that all scientific thinking is based upon pre-scientific, non-rational prejudices. Long before Kuhn, Michael Polanyi pointed out that all our scientific work almost systematically exhibits the traits of a hidden personal commitment. To this belong originality and intuition, scientific passions, but particularly the—partly non- or semi-rational—presuppositions, convictions, commitments and beliefs of the investigator. However, even Polanyi brought this up only twenty years after Dooyeweerd had pointed out the suprarational and supratheoretical, transcendent-religious root of thinking.

Not only that: Dooyeweerd broke more radically with the dogma of rational autonomy than Polanyi did. For Dooyeweerd, rational knowledge is only one out of various forms and kinds of knowledge, such as aesthetic knowledge, moral knowledge and pistical (or faith) knowledge. After Dooyeweerd, Thomas Kuhn was the *first* who really broke with the idea of the strict rationality of science. However, for Kuhn, knowledge is ultimately an *ir*rational, for Dooyeweerd a *supra*rational matter. The two kinds of knowledge could not differ more: the *suprarational*, which surpasses reason and is *transcendent*, is essentially different from the *irrational*, which goes against reason, and is *immanent*.

Kuhn and Dooyeweerd

Dooyeweerd was the first and the most thorough philosopher to point out that all pre-theoretical presuppositions ultimately are of a transcendent-religious character. The word "religious" here does not have the meaning that Kuhn attached to it. To him, "religious" is nothing more than—as Dooyeweerd would put it—only one of the immanent-modal-functional aspects of our empirical reality: the pistical modality. In other words, "religious" here only refers to facets of our immanent living and thinking.

For Dooyeweerd, however, the *entire* immanent-modal-functional life is religious in the sense that people have been called to serve God in every facet of their everyday life, including their scientific activity. This is because our entire immanent-modal-functional life converges in the *transcendent*-religious life of Man's supramodal and suprafunctional Ego. Beyond all immanent factors, of which the pistical is just one, there is the transcendent-*religious* heart, in which all these immanent functions are concentrated.

In Dooyeweerd's view, all scientific activity is ultimately determined by someone's ultimate commitment, which is always of a transcendent-religious nature. If indeed all science is rooted in some ultimate commitment—and I definitely believe it is—this could very well be a Christian commitment. We even believe that this is the most desirable commitment possible, both for theology and for any other "special science."

For the rest, also compare my chapter on psychology for a similar treatment of the underlying problems.

9

Reformed Scholasticism and Reformational Thinking

by Joseph Boot

The Root of Creation

THE NEW TESTAMENT reveals explicitly the role of Christ Jesus as the one *in whom* all things are created and held together and *for whom* all things exist (cf. Col. 1:15-20). The apostle Paul deepens our understanding of creation and redemption profoundly by showing that the triune God is the root and end of all things: "*for from Him and through Him and to Him are all* things" (Rom. 11:36).

Herman Dooyeweerd has taught us that it is not only the Christian worldview, but all human thought which is embedded in a religious ethos (ground-motive) oriented toward an idea of origin and law-order. In his *New Critique of Theoretical Thought* Dooyeweerd expressed this reality in philosophical terms:

> All meaning is from, through and to an origin, which cannot itself be related to a higher origin ... all genuine philosophical thought has therefore started as thought that was directed toward the origin of our cosmos.[1]

In the Greco-Roman cradle of Western civilisation, there was

---

1. H. Dooyeweerd, *A New Critique of Theoretical Thought*, Collected Works of Herman Dooyeweerd, Series A, vol. 1, General Editor D. F. M. Strauss. (Lewiston, NY: Edwin Mellen, 1997), 9.

no room in philosophical thought for a free *creation* by an infinite-personal God as revealed in the Bible. As noted in other chapters, this is because the Greek understanding of *nature* (as it comes to full flower in Aristotle) was ruled by a "form-matter" scheme that regarded reality as consisting of an *uncreated* amorphous *chaotic matter* which by a forming activity of an impersonal divine principle achieves a coherence of "form and matter." This duality, closely connected to the Greek idea of *substance*, had the effect of *dividing reality* into two realms – the sensory and supra-sensory – the former being the realm we can experience with our senses and the latter which we cannot. This latter realm was nonetheless thought to be knowable by the intellectual contemplation of rational souls – an idea which influenced the thought of Augustine, for whom the soul was conceived as an immortal substance.

In our understanding of what it means to be human, the eventual result of these ideas was that man came to be seen as assembled from two components, distinct in principle i.e., a mortal, material body, and an immortal, rational soul. Plato considered the soul-substance of the human being primary, whilst regarding the body as merely its "tool." For Aristotle, form is the divine, higher principle that is embedded in non-divine, chaotic matter as its essential unity. Together they make up a substantial unity in which the rational soul is considered the "essential form."[2]

This view is a radical departure from biblical revelation, in which there are no independent substances (uncreated soul substances, essences, or eternal chaotic material), over-against the all-conditioning Word of God. In Scripture creation is *distinct* from Christ but not *separated* from Him. The apostle Paul thus shocks the Greek philosophers in Athens with his application of

---

2. D. F. M. Strauss, "Scholasticism and Reformed Scholasticism at Odds with Genuine Reformational-Christian Thinking," in *Ned. Geref. Teologiese Tydskrif* 5, no. 2 (March 1969): 97-114.

this reality, "for *in him* we live and move and exist" (Acts 17:28). As Andree Troost puts it, "[Christ] is with God the Father, the creator and bearer of the entire cosmos which was created *in* him."³

Scholasticism

In the 13ᵗʰ century, Thomas Aquinas brought Roman Catholic scholastic thought to its apogee by officially interpreting Aristotle's views for the church. He attempts to build a formal *bridge* between the Greek dualistic worldview and Scripture. As Dooyeweerd notes, "Scholasticism seeks a synthesis between Greek thought and the Christian religion. It was thought that such a synthesis could be successfully achieved if philosophy, with its Greek basis, were to be made subservient to Christian theology."⁴ Aquinas thus tried to accommodate the form-matter dualism of the Greeks to the Christian faith. In this marriage, "matter" was the principle of imperfection, and the "rational form" was the "thinking soul" which participated in the divine.⁵ As a result, Aquinas divides the creation order into a *natural* and *supernatural* realm. That legacy has remained with us in various permutations ever since.

In the metaphysics of Aristotle, to which Thomas is so deeply indebted in every respect, "pure matter" and "pure form" are mutually irreducible original principles of being. Here "pure matter" has no real independent existence because it can never reveal itself without substantial form – Aristotle thereby giving primacy to the principle of form as essentially divine. But even when matter is thus regarded as a principle of imperfection (and so not divine)

---

3. Andree Troost, *What is Reformational Philosophy: An Introduction to the Cosmonomic Philosophy of Herman Dooyeweerd*, trans. Anthony Runia (Jordan Station, ON: Paideia Press, 2012), 166.
4. H. Dooyeweerd, *Roots of Western Culture, Pagan, Secular and Christian Options*. Collected Works of Herman Dooyeweerd, Series B, vol. 4, General Editor D. F. M. Strauss. Grand Rapids, MI: Paideia Press, 2012.
5. Dooyeweerd, *Roots of Western Culture*, 119.

the *divine nous* is only the Origin of the form of the cosmos, a kind of demiurge giving form to reality, but by no means the transcendent creator of heaven and earth as revealed in the Bible. Aristotle's first unmoved mover is at rest in total contemplation and bears no resemblance to the triune God who is always working.

To accommodate this view to the biblical teaching presented a major problem, but Aquinas set about trying to do so. He appears to affirm that God brings everything forth without pre-existing matter, but the polarity of the form-matter scheme keeps poisoning his efforts to be scriptural. The Bible presents an integral unity of God's creative work which completely excludes warring polar principles of being at work in creation. Yet Aquinas sees pure (prime) *matter* as a kind of original chaos whilst *form* is constantly lent a divine character. Dooyeweerd pointed out that:

> We can indeed call all of creation divine because of its Origin, but within creation we never distinguish between two ontological principles, one of which is honoured as "divine" while the other is not. God's work of creation is perfect and knows no principle of imperfection.[6]

The effect of Thomas' perspective on the scholastic view of the human person was far-reaching because it denied the radical religious unity of man. The human soul as the *anima rationalis* is said to be the form of body forming a substantial unity. The body therefore has a kind of existence as the substantial form of the soul, but all the "higher" functions of life are conceived as the functions of form derived from a *thinking* soul. This soul "substance" is thought to be able to exist detached from the body at death giving us a fundamental "higher-lower" dichotomy for hu-

---

6. H. Dooyeweerd, *Reformation and Scholasticism in Philosophy*, vol. 2, Collected Works of Herman Dooyeweerd, Series A, vol. 6, General Editor D. F. M. Strauss (Grand Rapids, MI: Paideia Press, 2013), 296.

man existence which conflicts with created integral unity of the human person taught in Scripture.

Eventually, in this accommodation, some scholastic theologians developed a *psycho-creationist* anthropology. This paradigm asserts that with each new life, God permits the implanting of an indestructible soul into a body from without – the body being prepared by an organic life principle. So again, instead of maintaining the biblical unity of the human person, what finally emerges is the uncomfortable assemblage of two independent substances – body and soul. This is true even with Aquinas. As Dooyeweerd explains:

> He has to take the *anima rationalis* simultaneously as the sole substantial form of the material body and as "immortal substance." At the same time the psycho-creationist standpoint carried him back with inner necessity to the traditional scholastic view of the body as a special "independent entity"... the traditional scholastic doctrine of the human being as a compositum of two substances.[7]

The flesh (non-divine earthly matter of the body) is consequently conceived as a shell for the noblest "part" of man – the immortal *soul* which escapes the corruptible *material* flesh at death. The rational soul (*anima rationalis*) is regarded as a spiritual complex of particular functions (i.e., thinking, feeling, willing etc.), the seat of true light, natural reason and spirituality, whilst the body is implicitly or explicitly denigrated in terms of lower desires and carnal appetites. Sin's root is then supposedly located in these "lower" fleshly desires. This teaching obviously entails the problematic notion that God creates and inserts sinful souls into each new body – hence the need to shift the seat of sin to the body's "lower" capacities. This helps account for the rise of the Medieval ascetic ideal and a monastic life as manifesting the fullest expression of devoted service to God. In the end nothing is gained by

---

7. Dooyweerd, *Reformation and Scholasticism*, 2:400–401.

asserting a unity of body and soul if these concepts remain entirely in the grip of the Greek religious motives of form and matter.

The religious superstructure built up around this philosophical dualism steadily divides *all of life* into two domains, the natural and the supernatural (spiritual) – a worldview expressed in the polarities of *nature and grace*. Nature is conceived as form and matter and grace (supernatural faith) as an additional gift to the intellect (hope and love being gifts to the will); grace will bring the immortal soul to perfection. The upshot of all this is that the scriptural reality of the creation of human beings as a *unity*, along with a *life-encompassing* apostasy in sin and rebellion at the Fall leaving humanity in need of an equally *life-encompassing* redemption at the root of our being, is hidden from view in this scholastic perspective. Instead, though our "rational soul" is wounded by sin and deprived of the gift of faith to the mind, human nature is not radically perverted and depraved by the Fall. Scholastic thought teaches instead that the Fall really robbed us only of a supernatural gift of grace (i.e., true faith, hope and love) which is restored through Christ and the church – the church being the one *supernatural* institution of grace.

Reformed Scholasticism

Though the Reformation broke with much of this mischaracterisation of life and sought a renewal of the biblical understanding of a life-comprehending Creation, Fall, Redemption and Consummation by the power of the Holy Spirit, it failed to completely destroy scholasticism's artificial bridge from Aristotle. Consequently, a "Protestant scholasticism" soon became entrenched and has persisted right through into modern evangelicalism. As Dooyeweerd explained, "Protestant scholastics thought they could strip Greek philosophy of its pagan features by depriving it of all independence and turning it into a handmaiden. Thus, it was put to so-called formal use in systematic theology and theological ethics."[8]

The Reformation had two basic streams. The great reformer, Martin Luther, openly claimed to be of William of Ockham's school – a perspective in which he was immersed whilst at Erfurt monastery. He was profoundly influenced by Ockham's complete separation of "natural life" from the "supernatural" Christian life of grace – thereby driving a radical wedge between creation and redemption. So-called "nature" was viewed exclusively in the light of sin, with "reason" regarded as the only guide in the natural domain, clearly entailing the ubiquitous and secularizing notion of a radical separation of "reason" and "revelation." Consequently, "[I]n matters of secular government, justice and social order, a person possessed only the light of reason."[9] This fundamental error also expressed itself in Luther's attempt to set law (nature) and gospel (grace) in opposition to each other. The law was an order for sinful *nature* which Luther began to regard as antithetical to *supernatural* grace. Gospel love must overcome the "rigidity" of law. As a consequence, the link between creation-law and God's grace was effectively severed. On this view, redemption came to imply the *death* of "nature" rather than its restoration and *renewal*. Though he vigorously attacked pagan philosophy, because of his lack of insight into the full implications of a biblical worldview, Luther was unable to direct people to a truly inner reformation of thought. "He did not see that human thinking arises from the religious root of life and that is therefore always controlled by a religious ground-motive."[10]

John Calvin, though clearly grasping the sovereignty of God over all creation and its life-encompassing character, was unable to entirely shake himself free from the persistent Greek dualism we have been describing because he lacked a truly scriptural-

---

8. Dooyeweerd, *Reformation and Scholasticism in Philosophy*, 2:46.
9. Dooyeweerd, *Roots of Western Culture*, 141.
10. Dooyeweerd, *Roots of Western Culture*, 141.

ly grounded ontology. As a result, the nature grace dualism of scholasticism strove to establish a beachhead within the reformed tradition from the beginning. Calvin follows Augustine (who unsuccessfully fought to shake off the remnants of Neo-Platonism), and this is apparent in Calvin's view of the human person where he conceives of the soul as the noblest "part" of man – an immortal (though created) "being." The flesh is a kind of prison so that soul and body stand over against each other in uncomfortable tension, never fully taking in the biblical unity of the human person. Calvin's reformational emphasis on Christ's rule over all of life is thus soon pushed aside by a protestantized scholasticism that follows him. This reformed scholasticism seeks a synthesis with the Greek concept of nature by trying to tie the "light of reason" with the "light of scripture." Because it is a contrived pseudo-synthesis between Christianity and the Greek view of reason (and thereby is always threatened with being exposed or broken down) reformed scholasticism seeks to bring secular philosophy under its wing and guide it via *theological* ideas to prevent the natural light of "reason" going rogue. As Dooyeweerd has shown, this leads to a strong secularizing tendency:

> The point of contact for the dualistic separation between nature and grace will be sought, in particular, in the doctrine of *common grace*, which in its relationship to "special grace" can easily degenerate into a doctrine of two separate realms. The Reformed practitioners of the non-theological sciences, finding in Scholastic theology no usable guidelines for their own branches of investigation, will appeal to common grace, in order to justify their alliance with the prevailing, supposedly neutral modes of thought. And insofar as they take care not to trespass on the perilous terrain of theology, Scholastic theology for the most part will not interfere with them. Indeed, in this view, theology supplies an external link between natural thought and the Scriptures. However, since this connection is completely dominated by the unscriptural ground-motive of nature and grace

and cannot lead, therefore, to an inner reformation of *scientific thought*, the latter will place more and more distance between itself and the Scriptural ground-motive of the Christian religion.[11]

So then, whilst wanting to honour biblical revelation, even a reformed scholasticism offers no true inner reformation of all thought and so Christ's kingship and scriptural authority are soon sequestered in the narrow realm of religious faith. Theology is consequently honoured as "queen" of the sciences, whilst philosophy and other disciplines must simply be "adapted" to the church's theological principles. The thought that philosophy, history, natural sciences etc., must be inwardly reformed from a scriptural worldview just doesn't occur. These disciplines supposedly belong to the lower realm of nature, natural reason, and natural law, whereas theology is concerned with the higher supernatural realm of faith, grace, and the church.

It is then no surprise to find the eventual development of dialectical theology in Protestantism which, "sharply opposes the religious antithesis in the area of worldly life, rejecting the idea of Christian politics, of a Christian political party … and of Christian scholarship."[12] Karl Barth continues the identification of nature (conceived humanistically) with sin, separating nature from the Word of God which he and his followers regarded as "wholly other." He rejects any point of contact between the Christian faith and natural life so that he completely repudiates the idea of Christian culture – including Christian art, political life, scholarship, and even social action. Here, the creation law and ordinances recede so far from view that Christian thought effectively begins with the idea of a Fall and then redemption – for Barth there

---

11. H. Dooyeweerd, *Reformation and Scholasticism in Philosophy*, vol. 1, Collected Works of Herman Dooyeweerd, Series A, vol. 5. General Editor D. F. M. Strauss (Grand Rapids, MI: Paideia Press, 2012), 38-39.
12. Dooyeweerd, *Roots of Western Culture*, 143.

could be no knowledge of creation law and norms.

With this continuation of Greek philosophical dualism in various branches of Protestantism, we can see the many ways in which a *division of life* into separate domains has stubbornly manifested itself. Consider some of these familiar polarities still emphasized to varying degrees by many reformed evangelical Christians and Protestants of all stripes:

Body/Soul: We *are* a "soul"; we *have* a "body." Human beings are made up of two separate substances, one higher the other lower, easily distinguishable and separable. The soul (a complex of higher functions including reasoning and feeling) is the "real" person; the body is merely a shell. The soul's destiny is Heaven or Hell, the body and the earth are relatively less important.

Material/Spiritual: The Christian life is a "spiritual" life consisting of spiritual disciplines. It is an inner battle against the desires of the lower part of us – stemming from the body. The material world is an incumbrance, lesser, or evil, and we will eventually escape it into Heaven. In the meantime, we must suppress the desires of our material nature.

Natural/Supernatural: Most life activities are just natural and about this world, but Christianity is about a supernatural world beyond this one, and therefore this natural life and creation are not as important as the supernatural world. The natural is mundane and boring and carries on largely in terms of its own impersonal laws, but sometimes God breaks in to do supernatural things like miracles, which are much more significant than everyday events.

Public/Private: Our spiritual life of faith is an essentially private matter of personal conviction and should not be imposed on anyone else. Our private faith is not for the public space as it does not involve publicly accessible knowledge and in any case, God's kingdom is not of this world.

Secular/Sacred: Most of life functions well in terms of neutral secular principles and concepts that everyone can agree on. Politics, education, law, science etc., are secular areas of life basically governed by man's common natural reason. The church, however, is a sacred institution of grace which, unlike these other areas, is ruled by biblical revelation. This revelation must not be imposed or applied to culture and society, for to Christianize culture is mixing the upper and lower storeys, secular and sacred.

Law/Gospel: Law is concerned with the earth, the material world, and sinful natural desires, whereas gospel freedom is spiritual and concerns grace for the soul. The church is the institution of grace, not of law – which is a matter for the state as a natural institution. Grace throws law aside because grace has no more need for the law than Heaven needs Earth, or the saved soul has real need for the body.

Common/Special Revelation: The natural creation is the realm of common grace, common principles, natural law. By contrast, Christ is the source of special grace and special revelation. The one is a ladder to the other, but we need the addition of faith and grace in special revelation to bring us to completion, salvation, and perfection.

Reason/Revelation: Human reason is sufficient for understanding most of life in the natural world and guides politics, education, culture etc., in terms of neutral, rational principles. Human reasoning, though prone to errors, is good as far as it goes and can offer high-probability proofs for God's existence acceptable to logical and right-thinking people. However, supernatural revelation to the soul is admittedly necessary for eternal salvation and to disclose certain spiritual doctrines.

Science/Faith: The sciences operate only in terms of objective natural reason and concern religiously neutral knowledge of the natural world. The sciences answer factual questions about how things happen in the world. Faith is unrelated to reason and is only concerned with the higher value judgments of why things happen. The only truly Christian academic discipline is theology, because it is concerned with studying religion and faith. There can be no distinctly Christian view of philosophy or science.

Culture/Kingdom: The kingdom of God is a purely spiritual and invisible reality that does not manifest itself outside the heart and supernatural institution of grace – the church. The kingdom of God fundamentally concerns a future heavenly reality, not the present earth and human culture. The earth is destined for total destruction so nothing in human culture has any abiding value. Getting souls into Heaven and preserving them in the institutional church through this veil of tears is our calling.

Dooyeweerd has shown us that these artificial separations of domains in life ruled by different principles follow logically from the dualistic conception of the human person derived from the *form-matter and substance concepts* in Greek religion and then synthesized with the Christian view of creation and redemption.

Reformational Response

Scripturally, we may conceptually distinguish an *inner* and *outer* man (the bodily function-mantle of our total existence; 2 Cor. 4:11,16), fully dependent in every way and at every moment upon the sustaining Word of Christ (Acts 17:28; Rom. 11:36). But there is no independent "essence" of human life, no higher and lower substances or "parts." The "I" or human ego cannot be identified simply with reasoning, feeling, willing, or any other aspect of our existence because these *functions* all presuppose a deeper unity that transcends them. The "I," our full human selfhood, the *depths of the heart*, is God's mystery transcending the temporal functions of our existence and is grasped only in relation to God who has placed in us a sense of the eternal (Eccl. 3:11). Critically, Christians shall one day follow Christ out of the grave (Col. 1:18; 1 Cor. 15:20). It is the full person that is raised to life (inner and outer man), just as it is the totality of creation which will be released from its subjection to futility when we receive the fullness of our adoption as sons, the redemption of our bodies (Rom. 8:19-23).

Reformational thought therefore resists every inclination to divide up created reality in terms of philosophical distinctions that are entirely foreign to the Bible. Our faith rests on the scriptural truth "that the mediating Word is the religious lifeline which links God and man together in a life-long, *all-embracing* covenant relationship of revelation and response."[13] All of creation in every part is governed by the *mediating Word* of Christ and in no domain of life do we escape the all-embracing relationship we have with Christ and His Kingdom. *All of life* is a religious response to that Word.

Dooyeweerd's reformational philosophy translates this all-embracing and mediating power of the Word of Christ in terms of "ontic normativity." This is simply the recognition of a law-Word *for* creation that provides a normative structure for all spheres of life and every entity within creation – it governs the law-conformity of all created reality. As such, Christ cannot be "uncoupled" from a so-called "natural" realm of factual "neutrality," an area of creation that can be withdrawn from the sovereign Lordship and authority of Jesus and His written Word-revelation. Christ Jesus, who holds all things together by the Word of His power, from whom, through whom and to whom all things exist, cannot be banished to a supposed upper storey of reality, a spiritual world of "grace," shunted out of history to a future age, nor imprisoned in the walls of the church institute so that the kingdom of God (*Basileia*) is limited to the institutional *ekklesia*.

The central direction of Scripture is the *unity* and *continuity* of God's creation and redemption within the rubric of the kingdom of God – an all-encompassing creation, fall and redemption of the whole of life. This inescapable revelation must be the *start-*

---

13. G. J. Spykman, *Reformational Theology: A New Paradigm for Doing Dogmatics* (Grand Rapids: Eerdmans, 1992), 94.

ing point for both our philosophical and theological activity and is not a theological *product* of human interpretation – it is the motive-force of the biblical message. The radical character of this religious motive, argues Dooyeweerd:

> …can only be revealed by the Holy Spirit, because he opens our hearts so that our faith will no longer be a mere acceptance of formal articles of our Christian confession, but a living faith, serviceable to the central working of God's Word in the heart – the religious centre of our life … In their radical meaning – as the ground motive of the Word-revelation and the key to true knowledge – creation, fall and redemption are no simple articles of faith; they are rather the Word of God itself in its central spiritual power, directed to the heart, the religious centre of our existence. Confronted by the Word of God in his heart, man can offer nothing, but only listen and receive… The Word of God … must penetrate to the root of our being and become the central motive-force of our whole Christian life.[14]

This means that Christ's restorative kingdom life cannot be restricted to a "part" of the human person nor any isolated terrain of human existence such as the church institute or our personal devotional lives. Rather, it breaks out in marriage and family, education and entertainment, science and arts, politics and law, business and economics. In each of these areas we are led either in terms of the kingdom of light or kingdom of darkness, obedience or disobedience. As Danie F. M. Strauss has noted, "It is impossible to speak of a neutral sphere within so-called common grace, where the total antithesis, for or against Christ, does not radically apply."[15] In all life aspects, in every activity, institution, and aca-

---

14. H. Dooyeweerd, *Wat is die mens?* Cited in D. F. M. Strauss, "Scholasticism and Reformed Scholasticism at Odds with Genuine Reformational-Christian Thinking," accessed June 23, 2022, https://vcho.co.za/wp-content/uploads/2018/05/Scholasticism-and-Reformed.pdf.
15. Strauss, "Scholasticism and Reformed Scholasticism."

demic discipline, we will be for or against the Lord.

At the deepest level of our humanity, at the *heart of our existence*, all of life is a *continuous response* to the *Word of God* (Rom. 12:1) All the laws and norms Christ Jesus has ordained for creation which stand above us and yet are bound to us, call us to conformity to the Word! The matchless beauty of this gospel is that Christ's Word is life and His total kingdom one of righteousness, peace, and joy in the Holy Spirit.

10

The Church, Society, and the Kingdom

by Willem J. Ouweneel

The Church of God

In the New Testament, we find at least *five* different meanings for the Christian church, which I briefly summarize here:

1. The *worldwide, transcendent church*, that is, the church from its origin (either in Genesis, or in Acts 2, depending on one's ecclesiology) unto Christ's second coming (see especially Eph. 3:9–11; 5:23–24, 32). This church, the body of Christ, the house of God, the bride of the Lamb, in its ideal meaning, surpasses time and history.

2. The *worldwide, immanent-historical church*, that is, the church that, here on earth, passes through a certain history, through a process of growth and development, of failure and restoration, of ruin and renewal. As such it is a "building" that "grows into a holy temple in the Lord" (Eph. 2:21 NKJV), a "body" that "grows" to full maturity (4:13, 16; Col. 2:19). This church contains all true believers of all places and times, and has spread over all the earth. "Catholicity" is a qualitative notion expressing unity and fullness. Following Augustine, the Reformers began speaking of the "invisible" (ideal) church and the "visible" church, which may be a mixture of good and bad elements (cf. Rev. 2–3). In some sense, the term "invisible" is a little unfortunate: in the midst of all confusion and division,

always something of God's church becomes visible, if only in the love and fellowship of believers beyond church walls.

3. The *worldwide momentaneous church*, that is, the totality of all believers who, at a given moment, are on earth. Throughout the ages, many members of the church in meanings 1 and 2 have passed away, others have not yet come to faith, or perhaps are not even born yet. Various practical admonitions, such as maintaining "the unity of the Spirit in the bond of peace" (Eph. 4:3), refer to the worldwide church as it exists right now on earth. When Paul "persecuted the church of God" (Gal. 1:13), this referred to the entire church of *that* moment.

4. The *local church*, that is, the totality of all believers in a certain city or village (cf. Acts 8:1; 11:22, 25–26; 13:1; 14:21–23, 27; 15:4, 22; 18:22; 20:17 etc.). In this sense, the word *ekklēsia* can also be used in the plural (1 Cor. 16:1, 19; 2 Cor. 8:1; Gal. 1:2, 22; Rev. 1:4). The word *ekklēsia* can also refer to the *meeting* of the local church (1 Cor. 11:18; 14:19, 28, 34–35; Eph. 3:21; Col. 4:16).

5. A church as a *part* of the local church, a term used when a local church meets at various places in a city or village ("house churches" or "home churches") (Acts 2:46; 3:1, 8; 4:4; 5:14; 6:6; 12:12, 17; Rom. 16:3–5, 10–11, 14–15, 23; 1 Cor. 1:11; 16:19; Col. 4:9–17; Philem. 1:1–2, 10, 12, 23–24).

Besides these five meanings, church history supplies us with two more meanings:

6. A local company of Christians, distinct from other such companies within the same locality because of doctrinal and historical differences. Such local companies may be totally independent from any other such companies on earth.

7. A number of local companies, united into a certain *denomi-*

THE CHURCH, SOCIETY, AND THE KINGDOM

nation, a "church" such as the Roman Catholic Church or the Protestant Church of the Netherlands; or they may refer to themselves as a collection of "churches," such as the Christian Reformed Churches or, if other terms are preferred, the "Assemblies of God," or the "Reformed Congregations."

The Kingdom of God

Besides the various meanings of the "church of God," let us also consider the various meanings of the "kingdom of God":

1. In its most universal sense, the "kingdom of God" is identical with the rule of God over the entire world as created by him. The first time it is mentioned in this sense is in Exodus 15:18, "The LORD shall reign [or, reigns, or shall be King, or, is King] forever and ever." Psalms such as 95, 97, and 145 describe this universal and everlasting reign of God.

2. More specifically, the "kingdom of God" is the rule that God has entrusted to humanity, first, to the first two humans, and ultimately, to Christ *and* all those who will reign with him; see, e.g., "[I]f we endure, we will also reign with him" (2 Tim. 2:12). God said to Adam and Eve, "Be fruitful and multiply and fill the earth and *subdue* it, and have *dominion* over the fish of the sea and over the birds of the heavens and over every living thing that moves on the earth" (Gen. 1:28).

3. At the Fall as described in Genesis 3, the first humans not only fell into sin but, in a sense, involuntarily also handed the kingdom that had been entrusted to them to the Serpent ("who is called the devil and Satan, the deceiver of the whole world," Rev. 12:9). Since that moment, there exists in this world such a thing as the "kingdom of Satan" (Matt. 12:26). Satan has the "power of death," and, "through fear of death," also over people, "subject to lifelong slavery" (Heb. 2:14–15).

4. In the Old Testament, the "kingdom of God" in its more limited sense, which is the kingdom of the Messiah, was only a thing to be looked forward to, as it was anticipated by the prophets. This kingdom entered into the world only when the "king of the Jews" was born (cf. Matt. 2:2). Jesus was this "king," although his kingdom was one that could not be captivated in the categories of "this world," that is, the domain of sin and Satan (John 18:33–37). Since Jesus' death, resurrection, and elevation at the right hand of God, he is the One to whom "all authority in heaven and on earth has been given" (Matt. 28:18). God "seated him at his right hand in the heavenly places, far above all rule and authority and power and dominion, and above every name that is named, not only in this age but also in the one to come. And he put all things under his feet and gave him as head over all things to the church, which is his body, the fullness of him who fills all in all" (Eph. 1:20–23).

5. Although Christians may be divided into a-millennialists ("there will be no future millennial rule of Christ"), pre-millennialists ("there will be a future millennial rule of Christ in peace and justice, after his second coming and before the eternal state"), and post-millennialists ("there will be a future millennial rule of Christ in peace and justice, before his second coming"), Christians may at least agree that, one day, "when all things are subjected to him, then the Son himself will also be subjected to him who put all things in subjection under him, that God may be all in all" (1 Cor. 15:28). And of the believers (God's "servants") it is said, "they will reign forever and ever" (Rev. 22:5).

Church *Versus* the Kingdom

How do these two, the church and the kingdom, relate to each other? Here, Dooyeweerd's philosophy can be of great help. This is, first, because of his distinction—*not* dualism!—between the immanent-temporal and the transcendent-supratemporal (or, as I would prefer to put it, plenitemporal: time in its everlasting fullness and unity). The kingdoms of this world always have an immanent-temporal meaning, as being part of immanent cosmic reality. However, the kingdom of God, taken in whatever sense, always has a transcendent-plenitemporal meaning, though at the same time *expressing* and *manifesting* itself within *all* the immanent-temporal societal relationships within our cosmic reality (see below).

With the church it is a bit different. In the first meaning mentioned, the church, God's *ekklesia*, is transcendent-plenitemporal, though at the same time *expressing* and *manifesting* itself within *all* the other meanings of "church" mentioned, these all being of an immanent-temporal nature. Among these other six meanings, there is another distinction to be made, namely, between the universal meanings 2 and 3 on the one hand, the local meanings 4 and 5, and the denominational meanings 6 and 7 where we have to do with "church" as a societal relationship—one out of many.

This brings us to the second part of Dooyeweerd's philosophy that is of great help here, namely, his theory of entities, and among them in particular his theory of societal relationships, such as a wedded couple, a family, a nation state, a local church (or, a church denomination), a company, a school, an association, a political party, and so on. The first two are embedded in God's creational order, but the others are rather products of historical processes. This distinction must not be overrated: on the one hand, the forms marriage and family are shaped by history, whereas at least the nation state and the local church cannot be severed from God's creational order.

Now, the first thing that we must clearly distinguish is that the kingdom of God *manifests itself equally in all societal relationships*, namely as far as the followers of King Jesus Christ are concerned (the non-followers ignore or defy the kingdom of Christ). And it is equally true that the kingdom of Satan *manifests itself equally in all societal relationships,* namely, as far as the enemies of King Jesus Christ are concerned.

As I explain in other chapters, especially the one on theology and the one on psychology, we must sharply distinguish between "pistical," which is an immanent term, and "religious" in the sense of a transcendent term. That is, among the societal relationships mentioned, only a local church, or a church denomination, and actually also an ideological (e.g., humanistic) association, are of a pistical qualification, whereas the others are not: they are more of a biological, or an economic, or (given the many different types of associations) of a lingual, or juridical, or aesthetic, or ethical qualification, and so on. *But they are all of a transcendent-religious nature*, because the members of a marriage, a family, a nation state, a company, a school, an association, and so on, are all either serving God in Christ within these societal relationships, *or* they are not (or their lives are mixtures of the two). That is, they are all religious beings in the transcendent sense, be it for or against God (or a mixture of both). They either dedicate their marriages, families, companies, schools, and so on, to the honor of God and the service of Christ, or they do not (or do even the opposite).

Let us bring in here the terms "church" and "kingdom" again.

As we saw, in its universal sense, all the true Jesus-believers living on the earth at this moment constitute the worldwide church as it exists right now on earth (see above, meaning 3). Whether I am a husband or wife, a family member, a citizen, a school teacher or pupil, an employer or employee, a member of one or several associations, I am all these things as a member of the worldwide church—or not. The gathering which I go to on Sundays, or whenever, is my local church, which is supposed to be a practical expression of the one, worldwide church. I am a member of a local church, but in all other societal relationships I can never forget to be a Christian, that is, a member of the worldwide body of Christ.

To describe the kingdom of Christ in relation to the believers' lives, we need a different formulation. On the one hand, the rule of Christ is universal: he has been given all authority in *all* domains of this world. On the other hand, *in concreto* he exerts this rule in the lives of those who are his disciples (followers), and as such acknowledge his rule, in their private lives and in public. In this respect, there is in fact no distinction between the various societal relationships. As a local church member, the disciple of Christ obeys the Lord as well as he/she can. But exactly the same is true for him/her as a husband or wife, a family member, a citizen, a school teacher or pupil, an employer or employee, a member of one or several associations. The believer is always, in all domains of life, in all societal relationships, a disciple of Jesus, that is, a subject of the kingdom of God as it has manifested itself in Jesus Christ. He/she serves his/her Lord, not only as a church member, but also as a husband/wife, a family member, a citizen, a school teacher or pupil, an employer or employee, a member of one or several associations. In every domain of life he/she serves God, and follows Christ—or he/she does not (or leads a mixed life).

Errors

"Christian" views that do not properly discern these things, easily fall into a collection of errors that may be summarized with the label of "pisticism," that is, absolutizing the pistical aspect (just like evolutionists absolutize the biotic aspect, rationalists absolutize the logical aspect, Marxists absolutize the social and economic aspects, and so on).

One of the forms of pisticism to be mentioned is one belonging to Hyper-Calvinism. In its severest form, this is the idea that a Christian lives in a personal relationship with the Lord, and within the community of his church, but with the other societal relationships (apart from marriage and the family) he has to do as little as possible. The strictest of these Hyper-Calvinists refrain from all political involvement, and from all forms of science and culture. They may be forced to become an employee in a "worldly" company, but they prefer to form their own companies and their own schools. This is a confusion of the immanent-pistical and the transcendent-religious. That is, it creates a "horizontal" division between the pistical on the one hand, and all the other aspects on the other hand, instead of honoring the "vertical" duality between the immanent-pistical and the transcendent-religious. The "world" (in the pejorative moral sense) is not a ("horizontal") collection of certain (non-pistical) domains, but rather, in the 'vertical" sense, all that is stamped by sin and Satan, whether it is within one's local church or denomination, or within any other societal relationship.

Such an attitude is far removed from, for instance, Abraham Kuyper's adage, "God's honor in all domains of life." In Dooyeweerd's terms, a person can serve Christ in all domains of life, including science, culture, the arts, economy, politics, and so on, as long as his/her heart is oriented toward God and his Word, and he/she, in the power of the Holy Spirit, avoids sin and Satan as well as he/she can. No societal relationship whatsoever is as such sinful or Satanic, although there *are*, of course, corrupt associations, such as criminal syndicates—it is only the human heart that may be in the grip of sin and/or Satan.

Another form of what I call "pisticism" is two-kingdom theology. I mention it here only briefly because I have extensively dealt with this error in my book *The World Is Christ's*. This erroneous view distinguishes between, on the one hand, the kingdom of God—containing what I call the pistical—and, on the other hand, a kind of "neutral" kingdom, including science, culture, the arts, economy, politics, and so on. The church is "Christian," all the other domains may stand under God's rule in some remote way, but basically they are "neutral," that is, they are *per se* neither consecrated to God, nor hostile toward God. Believers and unbelievers alike can work in such domains. The great correspondence with the previous view is—in Dooyeweerdian terms—absolutizing the pistical aspect and creating a division between this and the other aspect. The great difference between this and the previous view is that science, culture, the arts, politics, and so on, are not despised; on the contrary, they are highly regarded. Christians may, and should, definitely work in these areas—but they are "neutral," they do not belong to the kingdom of Christ.

I leave the matter here. It is enough to say that this view neither properly discerns the church of God, nor the kingdom of God. Dooyeweerd is of tremendous help in properly discerning these matters—but even without Dooyeweerdian thinking, every believer ought to see how far the two errors here are removed from biblical thinking.

11

Realism and Nominalism
Part 1

by Danie F. M. Strauss

An explanation of the terms *realism* and *nominalism* is best guided by an account of how they historically emerged and developed. As we do so, we learn how the problem of "universals" relates to the order for reality and the orderliness of creation.

What became known as the opposition between *realism* and *nominalism* is a conflict of thought that originated within Greek antiquity where it is primarily associated with Plato's theory of ideas (also designated as *ontic forms*) and the subsequent Aristotelian-Thomistic metaphysics of *essential forms*. As well, at the cradle of Western philosophical speculation, one certainly has to acknowledge the presence of Parmenides with his fundamental identification of *thought* and *being*.

The Threefold *Universalia*

In the meantime, the core issue in this legacy is centered in the notion of universality and the nature of truth. According to the ripened conception of medieval realistic metaphysics, as defended by Thomas Aquinas during the 13th century, *universalia* have a three-fold existence:

(i) as archē-typical forms in the divine mind (*ante rem*);

(ii) as the immanent (universal) essential forms inhering in entities (*in re*); and

(iii)   as the subjective universal concepts within the human mind (*post rem*).

Truth was supposed to be based upon the correlation between *thought* and *being* (*adequatio intellectus et rei*).

This realistic metaphysics assumed a chain of being in accordance with the Platonic scheme of ontic form and its copy (*Urbild* and *Abbild*), with God as the highest being (*ipsum esse*, or "*Die Form aller Formen*") at the top of the hierarchy of being.

Early modern philosophy soon replaced the classical legacy of metaphysical realism with a *nominalistic* approach. The artificial synthesis between Greek antiquity and biblical Christianity—sustained by the societal power of the medieval Roman Catholic Church with its ecclesiastically unified culture—did not survive the disintegrating effects of the nominalistic movement that emerged during the late 13th and early 14th centuries. Duns Scotus and William of Occam denied the primacy of the human intellect as opposed to the will, and particularly Occam opened up an avenue for an arbitrary creativity, by means of which the human intellect can acquire control over the surrounding world. Beck correctly points out that modernity caused a transformation in the understanding of human rationality. Human reason no longer accepts, but rather logically controls nature as an object in service of the human spirit with its self-determination and self-understanding as pure subject, directed at the experience of its own power and freedom.[1]

Instead of looking at the world from the perspective of a pre-ordained hierarchical order of being, with God as the highest being, the nominalistic attitude stripped reality (outside the human mind) of any and all forms of order-determination and of its

---

1. H. Beck, "Metaphysiche Implikationen im Konstruktiven Realismus," in *Konstruktion und Verfremdung*, Herausgeber F.G. Wallner and B. Agnese (Vienna: Universitäts-Verlagsbuchhandlung, 1999), 3.

entire orderliness. It thus leaves open a new domain of exploration manifested in the Renaissance urge towards the rational control and mastery of the world—which soon found a powerful ally in the rise of modern natural science. However, this development was in the grip of the modern humanistic ground motive of nature and freedom (the natural science ideal and the personality ideal).

In order to understand this development, it should be noted that Plato and Aristotle respectively unveiled two closely related features of our life-world (*Wirklichkeit*), namely the role of *an order for* or a *law for* entities (Plato) and an understanding of the *orderliness* or *lawfulness of* entities (Aristotle). The former discovery was transposed into the speculative and transcendent realm as static ideal forms of being in Plato's thought, while the latter was absorbed in Aristotle's problematic notion of substance. Aristotle also realized that universality plays a key role in human understanding, although he starts with the strictly individual *primary substance* (*proten ousian*) in his *Categories*. However, in its individuality it precludes conceptual knowledge—something Aristotle did not want to sacrifice. As a consequence, he introduced the secondary substance, which is supposed to be the universal substantial form of an entity. This secondary substance is designated as the *to ti èn einai*.[2] According to Aristotle, a concept is always focused upon what is *general* or *universal*. In this way, he wants to safeguard the universality of theoretical knowledge. But at the same time, he restricted knowledge to *conceptual* knowledge. For Aristotle, true knowledge is therefore always knowledge of the universal *form*. The counterpole of form, namely *matter* (which lacks any positive determination[3] is therefore outside the reach of conceptualization. As such, it is *unknowable*.

---

2. Aristotle, *The Basic Works of Aristotle,* ed. Richard McKeon (New York: The Modern Library, 2001), *De Anima,* 412 b 16 and *Metaphysics* 1035 b 32.
3. Cf. *Metaphysics* 1029 a 20–26.

The Shift to Nominalism

Nominalism took a radical stance in opposition to this realistic metaphysical legacy by denying the existence (the "reality") of *universalia ante rem* and *universalia in re*. The place where nominalism allowed universality to prevail was inside the human intellect—either as concepts or as words. The world as such lacks any universal traits; it is populated by individuals only.

Particularly Descartes, in his methodical skepticism, exemplified the new spirit of the Renaissance and the post-Renaissance era by affirming the autonomy of the thinking subject as the ultimate starting point for philosophical thought. He carried through the consequences of denying any universality outside the human intellect. The most important implicit consequence of this nominalistic orientation is that it does not acknowledge any order transcending the human being as such. A universal law order for creatures and also the orderliness of such creatures (in their subjection to such laws) are transposed into the human mind. His seemingly innocent remark that "number and all universals are only modes of thought"[4] demonstrates the radical reorientation caused by modern nominalism.

Without entering into a detailed analysis of the philosophical development from Descartes up to Kant, one key element ought to be highlighted, for it explains the background of the currently prevailing idea of *construction*. In the thought of Hobbes, we find a new motive, namely that of *logical creation* (construction). In his work *De Corpore*, he introduces a thought experiment by imagining that reality in its totality is broken down into a heap of chaos and that human understanding, with the aid of well-defined concepts, then creates a newly ordered cosmos. Being acquainted with Galileo's mechanics, it is understandable that Hobbes em-

---

4. R. Descartes, *The Principles of Philosophy*, in *A Discourse on Method, Meditations and Principles*, trans. John Veitch (London: Everyman's Library. [1644] 1965), LVIII.

REALISM AND NOMINALISM (PART I)

ployed the concept of a moving body as the basic tool in the logical reconstruction of reality. Cassirer explains that this stance no longer accounted for truth in terms of the relationship between thought and being. Truth does not inhere in the things, but is attached to the names and their comparison as they are employed in statements.[5]

Before Hobbes, Galileo also formulated a thought experiment and without taking account of any real sense-experience, he arrived at his law of inertia. If a body is in motion and the path is extended into infinity, the body will continue its motion indefinitely, unless some force affects it. Galileo realized that it is not motion, but only a change of motion that requires a cause. According to Drake, the astronomy of that period had the task of improving the "methods of describing and calculating the observed positions and *motions* of heavenly bodies, rather than to explain such motions physically."[6] To this, he adds that physics evolved along two distinct paths, a philosophical and a mathematical part, and that astronomical calculations "which fell to the mathematicians, remained strictly *kinematic*."[7]

Promoting Human Understanding to the Formal Law-Giver of Nature

Eventually Kant took the outcome of Galileo's thought experiment further: Galileo derived a law and prescribed it to moving entities out of the pure understanding of the human being in its spontaneous subjectivity. This represents the crucial modern epistemological turn, known as the "Copernican turn," in ascribing

---

5. E. Cassirer, *Das Erkenntnisproblem in der Philosophie und Wissenschaft der neueren Zeit* (Darmstadt: Wissenschaftliche Buchgesellschaft, 1973), II, 56.
6. S. Drake, *Essays on Galileo and the History of Philosophy of Science*, vol. 1 (Toronto: University of Toronto Press, 1999), 68; emphasis added.
7. Drake, *Essays on Galileo,* 68; emphasis added.

the primacy no longer to the object, but to the subject. Of course, the problem was now to explain how the human subject inherently furnishes us with *universal a priori forms*, making possible our knowledge of the phenomena. Just compare the context in which Kant wrote about the difficulty involved in this turn, namely to explain how "subjective conditions of thought can have objective validity, that is, can furnish conditions of the possibility of all knowledge of objects."[8] Clouser aptly captures the impasse of this subjectivist stance: "Unless there were already laws governing the mind that were not its creations, what would explain the uniformity of the ways the mind imposes laws on experience."[9]

Rationalism and Irrationalism

Kant's solution to this problem must be seen against the background of the ambiguous nature of modern nominalism. In spite of the radical differences between realism and nominalism, both orientations restrict knowledge to universals. This restriction of knowledge to universals is typical of what is known as *rationalism*. By contrast, one can define *irrationalism* as that epistemological approach that accentuates what is individual and unique (contingent) at the cost of any universal traits outside the human intellect. Of course, this irrationalistic side of nominalism is self-contradictory, at least when one rejects the influential Aristotelian dichotomy between quantity (as a category of matter) and quality (as a category of form). A chair with four legs unmistakably possesses this definite numerical (quantitative!) quality! Therefore, the being of each individual manifests an inherent *universal* structural trait.

When Kant struggles with the problem of how "subjective

---

8. I. Kant, *Critique of Pure Reason*, 2nd ed. Hamburg: Felix Meiner, [1787] 1956, 122.
9. Roy Clouser, *The Myth of Religious Neutrality: An Essay on the Hidden role of Religious Belief in Theories* (Notre Dame: Notre Dame University Press, 2005), 367 note 7.

conditions of thought can have objective validity,"[10] his attempted solution illustrates that, in line with the thought experiment of Galileo, he simply drew the radical modern subjectivistic conclusion of Humanism: the laws of nature are a priori contained in the subjective understanding of the human being. Kant elevated understanding with its categories to become the *a priori* (formal) law-giver of nature.[11]

It was merely a matter of pursuing this approach consistently that the so-called absolute freedom idealism after Kant (Hegel, Schelling, Fichte) believed that logic and dialectic embrace reality in its fullness and totality, and bring it forth. Cassirer remarks that only at this point does it seem as if the circle of philosophy is closed by reaching its aim in the identity of reality and reason—that is the point where Hegel believes his "Science of Logic" stands. In his early development, Ludwig Feuerbach, the Luther of modern Humanism, continued this emphasis on the identity of *thought* and *being*. In the spirit of Hegel, Feuerbach holds that thinking is not a capacity of the spirit, but is itself the spirit.[12] And in his dissertation Feuerbach asserts that only the universal, the whole, the absolute is completed and perfect.[13] Philosophy is simply concerned with what is universal and unconditionally necessary (*"unbedingt Notwendig"*), and whatever is individual and particular disappears as unreal in the "One and All" infinite reality.[14]

These consequences can only be properly understood when it is realized that nominalism (also in its conceptualist variants, in-

---

10. Kant, *Critique of Pure Reason*, 122.
11. See Kant, *Critique of Pure Reason*, 161, 163 and I. Kant, *Prolegomena zu einer jeden künftigen Metaphysik die als Wissenschaft wird auftreten können* (Hamburg: Felix Meiner, [1783] 1969), § 36, 320.
12. See S. Rawidowicz, *Ludwig Feuerbachs Philosophie; Ursprung und Schicksal.* 2nd ed. (Berlin: Walter de Gruyter & Co., 1964), 16.
13. Rawidowicz, *Ludwig Feuerbachs Philosophie*, 27.
14. Rawidowicz, *Ludwig Feuerbachs Philosophie*, 34.

cluding Kant's own position), in fact transposes the universal side of entities (accounted for by Aristotle as the supposed universal substantial form of things) into the human mind (understanding).

Yet, in our experience of the world, we always encounter the universal and individual sides of entities as being inseparably present at once. This atom is *an atom*—the individual side ("this") and the universal side ("an") are simply two sides of the same coin. The being an atom of this atom is nothing but the universal way in which this individual atom evinces its subjection to the law-for-being-an-atom. Consequently, by stripping an entity of its orderliness (its universal side), it is simultaneously stripped from being subjected to the applicable universal order for its existence, i.e., both its *orderliness* and the *order for* its existence are eliminated.

Yet the permeating effect of nominalism surely takes us beyond Kant. We may even jump to a key figure within the school of "postmodernity," Richard Rorty. Richard Bernstein defines the rationalistic tradition (which he calls "objectivism") as "the basic conviction that there is or must be some permanent, a-historical matrix or framework to which we can ultimately appeal in determining the nature of rationality, knowledge, truth, reality, goodness, or rightness."[15] Mary Hesse sees scientific revolutions as "metaphoric redescriptions."[16] In following her, Rorty remarks: "This account of intellectual history chimes with Nietzsche's definition of 'truth' as 'a mobile army of metaphors'."[17] Rorty views "intellectual history" as "history viewed as the history of metaphor."[18] "Old metaphors are constantly dying off into literalness, and then serving as a platform and foil for new metaphors."

---

15. R. J. Bernstein, *Beyond Objectivism and Relativism: Science, Hermeneutics and Praxis* (Philadelphia: University of Pennsylvania Press, 1983), 8.
16. Cf. R. Rorty, *Contingency, Irony and Solidarity* (New York: Cambridge University Press, 1989), 50.
17. Rorty, *Contingency, Irony and Solidarity*, 17.
18. Rorty, *Contingency, Irony and Solidarity*, 16.

What Caused the Shift to Language? Three Epistemic Ideals

This emphasis on metaphor reveals the effects of what became known as the linguistic turn—prompting us to ask what happened after Kant that led to this position? The key to answering this question is found in the transition from universality to change and what is individual. Whereas, roughly speaking, one can say that the 18th century is the period of extreme (conceptual) rationalism, the transition to the 19th century can be designated as an acute awareness of the historical dimension of reality. By the end of the 18th century this, first of all, was due to the pioneering work by Johann Herder, a contemporary of Immanuel Kant. Korff calls Herder the German Rousseau and Cassirer praises Herder as the Copernicus of the (science of) history.[19] Proß sees in Herder the key figure who, in rejecting the 'Aufklärung' (Enlightenment), prepared the rise of romantic historicism.[20]

Although early Romanticism transposes the universal to what is unique, it did not distance itself from the inherent atomism (individualism) of the 18th century.[21] The step to holistic irrationalism was eventually taken by Schelling, Fichte and Hegel—three prominent post-Kantian philosophers in Germany during and after the rise of Romanticism. We should observe that, although Herder believes that society is subject to thorough historical change, he does not want to advocate an anchorless relativism. To curb this unwanted consequence, Herder upholds the ideal of humanity, which guarantees, as a universally binding rule, the uni-

---

19. E. Cassirer, *Das Erkenntnisproblem in der Philosophie und Wissenschaft der neueren Zeit* (Stuttgart: Kohlhammer Verlag, 1957), 226.
20. Cf. Cassirer, *Das Erkenntnisproblem*, 226ff. See also the editor's introductory remarks in Johann Gottfried Herder, *Abhandlung über den Ursprung der Sprache*, ed. by Wolfgang Proß (Munich: Carl Hanser Verlag, 1978).
21. See Dooyeweerd's analysis of the rise of Romanticism in a Chapter of this work.

ty and the meaning of history.[22]

The tutor of Leopold von Ranke (who is perhaps best known for his statement that the science of history studies the past "as it actually was") was none other than Barthold Georg Niebuhr (1776–1831), the pioneering historian who illustrates the transition from the 18th to the 19th century in a remarkable way. It was from the romantic movement—which included literary figures like Goethe and Schiller in Germany, Bilderdijk and Da Costa in The Netherlands, and Shelley and Keats in Britain—that Niebuhr received his appreciation of mythical thought. Without relinquishing the imaginative exuberance present in myths and sages, Niebuhr wanted to treasure the historical way of thought in its own right.

With an obvious allusion to Plato's classical allegory in *The Republic* of people living in a cave, Niebuhr compares the historian to a person whose eyes adapted so effectively to the dark, that it is possible to observe things that would be invisible to the newcomer. In opposition to Plato, who acknowledges only knowledge directed at the true (static) being of things as worthwhile, Niebuhr is convinced that only historical change provides genuine knowledge. This kind of knowledge is the most appropriate type of knowledge for humanity, comprising the vital self-developing of human beings.

---

22. Cassirer, *Das Erkenntnisproblem*, 228.

12

Realism and Nominalism
Part 2

by Danie F. M. Strauss

From Historicism to Language as New Horizon

OVER AGAINST the deification of universal (conceptual) knowledge during the 18th century, the ensuing reaction to rationalism reminds us of the importance of historical change. However, this irrationalist and historicist reaction against Enlightenment rationalism contains hidden problems that would only become explicit during and at the end of the 19th century.

It is noteworthy that this process was anticipated by the first critical reactions to Kant's *Critique of Pure Reason*. It was in particular Jacobi, Hamann and Herder who pointed out that Kant neglected the nature of language.

Although Feuerbach in his early development still continued the rationalistic line of nominalism by emphasizing universality at the cost of individuality, he had a clear understanding of the fact that the sensory capacities of the human being exceed the possibilities of the acquisition of concepts, because the former (concepts) are strictly based upon universality, while the latter (the senses) cannot transcend what is individual.[1]

Karl Mannheim, one of the prominent sociologists of the first half of the 20th century and the founder of the sociological subdis-

---

1. See S. Rawidowicz, *Ludwig Feuerbachs Philosophie; Ursprung und Schicksal*. 2nd ed. (Berlin: Walter de Gruyter & Co., 1964), 18.

cipline known as sociology of knowledge, had a solid understanding of the romantic roots of Dilthey's irrationalistic historicism:

> Dilthey is borne by, and may be the most important exponent of, that irrationalistic undercurrent which first became self-aware in Romanticism, and which, in the neo-Romanticism of the present, is on the way, in altered form, to effecting its attack on bourgeois rationalism.[2]

Only what can be experienced in the context of an historical, world-encompassing coherence could serve as the immediately certain basis of knowledge acquisition – and only by means of empathy one can attain a genuine understanding (*Verstehen*) of spiritual reality. The natural sciences know, the humanities understand.[3] Dilthey no longer supports the positivistic science ideal seeking what is typically human in some facet of nature. The historical aspect now occupies this vacancy: to be human means to be historically conditioned.[4] Habermas furthermore mentions the implied linguistic framework in Dilthey's hermeneutic:

> We don't understand a symbolic expression without an intuitive pre-understanding (*Vorverständnis*) of its context, because we are not capable of freely transforming the presence of an unquestioned background knowledge of our culture into an explicit awareness.[5]

---

2. Karl Mannheim, *Structures of Thinking*, ed. and intro. David Kettler, Volker Meja, and Nico Stehr, trans. Jeremy J. Shapiro and Shierry Weber Nicholson (London and Boston: Routledge & Kegan Paul, 1982), 162.
3. Wilhelm Dilthey, *Der Aufbau der geschichtliche Welt in den Geisteswissenschaften*. Reprint of the Berlin Edition (*Gesammelte Werke*, Vol. V, 1927) (Göttingen: VandenHoeck & Ruprecht, 1927), 86.
4. Dilthey, *Der Aufbau der geschichtliche Welt*, 275; cf. H. Diwald, *Wilhelm Dilthey, Erkenntnistheorie und Philosophie der Geschichte* (Göttingen: Musterschmidt-Verlag,1963), 38 n.11.
5. J. Habermas, *Moralbewußtsein und kommunikatives Handeln* (Frankfurt

REALISM AND NOMINALISM (PART 2)

In an article on hermeneutics and the Dilthey school, Gadamer explains the transition to language as a new universal in the thought of Heidegger: "'Being' certainly does not mean the being of something, also not the authentic or divine, for it is rather like an event, a pathos, that opens up the space in which hermeneutics—without a final foundation—turns into a new universal. This space is the dimension of language."[6]

The Hybrid Nature of Nominalism

We mentioned that rationalism entails the absolutization of knowledge in terms of universal features, that is, it deifies conceptual knowledge, whereas irrationalism, on the other hand, focuses upon whatever is unique, individual, unrepeatable and contingent, thus restricting knowledge to the approximating understanding of concepts stretched beyond the limits of their natural application (concept transcending knowledge)—that is, to idea-knowledge.

The perplexing fact is that nominalism comprises both these elements: In respect of the typical structure of entities, nominalism does not accept any conditioning order (universal structures) for, or any orderliness (universal structuredness) of such entities. Every entity is strictly individual. In terms of the distinction between rationalism and irrationalism, nominalism surely represents an irrationalistic view of the nature of entities, since every individual entity is completely stripped of its universal orderliness (law-conformity) and conditioning order. This characteristic applies to both moderate nominalism, viz. conceptualism (Locke, Occam, Leibniz and others), and to extreme nominalism, that rejects all general and abstract ideas and only accepts general names (Berkeley and Brentano).

This irrationalistic side of nominalism, however, does not

---

    am Main: Surhkamp Verlag, 1983), 17.

6. H.-G. Gadamer, "Die Hermeneutik und der Diltheyschule," *Philosophische Rundschau* 38, no. 3 (1991): 172.

exhaust its multi-faceted nature, because universals are acknowledged fully within the human mind, at least as general words in the case of Berkeley's and Brentano's extreme nominalism. This restriction of knowledge to universals is typical of rationalism in the sense defined by us. Therefore, it is possible to see nominalism as being simultaneously rationalistic in terms of the universals – concepts and words – in one's mind, and irrationalistic in terms of the strict individuality of entities outside one's mind.

The inability of conceptual knowledge to grasp what is unique and individual caused philosophers to look at the senses (cf. the development of positivism and neo-positivism) and at language to bridge the gap. It seems as if language can indeed mediate between universality and individuality in a way that transcends the limitations of concept formation. Mannheim understood these issues for he clearly grasped something of the two-fold nature of nominalism:

> Nominalism proceeds from the unjustifiable assumption that only the individual subject exists and that meaningful contextures and formations have being only to the extent that individual subjects think them or are somehow oriented toward them in a conscious manner.[7]

As a consequence, we can speak of a general (and currently widely acknowledged) shift from concept to meaning, from thought to language.

The key historicistic claims of postmodernity derive from post-Kantian Romanticism, and its lingual emphasis was anticipated by nominalism from its very inception (cf. Occam and Hobbes), and was also suggested by Jacobi, Hamman and Herder, even before the end of the 18th century! The key figure in the genesis of the linguistic turn, insofar as we may see it as an attempt to overcome the limitations of concept formation with respect to

---

7. Mannheim, *Structures of Thinking*, 196f; see also 224.

what is unique, contingent and individual, was Wilhelm Dilthey, who actually lived the greater part of his life in the 19th century. To be sure, what is called postmodernity merely constitutes a new power concentration of the irrationalistic side of nominalism. This basic orientation even pre-dates modernity—the latter taken in the sense of the 18th century Enlightenment.

Yet, acknowledging these historical roots should not mislead us to underestimate the vastly permeating (and uprooting) effects of contemporary postmodernism. Although the features are not new, their current hegemony surely is. The claim that in a fragmented and ever-changing world every person is entitled to his or her own "story"—while negating any and all grand meta-narratives (Leotard)—has the pretension of being just one amongst many other "stories." Yet, without realizing it, this new orientation overemphasizes historicity and linguisticality at the cost of other dimensions of creation equally co-conditioning human existence. In fact, these postmodern claims operate as an alternative grand meta-narrative, namely the universal claim which holds that everyone only has his or her partial story without any "universal" truth.

From the fact that this statement itself rests upon a universal claim—enabling it to apply to "everyone"—its inherent self-uprooting nature is manifest in its very formulation. Without an inherent constancy and universality, even the exclusively elevated conditions of historicity and linguisticality lose their meaning.

The enemy of scholarship and culture is not universality and constancy, but the internally antinomic attempt to assert historical change and lingual ambiguity at the cost of constancy and universality. It is only when we take seriously the liberating biblical perspective that creation cannot be explained merely in terms of some or other aspect that we in principle can escape from the one-sidedness of orientations such as rationalism, irrationalism, historicism and "linguism"—all of them combined and fused in the contemporary fad of postmodernism.[8]

The over-estimation of rationality in the legacy of the West cannot be divorced from the all-pervasive nominalistic conviction that reality itself supposedly has a "rational" structure. Since nominalism denies both the God-given order for (law for) the existence of creatures and the universality of creaturely responses to those laws (evinced in their lawfulness or orderliness), it is quite "understandable" why modern secular humanism "loaded" the human subject with the additional "responsibility" of becoming the law-giver—the constructive agent—of its own world.

---

8. For a critique of the distinction between so-called linear and non-linear thinking, see S. Sokal and J. Bricmont, *Fashionable Nonsense: Postmodern Intellectuals' Abuse of Science* New York: Picador, 1998); cf. the German edition: *Eleganter Unsinn: Wie die Denker der Postmoderne die Wissenschaften missbrauchen* (Munich: C. H. Beck, 1999), 164–167.

13

The Distinction between Structure and Direction

by Danie F. M. Strauss

IF WE LOOK AT philosophy and the various academic disciplines from the depth perspective of worldview, the most remarkable given is that we are constantly confronted by what we could call a surrogate salvific appeal. In other words, in the multiplicity of non-Christian approaches to scholarship we are invited to a way of liberation, we are requested to move away from one terrain of creation to the "kingdom of freedom/virtue/self-perfection/goodness/autonomy" etc. This means that the directional antithesis between *good* and *evil* is understood in structural terms, i.e., is identified with specific opposed terrains.

To the later Greek philosophers, for example, evil is found in the material world. For the existentialist philosopher of the 20th century, it is found in societal structures that threaten the freedom of the individual. For the neo-Marxist and the social conflict theorist (cf. Hegel, Simmel, and Dahrendorf), evil is found concealed in the authority structure of social collectivities as such (super- and subordination). For other thinkers, it is found located in the supposed inevitability of natural causality. And for still others, evil appears in the emergence of freedom which an individual is supposed to possess.

This apostate style of doing science—in philosophy and in the special sciences—constantly indicates the way to the good, to the meaning of life, and to freedom. However, each of these ways to salvation rest on a wrong evaluation of a well-created part of creation which, with an inner inevitability, leads to a depreciation of something or some facet within creation (a fundamental characteristic already of the ancient heresy of gnosticism), while at the same time it leads to the idolization (absolutization) of something else within creation—a point of departure of all idolatrous service which brings honor, meant for the Creator, to a creature.

It is significant, however, that the Bible does not localize evil in a terrain, in some province of human life, but on the contrary, in the apostate *direction* of humankind's heart, while salvation according to the Bible is likewise a directional matter: seeking the kingdom of God—in every terrain.

The acknowledgement of the directing role of faith in scholarly, so-called "rational," activities surfaced anew in the emergence of the philosophy of science in the previous century. Karl Popper advanced the penetrating critical insight that *faith* in the rationality of reason is not itself rational. In his work *The Open Society and its Enemies* he speaks about "an irrational faith in reason."[1] A similar position is advocated by Wolfgang Stegmüller when he states: "A self-guarantee of human thought is excluded, wherever one may consider it. One can never reach a positive result without pre-suppositions. One has to believe in something in order to justify something else."[2]

In reaction to Immanuel Kant's famous thesis, expressed in the foreword to the second edition of his *Critique of Pure Reason* (1787), namely that one has to set aside knowledge in order to make room for faith, Stegmüller adds: "A person does not have to set aside knowledge in order to make room for faith. Much rather one already has to believe something if that person wants to speak

---

1. K. Popper, *The Open Society and its Enemies*, vol. 2 (London: Routledge & Kegan Paul, 1966), 231.
2. W. Stegmüller, *Metaphysik, Skepsis, Wissenschaft* (Berlin/New York: Springer, 1969), 314.

of knowing and science at all." He furthermore asserts that an ultimate certainty is required, for without that it would be impossible even to start: "Some form of an absolute knowledge must exist; without it we would not have been able to begin . . . We must already 'possess' absolute evidence; that is, we must already believe in it." Finally, and perhaps his most remarkable formulation in this regard reads: in science one believes, in religion one knows (or: one claims to know)![3]

In addition to this, we have to refer to the notion of a *paradigm* (i.e., a theoretical frame of reference) as introduced in the work of Thomas Kuhn entitled *The Structure of Scientific Revolutions* (2nd impr., 1970). In more general terms one can say that modern philosophy of science realized that no single intellectual discipline can operate without (implicitly or explicitly) proceeding from an underlying philosophical frame of reference, from a theoretical view of reality.

Dooyeweerd opened the way to an understanding of the history of philosophical problems such as those regarding the relationship between:

- unity and diversity;
- universality and individuality;
- constancy and dynamics;
- knowledge of what could be grasped conceptually and knowledge transcending the grasp of concept formation (idea-knowledge);
- and so on and so forth.

Dooyeweerd has shown that all theoretical thinking is directed by a basic (transcendental) idea in which one finds an idea concerning

---

3. Stegmüller, *Metaphysik, Skepsis, Wissenschaft*, 314.

- the mutually cohering diversity within reality;
- the totality of this diversity;
- the origin of the latter of the diversity.

All the while, the key elements in Dooyeweerd's account derive from at least seven basic biblical perspectives:

1. Accepting God's Law for Creation;[4]
2. Acknowledging the interrelatedness and dependence of created reality;
3. Confessing the rule of Christ over all domains of creation;
4. Subjecting oneself to the key to knowledge: namely, the biblical basic motive of creation, fall, and redemption;
5. Knowing Christ as the fullness of creation (Col. 1: 15–20; Heb. 11:3);
6. Upholding the distinctiveness of "structure" and "direction";
7. Avoiding any absolutization of something within creation.

This many-sided but integral and coherent biblical starting point motivates and underlies the reformational philosophical tradition. The elaboration of Kuyper's thought in Dooyeweerd's philosophy has demonstrated that the answers given to these perennial questions are determined by an underlying theoretical view of reality (a transcendental ground-idea) which, in turn, is directed by an ultimate commitment (called by Dooyeweerd a thinker's

---

4. Kuyper correctly emphasizes that observation and perception ("mere empiricism" as he puts it) does not yield scholarly results as such—the various disciplines emerge only when what is observed is related to a general law, and it is philosophy ("the queen of the sciences"), finally, that has to combine what is unveiled in this way in one encompassing grasp ("one organic whole." *Lectures on Calvinism* (Grand Rapids, MI: Eerdmans, 1931), 112f.

THE DISTINCTION BETWEEN STRUCTURE & DIRECTION

"religious ground-motive").

Kuyper first introduced the principle of sphere sovereignty in order to account theoretically for the diversity within creation. Dooyeweerd explored and deepened this insight by enriching it in two directions:

(i) the interrelationship between the different (sphere-sovereign) modal aspects of reality is accounted for in terms of the principle of *sphere universality* (modal analogies, present in anticipations and retrocipations). In doing so, Dooyeweerd widened the scope of the principle of sphere sovereignty beyond distinct societal zones to embrace the fundamental dimensions of created reality (modal aspects and entities);

(ii) the interlacements within the domain of concrete things, events and societal relationships are accounted for in terms of *enkaptic* relationships in which the internal sphere sovereignty of the interwoven structures in question remains intact.

In other words, in being human (universal side) every individual human being, in a universal way, exhibits its subjectedness to the (equally universal) God-established law for the existence of human beings.

The structure of creation is not "direction-less," and the direction is not "structure-less." Therefore, we should distinguish between God's direction-giving structure for creation and the structured direction manifest in man's God-obedient or God-disobedient response. These insights in principle free us from the one-sidedness of monistic "isms" (see the chapter on isms).

Universality characterizes God's law for creation. It also constitutes a side of whatever is subjected to God's law in creation. In its lawfulness, orderliness, or law-conformity, every individual entity, event or societal collectivity, in a universal way, shows that it is subjected to a correlating God-given law. The being human of this person, and the being alive of this plant are instances of this universal orderliness.

The humanistic ideal of autonomy, i.e., that the human being is a law unto himself or herself, proceeds from the antinomic assumption that the conditions for being human and the human being meeting these conditions coincide!

Dooyeweerd articulates the following kingdom perspective:

> All Christians who in their scientific work are ashamed of the Name of Christ Jesus, because they desire honor among people, will be totally useless in the mighty struggle to recapture science, one of the great powers of Western culture, for the Kingdom of God. This struggle is not hopeless, however, so long as it is waged in the full armor of faith in Him who has said "All authority in heaven and on earth has been given to Me," and again, "Take heart! I have overcome the world."[5]

---

5. H. Dooyeweerd, *Christian Philosophy and the Meaning of History*, Series B, vol. 13, Collected Works of Herman Dooyeweerd, General Editor D. F. M.Strauss (Grand Rapids, MI: Paideia Press, 2013), 104.

14

Dooyeweerd's Perspective on Early Greek Philosophy

by Danie F. M. Strauss

THE SENSE IN WHICH Plato and Aristotle employed the term "dialectic" reflects something of the underlying unity of Greek philosophy. In *The Sophist* Plato describes *dialectic* as the science whose function it is to divide according to Kinds, not believing that the same Form is a different one or vice versa[1] – compare the phrase διαλεκτικὴ ἐπιστήμη (*dialektikē epistēmē*). This view is directed at the unique human capacity to think in a logical-analytical way, that is, to identify and distinguish (normally done on the basis of discerning what is similar and different).

A similar situation is found in the thought of Aristotle who relates dialectic to the syllogism. [The classical example of a syllogism is: All human beings are mortal; Socrates is a human being; therefore, Socrates is mortal.] He holds that there is a difference between a demonstrative premise and a dialectical premise. In the former case the premise is laid down, while a dialectical approach entails a choice between two contradictories. Yet both types argue syllogistically: "But this will make no difference to the production of a syllogism in either case; for both the demonstrator and the dialectician argue syllogistically after stating that something does or does not belong to something else."[2]

---

1. Plato, *The Collected Dialogues of Plato; Including the Letters*, eds E. Hamilton and C. Huntington (Princeton: University Press, 1973), 253.
2. Aristotle, *The Basic Works of Aristotle,* ed. Richard McKeon (New York:

In both cases the term *dialectical* is related to the logical-analytical abilities of human beings – either to *discern* or to *infer*. It will turn out, however, that the kind of dialectic found on the level of ultimate commitments, not only *transcends* the realm of logical-analytical thinking but at the same time *informs* it. During the early medieval period the entire *trivium* (grammar, rhetoric and dialectics) became known as *logic* – a practice which lasted until the 17th century.[3]

Orientation

Most philosophers and courses in philosophy appreciate the significance of Greek philosophy for the development of Western civilization. The multiple orientations and even differences in view displayed by Greek philosophy prompted Dooyeweerd to ask if there is not perhaps an underlying *unity* that may serve as a justification for referring collectively to "Greek philosophy." It indeed seems quite difficult to discern a shared *motivation behind* all the multifarious stances found in Greek philosophy.

One reason may be found in the *interpretative* nature of investigating the history of philosophy, which may lead to diverging assessments. Copleston even suggests that the "point of view" or "standpoint" of the historian will have an effect on the outcome of historical investigations because the historian must "have a principle of selection." The "own personal philosophical outlook" of the historian is "bound to influence his selection and presentation of the facts" and to affect his search for an understanding of the directing "motif" manifest in the history under consideration.[4] A

The Modern Library, 2001), *Analytica Priora* 24a21-24b13; see also *Topica* 100a30 ff.; as well as 65 and 188.
3. W. Risse, "Die Geschichte der Dialektik im Überblick bis Kant," in *Historisches Wörterbuch der Philosophie*, vol. 2, eds. J. Ritter, K. Gründer and G. Gabriel (Basel-Stuttgart: Schwabe & Co., 1972), 166-167.
4. F. Copleston, *A History of Philosophy* (New York: Doubleday, 1985), v.

slightly different approach is found in the consistent *problem-historical method* employed by Vollenhoven. He holds that contemporaries mutually influence each other and also exert an influence upon subsequent generations of philosophers. He does not want to suggest that any chosen problem stood in the centre of all philosophical approaches, because such a view easily leads to a one-sidedness that cannot do justice to those schools of thought for which this problem was not central or in which it perhaps did not even feature.[5] Bril expanded the approach of Vollenhoven in confrontation with prominent scholars of the 20th century, such as Foucault, Van den Berg, Kuhn, Poortman, and Lovejoy (with his notion of "unit-ideas").[6]

Clearly, the historian of (Greek) philosophy has to respect the "data," the *sources* – and the cultural, historical and societal background cannot be ignored either. However, the aim of our current investigation is indeed to see if the approach of Dooyeweerd does not reveal an *underlying unifying motive*, even if this motive itself may turn out to be caught up in or be struggling with a basic *split*, *divide*. We will argue that this is not merely a *logical* issue, but one reflecting the role of ultimate commitments, for within this supra-rational sphere a radical and central dialectic is operative – in the sense that two ultimate poles are both threatening and presupposing each other.

Is There a Shared Concern during the Initial Phase of Greek Philosophy?

Copleston identifies something of extreme importance for the Ionian philosophers, the fact of *change*, of *birth* and *growth*, *decay*

---

5. D. Th. Vollenhoven, *Geschiedenis der Wijsbegeerte*. Eerste Band, Inleiding en Geschiedenis der Grieksche Wjsbegeerte vóór Platoon en Aristoteles (Franeker: T. Wever, 1950), 5-6.

6. K. A. Bril, *Westerse Denkstructuren* (Amsterdam: VU Uitgeverij, 1986), 11-109.

and *death*.⁷ Yet, so he continues a few pages further, these philosophers had the wisdom to discern "that, in spite of all the change and transition, there must be something permanent. Why? ... There must be something which is primary, which persists, which takes various forms and undergoes this process of change." *Change* therefore does not merely concern "a conflict of opposites," which explains why Ionian philosophy is characterized by the attempt to find out what this *basic stuff* (*Urstoff* in German) is, exemplified in the well-known respective choices of *water* (Thales), *air* (Anaximines) and *fire* (Heraclitus).⁸

Copleston argues that Ionian materialism was *abstract* in nature and displayed a philosophical inclination, because in their original elements they discerned "the notion of unity in difference and of difference as entering into unity."⁹ An acknowledgment of this inclination makes it understandable why Heraclitus at once affirmed the *changefulness* of the world and simultaneously accepted the world law (*logos*) as an *untransgressable measure*: "The sun will not transgress his measures: were he to do so, the Erinyes, abettors of Justice, would overtake him."¹⁰ The fact that the Erinyes, the abettors of Justice, will punish the sun is significant, because it highlights the dialectic of *order* and *transgression*. If one associates *order* with what is *limiting* and transgression with the *unlimited*, then the claims of Philolaus also fit the dialectical picture. He holds that the universe as a whole, with everything in it, is fitted together "from the Non-Limited and the Limiting."[11] [12]

---

7. Copleston, *A History of Philosophy*, 17.
8. Copleston, *A History of Philosophy*, 20.
9. Copleston, *A History of Philosophy*, 21.
10. T. Comperz, *A History of Ancient Philosophy* (London: William Clowes & Sons Ltd., 1964), 73.
11. K. Freeman, *Ancilla to the pre-Socratic Philosophers. A Complete Translation of the Fragments of Diels, Fragmente der Vorsokratiker* (Oxford: Basil Blackwell, 1956), 73-Fr.1.
12. One of the leading contemporary scholars within the domain of physical

Philolaus connects this also with *harmony* because he says the latter "is a Unity of many mixed (*elements*), and an agreement between disagreeing (*elements*)."[13] This kind of thinking is typical of a *dialectical* mode of thought, where the way in which opposites are united is informed by a supra-theoretical dialectic. Dooyeweerd mentions a writing erroneously ascribed to Hippocrates, *Perì Diaìtes*, in which such an approach is asserted: "For all things are alike in that they differ, all harmonize with one another in that they conflict with one another, all converse in that they do not converse, all are rational in being irrational; individual things are by nature contrary, because they mutually agree. For rational world-order [*nomos*] and nature [*physis*], by means of which we accomplish all things, do not agree in that they agree."[14]

The Apparent Ambiguity Present in Different Modes of Explanation

At this point we have to account for the employment of different *modes of explanation*. The term *mode* is derived from *modus quo* and it designates a *manner* of existence, the ways in which concretely existing entities and events *function* (see the *Introduc-*

---

    theorizing, Brian Greene, is convinced that the ideal to formulate a unified field theory could be accomplished by what is currently known as *super-string theory*. The view of Philolaus, namely that the *whole* is such that everything in it *were fitted together* is closely imitated by the belief of Greene that *super-string theory* will find a framework in which every insight is *fitted* into a "seamless whole," a "single theory that, in principle, is capable of describing all phenomena" (B. Greene, *The Elegant Universe* [New York: W.W. Norton & Company Inc., 2003], viii - also compare pages 364-370, 385-386).

13. Freeman, *Ancilla to the pre-Socratic Philosophers*, 75-Fr.10.
14. H. Dooyeweerd, *Reformation and Scholasticism in Philosophy*, vol. 1, Collected Works of Herman Dooyeweerd, Series A, vol. 5, General Editor D. F. M. Strauss (Lewiston, NY: Edwin Mellen, 2003), 45.

tion). Therefore these *modes of existence* are at once *functions* as well as *modes of explanation*. Initially Greek philosophy by and large explored the following four modes of explanation, namely number, space, movement and (physical) change. Greek mathematics wrestled with what Becker designated as the *abyss* between *integers* and *continuity*.[15] The Pythagoreans were impressed by the apparent possibility to *arithmetize* musical consonants and it prompted them to claim that *everything is number*.

However, the discovery of *incommensurability* (irrational numbers) caused Greek mathematics to explore an alternative mode of explanation, namely *space*. Since it is possible to construe irrational numerical relationships spatially, Greek mathematics became "geometrized," that is to say, it made a choice for a *spatial* mode of explanation in giving prominence to spatial problems. This does not mean that Greek philosophy now turned into geometry. What happened was merely that in exploring the spatial mode of explanation, key elements of the meaning of space were discovered, while at the same time specific spatial features obtained a *metaphysical connotation* because they were employed in service of a more encompassing understanding of reality as such.

Within the context of spatial continuity (coherence), the most primitive awareness of infinity, understood as endlessness, is turned "inwards" - any spatial continuum could be divided *ad infinitum*. Thus it was realised that *continuity* allows for an *infinite divisibility*. Aristotle claims that it is self-evident that "everything continuous is divisible into divisible parts which are infinitely divisible."[16] However, the meaning of spatial wholeness was also explored in order to deny that such a continuous whole entails a

---

15. O. Becker, ed., *Zur Geschichte der griechischen Mathematik*, Wege der Forschung, Band 43 (Darmstadt: Wissenschaftliche Buchgesellschaft, 1965), xix.

16. Aristotle, *The Basic Works of Aristotle*, ed. Richard McKeon (New York: The Modern Library, 2001), *Physica* 231 b 15 ff.

multiplicity of *parts*. But advancing this view required a *more-than-spatial use* of spatial terms.

In the current context we may leave aside the intriguing difference between mathematical space (which is continuous and infinitely divisible) and physical space (which is neither continuous nor infinitely divisible).[17]

Conceptual Knowledge and Concept-Transcending Knowledge

Particularly in the school of Parmenides the idea of *being* was largely articulated by employing spatial terms in a *twofold* way. Sinnige speaks of "spatial images":

> It is fairly clear that Parmenides gives us two distinct descriptions of Being. The first of these is intended to be understood in a metaphysical sense: Being is determined in all respects (B Fr.8 verses 26-42), the second is formulated in cosmological terms: Being is a spatial whole, kept in balance from within and not bordered upon by another Being (vs. 42-49). The two descriptions overlap each other to a certain extent, which means that most terms have at the same time a metaphysical and a spatial connotation.[18]

The chief point to be observed here is that understanding *Being* requires the employment of terms derived from the spatial aspect. Sinnige calls them *cosmological terms*. Claiming that *Being is a spatial whole* accounts for the way in which *Being* manifests itself within the boundaries of the spatial aspect. Instead of calling this mode of speech *cosmological,* one can rather discern in it a

---

17. P. Maddy, "Three forms of naturalism," in *The Oxford Handbook of Philosophy of Mathematics and Logic*, ed. S. Shapiro (Oxford: Oxford University Press, 2005), 455 - see where she refers to Burgess; and see D. F. M. Strauss, *Philosophy: Discipline of the Disciplines* (Grand Rapids: Paideia Press, 2009), 236 ff.
18. T. G. Sinnige, *Matter and Infinity in the Presocratic Schools and Plato* (Assen: Van Gorcum, 1968), 86.

conceptual use of spatial terms. However, what is important for a philosophical understanding of *Being* only surfaces when a *metaphysical connotation* is attached to spatial terms. In such instances spatial terms are stretched *beyond* the confines of the spatial aspect – and the best way to capture their meaning is to realize that they employ terms derived from the aspect of space in a *concept-transcending* manner. Concept-transcending knowledge can also be labelled as *idea-knowledge*. Parmenides has *static being* in mind, in the sense of not being subjected to change (*atremes*). It is supposed to be stripped of all *movement* and therefore to be *immutable*. This fully determined static reality is reflected in our thinking, for Parmenides actually was convinced that *thought* and *being* are the same.[19] Parmenides holds that being has no "coming-into-being and no destruction."[20] Although the implicit intention is to abstract from *phoronomic* and *physical* considerations, the metaphysical idea-use of spatial terms is inevitably connected to the intuition of *uniform motion* and *change* – the former is elevated to the metaphysical idea of *immutability* while the latter is metaphysically *negated*: *being* is not subject to *change*.

The apparent ambiguity in the use of a specific mode of explanation disappears when it is realized that this ambiguity simply reflects the difference between a conceptual and a concept-transcending use of modal (aspectual) terms. The conceptual and concept-transcending sides of the spatial coin are both present when Parmenides accounts for crucial features of being, for he believes that being "... was not and will never be because it is connected

---

19. H. Diels and W. Kranz, *Die Fragmente der Vorsokratiker*, Vols. I-III (Berlin: Weidmannsche Verlagsbuchhandlung, 1959-60), B Fragment 3.
20. Diels and Kranz, *Die Fragmente der Vorsokratiker*, B Fragment 8 vs. 4 - see K. Freeman, *Ancilla to the pre-Socratic Philosophers. A Complete Translation of the Fragments of Diels, Fragmente der Vorsokratiker*. (Oxford: Basil Blackwell, 1956), 43.

in the present as an indivisible whole, unified, coherent."²¹ Being *coherent* and *connected* conceptually applies to spatial configurations such as *line stretches*, *squares* and *circles*, but claiming that being is an *indivisible unified whole* exceeds the confines of the spatial aspect in employing spatial terms in a concept-transcending way. Shapiro correctly points out that *coherence* (being *connected*) is actually an undefined primitive (spatial) term, every attempt to define it therefore turns out to be circular: "coherence is not a rigorously defined mathematical concept, and there is no noncircular way to characterize it."²²

Within the vitalist tradition a truly living entity is also indivisible and it is not composed out of parts. This view derives from Aristotle's vitalism. In his definition of the soul the word "*organikon*" has always been misunderstood.²³ Aristotle's vitalism is still alive in the twentieth century in the thought of neo-vitalists such as H. Driesch, A. Haas, P. Overhage and E.W. Sinnott – as well as the more recent Intelligent Design movement.

When Parmenides articulates his idea of "... an indivisible whole, unified, coherent,"²⁴ he at once introduces a split between the "one" and the "many." The numerical awareness of one, another one, and so on, underlies the notion of the "one and the many" which could easily be expanded, in a concept-transcending way, to the idea of *unity and diversity*. Stokes wrote a work on the one and the many in Pre-Socratic philosophy in which he explores two themes:

---

21. Diels and Kranz, *Die Fragmente der Vorsokratiker*, B Fragment 8, 3-6.
22. S. Shapiro, *Philosophy of Mathematics, Structure and Ontology* (Oxford: Oxford University Press, 1997), 13.
23. A. P. Bos, *The soul and its instrumental body, a reinterpretation of Aristotle's Philosophy of Living Nature* (Leiden-Boston: Brill, 2003), 85 ff., 93-94, 107-108, 162, 174, 200.
24. Diels and Kranz, *Die Fragmente der Vorsokratiker*, B Fragment 8, 3-6.

> ... the precise place of the antithesis between 'one' and 'many' in early Greek (especially Ionian and Eleatic) thought, and the degree to which the early philosophers failed to recognize the distinctions between different kinds of unity and plurality.[25]

We noted that Aristotle acknowledged the infinite divisibility of continuity, which explains why he also realized that the one and the many are not necessarily antithetically opposed. He distinguishes two senses of the *one* and the *many*.[26]

Wholeness and Multiple Parts

An analysis of the interconnections between number and space shows that our traditional distinction of different kinds of numbers is actually dependent upon the imitation of basic spatial features. The designation *integers* imitates the element of *wholeness* of spatial continuity, while the *fractions* (rational numbers) reflect the many *parts* of a spatial *whole*, captured in the mentioned insight that continuity is *infinitely divisible*.

The assumed "oneness" of being as an *indivisible whole* inevitably clashes with the very nature of the infinite divisibility of a continuum. But it is precisely for this reason that Zeno advanced his metaphysical idea of *oneness*. His aim, after all, was to argue against *multiplicity* and *movement*. If each "one" is *divisible* it would have had *multiple* parts and therefore it would be a "many" and not a "one." Consider B Fragment 3 of Zeno where the following argument is advanced: "...if there is a plurality, it must contain both a finite and an infinite number of components: finite, because they must be neither more nor less than they are; infinite, because if they are separate at all, then however close to-

---

25. M. C. Stokes, *One and Many in pre-Socratic Philosophy* (Washington DC: Center for Hellenic Studies, 1971), 1.
26. Aristotle, *The Basic Works of Aristotle,* ed. Richard McKeon (New York: The Modern Library, 2001), *Physics*, 185b32 ff.

gether they are, there will always be others between them, and yet others between those, ad infinitum."[27] When plurality is accepted the contradictory conclusion follows that it contains at once both "a finite and an infinite number of components."

Surely a whole contains all its parts, as it is still positively affirmed by the 20th century mathematician, Paul Bernays. He holds that "wholeness" i.e., the *totality-character* of spatial continuity stands in the way of a "perfect arithmetization of the continuum."[28] If we understand the first argument of Zeno from the perspective of the whole-parts relation, then these parts must be limited in number, because they are constitutive for the world as a whole. Alternatively, if we argue from the whole to the parts, then the infinite divisibility evinced by these divisible parts will imply that "there will always be others between them" - and so on indefinitely. Fränkel indeed uses the relation between parts and the whole in explaining what Zeno had in mind in his third *Fragment*.[29] Zeno's B Fragment 3 may indeed be appreciated as the first analysis of the relation between the whole and its parts and the relation of the parts to the whole.

From a systematic point of view, it is clear that the spatial whole-parts relation turns infinity, in the primitive sense of endlessness, *inwards*, that is to say, embodied in the *successive infinite divisibility of a continuum*. Zeno's paradoxes directly follow from his metaphysical attempt to eliminate the aspects of number and movement, instead of realizing that one has to acknowledge both

---

27. W. K. C. Guthrie, *A History of Greek Philosophy*, vol. 2 (Cambridge: Cambridge University Press, 1980), 90-91.
28. P. Bernays, *Abhandlungen zur Philosophie der Mathematik* (Darmstadt: Wissenschaftliche Buchgesellschaft, 1976), 74.
29. H. Fränkel, "Zeno von Elea im Kampf gegen die Idee der Vielheit," in Um die Begriffswelt der Vorsokratiker, *Wege der Forschung*, Band IX, ed. HG. Gadamer (Darmstadt: Wissenschaftliche Buchgesellschaft, 1968), 430.

the *uniqueness* of each one of these aspects of reality as well as their *unbreakable mutual coherence*. Motion is interconnected with a path (*space*) and speed can only be specified by a *number*.

In the metaphysics of space found in the thought of Parmenides, the starting-point is given for Zeno's argument concerning a *unitary wholeness* excluding plurality. The effect is that Zeno attempted to deny the *part*-element of the spatial whole-parts relation, while at once holding on to the trait of *wholeness* entailed in it. In a different context Strauss compared this view of Zeno with those of Wittgenstein and modern intuitionistic mathematics as follows:

> Whereas Wittgenstein had to throw away the ladder after climbing it (*Tractatus*, 6.54), Zeno started on top, with wholeness, and then discarded the ladder of infinite divisibility supporting it. The reverse took place in intuitionist mathematics, which started with the original spatial whole-parts relation, but then distorted it by accentuating the part element (with its implied infinite divisibility) at the cost of the element of wholeness (with its givenness as a totality all at once). The intuitionistic theory of the real numbers and the continuum followed a similar kind of Wittgensteinean approach – it used the 'spatial ladder of wholeness,' but immediately discarded it while preserving the infinite divisibility it implied.[30]

---

30. D. F. M. Strauss, *Philosophy: Discipline of the Disciplines* (Grand Rapids: Paideia Press, 2009), 407.

15

The Scope of Sphere Sovereignty

by Danie F. M. Strauss

THE IDEA OF sphere sovereignty could be seen as a first response to the given unity and diversity within creation. Within philosophical circles it is often referred to as the problem of the *One* and the *Many*. Of course, the crucial question is what we mean when we refer to the diversity in reality. Psalm 104:24 praises this diversity: "O Lord, how manifold are your works! In wisdom have you made them all."

Of course, this initial account harbors an important assumption, namely that differently natured entities populate our experiential world, thus highlighting that God created everything after its kind. This diversity is reflected in the terms we use to characterize diverse entities and Dooyeweerd followed Kuyper by employing the phrase *sphere sovereignty*. The diversity of aspects is correlated with the diversity of entities which we can experience within our everyday lives. This diversity is also to be observed in the discontinuous paleontological record and the discontinuities evinced in the current Natural System (NS – the classification of currently living entities).

Coyne, a prominent neo-Darwinist, has a sound understanding of the problem of continuity and discontinuity. Compare his remark: "For years after the publication of The Origin, biologists struggled, and failed, to explain how a continuous process of evolution produces the discrete groups known as species."[1] "And at

---

1. J. A. Coyne, *Why Evolution is True* (Oxford: Oxford University Press,

first sight, their existence looks like a problem for evolutionary theory. Evolution is, after all, a continuous process, so how can it produce groups of animals and plants that are discrete and discontinuous, separated from others by gaps in appearance and behavior?"[2] Yet, similar to Darwin who gave prominence to the slogan of Leibniz, namely that nature does not make jumps ("*natura non facit saltus*") Coyne also subscribes to the primacy of the just-mentioned continuity postulate, because it is the continuous process of evolution that produces discrete groups.

Gould remarks that for Darwin "… gradualism stood prior to natural selection in the core of his beliefs about the nature of things. Natural selection exemplified gradualism, not vice versa – and the various forms of gradualism converged to a single, coordinated view of life that extended its compass far beyond natural selection and even evolution itself."[3]

Clearly, within this mode of thinking there is no room for an acknowledgement of the inner nature of things and for the irreducibility of aspects. Anyone who digested the results of the philosophy of science of the 20th century will know that "facts" are not untouchable. Gould, once again, pointed out that as a biologist he properly understood the philosophy of science of the early and middle 20th century: "Facts have no independent existence in science, or in any human endeavor; theories grant differing weights, values, and descriptions, even to the most empirical and undeniable of observations."[4]

The next step is to account for the deepest convictions giving shape and direction to our theoretical endeavours. The above-mentioned continuity postulate of Leibniz is a manifes-

---

2009), 186.
2. Coyne, *Why Evolution*, 184.
3. S. J. Gould, *The Structure of Evolutionary Theory* (London: The Belknap Press, 2002), 154-155.
4. Gould, *Structure of Evolutionary Theory*, 759.

tation of the modern natural science ideal which eliminates any limits or boundaries set to human thinking. According to this ultimate commitment, human reason can reconstrue the world at will, rejecting any threat to the assumed power or autonomy of human reason.

Sphere Sovereignty as Obstacle

However, it is precisely the principle of aspectual (modal) sphere sovereignty that stands in the way of the humanistic science ideal with its levelling continuity postulate. Gould disqualifies the continuity postulate as a dangerous mental trap: "The stories we hear," so Gould argues,[5] "begin from the same foundational fallacy and then proceed in an identical erroneous way. They start with the most dangerous of mental traps: a hidden assumption, depicted as self-evident, if recognized at all – namely, a basic definition of evolution as *continuous flux*." [Gould points out that the dominant pattern of the paleontological record is that a type abruptly appears fully formed, remains constant over millions of years and then equally abruptly disappears unchanged.[6]]

Since change presupposes constancy it must be clear that any theory that does not recognize this foundational coherence may end up in serious theoretical difficulties, particularly when entities and processes are contemplated that enter into cosmic later modalities, for example when it is contemplated that material entities (having their highest active function within the physical aspect), either produce the biotic aspect of reality or assume an additional subject function within the biotic aspect (see Diagrams 2 and 3 of the *Introduction*). Can a particular sphere-sovereign function change into another function? Just contemplate for a moment the conviction that physical entities were transformed into biotic (i.e., living) entities.

---

5. Gould, *Structure of Evolutionary Theory*, 913.
6. Gould, *Structure of Evolutionary Theory*, 999–1000.

Can Modal Aspects Evolve?

Regarding the diversity in creation, it is important to note that each activity of analysis or abstraction is always dependent on a given multiplicity of aspects or entities that had to be identified and distinguished. It is precisely due to this inherent diversity present within the whole of creation that we are able to analyze it. Therefore, analysis (abstraction) presupposes a given multiplicity transcending the limits of our analytical activity. In other words, were it not for the more-than-logical diversity within creation, it would in principle have been impossible to think analytically! The logical-analytical thinking of human beings presupposes the creational diversity.

However, the problem regarding the "evolution" of modal aspects reveals a serious theoretical impasse. For example, if we accept that the physical function can change (can 'evolve') into the biotic aspect, the next question is if there will still exist a physical aspect of reality after the physical evolved into the biotical? This seems to be impossible, for now the physical aspect would be gone together with elementary particles, atoms, molecules, macro-molecules and macro-systems.

A less rigorous version may contemplate the question whether or not it is in general possible for one aspect to give rise to the existence of another aspect? For in this case the continued existence of the initial aspect may be affirmed. Yet, if this transition does not eliminate the initial (or primary) aspect, it is incorrect to claim that it changed into a different aspect. While holding on to the idea of "transformation" the only other option seems to be to defend one or another view of emergence in terms of which it is claimed that an on-going process eventually gives rise to various new aspects of reality. It is often asserted that once these additional aspects emerged (came into existence) they are irreducible. Emergent evolutionism (such as defended by Lloyd-Morgan, Whitehead, Alexander, Woltereck, Bavinck, Polanyi and recent Intelligent Design theories) indeed wants to have it both ways: continuity in descent (in the process of origination) and discontinuity in existence (in structure). Structure thus becomes the product of the genetic process of becoming.

We have noticed that although the biotic meaning of evolution surfaces as soon as evolution is discussed, it is implicitly pushed towards the background when the presumed development from the first cell to humans is explained. The term "evolution" then once again assumes the (non-physical) meaning-nuance of "progressive (biotic) development." But even when this (inconsistent) leap is made back to biotic evolution, the meaning of the latter is speculatively extended beyond all boundaries. Just consider the following statement of Sir Julian Huxley at the occasion of commemorating the appearance of Darwin's *Origin* in 1859: "This is one of the first public occasions on which it has been frankly faced that all aspects of reality are subject to evolution, from atoms and stars to fish and flowers, from fish and flowers to human societies and values – indeed, that all reality is a single process of evolution" (Quote from his lecture "The Evolutionary Vision" presented at the Convocation Ceremony that took place on Thanksgiving Day 1959). He also said that religion is an "organ of evolving man" which is no longer needed. But note the discrepancy between the claim that "all aspects of reality are subject to evolution" and the statement that "all reality is a single process of evolution": the first one elevates "evolution" to an all-encompassing law to which all aspects of reality are subjected and the second one reduces all laws to what "all reality is," namely "a single process of evolution"! What contradicts the latter statement is the *constancy* in which the "law" of the combined effect of random mutation and natural selection is supposed to operate. It is only on the basis of this element of constancy that evolutionary change could be accounted for. Add to this a remark from the neo-Darwinian biologist Wright:

If mind is totally absent in the non-living universe its appearance will be inexplicable. "Emergence of mind from no mind at all is sheer magic": The only satisfactory solution of these dilemmas would seem to be "that mind is universal, present not only in all organisms and in their cells but in molecules, atoms, and elementary particles."[7]

---

7. Quoted by T. Dobzhansky, *The Biology of Ultimate Concern* (New York: New American Library, 1967), 28.

16

Dooyeweerd's Philosophy of Time

by Danie F. M. Strauss

WHEN PHILOSOPHERS reflect on the problem of *time* it is customary to refer to Augustine who said: "What then is time? I know well enough what it is, provided that nobody asks me; but if I am asked what it is and try to explain, I am baffled."[1] Time is normally associated with what is known as the "passage of time" – based on the implicit presupposition that the future passes through the present into the past.

Augustine also stated here: if the present was *always present* without moving on (to the past), it would not be time but *eternity*. This shows that he stands within the tradition of seeing eternity as the *timeless present*. Already before Augustine the distinction between *time* and *eternity* was articulated in terms of the difference between *succession* and *simultaneity*. It is found in the B Fragments of Parmenides (520-450)[2] and further explored by Plotinus[3] where eternity is viewed as the *timeless present* – a view that resounded via Boethius (430-524) in the thought of Kierkegaard (1813-1855) (eternity as the *nunc aeternum*) and Wittgenstein, who said: "If we take eternity to mean not infinite temporal duration but timeless-

---

1. Augustine, *The Confessions of Saint Augustine*, trans. E. M. Blaiklock (London: Hodder and Stoughton, 1983), XI:14.
2. See H. Diels and W. Kranz, *Die Fragmente der Vorsokratiker*, vols. I-III (Berlin: Weidmannsche Verlagsbuchhandlung, 1959-60), B Fr. 8:3-6.
3. Plotinus, *The Enneads*, trans. Stephen MacKenna (London: Faber & Faber, 1956), III:7.

ness, then eternal life belongs to those who live in the present."[4]

Although the Bible does not explicitly attribute infinity to God, the theological tradition deduces God's infinity from his *omnipresence* and *eternity*, with *immutability* and *timelessness* equally important, and related issues.[5] Eternity is understood in terms of two apparently opposing notions: an *endless period of time* or *timelessness*. These two notions, on the one hand, may be related to the so-called Platonic and Aristotelian traditions, but actually should be appreciated in close coherence with the two conceptions of infinity operative in the history of mathematics (and theology). What I have in mind is the opposition between what is designated as the *potential infinite* and the *actual infinite*. As alternative designations of the potential and the actual infinite, with a larger intuitive clarity, one may employ terms derived from speculations about God's infinity employed during the 14th century – the *successive infinite* and the *at once infinite*. Compare the expressions *infinitum successivum* and *infinitum simultaneum*.[6]

Given the seemingly elusive nature of time, an escape route appears to be available in the idea of *time measurement* (dating an event), for through it our civilization managed to develop more familiar concepts in order to "conquer" time. The history of time measurement provides the following picture. Initially time was "captured" through *counting* – the days, weeks, months and years.

---

4. L. Wittgenstein, *Tractatus Logico-Philosophicus*, 3rd ed. (London: Routledge & Kegan Paul, [1921] 1966), 6.4311.
5. B. Leftow, "Eternity and Immutability," in *The Blackwell Guide to the Philosophy of Religion*, ed. W. E. Mann (Oxford: Blackwell Publishing, 2005), 62 ff.
6. See A. Maier, "Diskussion über das Aktuell Unendlichen in der ersten Hälfte des 14. Jahrhunderts," in *Ausgehendes Mittelalter*, vol. 1 (Rome: Roma, Edizioni di storia e letteratura, 1964), 77-79. See also D. F. M. Strauss, *Philosophy: Discipline of the Disciplines*. (Grand Rapids: Paideia, 2009), 239 ff.

Numerical succession forms the basis of this practice. Then our awareness of *simultaneity* surfaced, such as employed in sundials where the relative positions of the sun, the dial and the shadows are explored. Subsequently, the constant movement of the pendulum "ticked" off time duration *uniformly* (constantly). Finally, *atomic clocks*, dependent upon the *irreversibility* of radio-active decay, emerged. This irreversibility is also known as the arrow of time. In all four instances of time measurement the implicit presupposition remains that the future passes through the present into the past.

Moreover, any attempt to determine the "event" of *creation* is impossible in principle, for *dating* the supposed primordial event (the "Big Bang") to almost 14 billion years ago appeals to *time measurement* and time measurement always involves the *duration of a process* as determined by a specific *time order*. Any *time duration* is always *delimited by* and *subject to* such a specific (correlated – determining and delimiting) *time order*. Therefore, since dating presupposes this *time order*, the origination of this order itself cannot be *dated*.

Universal Constants and Units of Measurement

The phases through which time measurement developed, reflecting different modes of explanation, can be correlated with the *units of measurement* identified by Lorenzen in his *protophysics*. He distinguishes four units which reflect the four *modes of explanation* operative in the just mentioned history of time measurement, namely *mass, length, duration* and *charge*.[7] This shows that the generally accepted understanding of time, linking it with *duration*, is actually embedded within a context embracing diverse modes of explanation.

---

7. P. Lorenzen, "Zur Definition der vier fundamentalen Meßgrößen," *Philosophia Naturalis* 16 (1976): 1 ff.

	Lorenzen	Heisenberg (a)	Heisenberg (b)
Physical	charge	quantum of action	
Kinematical	duration	c (velocity of light)	time
Space	length		length
Number	mass		mass

Our Time Awareness Exceeds *Physical Time*

Moreover, our awareness of time actually exceeds the confines of *physical time* (which is homogenous). The French-American biologist, Lecomte du Noüy, pointed out that the biotic phases of life are accelerating – birth, growth, maturation, adulthood, ageing and dying – thus showing that the life cycle of living entities is *heterogenous* and therefore differs from physical time.[8] Bergson introduced his understanding of *psychical duration*. Noteworthy is that Hegel and Fichte already introduced the concept of "geschichtliche Zeit" (historical time) – a theme that was followed up by Kierkegaard, Jaspers, Heidegger, and many others. In 1948 a Dutch professor in modern philosophy, discussing this new fashion, entitled his inaugural lecture as "De Mensch als Historie" (The historical nature of being human).[9]

Dooyeweerd noticed that all definitions of "time" are simply definitions of *diverse facets of time*. Therefore, the Augustinian question still remains to be answered: what then is time really? Against the foregoing background Dooyeweerd's alternative answer to this question will now be explored.

---

8. H. Dooyeweerd, *A New Critique of Theoretical Thought*, vol. 2, Collected Works of Herman Dooyeweerd, Series A, General Editor D. F. M. Strauss (Lewiston, NY: Edwin Mellen, 1997), 28.
9. S. U. Zuidema, *De Mensch als Historie* (Franeker: T. Wever, 1948).

Heisenberg (c)	Heisenberg (d)	Weinert
	energy	temperature
velocity	velocity	second
length	length	meter
mass		kilogram

Time and the Impasse of Positivism

Positivism holds that the ultimate source of knowledge and truth is found in sensory perception. However, as soon as this maxim is tested, for example with reference to time or to the successive descriptions of matter through the history of physics, it turns out that the Achilles' heel of positivism is unmasked. Initially, in Greek culture, matter is described in numerical terms ("everything is number"), then in terms of space (the starting-point of Greek space metaphysics and the medieval chain of being with God as *ipsum esse*), followed by movement as explanatory term (the classical mechanistic worldview of particles in motion), and finally concluded in the acknowledgement of the characteristic *physical* nature of material things. (See the Chapter on *matter* by Danie F. M. Strauss.)

The key question is whether these aspectual terms could be observed in a sensory way. Can these terms be *weighed, touched, measured* or *smelled*? Just contemplate questions such as: What is the *colour* of the numerical aspect? What does the spatial aspect *taste* like? What does the kinematic aspect *feel* like? and What does the physical aspect *sound* like?

Any answer to these questions will be absurd, showing that these *functional terms* as well as what is intended with the term *time* cannot be observed by the senses. The reason is that neither time nor the various aspects of reality are concrete things. It is not difficult to realize that aspectual terms refer to a dimension of reality that is different from that of concrete (natural and societal) entities and processes. These entities and processes function within all the aspects of our experiential universe. Dooyeweerd emphasizes that the *meaning* of creation is found in its universal referring and expressing way. Nothing is self-contained, everything and every aspect points beyond itself and ultimately to God from, through and to Whom everything has been created (cf. Col. 1:15 ff.).

Consequently, the first step positivism had to take in order to digest "sense data" theoretically, has already eliminated the restriction of reliable knowledge to *sense data*!

That time cannot be identified with any single aspect also follows from these considerations. It is perfectly meaningful to speak of *temporal reality*, but it does not make sense to characterize reality exclusively in terms of a single aspect (such as the mentioned Pythagorean conviction that *everything is number*, the materialistic belief that *everything* is physical, the historicist claim that *all of reality is historical*, or the postmodern view that *everything is interpretation*). Dooyeweerd first developed his theory of modal aspects and entitary structures (designated as individuality structures), and only afterwards (probably in 1929) arrived at his first (radically new) understanding of what he called *cosmic time*. Traditional conceptions of time are constantly identifying time with merely one *aspect of time* – for example when "true time" is seen as *physical*, *emotional duration* (Bergson), that it is *existential* in nature (where existence is understood in a *historical* sense – Heidegger), and so on.

According to Dooyeweerd, time can only be experienced in its relation to created eternity (the *aevum*), in opposition to the *aeternitas increate* (the uncreated eternity of God). He characterizes the aevum as follows: "As an actual condition the aevum therefore is nothing but the creaturely concentration of the temporal upon eternity in the religious transcendence of the boundary of time."[10]

---

10. H. Dooyeweerd, *Time, Law, and History: Selected Essays*, Collected Works of Herman Dooyeweerd, Series B, vol. 14, General Editor D. F. M. Strauss (Grand Rapids, MI: Paideia Press: 2017), 22.

17

Philosophical Reflection on Physical Entities

by Danie F. M. Strauss

PHILOSOPHY OF NATURE was always interested in the "stuff" the universe is made of. Modern physics advanced quite a way in detecting and naming micro entities.

The size of electrons and quarks is smaller than 10^{-18}; they are so small that they are described as point-like.[1] Hydrons include those fermions and bosons designated as *mesons*. Furthermore, hadrons are constituted by quarks. Those known as baryons in turn include nucleons (neutrons and protons) and hyperons. Whereas the hadrons are "heavy," the leptons are small, including the electron and particles such as the muon, tauton and their corresponding neutrinos. For more information on this micro-dimension consult Penrose.[2]

The matter of an atom is concentrated in a volume of less than a 0.00000000000000000001 part of the volume of the atom.[3] Some facts about the way in which atoms function within the kinematic aspect are equally astonishing. According to wave mechanics, we find quantified wave movements around the atom, and the electron of a hydrogen atom (in its lowest orbit) moves

---

1. S. Kiontke, *Physik biologischer Systeme, Die erstaunliche Vernachlässigung der Biophysik in der Medizin* (München: Mintzel, 2006), 27.
2. R. Penrose, *The Road to Reality. A Complete Guide to the Laws of the Universe* (London: Vintage Books, 2004), 645 ff.
3. Kiontke, *Physik biologischer Systeme*, 27.

around the nucleus at a speed of about 6.8 million km per hour.[4]

From this, it is evident that the distinct number of elementary particles within the internal atomic structure is joined into a typical spatial and kinematic order of electronic orbits that configure the atom as an individual physical-chemical micro-totality. The special spatial configuration manifest within the internal arrangement of the parts of an atom reflects the typical foundational function of atoms. Biochemistry discovered many *isomeric forms*; that is, they have identified chemical configurations that are constituted by the *same atoms*, viewed from a purely quantitative perspective, but that nonetheless, owing to different spatial arrangements, differ *chemically*.

Consider $C_4H_4O_4$. That the chemical difference between *maleic acid* and *fumaric acid* has its foundation in alternative spatial arrangements is self-evident. In other words, it is intuitively clear that molecules such as these have a *spatial* foundational function, and not a numerical foundational function. (See the diagram below.)

Maleic acid
cis

Fumaric acid
trans

---

4. Kiontke, *Physik biologischer Systeme*, 27.

Stafleu remarks that the electron is characterized by exactly determinable values for its charge, rest mass, the magnetic moment and the lepton number.[5]

Diverse Modes of Explanation
Historical Perspectives on Physical Entities

The early Greek philosophers have chosen one or another fluid element as principle of origin, such as water (Thales), fire (Heraclitus) and air (Anaximenes). Of course, the subsequent development should take into account the significant role of the school of Pythagoras. The contribution of this school is that it articulated the insight that rational knowledge cannot be divorced from numerical relationships. Naturally this school went too far in its claim that everything is number. This thesis rests on the conviction that with the aid of the relation between integers, i.e., by merely using normal fractions, it is possible to describe the "essence" of whatever there is in numerical terms.

However, soon the developments within Greek culture became sensitive to spatial configurations – such as the shape of the calyx leaves found in nature, for this shape appeared as an instantiation of a regular pentagram. An investigation of the geometrical properties of a regular pentagram led to the discovery that it is not possible to express the ratio between any side and any diagonal of the regular pentagram with the aid of normal fractions, i.e., in terms of the ratio of two whole numbers (integer)s: a/b. This limitation at once embodied the discovery of 'incommensurable' quantities – something completely unacceptable for the Pythagoreans because suddenly within the limiting and form-giving nature of number the *apeiron* (the unbounded-infinite) appeared, i.e., irrational numbers were discovered.

The alternative mode of explanation that entered the scene

---

5. M. D. Stafleu, *De Verborgen Structuur* (Amsterdam: Buijten & Schipperheijn, 1989), 91.

was found in space. The spatial aspect allowed for the acceptance of static forms and it also opened the possibility to observe any spatial figure at once, without any before and after. The implication was that the acquisition of concepts is enclosed within the now and in the school of Parmenides this resulted in the equation of *thought* and *being*.

Plato's dialogue Meno, where the leader of the conversation used leading questions in order to allow the conversation partner to produce a geometrical proof, caused Oskar Becker to remark that this gave birth to the appreciation of the a priori nature of mathematics.[6]

The effect of the discovery of irrational numbers was not only that mathematics was *geometrized,* for it also paved the way for a speculative theory of reality attempting to explain the entire universe in terms of a *spatial* perspective – as a substitute for the outdated arithmetical orientation of the Pythagoreans. The implication was that Greek thought now understood matter in terms of spatial extension. An entity is identified with the place it occupies. Something *is* its place.

In its denial of movement, the school of Parmenides, in particular the arguments of Zeno, merely formulated the consequences of over-emphasizing the spatial aspect as mode of explanation. If something indeed is its place then it can never move, for passing from one place to another place will entail a change of essence!

The metaphysical overextension of the static nature of space even motivated a remarkable denial of the spatial whole-parts relation.

In order to understand this properly we have to keep in mind that whatever is continuously extended in a spatial sense allows for

---

6. O. Becker, ed., *Zur Geschichte der griechischen Mathematik, Wege der Forschung,* Band 43 (Darmstadt: Wissenschaftliche Buchgesellschaft, 1965), x.

an infinite divisibility. The spatial whole-parts relation turns the original numerical meaning of succession – the successive infinite – "inwards," embodied in the successive infinite divisibility of a continuum. In terms of the inter-modal coherence between number and space and in the light of the foundational role of number it indeed belongs to the meaning of the spatial whole-parts relation that it contains the possibility of endless divisions.

The spatial metaphysics of Parmenides, for that matter, inspired Zeno to defend a view of unitary wholeness that excludes plurality. In other words, Zeno wants to deny the "part"-element of the spatial whole-parts relationship while at the same time holding on to the "wholeness" which entails it.

The original numerical meaning of the number one as an integer analogically appears within the spatial aspect. The unity of a spatial subject is found in its wholeness. In other words, a spatial unity is constituted as a genuine whole or totality, a unitary whole allowing an infinite divisibility. The speculative (metaphysical) idea of a unitary whole precluding multiplicity robs both number and space from their unique meaning as well as from their mutual coherence.

In respect of the nature of material things the most important consequence is that the Greek-Medieval legacy only acknowledges concrete material extension. Extension characterizes the nature of material things.

Within the Aristotelian legacy it was believed that celestial bodies obey laws that are different from those that hold for entities on earth. In addition, it was believed that the movement of anything required a cause. The problem of motion increasingly acquired a more prominent position, although it did not mean that the powerful influence of the classical space metaphysics immediately lost its hold. The power of this spatial orientation is indeed still evident in the thought of Descartes (1596–1650) and even Immanuel Kant (1724–1804). In their understanding of nature both these philosophers continued to assign a decisive role to spatial extension. For Descartes extension serves as the essential characteristic of material bodies – *res extensa*, for he writes: "That the nature of body consists not in weight, hardness, colour, and the like, but in extension alone."[7] Kant's characterization of material bodies is also oriented to space. When our understanding leaves aside everything accompanying their representation, such as substance, force, divisibility, etc., and likewise also separates that which belongs to sensation, such as impenetrability, hardness, color, etc., then from this empirical intuition something else is left, namely extension and shape.

It should not surprise us therefore that Descartes straightaway applied the feature of (mathematical) continuity to material things and even to atoms that since Greek antiquity were supposed to be the last indivisible material particles. He holds that there cannot be atoms or material particles that are inherently non-divisible.

The nature of inertial motion unveiled the unbridgeable gap between the impetus theory and the basic idea of inertia, namely the possibility of an everlasting rectilinear motion. The shift to a new mode of explanation followed from the way in which Galileo formulated his law of inertia with the aid of a thought experiment. Suppose a body moves on a friction-free path extended into infinity, then this movement will simply continue endlessly. Opposed to the traditional Aristotelian-Scholastic conception according to which the movement of a body is dependent upon a causing force, the law of inertia implies that motion is something given and that therefore instead of trying to deduce or explain it, it should be accepted as a mode of explanation in its own right. Motion is original and unique and indeed embodies a distinct mode of explanation different from those used by the Pythagoreans (number) and the Eleatic school of Parmenides (space).

---

7. R. Descartes, *A Discourse on Method, Meditations and Principles*, trans. John Veitch (London: Everyman's Library, 1965), 200 – Part I, IV.

If motion does not need a causing force, then at most it is possible to speak of a *change of motion* (acceleration or deceleration) – and this does need a physical force.[8]

Writing on the foundations of physics, David Hilbert refers to the mechanistic ideal of unity in physics but immediately adds the remark that we now finally have to free ourselves from this untenable ideal.[9]

The idea of a uniform (rectilinear) motion on the one hand expands the inherent limitations attached to number and space as modes of explanation, and on the other it at once opens the way to consider another problem that already captured Greek thought. This problem concerns the relation between persistence (think about the nature of inertia) and dynamics (consider the change of motion requiring a physical force). But this issue is discussed in the Chapter on identity and change.

At this point we should observe that the classical opposition between *being at rest* and *moving* is untenable, because from a kinematic perspective 'rest' is a state of movement.[10] Unique and original modes of explanation are not *opposites* – for they are mutually cohering and irreducible.

Although Descartes and Newton did employ the concept force, it may in general be said that modern physics since Newton is characterized by its mechanistic main tendency. The mechanistic view consistently attempts to reduce all physical phenomena to a kinematic perspective. However, already in the course of the 19th century modern physics started to explore the nature of *energy*.

---

8. See C. F. Von Weizsäcker, *Große Physiker, Von Aristoteles bis Werner Heisenberg* (München: Deutscher Taschenbuch Verlag, 2002), 172.
9. Cf. D. Hilbert, *Gesammelte Abhandlungen*, vol. 3, 2nd ed. (Berlin: Verlag Springer, 1970), 258.
10. Cf. M. D. Stafleu, *Theories at Work: On the Structure and Functioning of Theories in Science, in Particular During the Copernican Revolution* (Lanham: University Press of America, 1987), 58.

The founder of physical chemistry, Wilhelm Ostwald, developed his so-called *Energetik* (energetics) that even influenced the later views of Heisenberg. Vogel refers to Heisenberg's work *Wandlungen in den Grundlagen der Naturwissenschaft* (Stuttgart 1949) where the latter explicitly speaks of energy as the basic stuff that constitutes matter in its threefold stable forms: electrons, protons and neutrons.[11] Yet Ostwald's *Energetik* did not exert a lasting influence upon the physics of the 20th century, probably because it was attached to a specific view of continuity opposed to an atomistic approach. Niels Bohr particularly mentions the excessive skepsis found in the thought of Mach regarding the existence of atoms.

The last prominent physicist who consistently adhered to the mechanistic approach was Heinrich Hertz. Soon after Hertz's death in 1894, the work in which he attempted to restrict the discipline of physics to the concepts mass, space and time, reflecting the three most basic modes of explanation of reality, namely the modes of number, space and movement, appeared: *The Principles of Mechanics developed in a New Context*. This caused him (and Russell) to view the concept of *force* as something intrinsically antinomous.

The Latin designation of mass during the medieval period was "*quantitas materiae.*"[12] From this it appears that number (*quantitas*) plays a key role in the concept mass. Mass actually concerns a physical *quantity*, but it is also possible to observe the quantity of energy from the perspective of the kinematical modality. In this case the technical expression is *kinetic energy* that indicates the action capacity inherent to a moving body.[13]

As soon as the physical aspect of reality surfaced it opened up

---

11. H. Vogel, *Zum Philosophischen Wirken Max Plancks. Seine Kritik am Positivismus* (Berlin: Akademie-Verlag, 1961), 37.
12. See A. Maier, *Die Vorläufer Galileis im 14. Jahrhundert* (Roma: Edizioni di Storia e letteratura, 1949), 144.
13. See Maier, *Die Vorläufer Galileis*, 142.

the way for 20th century physics to explore it as an independent mode of explanation and to arrive at an even more nuanced understanding of reality. For example, in his protophysics Paul Lorenzen distinguishes four units of measurement reflecting the first four modes of explanation: mass, length, duration and charge.[14]

A decade after Max Planck discovered his "Wirkungsquantum" he explicitly addressed the intrinsic untenability of the mechanical understanding of reality.

> The conception of nature that rendered the most significant service to physics up till the present is undoubtedly the mechanical. If we consider that this standpoint proceeds from the assumption that all qualitative differences are ultimately explicable by motions, then we may well define the mechanistic conception as the conviction that all physical processes *could be reduced completely to the motions* of unchangeable, similar mass-points or mass-elements.[15]

Einstein is equally explicit in his negative attitude towards "the mechanistic framework of classical physics."[16]

Eventually the distinction between the kinematic and physical aspects of reality thus became common knowledge. According to Janich the scope of an exact distinction between phoronomic (subsequently called kinematic) and dynamic arguments could be explained in terms of an example. Modern physics has to employ a dynamic interpretation of the statement that a body can alter its speed only continuously. Given certain conditions a body can

---

14. P. Lorenzen, "Zur Definition der vier fundamentalen Meßgrößen," *Philosophia Naturalis*, 16 (1976): 1 ff., emph. added. – see the Diagram in the chapter on time.
15. M. Planck, "Die Stellung der neueren Physik zur mechanischen Naturanschauung" in *Vorträge und Erinnerungen*, M. Planck, 5th ed. (Darmstadt: Wissenschaftliche Buchgesellschaft, 1973), 53.
16. A. Einstein, *Relativity, the Special and General Theory* (Bristol: Arrowsmith, [1920] 1985), 146.

never accelerate in a discontinuous way, that is to say, it cannot change its speed through an infinitely large acceleration, because that will require an infinite force.

The idea of an attracting force, initially conceived of in connection with magnetism, eventually brought Newton to the insight that magnetism is a force that cannot be explained through motion, although in its own right, foundational to the physical aspect, motion is a mode of explanation. Stafleu points out that the rejection of the Aristotelian distinction between the physics of celestial bodies and the physics of things on earth paved the way, in the footsteps of Galileo and Descartes, to realize that the same physical laws apply to both domains, i.e., that physical laws display *modal universality* (i.e., they hold universally).[17] He also remarks that Newton (just as Kepler) indeed already appreciated force positively as a principle of explanation that is distinct from motion as an original principle of explanation.[18] Stafleu summarizes this process through which the physical aspect emerged as an equally original mode of explanation as follows:

> In Newtonian mechanics, a force is considered a relation between two bodies, irreducible to other relations like quantity of matter, spatial distance, or relative motion. Though an actual force may partly depend on mass or spatial distance, as is the case with gravitational force, or on relative motion, as is the case with friction, a force is conceptually different from numerical, spatial or kinematic relations.[19]

Since the introduction of the atom theory of Niels Bohr in 1913, and actually already since the discovery of radio-activity in

---

17. M. D. Stafleu, *Theories at Work: On the Structure and Functioning of Theories in Science, in Particular during the Copernican Revolution* (Lanham: University Press of America, 1987), 73.
18. See Stafleu, *Theories at Work*, 76.
19. Stafleu, *Theories at Work*, 79.

1896 and the discovery of the energy quantum *h*, modern physics realized that matter is indeed characterized by physical energy operation. It is therefore understandable that 20th century physics eventually had to come to a general acknowledgement of the decisive significance of energy operation for the nature and understanding of the physical world, as it is strikingly captured in Einstein's famous formula:

$$E = mc^2$$

It was also realized that physical processes are irreversible. In itself this observation also justifies the distinction between the kinematic and the physical aspects of reality. Both Planck and Einstein knew that in terms of a purely kinematic perspective all processes are reversible. Einstein refers to Boltzmann who realized that thermodynamic processes are irreversible. Already in 1824 Carnot discovered irreversible processes – a discovery that was elaborated independently from each other in 1850 to the second main law of thermodynamics (the law of non-decreasing entropy). This law accounts for the fundamental irreversibility of natural processes within any closed system. The term entropy itself was introduced by Clausius only in 1865. In 1852 Thomson explains that according to this law all available energy strives towards uniform dissipation.[20] Planck remarks that "the irreversibility of natural processes" confronted "the mechanical conception of nature" with "insurmountable problems."[21]

It is only on the basis of an insight into the foundational posi-

---

20. See A. Apolin, "Die Geschichte des Ersten und Zweiten Hauptzatzes der Wärmetheorie und ihre Bedeutung für die Biologie," *Philosophia Naturalis* 4 (1964): 440 and H.J. Steffens, *James Prescott Joule and the Concept of Energy* (Folkstone, Eng.: Dawson; New York: Science History Publications, 1979), 140 ff.
21. M. Planck, *Vorträge und Erinnerungen*, 5th ed. (Darmstadt: Wissenschaftliche Buchgesellschaft, 1973), 55.

tion of the kinematic aspect in respect of the physical aspect that an appropriate designation of the first law of thermodynamics is made possible. Although we are used to employ the familiar designation of it as the law of energy conservation there is an element of ambiguity attached to the term "conservation" – as if energy is "held on to." When, on the law-side, the retrocipation from the physical aspect to the kinematic aspect is captured by the phrase *energy constancy* this ambiguity disappears and then we have at hand a concise and precise formulation of this law.

18

Dooyeweerd: Enriching our Understanding of Number and Space

by Danie F. M. Strauss

Weyl: *Mathematics as the science of the infinite*

Hilbert: *No one will expel us from the Paradise created for us by Cantor*

Succession

MOST CULTURES INCORPORATE in their awareness of multiplicity the ability to use the 10 human fingers in counting activities: 1, 2, 3, 4, 5, 6, 7, 8, 9, 10. Dooyeweerd designates this as the reversible numerical *time-order* of succession which at once ensures that every number is unique, subject to the core meaning of the numerical aspect, *discrete quantity* (see *Diagram* 1 of the *Introduction*).

Endlessness

Extending this succession indefinitely gives rise to endlessness, the view that it can be continued indefinitely, without an end. Since Aristotle this kind of infinity is known as the *potential infinite* and opposed to the so-called *actual infinite*, the infinite given at once as a totality. These natural numbers are lying at the basis of what should be called the *successive infinite*. However, the natural numbers could also be seen as an infinite totality given at once, i.e., as an instance of the *at once infinite* (the actual infinite).

Number and Space

Dooyeweerd points out that space, with its core meaning of *continuous extension*, presupposes the meaning of number, because spatial extension is specified by a number (magnitude), while the *order of extension* (dimension) is also specified by using a number: 1-dimensional extension (a line), 2-dimensional extension (a surface), and so on.

Dooyeweerd's brother-in-law, D. Th. Vollenhoven (who completed his PhD dissertation on the foundation of mathematics in 1918), argues that whoever says *space* speaks about a multiplicity of dimensions and points out that *multiplicity* presupposes the arithmetical with its "more" and "less." What is more, the possibility of *measuring* shows that within space number is pre-supposed – but the opposite is not true, for although a number is needed to specify the length of a line, it does not make sense to speak about *parallel numbers* or *intersecting numbers*.

Who Made the Integers (The Whole Numbers)?

Dooyeweerd mentions Kronecker (1823–1891) who said "God made the whole numbers [integers] and that everything else is the work of humans." On the same page he adds the following remark of Hermann Weyl (1885–1955): "Mathematics is totally dependent on the character of the natural numbers, …"[1] Kronecker held the prestigious Mathematics Chair in Berlin while Weyl was one of the brilliant students of David Hilbert (1862–1943). Weyl left the axiomatic school of Hilbert and became an adherent of the intuitionistic mathematics of the Dutch mathematician L.E.J. Brouwer (1881–1966). Hilbert became the foremost mathematician of the 20th century after Henrí Poincaré (1854–1912) passed away.

Yet the integers are not created by God. Number names and

---

1. H. Dooyeweerd, *A New Critique of Theoretical Thought*, vol. 2, Collected Works of Herman Dooyeweerd, Series A, General Editor D. F. M. Strauss (Lewiston, NY: Edwin Mellen, 1997), 88.

numerals are "man-made" – only *naming* diverse individual entities or traits generates number names – such as one, two, three . . . or the numerals 1, 2, 3, ...

The Paradise Created by Cantor

During the last 25 years of the 19th century Georg Cantor (1845–1918) designed *set theory* (German: *Mengenlehre*) including his theory of transfinite cardinal and ordinal numbers (cardinal: *how many* and ordinal: the *order or position*). Cantor's transfinite arithmetic prompted Hilbert to praise his purely intellectual achievement which created for us a Paradise out of which no one will drive us.

What is a Set?

Cantor defines a set with the aid of terms derived from our awareness (intuition) of *number* and *space*: A set is the collection *M* of a *multiplicity* of properly distinct objects *m* (the elements of *M*) brought together into a *whole*.

The key terms are *discreteness* (a *multiplicity* of elements) and *wholeness* (entailing the whole-parts relation). Laugwitz notes that in Cantor's definition of a set, "The discrete rules!"[2]

Law-Conformative Facts

Numerical and spatial facts are *law-conformative* for they follow the measure of numerical and spatial operations on the law-side of these aspects, such as *addition* (Dutch and Afrikaans: *wet-matig* = *measure* of the *law*). The next numerical operation on the law-side is *multiplication*. Operations on the *law-side* of the numerical aspect are strictly correlated with *numerical subjects*.

The operations of addition (+) and multiplication (×) are closed over the *set* of natural numbers *N*. It means that adding or multiplying any two numbers, such as 5 and 7, will always yield

---

2. D. Laugwitz, *Zahlen und Kontinuum. Eine Einführung in die Infinitesimalmathematik* (Mannheim: B.I.- Wissenschaftsverlag, 1986), 9.

another natural number – in this case respectively 12 and 35. This constitutes the *system* of natural numbers. Introducing further operations, such as *subtraction* and *division*, requires an expansion of numerical subjects, respectively the (positive and negative) *integers* and the *fractions* (rational numbers).

Restricting Mathematics to the Successive Infinite?

The Prince of mathematics, Carl Friedrich Gauss (1777–1855), only acknowledges the potential infinite (preferably designated as the *successive infinite*) and protests in 1831 against the use of the infinite as something completed. Nonetheless, during the last quarter of the 19th century Weierstrass, Dedekind and Cantor explored the actual infinite in order to account for what mathematicians call the *real numbers* (in addition to integers and fractions, also including irrational numbers such as $\sqrt{2}$ or π – with non-repetitive decimal expansions). The intention of these mathematicians was to *arithmetize* mathematics fully, i.e., to reduce space to number (continuity to discreteness) thus reviving an element of Pythagoreism. Mathematicians today still designate the real numbers as "the continuum."

The implications of this approach could be read in my article on the *Main Contours of the History of Mathematics*.[3]

Unfortunately, Bertrand Russell considered a set *C* with sets *A* not containing themselves as elements. The upshot is perplexing.

(i) If C is an element of C, it must conform to this condition, i.e., that it does not contain itself as an element.

(ii) If C is not an element of C, then it meets the condition for being an element of C

Therefore,

C is an element of C if and only if it is not an element of C!

[that is, $C \in C \Leftrightarrow C \notin C$]

---

3. *PONTE*, Vol. 75 | No. 1/1 | Jan. 2019, DOI: 10.21506/j.ponte.2019.1.11

The apparently innocent combination of *multiplicity* and *wholeness* therefore caused havoc within the discipline of mathematics, giving rise to the third foundational crisis and to conflicting schools of thought within this special science. For the logicism of Russell mathematics is logic, while the intuitionist school and that of axiomatic formalism accepted a pre-logical or extra-logical subject matter. Intuitionism reacted both to logicism and formalism and generated a whole new mathematics.

The hope to demonstrate the consistency of mathematics – Cantor's Paradise – was shattered in 1931 by the 25-year old Kurt Gödel, who has shown that any formal theory that is adequate to include the theory of whole numbers is either inconsistent or incomplete.

This outcome is consistent with Dooyeweerd's claim that the core meaning of an aspect, its meaning-nucleus, is indefinable, an insight even acknowledged beyond intuitionistic mathematics.

The Dutch mathematician Roos remarked in 2010 that Hilbert never recovered from this blow. The remarkable fact is that the intuitionistic school of Brouwer created a whole new mathematics which find no counterpart in classical mathematics – Stegmüller states: "The special character of intuitionistic mathematics is expressed in a series of theorems that contradict the classical results."[4]

Brouwer declares: "theorems holding in intuitionism, but not in classical mathematics flow from the special way … of development from the basic intuition, [from which] properties ensue which for classical mathematics are false."[5]

---

4. W. Stegmüller, *Main Currents in Contemporary German, British and American Philosophy* (Dordrecht: D. Reidel Publishing Company, 1969), 331.
5. L. E. J. Brouwer, "Consciousness, Philosophy, and Mathematics," in *Philosophy of Mathematics, Selected Readings*, eds. P. Benacerraf and H. Putnam (Oxford: Basil Blackwell, 1964), 79.

Weyl summarises the situation succinctly: "It must have been hard on Hilbert, the axiomatist, to acknowledge that the insight of consistency is rather to be attained by intuitive reasoning which is based on evidence and not on axioms."[6]

The irony is that although Dooyeweerd developed a theory of modal law-spheres which accounts for infinite totalities, he opted to follow Brouwer and Weyl by merely acknowledging the potential infinite.[7] In the absence of a theory of modal aspects Bernays approximates Dooyeweerd's idea of a numerical anticipation to space as follows: "The idea of the continuum is a geometric idea which Mathematical Analysis expresses in an arithmetic language."[8]

---

6. Quoted in C. Reid, *Hilbert* (New York: George Allen & Unwin, 1970), 269.
7. See D. F. M. Strauss, "The Philosophy of the Cosmonomic Idea and the Philosophical Foundations of Mathematics," *Philosophia Reformata* (2020): 1-19.
8. P. Bernays, *Abhandlungen zur Philosophie der Mathematik* (Darmstadt: Wissenschaftliche Buchgesellschaft, 1976), 74.

The Uniqueness of and Interconnections between Number and Space

Types of number		Spatial features
(reflecting in their multiplicity the qualifying role of discrete quantity as meaning-nucleus of the quantitative aspect)		(imitated, i.e. analogically reflected in the anticipatory coherence between number and space)

	Not-yet-disclosed characterization	
Natural Numbers (subject to the primitive numerical time-order of succession)	SERIAL	The Spatial Order of Extension
	Semi-Disclosed characterization	
Integers (imitating spatial wholeness)	WHOLENESS ⎯⎯⎯⎯⎯→ *anticipatory coherence*	The Factual Whole-Parts Relation
	Semi-Disclosed characterization	
Fractions (imitating the infinite divisibility of spatial wholeness)	DENSE ⎯⎯⎯⎯⎯→ *anticipation to a retrocipation*	The Infinite Divisibility of a Continuous Whole
	Fully Disclosed characterization	
Real numbers (imitating spatial continuity on the basis of the *at once infinite*)	PERFECTLY COHERENT ⎯⎯⎯⎯⎯→ *fully disclosed anticipation* ('continuous')	The Spatial Time-Order of At Once Determining every Factually Extended Spatial Continuum

19

Modal Universality

by Danie F. M. Strauss

WHEN WE DIRECT our theoretical attention toward the modal aspects or functions of reality—such as the spatial aspect, the physical facet, or the social function mentioned in the *Introduction*—we are no longer involved in the classification of entities according to the kinds or types to which they belong, and are therefore also not interested in the "kind laws" or "type laws" for entities. The mere distinction between economic and un-economic, for example, is not specified in any typical way. Both a state and a business can waste their money (and thus act *un-economically*) and both are called to function under the guidance of economic considerations of frugality. But it is only possible to articulate these perspectives when the economic aspect is understood in its modal universality, i.e., when the typical nature of the business and the state is disregarded. Modal laws hold universally without any specification—universities, businesses, states, families, and sport clubs all have to observe the general meaning of economic norms. In his discussion of "theories about everything," Breuer approximates the idea of modal universality when he states that a theory is universally valid if it holds for the "entire material 'world'," i.e., when "no part of the material world is excluded from its domain of validity."[1] However, he does not realize that the intended universality of a theory presupposes modal universality.

The physicist Von Weizsäcker approximates the universal va-

---

1. T. Breuer, "Universell und unvollständig: Theorien über alles?" *Philosophia Naturalis* 34 (1997): 2.

lidity of physical laws because he is convinced that the laws of quantum physics hold for all possible objects: "Quantum theory, formulated sufficiently abstract, is a universal theory for all *Gegenstandklassen* (classes of objects)."[2] When he explains, on the next page, that one cannot deduce the kinds of entities of experience from the universal scope of quantum theory, he implicitly alludes both to universal modal laws and type laws (the latter with their specified universality).

The law holding for a specific kind or type of entities still has its own universality, but this universality is *specified*. The law for being a state is universal in the sense that it holds for all states. But because not everything is a state, this *type law* is specified—it only applies to states. Likewise, businesses and states belong to different kinds of societal entities, and this typical difference is seen in the typical differences between the function of a state and the function of a business within the economic aspect—business economy differs from state economy (a business cannot "tax" its clients, but the state can tax its citizens). In general, one can say that modal laws encompass all possible entities, whereas typical laws (type laws) only hold for a limited class of entities.

Once the universality of every modal aspect is acknowledged, another avenue for the distinction between these two dimensions of reality is provided. The immediate implication of the modal universality of the aspects of reality is that no single (natural or social) entity or process can "escape" from functioning within every aspect of reality. It will turn out that this statement is only sound if a distinction is made between subject functions and object functions. For example, although material entities (like coins or stones) cannot buy and sell, they may have an object function within the economic aspect as a coin, or simply as a precious stone found in nature.

---

2. C. F. Von Weizsäcker, *Der Mensch in seiner Geschichte* (München: Deutscher Taschenbuch Verlag, 1993), 128.

In this sense, the modal laws of every aspect apply to every possible entity and process. Modal laws therefore apply universally; their scope is not limited to any class or any specific kind of entities. Quantitative laws do not merely hold for apples and oranges, or for that matter human beings: they apply to any multiplicity (plurality) of whatever kind.

Conversely, the laws for any specific kind of entity are solely applicable to those types of entities. The law for being an atom (e.g., having a nucleus) does not apply to mammals or states alike. Similarly, the structural principle for the state as a public legal community does not apply to other kinds of societal institutions, such as ecclesiastical communities or business firms.

In general, it can be said that modal laws hold for all possible classes of entities, whereas type laws hold for a limited class of entities only. This explains why even Kant was compelled to make a distinction between his (supposedly universally valid a priori) thought categories on the one hand, and so-called empirical laws of nature on the other:

> We rather have to distinguish empirical laws of nature, which always presuppose particular perceptions, from the pure or general natural laws, which, without having a foundation in particular perceptions, only contain the conditions of their necessary connection in an experience. In respect of the latter nature and possible experience are entirely the same; and since within these the law-conformity of the necessary connection of appearances in an experience (without which we are totally incapable of knowing any object of the world of sense), actually is based upon the original laws of the understanding, so it initially does sound strange, but it is nonetheless certain, when I state with respect to the latter: understanding creates its laws (a priori) not out of nature, but prescribes them to nature.[3]

---

3. I. Kant, *Prolegomena zu einer jeden künftigen Metaphysik die als Wissenschaft wird auftreten können* (Hamburg: Felix Meiner, [1783] 1969), par. 320.

This distinction runs parallel with the one we have drawn between modal laws and type laws. Although misdirected by the rationalistic assumptions of his epistemology, we note that Kant, in his search for the synthetic a priori, actually struggled with the nature of modal universality. Positivism and neo-positivism ought to be acknowledged for their emphasis on experimental testing and confirmation (which is not the same as *verification*). Only through studying the *orderliness* or *law-conformity* of entities, is it possible to arrive at an understanding of the type laws holding for that limited class of entities conforming to their peculiar type laws. In the case of physics, it requires empirical research through experimentation.

In order to appreciate Kant's position better in this regard, we have to look at the historical background of the distinction between modal laws holding for whatever there is and type laws applicable to a limited class of entities only.

By modally abstracting a particular aspect one gains access to the (unspecified) universality of modal-functional relationships. Since modal aspects are not concrete entities or events, they cannot be treated as if they are entitary in nature, because that would simply amount to a reification of modal functions. A widespread and well-known example of such a reification is the reference to the origin of "life." Of course, the intention is to refer to living things, yet no single living entity is exhausted by its biotic (life) function, since living entities also display, among others, a physical aspect, and both physicists and biologists know that the physical-chemical constituents of living entities are not "alive."

If one really wants to gain an understanding of the type law of any particular kind of entity, one has to investigate that entity empirically. One cannot derive the typical nature of different kinds of physical entities merely from modal analysis or abstraction—what is required, is empirical testing through experimentation—the legitimate facet of the positivist claim.

The fact that modal laws—such as those of quantum physics—hold for all possible "objects" is clearly seen by Von Weizsäcker where he observes: "Quantum theory, formulated sufficiently abstract, is a universal theory for all *Gegenstandklassen* (classes of objects)."[4] When he explains, on the next page, that one cannot deduce the kinds of entities of experience from the universal scope of quantum theory, he implicitly alludes both to universal modal laws and type laws (the latter with their specified universality).

Weyl also implicitly makes an appeal to the distinction between modal universality and typicality: "But what is connected with the a priori construction is experience and an analysis of experience through the experiment."[5]

Discussing the nature of an a priori synthetic element in the "empirical sciences," Stegmüller raises the following possibility—alluding to the same issue:

> Surely, this cannot imply that the totality of law-statements present in a natural science could be of an a priori nature. Much rather, such an apriorism should limit itself to the construction of a limited number of a priori valid law relationships, while, furthermore, all more specific laws of nature should be dependent on empirical testing.[6]

Note the similarity between Stegmüller's statement and the following explanation given by Stafleu (related to the distinction between modal laws and typical laws):

> Whereas typical laws can usually be found by induction and generalization of empirical facts or lower level law statements, modal laws

---

4. Weizsäcker, *Der Mensch*, 128.
5. H. Weyl, *Philosophie der Mathematik und Naturwissenschaft*, 3rd rev. ed. (Vienna: R. Oldenburg, 1966), 192.
6. W. Stegmüller, *Metaphysik, Skepsis, Wissenschaft* (Berlin/New York: Springer, [1954] 1969), 316.

are found by abstraction. Euclidean geometry, Galileo's discovery of the laws of motion . . . , and thermodynamic laws are all examples of laws found by abstraction. This state of affairs is reflected in the use of the term "rational mechanics," in distinction from experimental physics.[7]

Another example of what modal universality (a modal law) is all about is found in a telling remark by the 19th-century British philosopher, John Stuart Mill, aptly illustrating the scope of "numerosity":

> All numbers must be numbers of something: there are no such things as numbers in the abstract. But though numbers must be numbers of something, they may be numbers of anything. Propositions, therefore, concerning numbers, have the remarkable peculiarity that they are propositions concerning all things whatever; all objects, all existences of every kind, known to our experience.[8]

Particularly widespread is the confusion of modal universality and typicality when it comes to art works and an appreciation of the "aesthetic." Entities characterized by their aesthetic aspect should certainly be known to us as art works—the universal scope of the aesthetic also embraces those entities that are not characterized by the aesthetic mode, but still have a function within this aspect, owing to its modal universality. Therefore, aesthetics should not be restricted to those things dominated by their aestheticity, but also leave room for the aesthetic function of those entities that are not typically aesthetic. Zuidervaart lucidly explains this state of affairs:

---

7. M. D. Stafleu, *Time and Again: A Systematic Analysis of the Foundations of Physics* (Toronto: Wedge, 1980), 11.
8. Quoted from J. S. Mill, *A System of Logic*, Bk II, Ch 6/2, in E. Cassirer, *Substance and Function* [trans. of *Substanzbegriff und Funktionsbegriff*, 1910; repr. 1923] (New York: Dover, 1953), 3334.

I cannot avoid viewing the structure of aestheticity from both typical and aspectual angles. In the first place, much of that which is called aesthetic is typically artistic. There exist countless things and manners of functioning that cannot be explained except as members of an artistic type of existence that is dominated by its aestheticity. For example, the concrete existence of an art work is experienced as a typically aesthetic object. On the other hand, much aestheticity is not typically aesthetic. For example, a human being and a "beautiful" landscape are present to one another through certain aesthetic relations and functions. Neither the human nor the landscape is typically aesthetic. Their aesthetic relationship is certainly not artistic. Rather it is one instance of the fact that an aesthetic aspect permeates all creaturely existence.[9]

The classical humanistic science-ideal in this sense aimed at a consistent functionalization of what is given in our naive experience (consider the way in which the main tendency of classical physics attempted to reduce all physical phenomena to mathematical-kinematical motion). It also acquires a striking manifestation in the logical ideal that should guide natural scientific endeavors according to Rickert.

Whenever a function or aspect of reality is treated as if it is an entity, such an aspect is *reified* (or "hypostatized"). Conversely, if an entity is treated as if it is an aspect or function, it is *functionalized*. The neo-Kantian philosopher, Heinrich Rickert, explains:

> Whatever the role the category of a thing may fulfill in a theory of the thing world, envisaged as closed, at bottom there is no doubt that the natural sciences have to strive to resolve the rigid and fixed things increasingly, ... and this means nothing else but transforming as far as possible all thing concepts into relation concepts.[10]

---

9. L. Zuidervaart, *Explorations into a Philosophical Aesthetics*. Stenciled Paper (Toronto: Institute for Christian Studies, 1977), 6f.
10. H. Rickert, *Die Grenzen der naturwissenschaftlichen Begriffsbildung* (Tübin-

When biologists speak about the origin of "life" they treat the biotic function as if it is an entity.

Universality in this sense entails that it underlies and makes possible the functioning of every entity within every aspect. Philosophically speaking, the technical term designed to capture the nature of those conditions making possible the existence and functioning of something, is *transcendental*. This term acquired a particular meaning in the philosophy of Kant, for in his *Critique of Pure Reason* the word *transcendental* is employed to account for that which provides the basis of all experience in the sense that it makes possible what we experience.

Unfortunately, Kant did not accept any *ontic* universality, for according to him the formal source responsible for the ordering of the chaotic sensory impressions presented to us in experience, is found within the human subject itself—in what he calls the (a priori) forms of intuition (space as outer and time as inner forms of intuition).

In this brief chapter the biblical creation motive opens the way to the alternative distinction between modal universality and type laws.

---

gen: J. C. B. Mohr, 1913), cf. pp.68-69, 173, 197.

20

Philosophical Roots of Psychology

by Willem J. Ouweneel

Sometimes I think that, in the end, just two disciplines have been really important in my theoretical thinking: psychology and the philosophy of science. Psychology is one of the so-called "special sciences" (German: *Fachwissenschappen*; Dutch: *vakwetenschappen*), and the philosophy of science (German: *Wissenschaftsphilosophie*; Dutch: *wetenschapsfilosofie*) is the universal discipline underlying all the "special sciences". In a sense, these two have been even more important—not than the Bible of course but—than theology, viewed as a scholarly enterprise, that is, as one of the many "special sciences." This is because scientists and scholars, including theologians, are just like all other humans: in essence, they usually believe what they wish to believe, and reject what they do not wish to believe. There is no knowledge without prejudices, and this is "even" true for scientific knowledge.

It is a naïve (so-called "positivistic") view that science, including theology, is neutral, objective, unprejudiced; in short: is based on pure "facts." As my teacher, Dooyeweerdian philosopher Andree Troost, often said, the so-called facts are always "facts-for-people." That is, what we call "facts" are always humans, animals, plants, inanimate things, events and states of affairs as functioning within the minds of the people who perceive them.

Psychologists have made an important distinction between "sensation" (German: *Empfindung*, Dutch: *gewaarwording*) and "perception" (German: *Wahrnehmung*; Dutch: *waarneming*). Take, for instance, sight: what we "sense" with our eyes are not much more than colors and forms; what we "perceive" with our minds, however, is these colors and forms as they are shaped by our affections, emotions, volitions, reasonings, preferences, preceding knowledge that we have collected. We would not recognize a chair as a chair if we had no such preceding knowledge of chairs in general. But it goes even further: if we observe a certain young lady, it makes a tremendous difference whether we are the mother of this young lady, or her little son, or her teacher, or her lover, or her physician, or her boss, or a man with evil desires. Each of these seven persons observes a different young lady. There is no such thing as an "objective" lady who could be isolated from all our various perceptions.

"Objectivity"

Here we have a vital term: "objective." There is no doubt that all science must be "objective" in the sense that the outcome of any experiment or investigation must never be influenced by our preconceived ideas. But that same science can never be "objective" in the sense that science can be done by reason alone, apart from our feelings, volitions, reasonings, preceding knowledge, etcetera. Science is done by *humans*, not by *robots*, and humans always bring along their affections, emotions, volitions, reasonings, preferences, and preceding knowledge that they have collected.

The positivistic view of some "objective facts" and of "objective science" in the sense just described is outdated, at least among philosophers. Yet, I know of at least two categories of science where this obsolete view is still rather strong; these are the two—very different—domains of theoretical physics and theology. Theoretical physicists generally seem to still strongly believe in the "objective facts," and thus are often people who wish to have to do with philosophy as little as possible. The latter is equally true for that very different category of scholars: theologians. Throughout the centuries, they too have usually been quite afraid of philosophy.

Indeed, too many theologians still believe that, if you would simply stick to the "facts" of the Bible, you would easily see that *they*—*these* theologians—are right. Over against these "objective facts" they like to place the "unbiblical prejudices" of their theological opponents—as if unprejudiced theology were at all possible. They really believe that *they* are free of any sort of (theological or philosophical) prejudices—"they just stick to the Bible"—whereas their opponents do not. They have never learned to see that *all* theologians view the Bible through the glasses of their various worldviews, church confessions, and preconceived ideas (see my chapter on theology). This is no problem; *all* scientists and scholars are in the same boat, when it comes to such biases toward their respective subject fields.

This is where psychology comes in; some psychologists are highly interested in the emotions, volitions, (ir)rational arguments, and prejudices that play a role in the way people shape their views, creeds, hypotheses, and theories. Interestingly, they themselves necessarily do so within the framework of their own psychological paradigms. There is no way we can ever escape from such a "hermeneutical circle": we can speak of the prejudices of certain scientists only with the paradigm of our own prejudices.

The philosophy of science, which investigates (among many other things) the way scientific hypotheses and theories come about, is equally interested in the matter of the scientists' prejudices. One great pioneer in this respect was Karl R. Popper (1902–1994); but in his view the rational component was still dominant. It was different with Thomas S. Kuhn (1922–1996) in his book *The Structure of Scientific Revolutions* (1962). This work became world famous because of his idea of the leap-wise progress of science and his idea of "paradigms," scientific and pre-scientific thought-frameworks that dominate periods of "normal science" (see on this, my chapter on theology). But for our purpose, a third idea was equally important, namely, that a "paradigm" is never a purely rational totality, but also contains irrational, sensitive, volitional, social, historical, economic elements, and even "religious" elements.

The Double Sense of "Religious"

These ideas were very important and very influential. However, as I argued in my theology chapter, Kuhn used the word "religious" in the same way as Dooyeweerd used the word "pistical," namely, as just one of many *immanent* aspects of our cosmic reality. And to be sure, "paradigms" generally do contain such pistical elements. But what Kuhn did not see, is "religious" in its *transcendent* sense, as "something" that precedes and surpasses *all* immanent aspects of reality, including the pistical one. Dooyeweerd never became as famous as Kuhn became; he did not even come near. Nevertheless, he was much *earlier* than Kuhn, and in some important respects his view was *better* than Kuhn's view. Long before Kuhn, Dooyeweerd, in his *Wijsbegeerte der wetsidee* (1935–36), and the extended English version of this, *A New Critique of Theoretical Thought* (1953–1958), presented the notion of not only the rational, but also the irrational, sensitive, volitional, social, historical, economic, and pistical elements of all theoretical thinking. But beyond this, Dooyeweerd, in contrast with Kuhn and so many other "secular" philosophers, discerned the *transcendent-religious* determinedness of all practical as well as theoretical thinking.

To my mind, we have to do here with one of the most fruitful elements in Dooyeweerd's thinking. He thought of this transcendent-religious determinedness of all human thinking not so much because he was "cleverer" than other philosophers, but because his thinking was drenched in *Christian*-theoretical thinking.

Notice here the distinction between "Christian" and "theoretical": Christian is the opposite of non-Christian (or even anti-Christian), and theoretical is the opposite of practical. There is Christian-theoretical and Christian-practical, and non-Christian-theoretical and non-Christian-practical. Christian thinking is inspired by biblical thinking, but the latter is always *practical* thinking. That is, it is of a universal nature, in which all aspects of cosmic reality function at the same time, without being consciously distinguished. In theoretical thinking, however, human attention is focusing upon, and strongly limited to, just one such aspect. In psychology, the attention is focusing upon the psychical aspect (in my view, aspect*s*: the sensitive and the perceptive aspect), just as, in sociology, the scientist focuses upon the social aspect, and in ethics upon the moral aspect of cosmic reality.

At the same time, all these cosmic aspects are closely interlinked. This matter is investigated in philosophy, which is a "totality-science," underlying all the various disciplines. But moreover, it is (Christian) philosophy that is aware of the *unity* of all these cosmic aspects. Psychology has often been tempted to reduce the totality of reality to the psychical aspect(s) (psychologism, psychical monism), just as physics has often tried to reduce reality to the physical aspect (materialism), and sociology to the social aspect (socialism), and so on. I am not aware of any other philosophical school than the Dooyeweerdian one that has grasped the fundamental notion of all cosmic aspects to be of equal value, and to find their unity and coherence within the *transcendent-religious*.

Philosophical Anthropology

This is where a specific branch of philosophy comes in, namely, philosophical anthropology: the philosophical doctrine of Man, or, to avoid gender biases, of humanity. Philosophical anthropology is the branch of philosophy that underlies all "humanities" (special sciences occupied with humanity), just as "natural philosophy" (the philosophy of nature) underlies all the natural sciences, and "cultural philosophy" (the philosophy of culture) underlies all the cultural sciences. All these branches of philosophy form together what has been called "ontology," or, as we prefer to say (to avoid ancient-Greek connotations), philosophical cosmology. All these branches mentioned so far are of a *theoretical* nature—but in the end, they find their roots in something that is of a *practical* nature: a human view of cosmic reality, a "worldview," no matter how unarticulated such a worldview may be with many people.

This helps us to understand what "Christian psychology" is. This is not some mixture of secular psychological insights, interlarded with Bible verses (as has so often been the case). A Christian psychology is a psychology rooted in a Christian philosophical anthropology, which itself is rooted in a (pre-theoretical) Christian worldview, which as such is rooted in the Bible. This is a difficult point, but of the greatest importance: Christian psychology is *not* based upon Bible passages, it is *not* based upon theology (this is another common misunderstanding), but on a Christian philosophical anthropology, which itself is rooted in a (pre-theoretical) Christian worldview—and the latter can be called truly Christian only if it is drenched in biblical thinking.

Dooyeweerd has chosen here a biblical notion that has turned out to be very helpful, namely, the human heart. We may use this as an example to explain the differences between the Bible and theology, as well as between the Bible and theology on the one hand, and philosophical anthropology on the other. In the Bible, the term "heart," both in the Old and the New Testament, has a large array of meanings; here, higher animals also have hearts, as biology would underscore (cf. Dan. 4:16 KJV etc.). Theology has the task of mapping out these various meanings, and to suggest what is the preponderant sense of this biblical notion. In this way, it may certainly be helpful to philosophical anthropology. However, the latter has quite a different task: it must endeavor to describe the human "heart" in a way that is, and remains, thoroughly biblical (i.e., in line with broad biblical thinking, or with the "spirit of Scripture"), and at the same time is useful for a Christian-philosophical foundation for the humanities.

This is not an easy task. No Christian philosopher has ever

the right to claim that he has fully "succeeded" in this respect. Not only Christian psychology but also Christian theology and Christian philosophy always remain fallible human enterprises. God's Word is infallible, all human thinking, including theology, psychology and philosophy, are fallible. In even the "most Christian" theology, psychology, or philosophy, we have to do with all the (fallible) (ir)rational, sensitive, volitional, social, historical, and pistical elements that are characteristic of all human thinking. However, this does not prevent us from stating that some philosophies are—though strictly theoretical—more "in the spirit of Scripture" than others. If we accept this, I must add that I do not know of any Christian philosophical anthropology that is more appropriate to serve as a basis for a Christian way of doing the humanities than the Dooyeweerdian anthropology.

The Human Heart

To summarize, I believe the latter to be true because Dooyeweerdian anthropology is aware of the transcendent-religious orientation of all human thinking—and the notion of such an orientation is closer to biblical thought than other such orientations. The fact that Dooyeweerd has linked this transcendent-religious orientation with the biblical notion of the human *heart* is, in my view, a "big hit." Of course, Dooyeweerd's philosophical-anthropological notion of the heart is not *identical* with the biblical notion of the heart: the former is theoretical, the latter is practical. That is, the former has a limited, carefully described meaning (something like "the transcendent-religious concentration of all human existence"), and the latter contains a large array of common-speech meanings. But at the same time, I firmly believe that Dooyeweerd's *theoretical* notion of the heart is in line with the practical biblical way of speaking (see further in my chapter on "Adam, Where Are You?").

Dooyeweerd sometimes quoted Eccl. 3:11, which says that God "has put eternity [others: a sense of eternity, awareness of time, or, the world] into man's heart," to suggest that the way he used the notion of the "heart" was in line with the Bible. Later, he regretted such quotations, because they might suggest that he had "derived" a philosophical notion from the practical parlance of Scripture, which was not his intention at all. Psychological, philosophical, and even theological theories can never be "derived" from the Bible, simply because the Bible does not contain any theories, waiting to be taken out from it. Theories (as Popper put it) are nothing but creative *inventions* of the human mind, but such that they are believed to account for states of affairs encountered in reality. It may be hard to swallow for some, but even the finest Christian (or "Christian") psychological, philosophical, and theological theories are *man-made*, though designed to account for reality. How little this is often understood is obvious from the fact that theologians whose theories are attacked often respond as if it is the Bible itself that is being attacked.

Actually, Christian psychologists or philosophers might fall into the same snare. Those who attack Dooyeweerdian thinking do *not*, in this way, necessarily attack Christianity—although I am still waiting to find attackers who have come up with a more satisfactory form of Christian philosophy. Dooyeweerdian philosophy is not absolute truth—the point is only that I do not know of any more appropriate and useful form of Christian thinking. Some may say, So what? What does it matter? This question would be correct if it were only a matter of theoreticists, a game for scholars. In reality, we have to do with a very practical matter: we badly need a Christian approach to the humanities, and this is only possible if we develop a Christian-philosophical anthropology, firmly rooted in a (pre-theoretical) Christian worldview, in which a biblical view of humanity takes the central place. I am not aware of a more appropriate and useful Christian-philosophical anthropology than the one offered by the Dooyeweerdian school.

21

Galileo and Einstein

by Danie F. M. Strauss

EVER SINCE THE development of Galileo's mechanics, classical physics attempted to understand all bodies in terms of the denominator of *mechanical movement*. The law of inertia assumes the constancy of motion if no *physical forces* interact with this movement. From Newton up to the beginning of the 20th century this *mechanistic* tendency characterized the main development of modern physics. Max Plank described this mechanistic orientation as follows in 1910:

> The conception of nature that rendered the most significant service to physics up till the present is undoubtedly the mechanical. If we consider that this standpoint proceeds from the assumption that all qualitative differences are ultimately explicable by *motions*, then we may well define the mechanistic conception as the conviction that all physical processes could be reduced completely to the *motions* of unchangeable, similar mass-points or mass-elements.[1]

In kinematics all processes are *reversible* in principle. This reversibility concerns the *kinematical time order of uniformity (constancy)*. This time-order of reversibility is analogous to numerical succession and spatial co-existence—both of which are also *reversible*. The reversibility of the numerical time order first of all flows from the reversibility of the + and − directions in the system of

---

1. M. Planck, *Vorträge und Erinnerungen*, 5th ed. (Darmstadt: Wissenschaftliche Buchgesell-schaft, 1973), 53; ital. added. Also see the earlier chapter on physical entities.

integers. Although concrete events in physical reality are unidirectional, the time order within the numerical aspect could be experienced both in the positive and the negative directions.

As such it lies at the foundation of the *dynamic* changes discernible within physical processes of *energy transformation*. As early as 1824, Carnot discovered fundamentally irreversible physical processes. During the 19th century the implication of this discovery was further explored by Clausius and Thompson in their formulation of the *second main law of thermodynamics*. In 1865, Clausius introduced the term *entropy*. This law accounts for the *irreversibility* of physical processes since it determines the *direction* of a physical (or chemical) process in a *closed system*.

Thus, the law of non-decreasing entropy was established as the second main law of thermodynamics. At the same time, the classical mechanistic reduction to pure motion was uprooted. Justifiably, therefore, Max Planck (in the 1910 article quoted) remarks that the "irreversibility of natural processes" confronted the "mechanistic conception of nature" with "insurmountable problems."[2] The effect was that physicists had to acknowledge that *physical time* is irreversible. This *irreversibility* is manifested in the *a-symmetrical* relation of *causality*, for it stands to reason that the *cause* precedes the *effect*. Kant already realized that *causality* is not identical to *succession*, because although day and night (and: night and day) are succeeding each other, it is incorrect to say that either one is the *cause* of the other.

In a different context, Janich draws a clear distinction between *phoronomic* and *dynamic* statements. He states that the scope of the strict distinction between phoronomic (subsequently called kinematic) and dynamic arguments could be explained in terms of an example. Modern physics has to employ a *dynamic* interpretation of the statement that a body can alter its speed continuously only. Given certain conditions a body can never accelerate

---

2. Planck, *Vorträge und Erinnerungen*, 55.

in a discontinuous way, that is to say, it cannot change its speed through an infinitely large acceleration, because that will require an infinite force.

Since the discovery of radioactivity, it turned out that within micro-structures themselves there are irreversible processes present that proceed spontaneously in one direction only. In addition, this state of affairs, straightaway, confirms the irreducibility of the physical aspect to the kinematical aspect (with its reversible time order). It is therefore incorrect to say that "change" is the only "constant."

Already in his *Isagogè Philosophiae* of 1930, Vollenhoven, distinguished between the mechanical and the physical aspects. However, in the edition of 1936 this distinction no longer appears. By contrast, his colleague, Dooyeweerd, initially maintained the order: numerical, spatial, physical—thus identifying the kinematical aspect with the physical aspect. Round about 1950 Dooyeweerd realized that this distinction is necessary to account for the fact that kinematics (phoronomy) can define a uniform motion without any reference to a *causing force* (compare Galileo's law of inertia).[3] In an article of 2003, I included an account of the *ontic status* of the various modal aspects of reality, with special reference to the numerical and spatial aspects.[4]

That physical laws pre-suppose the meaning of the kinematic aspect could be demonstrated with reference to the first main law of thermodynamics, currently known as the law of the *conservation of energy*. Already in 1847, at the youthful age of 26, Helmholtz presented a formulation of this first main law of phys-

---

3. See H. Dooyeweerd, *A New Critique of Theoretical Thought*, vol. 2, Collected Works of Herman Dooyeweerd, Series A, General Editor D. F. M. Strauss (Lewiston, NY: Edwin Mellen, 1997), 99.
4. D. F. M. Strauss, "Frege's Attack on 'Abstraction' and his Defense of the 'Applicability' of Arithmetic (as Part of Logic)," *South African Journal of Philosophy* 22 (2003): 63–80.

ics to the *Physics Society* of Berlin. He began by pointing out that nobody had succeeded in building a successful *perpetual motion machine*. This was a logical consequence of the *indestructibility* of energy. Up to this day physicists recognize this law as the law of energy conservation which means that energy cannot be created or destroyed. What is at stake here is the *constancy* of energy. But the nature of constancy is precisely what Einstein employed in his special theory of relativity. One can indeed say that the crux of Einstein's theory of relativity is to be found in the nature of the (kinematic) *order of constancy* which it presupposes.

Bryon and Spielberg correctly emphasized that Einstein's theory concerns "invariance"—i.e., constancy—but unfortunately, they confused the terms *absolute* and *unchanging*. Indeed, Einstein originally developed his theory in order to find those things that are invariant ("absolute" and unchanging) rather than the *relative*. He was concerned with things that are universal and the same from all points of view.[5] The term *unchanging* is simply the denial (negation) of *change*—a *physical* term. The physical aspect must not only be distinguished from its foundational kinematic aspect, since there is also an indissoluble coherence between these two aspects. For this reason, we shall find within the physical aspect a structural moment which reminds us of the foundational meaning of the kinematic aspect. Constancy appears in the physical aspect as a structural reminder of the meaning of motion. In philosophical terms we may say that we find an *analogy* of the kinematic aspect at the law side of the physical aspect.[6]

A formulation of the first main law of thermodynamics which intends to be true to reality would therefore have to refer to *energy*

---

5. D.A. Bryon and N. Spielberg, *Seven Ideas that Shook the Universe* (New York: John Wiley & Sons, Inc., 1987), 6.
6. Cf. D. F. M. Strauss, "Kant and Modern Physics. The Synthetic a priori and the Distinction Between Modal Function and Entity," *South African Journal of Philosophy* 19 (2000): 26–40.

constancy. Strictly speaking, the use of the term "conservation" is inadequate, since the activity of retention itself requires an input of energy – as in the case of thermodynamic "open systems" (or "steady states"). The law of *energy constancy* illustrates not only the distinct uniqueness of the kinematic and physical aspects, but, while taking into account the distinction between law side and factual side, also the indissoluble coherence between them: without the foundational position of the kinematic aspect in the order of the various cosmic aspects we would have no grounds for discerning an analogy of the aspect of movement within the physical aspect, that is, the analogy of *energy constancy*. The distinctness and mutual coherence of constancy and change renders the statement that change is the only constant meaningless.

This foundational relation between constancy and change (the kinematical and physical aspects) is also significant for a meaningful account of our awareness of *identity*. Read the chapters on physical entities.

22

Modes of Explanation Making Identity Understandable

by Danie F. M. Strauss

THE IDEA OF AN ENTITY transcends any particular mode of explanation through which knowledge of entities is obtainable. One can explore different *modes of explanation* to demonstrate this perspective. But whenever any specific mode of explanation is used two things ought to be kept in mind.

(i) Approaching an entity from one functional (aspectual) perspective only can never exhaust the full, many-sided existence of such an entity;

(ii) Terms from any specific mode (aspect/function/facet) of reality could be used in a way stretching beyond the limits of the mode under consideration – in which case it is used in a concept-transcending way to refer to the entire existence of an entity.

When we speak about the *unity* of an entity, the fact that it is *one*, a straight-forward appeal is made to the *quantitative function* of such an entity (in which case the numerical terms 'one' and 'unity' are used conceptually, i.e., they are employed to refer to the way in which an entity functions *within* the arithmetical aspect). But the philosophical legacy of the West also explored our numerical intuition by using it to refer to *more than* the merely quantitative aspect of an entity. The acknowledgement of the *individuality* and *uniqueness* of an entity is quantitatively conditioned in that it is *distinct*. But this awareness of the individuality of an entity (its *being distinct*) does not merely capture the numerical qualities of an entity since it at once alludes to all other features of it as well. In other words, functional terms, such as those having their seat within the quantitative mode of reality, can be used to refer to the way in which an entity functions within the boundaries of a specific aspect (the conceptual use of the terms 'one' and 'unity'), or our numerical intuition can be stretched in concept-transcending ways to refer to the total existence of an entity in terms of the *idea* of its uniqueness or individuality.

Therefore, when an entity is seen as an *individual* entity, i.e., as *being distinct* from other entities, the (co-conditioning) role of the quantitative aspect is at stake. Yet this fact does not justify the elevation of number to become the "principle of individuation" as it is found in Aristotle who connected the category of *quantity* with *matter*: "But all things that are many in number have matter."[1]

In addition to the just mentioned numerical mode of explanation, the description of an entity may explore the *spatial mode* by adding a different specification, for instance when an entity is designated as an individual *whole* (*totality*). But it is only when we explore the points of entry offered by the kinematical and physical aspects of reality that we are capable of articulating a well-founded intuition of *identity*, for then we can add further specifications in saying that an entity is an *enduring* individual whole in spite of any *changes* to which it may be subjected. The term *identity* acquires a concept-transcending meaning in the sense that it stretches the original kinematical meaning of movement beyond its modal (aspectual) limits to refer to the entity in the totality of its persistence (enduring existence). This *idea* of identity presupposes the core kinematical meaning of a *uniform motion* (constancy) but it cannot

---

1. Aristotle, *The Basic Works of Aristotle*, ed. Richard McKeon (New York: The Modern Library, 2001), *Metaphysics* 1074a33-34.

be reduced to it. Once more we have to point out that Einstein did not develop a theory of *relativity*, but rather a *theory of constancy*.

In general, one can say that terms residing within a particular modal aspect may therefore be applied in a *twofold* sense, either as referring to phenomena functioning within the aspect concerned, or terms like these may be employed in such a way that they stand in the service of an understanding *transcending* the limited context of a specific mode of explanation. When the awareness of *uniform motion* is applied to the description of a uniformly moving body in a purely (abstract) kinematic sense, we may say that such a term is used in a *conceptual way*. However, the moment we expand our scope and use the term "constancy" in order to refer to the *identity* of an entity over time in spite of changes it may experience, then the intuition of constancy is expanded in a *concept-transcending* way that is manifest in speaking about the *identity* of such an entity.

The phrase *concept-transcending knowledge* can be designated as *idea-knowledge*, where it is assumed that a *form of thought* is needed in order to capture that kind of knowledge *transcending* the limits of concept formation. Nicolai Hartmann therefore aptly explained Kant's notion of the ideas of reason in a similar fashion. The thought-form required to *think* of an unknowable "thing-in-itself" ("Ding an sich") is what a "Grenzbegriff" intends to capture (*Grenzbegriff* = concept-transcending knowledge).[2] In passing, it should be noted that *conceptual knowledge* is constituted by *universality* whereas *idea-knowledge* approximates what is unique, individual and contingent.

In general, therefore, our talking about the identity of things rests upon the basis of a *concept-transcending idea* of the trans-modal reality of entities. Dooyeweerd writes: "The transcendental Idea of the individual whole precedes the theoretical analysis of its

---

2. See D. F. M. Strauss, "Popper and the Achilles Heel of Positivism," *Koers* 68, no. 2 and 3 (2003): 254.

modal functions. It is its pre-supposition, its cosmological a-priori."[3] It entails that entities belong to a distinct dimension of reality intimately cohering with another dimension of reality, namely that of modal functions (aspects) as explained in the *Introduction*. We only have access to entities because these aspects not only serve as modes of being and modes of explanation, but also as *experiential points of entry* to entities.

Lowe is justified in distinguishing between *identity* and *unity*: "A principle of individuation, we might say, is not so much a criterion of *identity* as a principle of *unity*."[4] But instead of exploring the kinematical meaning of uniform motion and its expansion to the idea of the *identity* of an entity, Lowe reverts to the logical-mathematical criterion of identity advanced by Frege.[5] Our basic concern is with the *ontic identity* of entities – mindful of the Quinian slogan mentioned by Schulte: "No entity without identity."[6]

Frege certainly employs an appropriate expression when he speaks about "Identitätsurteile" / "identity propositions."[7] But while he immediately relates such propositions to the logical principle of identity, our argument opts to account for the given ontic reality of *enduring entities*.

We are now in a position to understand why Von Kibèd got stuck in a static logic of identity. It is because he disregarded the

---

3. H. Dooyeweerd, *A New Critique of Theoretical Thought*, vol. 3, Collected Works of Herman Dooyeweerd, Series A, General Editor D. F. M. Strauss (Lewiston, NY: Edwin Mellen, 1997), 65.
4. E. J. Lowe, *The Possibility of Metaphysics, Substance, Identity and Time* (Oxford: Clarendon, 1998), 33.
5. Lowe, *The Possibility of Metaphysics*, 41.
6. J. Schulte, "Nachwort," in *Die Grundlagen der Arithmetik: Ein logisch mathematische Untersuchung über den Begriff Zahl*, G. Frege (Stuttgart: Reclam, 1987), 149.
7. G. Frege, *Schriften zur Logik und Sprachphilosophie: Aus dem Nachlaß* (Hamburg: Felix Meiner, 2001), 15.

kinematic and *physical* points of entry to entitary reality. In other words, he did not acknowledge the *uniqueness* and *coherence* between *constancy* and *dynamics*. A fruitful ontology requires an articulated awareness of the multiple modal aspects of reality – such as it is found in the philosophical legacy of Dooyeweerd and Vollenhoven. Carnap proceeds from a fairly simplistic and reduced view when he discusses five basic relations as 'categories': "identity, similarity, intensity, time, and space."[8] With these terms Carnap intends the numerical ('identity'), the spatial ('similarity', 'space'), the kinematical ('time') and the physical ('intensity').

Mechanistic Biology and the Identity of Living Entities

The immense successes of organic chemistry and biochemistry in unravelling the intricate physico-chemical functioning of living entities tempt modern biologists who are inclined to a *physicalistic* approach to over-accentuate the dynamic flow of the physical-chemical constituents of living entities.

Just consider the fact that all the atoms of our body, even of our bones, are exchanged at least once every seven years; all the atoms in our face are renewed every six months; all our red blood cells every four months; and 98% of the protein in the brain in less than a month. Add to this that our white blood cells are replaced every ten days and one-thirteenth of all our tissue proteins are renewed every 24 hours,[9] then we may justifiably ask the question: what guarantees the *identity* of a living entity if all the candidates are caught up in constant flux?

From a purely mechanistic or physicalistic point of view a living thing is explicable in physical terms only. But then it must display a physico-chemical identity constituted by its atoms, mol-

---

8. R. Carnap, *The Logical Structure of the World: Pseudoproblems in hilosophy* (London: Routledge & Kegan Paul, 1967), 135.

9. A. Jones, ed., *Science in Faith: A Christian Perspective on Teaching Science* (Essex: Romford, 1998), 40.

ecules, and macro-molecules. The problem, however, is that all these constituents are constantly changing! Which of these physico-chemical components could then constitute this supposedly purely physico-chemical identity of living things? Will it be those atoms, molecules, and macro-molecules currently present within it, those present years ago, or those that will be present a few years hence!?

When living things are *physicalistically* reduced to their *material constituents*, their *biotical identity* is necessarily lost – since the supposed elements of identity continually vary. Plato discusses the example of a wooden ship of which all the constitutive parts are replaced on sea.[10] See the discussion by Van Woudenberg.[11]

Yet, once the unique biotical function of living things is taken into account, it is even possible to claim that a living thing, considered in terms of the biotic mode of explanation, is in a *stable state* (referred to as *health*), while at the same time the claim can be made – without any contradiction – that, considered in terms of a physico-chemical mode of explanation (with a view to the flowing equilibrium of its physical-chemical constituents), it exists in an *unstable state*. We should keep in mind that Von Bertalanffy [on the basis of his idea of the dynamic equilibrium (*Fliessgleichgewicht*)] generalized the second main law of thermodynamics to *open systems*.[12] If the physical-chemical substratum of living things approaches a state of *higher statistical probability*, biotical *instability* increases as a sign of the final process of *dying*. Heraclitus must have understood something of *open systems* with his idea of flux, because his thought exhibits an awareness of the reciprocity

---

10. Plato, *The Collected Dialogues of Plato; Including the Letters*, ed. E. Hamilton and C. Huntington (Princeton: University Press, 1973), *Phaido*, 58.
11. R. van Woudenberg, *Het Mysterie van de Identiteit, Een Analytisch-Wijsgerige Studie* (Nijmegen: SUN, 2000), 28.
12. D. F. M. Strauss, "The Scope and Limitations of Von Bertalanffy's Systems Theory," *South African Journal of Philosophy* 21, no. 3 (2002), 163-179.

between persistence and change.[13]

From our preceding considerations important consequences follow.

(i) Whenever an idea of *identity* is formulated, the decisive clue is always given in the *mode of explanation* involved. For example, compared to the *physical* identity of material entities, living entities display a *biotical* identity.

(ii) Furthermore, whenever *identity* is the theme, at least an implicit awareness of the foundational relationship between constancy and dynamics is entailed.

(iii) Finally, since an entity is more than the sum of its different modes of explanation, no single (entitary) identity-claim can exhaust the uniqueness of any entity.

Sometimes a distinction is made between living and non-living entities: the first category applies to entities that retain their identity in spite of changes, whereas the second category refers to material things. Van Woudenberg remarks that the latter groups of entities can only be maintained through *external* intervention.

It is clear that he did not realize that what von Bertalanffy designated as a *flowing equilibrium* (*Fliessgleichgewicht*) – exemplified in a fire or glacier – does not require external maintenance (such as in the case of Plato's ship). Consequently, there ought to be no objection to speak about the identity of physical entities as well. But endurance over a period of time may be questioned in terms of what is known as the "principle of the inderscernability of identicals" of Leibniz, entailing that only when we restrict ourselves to a specific moment in time is it possible to affirm the identity of entities. However, as van Woundenberg[14] remarks, the idea of

---

13. H. Diels and W. Kranz, *Die Fragmente der Vorsokratiker*, Vols. I-III (Berlin: Weidmannsche Verlagsbuchhandlung, 1959-60), B Fr.90.
14. R. van Woudenberg, *Het Mysterie van de Identiteit, Een Analytisch-Wijs-*

temporal parts does not side-step the awareness of identity over time, but presupposes it.

---

gerige Studie (Nijmegen: SUN, 2000), 43.

23

Understanding Enkapsis As Contrasted with the Chemical Bond

by Martin A. Rice, Jr.

THE NOTION OF enkapsis is central to understanding Dooyeweerd's theory of individuality structures. In other words, it is central to understanding what *an individual thing* is in the context of the overall theory of the modal spheres as it is explained in the *Introduction*. Let me distill what Dooyeweerd has to say without referencing lengthy quotes. The interested reader may then follow up with the references provided.

For our purposes we will deal with just two individuals, one enkaptically contained in the other (although it is possible for several individuals to be enkaptically contained in one or more individuals). Firstly, the relationship is a kind of *containment*. The two individuals are structurally "interlaced," to use Dooyweerd's term. If you were to "pick up" the enkapsulating individual you would "pick up" the enkapsulated individual. Dooyeweerd uses the phrase "individuality structures" to denote that we are considering individuals by the type or *kind* of thing they are.[1]

Secondly, the enkapsulating individual depends necessarily for its existence on the enkapsulated individual. This is an ontological

---

1. H. Dooyeweerd, *A New Critique of Theoretical Thought*, vol. 3, Collected Works of Herman Dooyeweerd, Series A, General Editor D. F. M. Strauss (Lewiston, NY: Edwin Mellen, 1997), 636.

dependence. Eliminate the latter and you eliminate the former.[2]

Thirdly, both individuals still exhibit their own functions as individuals. In Dooyeweerd's parlance, their individuality functions are not "overridden."[3] The enkapsulated individual can still be identified as what it is, before or after enkapsulation, without needing to destroy the enkapsulating individual. If something was, say, a chemical substance of a certain kind before being enkapsulated in a more complex structure, it can still be identified as that chemical substance afterward.

Fourthly, and finally, the two individuals involved have different leading or qualifying functions. They are two different *kinds* of objects whose nature according to *kind* is determined by different modal aspects. If they were to be the same *kind* of object as determined by the same modal aspects, i.e., have the same leading or qualifying function, then the relationship would not be enkaptic. It would be a part-whole relation according to Dooyeweerd's definition of the part-whole relation.[4] Let's see how this plays out in an example.

Dooyeweerd illustrates enkapsis using the statue *Hermes* by the Ancient Greek sculptor Praxiteles.[5] The enkapsulated "individual" is the marble (one of the forms of limestone or calcite). The enkapsulating individual is the actual sculpture, *Hermes*.

Obviously, the two are intricately interlaced (that is connected) such that the statue necessarily is ontically dependent on the marble. Destroy the marble and you destroy the *Hermes*. Our first two conditions on enkapsis are met.

As for the third condition, the marble is still identifiable clearly as marble. Its internal functioning is not overridden. The chem-

---

2. Dooyeweerd, *New Critique*, 3:640.
3. Dooyeweerd, *New Critique*, 3:640f.
4. Dooyeweerd, *New Critique*, 3:636, 638f.
5. Dooyeweerd, *New Critique*, 3:638.

ical functioning of the marble remains unchanged by its inclusion in the sculpture. It can still be attacked by HCl and will still melt at its original melting point. Its hardness remains unchanged, as does its tensile strength and density.[6] Such properties can still be used to destroy the statue in exactly the same way they can destroy any slab of marble. The whole will be obedient to laws governing the enkaptically contained object. In short, marble will still behave like marble.

Moreover, the fourth condition is met. Both individuals have different qualifying functions. The statue is aesthetically qualified as an aesthetic object. Its leading function is found in the aesthetic modality. The marble is physically qualified as a physical object. Its leading function is found in the physical modality. Let's now turn to see if the idea of enkapsis will help us in clarifying the nature of the chemical bond.

One problem the introductory chemistry student faces is the difference between substances chemically bonded and mere mixtures. Introductory textbooks offer quick and facile definitions of a mixture and leave it at that. In back of the author's mind is the typical example of sugar and sand, or salt and sand, motivating the definition. The following is a typical textbook definition of a mixture.

> If two or more different substances are mixed and each retains its identity and specific properties, the result is a mixture.[7]

The notion of substances in a mixture retaining their separate identities and specific properties is a common theme in textbooks. It also leads us to suspect, given the previous discussion, that certain mixtures are perfect examples of enkaptic relations, given what the above definitions say about how each substance in the

---

6. Dooyeweerd, *New Critique*, 3:640f.
7. Donald Gregg, *Principles of Chemistry*, 3rd ed. (Boston: Allyn and Bacon, 1968), 4.

mixture "retains its identity and specific properties." But there are conceptual problems here.

Mixtures also exhibit new properties not exhibited by the substances that compose them. Melting, freezing, and boiling points change remarkably, as when electrolytes are added to water to increase its boiling point. Hence, original properties of the components of the mixture are not retained, which makes it problematic to say (if we identify things by their properties) that the identity of the components is retained as well. (But in the example of the *Hermes* one can get the marble to display the properties of calcite!)

Even more problematic is the omission in introductory texts of any discussion of metal alloys which are generally considered mixtures. In what sense can the components of bronze and brass be said to retain their separate identities? Treating the chemical bond as enkapsis is just as problematic. Concerning the "enkapsis" of sodium and chlorine in salt, Strauss writes:

> In this case, the internal sphere of operation of the atoms remains intact although, through a chemical bond, they were taken into the table salt molecule. When the internal sphere of operation of interwoven entities is retained, the term enkapsis is employed. Does this imply that the atoms become part of the chemical bond that exists within the molecule? Not at all, because the bond applies only to the binding electrons and not to the whole atom.[8]

Certainly, current theory puts the "work" of ionic chemical bonding on the electron shells of the atom. But in what sense are the original identities of the atoms retained?

Their original properties are certainly *not* identifiable in the behavior of the molecule and its properties, *qua* molecule. It seems impossible to say that the identities of the so-called enkapsulated identities are retained. If they are, in what sense are they retained?

---

8. D. F. M. Strauss, *Philosophy: Discipline of the Disciplines* (Grand Rapids, MI: Paideia Press, 2009), 466.

In the sense that the marble clearly retains its identity in the example of the *Hermes* while the atoms of the molecules do not so retain their identities. Furthermore, to say that the nucleus is the internal structure of the atom and neglect the electron shells is also misleading. This requires some parts to be more "internal" than others.

The nucleus is certainly responsible for the strong positive charge of the sodium anion. Without the positive charge contributed by the nucleus the ionic bond would not exist. The electrons are just as much internal parts of the atom as is the nucleus. Additionally, they are layered in "shells."

From the macroscopic point of view there is just no way to say or to ascertain that the original identities of the sodium or chlorine atoms are retained. It is certainly not as crystal clear as it is in the case of the marble in the *Hermes*. The original identities of the sodium and chlorine emerge in any sense only after the destruction of the molecule. To think we can say that the atoms retain their identities is merely a *misleading artifact of how we write their formulae and theoretically conceive of the chemical bond*. Once in the chemical bond, neither sodium nor chlorine behave like sodium or chlorine. This is the same with the atomic components of any other true molecule.

In order to distinguish enkapsis from the part-whole relation, the leading function of the enkapsulated entity must be different from that of the enkapsulating entity. (Otherwise, the relation devolves to the part-whole relation.) If we accept the current account of the modal spheres, the qualifying function of atoms in a chemical bond is exactly the same as that of the enkapsulating molecule. The atoms and the molecule they form are of *the same modal kind, i.e., physical*. This is just what Dooyweerd expects in the part-whole relation. It is what enables him to say that the torso is a part of the *Hermes*, but not the marble. Unless this is the case enkapsis cannot be distinguished from the mere part-whole relation. In fact, the whole distinction would fall apart. Hence, the chemical bond must be accepted as a part-whole relation, or Reformational philosophy must countenance chemical bonding as a brand-new species of modal functioning.

24

Antinomy and Contradiction

by Danie F. M. Strauss

As A RULE SCHOLARS do not distinguish between *contradictions* and *antinomies*. Consider the statement that there is a *square circle* (used by Kant, Russell, and Cassirer). Now consider the equally well-known statement used by Zeno in his argumentation against the reality of motion:[1] *Something moving neither moves in the space it occupies nor in the space it does not occupy.*

As long as one merely considers the well-known logical principles of *identity* and *non-contradiction* (whether or not amended by the principle of the *excluded middle*), no *material* criterion of truth is available – namely regarding the *content* of an argument, for in terms of these principles, one can at most (formally) affirm that two contradictory statements cannot both be true at the same time and within the same context. Kant clearly understood this:

> Therefore the purely logical criterion of truth, namely, the agreement of knowledge with the general and formal laws of the understanding and reason, is no doubt a condition sine qua non, or a negative condition of all truth. But logic can go no further, and it has no test for discovering error with regard to the contents, and not the form, of a proposition.[2]

What refers thought irrevocably beyond logic is the *principi-*

---

1. H. Diels and W. Kranz, *Die Fragmente der Vorsokratiker*, Vols. I-III (Berlin: Weidmannsche Verlagsbuchhandlung, 1959-60), B Fragment 4.
2. I. Kant, *Kritik der reinen Vernunft*, 2nd ed. (Hamburg: Felix Meiner, [1787] 1956), 84.

um rationis sufficientis (also known as *principium rationis determinantis* and *principium reddendae rationis*) – in English formulated as the "principle of sufficient reason."

This principle, originally formulated by Leibniz, was subjected to an extensive investigation by A. Schopenhauer in 1813. He called it the principle of sufficient ground of knowledge (*principium rationis sufficientis cognoscendi*):

> As such it asserts that, if a judgement is to express a piece of knowledge, it must have sufficient ground or reason (*Grund*); by virtue of this quality, it then receives the predicate true. Truth is therefore the reference of a judgement to something different therefrom. This something is called the ground or reason of the judgement ...[3]

The general legacy of Leibniz is captured in the phrase: there is nothing without a sufficient ground (*nihil est sine ratione sufficiente*). Of course, Plato affirmed that assertions require a foundation,[4] whereas Aristotle distinguished amongst the *aitiai* four causes: material, formal, effective and final.

In his *Monadology*, Leibniz formulates his view as follows:

> ... and the second the principle of sufficient reason, by virtue of which we observe that there can be found no fact that is true or existent, or any true proposition, without there being a sufficient reason for its being so and not otherwise, although we cannot know these reasons in most cases.[5]

---

3. A. Schopenhauer, *On the Fourfold Root of the Principle of Sufficient Reason*, trans. E. F. J. Payne (La Salle, IL: Open Court, 1974), 156.
4. Plato, *The Collected Dialogues of Plato; Including the Letters*, ed. E. Hamilton and C. Huntington (Princeton: University Press, 1973), *Timaeus* 28a.
5. G. W. L. Leibniz, *Philosophical Papers*, ed. Leroy E. Loemker, Synthese Historical Library, vol. 2 (Dordrecht-Holland: D. Reidel, 1976), 646 – see Sections 44 and 196.

ANTINOMY AND CONTRADICTION

People are often tempted to think that logic is decisive when a "good argument" is mentioned. Since an argument by itself merely links premises and conclusions—either in a valid or in invalid way—the "goodness" of an argument does not convey an assessment regarding the reliability of the premises or the conclusions. The latter requires proper distinctions in respect of the ontic nature of the diversity within reality – and the said distinctions ultimately reflect the worldview of a person.

If the *principium rationis sufficientis* refers to thinking beyond the limits of pure logicality, the logical principle of non-contradiction is founded in an underlying *ontical* principle, namely the principle forbidding inter-modal reductions – where the latter invariably result in *antinomies*.[6] This principle is *ontic* in nature and should be called the ontical principle of the excluded antinomy (*principium exclusae antinomiae*).

The perennial philosophical problem of explaining the coherence of what is unique and irreducible (the "coherence of irreducibles") therefore opens the way to an acknowledgment of the foundational position of the *principium exclusae antinomiae* in respect of the logical principle of non-contradiction – and at once explains why the distinction between antinomy and contradiction is not purely logical. The *principium exclusae antinomiae* not only depicts the limits of logic, but also underscores the significance of a non-reductionistic ontology transcending the confines of logic. Ontological reductionism violates the *principium exclusae antinomiae* and it leads to disastrous consequences, entailing all kinds of logical contradictions. Even if we disregard possible underlying antinomies, a negation of the principle of non-contradiction is equally devastating. Hersh remarks: "From any contradiction, all propositions (and their negations) follow! Everything's both true

---

6. H. Dooyeweerd, *A New Critique of Theoretical Thought*, vol. 2, Collected Works of Herman Dooyeweerd, Series A, General Editor D. F. M. Strauss (Lewiston, NY: Edwin Mellen, 1997), 36 ff.

and false! The theory collapses in ruins."[7]

The alternative to (antinomic) reductionism is given in an analysis of inter-modal connections presupposing their irreducibility. One of the richest implications enclosed in such an analysis is the fact that it is possible to come to a theoretical articulation of modal norms on the basis of analyzing analogies (retro- and anticipations) on the norm side of the normative aspects of reality.

Critical Thinking versus Critical Solidarity

In practice, being critical more often than not simply means that when you read a scientific article or book or when you listen to a scholarly presentation that you then notice differences of opinion. Picking up a book and finding something you do not agree with within the first couple of pages is not all that difficult. However, in order to be able really to benefit from the exercise of a critical spirit, one has to observe something more fundamental than critique, namely what is designated as *showing solidarity*.

The acknowledgment of supra-individual and supra-arbitrary principles enables all forms of rational interaction and scholarly communication. Those who have published on the theme of critical thinking normally enter into a discussion of modern (informal and formal) logic. The standard textbook on *Logic* by Copi immediately comes to mind,[8] or even a typical work on critical thinking (such as the one written by Bowell and Kemp).[9] Implicit in works such as these is the acceptance of the basic logical principles of identity, non-contradiction and the excluded middle (*tertium non datur*). Without these principles both classical predicate (syllogistic) logic and modern symbolic logic (propositional logic)

---

7. R. Hersh, *What is Mathematics Really?* (Oxford: Oxford University Press, 1997), 31.
8. See I. M. Copi, *Introduction to logic*, 9th ed. (New York: Macmillan, 1994).
9. T. Bowell and G. Kemp, *Critical Thinking, A Concise Guide* (London: Routledge &Kegan Paul, 2005).

collapses. The logical validity of particular modes of inference depends upon the logical principle of non-contradiction.

Logical Principles and Christian Scholarship

Consider the following argumentation against the possibility of divergent standpoints within scholarly disciplines (mathematics included) – an argument rooted in the belief that scholarship ought to be "objective" and "neutral." It runs as follows - with an implicit appeal to the later Wittgenstein's idea of "language games":

> Only those participants who accept the "rules of the game" are allowed to join the realm of science. When it is asked which "rules" ought to be followed, the mentioned three logical principles are specified.

However, intuitionistic logic does not accept the universal applicability of the logical principle of the excluded middle. The first two principles are embedded in the unity and diversity within reality because the latter make possible all identification and distinguishing. The normative demand of the principles of identity and non-contradiction is to identify A with A and to distinguish A from non-A. The crucial question is therefore: does intuitionism (with its logic) constitute a valid standpoint in mathematics?

Suppose we apply the yardstick of the three mentioned logical principles to this situation, that is, let us assume that only those who accept all three logical principles qualify to play the game of science. Then the principle of the excluded middle implies that intuitionism either is or is not a valid mathematical standpoint - there is no third possibility. Yet what is presupposed in this application is an implication of the principle of non-contradiction, namely that affirming and negating the scholarly status of intuitionism cannot both be true at once. However, on the basis of the three given logical principles one does not find sufficient grounds for the truth or falsity of two contradictory statements. The moment grounds are needed we are irrevocably referred beyond the boundaries of logic. On the basis of the initial argument, holding on to the first three logical principles, the only other option left (next to disqualifying intuitionism as an acceptable mathematical standpoint), is to accept it as a valid standpoint in spite of the fact that it partially truncates the principle of the excluded middle (thus implicitly applying the principle of the excluded middle, for here there is no reference to an infinite totality). In other words, if the answer to the question: whether or not intuitionism is a valid standpoint in mathematics? is affirmative, then the principle of non-contradiction is violated, and when it is negative, a new problem arises. Why is it not the case that intuitionism represents the valid mathematical standpoint rather than the Cantorian (or axiomatic formalistic) orientation? Is it unacceptable because the majority of mathematicians are not intuitionists?

Unfortunately, this option introduces a new 'principle', namely the *majority*. However, it is simply impossible to provide a justification for the majority principle. At most, recourse could be taken to a *regressus in infinitum* (treated in textbooks on logic as the *majority fallacy*):

> Did the majority decide that what the majority believes is true?
> And:
> Did the majority decide that the majority decides that what the majority decides is true?!
> .... and so on *ad infinitum*.

Amongst the "rhetorical ploys and fallacies" discussed by Bowell and Kemp, the "fallacy of majority belief" is also mentioned.[10]

Clearly, accepting the existence of universal principles for thinking as inevitable, does not entail that there is no room left for disagreement about specific principles of reasoning. Our argu-

---

10. Bowell and Kemp, *Critical Thinking*, 131 ff.

mentation not only demonstrates that the claim concerning the objectivity and neutrality of scholarship is self-defeating, but at the same time it also opens up space for a distinctively Christian approach to scholarship guided by the principle of the excluded antinomy and rooted in the ultimate conviction that nothing within creation ought to be deified or absolutized.

We may mention that the mathematician Hersh also questions the supposed infallibility and objectivity of mathematics.[11]

It is noteworthy that Wittgenstein followed Brouwer[12] and that the well-known analytical philosopher Dummett also supported the intuitionistic approach[13] – not to mention prominent mathematicians such as Weyl, Heyting, Van Dalen and Troelstra who continued to work within the legacy of the intuitionistic mathematics of Brouwer.[14]

A *Square Circle* and Spatially *Static Motion*

In conclusion we may return to the *square circle* and "static motion" mentioned in the first paragraph of this chapter. Confusing two spatial figures, namely a *square* and a *circle*, concerns only *one* modal aspect and is therefore merely an *intra-modal contradiction*. However, when it is attempted to confuse two different sphere-sovereign modal aspects, a genuine antinomy surfaces. An antinomy is *inter-modal in nature*, always entailing a contradic-

---

11. See R. Hersh, *What is Mathematics Really?* (Oxford: Oxford University Press, 1997), Part One, Chapter 3 – 35-47.
12. L. Wittgenstein, *Philosophical Investigations*, 3rd ed. (Oxford: Basil Blackwell, 1968), 112 (par.352); cp. 127 (par.426).
13. See M. A. E. Dummett, *Elements of Intuitionism* (Oxford: Clarendon Press, 1978) and M. A. E. Dummett, *Frege, Philosophy of Mathematics* (Cambridge: Harvard University Press, 1995).
14. See L. E. J. Brouwer, "De Onbetrouwbaarheid der Logische Principes" in L. E. J. Brouwer, *Wiskunde, Waarheid, Werkelijkheid* (Groningen: Noordhoff, 1919).

tion. It embodies an attempt to reduce one or another aspect to others, such as is found in Zeno's attempt to reduce motion to space, entailing the contradiction that something moving can move *if and only if* it cannot move.

25

Different Kinds of Criticism

by Danie F. M. Strauss

CLEARLY, ALTHOUGH it is inevitable to accept the existence of universal principles for thinking, this does not entail that there is no room left for disagreement about specific principles of reasoning (see the Chapter on contradiction and antinomy).

The argumentation that we have pursued demonstrates an instance of immanent criticism, for it has shown that the claim concerning the objectivity and neutrality of scholarship is self-defeating. Let us now explore the different types of criticism that ought to guide meaningful scholarly communication in some more detail. At the outset we mention the following types of criticism in order to elucidate the requirements of meaningful and constructive *scholarly communication*: (a) immanent criticism; (b) factual criticism; and (c) transcendental criticism.

Immanent Criticism

The first and most basic meaning of immanent criticism is given in the task to put yourself, so to speak, "in the shoes" of your conversation partner or opponent and then attempt to highlight the inconsistency or inconsistencies of that position.

It frequently happens that intellectual communication derails on the basis of what is known as *transcendent criticism*. It amounts to critique formulated in terms of one's own perspective without an attempt to involve the perspective of one's conversation partner in the argument. The fruitless outcome of transcendent criticism is aptly captured in the proverbial: "You say this, and I say that, so what?"

Let us rather briefly discuss a few examples of immanent criticism.

Example 1: Descartes' Proof for the Existence of God

In his Meditations III Descartes posits as a general rule, *that all that is very clearly and distinctly apprehended (conceived) is true.* To the question, what guarantees the truth of clear and distinct thought? Descartes answers that God will not deceive us, and he then proceeds to argue that of all the ideas in the human mind the idea of God is the clearest and most distinct.[1] This results in *begging the question (circular reasoning)*, for the existence of God is dependent upon the truth of clear and distinct thinking, while the truth of clear and distinct thinking depends upon (the existence of) the non-deceiving God. This kind of argument, where the conclusion is presupposed in one of its premises, is also known as a *petitio principii*.

Example 2: The Attempt of (Biological) Vitalism to Negate the Physical Basis of Living Entities

Since ancient Greece biological thought explored a vitalistic mode of thought, claiming that there is an immaterial "life-principle" (designated by Aristotle as *entelecheia*) operative in all living entities. The German biologist Hans Driesch continued this tradition in his neovitalist biology that dominated the scene by the end of the 19th century and during the first couple of decades of the 20th century – supported by the experimental study of regenerative phenomena.[2] It caused him to believe that the *entelechie* can

---

1. R. Descartes, *A Discourse on Method, Meditations and Principles*, trans. John Veitch (London: Everyman's Library, 1965), 95-96; 100.
2. He did research on phenomena of regeneration and discovered that animals are capable, when divided at an early stage of their development, to regenerate the entire living entity. Later on it was shown that in the case

"suspend" physical laws (such as the second law of non-decreasing entropy).³ Yet the mere fact that this immaterial factor is also described as a *vital force* shows that the physical substrate of living activities supposed to be transcended is still present in the term "force."

Example 3: Postmodernism

The motive of *logical creation* was dominant in *nominalistic* trends of thought since Thomas Hobbes and Immanuel Kant explored its rationalistic implications.⁴. Early modern philosophy elevated human reason to become the (formal) law-giver of the world. Impressed by Galileo's ability to derive the law of inertia from a thought-experiment — concerning a body in motion that will continue its motion endlessly if the path is extended into infinity — Immanuel Kant drew the radical conclusion: if, from the spontaneous subjectivity of human thought, one can derive the law of inertia and apply it to the moving "objects" in nature, then the laws of nature must be present in human thought *a priori* (i.e., before all experience). Kant explicitly states: "Understanding creates its laws (a priori) not out of nature, but prescribes them

---

of certain animals even a part as tiny as 1/280th can regenerate the entire animal. In general, the mere occurrence of processes of growth seem to contradict the second main law of thermodynamics, stating that within a closed system the most probable condition would be an increase in chaos, i.e., disorder.

3. We shall show below, in the context of *factual critique*, why this Neovitalist view is mistaken.
4. Thomas Hobbes is particularly known for his totalitarian view of the state as it is developed in his book *Leviathan* (1651). Immanuel Kant, the giant of the 18th century, is best known for his influential *Critique of Pure Reason* (1781, 1787). We take rationalism to be an over-estimation of universal conceptual knowledge.

to nature."⁵ The irrationalistic side of nominalism, emphasizing the unique individuality of events, inspired the idea of the "social *construction* of reality" – a line moving from Kant and Husserl to Schutz, Berger and Luckmann.⁶ Consequently, the contemporary "postmodern" idea that we create the world we live in (either through thought or through language) merely continues core elements of (*early*) *modern* philosophy!

This entire development hinges on the ambivalent nature of modern nominalism – outside the human mind it rejects all universality – universality is only immanent to human consciousness, either as universal concepts or as universal words. Outside the human mind things and events in their unique contingency and individuality are found (see the Chapters on nominalism).

The following *immanent criticism* can be raised against the stance of nominalism. In order to make its claim nominalism implicitly had to hang on to one element of universality outside the human mind – the *being individual* of everything! *Being individual* is a universal property applying to every individual.⁷

Example 4: Relativism and Historicism

The relativist statement: "There is no truth" is famous for its self-defeating nature. Ernst Gellner underscores it with his remark: "Notoriously there is no room for the assertion of relativism itself

---

5. I. Kant, *Prolegomena zu einer jeden kunftigen Metaphysik die als Wissenschaft wird auftreten können* (Hamburg: Felix Meiner, [1783] 1969), II:320; § 36.
6. In Husserl this idea of *construction* was still conceived of in a *rationalistic* way. Existential phenomenology, on the other hand, transformed Husserl's rationalism into an *irrationalistic* perspective.
7. When historicism mounted its intellectual forces at the beginning of the 19th century it also claimed that all historical events are unique, individual and irrepeatable, without realizing that these three features are *universal* because they apply to *all* historical events!

DIFFERENT KINDS OF CRITICISM

in a world in which relativism is true."[8]

The position of relativism is reinforced by modern historicism in its claim that everything is caught up in the never-ceasing process of (historical) change, including legal practices, moral convictions, aesthetic standards, and economic principles. However, immanent criticism points out that only that which is not intrinsically *historical* in nature can *have* a history. Therefore, if everything *is* history, nothing is left that can *have* a history and thus historicism achieves the opposite as that for which it has aimed. Instead of historicizing everything nothing historical is left.[9]

Example 5: Moral Commandments and Natural Law

Within modern Roman Catholic moral philosophy, the conviction is found that from the moral law (the "decalogue") rules of "natural law" could be derived. Thomas Aquinas (1225–1274) holds that derivations such as these could be made by using commandments like "You shall not murder," "You shall not commit adultery," and "You shall not steal." What he did not realize is that the concepts *murder*, *adultery* and *steal* presuppose unlawfulness in a jural sense. The prohibition of murder requires that one ought not to show such a lack of love and care towards one's neighbour that the desire to intentionally slay such a person arises. But when it is attempted to reduce the *moral* meaning of this commandment

---

8. E. Gellner, *Relativism and the Social Sciences* (Cambridge: Cambridge University Press, 1985), 85.
9. A comprehensive critique of historicism and pragmatism is found in R. Clouser, *The Myth of Religious Neutrality: An Essay on the Hidden role of Religious Belief in Theories* (Notre Dame: Notre Dame University Press, 2005). His closing statement reads: "Therefore I find that Rorty has failed to rescue historicism from the incoherencies native to it. Its central claims are still self-referentially, self-assumptively, and self-performatively incoherent, and Rorty's additions to them only compound the difficulties by being mutually inconsistent." Clouser, *Myth of Religious Neutrality*, 19.

to the jural an antinomy appears, since the meaning of morality presupposes the jural sense of unlawfulness. In order to side-step this antinomy, Victor Cathrein suggested that it is forbidden to murder unlawfully.[10] However, since the concept "murder" presupposes the jural element of unlawfulness (murder = unlawful killing), this escape-route continues to be antinomic. The possibility of an unlawful "murder" entails that its opposite is also possible: "lawful murdering." But since *murder = unlawful killing* the construction of "lawful murdering" boils down to the following entailed logical contradiction: "lawful-unlawful killing."

The last example introduced a new term, the term *antinomy*, to our discussion. It is not meant to be synonymous with a *contradiction*. As an example of a contradiction Cassirer refers to a "rundes Viereck" (a "round square"),[11] thus slightly altering the original example given by Kant in 1783.[12] Confusing two *spatial* figures is merely contradictory, because circles, squares and triangles are all appearing within *one* aspect of our experience – the spatial aspect. (Compare the Chapter on contradiction and antinomy.)

However, when two distinct aspects are confused something worse happens, for then we meet a *clash of laws*. For this reason, the attempt to reduce one aspect to a different one inevitably results in an *antinomy* (anti = against; nomos = law). An antinomy necessarily expresses itself in contradictions, but not all contradictions presuppose an antinomy. Since we can refer to the aspects of

---

10. V. Cathrein, *Recht, Naturrecht und positives Recht. Eine kritische Untersuchung der Grundbegriffe der Rechtsordnung*, 2nd ed. (Freiburg im Breisgau: Herder, 1909), 223.
11. E. Cassirer, *Substanzbegriff und Funktionsbegriff* (Darmstadt: Wissenschaftliche Buchgessellschaft, [1910] 1969), 16.
12. Immanuel Kant mentions the illogical concept of a "square circle" (Kant, *Prolegomena*, 341; § 52b). We have noted that contraries like logical – illogical, polite – impolite, legal – illegal, etc. are all founded on the logical principle of non-contradiction.

our experiential world as *modes of being* or as *modalities* it is clear that whereas a contradiction is always intra-modal in nature, an antinomy is always *inter-modal*. Moreover, recognizing an antinomy presupposes an insight into unique (and irreducible) *modal aspects* – without denying their *mutual coherence*. However, these considerations transcend the scope of the first three logical principles for they make an appeal to the *ontological* principle of the *excluded antinomy*.

By introducing this principle, we have already moved towards one instance of the nature of *factual criticism*.

Factual Criticism

It frequently happens that a position is assumed on the basis of allegedly sound "facts" but that closer scrutiny reveals the opposite.

Example 1: 'Soul' and 'Body'

Since Plato advanced his 'proofs' for the immortality of the soul in his dialogue *Phaido*, medieval scholasticism continued the idea that the human "rational soul" can operate in independence from the human "material body."[13] Thomas Aquinas writes: "Therefore, if the intellectual principle contained within itself the nature of any body, it would be unable to know all bodies."[14] However, in terms of *factual critique*, it should be pointed out that in all thought activities

---

13. Plato believed that when the soul investigates without the mediation of the body, it is directed at the world of the pure and eternal, immortal and unchanging, constant and equally natured things (Plato, *The Collected Dialogues of Plato; Including the Letters*, ed. E. Hamilton and C. Huntington [Princeton: University Press, 1973], *Phaido* 79 d). The soul exhibits the greatest similarity to the divine, immortal, conceivable, simple indissoluble, constant and "self-identical," while the body bears the greatest similarity to the human, mortal, multifarious, non-conceivable, dissoluble and never-constant (*Phaido* 80 b 1-6).
14. A. C. Pegis, *Basic Writings of Saint Thomas Aquinas*, vol. 1 (New York: Random House, 1945), 685.

of humans physical-chemical processes take place in the fore-brain. Although the total mass of an adult brain is a mere 2% of its total mass, 25% of the total metabolism occurring within the human body is found in the brain.[15]

Example 2: Suspending Physical Laws

We noted above that the neovitalism of Driesch believed that the "immaterial vital force" (*entelechie*) can 'suspend' physical laws, such as the law of non-decreasing entropy (because apparently a living entity builds up more and more order, thus seemingly "side-stepping" the increase in disorder prescribed by this law).[16]

By providing his generalization of the second main law of thermodynamics, Von Bertalanffy abandoned this notion of the "suspension" of physical laws by an assumed immaterial *entelechie*. The implicit assumption in Driesch's argument was that one can view a living entity as a physically *closed system*. Through his generalization Von Bertalanffy accounted for *open systems* – such as a glacier, fire or living entities viewed from their physical aspect – which means that a living entity does build up more and more order "at the cost" of extracting it from its environment (Schrödinger calls it *negentropy*).[17] The current *factual state of affairs* therefore uprooted the neovitalist idea of suspending physical laws.[18]

---

15. Cf. M. Plamenac, "Bio-physical Analysis of Vital Force of Living Matter," *Philosophia Naturalis*, 12 (1970), 444.
16. See H. Driesch, *Philosophie des Organischen* (Leipzig: Engelmann, 1921), 434 ff.
17. See E. Schrödinger, *What is Life? The Physical Aspect of the Cell* (New York: University Press, 1955).
18. After Von Bertalanffy generalized the second law for *open systems* (see L. Von Bertalanffy, *General System Theory* [Penguin University Books, 1973]) the followers of Driesch accepted it but continued their altered Neovitalism (see E.W. Sinnott, *The Problem of Organic Form* [London: New Haven, 1963] and E.W. Sinnott, *Matter, Mind and Man, The Biology of Human*

Example 3: Marx's View of the Sub- and Superstructure of Society

Karl Marx advanced the view that the historical-economical substructure of society provides the basis for (in the sense of one-sidedly determining) the ideological superstructure of law, morality and religion. However, *factually* it turned out that within societies with practically the same historical-economic substructure large differences in law, morality and religion are present, thus making the causal connection suggested by Marx invalid.

Transcendental Critique

The preceding discussion highlighted the importance of immanent criticism and factual criticism for meaningful and constructive scholarly communication. But it remained enclosed within the realm of theoretical views of reality, such as that of (neo-)vitalism or historicism. The positive outcome of what has been discussed is that the undeniable presence of alternative and sometimes even conflicting standpoints in various academic disciplines invalidates the idea of an "objective and neutral reason."

As mentioned in the Chapter on ultimate commitments, competent scholars in the domain of philosophy of science acknowledge that the traditional appreciation of human thought and of the power of reason are rooted in deeper convictions. The prevailing implicit trust in reason did not realize that such a *trust* or *faith* in reason is not itself rational! We have noted earlier that the well-known philosopher of science, Sir Karl Popper, radically attacks an uncritical or comprehensive rationalism which is based

---

Nature [New York: Atheneum, 1972], J. Haas, *Sein und Leben, Ontologie des organischen Lebens* [Karlsruhe: Badenia Verlag, 1968], W. Heitler, *Ueber die Komplementarität von Lebloser und lebender Materie.* Abhandlungen der mathematisch-naturwissenschaftlichen Klasse, Nr.1. [Mainz, 1976], P. Overhage, *Die biologische Zukunft der Menschheit* [Frankfurt am Main: Joseph Knecht, 1977] and contemporary Intelligent Design).

upon "the principle that any assumption which cannot be supported either by argument or by experience is to be discarded."[19] He argues that this kind of rationalism is demonstrably inconsistent, i.e., in terms of its own criteria: since "all arguments must proceed from assumptions, it is plainly impossible to demand that all assumptions should be based on argument."[20] Popper is aware of the fact that behind the idea of an "assumptionless" approach a huge assumption hides itself – something eventually also criticized by the prominent hermeneutical philosopher, Hans-Georg Gadamer, in his mocking of the prejudice of Enlightenment against prejudices.[21]

Popper's own position unequivocally demonstrates his insight into the self-insufficiency of "rationality." He knows that the rationalistic trust in reason is not rational itself and as mentioned he explicitly speaks of "an irrational faith in reason" – which means that according to him "rationalism is necessarily far from comprehensive or self-contained."[22]

Stegmüller, an equally formidable philosopher of science from the second half of the 20th century, holds, as we noted, a similar conviction. He says that there is no single domain in which a *self-guarantee* of human thinking exists – one already has to believe in something in order to justify something else.[23] [24]

---

19. K. Popper, *The Open Society and its Enemies*, vol. 2 (London: Routledge & Kegan Paul, 1966), 230.
20. Popper, *The Open Society*, 230.
21. Cf. H-G. Gadamer, *Truth and Method*, 2nd rev. ed. (New York: The Continuum Publishing Company, 1989), 276.
22. Popper, *The Open Society*, 231.
23. W. Stegmüller, *Metaphysik, Skepsis, Wissenschaft* (Berlin: Springer, 1969), 307.
24. This position is reminiscent of a remark made by Max Planck, the famous physicist who discovered the quantum of energy h (6.62×10^{-34} joule sec), in his rectorial oration of 1913: "One should not believe that it is possi-

DIFFERENT KINDS OF CRITICISM

From an anthropological perspective this implies that one has to understand that it is not 'thinking' that thinks, but the concrete human being who is more than thinking. Scholarly thinking is made possible by a supra-theoretical commitment that gives *direction* to scientific thought. The word *transcendental* is employed in this sense – it intends to capture those conditions (both theoretical and supra-theoretical) that make theoretical thinking possible. When transcendental critique is exercised an account is required of the theoretical view of reality of a thinker and of the deepest, direction-giving commitment lying at the root of a particular theoretical view of reality.

Theoretical orientations such as (neo-)vitalism, historicism, dialectical Marxism, arithmeticism, and so on are all instances of theoretical views of reality in which a specific account is given of the unity and diversity found in reality. Applying the principle of the *excluded antinomy* opens up the possibility to show that such *ismic* orientations are untenable because they harbour insoluble *antinomies*.

Yet there is more to scientific paradigms (theoretical views of reality) since the (supra-theoretic) root-commitment of a scholar ultimately reveals the deepest basic motive (ground-motive) operative in such paradigms. We will give merely a brief indication of what this entails – by looking at some of the issues discussed above in terms of *transcendental criticism*. In line with the first chapters of this work we can note that although Greek thought

---

ble, even in the most exact of all the natural sciences, to make progress totally without a world view, that is to say, completely without improvable hypotheses. Also, for physics the statement is true that one cannot attain salvation without faith, at least faith in a certain reality outside ourselves" (M. Planck, "Neue Bahnen der physikalischen Erkenntnis [Rede, gehalten beim Antritt des Rektorats der Friedrich-Wilhelms-Universität]," in *Vorträge und Erinnerungen*, M. Planck, 69-80. 5th ed. [Darmstadt: Wissenschaftliche Buchgesellschaft, 1973], 78.)

by and large is characterized by a realistic orientation, it did know nominalist thinkers as well – such as Callicles and the *Sophist* Protagoras. Both philosophers thought within the context of the deepest motivation of Greek thought and culture, expressed in the concern for *immutability* within a world of *change*. Aristotle eventually captured this tension by using the terms *form* and *matter*. The view of the human person found in the thought of Callicles and Protagoras is in the grip of the matter motive, for human subjectivity is seen as constantly changing and it cannot be grasped in any fixed form or measure. Only the *polis*, the Greek *city state*, as bearer of the Greek form motive, is capable of supplying the human being with a cultural garb through education and obedience to positive laws – thus demonstrating the primacy of the form motive in the thought of Protagoras. This explains why he holds that human beings, coming from a condition in nature where the state is absent, have those properties that are necessary for the formation of a state – but not on the basis of (the modern idea of) a "social contract."[25]

Modern nominalism, since the Renaissance, emerged within a different context. It was inspired by the urge to be liberated from the medieval unified ecclesiastical culture – humankind wanted to establish its own freedom and autonomy and it found in the rising successes of the new natural sciences the required control instrument. This implied that the ideal of a free and autonomous personality gave birth to the Renaissance natural science ideal, aimed that the reduction of all of reality to the determinism of mathematical-physical categories. Yet, as soon as all of reality is reduced to such a determined mathematical-physical condition, the assumed free and autonomous human personality falls prey to its own creation, the natural science-ideal, that now reveals

---

25. See A. Menzel, *Beiträge zur Geschichte der Staatslehre* (Vienna & Leipzig, 1929) and A. Menzel, "Griechische Staatssoziologie," *Zeitschrift für öffentliches Recht*, XVI (1936).

its Frankenstein-effect: in a world fully determined by the law of causality there is no room left for the freedom of the human person. *Nature* and *freedom* turned out to be a different basic motive (ground-motive), not only giving direction to modern nominalism but to modern post-Renaissance thought in general.[26]

The view of Kant mentioned above, regarding human understanding as the *a priori* (formal) law-giver of nature, represents his restriction of the natural science ideal to the world of phenomena (sense impressions), for behind appearances the freedom of the human soul is concealed (as a "thing-in-itself").[27] Kant indeed simply used the age-old distinction between "essences" and "appearance" in order to safe-guard a supra-sensory domain of moral freedom where the human being could be appreciated as an ethical aim-in-itself (Selbstzweck).[28] Kant explains: "*For if appearances*

---

26. Dooyeweerd's analysis of the dialectical development of modern philosophy, alternating between giving primacy either to the nature pole (Descartes, Hobbes, Leibniz, Locke, Berkeley and Hume) or to the freedom pole (Rousseau as transitional figure, Kant and post-Kantian freedom idealism: Schelling, Fichte and Hegel) provides an unparalleled understanding of modern philosophy (see H. Dooyeweerd, *A New Critique of Theoretical Thought*, vol. 1, Collected Works of Herman Dooyeweerd, Series A, ed. D. F. M. Strauss [Lewiston, NY: Edwin Mellen, 1997], 216-495.)
27. See I. Kant, *Kritik der reinen Vernunft*, 2nd ed. (Hamburg: Felix Meiner, [1787] 1967), XXVII-XXVIII.
28. The following words of Kant explicitly reveal his awareness of nature and freedom as the deepest motivating power of the critique of pure reason: "My purpose has only been to point out that since the thoroughgoing connection of all appearances, in a context of nature, is an inexorable law, the inevitable consequence of obstinately insisting on the reality of appearances is to destroy all freedom. Those who thus follow the common view have never been able to reconcile *nature and freedom*" (my italics – D. F. M. S, I. Kant, *Kritik der reinen Vernunft* [Hamburg: Felix Meiner Verlag, (1781) 1967], 537; I. Kant, *Kritik der reinen Vernunft*, 2nd ed. [Hamburg:

*are things in themselves, freedom cannot be upheld."*²⁹

The understanding of causality in the biology of Driesch actually attempted to apply the classical science-ideal to biotic phenomena as well. But his *negative* view of *entelechie*, circumscribed as non-spatial, non-mechanical, indivisible and non-energetic provided a starting-point for Arnold Gehlen – with an appeal to the idealism of Schelling and Hegel – to explore *freedom*. In order to achieve this Gehlen had once more to restrict causality to *mechanical* causality. "Because causality is only thinkable as mechanic causality, *entelechie* is *free* in a negative sense, that is it is spontaneous and primary in a sense that is incapable of closer determination."³⁰ This dialectical relation between *nature* and *freedom* is further elaborated in Max Scheler's work on the place of the human being within the cosmos³¹ and the freedom motive is also embodied in the idea of *Weltoffenheit*, developed in the thought of Gehlen, Portmann (a biologist) and Pannenberg (a theologian). In his PhD on the thought of Portmann this legacy is summarized by R. Kugler: "The innermost essence of the human being is freedom ..."³²

Finally, Karl Jaspers, who is well-known within the circles of the discipline of communication, expressed his own indebtedness

---

Felix Meiner, (1787) 1956], 565.)

29. "Denn, sind Erscheinungen Dinge an sich selbst, so ist Freiheit nicht zu retten." I. Kant, *Kritik der reinen Vernunft*, 2nd ed. (Hamburg: Felix Meiner, [1787] 1967), 564.

30. A. Gehlen, *Theorie der Willensfreiheit und frühe Philosophische Schriften*, (Berlin: Luchterhand, 1965), 60.

31. M. Scheler, *Die Stellung des Menschen im Kosmos*, 6th ed. (Bern-München: Francke, [1928] 1962), 38, 40.

32. R. Kugler, *Philosophische Aspekte der Biologie Adolf Portmanns* (Zürich: EVZ-Verlag, 1967), 81.

to the motive of nature and freedom as follows: "Because freedom is merely through and in opposition to nature, it must fail as freedom. – Freedom is only when nature is."[33]

---

33. K. Jaspers, *Philosophie* (Berlin: Springer Verlag, 1948), 871.

26

The Significance of Dooyeweerd's Work for the Natural Sciences

by Richard Gunton

Introduction

HERMAN DOOYEWEERD's Dutch frame of reference may have led to some disappointment when natural scientists have turned to his legacy for insight. The word translated "science," for him, means one or all of the scholarly disciplines, from maths through physics and sociology to theology, where English speakers understand only the natural sciences – especially physics, chemistry and biology. Many thinkers in Dooyeweerd's tradition continue to use "science" as widely as he and indeed other speakers of Germanic languages naturally use their equivalent, *wetenschap* (German: *Wissenschaft*), no doubt because Dooyeweerd's philosophy itself contains an important justification for this broad connotation. But we should start by asking how philosophy can possibly be significant for the natural sciences. Having seen Dooyeweerd's agenda, we will know what kind of significance to look for, and how to understand his conception of science.

A common view is that scientists need philosophy about as much as birds need ornithology – that is, not at all. On this view, science is an autonomous practice: it builds its own foundations and justifies its own assumptions. The unity of science is essential here, because diverse areas are interrelated so that any particular scientific investigation proceeds on the basis of assumptions and knowledge justified elsewhere – often historically in physics. A demarcation then comes easily, because the foundations and methodologies of physics do not reach far into the human sciences, where experiments are rarely feasible and many practitioners hold dear the principle of human freedom. So we find that 'science' commonly refers to a supposedly autonomous constellation of natural sciences.

In recent decades, historians of the sciences have increasingly scrutinized the wider social and ideological contexts in which scientists work. This trend is nevertheless characterized by attention not only to socioeconomic circumstances but also to personal and cultural philosophies. Acknowledging the work of scholars such as Steven Shapin,[1] Simon Schaffer[2] and Patricia Fara,[3] a flavor of this contextual approach may be evoked as follows. Certain people in various societies have enjoyed some combination of personal satisfaction, social prestige, economic benefit and political accolade from offering innovative accounts of features of the world that they can explain, predict, demonstrate or reproduce – thus persuading others of their own original contributions to knowledge and earning the title of "scientist." Such success depends on some kind of fit between the intellectual and existential frameworks in which these scientists operate and relevant features of the world, including their socio-cultural contexts. To this we can add the observation that intellectual and existential frameworks, commonly called worldviews in the neo-Calvinist tradition, can be related to more explicit paradigms and philosophies. So philosophy surely matters, at some level.

1. S. Shapin, *The Scientific Revolution* (Chicago: University of Chicago Press, 1996).
2. S. Naylor and S. Schaffer, "Nineteenth-century Survey Sciences: Enterprises, Expeditions and Exhibitions," *Notes and Records* 73 (March 2019): 135–147, doi: 10.1098/rsnr.2019.0005.
3. P. Fara, *An Entertainment for Angels: Electricity in the Enlightenment* (Duxford: Icon Books, 2002).

By developing this contextual approach, we reach Dooyeweerd's view of the role of philosophy in the sciences (that is, in all areas of scholarship). Philosophies are driven and shaped by religious ground-motives: deep-rooted cultural convictions about what reality is based on. Because these ground-motives can shape and direct scientists' work, their formal articulation (perhaps as worldviews) in philosophical terms might hold a key not only to understanding historical directions in the development of scientific fields, but also to orienting scientific work to make it more fruitful and reliable in the present. To hold out this prospect is, of course, to assume that a philosophical analysis of scientific worldviews can be successfully oriented towards the actual constitution of the world. Most secular thinkers would probably part company with us at this point: surely 'science' itself has the most successful methodology and track record of any discipline for discovering the constitution of the world? But Dooyeweerd sees a fundamental mystery in the nature of reality such that it can only partially be analyzed, with different scholarly disciplines complementing each other. Moreover, his version of philosophy is not at all alien to the sciences. It employs what he calls a transcendental-empirical method, yielding a theory about the general structure of creation that is informed by experience and subject to revision. Furthermore, it accounts for the nature of human reasoning and inquiry into the world using the same categories as those which it uses for the world as a whole. This philosophy is offered as a meta-science: a systematic empirically-grounded framework within which to situate and indeed integrate the diverse sciences – not just the natural sciences, but scholarly disciplines from maths to theology. Dooyeweerd's conception of philosophy has been dubbed "the discipline of the disciplines."[4]

We see, then, that Dooyeweerd's own worldview differs from

---

4. D. F. M. Strauss, *Philosophy: Discipline of the Disciplines* (Grand Rapids: Paideia Press, 2009).

prevailing views of the nature and role of both philosophy and the sciences, yet resonates at times with contemporary historiography and sociology of the sciences. It is a fundamentally pluralistic view that attempts to understand the diversity of worldviews of scholars, the diversity of disciplines that they follow and the rich diversity of the world that they study. And it offers to accommodate and elucidate the structure of other scholarly disciplines while respecting their distinctive characters and approaches. Dooyeweerd's view of the sciences may be portrayed as a unified patchwork of disciplines with their diverse works in progress, co-created by researchers using distinct ideological fabrics that derive from a number of cultural ground-motives. What, then, unites them?

Aspects and Sciences

As will be clear from other chapters in this volume, the most characteristic theme of Dooyeweerd's philosophy is his theory of modal aspects. Each of the aspects has its corresponding special science(s), including many of the academic disciplines that may be found in a university. Two pitfalls must be avoided in appreciating the significance of this hypothesis. First, an aspect is, on Dooyeweerd's hypothesis, not merely a mode of human experience but also a mode in which reality actually functions. Second, no aspect should be taken as more real than any other, nor any science as giving an ultimate account of the nature of reality. Contemporary discourse (now as in Dooyeweerd's time) tends to construe the "physical" as constitutive of reality, and to see the explanatory and predictive success that many theories have achieved through reducing phenomena to constituent parts as validating a mechanistic hypothesis whereby particles are the ground of being. But according to Dooyeweerd's transcendental critique, purely physical particles are an inconceivable concept and thus a meaningless hypothesis. By contrast, Dooyeweerd paints scientific analysis as abstracting a single mode from real phenomena and entities so that the scientist loses sight of real *things* in order to investigate real *modes of functioning*, in the abstract. Most natural sciences also engage in another kind of abstraction, by which we perceive types of entity – such as kinds of particle, chemical or species – but this is done separately from modal abstraction. With these options in mind, Table 1 lists the 15 aspects and some corresponding sciences.

Table 1: *The modal aspects of Dooyeweerd's framework, with corresponding academic disciplines.*[5]

Aspect	Discipline
Numerical	Arithmetic, Algebra
Spatial	Geometry
Kinetic	Dynamics, Mechanics
Physical	Physics, Chemistry, Materials science, Geology, Astronomy
Biotic	Life sciences, Physiology, Biology
Sensitive	Psychology, Sensory sciences, Animal behaviour
Analytical	Logic, some of Cognitive psychology
Formative	Design science, History, Technology, Engineering
Lingual	Linguistics, Semiotics, Exegesis, Hermeneutics, Translation studies
Social	Sociology, Organisational science
Economic	Economics, Management science
Aesthetic	Aesthetics, Musicology, etc
Jural	Juridics, Legal science, Political science
Ethical	Ethics
Certitudinal	Theology, some of Anthropology

---

5. Abbreviated from A. Basden, "Understanding the Relationships between Fields of Research," *The Electronic Journal of Business Research Methods* 19, no. 1 (2021): 27-41.

The first seven aspects correspond quite well with core disciplines to be found in the science faculty of a contemporary university. Table 2 attempts the classification the other way round, indexed by the science departments at a notable traditional university in England. The physical and biotic aspects appear in many different departments, probably because of the diversity of specific types of entities and systems characterized by these aspects. Indeed, Dooyeweerd would have us note that the scope of any science can only be defined using concepts and methods taken from outside that discipline. To define physics in terms of, say, matter and energy or biology in terms of life immediately requires clarification about the physical or biotic aspects of those concepts, abstracting them from their everyday connotations. In the end, 'physical' or 'biotic' must be explained (not defined) by contrasting it with other aspects, and the discipline that can help us to do this is philosophy.

Table 2: *Natural science (including mathematics but excluding medical) departments at the University of Cambridge,[6] with suggested corresponding modal aspects.*

Department (discipline)	Focal aspect(s)	Comments on discipline
Pure Mathematics and Mathematical Statistics	Numerical; Spatial	These two aspects in maths were largely separated up to medieval times but are now integrated
Applied Mathematics and Theoretical Physics	Numerical to Biotic	This department is notably interdisciplinary, hence multi-aspectual

---

6. "Department A – Z," University of Cambridge, accessed October 27, 2021, https://www.cam.ac.uk/colleges-and-departments/department-a-z.

Astronomy	Kinetic; Physical	Studying specific types of physical entity
Physics	Physical	In its pure form, focuses on universal relations of the physical aspect
Materials Science and Metallurgy	Physical	These physical sciences focus on specific types of physical entity
Chemistry	Physical	
Earth Sciences	Physical; Biotic	Multi-aspectual
Biochemistry	Physical; Biotic	The enkapsis of physical entities (molecules) within living tissues
Genetics	Biotic	Universal relations of the biotic aspect
Plant Sciences	Biotic	
Pharmacology	Biotic	These disciplines all tend to focus on animals (at Cambridge, their botanical equivalents are studied in Plant Sciences)
Physiology, Development and Neuroscience	Biotic; Sensitive	
Pathology	Biotic; Sensitive	
Zoology	Biotic; Sensitive	
Psychology	Sensitive	

Although Dooyeweerd's aspects themselves defy rigorous definition, philosophers in the tradition have offered some helpful articulation. Notably, M. D. Stafleu construes aspects as relation-frames, focusing on how each one provides a set of ways in which entities (particulars) can relate to each other.[7] The numerical

---

7. M. D. Stafleu, *Time and Again: A Systematic Analysis of the Foundations of Physics, Philosophy of Dynamic Development*, 2019, http://www.mdstafleu.

relation-frame is the set of possible relationships among numbers (so it concerns forms of equality and inequality), while the spatial relation-frame is the set of possible spatial relationships (concerning relative location and equivalence). The kinetic relation-frame concerns relationships jointly over space and time (constancy and movement), while the physical relation-frame concerns interactive relationships (cause and effect). The biotic relation-frame then concerns the vast diversity of relationships among living things at many levels of organization, while the sensitive relation-frame is about animal–environment relationships mediated by stimuli. In each case there are types of entity (e.g., numbers, particles, organisms), and modes of relating (numerically, physically, etc.). A science, then, is a study of relationships in one of the relation-frames (aspects), and it may focus on universal (modal) relationships, as happens in mathematics and much of physics, or on types and structures, as is more characteristic of chemistry and the biological sciences.

Defining Science

We now return to the meaning of "science" itself. Here again a Dooyeweerdian view can enrich the prevailing discourse. While science is commonly defined in terms such as "systematic study of the structure and behaviour of the physical and natural world,"[8] there is considerable variation on this theme, with varying emphasis among methods (e.g. testing hypotheses), values (e.g. unbiasedness) and results (e.g. secure knowledge). Philosophical definitions attempt to be normative, and Dooyeweerd's is no exception: a science should be a body of theory relating to abstract relations that hold in one of the aspects. This means a system of law-like generalizations about the relationships that hold among individual creatures of appropriate kinds, or in short, an endeavour to seek out the law structure of creation in some aspect.

---

nl/421197815.
8. *New Oxford Dictionary of English* (Oxford: Oxford University Press, 2001).

In this conception, each science will need peculiar kinds of data, tools and techniques in order to discover the characteristic forms of the abstract relations and entities it studies. Yet Dooyeweerd says little about how scientists should work. At this level of generality, indeed, most philosophers struggle to find much in common between the methods appropriate to such diverse disciplines as mathematics, chemistry, history, sociology and theology, all of which are sciences to Dooyeweerd. In fact, even for the natural sciences, descriptive accounts find little to say about a unified scientific method (what is the shared approach of cosmology, polymer science and zoology, for example?). Nevertheless, the normative tone of Dooyeweerd's philosophy surely ought to lead to some guidance.

Enriching the Sciences

How can particular scientific areas be enriched by Dooyeweerd's Reformational approach? The answer surely concerns methodology, but at a wide range of levels. Starting from the most general, we will look at three: the scope of the sciences, general scientific method, and discipline-specific methodologies.

Dooyeweerd's critique of the scope of the sciences has already been hinted at. Science is concerned with general laws: relations and structures that may be found to underlie particular instances. The latter are the data for a science; the former are what it seeks to uncover. This concurs with a form of critical realism. But the data/laws distinction also suggests a circumscription of the kinds of hypotheses that are truly scientific. All proposed scientific laws can be taken as hypotheses about laws of nature. But when scientific theory and methods are directed to evaluate hypotheses about particular events or instances, these applications of a science do not themselves contribute to the body of theory. There is no progress in theory of physics, chemistry or biology from evaluating hypotheses about when or how a particular murder took place, although practitioners of forensic science may draw on their problem-solving experience to make theoretical contributions. And similarly, there is no progress in cosmology, geology or evolutionary biology from evaluating hypotheses about when or how a certain planet or rock formed, or a certain speciation event occurred. Again, addressing such particular questions may help contribute to theory development, but conclusions about particular entities or events are not themselves theoretical. This exclusion may seem an unwelcome incursion, but it is an important restriction in a worldview where each particular individual has its own nature and human knowledge is not exhausted by scientific analysis. Moreover, it is not to deny that scientific theoretical components can be closely allied with such investigations, such as theories of stellar and planetary formation, rock cycles, speciation and so on, alongside the particular hypotheses that often attract more public attention.

Regarding general scientific method, Dooyeweerd's framework has provided a foundation for development by subsequent thinkers. The sequence of modal aspects is woven throughout the special sciences, inasmuch as every real situation functions within all the aspects. For example, the physical and kinetic relations that physicists seek to embody in theories are mostly expressed in numerical formulas that refer to spatial and kinetic metaphors (field, orbit, wave, vibration, current, etc.). Moreover, physicists rely on their senses to collect data, usually with the aid of invented measuring devices, and, as with all scholarship, the theories they form have a primarily logical nature. Then theories are expressed in natural language, developed in social collaborative communities under economic constraints, and expected to have aesthetic qualities. Whereas some philosophers have attempted to impose narrowly logical criteria on scientific method, as did Karl Popper, a Dooyeweerdian approach can be both richer and truer to reality. Stafleu has posited an "opening process"[9] describing how scientific

---

9. M. D. Stafleu, *Time and Again: A Systematic Analysis of the Foundations of*

theories can be developed (not just tested, as in the Popperian framework) in several alternative directions lying on two main axes. One axis describes opposite directions along the sequence of modal aspects, either (1) towards mathematization, seeking quantitative accounts of phenomena or (2) towards complexity, seeking novel phenomena with the aid of invented instruments. The other axis describes the opposite directions (3) towards unifying general laws, by discovering analogies that hold between aspects, or (4) towards increasingly accurate description of specific structures and types. Both (1) and (3) concern discoveries of analogies between modal aspects, an insight that can help explain recurring features of scientific progress and potentially suggest fruitful lines of investigation for scientists. Direction (1) is elucidated by Stafleu as objectification[10] in a bold move that connects Dooyeweerd's insights about retrocipations to the hitherto poorly-defined concept of objectivity. Direction (3) can be seen in some paradigmatic advances in various sciences, such as the realization by physicists that heat, light and gravity might each be founded in kinetic phenomena, or the realization by biologists that evolution might (through natural selection) be founded in a quantitative phenomenon. There is certainly scope for philosophical development of a Dooyeweerdian theory of scientific progress, and the fruit of such a project could be of great interest to practicing scientists.

Finally, looking at discipline-specific methodologies is a further step towards application of Dooyeweerdian thinking to of-

---

Physics (Toronto: Wedge, 1980), sec. 1.7.

10. M. D. Stafleu, *Time and Again: A Systematic Analysis of the Foundations of Physics* (Toronto: Wedge, 1980); M. D. Stafleu, *Time and Again: A Systematic Analysis of the Foundations of Physics, Philosophy of Dynamic Development*, 2019, http://www.mdstafleu.nl/421197815; R. M. Gunton, M. D. Stafleu and M. J. Reiss, "A general theory of objectivity: Contributions from the Reformational philosophy tradition," *Foundations of Science* (2021), doi: 10.1007/s10699-021-09809-x

fer insights and potentially enrichment to the natural sciences. A handful of scientists working with a Dooyeweerdian approach have proposed methodological guidance or research programmes for their disciplines, and here we can do no more than cite some of those that pertain to natural sciences. For statistics, Andrew Hartley has argued in favour of Bayesian inference.[11] For physics, Stafleu has made a range of proposals including that theoreticians should not attempt to subsume gravitation, which is a modal law, under the same theory as the other known forces, all of which are specific to certain types of entity.[12] Strauss has also shed light on the so-called wave–particle paradox with reference to the need for a concept-transcending idea: the distinct concepts of particle and wave cannot be reduced to each other because each refers to a different aspect, yet experimental evidence compels us to accept a richer reality that transcends scientific abstraction.[13] For biology, Klapwijk has outlined a non-reductionist theory of emergent evolution.[14] For ecology, Gunton and Gilbert[15] have outlined four fruitful aspectual paradigms coexisting in contemporary research. For psychology, Harry Van Belle has argued for the conscious in-

---

11. A. M. Hartley, *Christian and Humanist Foundations for Statistical Inference: Religious Control of Statistical Paradigms* (Eugene, OR: Resource Publications, 2007).

12. M. D. Stafleu, *Time and Again: A Systematic Analysis of the Foundations of Physics, Philosophy of Dynamic Development*, 2019, sec. 11.1, http://www.mdstafleu.nl/421197815.

13. D. F M. Strauss, *Philosophy: Discipline of the Disciplines* (Grand Rapids: Paideia Press, 2009).

14. J. Klapwijk, *Purpose in the Living World? Creation and Emergent Evolution*, ed. H. T. Cook (Cambridge: Cambridge University Press, 2008).

15. R. M. Gunton and F. Gilbert, "Laws in ecology: diverse modes of explanation for a holistic science," *Zygon* 52 no.2 (2017): 538–560, doi: 10.1111/zygo.12334.

volvement of human subjects in experiments.[16] No doubt there are other attempts to enrich particular natural scientific fields using themes inspired by Dooyeweerd's work, as there are also in other disciplines. But there is surely great scope for further contributions by scientists who may yet come to appreciate the richness, beauty and openness of this framework.

---

16. H. Van Belle, *On being a Christian academic psychologist* (1997) Available at: https://www.allofliferedeemed.co.uk/vanbelle.htm.

27

What Happened to "Evolution"?

by Danie F. M. Strauss

Introductory Remark

THIS CHAPTER WILL focus on the fluctuating meaning which the term *evolution* obtained within (neo-)Darwinism. We shall see that *evolution* in the biotic sense of the word has been reduced to *physical change*, to the idea of *continuous flux* (gradualism) – and that this view even overrules Darwin's idea of natural selection. In order to show that the problems involved are super-imposed by a preconceived conception of continuous change, multiple key quotations are extracted from the works of acknowledged biologists.

Physical Change versus Biotic Development

As physical entities atoms, molecules and macromolecules are not alive. Only plants, animals and humans actively function within the biotic aspect of reality. When this distinction between the physical and biotic aspects of reality is accepted, it entails that normally the term *evolution* is used to designate progressive (increasingly higher) biotic development. Yet, when Darwin published his famous work on the *Origin of Species* in 1859, the term *evolution* instantly lost its unique biotic sense. It was no longer employed to designate progressive organic development.

Darwin in fact proceeds from a radical physicalist (materialist) starting-point which fully emasculates the term "evolution." This is not realized by most supporters of (neo-)Darwinism. Of course, it is also not understood by the general public which continues to think that the (Darwinian) theory employs the term evolution in the sense of progressive biotic development without being aware of the fact that the authentic meaning attached to the term *evolution* within (neo-)Darwinian circles, is given by equating it with physical change.

The Ambiguity of *Evolution* within Neo-Darwinism

Although the biotic meaning of evolution surfaces as soon as evolution is discussed, it is implicitly pushed towards the background when the presumed development from the first cell to humans is explained. The term "evolution" then once again assumes the (non-physical) meaning-nuance of "progressive (biotic) development." But even when this (inconsistent) leap is made back to biotic evolution, the meaning of the latter is speculatively extended beyond all boundaries.

Does Darwin's Theory Allow for Progress?

The biologist who clearly realized that Darwin's position in 1859 does not allow for progress (understood as biotic development across all boundaries), is no one other than Stephen Gould. In a 1996 work on the grandeur of life he relates this to the fossil record:

> I believe that the most knowledgeable students of life's history have always sensed the failure of the fossil record to supply the most desired ingredient of Western comfort: a clear signal of progress measured as some form of steadily increasing complexity for life as a whole through time. The basic evidence cannot support such a view, for simple forms still predominate in most environments, as they always have. Faced with this undeniable fact, supporters of progress (that is, nearly all of us throughout the history of evolutionary thought) have shifted criteria and ended up grasping at straws.[1]

---

1 S. J. Gould, *Life's Grandeur: The Spread of Excellence from Plato to Darwin* (London: Jonathan Cape, 1996), 167.

WHAT HAPPENED TO "EVOLUTION"?

In a different context he explains this as a paradox:

> The problem that spawns this confusion within the Darwinian tradition may be simply stated: The basic theory of natural selection offers no statement about general progress, and supplies no mechanism whereby overall advance might be expected. Yet both Western culture and the undeniable facts of a fossil record that started with bacteria alone, and has now exalted us, cry out in unison for a rationale that will place progress into the centre of evolutionary theory.[2]

Keep in mind how Gould explains natural selection in 1996: "Natural selection—a mechanism that yields only local adaptation to changing environments, not general progress."[3]

Gradualism: The Continuity Postulate of Modern Philosophy

This situation is further complicated because Darwinism and neo-Darwinism not only reduced the biotic meaning of evolution to *physical change*, but also assumed that this physical change is *continuous*. This conviction that evolution means continuous change (flux) is also known as *gradualism*. According to Stephen Gould the embarrassment caused by the idea of progress is actually an outcome of Darwin's prior (*a priori*) commitment to the continuity postulate of modern philosophy. This postulate entails that human thought can bridge all boundaries (discontinuities) encountered within reality. It is generally known in the form of the slogan: nature does not make jumps (*natura non facit saltus*), which goes back to the so-called *lex continui* of Leibniz (in the 17th century). Geology does not reveal the expected finely-graduated organic chain.

---

2. Gould, *Life's Grandeur*, 136.
3. S. J. Gould, *Full House: The Spread of Excellence from Plato to Darwin* (New York: Harmony, 1996), 174.

The "Imperfection" of the Fossil Record

The belief that nature does not make jumps underlies Darwin's view that geology must reveal a finely-graduated organic chain – and if it does not, the only explanation would be that the fossil record is "imperfect." Although this conviction appears to be nothing but a "neutral statement of fact," the use of the word "imperfection" in the subsequent "explanation" demonstrates the hidden assumption of gradualism (the just-mentioned continuity postulate) expressed in it.

Yet Darwin was honest enough to concede: Geology assuredly does not reveal any such finely-graduated organic chain; and this, perhaps, is the most obvious and serious objection which can be urged against the theory. The explanation lies, as I believe, in the extreme imperfection of the geological record. Darwin believes in the "imperfection" of the fossil record. When Darwin says that he believes in the "extreme imperfection of the geological record" it means that he believes that there has been a perfectly continuous development but that this perfect continuity is simply not displayed in the fossil record. Therefore, he maintained the hope that these intermediate (or transitional) forms will still be found. But we continually overrate the perfection of the geological record, and falsely infer, because certain genera or families have not been found beneath a certain stage, that they did not exist before that stage. He phrases this gradualistic continuity postulate also in the following terms: "Natural selection acts only by the preservation and accumulation of [infinitesimally – new insertion[4]] small inherited modifications."[5] Clearly, Darwin's belief embodied the

---

4. C. Darwin, *On the Origin of Species by Means of Natural Selection or the Preservation of Favoured Races in the Struggle for Life*, ed. J. W. Burrow (Hardmondsworth: Penguin Books, [1859] 1968), 142.
5. C. Darwin, *On the Origin of Species by Means of Natural Selection or the Preservation of Favoured Races in the Struggle for Life*, 56, accessed October 29, 2005, http://www.infidels.org/library/historical/charles_darwin/origin_

hope that fossils of the continuously changing transitional forms will be found through continued paleontological research and the discovery of new fossils.

This raises the question: What happened to this expectation during the subsequent more than 150 years? In 1999 Jones reiterates the problem as follows:

> The fossil record – in defiance of Darwin's whole idea of gradual change – often makes great leaps from one form to the next. Far from the display of intermediates to be expected from slow advance through natural selection, many species appear without warning, persist in fixed form and disappear, leaving no descendants.[6]

As mentioned earlier, Darwin conceded that geology assuredly does not reveal any finely graduated organic chain, and this is the most obvious and gravest objection which can be urged against the theory of evolution. Let us see what Ernst Mayr, one of the key figures in the "New Synthesis" of Darwinism (that gave rise to the label neo-Darwinism) had to say in 1991:

> Paleontologists had long been aware of a seeming contradiction between Darwin's postulate of gradualism ... and the actual findings of paleontology. Following phyletic lines through time seemed to reveal only minimal gradual changes but no clear evidence for any change of a species into a different genus or for the gradual origin of an evolutionary novelty. Anything truly novel always seemed to appear quite abruptly in the fossil record.[7]

---

of_species/Intro.html.

6. S. Jones, *Almost Like a Whale: The Origin of Species Updated* (Doubleday, 1999), 252.
7. E. Mayr, *One Long Argument: Charles Darwin and the Genesis of Modern Evolutionary Thought* (Cambridge: Harvard University Press, 1991), 138.

The Dominance of a Philosophical Presupposition in Neo-Darwinism

The fact that the continuity postulate (gradualism) occupies the central position in Darwin's thought shows that an a priori speculative philosophical view overrules the available data. This is confirmed by Gould:

> (i) "Gradualism may represent the most central conviction residing both within and behind all Darwin's thought";[8] and:
>
> (ii) "I believe, therefore, that Darwin's strong, even pugnacious, defence of strict gradualism reflects a much more pervasive commitment, extending far beyond the simple recognition of a logical entailment implied by natural selection – and that this stronger conviction must record such general influences as Darwin's attraction to Lyell's conflation of gradualism with rationality itself, and the cultural appeal of gradualism during Britain's greatest age of industrial expansion and imperial conquest."[9]

According to Gould the continuity postulate represents the core conviction of Darwin. From the foregoing the astonishing position is clear: for Darwin natural selection does not represent his core conviction – this position is occupied by the *continuity postulate*. Moreover, it is important for those interested in intellectual history ("the history if ideas") to realize that the primacy given in Darwin's thought to the continuity postulate (nature does not make jumps), evinces the rootedness of his thought in the modern humanistic science ideal which surfaced during and after the Renaissance.

---

8. S. J. Gould, *The Structure of Evolutionary Theory* (London: The Belknap Press of Harvard University Press 2002), 148.

9. Gould, *Structure of Evolutionary Theory* (London: The Belknap Press of Harvard University Press, 2002), 151.

WHAT HAPPENED TO "EVOLUTION"?

Evolution as Continuous Flux Questioned

Gould connects this a priori postulate regarding incremental continuous change to the widespread and generally defended neo-Darwinian basic definition of evolution as *continuous flux*:

> The stories begin from the same foundational fallacy and then proceed in an identical erroneous way. They start with the most dangerous of mental traps: a hidden assumption, depicted as self-evident, if recognized at all – namely, a basic definition of evolution as continuous flux.[10]

Gould understood Darwin's commitment to the boundary-*levelling* modern humanistic science-ideal. He writes: "We often fail to recognize how much of the Origin presents an exposition of gradualism, rather than a defence of natural selection."[11] And: "In fact, I would advance the even stronger claim that the theory of natural selection is, in essence, Adam Smith's economics transferred to nature."[12] To this we may add what Marx wrote to Engels in a famous letter of 1862:

> It is remarkable how Darwin recognizes among beasts and plants his English society with its division of labor, competition, opening up of new markets, 'invention,' and the Malthusian 'struggle for existence.' It is Hobbes's '*bellum omnium omnes*' [war of all against all] and one is reminded of Hegel's Phenomenology, where civil society is described as a 'spiritual kingdom,' while in Darwin the animal kingdom figures as civil society.[13]

---

10. Gould, *Structure of Evolutionary Theory*, 913.
11. Gould, *Structure of Evolutionary Theory*, 151.
12. Gould, *Structure of Evolutionary Theory*, 122.
13. Quoted in S. J. Gould and Niles Eldredge, "Punctuated Equilibria: The Tempo and Mode of Evolution Reconsidered," *Paleobiology* 3, no. 2 (Spring 1977), 145.

An Increasing Challenge to the Idea of Continuous Transition

The last fifty to sixty years witnessed an increasing challenge to the classical Darwinian conception of a gradually and continuous transition through numberless incrementally small changes over millions of years. This challenge flows from what Gould and Eldredge (already in 1972) characterized as the dominant theme of the fossil record, namely stasis (constancy or fixity). Two years later the paleontologist Kitts categorically in the neo-Darwinist Journal *Evolution* states: "Evolution requires intermediate forms between species and paleontology does not provide them."[14]

Stasis Is Data

One may capture the core of this issue by employing the opposition of continuity versus discontinuity, as it is explained by McGar in a work on Gould (2006):

> The clear predominance of an empirical pattern of stasis and abrupt geological appearance as the history of most fossil species has always been acknowledged by paleontologists, and remains the standard testimony… of the best specialists in nearly every taxonomic group. In Darwinian traditions, this pattern has been attributed to imperfections of the geological record that impose this false signal upon the norm of a truly gradualistic history. Darwin's argument may work in principle for punctuational origin, but stasis is data and cannot be so encompassed.[15]

Gould is therefore justified in asking (in 2002): "So if stasis could not be explained away as missing information, how could gradualism face this most prominent signal from the fossil re-

---

14. D. B. Kitts, "Paleontology and Evolutionary Theory," *Evolution* 28, no. 3 (September 1974): 467.
15. P. McGarr and S. Rose, *The Richness of Life, The Essential Stephen Jay Gould* (London: Jonathan Cape, 2006), 242.

cord?"¹⁶ In 2006 Van den Beukel mentioned that Gould and Eldredge claimed that stasis (= immutability, stand-still), and not change, is the dominant theme of the fossil record. He adds a remark from Eldredge, namely that this destroys the backbone of the most important argument of the modern theory of evolution.¹⁷ Berlinski also affirms that most species "enter the evolutionary order fully formed and then depart unchanged."¹⁸

Conclusion

In its original biotic sense, the term *evolution* (biotic development) merely designated the growth (development) of a living entity from birth to maturity. Within (neo-)Darwinism two important things happened to the term evolution. (i) It was first of all reduced to physical change in order to avoid the idea of progressive development. (ii) Secondly, neo-Darwinists (inconsistently) continued to switch to a biotic perspective in order to express their belief (faith) in the speculatively assumed continuous evolutionary process of infinitesimal, incremental change – a process in which new and "higher" forms allegedly "evolved" while bridging the gap between the level of bacteria and that of humans. In the Prologue of his recent book, *Darwin's Doubt* (2013), Stephen Meyer states the following in connection with the assumed origination of the first living entities:

> The type of information present in living cells – that is, 'specified' information in which the sequence of characters matters to the function of the sequence as a whole – has generated an acute mystery. No undirected physical or chemical process has demonstrated

---

16. Gould, *Structure of Evolutionary Theory*, 759.
17. A. van den Beukel, "Darwinisme: wetenschap en/of ideologie?" in *Schitterend ongeluk of sporen van ontwerp*? ed. C. Dekker, R. Meester and R. van Woudenberg (Kampen: Ten Have, 2005), 106.
18. David Berlinski, "The Deniable Darwin," Discovery Institute, June 1, 1994, https://www.discovery.org/a/130/.

the capacity to produce specified information starting 'from purely physical or chemical' precursors. For this reason, chemical evolutionary theories have failed to solve the mystery of the origin of first life – a claim that few mainstream evolutionary theorists now dispute.[19]

This book of Meyer is dedicated to the mystery of the Cambrian explosion (initially estimated to have occurred in 20 to 40 million years, but now reduced to 5 to 6 million years).[20]

---

19. S. Meyer, *Darwin's Doubt* (New York: Harper Collins, 2013), vi.
20. Meyer, *Darwin's Doubt*, 72.

28

Of History and the Science of History

by Harry Van Dyke

REFORMATIONAL PHILOSOPHY as pioneered by Herman Dooyeweerd stands out for its recognition of the rich diversity in the creation of unique and irreducible modes of being ("modalities"), such as the physical, psychical, logical, jural, and ethical. Corresponding with that, it recognizes a rich diversity of things ("individuality structures" and "social collectivities"), such as families, firms, schools, and churches, each uniquely characterized ("qualified") by one of the modalities. This twofold diversity enables one to sort through the ocean of historical literature, each branch or genre representing a subdiscipline—specializations that can be classified according to either modality or structure.[1] Such classification reminds one, for example, that autobiographies are not intellectual biographies, that church history is not the same as the history of Christianity, and that the history of natural disasters must not be confused with the history of epidemics like the cholera or the COVID virus.

Again, as the present volume tangibly illustrates, reformational philosophy in many instances links the special sciences or academic disciplines to a particular modality as the leading focus of

---

1. Appended to this chapter is a tentative *Taxonomy of Historical Writings*, divided over genres and branches, in part following the two diversities mentioned above.

that discipline. The historical modality at its core is defined as the mode of control, power, or mastery in cultural power formation. Dooyeweerd describes this core as giving form to material "in free control over the material"[2] or "according to a free design."[3] Examples are found in subject-subject relations such as a general and his army and a teacher and his pupils. Of subject-object relations examples are a carpenter crafting a bench and a legislator drafting a statute. The science of history, if we are to define it, with Dooyeweerd, in terms of the "historical" or "culturally formative" modality, might also be called *culturology*, a kind of history of more limited scope.[4]

When the scientific historian studies the phenomena, events, and processes over time in the life of humankind, he is keenly aware that many of these things have a culturally formative side to them—the very side (facet, aspect, mode) that characterizes the phenomena, events, and processes that spark his interest as a historian. Meanwhile, the meaning of words like power, control, and mastery at the core ("nucleus") of the historical modality should not be inflated. For Dooyeweerd, the day of June 18, 1815 concerns the historian only and exclusively because the Battle of Waterloo which then took place restored a kind of balance of power in Europe. The culturologist would nod in agreement, but the historian would protest. For he is also interested in the sight of peasants at dawn of that fateful day, hurriedly gathering

---

2. H. Dooyeweerd, *Christian Philosophy and the Meaning of History* (Lewison, NY: Edwin Mellen, 1996), 56.

3. H. Dooyeweerd, *Roots of Western Culture, Pagan, Secular and Christian Options*, Collected Works of Herman Dooyeweerd, Series B, vol. 4. General Editor D. F. M. Strauss (Grand Rapids, MI: Paideia Press, 2012), 66.

4. The term *culturologists* was first suggested by Professor L. A. White of the University of Michigan to designate "theoreticians of civilization" like Arnold Toynbee; see H.-I. Marrou, *De la connaissance historique* (Paris: Éditions du Seuil, 1954), 174n.

in what they can of their rain-drenched standing crops, dreading the awesome and alarming troop movements of the previous day as Wellington's forces assembled to the north and Napoleon's forces lined up to the south. Those scurrying peasants—a "non-historical" event, writes Dooyeweerd in a self-consistent way[5]— are nevertheless of keen interest to the historian *of peasant life through the ages*. The historian of European agriculture may well find it a factoid of curious interest as well. And, to mention no more, the historian of wars and their collateral damage—and today the historian *of climate and climate change*—may possibly wish to include details of this sort in their investigations and their resulting reports and narrative accounts. Indeed, the historical discipline has a wider reach than culturology, given its sometime preoccupation with "non-historical" topics like marginalized minorities or "lost causes" or newly discovered tribes: little of culturally formative power there, but plenty of history.

* * *

Yet we shall not spurn culturology. As distinguished from conventional history, it can serve as a kind of ancillary science. Culturology can lay bare fascinating "patterns" and "mechanisms" of human life in society, such as challenge-and-response, rout-and-rally, rise-shine-decline. In the course of studying the past, the historian can raise at least four key questions in his capacity as a culturologist.

First, does culturology help distinguish between progressive and reactionary tendencies? As the historian analyzes the deeds and decisions, the trends and events that he comes across, he wonders: Are these new initiatives and developments in line with the

---

5. Dooyeweerd, *In the Twilight of Western Thought* (Philadelphia: The Presbyterian and Reformed Publishing Company, 1960), 95; see also H. Dooyeweerd, *A New Critique of Theoretical Thought*, vol. 2, Collected Works of Herman Dooyeweerd, Series A, General Editor, D. F. M. Strauss (Lewiston, NY: Edwin Mellen, 1997), 230.

historical laws of differentiation and integration? Do they open up or close down the cultural zone in question? Do they uncover and unfold new possibilities and new potentials in human culture, or do they send humanity up a blind alley, resurrecting or repristinating a situation or condition that is no longer viable? Are we looking each time at an act, trend or pattern that must be characterized as revolutionary or reactionary, or instead as reformational, simultaneously respecting both change and continuity? Whichever it is, it is bound to have certain consequences as history moves on. The historical researcher is prepared and forewarned, armed as he is with helpful culturological insights.

Second, does this or that event confirm or upset the balance of power among people and nations? That can make the difference between continued peace or unsettling strife.

Third, does the matter under investigation evolve in relative isolation, or does it evidently function in all modalities through analogical retrocipations and anticipations (see the relevant chapter in this volume), so that neglect of these other modalities would impoverish the understanding of the matter being investigated. The social historian, for instance, must realize that his topic is not isolated from its economic aspect, and the political historian must not forget that his topic cannot be separated from its tie-in with the moral aspect.

Fourth, can the concept of "ground-motives" (basic religious motives) be a useful heuristic tool? In the back of his mind the historian is aware of at least four ground-motives that have helped shape western civilization since the ancient Greeks. This knowledge can be quite helpful to him. Long before Thomas Kuhn and his followers, Dooyeweerd's students knew about "reigning paradigms" in their most concentrated forms: the mental disposition and basic drives of form and matter, nature and grace, nature and freedom, and creation, fall, and redemption. Admittedly, historians, intent as they are on finding empirical evidence, are little accustomed to dealing with supra-personal spirits in ever so many varieties that move—nay drive—people as they act and give shape to their personal and communal lives. And until recently[6] historians have been far from familiar with fathoming the hidden players on the will, the consciousness and—not to forget—the subconscious of human actors on the stage of history. None the less, knowledge of ground-motives can be fruitful for research.

Let's take an example from the closing days of the Old Regime. The culture of the *ancien régime* in the eighteenth century was dominated and animated by a deep-seated worldview characterized by a tension between nature and freedom. This tension can be illustrated from the storming of the Parisian prison fortress the Bastille, 14 July 1789. At bottom this mob act can be seen as a protest of the *free* human personality against the oppressive might of the establishment that was assumed to be an order for society dictated by *nature* itself.[7]

But back to where we began. The foregoing explorations about the utility of culturology does not diminish the value of how Dooyeweerd chooses to define the science of history. After all, the great value of making a special study of the past with the focus on things "qualified" by the *historical law-sphere* is that one is reminded time and again that the historical law-sphere is the pivot between the earlier, natural law-spheres and the later, normative law-spheres. Throughout history, humans have been privileged, but also obliged, to give shape, in free design, to the normed zones

---

6. Modern "mentality history" approximates it.
7. Here I disagree with an astute critic of Dooyeweerd's approach to history; see the chapter by Dale K. Van Kley ("Dooyeweerd as Historian") in George Marsden and Frank Roberts, eds., *A Christian View of History?* (Grand Rapids, MI: Eerdmans, 1977), 139–79. Professor Van Kley heaps scorn on the very idea that a ground-motive might help explain the storming of the Bastille; he calls the notion "too preposterous on the face of it to merit serious consideration" (p. 160).

of life as they "positivize" (actualize, realize) these zones in accordance with normative principles that are to obtain in them, each time in shapes and forms that are serviceable to the needs of the time.

* * *

Finally, quite apart from the systematics of Dooyeweerd's philosophy, one might argue that most helpful for historians, providing their research and writing with deeper understanding and clarifying insights, are the ideas that Dooyeweerd has in common with "Dooyeweerdians," reformationalists, and neo-Calvinists in general. Bear with me as I repeat them, for they bear repeating. Those basic ideas can be summarized as follows:

- That world history is the drama of the antithesis between the community of those who are marked by love of God and the community of those who are stamped by love of self—in the terms of St. Augustine: between the *civitas Dei* and the *civitas terrena*.[8]
- That the God of the Scriptures is the Lord of history and works out his will according to his good pleasure.[9]
- That the course of history is not meaningless, but that it is guided purposefully by God and made to pass through creation/fall/redemption/consummation.
- That God is a God of life, of love, of order, and that God therefore maintains and sustains orderliness in the world.
- That life on earth is subject to a regime of regularity—a law order which protects and promotes human well-being and which humans may deny or defy yet can never undo.

---

8. H. Dooyeweerd, *The Struggle for a Christian Politics*, Collected Works of Herman Dooyeweerd, Series B, vol. 17, General Editor D. F. M. Strauss (Grand Rapids, MI: Paideia Press 2012), 14.
9. Cf. K. J. Popma, *Evangelie en geschiedenis* (1972); Eng. trans., *Gospel and History* (Aalten, Neth.: WordBridge, 2021), 207f.

- That to go against the world-order is to court disaster, for whoever crosses it will face the consequences of disorder, disruption, chaos, and misery, in which life does not thrive and culture stagnates and eventually shuts down from internal tensions and contradictions.[10] Often, the ultimate calamity is escaped only when men repent of their evil ways: then God in his grace "repents of the disaster he said he would do to them" (Jonah 3:10). God mercifully grants people "times of refreshment" (Acts 3:20), for in his patience God is not willing "that any should perish, but that all should come to repentance" (2 Pet. 3:9) and "that all people should be saved" (1 Tim. 2:4).
- That all events can be said to have a dual origin. *Secondarily*, events arise from that which precedes them, their temporal antecedents (the usual concern of historians). *Primarily*, events are grounded in that which proceeds from the hands of God, the Creator and Sustainer of the cosmos (the usually neglected concern of historians).[11]

  This dual perspective eviscerates historicism, which holds (in the definition of Vollenhoven) that all events find their explanation in their historical antecedents, and only in their antecedents, thus shutting God out of his own creation and locking humanity up in a closed world.
- That history cannot be explained purely in terms of itself: that events cannot be fully explained in terms of preceding events, but that at every step, at every moment between what has been and what will happen next, there is the wondrous mystery of God's invitation to act and man's free re-

---

10. See H. Van Dyke, "Professing God in History," inaug. address, Redeemer University College, 2002.
11. This way of formulating "the divine mystery in history" was worked out by reformational philosopher Meyer C. Smit in his *Writings on God and History* (1987; repr. Dordt College Press, 2021), 217–234.

sponse to that inescapable invitation.[12]

- That the disclosure or opening-up of culture always happens under the guidance of a religious faith, whether biblical or apostate.[13]
- That history is neither self-driven nor propelled by socio-economic, intellectual, geographical, and similar historical forces, but that, even as these forces exert their influence, human beings, their deliberations and decisions, are always the requisite factor behind events.
- That excessive expansion of one sphere in society inevitably calls up reactions from one or more of the other spheres, resulting in tensions that will be resolved of themselves or else through crises, not seldom accompanied by violence.
- That all men, all cultures, and all time periods participate in the one universal history, and that they are all played out before the face of God.[14]
- That all historians, being human, when they enter their field and practice their profession in the quest for truth about the past, do so with fundamental prior commitments, commitments that are not only stamped by their personality, age, social status, life experience, and so on, but especially by their (not always conscious, though deeply held) beliefs about the meaning and destiny of human existence.
- That it is the sacred duty of the historian *to do right* by those who went before him, because they are his "neighbors" in

---

12. Smit, *Writings on God and History*, 63–89, 217–234; see also Popma, *Gospel and History*, 180–207.
13. Cf. Dooyeweerd, *A New Critique*, 2:298–323.
14. Cf. K. J. Popma, *Calvinistische geschiedenisbeschouwing* (1945); Eng. trans., *Scriptural Reflections on History* (Aalten, Neth.: WordBridge, 2020), 17–21.

the deeply religious sense of the word.[15] His hermeneutics of suspicion needs to be balanced by a hermeneutics of charity.

Conclusion

We can be thankful that the neo-Calvinist tradition, in which reformational philosophy and the reformational worldview[16] have come to fruition, has great practical relevance for the academy as well as for the practice of life, embracing both the discipline of history and our everyday awareness of being historical creatures living *coram Deo*, in the presence and before the face of God.

---

15. This is a recurring theme in the historiographical essays by Professor A. Th. van Deursen of the VU University Amsterdam; see for example his *De Geest is meer dan het lichaam* (Amsterdam: Bert Bakker, 2010), 136–41 and *De Eeuw in ons hart* (Franeker: Van Wijnen, 1991), 87.
16. For the latter, see esp. Albert M. Wolters, Creation Regained: Biblical Basics for a Reformational Worldview (Grand Rapids, MI: Eerdmans, 1985).

APPENDIX
A TAXONOMY OF HISTORICAL WRITINGS

Categories for Classifying Works of History

A. **GENRES:** Histories of Cultural Entities

1. **History of Nature** (as it impacts on man)
   - 1.1 history of a geographical region
   - 1.2 history of climate
   - 1.3 environmental history
   - 1.4 history of natural disasters
   - 1.5 history of disease; of an epidemic
   - 1.6 history of diet; of nutrition

2. **Lives of History-Makers**
   - 2.1 Autobiography; apologia; memoirs; confessions
   - 2.2 biography; hagiography
   - 2.3 psychohistory (individual)

3. **Art History**
   - 3.1 history of architecture; visual and performing arts; graphic design; cinema; etc.
   - 3.2 history of styles; of schools
   - 3.2.1 history of an artist's works and development

4. Literary History
- 4.1 history of a literary movement; of a literary style
- 4.2 biography of authors; of novelists; of poets
- 4.3 reception history

5. Institutional History
- 5.1 history of a concrete entity, such as:
- 5.2 an association, a club; a lodge; a religious order; a university, an academy
- 5.3 an international organization; a museum, art gallery; a troupe, orchestra; an art festival; a business firm, a manufacturing company; a bank; a foundation
- 5.4 a ruling dynasty; a police force; etc., etc.
- 5.5 urban history
- 5.6 family history
- 5.7 colonial history
- 5.8 history of an empire
- 5.9 history of sports
- 5.10 church history
- 5.11 cultural history (see also B.11.3.)

6. World History (universal history)

B. BRANCHES: Histories of Cultural Dimensions

7. Psychohistory (collective)

8. Intellectual History
- 8.1 history of climates of opinion; of intellectual trends
- 8.2 history of mentalities

A TAXONOMY OF HISTORICAL WRITINGS

- 8.3 history of ideas, notions, concepts
- 8.3.1 history of bodies of knowledge
  history of science, pedagogy, medicine, history of philosophy
  history of dogma
- 8.3.2 history of branches of learning
  history of mathematics
  history of physical sciences
  history of psychology
  history of historical science and history-writing
  history of literary criticism
  history of political / economic aesthetic / ethical theory
- 8.4 history of an ideology
- 8.5 history of a thinker: intellectual biography

9. History of Culture-Making Forces

- 9.1 agricultural history
- 9.2 military history
- 9.2.1 history of warfare, of conquest
- 9.2.1.1 history of a war, a campaign, an operation, a battle
- 9.2.2 history of a branch of the armed forces
- 9.2.3 history of a fighting unit
- 9.3 history of technology
- 9.3.1 history of inventions
- 9.3.2 history of industrial design
- 9.3.3 history of inventors ("scientists")
- 9.3.4 history of printing
- 9.4 history of transportation

9.5	history of schooling (education)	
9.6	history of missions	
9.7	history of brainwashing, torture, etc.	

10. History of a Language

11. Social History

11.1	history of social manners, customs, etiquette, everyday life
11.2	labor history
11.3	history of society
11.4	history of travel, exploration, discovery

12. Economic History

12.1	business history
12.2	history of commerce, of trade relations
12.3	history of banking
12.4	history of industrialization

13. Political History

13.1	domestic political history
13.1.1	history of a state, of a country as a political unit
13.1.1.1	history of a coup, uprising, insurrection, revolt, revolution
13.1.2	constitutional history
13.1.3	parliamentary history
13.2	diplomatic history
13.2.1	history of foreign affairs
13.2.2	history of international relations
13.2.3	history of war and peace
13.3	legal history
13.3.1	history of law

13.3.2 history of legislation
13.3.3 history of a judicial system

14. History of Aesthetic Perception
14.1 iconography
14.2 social history of art

15. History of Morals, Ethics

16. History of Religious Faith, of Beliefs; Mythology; Magic

29

Constitutive and Regulative Historical Principles

by Danie F. M. Strauss

Conservatism and Revolution

THE NORMATIVE CONTRARY *historical-unhistorical* uproots the positivistic preoccupation with historical *facts*, for without the implicit application of a historical norm of development, it would be impossible to speak of *reactionary* or *revolutionary* historical events. Reaction and revolution presuppose the normative meaning of *historical constancy* (*continuity*) and *historical change* – revealing on the norm side the coherence between the historical aspect and the *foundational* role of the kinematic and physical aspects. Reactionary movements cling to the status quo without any flexibility or willingness to face the challenge of *changing* historical circumstances. Revolutionary movements, by contrast, take such challenges so seriously that no room is left for any *historical continuity*.

Historical Continuity

It is only when a sound application of the (constitutive) norm of historical continuity prevails that constructive *reformation* takes place, avoiding the historically antinormative extremes of reaction and revolution. Historical development is always confronted with a struggle between *progressive* and *conservative* forces, but only through *continuity-abiding reformation* is it possible to bend these opposing forces into the pathway of historical norm-conformity.

Tradition

Tradition, as the guardian of historical continuity, not only embodies the worthwhile legacy of the past, but also calls for continued reformation. But when a responsible reformation takes place, it only brings about *changes* on the basis of historical continuity and not at the cost of it.

Biotic Analogies

The biotic analogy within the structure of the historical aspect is particularly responsible for many controversies. The original biotical meaning of *growth* and *development* provides the source for analogical and even metaphorical usages. In the original, biotic sense, the normal life cycle of any living entity follows the path of the biotic time order of *birth, growth, maturation, ageing* and *dying*. Biotic growth proceeds along the lines of *differentiation* and *integration*. Diverse organs *differentiate*—but if the living entity does not manage to *integrate* this differentiating growth process, it will *disintegrate* and *die*. Interestingly, in 1931 Dooyeweerd still related the term *integration* to the mathematical "infinitesimal calculus."[1]

The Calling to Formative Control

In the context of the historical aspect, the task-setting nature of historical principles entails that the calling to (formative) control – over fellow human beings (the competence vested in some or other societal office) and over cultural objects made by humankind – comes to expression in processes conforming to or violating

---

1. H. Dooyeweerd, *The Crisis in Humanist Political Theory: As seen from a Calvinist cosmology and epistemology*, Collected Works of Herman Dooyeweerd, Series B, vol. 7, General Editor D. F. M. Strauss (Grand Rapids, MI: Paideia Press, 2010), 65.

the fundamental historical principles of historical differentiation and historical integration. These principles are *functional* principles exhibiting the *modal universality* of the cultural-historical mode. Although Griffioen highlights factual mistakes in Dooyeweerd's account of undifferentiated societies, he does not question the constitutive normative meaning of historical differentiation and integration. He points out that Dooyeweerd's view of totem cultures is dependent upon the interpretation of Cassirer. Instead of *identifying* human beings with plants or animals, one rather has to discern a parallelism between a *natural series* and a *cultural series* within such cultures.[2]

He also correctly emphasizes the distinction between a *constant principle* and its *variable form-giving*, although he does not reveal insight into the meaning of *modal principles* as distinct from *structural (typical)* principles, for he only discusses *norms* as *structural principles*.[3]

Unfortunately, Griffioen nowhere in this illuminating and penetrating article *explicitly* undertakes the task of "locating" the "modal seat" of the term *differentiation* (and its correlate: *integration*) — which is found solely in the *biotic mode of reality*. In addition, he also does not *explicitly* account for the fact that the inter-modal coherence between the normative aspects and their foundational connection with the biotical (and other natural) mode(s) actually highlights fundamental *modal norms* requiring positivization within the process of cultural development. But not even Dooyeweerd himself realized that *differentiation* and *integration* represent *biotical* analogies within cosmic later aspects

---

2. Cf. S. Griffioen, "De Betekenis van Dooyeweerd's Ontwikkelingsidee," in *Philosophia Reformata*, 51, no. 1 and 2 (1986): 91 note 1 – where he refers to more recent ethnological research and to some writings of E. Leach, C. Geertz and Claude Lévi-Strauss.

3. S. Griffioen, "De Betekenis van Dooyeweerd's Ontwikkelingsidee," in *Philosophia Reformata*, 51, no. 1 and 2 (1986): 103 ff.

(including the historical aspect) — although he did discuss the acknowledgment of vital and dead elements in the tradition in connection with the biotical analogy within the historical aspect.[4]

Constitutive and Regulative Historical Principles

Constitutive historical principles are not eliminated when a deepening or disclosure of the meaning of the historical aspect takes place. The first element of deepening the meaning of the historical aspect is found when the awareness of what is historically *significant* materializes in inscriptions, monuments, written historical accounts, and so on. The latter serve as *sources* for the historian. The difference between what is *historically significant* and what is *insignificant* is made possible by the anticipatory coherence between the cultural-historical aspect and the sign mode. Cultures in which this anticipatory moment is not yet disclosed do not, strictly speaking, participate in *world history*, as Hegel realized.

Constitutive meaning-moments within the cultural-historical aspect acquire new meaning under the guidance of regulative moments. For example, an articulated understanding of what is historically significant enables a more nuanced *identification* of a cultural community with its historical past and at once highlights avenues through which what is fruitful in its tradition could be pursued in further historical development. Once the social anticipation is opened up, intercourse with other cultures leads to an equally articulated development of the *national identity* of communities. The uniqueness and individuality of cultures are thus recognized. But since the contours of the normative aspects of reality embrace the multi-faceted nature of all cultures, their uniqueness and individuality can only be manifested within shared dimensions of normativity, for individuality and universality are not

---

4. See H. Dooyeweerd, *Encyclopedia of the Science of Law*, vol. 1, Introduction, Series A, vol. 8, General Editor D. F. M. Strauss. Special Editor A.C. Cameron (Grand Rapids, MI: Paideia Press, 2012), 157-158.

opposites, but *mutually cohering traits* of every concretely existing creature or societal reality.

Logic and Culture

Prinsloo[5] approaches this problem from the angle of the relationship between *logic* and *culture*. He discusses examples by thinkers such as Peter Winch and Evans Pritchard. Whereas these thinkers want to demonstrate that *consistency* is something different for Westerners and 'primitives', he successfully shows that both actually observe the (underlying, universal, logical) principle of *non-contradiction*.

The Process of Disclosure

The applicability of this principle, however, presupposes the nature of *logical concept formation* and concept formation, in turn, rests on the nature of *universality*. It was exactly this problem – the relationship between universality and what is individual – that haunted the new claims by historicism during the 19th century. Acknowledging cultural diversity and historical uniqueness does not eliminate universality, but *presupposes* it. Only if the phenomenon of culture is something *universally human*, will it be possible to differentiate between the peculiarities of *different* cultures and to gain insight into the process of differentiation and integration occurring within societies. The process of differentiation and integration taking place within a developing society soon discloses the requirement for observing the historical norm of *cultural economy*. The internal sphere of competence of every newly differentiated societal community and collectivity demands respect, but whenever this is not obtained, history tells the story of the many one-sided abuses of power, leading to situations where one sector of society violates the internal sphere sovereignty of another. During the Middle Ages the Roman Catholic Church exceeded

---

5. E. D. Prinsloo, "Logic and culture," *South African Journal for Philosophy* 8 (1989): 94-99.

the limits of the church as an institution and excessively impinged upon the spheres of competence of the non-ecclesiastical domains of life. Likewise, after the Renaissance, the modern humanistic science ideal breached the integrity of every non-scholarly domain of life – just recall how Kant, in his *Critique of Pure Reason*, claimed that even *law* and *religion* cannot withdraw themselves from the critical scrutiny of reason.[6]

These anticipatory moments within the modal structure of the cultural-historical aspect must be distinguished from the *original function* of communal and collective activities of a differentiated society within the post-historical modalities. It is only within the latter context that one can for example speak of "love for culture" or even about the guiding role of faith in the (harmonious or disharmonious) disclosure of culture. Although Dooyeweerd does not properly distinguish between this internal and external coherence, he does provide us with an extensive analysis of the process of disclosure and particularly of the guiding role of faith in this process.[7]

It should be kept in mind that Dooyeweerd does not pursue an ideal of *progress*, for he acknowledges merely that an increasing historical process of differentiation and integration could be appreciated as progressive. By and large he opposes reactionary and revolutionary events while holding that both are disobeying the cultural norm of *historical continuity*. Dooyeweerd emphasized that within all societies there is always a clash between conserva-

---

6. I. Kant, *Kritik der reinen Vernunft* (Hamburg: Felix Meiner Verlag, [1781] 1967), 12.
7. See H. Dooyeweerd, *A New Critique of Theoretical Thought*, vol. 2, Collected Works of Herman Dooyeweerd, Series A, General Editor D. F. M. Strauss (Lewiston, NY: Edwin Mellen, 1997), 180-365 and H. Dooyeweerd, *Roots of Western Culture, Pagan, Secular and Christian Options*, Collected Works of Herman Dooyeweerd, Series B, vol. 3, General Editor D. F. M. Strauss (Lewiston, NY: Edwin Mellen, 2003), 89 ff.

tive and progressive tendencies. When the former gains the upper hand history takes on a *reactionary* direction and when the progressive tendencies dominate a *revolution* is at hand.

Moreover, when such a clash surfaces the norm of *historical continuity* ought to mediate a process well-known to us, *reformation*.

30

The Significance of Dooyeweerd's Philosophy for Understanding the Complexity of Technology: A Case Study About the Energy Infrastructure of the Future

by Maarten J. Verkerk

Introduction

THE ENERGY INFRASTRUCTURE plays a crucial role in the development of the world. It is a life-sustaining system that supports all main activities of human beings. The use of fossil fuels leads to irreversible changes of the climate, threatening the existence of humans, animals, and plants. The main challenge of the present time is to transform the present energy infrastructure into a sustainable one.

The energy infrastructure is very complex. It is not "one" infrastructure but consists of different energy infrastructures that interact in a complex way, e.g., the oil infrastructure, the gas infrastructure, the coal infrastructure, electrical infrastructure, the hydrogen infrastructure, and so on. Each infrastructure consists of different actors that interact in a complex way. Some interactions are orchestrated, others are not. The energy infrastructure is not only about physical principles of energy generation but also about social, economic, political, juridical, and moral issues. In addition, this is interwoven with all sectors of society, e.g., mobility, living, health care, food, finance, industry, and cyber. Each of these sectors has its own characteristics and dynamics.

The key question of this chapter is: How to understand the complexity of technology and technological infrastructures? In this chapter I will show that Herman Dooyeweerd offers some key concepts to understand this complexity. In the next chapter I will show that these key concepts help us to understand human responsibility in developing sustainable infrastructures. To make the philosophical concepts more concrete, I will make use of a case study: the energy infrastructure of the future.

Key Concepts

Human beings have a natural tendency to translate complex problems into simple models. The main reason is that people have difficulty understanding complexity and that simple models induce the feeling that they can solve these problems. However, there is a danger that simple models overlook important features, which means that the solutions do not work. To put it in a popular way: too simple models lead to too simple solutions, and too simple solutions lead to big disasters.

How to prevent too simple models and too simple solutions? The discipline that deals with such questions is the philosophy of technology. In this section we borrow three key concepts from the philosophy of Herman Dooyeweerd to analyze and to understand the complexity of technology and technological infrastructures.

Aspects

The first concept is the idea of aspects. Dooyeweerd argues that every whole in this reality functions in different aspects. For example, a pair of glasses consists of different materials (physical aspect), has a specific shape (spatial aspect), strengthens my eyesight (sensory aspect), represents an economic value (economic aspect), and is beautiful or ugly (aesthetic aspect). Also, a windmill functions in different aspects. The most striking are the physical aspect (transition of energy), the formative aspect (design), the economic aspect (costs), and the moral aspect (sustainability, safety). The great discovery of Dooyeweerd was that every whole functions in different aspects. In total, he distinguishes fifteen different aspects.

Wholes

The second concept is the idea of wholes. Dooyeweerd argues that there are different kinds of wholes. For example, there are "living wholes" like human beings, animals, and plants, "technical wholes" like cars, houses, windmills, and solar panels, and "societal wholes" like states, households, hospitals, churches, enterprises, and museums. Dooyeweerd argues that all these wholes have their own nature or identity. For example, a windmill is characterized by the formative or technological aspect (controlled energy generation), a hospital by the moral aspect (care for patients), and a church by the faith aspect (honoring God).

Enkaptic Structures

The third concept is the idea of enkaptic structures. In enkaptic structures wholes are connected to each other without losing their own identity. An example of an enkaptic structure is the electrical energy infrastructure of the future. In this infrastructure quite different wholes are connected to each other: power stations, windmills, solar panels, transmission networks, distribution networks, households, hospitals, churches, factories, and so.

Case Study: The Energy System of the Future

The concepts of aspects, wholes, and enkaptic structures provide an in-depth insight into the complexity of the energy system of the future.

Aspects

Let us start with the key concept of aspects. According to Dooyeweerd every aspect has the following properties:

1. Every aspect has its own nature, quality, or modus. For example, the nature of the physical aspect differs from the biological aspect, the nature of the biological aspect differs from the moral aspect, and the nature of the moral aspect in turn differs from the faith aspect.
2. Since each aspect has its own nature, quality, or modus, it cannot be reduced to another one. For example, the biological aspect cannot be reduced to the physical aspect, the economic aspect not to the social aspect, and the faith aspect not to the moral aspect.
3. Each aspect has its own normativity. For example, there are physical and biological laws and there are social and moral norms. Laws cannot be violated, but norms can. For example, human beings can never escape the laws of gravity, but they can violate moral norms.

In the foregoing section I have argued that in the energy infrastructure of the future different wholes are connected to each other. Each of these wholes can be described in more detail by using the key concept of aspects. I would like to illustrate that with an aspectual analysis of a windmill as a source of renewable energy (see Table 1).

Table 1: An aspectual analysis of windmills

Aspect	Nature	Type of Normativity	Illustration
arithmetic	number, quantity	laws	measurable quantities like height of the tower, the length of the blades, and the amount of generated electricity
spatial	extent	laws	size and form of the foundation, tower, turbine, and blades
kinematic	movement	laws	speed of the wind; rotational speed of the blades; different types of vibrations
physical	energy, interaction	laws	materials and properties of the foundation, tower, turbine, and blades; conversion of wind energy into electrical energy
biotic	life, organic, vital	laws	influence of electromagnetic fields and waves on life; influence of offshore windmills on sea life

psychic	sensitive, sensorial, primary psychic reactions	laws	influence of windmills on sensorial and psychic experiences; reported symptoms include headaches, nausea, sleep problems, tinnitus, and anxiety ('wind turbine syndrome')
analytical	logic, rational, analytical distinction	norms	rational design of the windmill; sharp definitions of relevant concepts
formative	shaping, power, control	norms	design of the windmill; control of power generation; influence of residents on the location of windmills
lingual	meaning, symbolic meaning	norms	name of the windmill park; framing of windmills in the daily papers and social media ('energy source of the future' or 'destruction of the landscape')
social	intercourse, communion, interconnectedness	norms	influence of the windmill park on the social life of residents

economic	control of rare goods, stewardship, productivity	norms	investments; costs per kWh; efficiency; loss of value of houses in the direct neighborhood
aesthetic	harmony, beauty	norms	visual appearance of windmills; harmonious integration of a windmill park in the natural environment
juridical	justice, law	norms	ownership; liability in case of incidents; complaint procedures
moral	love, care, willingness to serve	norms	care for passing birds; limiting the influence of the shadow of blades on animals and humans; safety
certitudinal (faith)	certainty, reliability, faith	norms	reliability of the windmill; windmills as expression of faith in sustainable energy

Table 1 clearly expresses the complexity of windmills: engineers and managers must consider fifteen different aspects!

Wholes

In the energy infrastructure of the future different wholes are connected to each other. According to Dooyeweerd a whole has the following properties:

1) Every whole has an its own identity. For example, the identity of a church building is different from the identity of a court house, and the identity of a marriage is different from the identity of a bridge club.

2) The identity of a whole can be determined by means of an aspectual analysis. For example, the identity of a church is expressed by the faith aspect and the identity of a courthouse by the juridical aspect. The identity of a marriage is characterized by the moral aspect and the identity of a bridge club by the social aspect.

3) Each whole functions in fifteen aspects, in some active and in others passive. For example, a windmill functions in the aesthetic aspect passively for it cannot experience beauty but only be experienced as beautiful. People, on the other hand, do function actively in the aesthetic aspect: they can experience a windmill as beautiful (or ugly).

In the energy infrastructure of the future quite different wholes are connected to each other. First, technical wholes like ships that transport oil, refineries that convert oil into fuel, cars that use gasoline, and so on. Further, technical wholes like windmills and solar panels that generate renewable electrical energy; transmission and distribution networks that transport electrical energy; equipment that uses electrical energy for transport and heating; and so on. Second, different types of societal wholes like companies that are active in the energy sector, local and national authorities that make policies and regulations, and institutions that enforce legislation. Thirdly, there are quite different societal wholes that use energy, e.g., households, hospitals, churches, factories, shops, and so on. Each user of energy has its own justified interests.

In summary, the energy infrastructure of the future is more than a set of new technologies. It also cannot be interpreted as an advanced technological system. It must be understood as a medley of technical and societal wholes.

Enkaptic Structures

How now to understand the energy infrastructure of the future? Inspired by the philosophy of Dooyeweerd, I would like to coin the concept "enkaptic structure." This type of structure has the following properties:

1) Enkaptic structures have a 'common denominator'. The energy infrastructure of the future is about sustainable energy. It is not only about the generation and transport of energy but also about the use of energy. All technical wholes in this infrastructure are designed — better: ought to be designed — in such a way that a sustainable infrastructure develops. All societal wholes (parties) in this infrastructure act and interact — better: must act and interact — in a such way that ultimately a sustainable infrastructure is developed.

2) The common denominator has a normative component. This normative component came in the forgoing sentences to the fore in the words that are used: "must be designed," "must act and interact," and "sustainable infrastructure."

3) In an enkaptic structure, wholes keep their own identity. For example, the identity of windmills remains the controlled generation of sustainable energy, and the identity of transmission and distribution lines remains the controlled transport of electrical energy. The identity of local and national authorities continues to be determined by the juridical aspect (legislation and enforcement), and the identity of a hospital that uses energy continues to be determined by the moral aspect (caring for patients).

4) Every whole must contribute to the flowering of the whole infrastructure and to the flowering of the users of sustainable energy.

In conclusion, the energy infrastructure of the future is a medley of technical and social wholes that interact with each other in such a way that every whole keeps its identity and a sustainable infrastructure develops.

Summary

Dooyeweerd's philosophy offers three key concepts for understanding the complexity of technology and technological infrastructures: aspects, wholes and enkaptic structures. The relevance of these concepts can be illustrated by exploring the energy infrastructure of the future. Each of these concepts identifies a specific type of complexity. The concept of aspects highlights that energy technology is multi-aspectual; the concept of wholes shows that the energy infrastructure must be understood as a medley of technological and societal wholes; and the concept of enkaptic structures emphasizes that the energy infrastructure has a normative denominator: the generation, transport, and use of sustainable energy.

31

The Significance of Dooyeweerd's Philosophy for Understanding Human Responsibility in Technology

by Maarten J. Verkerk

Introduction

THE CASE STUDY in the previous chapter makes the question of human responsibility super clear. Who is responsible for global warming? Who is responsible to address this issue? Is ethics first and foremost something for politicians and policy makers? Or is it something especially for engineers and citizens? I would like to start with four statements which illustrate the way people in our culture think about the relation between the climate crisis and ethics:

> "As an individual citizen, I cannot contribute to limiting global warming because I have no power or influence."

> "As an engineer I develop what my bosses tell me. It is the responsibility of society whether or not they use products that emit CO_2."

> "As a company, we recognize the problem of global warming. But measures can only be taken internationally, otherwise our competitive position will deteriorate."

"The government must take the lead in the transition to a sustainable society."

Each of these statements has a certain plausibility. Indeed, individual citizens have little influence, engineers have bosses who decide what to do, companies operate in a competitive playing field, and governments play an important role in development. But does this mean that these statements give a good description of the responsibilities of the different actors?

In this chapter I would like to defend the proposition that every actor in society has its own responsibility regarding the climate crisis. I also want to make it plausible that the transition to a sustainable society requires shared values and shared visions for the future.

Three Classical Ethical Approaches

Let's look at history first. In philosophy, three main ethical theories have been developed to provide a first handle for the responsibilities of the various actors in society: virtue ethics, duty ethics, and consequentialism. Each of these theories has its own approach: virtue ethics focuses on the person who acts, duty ethics on the quality of the act itself, and consequentialism on the result.

The father of virtue ethics is the Greek philosopher Aristotle. Virtue ethics is primarily interested in the personal qualities of the person who acts. It's about the development of virtues and using these virtues in a good and balanced way. In health care, for example, it is about the virtues of empathy and involvement, in politics about integrity and justice, and in society of respect and a sense of community. The idea is that a virtuous person always and everywhere, acts virtuously. Popularly expressed, if the right people are at the wheel, things will be fine.

A fine example of duty ethics can be found in the Bible. The Ten Commandments summarize the rules and commandments for the people of Israel with respect to God and society. Duties always take the form "thou shalt..." or "thou shalt not...." The main example of philosophical duty ethics is Kant's ethics. According to him, the core of morality is to act out of respect for and in accordance with duties. In his view, duties must be respected in every situation.

Consequentialism concentrates on the morality of the objectives of an action. The best-known version is the utilitarianism of Jeremy Bentham and John Stewart Mill. According to this approach, the goal of morality is "to make as many people as happy as possible." This form of ethics states that the consequence or result of an action is the most important criterion for judging it.

These three approaches are often seen as competitive. That is incorrect. It is better to regard them as complementary. After all, they address different aspects: the person acting, the nature of the act, and the result of the act. In one situation one approach is more obvious, and in another situation another one.

Different Types of Normativities

The three classical ethical approaches focus on human actions. However, a condition to act in a responsible way in a concrete situation requires insight in the norms that apply to this situation. Again, I want to make this clear based on a case study.

In the previous chapter, the complexity of the energy infrastructure of the future has been analyzed. Three different kinds of complexities were identified: aspects, wholes, and enkaptic structures. The aspectual complexity of the energy infrastructure of the future has been elaborated for technology. Every technical whole functions in fifteen different aspects. In five aspects there is normativity in the form of laws and in ten aspects in the form of norms. This means that citizens, engineers, companies, and politicians must take these laws and norms into account. This means that in the generation, transport, and use of sustainable energy not only technical and economic aspects have to be addressed, but also social, esthetic, and moral issues.

The key concept of wholes shows that the energy infrastructure cannot be interpreted as a superstructure that is controlled from a central point but must be understood as a medley of technological and societal wholes. Every whole has its distinct identity. This is where a normative component comes into play. In the policy on, design and use of the infrastructure of the future, the own identity of technical and societal wholes must be respected. That means, no actor is allowed to control other actors. No actor may exercise power over other actors in an unauthorized manner.

The idea of enkaptic structures emphasizes that the energy infrastructure has a normative de-nominator. It is about the generation, transport, and use of sustainable energy. Each actor must contribute to the flourishing of the infrastructure and the infrastructure in turn must contribute to the flourishing of each actor. All technical wholes must be designed in such a way that the infrastructure and its actors are shown to their full advantage.

Maybe some readers will breathe a sigh now. Do we really have to consider so many laws and norms? Can't we make do with a simple list that we can tick off? The answer is 'no'. The reason is that reality is so complex.

A Web of Responsibilities

The statements in the introduction are a wonderful example of the discussion about the responsibilities of individuals and organizations with a view to a sustainable future. I would like to elaborate these responsibilities in general. First, I will discuss the responsibility of an engineer in a company. Second, I will argue that the responsibility of organizations is dependent on their identity.

Organizations are made up of people. When we say that organizations bear responsibility, we mean that people in organizations can be held accountable for their behavior. To gain more insight into the responsibilities of individuals in organizations, it is important to look at their position in the organization. Take, for example, the responsibility of engineers in the Research & Development (R&D) department of an oil refinery or an electricity company. Are they responsible for developing sustainable products and installations? And exactly how far does their responsibility extend? Engineers can be expected to use all their professionalism and creativity to achieve breakthrough innovations that lead to a sustainable society. At the same time, it must be recognized that more is needed than motivated engineers. After all, engineers are part of a larger organization. Each of the hierarchical layers in that organization must contribute. The R&D manager must ensure a good project plan and a good innovative climate in the R&D department. The business unit manager must allocate sufficient resources to execute that plan and is responsible for relationships with stakeholders. The CEO is responsible for a sustainable policy. In other words, there is a "web of responsibilities"; a web that is organized to a high degree "vertically." The statement in the introduction about the responsibility of the engineer is true to the extent that an engineer is highly dependent on the decisions of management. But that statement is so far untrue that within the whole of the organization an engineer has his own responsibility, and if an organization does not take on its responsibility, an engineer does not have to continue working there.

In Dooyeweerd's view, society cannot be seen as a hierarchical structure with the state at the top and other social structures subordinate to it, but they are all structures at the "same level." All structures have their own identity which is expressed in the so-called qualifying function. For example, the identity of the state is juridical (law, justice), a family moral (care for each other), a company economic (profit motive), a church religious (worship of God), and so on. Each of these societal structures has its own responsibility with respect to a sustainable energy infrastructure of the future. The state plays a key role: it is the only structure that has the responsibility to make and to enforce laws to facilitate the transition to a sustainable society. Additionally, the state must take care that the development of a sustainable energy infrastructure is inclusive: all citizens must have access to energy. Companies in the field of generation, transport, and distribution of energy have the responsibility to cooperate so that a sustainable energy infrastructure will evolve. Organizations that use energy have the responsibility to do as much as possible to conserve energy, to produce sustainable energy as much as possible (e.g., solar panels), and to contribute to a stable energy infrastructure. In summary, the Dooyeweerdian analysis of society shows that not one actor (e.g., the state or the energy sector) is responsible for the development of a sustainable energy infrastructure but that there is a "web of responsibilities"; a web that is organized to a high degree "horizontally."

How to Guide the Energy Transition

The energy infrastructure of the future is of enormous size. It connects regions, countries, and continents in one global system. By that, it also connects different cultures, economic systems, and political structures. In the worst-case scenario, every country will have its own policy and legislation with respect to this infrastructure. These observations raise the question: How to guide the transition of the present energy system to a sustainable energy system? Negatively formulated: How to prevent the energy infrastructure of the future from becoming a patchwork that in the end does not meet any of its requirements? I would like to add: How to ensure that the energy system of the future serves the global society as a whole and not only the interests of rich people, rich companies, and rich countries?

The above analysis leads to a couple of strategies that must be addressed simultaneously. First, the government has a major responsibility in co-developing a vision of a sustainable society, in co-developing an energy infrastructure, in enacting adequate legislation, and in facilitating the transition. Governments must cooperate internationally with respect to policies and standards. Second, energy companies should work together as much as possible to transform the current energy system into a sustainable system. Especially, we would like to emphasize the power of shareholders and banks to force a shift to a sustainable system in the energy sector. Third, engineers have a personal and a professional responsibility to develop infrastructures that meet relevant values and norms. Generally, this role has been taken up by professional engineering associations. Four, users of energy must be stimulated to conserve energy and to make the transition to using sustainable energy. They can exert a certain power on their suppliers to accelerate the process. Finally, it must be stressed that the energy transition is not only a matter of 'ratio' and 'technology' but is also a matter of values, mind-sets, and basic beliefs. Societal dialogues are necessary to make values, mind-sets, and basic beliefs explicit.

Conclusions

This paper investigates the responsibility of individuals and organizations in the development of the energy infrastructure of the future. It is argued that there is a web of responsibilities. This web has a vertical dimension expressing the different responsibilities of the various hierarchical layers in organizations, and it has a horizontal dimension expressing the different responsibilities of different organizations depending on their identity.

32

Understanding One's Own Professional Practice: The Triple I Model

by Maarten J. Verkerk

Introduction

SEVERAL YEARS AGO, I met Fred Holtkamp, a man in his late forties or early fifties. He worked at a college and researched the design and use of orthopaedic devices. He was eager to understand why so much went wrong in his field and why it was not possible to make significant progress in improving the quality of the aids. So, he contacted a philosopher of technology. As an illustration of everything that went wrong, he told me the story of a nun who was prescribed an expensive device to reduce pain when moving. After a week – despite pain during walking without the device – she put the device in the closet and never used it again. This story was the beginning of a long collaboration.

I told Fred about the practice approach in general and the Triple I model specifically. This model supports professionals to reflect on their own practice. Everything showed that Fred had no aptitude for philosophy, but gradually he began to understand this model. He even got excited about it. He learned a new language and began to look at the problems in his field in a different way. And not only Fred, but also some of his colleagues saw the value of the Triple I model.

In this chapter the Triple I model is introduced partly based on the collaboration with Fred. I note that the model can be used not only to analyse the situation but also to improve the quality of practice. Both applications are discussed in this contribution.

Case Study: Ankle Foot Orthoses

One of the devices in the field of orthopaedics is the ankle-foot orthosis (AFO). This orthosis is externally applied and intended to control position and motion of the ankle. Reasons for the use of AFOs vary from congenital malformations to diseases and traumas such as poliomyelitis, multiple sclerosis, cerebrovascular accident, or head injuries resulting in an aberrant gait pattern. An AFO is a piece of medical technology that is generally constructed of lightweight polypropylene-based plastic in the shape of the letter "L," with the upright part, depending on the function of the AFO, behind the calf or in front of the shank, and a lower part running under the foot. They are attached to the calf with a strap and are made to fit inside accommodative shoes.

Fred Holtkamp et al.[1] conducted a survey to obtain insight in the use, non-use, satisfaction, and dissatisfaction of AFOs. This survey showed that one out of fifteen participants did not use the AFO at all. This result is striking because these people were dependent on this device for daily functioning. Evidently, the use of this device generated more discomfort than the non-use! Further, the survey showed that one quarter of the AFO users was dissatisfied. The highest level of dissatisfaction was reported for "comfort."

What are the causes of non-use of and dissatisfaction with AFOs? These questions were addressed with the Triple I model.

The Triple I model

Fred knew the world of orthopaedics like the back of his hand. He

---

1. F. C. Holtkamp, E.J.M. Wouters, J. van Hoof, Y. van Zaalen and M.J. Verkerk, "Use of and Satisfaction with Ankle Foot Orthoses," *Clinical Research on Foot & Ankle 2*, no. 2 (2015): 1-8..

knew how the orthopaedic doctor and the orthopaedic engineers worked together. He also knew that there were significant quality differences between the various companies that made AFOs. I suggested to Fred to define the different places where patients meet professionals as practices.

Let us explore the word "practice." The philosopher Alisdair MacIntyre[2] has coined the word "practice" in his book *After Virtue. A Study in Moral Theory*. In his view, practices are about morality. This is expressed in, among other things, the way in which people in those practices collaborate and the "standards of excellence" they use. The sociologist Nicolini[3] emphasizes that the study of practices must start in the middle of the action. In his view, practices are always about what people are doing and saying. He believes that practice theories can offer radically new ways of understanding the work of professionals. Finally, Christian philosophers have developed the so-called normative practice approach that focusses on the normative aspects of the actions of professionals.[4]

I have developed the so-called Triple I model in close collaboration with professionals from different disciplines[5] (see Figure 1). This model can be seen as a practical translation of the aforementioned normative practice approach. The first "I" refers to the "identity and intrinsic values" of a practice. For example, the identity of a health care practice is characterized by "caring

---

2. A. MacIntyre, *After Virtue. A Study in Moral Theory*, 2nd ed. (Notre Dame: University of Notre Dame Press, 1984).
3. D. Nicolini, *Practice Theory, Work, & Organisation, An Introduction* (Oxford: Oxford University Press, 2012).
4. M. J. Vries and H. J. Jochemsen, *The Normative Nature of Social Practices and Ethics in Professional Environments* (Hershey, PA: IGI Global, 2019).
5. M. J. Verkerk, "A Philosophy-based 'toolbox' for Designing Technology: The Conceptual Power of Dooyeweerdian Philosophy," *Koers – Bulletin for Christian Scholarship* 79, no. 3 (2014): 1-7, Art. #2164.; M.J. Verkerk, F. C. Holtkamp, E. J. M. Wouters, and J. van Hoof, "Professional Practices and User Practices: An Explorative Study in Health Care," *Philosophia Reformata* 82, (2017): 167–191.

for." All activities in the practice must be focussed on the well-being and health of the patient. The intrinsic values of the healthcare practice are values like empathy, involvement, altruism, and caring. The second "I" refers to the "interests of stakeholders" of a practice. The most important stakeholders of health care practices are the insurance companies, patient organizations, professional associations, and authorities. Every stakeholder has its own *justified* interests. The third "I" refers to the "ideals" and "basic beliefs" of society that influences health care practices. For example, views on patient autonomy and health insurance coverage.

Analysis of the Orthopaedic Chain

One of the first things we did was to investigate the health care chain from the patient's perspective. This is also known as the patient's journey. Figure 2 shows the patient journey of an AFO-user. This journey consists of seven steps: awareness of the patient or his or her caregiver, assessment by a physician, examination and tests by a physician, specifications made by an orthopaedic engineer, manufacturing of the device, evaluation of the device by the orthopaedic engineer and the patient, and acceptance and use by the patient. This figure also describes the actions and outcomes for every step.

We sat for a while watching this patient's journey. We looked at each other and said: really you should see every step of this journey as a practice. And if you do that, what do you see? The most important observation is that the whole patient journey starts and ends with the patient. The journey starts with a care question (complaint) of the patient: difficulties in daily movements. The journey process also ends with the patient: the acceptance and actual use of a device that supports the patient in mobility. Therefore, we decided to coin the term "user practice" to address the daily life of the patient. The second observation was that patients use their devices in quite different situations, e.g., daily life at home, at work, and during sport or societal activities. That means there are different user practices. The last observation was that there was not one professional practice, but four: the general practitioner who assesses the complaints of the patient, the health care specialist who makes a diagnosis and prescribes an orthopaedic device, the orthopaedic engineer who translates the prescription in a specification and evaluates the device with the patient during delivery, and the operators and engineers who work together to produce the orthopaedic device (see Figure 3).

User Practices

When we zoomed in on user practices, it became clear how important it was to coin that term. Fred's experience was that neither the specialist nor the orthopaedic engineer systematically analyzes the various practices in which the patient is active and makes explicit their importance of their input for the design of the device (see figure 4). This experience would later be substantiated by data.

At first glance, an AFO should reduce a mobility problem. So, you can say that the most important function of an orthopaedic device is to promote movement. However, there is a big difference in the movements made when cleaning the house, when using public transport, when climbing a ladder if you are a window cleaner, and in sports such as cycling, jogging and mountain climbing. In other words, the context of the movement plays a major role.[6]

We found that four general user practices are relevant for specifying AFOs: daily life at home, transport, work, and leisure.[7] "Daily life at home" consists of movements like walking indoors,

---

6. M. J. Verkerk, F. C. Holtkamp, E. J. M. Wouters, and J. van Hoof, "Professional Practices and User Practices: An Explorative Study in Health Care," *Philosophia Reformata* 82, no. 2 (2017): 167–191.
7. F. C. Holtkamp, M. J. Verkerk, J. van Hoof and E. J. M. Wouters, "Mapping user activities and user environments during the client intake and examination phase: an exploratory study from the perspective of ankle foot orthosis users," *Technology and Disability* 28, no. 4 (2016): 145–157, DOI: 10.3233/TAD-160452.

manoeuvring in the kitchen, walking the stairs, crossing thresholds, and using the bathroom. "Transport" involves for instance walking, cycling, public transport, and car driving. "Work" consists of movements related to one's daily work. Often, the working environment is characterized by specific conditions like temperature, humidity, bumpiness of the floor, and so on. Finally, "leisure" might consist of a couple of quite different movements in various environments. For example, the movements and conditions of playing bridge are quite different in comparison with that of mountain hiking.

In conclusion, our reflection on user practices opened our eyes to the fact that professionals do not systematically map the different environments in which their patients live and do not analyze the various sets of movements that take place within these environments. This observation reveals the first cause why some patients do not use the AFO at all and why other patients are dissatisfied with their AFO: it does not fit their daily life.

Professional Practices

Next, we zoomed in on the professional practices. We concluded that professionals in the chain do not cooperate optimally. The Triple I model helped us to identify possible causes (see Figure 5).

Every professional practice has its own identity and its own intrinsic values. Let us focus on the intrinsic values. Generally, the intrinsic values of the health care practice are values like empathy, involvement, altruism, and caring. Also, the orthopaedic engineering practice is based on core values like empathy, involvement, altruism, and caring, but also on technological values like control and creative design. Finally, the intrinsic values of the manufacturing practice are technological values like discipline, cleanliness, quality, and control.

Every professional practice involved has its own specific network of stakeholders. The networks of stakeholders will partly overlap and partly be specific. Generally, it cannot be taken for granted that the influence of these parties is all borne by the same intention: the well-being and interests of the patient.

Finally, it cannot be assumed that each professional practice is influenced in the same way by the societal ideals and basic beliefs. For example, health care practice can be influenced by the social value of providing tailor-made solutions for each patient. But manufacturing practice can be influenced by the same society to generate more profit by standardizing which can be at odds with the value of customizing.

In conclusion, the Triple I model revealed three possible mechanisms for why professionals do not cooperate optimally: a misfit of intrinsic values, the influence of the various stakeholders, and the influence of basic beliefs in society. This analysis reveals the second cause why some patients do not use the AFO at all and why other patients are dissatisfied with their AFO: professionals fail in cooperating to put the well-being of the patient at the centre. A solution is "to integrate" the different professional practices (see Figure 5).

Conclusions

At the beginning of this chapter, I introduced the orthopaedic engineer, Fred Holtkamp. The aim of our collaboration was to improve the quality of orthopaedic aids. The Triple I model taught us to look at these tools in a different way to identify the main problems and to suggest solutions.

Finally, I come back to the story of a nun who after a week put her expensive orthopaedic shoes in the closet and never touched them again. It turned out that she could not kneel in her expensive shoes, a capital design flaw that was caused by the fact that the orthopaedic engineer was not aware of the daily life of a nun and did not analyze it systematically.

Figures and Captions

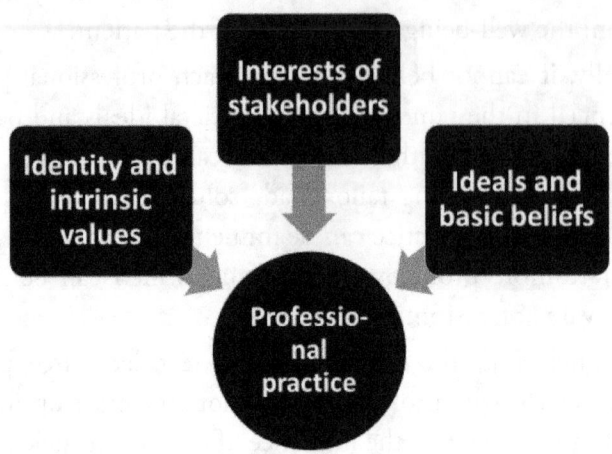

Figure 1: Triple I model for professional practices

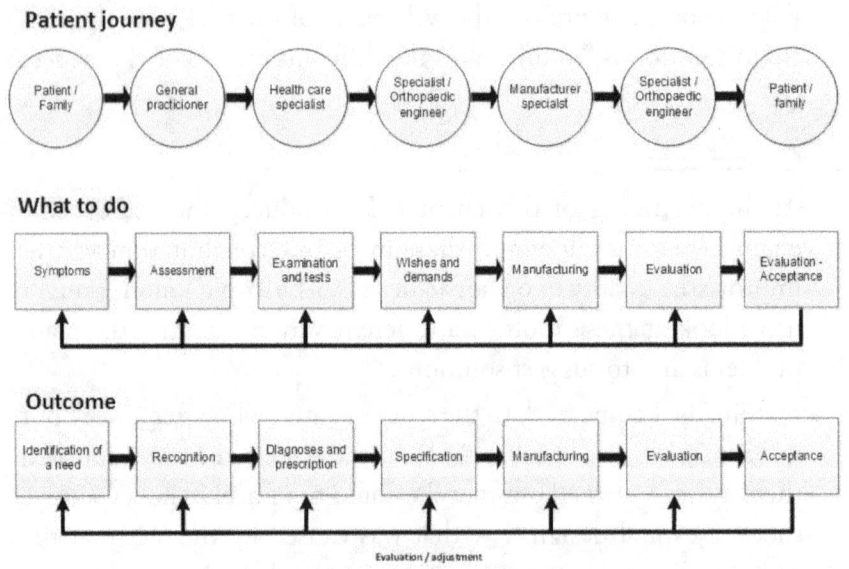

Figure 2: Patient journey of an AFO-user.

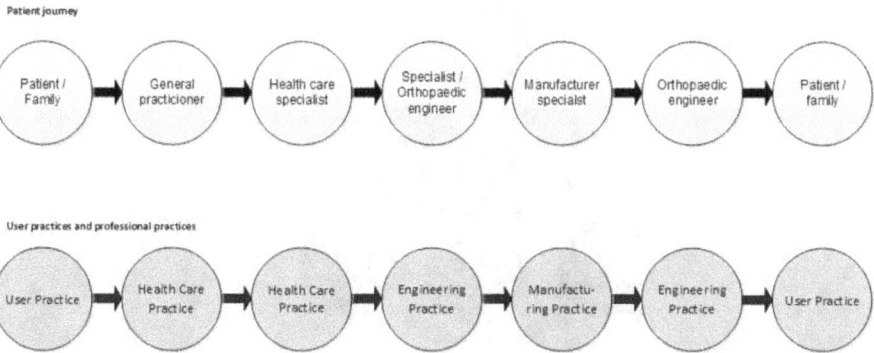

Figure 3: Different practices in the patient journey of an AFO user.

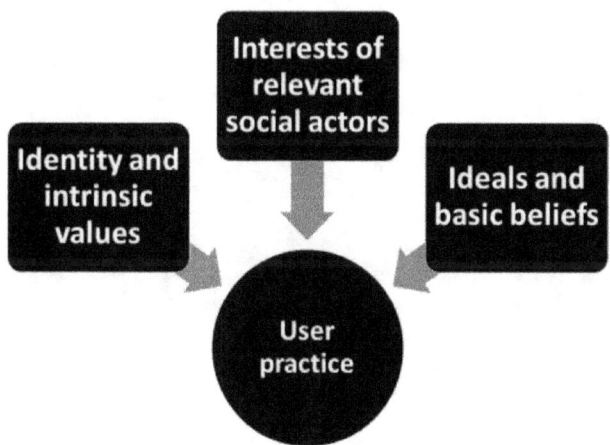

Figure 4: Triple I model for user practices

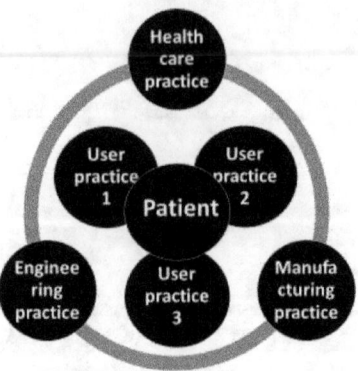

Figure 5: Integration of professional practices around the patient and its user practices

33

BASIC AESTHETICS
as Dooyeweerd could have written it

by Calvin Seerveld

AESTHETICS IS UNDEVELOPED in Dooyeweerd's philosophy. But his vision for aesthetics as a prime theoretical study of an irreducible aspect of creatural reality in the encyclopedia of the sciences is a pivotal idea that deserves careful attention. So I extrapolate from Dooyeweerd's basic suggestions and consciously speak in a Dooyeweerdian view what follows.

It is a basic thought in Dooyeweerd that just as a prism will break white light up into several different but always ordered colours, just so our cohering temporal reality is a framework with a rainbow of ways creatures can be understood in it.

For example,[1] cigars can be approached[2] economically (cost too much), sensitively (satisfying aroma), ethically (unhealthy), legally (taxed contraband), and also aesthetically (looks *like* a slim hot dog, a bulky writing instrument, or a penis). Not only cigars but all things in our earth world can be examined in each of these rainbow-coloured ways. Each way of examining things — cigars,

---

1. H. Dooyeweerd, *In the Twilight of Western Thought* (Philadelphia: Presbyterian and Reformed Publishing Company, 1960), 6-8,122,130.
2. H. Dooyeweerd, *Encyclopedia of the Science of Law*, vol. 1, Introduction, Series A, vol. 8, General Editor D. F. M. Strauss. Special Editor A. C. Cameron (Grand Rapids, MI: Paideia Press, 2012), 13-15.

trees, bugs, important officials, volcanic rock, dreams, thoughts — is legitimate; but each kind of approach — economically, sensitively, ethically, legally, or aesthetically — does not give you by itself full knowledge of the object of your subjective attention.

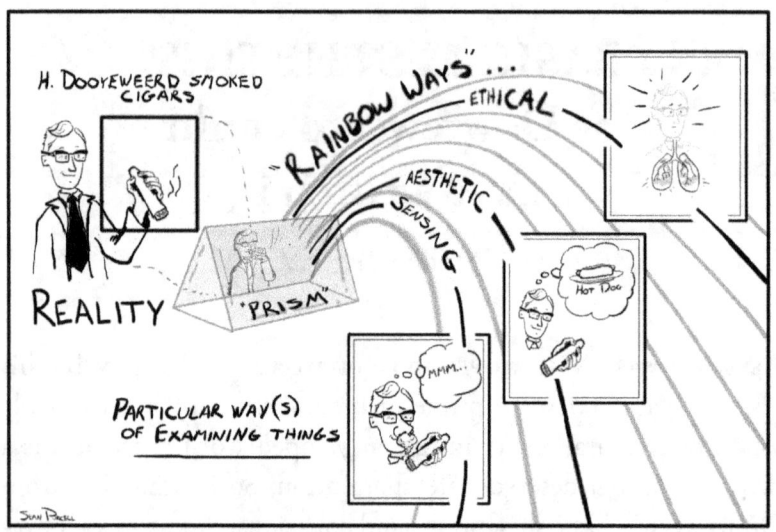

Aesthetic Life

A shorthand formulation for understanding the aesthetic way of approaching things is this: what does it seem *like?* Don't think about the object, but use your *imagination*.

A tree is *like* a sentinel, *like* an old person losing its leaves, *like* a friend on a hot day in whose shade you would like to rest. Such ruminating activity we may call "aesthetic life."

"Making believe" is being busy aesthetically. When children "dress up" in fancy clothes or "play house," they are acting aesthetically. If you notice the quirks in what's happening around you that are not obvious but betray covert subtleties of what's going on, you are on aesthetic alert. Unlike a blink, a wink between friends alludes to something, and is a subtle imaginative way to communicate secrets. Being witty or telling well an ingenious, self-reproaching joke can be an aesthetic effort to relieve an argumentative tension in a social gathering. Noticing while sitting in your canoe on a large lake a lovely solitary loon's call in the silence before an approaching thunderstorm tells you aesthetically to get back to land quick. When you are walking on stilts to pretend to be a giant, you are aesthetically active. The beautiful contour of trees silhouetted against a setting sun in the jungle is an aesthetic smorgasbord asking for your imaginative acceptance.

That is, the *peculiarly nuanceful properties* of things and the *imagining doing as-if quality* of actions telltale the aesthetic dimension of our creatural reality.

Dooyeweerd's thesis that the aesthetic is a prime legitimate side of reality is very important. Then humans do not have to apologize for their aesthetic activity. It's one way you were created to be in this world. And imaginative activity is as relatively important as thinking or loving or paying taxes to a grown-up in North America, Asia or Africa. It is so that all the other ways a person exists—health-wise, (un)educated, proud, (in)competent—colours how you practise aesthetic life. A person's aesthetic life can be threadbare, brimming over with joy, pedestrian, or enriching one's self and neighbours. Somewhat like a thoughtless person who doesn't think when he speaks, anybody who doesn't have a sense of humour or much imagination can become like a bore in the company of one's neighbours. The ability to make-believe may not be as urgent as breathing with a heart pumping blood or as critical to Life and Death as to Whom or What you are deep down committed to and live for, but to have aesthetic life percolating and subliminally at work in all the other ways you also exist is as vital for a human person in society as infrared rays are to warming sunlight.

Aesthetic Ordinance as Godly Imperative

Humans, according to Dooyeweerd, are called to obey God's

Word.³ The Almighty Creator God revealed in Jesus Christ has not spoken just in the Bible. God calls us also to follow the good ways God created us to exist: to be (organically) healthy, non-contradictory (logical) in thinking, to be aware of gravity (physically) in standing and walking, clarity in speech (lingually), frugal and generous in spending resources (economically)—God even asks us humans to be reverent, respectful of authority (confessionally). It's true, we humans do not always respond to these creatural ordinances God has quietly laid down for us to practice. That's why there is often sickness, confusion, accidents, dispute, greed, revolutionary activity afoot. But God's creational laws for *clear* speech and *sound* thought and *just* governance, *relaxing* emotions and *humble* service are not reprimanding divine prohibitions which box you in: God's creative ordering bounds to our different kinds of activities are invitations to open up and fill out one's several human abilities to mature and blossom fruitfully. God's Words and Spirit offer demarcated opportunities for blessing.⁴

God's Word for aesthetic life is: *be metaphoric!* Fool around purposefully; be whimsically entertaining without calling attention to yourself; dare to be congenially ironic to get at the truth; enjoy doing odd things that spark something new for others; be amazed at what is beautiful but hidden; value what is puzzling, and carefully reflect even on what seems ugly or awful. That is, God's good Word for aesthetic human life is: do not always simply be straight-forward, but throw a curve ball, do the unexpected, see strange connections, play around with differences.

And this aesthetic imperative from the Creator God to notice and even be metaphoric has the character of a stimulating limit. If you overdo the call to be metaphoric, you can become extrava-

---

3. H. Dooyeweerd, *A New Critique of Theoretical Thought*, vol. 1, Collected Works of Herman Dooyeweerd, Series A, General Editor D.F.M. Strauss (Lewiston, NY: Edwin Mellen, 1997), 506-508.
4. Dooyeweerd, *In the Twilight*, 185-187.

gant, flagrant, pretentious, foolish. And if a person cannot muster the effort to respond to God's call to be metaphoric, you can become banal, insipid, jejune, as pernicious as an anaesthetic kill-joy.

Artists are Professional Imaginators, Not Saviours

Some persons develop the skill to turn their native metaphoric gifts into special objects or events like sculptures, paintings, theatre, poetry and dance. Because Dooyeweerd recognizes the importance of ordinary thinking ("naive experience")[5] he does not idolize professional thinkers like philosophers and scientists.

Naturally he does honour the cultural contributions made by figures like Kant, Cassirer[6] and Hannah Arendt. Somewhat similarly, anybody in the thought tradition of Dooyeweerd who recognizes the underlying blessing of ordinary imaginativity, the ludic (playful) lift aesthetic life gives to our daily mortal existence, will not idolize professional artists and artistic geniuses.

H. R. Rookmaaker assumed his university professorial office by rigorously calling into question the long-standing Humanist tradition of cheering on artists as the prophets who can save the world with Beauty.[7]

I too should like to embody and accent Dooyeweerd's careful and appreciative assessment of artistry which intensifies and squares, so to speak, aesthetic life into a crafted symbolic, stand-alone object or event subject first of all to the aesthetic ordinance, by comparing artwork to the task of plumbers and their worth in society. Plumbers craft vehicles out of stone (aqueducts) or metal

---

5. Dooyeweerd, *In the Twilight*, 13-16.
6. H. Dooyeweerd, *A New Critique of Theoretical Thought*, vol. 2, Collected Works of Herman Dooyeweerd, Series A, General Editor D.F.M. Strauss (Lewiston, NY: Edwin Mellen, 1997), 346-351.
7. H. Rookmaaker, "The Artist as Prophet?" in *The Complete Works of Hans Rookmaaker*, vol. 5, ed. Marleen Hengelaar-Rookmaaker (Carlisle UK: Piquant, 2003), 169-187.

pipes (modem toilets) to carry water safely for human use, and prevent disease. Artists form materials like wood, catgut, paint, gestures and voices into visible or audible suggestion-rich symbols to invigorate human imagination, and avert a dumb herd mentality. But neither sanitation nor artwork experiences give you a free ticket to heaven and a carefree existence. Both water-carrying instruments and allusive symbolic forms can facilitate and enrich human life, *or* mess up society, depending on their character and quality. They do not replace the death and resurrection of Jesus Christ. Those who believe ART actually helps people transcend ordinary reality and provides a salvific serenity may tempt others to become devout mystics, but such spiritualistic escapism, often promoted in the Name of BEAUTY, it seems to me, turns its back on reforming and redeeming the muck and misery in which many of one's neighbours are immersed, and is not a fruitful conception of artistry but tends to overrate artists as priestly mediators of salvation.

Bona Fide Art Works Betray the Art Makers' Slant on What Life is For, so Beware!

Dooyeweerd thinks all human artefacts are permeated and normed by the deep-going Spirit at work in a given age (Zeitgeist, "ground-motive")[8] which both stamps one's artwork with a vision of the world and provides the rationale for one's life activity in society.

The ancient pagan Graeco-Roman powerful public theatre of Sophocles and Seneca was driven by a deep allegiance, Dooyeweerd would say, to design a perfect harmonious *form* in durable *matter* (tragic circumstances) to elicit cathartic relief for the women and men who attended. Medieval European architects of towering cathedrals with an expensive, awe-inspiring rose window, which dispensed *grace* in the city were

---

8. Dooyeweerd, *New Critique*, 2:240; Dooyeweerd, *In the Twilight*, 32-39ff.

praised by the Church, while the *nature* of feces and garbage were allowed to run amok in the streets—you inhabited a split two-decker universe. Modern secularized culture insures there be the *necessity* of fated factual events which artists are driven by *freedom* to surmount or dialectically struggle with.

Such a broad-brush orientation in approaching artworks, however, must not degenerate into stigmatism, since particular artists can twist and turn their spirited milieu and chosen visionary tradition so as to modify, complicate and correct their inheritance. God's ordered world (including an aesthetic ordinance) is a common gift to humans of all ages—ancient, medieval, modern—so artists of all stripes, times and faiths (or lack thereof) can produce solid artwork.[9]

Etruscan red-and-black decorated vases by menial potters still ennobled flowers and enhanced a home. Haunting Gregorian chants in the phrygian mode can turn laments like Psalm 51 into unforgettably sad melodies voicing trust in the faithful Covenant God. Enlightenment painter Antoine Watteau is able, despite his rococo frivolous milieu in France, to offer a breath-taking critique of Louis XV's mores. Gerald Manley Hopkins can arrest the attention of anyone in our current disbelieving fast-paced digital environs with his sprung-rhythm consecrated poetry, and posit a wondrous hope. That is, producers of art's symbolic form are not stereotypes of philosophical positions, but usually are incisive imaginative providers of masked meanings.

Goethe's *Faust* (1808/1832) or *Leiden des Jungen Werthers* (1774) can beguile readers into trying themselves to outwit God or sacrifice everything they be for an all-consuming illicit love. Ingmar Bergman's intriguing *Seventh Seal* (1957) or Robert Bresson's mesmerizing *Un condamné à mort s'est échappé ou Le vent souffle où il veut* (1956) can make you wonder existentially wheth-

---

9. Dooyeweerd, *In the Twilight*, 54-56.

er your life is "nasty brutish and short" or worth a Pascal wager to believe in God's unfathomable grace. Put Hieronymous Bosch's fantastic *The Garden of Earthly Delights* painterly art (ca. 1510–1515) next to a Rothko wavering colour-field canvas (1950s) and you have a riveting choice between a bizarre heaven and hell or a gesture toward a Buddhist mystical transcendence. Artistry, if you know how to read its spirit and symbolic allusivity, has the power to get under your skin and shape your shalom *or* mislead your very stance on what is meaningful.

Godly Style

Dooyeweerd goes for the jugular in his thetical and critical philosophical analysis: pretheoretical human activity not only conditions our theoretical and multiple cultural contributions but signals where we stand in God's world.[10] Your *style* of daily activity, which is a definite subliminal response to the Creator God's aesthetic imperative Word, bespeaks your response to the Lord of the universe as much as your explicit verbal confession does or the theological dogma you hold. Is your style of speech and your intimate caresses and your style in fixing broken objects godly? There is more than one style, I believe, to show you are an adopted child of God. You can be Puritanically ascetic or Reformationally curious, characteristically skittish, strict or exuberant, basically anxious or hopeful as a person, but to be godly in style, one needs to avoid being rough and harsh or prim and sanctimonious, and act normally sure with laughter and with weeping.

Once upon a time in Dooyeweerd's home for conversation with a dozen American students (1957), we were served a delicious white German Mosel wine with the sweets. As Professor Dooyeweerd himself served each of us with a second glass full, he smiled, and said "*Gevaarlijk lekker!*" (dangerously delicious).

---

10. Dooyeweerd, *New Critique*, 2:345; Dooyeweerd, *In the Twilight*, 120-125.

That models, I think, that there can well be a moment of festive leisure in our intense rigour of service to God and neighbour with whatever talents we have been outfitted. Godly style has the mark of joyful carefulness in God's world.

Dooyeweerd is not like a weird dodo ("Dodoweird"), an extinct pigeon which could not fly. Dooyeweerd and Vollenhoven are more like the raven and dove sent out by Noah from the ark to bring back surprising fresh news that God's troubled world needs aesthetic gardening to brighten up all the other (modal) human tasks waiting for our willing work, like thinking (hypothetically) wisely, feeling (empathetically) sensitive, caring (winsomely) with mercy for others, and guiding governing societal relations (diplomatically) into peace.

Professional Note:

If Dooyeweerd had not taken the numerical analogue within the aesthetic aspect (viz., *schoone harmonie,* beautiful harmony) to be the kernel of the aesthetic mode, he would have explored more fully the complex richness of aesthetic life reality, as this chapter on Basic Aesthetics tries to do.[11]

---

11. Cf. C. Seerveld, "Christian Aesthetic Bread for the World," in *Normative Aesthetics*, ed. John Kok (Sioux Center: Dordt College Press, 2014), 152.

34

Is Language Uniquely Human?

by Danie F. M. Strauss

DOOYEWEERD'S THEORY of modal aspects conjectures that humans and non-human entities – such as material things, plants and animals – in principle function in all aspects of reality, either actively (as subjects) or latently as objects. The speech sounds produced by humans are functioning subjectively in the aspects of number, space, movement and the physical, but within all the post-physical aspects they display latent object functions. Subjects within the post-physical aspects can make these latent object functions *patent*, for example when a person hears speech sounds and understands what they mean.

What, However, Is Unique About Humankind?

Some thinkers are of the opinion that *language* is the particular characteristic that distinguishes humankind from animals. By means of language humanity owns and utilizes an awareness of the past and the future, a consciousness including the knowledge of the individual person's limited lifespan. Von Bertalanffy says that symbolism "if you will, is the divine spark distinguishing the most perfectly adapted animal from the poorest specimen of the human race."

Some Distinctive Features of Human Language

Animal communication does not refer to the past or the future. It refers to the vital here and now. For this reason, animal signs strictly have one content for every single sign. All human utterances, by contrast, can signify a number of different things, depending on the context, intention, or even, in the case of written language, the punctuation. It presupposes a responsible free human activity, which requires accountable choices. Eibl-Eibesfeldt categorically states that that "which, by contrast, regarding animals, is generally designated as 'language', exclusively moves within ... the domain of interjection, of the expression of moods lacking insight."[1]

Compare this with the famous dance of the bees that always indicates by means of the (i) tempo, (ii) direction and (iii) angle of the figure eight executed, the (i) distance, (ii) location, and (iii) direction of the source.[2] This is why there is a difference in principle between the learning of certain signs by chimpanzees and gorillas and all human language usage – these animals are simply not free to react in response to norms.

In the *Introduction* we mentioned that according to Dooyeweerd the normative contraries of the post-psychical aspects presuppose the logical principle of non-contradiction, reflected in other contraries, such as logical – illogical, reaction and revolution versus reformation, clear and ambiguous, polite – impolite, legal – illegal, and so on. Animals are incapable either to obey or to disobey norms, because they do not have subject functions in the normative aspects.

Vocal Capacities

Mammal's sounds simply do not compare with, for example, birdsong. The vocal potential of the gorilla and orangutan is exceptionally poor. The chimpanzee is somewhat better, and the gibbon can produce sounds covering almost an octave. All these anthropoids,

---

1. I. Eibl-Eibesfeldt, *Grundriß der vergleichenden Verhaltensforschung, Ethologie*, 8th rev. ed. (Vierkirchen-Pasenbach: Buch Vertrieb Blank GmbH, 2004), 214.
2. See Eibl-Eibesfeldt, *Grundriß der vergleichenden Verhaltensforschung*, 258 ff.

IS LANGUAGE UNIQUELY HUMAN?

however, completely lack the playful sounds produced by the human suckling. The unprecedented possibilities of human sound production transcend that of the anthropoids by far. In addition, this sound production displays an exceptionally rich modifiability.

Speech Organs?

The "humanlike" apes (anthropoids, i.e., the orangutan, gorilla, chimpanzee, and gibbon), are, as a result of anatomical shortcomings, born incapable of speech. In order to provide the newborn human suckling with a milk tract separate from the respiratory tract, the position of the human larynx at birth is the same as that of mammals. In the period between the first and second year, this highly positioned larynx starts its descent in the neck. This downward movement creates the pharynx cavity, necessary for the articulation of the richer voice disposition in human beings. Laitman declares that the precise time this shift occurs, as well as the physiologic mechanisms that underlie it, are still poorly understood.[3]

As soon as the larynx reaches its destined low position, it can no longer lock into the nasopharynx. Consequently, the respiratory and digestive pathways cross above the larynx. This creates the possibility of suffocating, which surely is, evaluated in itself, something negative. However, it is precisely this expanded pharynx that provides human beings with the unique potential to produce a rich variety of speech sounds. The palate between the mouth and nose cavities serves as basis for the resonance of the sounds produced. Goerttler even mentions the fact that, in the third month after conception, a distinctively human structural element develops (the vocal chord 'blastem').[4]

It is interesting in this connection that Laitman informs us

---

3. J. T. Laitman, "Evolution of the Upper Respiratory Tract: The fossil Evidence," in *Hominid Evolution*, ed. P. V. Tobias (New York: Liss, 1985), 282.
4. K. Goerttler, "Morphologische Sonderstellung des Menschen im Reich der Lebensformen auf der Erde," in *Neue Anthropologie*, vol. II, H-G Gadamer and P. Vogler (Stuttgart: Georg Thieme, 1972), 250.

that the basicranial similarities between the Australopithecines (the Southern apes) and extant apes suggest that their upper respiratory tract was also similar in appearance. Consequently, as with living non-human primates, the pharynx portion for sound modification in these early hominids would have been greatly restricted:

> If we define a *speech organ* as that bodily part which exists solely in service of the production of speech sounds, then the surprising fact is that there are no human speech organs. Let us enumerate possible candidates: the lungs, larynx, mouth cavity, palate, teeth, lips and nose cavity. Without exception, all these organs perform primary functions that would continue to function in their normal way even if human beings never uttered a single word! Human language simply takes hold of all these different organs in the production of speech sounds.[5]

This highly developed and subtle cooperation, especially of three organs so heterogeneous in character as the mouth, the larynx and the brain, integrated in the production of human speech sounds, makes it rather difficult, if not hopeless, to provide us with a causal evolutionistic explanation of this astonishing phenomenon.

Such an unfathomable process of change affecting so many differently structured organs and organ complexes, closely correlated with each other, should have proceeded harmoniously as a total change, if it was to come to the unprecedented perfection of human speech.[6]

The German zoologist, Bernard Rensch, who believes that animals can form a-verbal concepts (concepts without words), admits that only a human being can form a concept of causal relation-

---

5. P. Overhage, *Der Affe in dir* (Frankfurt am Main: Josef Knecht, 1972), 243.
6. Overhage, *Der Affe in dir*, 250.

ships. Only a human being can make deductions, accompanied by parts of speech such as "in consequence of," "because," "in case," etc. The human ability to come to logical conclusions is lacking in animals.

If it is possible to show that animals can locate similar entities and afterwards act accordingly, are we then justified in concluding that they have averbal concepts? What do we mean with the term: *concept*? This question becomes more urgent when Rensch stresses that his use of the term "averbal" is meant to emphasize that "averbal concepts" in animals do not proceed from *logical operations*.[7]

For this reason, he claims that the trait determining the gap between humans and anthropoids is *logical thinking*.[8]

On the basis of their sensitive intelligence, animals are capable of seeing similarities and differences. Certainly, human beings share this *perceptive* dimension with animals – but humans are not confined to or qualified by this sensitive way of negotiating similarities and differences.

Portmann characterizes animals as *Umweltgebunden* (constrained by environment) and *Instinktgesichert* (protected by instinct).[9]

From a Dooyeweerdian perspective one can say that his argumentation implicitly supports the view that the lingual capacity of humans confirms the ontic status of the sign-mode of reality.

---

7. B. Rensch, Gedächtnis, *Begriffsbildung und Planhandlungen bei Tieren* (Hamburg: Parey, 1973), 118.
8. B. Rensch, *Biophilosophy* (New York: Columbia University Press, 1971), 147.
9. A. Portmann, *A Zoologist Looks at Humankind*, trans. Judith Schaefer (New York: Columbia University Press, 1990), 79.

35

The Prevalent Technicism in Society

by Egbert Schuurman

ACCORDING TO DOOYEWEERD[1] the humanistic ground-motive after the Middle Ages influences "the whole development of Western culture." It is surprising however that although Dooyeweerd speaks about the cultural influence of the religious ground-motive, he nevertheless restricts his discussion of that cultural influence mainly to the field of philosophical and scientific thought. Perhaps he does so because, especially later on, he deals with the religious ground-motives in his transcendental critique. In that critique he argues that every philosophical thought is founded in a religious motive.

In this light it is clear that Dooyeweerd devoted great attention to the pervasive influence of the religious ground-motives in philosophical thought in all its variety. But although these motives were radical and integral in character, their *cultural* implications remained mainly unelaborated in his discussions. Still, the important question is: what influence does the humanistic ground-motive have on the health and wholeness of our culture, a culture which philosophy and science influence greatly through technology and economy.

Dooyeweerd speaks about the ground-motive of the Western culture as the motive of *nature* (with its natural science ideal) and *freedom* (with its ideal of a free and autonomous personali-

---

1. H. Dooyeweerd, *A New Critique of Theoretical Thought*, vol. 1, Collected Works of Herman Dooyeweerd, Series A, General Editor D.F.M. Strauss (Lewiston, NY: Edwin Mellen, 1997), 169.

ty). Stressing the *cultural* influence of the ground-motive, I like to speak about the *scientific-technical ideal of control,* or *technicism.*[2]

The interpretation of Western philosophy and history as technicistic is very close to what the father of Reformational philosophy, Herman Dooyeweerd, has designated as the driving force of Western culture. His position is that from the beginning of the modern age, Western philosophy has been controlled by the ideal of attaining absolute freedom of the human person in the scientific domination of all of reality — an outlook also called *scientism*. I would like to take a further step and say this ideal is actually the ideal of scientific-technical control. In taking this step, I think that I am deepening and broadening Dooyeweerd's view and at the same time bringing his philosophy up to date. The ideal of control relates not only to science and philosophy, but seeks to subordinate all of culture. The broadening then is that the conflict, as Dooyeweerd has described it, does not just take place between the absolutized freedom of the thinker and the absolutized science which results, but that the scientific-technical ideal of control puts the whole of reality under pressure. The ideal of technical control threatens not just man in his freedom but also nature and the social structures within which people function. As a result of the ideal of control, people reduce reality, and so culture, to scientific-technical categories and deny the distinctive character of things.

In other words, while Dooyeweerd deserves much credit for pointing out the tension in Western philosophical and scientific thought, I would want to emphasize that the tension or inner conflict is one which encompasses Western culture as a whole and does not just concern the intramural world of science. Dooyeweerd, I believe, would agree completely with this view. He just did not get around to making a full analysis of the cultural impact of the polar tension between the ideal of freedom and the ideal of

---

2. E. Schuurman, *Faith and Hope in Technology* (Toronto: Clements Publishing, 2003), 63-93.

science.

Perhaps the reader might wish to counter my interpretation by saying that not technicism but economism — as a reduced and at the same time absolutized economy — is the basic ailment of our culture. There is some merit to this view. But if we do some historical research, we quickly discover that in wartime and, for example, in the development of space travel in the era of the Cold War, the spirit of technicism demanded numerous economic sacrifices rather than bringing economic prosperity. We have learned meanwhile that the population of the Soviet Union was starved in the interest of realizing the ideals of technicism. For the sake of the geopolitical power and name of the Soviet Union, everything was made subservient to space travel technology at the expense of the population. Accordingly, when today the liberal market economy — i.e., capitalism — is singled out as the cause of much misery, that analysis is inadequate. Such an analysis, one to which especially Bob Goudzwaard[3] has devoted his attention, is indeed fruitful. Yet I believe that working in the background of capitalism is the ideal of technical control. Today's free market economy is possible only on the drive to achieve technical control. In other words, capitalism's lifeline is technicism.

Especially governments are driven by technicism in their plans to control society. While the power of technical control may be pivotal for industrial enterprises, they still have to take account of what consumers want. The liberal market economy cannot thrive without the approval of consumers. For this reason, it can also be said that economism as capitalism in turn strengthens technicism. The two are, as it were, Siamese twins. Both suffer from a contraction of their outlook. As a result, in part of the dynamism evoked and the enormous scale of it (there is good reason why we speak of the globalization of technology and the economy), the concur-

---

3. B. Goudzwaard, *Capitalism and Progress: A Diagnosis of Western Society* (Toronto/Grand Rapids: Wedge/Eerdmans, 1997).

rence of an overestimated technology and a contracted economy is dangerous to humanity, society, and the environment.

Technicism is a very ancient pretension. We already encounter its hubris in the building of the Tower of Babel: humans, viewing themselves as gods, want to storm the heavens: "nothing they propose to do will now be impossible for them" (Genesis 11:6). The same mentality arises after the Middle Ages when the development of the natural sciences gains momentum and is united with a philosophy from which God has disappeared and in which man is enthroned. Once this occurs, the original bond between humanity and nature is broken and nature is regarded as a mechanism to be controlled.

In the light of the fundamental attitude sketched above, I can more accurately describe what technicism is. *Technicism is the pretension of humans, as self-declared lords and masters using the scientific-technical method of control, to bend all of reality to their will in order to solve all problems, old and new, and to guarantee increasing material prosperity and progress.* By means of their technology humans want to control and safeguard the future. This technicism answers to two important norms as though they are the two great commandments: the norm of technical perfection or effectiveness and the economic norm of efficiency. In other words, by means of the scientific-technical method of control the stated goals must be reached as directly and efficiently as possible. The entire technical process, therefore, is clearly set within a narrow framework. *Everything outside that narrow framework is denied recognition.* This concerns the value of human freedom, nature and the distinctive character of plants and animals. The whole of reality is seen as a mechanism or machine which we have to control. The cultural paradigm under the influence of technicism is the *machine-model*. Norms as that of appreciation, care, love, harmony, doing justice, and so forth are, accordingly, discounted (see Chapter 51 on the meaning of technology).

Thus, when I speak of '*technicism*' I especially have in mind the overestimation of the scientific method of technical control. Hence technologies in which that method remains in the background (as in civil engineering) also produce fewer problems; but precisely those technologies which cannot exist without this method give rise to more uneasiness (such as chemical technology, electronic technology, information technology, biotechnology, and so forth). In addition, the method of those technologies is also being introduced in non-technical areas. Especially the method employed by modern technology in the designing phase inspire people to apply it also outside the realm of technology. The economical praxis is more than once marked by excessive scientific control, being dominated by a scientific-technical model: we hear of the *mechanism* of the market place. I suspect besides that more organizations are also stamped by technicism which thereby causes huge problems for the world of labor relations and the role of responsible people in that world.

This "evil" is not inherent in the method itself, of course, but in its overestimation and imperialism. It is inherent in the conviction that with this scientific-technical method of control humans can accomplish ever better and bigger results both in technology itself (where the method is appropriate) and outside of it.

The dark side of technicism becomes more and more clear in our days. When in the post-World War II era the results in the form of growth in prosperity became truly impressive, consumers too began to venerate modern technology. For a long time this veneration made people blind to its negative aspects. In the meantime, we have discovered that the world surrounding us — plants, animals, but also humanity itself — can easily become a victim of modern technology. Present-day technical developments are in many ways very threatening. The very basis of our existence is being ruined.

In thinking of dangerous manifestations of technicism, I do

not just have in mind the threat of nuclear weaponry or the radioactive waste generated by nuclear power plants, but equally certain phenomena of our technological culture such as deforestation, desertification of large parts of the earth, depletion of the ozone layer, the emission of greenhouse gases along with climate changes, the destruction and pollution of nature, the overestimation of genetic manipulation techniques and of the latest information and communication technologies which produce increasingly less information and communication among people. An overvalued technology makes for mutual estrangement and social disintegration. Under the influence of technicism and economism, man becomes the prisoner and victim of his own culture. Present-day technical and economic culture is clearly paradoxical or dialectical. How can we overcome this deep crisis?

36

Popular Sovereignty
by Danie F. M. Strauss

THE IDEA OF *popular sovereignty* surfaced prominently in the writing of Marsilius of Padua and Jean of Jandun in 1324 with *In Defense of Peace* (*Defensor Pacis*). This invited reflection on the nature of *sovereignty* which was later undertaken by Jean Bodin in his discussion of the nature of governmental sovereignty. In 1576 Bodin still designated a state as a *republic* while using the word état for *specific forms* of the state. He introduced the concept of *sovereignty* in service of an understanding of the *authority* (power) of a government. Unfortunately, he failed to rid his mind of the traditional universalistic perspective that proclaims the state to be the *all-encompassing whole of society*. In Book III Chapter 7 of his work on the state, he portrays the relationship between the family, corporations and colleges to the state as that between the whole (the state) and its parts.[1]

This comprehensive view hampered his understanding of the process of differentiation because he viewed the legal competence of law-making societal entities, distinct from the state, as a threat to the sovereignty of the state. Of course, exactly the opposite is the case, for without the crystillization of distinct societal spheres with their peculiar (non-political) legal interests, the state would

---

1. "... sowie zwischen diesen und dem Staat verhält es sich ähnlich wie mit dem Unterschied zwischen dem Ganzen und seinen Teilen." J. Bodin, *Sechs Bücher über den Staat*, Buch I-III, trans. Bernd Wimmer, ed. P. C. Meyer-Tasch (München: Verlag C. H. Beck, 1981), 521.

not have the task to integrate a diversity of legal interests into one public legal order. Whereas his idea of *sovereignty*, as the characteristic feature of the government of a state, forms part of the significant process of differentiation that took shape after the Middle Ages, his ungrounded fear that newly emerging spheres of legal competence would threaten the sovereign law-making competence of the state stood in the way of positively appreciating societal differentiation.

Next to the differentiation of church and state, the Industrial Revolution accomplished the differentiation of the nuclear family and the modern business enterprise. It is therefore not surprising that the 19th century gave rise to the prominent modern democratic states, such as Germany, the Netherlands, France and Britain as well as Australia, New Zealand, the USA and Canada.

Does Sovereignty Belong to the People or to the Monarch?
Unfortunately, modern political theories were mainly interested in the *power* of the state. Their basic problem was: Does the highest power within the state belong to the *people* or to the *monarch*? This gave rise either to the idea of *popular sovereignty* or to the *sovereignty of the monarch*. Therefore, since Machiavelli, the established distinction drawn was that between a *kingdom* and a *republic*. This practice could not do justice to the *public-legal* character of the state, because it does not leave room for the insight that the concern for the *res publica* as such does not yet say anything about the *form* in which it should be realized. The idea of the *public interest* solely underscores that the state, in the true sense of the word, is a *republic* (a *res publica*). Its sole concern is the "res" of the "publica"—the *res publica*. Apart from a *parliamentary democracy* (such as the USA) and a *monarchical democracy* (such as Britain and The Netherlands), pre-1991 Russia was justified in designating its totalitarian member states as "people's republics"— just recall the acronym USSR, which stood for the *Union of Soviet Socialist Republics*.

The Limitations of Undifferentiated Societies

It follows from our preceding analysis that *undifferentiated societies* are incapable of giving shelter to a state in the *public-legal* sense of the term. Within such societies there is no room for an exclusive legal *competence* or *jurisdiction* over a *limited cultural area*, familiar to us as the *territory* of the state.

Once the public-legal character of the state is acknowledged, two issues require attention:

(1) To give an account of the uniqueness of the state within a differentiated society; and
(2) To illuminate the relationship between the state and the diverse non-state societal entities present on the territory of the state.

The Uniqueness of the State Within a Differentiated Society

Undifferentiated societies lack a proper understanding of the state as a distinct legal institution. Such an idea includes the insight that governmental authority cannot be deemed the *private property* of one or another this or that (private) person (as absolute monarchs sometimes claimed) and that for this reason it also cannot be restricted to a formal recognition of existing legal privileges and customs. Only when these privileges are eliminated will it be possible for the true *parts* of the state, such as provinces and municipalities, to support the typical *res publica* nature of the state. It must be clear that the whole-parts relation is of critical importance. Applying the whole-parts relation to human society will also lead to an erroneous understanding of sovereignty and different spheres of competence within a differentiated society. Just recall Bodin's view of sovereignty: although the sovereignty of the government of a state pre-supposes differentiation, Bodin in fact conceived it as standing in opposition to societal differentiation. He saw sovereign power as *summa in cives ac subditos legibusque soluta potestas*, i.e., "as supreme power, unbound by law, over citizens and subjects."

The main reason for this shortcoming is found in the affinity of his ideas with the "classical formula of political absolutism" according to which sovereignty is not only *absolute* but also *indivisible*.[2] Although Bodin supports the long-standing principle of natural law, *pact sunt servanda* (contracts must be kept), his understanding of sovereign power shows an element of the *potestas Dei absoluta* (the despotic arbitrariness of God) advanced by William of Ockham. Esmain notes that the adage "Princeps legibus solutus est" (*the monarch is elevated above the law*) was derived from Ulpian, one of the classical Roman jurists who lived ca. A.D. 170–228.[3]

Ancient Greece as well as the medieval era and modernity since early modern times since the Renaissance, did not know the "state," for this term only emerged by the end of the 18th and the beginning of the 19th century. Traditionally the term *Politeia* (the title of Plato's *Republic*) was used alongside the well-known legacy to speak of a *Kingdom* or, if one wants to conform to inclusive (politically correct) language, a *Realm* (*regnum*). Plato held the view that the two highest political estates, the philosophers and soldiers, shared communal ownership but did not partake in private marital life and family life. The lowest estate of manual labourers is stripped of *all rights*. The upshot is a typical totalitarian structure. In a similar fashion, Aristotle conceived of the *polis* as the all-embracing political community that aims, to a greater degree than any other, at the highest good: "Every *polis* is a community of some kind,[4] and every community is established with a view to some good; for mankind always acts in order to obtain that which they think good. But, if all communities aim at some good, the

---

2. See P. C. Meyer-Tasch, "Einführung in Jean Bodins Leben und Werk," in J. Bodin, *Sechs Bücher über den Staat,* Buch I-III, trans. Bernd Wimmer, ed. P. C. Meyer-Tasch (München: Verlag C. H. Beck, 1981), 35.
3. See A. Esmain, "La Maxime Princepts Legibus Solutus Est L'ancien Droit Public Français," in P. Vinogradoff, *Essays in Legal History* (New York: WM. W. Gaunt & Sons, Inc., 1993), 202.
4. Ἐπειδὴ πᾶσαν πόλιν κοινωνίαν... (i.e., every polis is a community of some kind).

polis or political community, which is the highest of all, and which embraces all the rest, aims at good in a greater degree than any other, and at the highest good."[5]

The Middle Ages continued the conception of Aristotle with a qualification, because according to the view of Thomas Aquinas the state only leads to temporal perfection, overarched by the supra-natural accomplishment of the church. His view of the function of the church as a supernatural institution of grace continued to exert an influence on the official position assumed by the Roman Catholic Church. The well-known papal encyclical, *Quadragesimo anno* (15 May 1931) explicitly states: "Surely the Church does not only have the task to bring the human person merely to a transient and deficient happiness, for she must carry a person to eternal bliss."[6] Zippelius illuminates this point with reference to the whole-parts relation: "Parts are standing in a proper relation to the whole when one and the same principle rules them."[7]

The implication of this insight is that societal entities distinct from the state cannot participate in the same structural principle as the state. Perhaps the first thinker who realized this was the Calvinistic legal scholar, Johannes Althusius, in his work from 1603: *Politica Methodice Digesta*. He accepted *proper laws* for different societal entities, which imply that churches, families, business enterprises and the like cannot be *parts* of the state—only provinces

---

5. Aristotle, Politica, text edition by F. Susemihl and R. D. Hicks, *The Politics of Aristotle: A Revised Text, With Introduction, Analysis and Commentary* (New York: McMillan & Co., 1894): 1252 a 1-7; Aristotle, *The Basic Works of Aristotle*, ed. Richard McKeon (New York: The Modern Library, 2001), 1127.
6. Cf. H. Schnatz, ed., *Päpstliche Verlautbarungen zu Staat und Gesellschaft, Original dokumente mit deutscher Uebersetzung* (Darmstadt: Wissenschaftliche Buchgesellschaft, 1973), 403.
7. R. Zippelius, *Geschicte der Staatsideen, Vierte, verbesserte Auflage* (München: Beck, 1980): 67, "Teile stehen aber dann in einem rechten Verhältnis zum Ganzen, wenn ein und dasselbe Prinzip sie regiert."

and municipalities qualify for this privilege.[8]

It is precisely the uncritical application of the whole-parts relation to human society that obstructed a proper understanding both of the state as such and of its place within a differentiated society.

---

8. See H. E. S. Woldring, "The Constitutional State in the Political Philosophy of Johannes Althusius," *European Journal of Law and Economics* 5 (1998): 129-132.

37

The Intriguing Nature of Firms and/or Markets and/or Workers

by Frederick C.v.N. Fourie

A QUESTION LIKE "what is a firm?" or "what is a market?" may intuitively appear to be relatively simple and obvious. However, they can become unexpectedly muddled if left to the analytical-ideological designs and conceptual constructs of, for example, theoretical economists and labour organizations. Similarly, managerial economists or corporate lawyers contribute to the complexity in their analysis of, for example, the ownership and control of an incorporated firm (i.e., a corporation).

For me, the Dooyeweerdian analytical framework for the characterization of societal institutions is extremely valuable to avoid confused or distorted thinking when confronted with such issues. A cardinal proposition from this framework is that, in a differentiated society, a societal institution such as the firm has an intrinsic nature that endures over time amidst and despite changes in its factual form in a particular situation, country, legal system, stage of development or historical period. Once one is alerted to this idea, such an intrinsic nature can be intuitively recognized in the observation of the various shapes and sizes, as well as organizational and legal forms, of business enterprises over time and across place/countries.[1]

---
1. An interesting analytical twist is that, to recognize the *typical differences between different types* of institutions (e.g. between a firm and a social club), it is required to simultaneously recognize the *commonalities amongst different forms* of each of the compared institutional types. Therefore, an element of constancy (= the typicality) is necessary to recognize changes in form,

This basic insight is found in Dooyeweerd's exposition of the *typical nature* of societal structures or institutions — he calls them "structures of individuality of human society" — which he robustly demonstrates in his systematic analysis of the State, the church, voluntary associations, societal inter-relationships, and so forth.[2]

The existence of a variety of *typical* institutions appears to have been a key element in the unfolding and development of human society, a process in which a variety of distinct, more-or-less durable, organised, societal collectives or communal institutions have evolved, e.g., states, churches, schools, social clubs, firms, labour unions. (This occurred amidst the existence of *natural* communities such as the family.) These communal institutions have "the character of a whole joining its members into a social unity, irrespective of the intensity of the communal bond."[3]

In the case of the State, its individuality, or typicality, centers around its *foundation* in organised security-police-military power (the "power of the sword") being coupled inextricably with its *qualifying/leading* function, which is of a legal-juridical nature: organizing and maintaining a public legal order. The latter requires, and is based on, having organised security-police-military power.[4]

Recognizing the idea that a societal institution has a discernable *typical nature* is a powerful instrument in understanding the functioning of, and changes in, the variety of societal institutions — from both a normative and a positive perspective. Changes (good as well as bad) gain significance once one recognizes that, amidst the changes in *form*, the intrinsic nature remains unchanged — unless

---

complexity and operation (of firms, say), whether over time or existing at a point in time. Put differently: *it is the element of constancy that enables the comparisons and analysis of change – and simultaneously is the clue to the typicality.*

2. H. Dooyeweerd, *A New Critique of Theoretical Thought*, vol. 3, Collected Works of Herman Dooyeweerd, Series A, General Editor D.F.M. Strauss (Lewiston, NY: Edwin Mellen, 1997), part II.
3. Dooyeweerd, *New Critique*, 3:177.
4. See Strauss, Introduction chapter; Dooyeweerd, *New Critique*, vol. 3, part II, chapter III.

distorted beyond recognition, of course.

In the case of the firm, a revealing, indeed tantalizing, exercise is to examine the variety of forms of the business enterprise found currently as well as in history – for example during the approximately 200 years in which the business enterprise in the United States developed from the simple family farm, artisan shop and general merchant of the colonial era, to the modern, complex, integrated mass-producer/distributor corporation of the 21st century.[5] Can one identify *common characteristics* that are intuitively *intrinsic to and shared by* these different organizational forms? My careful studies of this period prompted a detailed derivation and extraction of the "intrinsic nature of the firm" from the historical progressive development of the firm.[6]

My proposition is that – analogous to the leading and foundational functions of the State – the typical nature, or intrinsic nature and individuality, of the firm (business enterprise) is the following:

(a) its *foundational function* is to be found in *capital formation* and
(b) its *leading function* is to be found in *managing* the production and sale/distribution of goods and services for clients/customers.

Where it differs fundamentally from the State, is that it is a voluntary association.

Together these two capture the essence of the typical nature of the firm or business enterprise, whatever its form and degree of development, complexity and sophistication. Moreover, there is a crucial coherence between these two characterizing functions:

(a) Possessing *capital power* (financial resources, economic power) is the *foundation that enables* the manager(s) of a firm to

---

5. See A.D. Chandler, *The Visible Hand* (Cambridge, MA: Harvard University Press, 1978).
6. See F.C.v.N. Fourie, "A structural theory of the nature of the firm" (PhD diss., Harvard University, 1981), chapters 2 and 3.

acquire, employ and organise factors of production in a production/distribution/commercial process. The establishment, expansion and development of a firm can occur only insofar as capital formation takes place in sufficient quantities.

(b) The *managing function* has the *leading (or guiding) role* with respect to how capital formation, and thus the *economic power* embedded in capital, is unlocked and harnessed towards utilising people/workers and material inputs in productive processes – and indeed all activities of the business enterprise in pursuit of chosen goals (which can, but need not be, profit maximisation). The managing function also implies and presupposes that an internal authority structure is integral to the firm/organization.

Note the deep-seated, indissoluble coherence: The economic power inherent in financial resources is the *foundation* that *enables* the firm to *manage* a production/distribution process. The managing function is what *unlocks* the potential of capital power to employ and organise workers, land, capital goods and materials in commercial production or distribution activities.

What is fascinating is to realize that a small, single-owner business possesses these founding and leading functions (and all the actions inherent in their interactions and enablement) as much as a large corporation does. The modern corporation has differentiated and split up these functions into complex hierarchical organizational structures and specialized tasks with numerous employees and managers — increasing the scope and complexity of the management task exponentially; simultaneously the capital foundation has evolved and "unfolded" to encompass complex shareholding and debt structures as well as financing mechanisms. However, this does not intrinsically change the typicality of the firm, only its form.

- Whether it is a one-person enterprise, a small business partnership, a medium-size public company, or a complex corporation or conglomerate, these two *characterizing functions* (in their coherence) can always be seen to shape, guide and enable the existence, operation and growth of the firm as a societal institution.

A note on capital supply and corporate shareholding: In the one-person firm, the founding capital is likely supplied by the "owner-manager"; in the corporation, capital is supplied by often unrelated, anonymous shareholders (who earn dividends and investment growth in return). This is part of the development and "unfolding" of the firm from small-and-simple to large-and-complex, combined with the development of stock exchanges. In the one-person firm the "owner-manager" also functions as the "board of directors" of the "organization."

The relationship between the firm and the family is worth reflecting on. In the one-person "family business" (note the interwovenness in that expression) with the head of the household likely the owner-manager, the scope is constrained by the access to personal capital (and perhaps also personal management skills or capacity). A partner from another household can then be brought in to strengthen the capital base of the enterprise. Though less hampered, the capital foundation is still enmeshed with the household — *and* the household carries the risk if the firm were to go bankrupt. This constrains the scope and expansion of the firm. However, the legal form of the company — where limited liability protects the founder's household from loss by separating personal property from the firm's property/assets — provides (and has historically provided) the vehicle to break loose from this constraint. This differentiation and, indeed, emancipation of the firm from its earlier interwovenness with the family/household enabled it to come into its own as typical societal institution/organization in the economic sphere. Historically this has enabled the remarkable spread and growth of the corporation in the world economy.

Note that the typicality of the firm involves a necessary *interlacement with the market*: the production of goods and services is for the purpose of selling (or bartering) it to customers in market transactions. Therefore, the *internal* organization and management of the firm and its economic/capital resources are geared towards an *external* transactional relation with a customer — an *inter*-relationship. (These can be firm-to-firm or firm-to-person inter-relationships.) This means that the rationale, existence and viability of a firm is inextricably linked to markets, whence come the revenue that sustains the business and its capital foundation. But the firm still is to be distinguished from the market.

Markets as such intrinsically are *inter-relational* phenomena: they link and coordinate firms/sellers and customers/buyers in momentary (if repeated) transactions — but, note, do not integrate or bind them together in any kind of durable, cohesive whole. Markets cannot exist without firms that produce and sell, and vice versa. Markets involve exchange relations (between buyer and seller) as well as rivalry relations between sellers.[7] Dominant firms can exercise market power, but there is no relation of authority in market relations.

Distortion 1: Employees or workers? Because "labourists" and "workerists" — and others who have an ideological anti-business predisposition — apparently have an aversion to the entire idea of a firm, they cannot "see" that the firm is an *organization* of people, nor can they perceive the leading and foundational functions. As a result, all they see are the *individual workers* (and specifically not the managers) — a distorted and indeed reductionist view of a societal organization that is there for anyone to observe in its wholeness. It also is individualistic: reducing firms to a multitude of individual workers. A notable case where this view is applied, is regarding small informal firms (in the informal sector[8]) in developing coun-

---

7. See F. C.v.N. Fourie, "The Nature of the Market: a Structural Analysis," in *Rethinking Economics: Markets, Technology and Economic Evolution*, ed. G. Hodgson and E. Screpanti (Aldershot: Edward Elgar, 1991).
8. The informal sector comprises all informal firms, which are those that are not officially registered as businesses or for taxation. This is not the same as the illegal or underground economy, which involves trading in illegal goods (irrespective of whether by registered or unregistered businesses). In South Africa, the informal sector accounts for approximately 18% of total employment. About 80% of informal firms are one-person enterprises, i.e. without employees; the remaining 20% provide jobs for almost

tries. When it comes to economic policy in this context, workerists typically do not want *enterprise-based* policy support for enterprise development and job creation, say. They tend to argue exclusively for *individual-worker based* support policies such as State-provided medical and pension benefits for informal workers.

The one-person firm is a particularly and sobering analytical case for all participants in the debate. The key is to recognize it as an embryonic, less-unfolded form of the fully developed, internally differentiated, complex and mature corporate enterprise. All the functions and aspects are present, but they are concentrated and coincident in one individual. But it still is a firm. Therefore, the appropriate form of policy support is an enterprise support programme – not worker rights programs, which relate to the lack of employment contracts, medical benefits and pension benefits (also found, frequently, in the *formal* sector of economies).

Distortion 2: In the beginning there were markets? Transactions analysis can be useful to understand mergers between firms. The decision to internalize a prior market relationship — e.g., between a firm and its supplier — by merging with a supplier firm, is likely to be based on the cost of an external transactional relationship compared to what the cost would be if it were to become an intra-organizational supply relationship. Such cost analyses can explain the size (or boundary) of large commercial enterprises.[9]

However, taken too far (neo-classical economists are somewhat besotted with the market), it has been argued that transactions-cost analysis explains the *existence* of firms.[10]

---

half of those working in the informal sector (2013 data; Fourie 2018). On another note: a major hindrance identified in these enterprises is that their enterprise money and finances often are not kept separate from those of the household/family – thwarting the proper financial (and overall) management and recordkeeping of the enterprise (Fourie 2018).

9. O.E. Williamson, *Markets and Hierarchies: Analysis and Antitrust Implications* (New York: The Free Press, 1975).
10. R. H. Coase, "The Nature of the Firm," *Economica* 4, no. 16 (November 1937): 386-405.

The assumption is that "in the beginning there were markets" in which market trading between producers took place. An awareness of transactions costs then led to a preference to avoid having to co-ordinate production through market exchange — leading to the combination (or merger) of producers, thus "creating firms".[11] The distortion here is that markets cannot produce and that economic production activities cannot be reduced to markets. The intrinsic nature of the firm cannot be explained in terms of another, typically different societal relation. Coase's "producers" in fact are one-person firms that produce and trade (in a market context, of course). A related distortion is to deny the existence of firms as organizations and describe them — in extreme individualistic fashion — as a multitude of market transactions between autonomous individuals.[12]

Distortion 3: Who owns the firm? Shareholders' rights? In managerial theory, the so-called separation of ownership and control has been quite an issue: it is lamented that, in the modern corporation, the "owners" (shareholders) of the firm are not in control of the management of the/their firm — the board and executive team are. This contrasts with earlier, simpler forms of the firm, with the one-person firm as purest form, the capital owner/supplier also being the chief executive/manager.

First, clearly the idea of "ownership of the firm" has emanated from simpler forms of the firm, where it seemed obvious that the founder of the firm, who supplied the capital, runs and actually *owns* the business. However, in the corporate form of the firm, the function of supplying capital has been differentiated out to external, unrelated, usually anonymous shareholders (and bondholders).

---

11. It seems that Coase's is thinking mainly in terms of the emergence of corporations (or large firms). It suggests that he would not (or did not) consider a one-person business as a 'firm'. It is a common analyst mistake to confuse the factual *form* of observed firms with the intrinsic *nature* of firms.
12. Compare A. A. Alchian and H. Demsetz, "Production, Information Costs, and Economic Organization," *American Economic Review* 62, no. 5 (Dec. 1972): 777-795; Williamson, *Markets and Hierarchies.*

The question is: do the shareholders own the firm, or just its shares (which normally are bought and sold without an intention to influence the operation of the firm)? Is the concept of ownership of the firm (still) appropriate?

Secondly, given that the corporate firm is an *organization of people* (managers *and* employees): is it appropriate to think that it can be owned (with all the power-and-disposal implications of the ownership of private property)? I would argue that it is not, and that shareholders rights, e.g., regarding the election of the board of directors, should be derived not from the concept of firm ownership, but from the intrinsic nature of "capital-suppliership" — and could be exercised in a shareholder association with specified rights. Surely this matter requires in-depth reconsideration.[13]

Distortion 4: Are employees labour inputs or members of the organization? If the firm is a voluntary association and organization, how is its membership determined? My question is whether employees should be regarded as "labour inputs," hired and dismissed in labour markets, or — like managers — as *members* of the firm (as an "organization of people")? This implies membership contracts, rights and obligations — including entry and exit conditions. This suggests a new way of thinking about hiring and firing, employment and unemployment. It is about finding a new model for apportioning, or balancing, the risks (and rewards) faced by shareholders, managers and employees/workers amidst variable business conditions and market rivalry.

Conclusion: A Personal Note

In the 21st century, political-economic systems continue to compete for supremacy; economic concentration and market dominance steadily increase; employment levels are inadequate to reduce unemployment and poverty in the world; executive remuneration in the corporate world reach astronomical heights while billions of

---

13. See F. C.v.N. Fourie, "Separation of Ownership and Control: What is the Problem?" *South African Journal for Economic and Management Sciences* (1996).

people live alongside in poverty; in developing countries formal and informal micro-enterprises struggle to survive, grow and create employment.

To conceptualize and implement appropriate policies to increase employment, especially in developing countries, a clear and consistent understanding of the nature of firms and markets in a particular context is essential (among many other things). Whether current economic and management theory or government policies do that, is doubtful. What I can say, is that Dooyeweerdian insights such as those sampled above — linked to a desire to *avoid distorted analyses* – have greatly assisted me in thinking about, researching and proposing appropriate policies for job creation in the townships of South Africa. A key intervention that has been indicated is to help informal enterprises to keep the firm (and its money) separate from the household (and its money) — aided by keeping at least a rudimentary record of flows between them and of the firm's revenue and expenditures as such. Additionally getting business premises that are separate from the household dwelling — spatial differentiation — appears to be a vital complement to such financial differentiation and emancipation of the firm.

38

Developments within Roman Law

by Danie Strauss

THE INITIAL FOLK LAW in ancient Rome (*ius civile*) was restricted to the Roman tribe, hence was *exclusive* since it applied to members of the Roman tribe only. Germanic folk law, too, was basically tribal law based on blood feud, with ordeals, oath-helping, and other procedures.[1] Owing to the nature of tribal law, the legal status of a person was completely dependent upon membership in the tribe—in the case of Rome, upon membership of the Roman *populus*. People living outside this circle were lawless (*exlex*) and also designated as barbarians. Yet there also existed laws of the barbarians (*leges barbarorum*). The oldest forms of this kind of law, which was distinct from Roman law (*leges Romanae*), is found in the law of the Salic Franks and the *Lex Salica* which was issued by the Merovingian king Clovis after his conversion to Christianity in A.D. 496.[2]

As Roman folk law, the *ius civile* from its very inception was reminiscent of the undifferentiated, tribal background of Roman life. However, during the expansion of the Roman empire non-Romans were soon present on Roman territory. This situation increasingly called for some kind of a legal arrangement in order to make legal provision for the non-Romans within the Roman empire. This was done in what emerged as the *ius gentium*. Although this new legal development is sometimes seen as the starting-point of what later became known as the *law of nations*, it should actually rather be seen as the starting-point of civil private law and therefore not as the legal source of the law of nations. The subsequent legal devel-

---

1. H. J. Berman, *Law and Revolution. The Formation of the Western Legal Tradition* (London: Harvard University Press, 1983), 51.
2. Berman, 53.

opment superseded the artificial intermediate position of *Latini* as a class between foreigners and Roman citizens: Mackenzie remarks: "Finally, Caracalla bestowed the citizenship on all . . . subjects of the Roman empire."[3]

Feudo-Vassalism, Guilds and Manors

During the Middle Ages the societal arrangement of Western Europe, which lasted from the 9th to the 15th centuries, was designated as *feudalism*.

Feudalism. As can be expected, during such a vast period of time changes occurred throughout society. For example, mere tenancy developed into tenancy for life and eventually it was extended into a heritable holding. Medley identifies two properties as defining features of the feudal era:

> . . . characteristic of the whole period was what has been described as the union of two relationships of lord with man and lord with vassal. Thus feudalism, or feudo-vassalism, as it has been more correctly called, contained both a social element based upon land-tenure, and a political element expressed by homage and fealty [i.e., a pledge of allegiance of one person to another].[4]

These two elements were intertwined in a relatively undifferentiated manner within the feudal system. The latter increasingly accommodated owners of large pieces of land, which they had received as reward for their support to the King in times of threats to the realm. An important supposition of the feudal system was that portions of governmental authority were still spread over cities, guilds, and market communities.

Guilds. During the 9th century the powerful counts and dukes combined forces with the church and thus generated the genuine

---

3. Lord Mackenzie, *Studies in Roman Law with Comparative Views of the Laws of France, England, and Scotland*, 7th ed., ed. J. Kirkpatrick (Edinburgh: William Blackwood & Sons, 1898), 79.
4. J. D. Medley, *A Student's Manual of English Constitutional History* (Oxford: Blackwell, 1925), 24-25.

bearers of governmental authority during the subsequent medieval era. Although these guilds did integrate religious interests and professional interests, they still merely formed a relatively *undifferentiated* societal unit. Even the influential international traders (merchant guilds) of the 12th and 13th centuries were succeeded by craft guilds with a similar undifferentiated structure. The Medieval guilds were undifferentiated with structures similar to those of the extended family and sib, but without any real or fictitious common descent.[5]

Probably as a continuation of the Germanic guilds, the 11th and 12th centuries witnessed the rise of the guild system in various towns. They often originated as sworn brotherhoods binding their members by oaths regarding mutual protection and service. Berman points out that the multifarious forms displayed by various types of guilds are all normally designated by the word *guild*, while in fact this term encompasses entities as diverse as: "*ars, universitas, corporatio, misterium, schola, colleguim, paraticum, curia, ordo, matricola, fraglia*, and, for the merchant guild *hansa* or *mercandancia*"—yet "the ordinances of all the dozens of guilds that might exist within a city had many features in common, and these common features existed throughout the West."[6]

Our interest in the difference between undifferentiated societies and differentiated societies invites us to observe how, during the Middle Ages, non-ecclesiastical society continued to function within *undifferentiated structures*. Troeltsch notes that this medieval period also knew a large number of *authorities* ("*Obrigkeiten*"), but points out that they are superseded by the power of the all-embracing, supra-natural, spiritual world empire of the Church. The latter has its own structure of super- and subordination. However, medieval society does "not know a state as a unified, sovereign will-organization of the whole, where it is irrelevant who exercises this sovereignty."[7]

---

5. Berman, 290–292.
6. Berman, 391.
7. Cf. E. Troeltsch, *Aufsätze zur Geistesgeschichte und Regiossoziologie*, Hrsg. Hans

The Manor. In 13th-century English law, a typical undifferentiated community is found in the landed *estate* known as a *manor*. Although it was not a technical legal term, it was characterized by the recognition of the right of a lord to hold a court as a unit for the exercise of jurisdiction, although it might have evolved as an economic unit. In the course of the subsequent centuries the on-going emergence of new estates divided the *vills* into several *manors* without establishing an exclusive jurisdictional territory, for the boundaries of *vill* and manor may partially overlap.[8] In addition, as Dooyeweerd points out, the legal competence of a manor included the capacity to issue legal summonses and ordinances which embraced almost all spheres of society:

> The owner of large feudal land holdings was endowed with privileges which gave him the legal right to act as lord over every person domiciled on his estate. In the medieval cities the guilds were the undifferentiated units which simultaneously displayed an ecclesiastical, industrial, and at times even a political structure. These guilds were often based on a kind of fraternity which, as an artificial kinship bond, embraced its members with their families in all their activities ... It is important to note that at a higher level feudal lords exercised governmental authority as if it were private property, which they could indeed acquire and dispose of on the basis of private legal stipulations. All of these undifferentiated legal spheres possessed autonomy, i.e., the legal competence and right to act as government within their own sphere without the intervention of a higher authority.[9]

Baron (Tübingen: J.C.B. Mohr [Paul Siebeck], 1925), 302: "The Medieval era knows numberless authorities and an authority which determines these authorities while itself being conditioned by strong forces, and adjacent to them the spiritual world empire of the church super-ordained over all of them, which with its indebted dignitaries constitute themselves a part of the authorities and then on the whole, in addition, is an order embracing all together. But it does not know a state as a unified, sovereign will-organization of the whole, where it is irrelevant who exercises this sovereignty."

8. Medley, 44.
9. Dooyeweerd, *Roots of Western Culture*, p. 54;, 54; see also Berman, 316–332.

39

Dooyeweerd's Critical-Empirical Theory of Law

by Alan Cameron

IN THE SECOND HALF of the 20th century a revival of interest in legal philosophy took place attributable to the publication in 1961 of H. L. A. Hart's *The Concept of Law*, "probably the most important work of legal philosophy produced this [20th] century."[1] Hart's theory of law sits within the school of analytical legal philosophy associated with the theory of legal positivism that has insisted on maintaining a strict analytical distinction between law "properly so-called" and morality. Following in the English tradition of Jeremy Bentham and John Austin, Hart set out to correct flaws in its positivist theory of law. He abandoned the Austinian idea of law as the command of a sovereign in favor of a theory of law as rules, while maintaining the strict distinction, if not complete "separation," of (the concept of) law and (the concept of) morality.[2]

Hart's theory of law as rules enabled a revision of English legal positivism in keeping with its *empirical-factual* orientation. This contrasted with continental legal positivism's leading exponent Kelsen, who had propounded a theory of law based on the *Grundnorm* (basic norm) as a *hypothetical-logical* foundation for law as a *normative* system.[3] Hart thought that through his theory of the

---

1. Hart, *The Concept of Law*, 2nd ed. (1994), blurb on dustjacket.
2. Ibid., 79–99, 185–212.
3. Lloyd, *Introduction to Jurisprudence*, 318–321, containing an extract from

"social sources" of law as rules he had overcome the persistent and perplexing problem of legal theory—namely, to account for *both* the normativity *and* factuality ("positive") quality of law.[4] Hart also defended his positivist theory against the moral criticism of positivist theories by traditional natural law theory that became acute with the rise of national socialism and the horrors perpetrated by Hitler's regime facilitated by its brutal laws.[5]

It is a testament to the seminal importance of Hart's *Concept* that it provoked critical responses from many different quarters, including those from within the analytical school itself. There have been defenses of Hart's basic "analytical" analysis of law as comprising primary and secondary rules with some revision, for example, in the work of Neil MacCormick.[6] Some within the analytical tradition to which Hart belonged, in their theories of different forms of positivism, did not think it necessary to abandon positivism altogether in order to accommodate some necessary (substantive) moral element in their concept of law.[7] From within the Thomist Roman Catholic natural law tradition, John Finnis, in the style of the analytical school of jurisprudence, imaginatively turned some of Hart's own innovative insights against its author to defend a revised Thomist theory of natural law.[8] Lon Fuller at Harvard countered Hart's positivism with his idea of the inner morality of law.[9] However, Fuller's process-focused inner moral requirements for the existence of valid law of a legal system still remained oriented towards requirements of "positive" *state* law. Ronald Dworkin's *Law's Empire* on the other hand, in keeping with the Anglian

---

Kelsen, *General Theory of Law and State.*
4. Hart, *The Concept of Law* (1961), 86.
5. Ibid., 185–212.
6. MacCormick, *H.A.L Hart* (1981).
7. See https://iep.utm.edu/legalpos/, "Inclusive vs Exclusive Positivism."
8. Finnis, *Natural Law and Natural Rights* (1980).
9. Fuller, *The Morality of Law*, rev. ed. (1969).

liberalist tradition, but without resorting to natural law theory, rejected legal positivism and insisted on a necessary substantive moral content for law in his idea of law as integrity.[10]

These responses to Hart within established Anglo-American traditions came under attack, along with Hart's work itself, as being reflective of an approach to the analytical study of law that was based on Enlightenment assumptions associated with a belief in a neutral objective human reason. Drawing on continental critical theory, the Critical Legal Studies movement (CLS) focused on exposing the ideological "tilt" (bias) in the dominant liberal legal and social theory that covered all of the aforementioned theorists, including Hart.[11] Less interested in expounding the doctrines of the various branches of the law in an "objective" rational and purportedly (politically) "neutral" way divorced from political, social theories and from critiques found in the philosophy of social and natural sciences, CLS set out to show the hidden political and social bias in the dominant liberal approach to the study and practice of law and politics that favored powerful elites over the disadvantaged.[12] Postmodern legal theory under the influence of leading lights such as Foucault, Derrida, et al., further undermined the rational neutral analyses of law and debates about what was the best rational account of law. In contrast to Hart's ordinary language approach to legal analysis we find language discourse theory, hermeneutical theory, semiotics and the like bolstering the critical, post-modern and feminist assaults on liberal legal theory.[13]

---

10. Dworkin, *Law's Empire* (1986).
11. Unger, *Knowledge and Politics* (1975); idem, *Law in Modern Society* (1976). On "tilt," see Caudill, *Disclosing Tilt: Law, Belief, and Criticism* (1989). For an assessment of Caudill's "unique" reformational contribution, see Cameron, "Legal Ideology and Ideology Critique."
12. For a "liberal" view of CLS, see Altman, *Critical Legal Studies* (1990).
13. Hunt and Wickham, *Towards a Sociology of Law as Governance* (1994); Morgan, "Feminist Theory as Legal Theory" (1988).

The above incomplete account of trends in legal philosophy, around the time Dooyeweerd was developing his general philosophical and jurisprudential works, and which developed later, indicates the central problems that Dooyeweerd was trying to address in his theory of law and that have persisted to the present day. These might be summarized as two inextricably interconnected questions—A: the critical-theoretical question; and B: the empirical question.

A. The Critical-Theoretical Question

The critical-theoretical question concerns the nature of legal knowledge and how it is attained through the academic study of law. During Dooyeweerd's formal legal studies culminating in his doctoral dissertation of 1917 on the Cabinet in Dutch Constitutional Law, he encountered chaotic disagreements amongst jurists in their attempts to explain the conceptual basis not only of constitutional law but of law in general.[14] A fundamental question concerned the relationship between the factual and normative elements of law. Dooyeweerd's jurisprudence (legal theory), with its legal ontology (theory of legal phenomena) captured in the elementary and complex basic concepts of law, is based upon a unique legal epistemology that claims to have overcome this enduring theoretical conundrum. Our discussion of the empirical question (see at B below) points to the role of these concepts in analyses of concrete (empirical) law both in relation to its normativity and factuality.

To get at the roots of the apparently irresolvable conflicts in theoretical accounts of law mentioned above, Dooyeweerd undertook an examination of the history of Western philosophy.[15] This broad philosophical-historical analysis is the basis of his history of

---

14. See Henderson, *Illuminating Law: The Construction of Herman Dooyeweerd's Philosophy*, 24–25, 52–87.
15. Dooyeweerd, *A New Critique*, II, 169–495.

legal philosophy connected to the history of legal concepts as they were taught within the special discipline of law in all of its branches, mainly within continental jurisprudence.[16] It is explained elsewhere how Dooyeweerd was influenced by the Dutch Reformed Christian teaching and, in particular, the Kuyperian idea that *all of life* has a religious root. The pervasiveness of religion extends to all academic work including concept-forming within the disciplines and their theoretical-philosophical basis. Dooyeweerd set out to provide an account of the religious roots of theorizing in the dominating Western traditions of philosophy and theory, and of Western culture in general.[17]

In his *Encyclopedia of the Science of Law*[18] Dooyeweerd connects his philosophical system, with its account of the religious roots of human existence, to a philosophical exposition of the discipline ("science") of law and its concepts. This is done through a revival of the historical idea of an encyclopedia of the science of law as a universal philosophical introduction to the discipline of law.[19] This historical idea of an encyclopedia of the science of law is transformed through the "transcendental ground-Idea" rooted in the biblical religious ground-motive of creation, fall, and redemption. The biblical religious (Christian) ground-motive is viewed in opposition to the other major ground-motives in world history with their respective ground-ideas operating within the science of law and other theoretically based disciplines.[20]

Fundamental to his philosophical account of the discipline of law is the distinction between our primary way of knowing of the

---

16. Dooyeweerd, *A New Critique*, 4 vols. (1953–58; repr. 1984, 2015).
17. Dooyeweerd, *Roots of Western Culture* (1979).
18. Translation of *Encyclopaedie der Rechtswetenschap* (course syllabi, five vols.).
19. Dooyeweerd, *Encyclopedia of the Science of Law*.
20. Dooyeweerd, *Encyclopedia of the Science of Law*, I, 48–75 for ground-motives; see also 75–94 for Christian ground-idea and encyclopedic concept of law.

entirety of experienceable reality (our "naïve" experience) and our theoretical experiencing and knowing of the same cosmic reality.[21] No academic discipline can carry out its disciplinary academic work to provide a scientific conceptually-framed knowledge without a *philosophical-theoretical demarcation* of its area of study under the guidance of a theoretical ground-idea that is directed by a religious ground-motive. Dooyeweerd's arrived at this demarcation of the sciences by reforming the Kantian idea of the *Gegenstand-relation* via his unique theory of cosmic modal aspects.[22] These *modal aspects* are the elementary (ontic) spheres of the cosmic divine creational law that governs the entire human experiential horizon.[23] The (normative) jural aspect *theoretically* abstracted from the given coherence of all the modal aspects provides the modal perspective that orients the discipline, the ("social") science of law *and its concepts*, towards its disciplinary subject-matter, its scholarly field of research and higher learning.[24] The following summary concludes this brief overview of the *critical-epistemological element* of the Dooyweerdian jurisprudence (theory or philosophy of law).

All of created reality, including human creatures and all of their activities, is ordered and upheld by God's constant, dynamic cosmic Word of Law (Law-Word). The conceptualizing activity of forming concepts employed by scholars and practitioners of law to account for human experience in respect of its jural/legal dimension involves a subjective religiously-rooted activity that presupposes a prior epistemological (theoretical thinking) act of *abstracting*. This abstracting is a *theoretical* setting aside of the (ontic) jural aspect from all non-jural aspects of reality within the creationally-given intermodal coherence of all the aspects of reality. This is

---

21. Dooyeweerd, *Encyclopedia of the Science of Law*, I, 23–24.
22. Ibid., 38ff for *Gegenstand-relation;* for critique of Dooyeweerd's *Gegenstand-relation*, see Strauss, *Philosophy: Discipline of the Disciplines*, 361–368.
23. Dooyeweerd, *A New Critique*, I, 3–4.; II, 331–34.
24. Dooyeweerd, *Encyclopedia of the Science of Law*, I, 23.

no "objective" *merely* "rational" activity but is of a subjective-philosophical character rooted in the central religious dimension of the human heart, "the undivided center of all temporal human existence."[25] All of the "isms" in legal philosophy are accounted for by the differing and often incompatible religious commitments that underlie their answer to the philosophical question, what is the nature of jural/legal phenomena?[26] These religious commitments also shape the answers to basic jurisprudential questions: What are the concepts of law? What are the particular *conceptions* (content) of those concepts (even assuming a considerable degree of agreement on what these jural concepts are)?

No theory of law, nor the scholarship *within* the discipline of law with its legal concepts, is able to proceed except on the basis of a *prior* religiously-rooted *theoretical/analytical identification of the legal/jural* aspect from all non-jural modal aspects of reality. Within Dooyeweerd's encyclopedic idea of the science of law, it is the task of philosophy of law, in partnership with the discipline of law itself, to theoretically-philosophically account for the basic concepts of law which constitute the overall concept of law. This conception of philosophy and philosophy of law can be radically contrasted with the Kantian idea that has been so influential in mainstream jurisprudence and within the discipline of law—the assumption that legal reality, legal factuality, is an unordered chaotic datum to which the human categories of the mind subjectively provide a rationally ordered conceptual account.[27] On the other hand, the encyclopedic conception of the science of law and role of legal theory, while fully acknowledging the subjective character of legal conceptualizing, also rejects the historicism and irrationalistic relativism of postmodern approaches to the discipline of law under the influence of humanistic philosophies of law.

---

25. Dooyeweerd, *Encyclopedia of the Science of Law*, I, 37, 46.

26. For "isms," see Dooyeweerd, *Encyclopedia of the Science of Law*, I, 36.

27. Dooyeweerd, *A New Critique*, II, 41.

B. The Empirical Question

H. J. van Eikema Hommes, the successor to Dooyeweerd in the chair of legal philosophy, encyclopedia of law and old Dutch law in the Free University at Amsterdam describes Dooyeweerd's jurisprudential method of analysis as "transcendental-empirical."[28] Under *A* (the theoretical-critical question), I referred to the ground-ideas rooted in the religious ground-motives that give direction to theoretical thinking in philosophy and the scholarly disciplines including the discipline of law. There the ground-idea of the Philosophy of the Cosmonomic Idea was described as "transcendental," a reference to the transcendental critique that seeks to uncover the most fundamental questions for philosophy.[29] However, the empirical element of the encyclopedic method also is implicit in Dooyeweerd's account of the transcendental critical character of the theoretical attitude of analytical thinking. This is because the theoretical idea of the jural aspect of reality that is central to Dooyeweerd's unique theory of law refers to an aspect of reality that is (ontically) *given* as a transcendental mode of reality of God's ordering law for Creation. As a normative aspect amongst all other normative and non-normative ('natural') aspects of given experienceable reality it expresses itself in empirical legal phenomena as normative jural facts such as concrete laws as well as jural acts of law-making (e.g., the process of statutory legislating), or in the transference of legal ownership, the formation of a legal contract, and so forth.

Dooyeweerd's encyclopedic jurisprudence may not be the only legal theory to resist reducing the factuality of legal phenomena

---

28. Hommes, *Major Trends in the History of Legal Philosophy*, 372. On Dooyeweerd's professorship, see Verburg, *Herman Dooyeweerd: The Life and Work of a Christian Philosopher*, 87–150.
29. Cf. Dooyeweerd, *A New Critique*, I, 3–21, for the "first way," "from above"; cf. 34–38 for the second, "immanent" way.

to "natural facts."[30] However, the encyclopedic method is unique in finding the normative source of legal factuality in pre-positive jural normativity within a creationally given aspect of reality. In the *Encyclopedia of the Science of Law* the "empirical" side of the theory is expressed in the basic concepts of law that are no mere rational construction of brute legal facts. They aim to capture the internal complexity of the jural aspect of reality as it is subjectively realized in human actions and cultural-social formations by providing a conceptual basis for the best theoretical explanation of reality viewed from the disciplinary standpoint of the jural aspect.

In Dooyeweerd's encyclopedic conception of jurisprudence as philosophy of law there is an intimate relationship between the discipline of law and the philosophy of law which is required to provide the basic concepts for the legal discipline. The discipline of law as the normative science of law cannot within itself provide those concepts which it needs to carry out its disciplinary enquiries, explanations and expositions of legal reality. The reverse is also true. Without constantly drawing on the "empirical" work—the research and applications of the discipline—legal philosophy lacks the necessary empirical basis for forming and refining the theoretical-philosophical conceptual foundations it provides for the discipline (science of law). This interrelationship will be elaborated in the following chapter that gives an overview of the conceptual structure of the *Encyclopedia of the Science of Law*.

---

30. See MacCormick and Weinberger, *An Institutional Theory of Law*, 95–97 for MacCormick's positivist "institutional facts."

40

The Relationship between Dooyeweerd's Systematic Philosophy and his Theory of the Basic Concepts of the Science of Law

by Alan Cameron

Introduction

DOOYEWEERD'S JURISPRUDENCE is grounded in the theory of the modal aspects. The modal theory is only one component of the Philosophy of the Cosmonomic Idea along with the theory of individuality-structures and enkaptic interlacements. However, it is the modal theory that is the unique basis for Dooyeweerd's jurisprudence with its encyclopedic (interdisciplinary) method of analysis intended for application within the discipline (science) of law. The idea of the juridical, or jural, modal aspect embedded in the coherence of all modal aspects of reality is the "primary foundation" and the key to the entire conceptual framework of the *Encyclopedia of the Science of Law*.[1]

This chapter provides an overview of how the idea of the jural aspect is applied in Dooyeweerd's encyclopedic jurisprudence with its "basic concepts" framework.[2] Before we consider these con-

---

1. Dooyeweerd, *Encyclopedia of the Science of Law*, I, 11: heading title to Pt 1.
2. Ibid., Vol. 10/3: *The Elementary and Complex Basic Concepts of Law* (forthcoming).

cepts there is the question, What is the jural aspect?

The Jural Aspect

What differentiates this aspect from other aspects of reality? From the general theory of the modal aspects, we know that any account of a modal aspect must capture its modal core ("kernel" or "nucleus") along with its analogical structure. In the analogies lies the modal basis of the *Encyclopedia*'s full concept of law, even though it is the jural modal core that *characterizes or qualifies* the analogies.[3] The attempt to account for the (normative) modal core meaning of the jural aspect therefore always requires an appeal to the analogical structure of the aspect. Dooyeweerd found it "very difficult" to find a suitable term that grasps intuitively the modal core of the jural aspect.[4] Only "retribution" could do that, notwithstanding its liability to be misinterpreted and overly narrowly construed especially in a criminal or penal sense.[5] But this meaning kernel, however described, cannot be understood apart from the analogical structure of the aspect itself – the modal connections to aspects that both precede and succeed it in the temporal order of the modal aspects. Whatever term is used to capture the modal kernel, it is the modal jural analogies that are the basis for the "elementary" basic concepts of human laws.[6]

Jural Analogies and Elementary Basic Concepts of Law

No attempt is made here to even summarise all of the elementary basic concepts of law that are analysed in depth in the *Encyclopedia*.[7] Some of them will be discussed to indicate how they arise out of the analogical structure of the aspect and illustrating their

---

3. See the description or "circumscription" in *A New Critique*, II, 129.
4. Ibid.
5. Chaplin, *Herman Dooyeweerd: Christian Philosopher of State and Civil Society*, 193, suggests "tribution" as an alternative.
6. Dooyeweerd, *Encyclopedia of the Science of Law*, Vol. 10/3.
7. Ibid., 11–34.

connection to "empirical" legal phenomena.

The jural concept of unity-in-a multiplicity is a jural analogical concept that corresponds to the numerical retrocipatory analogy within the jural aspect. It looks back to the aspect of discrete quantity, the first in the temporal order of the aspects.[8] As a concept it is basic in the discipline of law because it appeals to a universal feature of all law and all jural phenomena. Lawmakers must always consider the *multiple* relevant interests of each member of the relevant community or societal relationship and integrate them into a jural *unity* of jural norms applicable to the factual context. This is the case, whether at the state legislative and judicial level, or in the "private" sphere, for example, voluntary organizations formulating "codes" or "rules" to regulate their members.[9] This is not a unity in an original modal numeric sense, nor in a physically qualified sense, but in a jurally qualified sense. It requires bringing into a jural one-ness (unity) the multiple jural interests of every member according to jural norms and principles that ensure each is given his or her due within the jural unity.

Jurisdiction, the *area* over which law and its norms *extends*, is captured within the discipline of law as a jural *spatial* concept. So is jural *location* when it applies to the *place* where, for example, a contract in law is formed – not necessarily the "physical" location where the goods are located.[10]

There are countless empirical instances of *jural movement* that can be given.[11] A consumer purchase of an item at a book shop, whether in person at a physical location or online, involves a *ju-*

---

8. Ibid., 11-13.
9. On the application of encyclopedic jurisprudence to internal professional organizational codes, see Cameron, "Dooyeweerd on Law and Morality."
10. Dooyeweerd, *Encyclopedia of the Science of Law*, Vol. 10/3, 13-15.
11. The reason why the *Encyclopedia* does not distinguish jural movement from jural ground, or from cause and effect, is explained in vol. I, 18 (editor's note).

ral movement, a *trans*-action. This is not referring to the "physical" book itself being passed to the buyer but the *ownership* of the book.

Movement of legal title entails a jural *change* in the legal relation of each party to the consumer purchase transaction implied in the word "transaction" itself. Jural change here refers to the *physical analogy* within the jural aspect of a jural *cause and effect*. Jural causation implies a jural *ground* for a jural effect or consequence.[12] This is quite different from physical cause and effect such as involved in a chemical reaction. The breach of a legal norm such as a criminal act involves a *jural reaction* with legal effects (consequences) such as a fine or imprisonment.

Other physical-jural analogies are at play in *weighing* the different (individual and communal) jural interests involved in making law or in judicial decision-making in a court case. This always involves a jural *balancing* process. But the balancing "scales" of the law is not like a simple weighing of physical things with physical scales. It involves a weighing and balancing using a "standard of proportionality" in accordance with weight attributed to each of the jural interests and avoiding giving *excessive* weight to any one jural interest. Over and above balancing in a proportionate jural way it also requires jural *harmonizing* of all those interests.[13] Proportionate balancing and avoidance of excess involve an analogical retrocipation to the normative economic aspect of *frugality*. This is the jural elementary concept of *jural economy*.[14] However, avoiding excess, either in weighing legal norms embodied in legal rights, or in weighing legal facts in a court decision, is merely part of the process of *jural harmonization,* in Dooyeweerd's view, a dis-

---

12. Dooyeweerd, *Encyclopedia of the Science of Law*, Vol. 10/3, Part 2, 35ff. See also Cameron, "Dooyeweerd's Jurisprudential Method," for a comparison with Hart and Honoré, *Causation in the Law* (1985).
13. Dooyeweerd, *A New Critique*, II, 129.
14. Dooyeweerd, *Encyclopedia of the Science of Law*. Vol. 10/3, 30–31.

tinct (normative) aesthetic retrocipation.¹⁵

Jural Anticipations and "Opening Up" Jural Concepts

The elementary concepts of law are "constitutive" for the concept of law.¹⁶ The implication of this is that it is possible for law or whatever type of source of law to exist without *all* of the analogies within the jural aspect coming to concrete historical expression. The *legal* principles of good faith, trust, "good morals" and their corresponding concepts that are found, for example, in Civil Law and Common Law traditions are not necessarily found in all societies' legal systems or in all societies in the history of their laws. They only came into being through an *idea of justice* under the influence of the Christian faith that led the historical "opening process" in the development of Western culture including its laws and legal systems.¹⁷ In the *Encyclopedia* there is extensive analyses of how the moral anticipatory analogy within the jural aspect came to expression in the law through the principles of guilt or fault.¹⁸

There is no better example of the faith-led nature of the moral opening up of the jural sphere of life than in the development of the concept of duty of care in the English common law of civil law obligations ("tort") which the English judge Lord Atkin famously stated as being based on the biblical injunction to love one's neighbour.¹⁹ Dooyeweerd's modally-based conceptual framework brilliantly explains how this moral-religious principle becomes a moral-legal principle in concrete law by opening up what had

---

15. Ibid., 32–34; see Chaplin, *Herman Dooyeweerd*, 189–190 for a critique of these concepts.
16. Hommes, *Major Trends*, 374, 375.
17. Dooyeweerd, *Encyclopedia of the Science of Law*, I, 123 ff.
18. Ibid., 123–33; cf. *Encyclopedia of the Science of Law*, Vol. 10/3, 89–107.
19. *Donoghue v Stevenson* 1932: 100; see Lord Atkin's famous statement of "the neighbour principle": https://en.wikipedia.org/wiki/Donoghue_v_Stevenson#House_of_Lords/.

been a restricted legal duty in a moral way without itself being a purely moral or ethical principle.[20]

Elementary Basic Jural Concepts as Foundation for Other Components of the Encyclopedic Jurisprudential Structure

Complex Basic Concepts

The elementary basic concepts based on the retrocipatory analogies within the jural aspect, along with the complex or compound basic concepts of law, constitute the overarching concept of law.[21] Each of the complex concepts are founded on all of the elementary concepts – those discussed above and others such as jural life (biotic analogy), jural intention or will (sensory-psychical), jural attribution/imputation (logical), jural formation and power (historical) jural or legal interpretation (lingual/symbolic), and legal/jural intercourse (social analogy).[22]

The complex concepts include the standard concepts of jurisprudential scholarship such as sources of law, rights, legal personality and corporation, which are connected to the complex concepts of legal subject(ivity) and object(ivity) arising out of that part of the general modal theory of the subject-object relation.[23] So the complex concepts include relational ("categorial") concepts: the relation of law-or norm-side (legal norms) and fact- or subject-side (legal facts) the jural subject-object relation, and the temporal relation of coming into being (legal origination) and passing away (legal termination) connected to the complex basic

---

20. See Bigwood, *Exploitative Contracts*, 485ff for a more recent application of the principle as a contractual *duty of care*, reviewed in my article "Liberal Foundations of a Liberal Conception of Exploitative Contracts – A Challenge," 127–139.
21. Dooyeweerd, *Encyclopedia of the Science of Law*, Vol. 10/3, 9.
22. Ibid., 11–34.
23. Ibid., 108 ff.

concept of jural time.[24]

The Jural Aspect, Individuality-Structures, and Enkaptic Interlacements in the Encyclopedic Jurisprudence

The general modal theory, which includes an account of the irreducible, universal, jural aspect of reality, provides the "primary" foundation for the jurisprudential account (encyclopedia) of the discipline of law. It is immediately and directly expressed in the elementary and complex basic concepts of law. On its own, however the theory of the jural modal aspect is insufficient as a comprehensive theoretical framework for the discipline of law. The other main conceptual components of the encyclopedic jurisprudence — the typical-structural basic concepts of law tied to the complex concept of sources of law — require a "second foundation" in the general philosophical theory of individuality-structures and enkaptic interlacements.[25]

This part of the encyclopedic jurisprudence, building on the idea of the jural aspect and its analogical structure expressed in the elementary and complex jural concepts, provides a unique theory of legal pluralism. The theory of different sources of law not only accounts for how the jural aspect can express itself in every societal sphere and human relationship but how that expression also provides an internal sphere of law of a different structurally irreducible *type*. The explanation for these irreducible *types* of law arises from the theory of individuality-structures, or as Strauss and others now prefer the theory of *type laws*, that is, *structural types* that apply to entities.[26] This provides the foundation for explaining the structural basis of the different branches of law and their

---

24. Ibid., 109–112.
25. Dooyeweerd, *Encyclopedia of the Science of Law*, I, vii, ix: heading titles for Parts 1 and 4.
26. Strauss, *Philosophy: Discipline of the Disciplines*, 25; "law" and "type" here have a cosmic, not jural, sense.

sources, including the very important distinction between private and public law, and their subcategories.[27]

The theory of the forms of enkaptic interlacements of the individuality structures is necessary in order to explain the sources of law and the complex ways in which different types of human laws interconnect with one another.[28] The following is a summary explanation of the way in which Dooyeweerd's theory of enkaptic interlacements of societal structures applies to types of human law, their sources, and interweaving in a developed (differentiated) society.[29]

All state law, comprising the law generated by the state's main law-making organs, the legislature and courts, is of a *public* type. This includes what lawyers and legal scholarship refer to as private law, that is a common state law governing, for example, private property (property law) contractual relations (contract law) and other societal co-ordinational relationships of members of society (law of civil law obligations such as the law of civil wrongs ("delicts" or "torts"). This public type of law is not the only type of human law that exists. The state *public type* of law itself could not exist or have any purpose without there being other non-state types of human law. The reason for this is explained in the following summary.

It is the (universal) jural modal aspect of the state which plays the role of qualifying/leading modal aspect in its type (structural) law. This practically means that it has its own internal sphere of human law, its "public" law, to govern its own internal activities and functions such as found in its constitutional and administra-

---

27. Hommes, *Major Trends,* 390 ff; covered by Dooyeweerd in *Encyclopedia,* Vol. 4/11, yet to be published.
28. On "nodal point of legal interlacements," see Hommes, *Major Trends,* 390–392.
29. The part of the Encyclopedia that deals with "typical" basic concepts is yet to be published in Vol. 4/11.

tive law. It also has a vast array of laws for public health, welfare, state economic policy and other activities in society. The state, through its law, serves the *public interest* that includes the interests of all citizens of the state and all societal institutions within its *legal* territorial jurisdiction. This is not confined to what is understood as "civil rights" and freedoms. The state in addition is required to *integrate in a public legal way* all other non-state societal spheres and relationships *through the regulation of their internal jural spheres of law according to norms of public legal justice*. For example, "private" sports, cultural and other voluntary, economic/commercial and professional organizations are encompassed by this public legal regulation. This is not a merely aspirational normative goal, but is an empirical description of what state law does in different domestic jurisdictions – certainly in those based in the Civil Law and Common law traditions. The following are two examples of the plurality of different types of law and their sources and the state law's integrating function with respect to them.

The inner jural aspect of "private" commercial and consumer relationships comes to *formal* expression in the economic-jural practice of individual contractual agreements. According to the encyclopedic jurisprudence the individual contracts themselves have their jural source as law in the non-state sphere (jural aspect) of co-ordinational economic relations. What is known to practising lawyers and jurists as the "law of contract" is a state common law that integrates all instances of "private" *economically qualified* co-ordinational jural agreement-based formations in a public legal way. It does this by setting general state law-sanctioned requirements for contractual formation, public legal norms of contractual justice and state-sanctioned remedies for breach of those norms in private contractual interactions.[30]

---

30. For an encyclopedic account of the contract and contract law as two sources of law, see Cameron, "The Jural Aspect in Dooyeweerd's Philosophy of Law," 279–308, at 296–301.

Another example of this state common "private" law regulation is the requirements of voluntary and professional organizations to ensure their internal "rules" cover specific areas of internal regulation according to common standards, and, in case they have no rules at all, that they formulate a set of compliant rules. All of these state law requirements are to promote the public interest in ensuring associational justice within their internal processes, that is, for the interests of society at large. The original ("genetic") source of all of the internal spheres of laws, rules, or codes of non-state associations, institutions and co-ordinational relationships is *not* the state law that regulates them but is found in those "sovereign" societal spheres themselves which the state may try to usurp but cannot actually disregard without a societally damaging effect.

From the primary foundation of the theory of the jural aspect, in combination with the secondary foundation of theory of structures of human entities and relationships and their interweavings, there emerges an extraordinary theory of legal pluralism fit for application in highly complex contemporary societies with all of their demands for better forms of legal justice.

41

Civil Private Law[1]

by Herman Dooyeweerd

The Nature of Civil Law

CIVIL LAW PROPER, as it has found expression in modern law codes, is the outcome of a long-standing historical process. It presupposes a high degree of differentiation and integration of legal life and is geared to one structure in human society only, namely that of co-ordinational civil relationships that fall outside the internal communal and collective spheres of marriage, family, the business firm, organizations, and so on, thus to relationships in which individuals do not exercise any authority over one another.

On the one hand civil law presupposes the existence of a genuine state, one in which civil cases are decided by an impartial judiciary, and decisions arrived at by the civil judge are executed by officers of the state. On the other hand, it presupposes the development of individualized private societal relationships where people participate in coordinated interaction as individual legal subjects with juridical equality. Distinct from the specific private communal law obtaining within particular societal collectivities such as the family, church, school, business, social club, etc., the sole purpose of civil law is to apply the demands of social justice in the reciprocal private interactions between individuals. In this respect civil law is also clearly distinct from constitutional law, although it is necessarily interwo-

---

1. Extracts from H. Dooyeweerd, *Time, Law, and History: Selected Essays, Collected Works of Herman Dooyeweerd*, Series B, vol. 14, General Editor D.F.M. Strauss (Grand Rapids, MI: Paideia Press: 2017), 345–348.

ven with the inner law of the state. Constitutional law, taken in a broad sense, is typically organized communal law of a distinct character: it comprehends the legal organization and arrangement of relationships of authority and compliance between government and subjects. This organization is founded on the sword power of the government and is intended to bring to expression the public-legal idea of the common good. Civil law, by contrast, regulates private coordinational relationships as such, displaying no relationships of authority and subordination. It is governed by the idea of civil private law.

In modern civil law the worth of the individual person comes to juridical expression independently of race, ethnicity, religion, membership in a specific interest group, etc. Although its legislative origin is inextricably intertwined with the state, yet civil law as such is not *communal law*[2] and cannot be made into communal law without affecting its inner nature.

Nevertheless, civil law by its very nature does not exist in isolation but only in indissoluble intertwinement with all the other jural spheres of human society: with private communal law in the distinct structures of marriage, nuclear family, extended family, church, business firm, school, voluntary organizations and associations, etc. etc. Civil law is also intertwined with the public law of the state as an organized community; with international law; with the non-civil, free coordinational law of normal social interaction.

When, for example, our Civil Code makes the introductory remark regarding marriage: "The law treats marriage only with respect to its civil relationships," then it proceeds from the assumption that marriage functions in numerous other relationships and that this intimate societal form of life has an *internal* communal sphere without which the merely civil-legal relationships would not be able to function *externally*.

---

2. Not even in its regulation of the external civil-legal relationships between family members, or members of other communities.

Civil law, according to its entire structure as a differentiated legal system, is the asylum of the individual person, the fortress for the protection of the individual person within legal life.

Civil Law and Non-Civil Law

Civil law can fulfill this role only in unbreakable coherence with the communal and collective jural spheres[3] in which the solidarity of the members in relationships of authority and subordination is maintained.

Within these communal and collective spheres, a person is only a member of the collectivity and is not considered according to his private sphere as an individual. In civil-legal relationships, however, the government has to ensure that every person receives his due as an individual.

Precisely to prevent overstraining society's communal and collective spheres, civil law functions as a beneficial bulwark insofar as an individual's civil rights ought to be protected against infringements by collective and communal organs—including the organs of the state.

However, as we shall see later, civil law cannot accomplish this task alone. On the one hand it needs the counterbalance of the state's social legislation guided by the public-legal idea of community which prevents private individuals or organized communities from usurping power. On the other hand, it needs the counterweight of private communities which ought to protect their internal spheres against usurpation by the state.

---

3. Every societal collectivity (*"verband"*) embraces a community, but not every community is a societal collectivity. A societal collectivity always has organs endowed with power. The family community, to the extent that it is built solely upon a cognate basis, lacks such an organ. On the other hand, a societal collectivity has relative continuity independent of changes in its membership. For that reason, for example, marriage as a community is not a societal collectivity.

When the principles of civil law are overemphasized the inevitable effect is an individualistic conception of law. But this does not justify the view that civil law itself is individualistic just because it cannot fulfill the role of a communal law.

Civil Property Right

All of this should be kept in mind when evaluating civil property right. *Civil law* should never—as so frequently happens in legal science—be equated with all of *private law* understood as all law falling outside the domain of *public law*. After all, as we have seen, private law encompasses many spheres of law which as such do not display a civil-legal character.

What falls outside the domain of civil law is all the specific law of private communities and collectivities which serve their inner structure, guided by a destination lying outside the jural domain. This is the case in internal marriage and family law, internal business law, internal associational law, internal church law, and so on. The same goes for those branches of private law which, although they do not display a communal or collective character, are typically guided by an extra-jural destination. An example would be the commercial rules that arose in society to deal directly with the economic destination of business and industry, such as conditions commonly used in the insurance business like the exclusion of particular risks, a condition that makes sense only for reasons of business economics.

Non-civil private law in real relationships must be taken into account in the formation of civil law only to the extent that it is intertwined with civil law. But then it is done solely for the protection of the sphere of civil law itself and not for interfering in the internal domain of non-civil private law.

42

The Theory of an International Legal Order

by Romel Regalado Bagares

Theorizing the 'International Community'

IN A GLOBALIZED WORLD, the idea of an international community "appears omnipresent" but "the frequent use of the concept...is not matched by any clarity of content."[1] Yet the concept of an international community is a "constructive abstraction"– one that is packed with a "powerful and privileged meaning" such that it "establishes the international community as a legal agent that is personified empirically in relevant decisions and actions."[2] The distinction made between international society and international community – popular in international legal writing – echoes the thought of the German sociologist Ferdinand Tönnies.[3] Yet for Herman Dooyeweerd, this is an uncritical appropriation of Tönnies' terminology, as it neglects the former's romanticist tendencies: in Tönnies' pessimistic theory, modernity leads to *Gesellschaft*, into a societal differentiation (if not decline) marked by contractual relations, at the expense of an organic unity of the *Gemein-*

---

1. Andreas Paulus, "From Territoriality to Functionality? Towards a Legal Methodology of Globalization," in Dekker and Werner, eds., *Governance and International Legal Theory* (Leiden: Brill, 2004), pp. 42, 60.
2. Nicholas Tsagorias, "The Will of the Community as a Normative Source of International Law," in ibid., pp. 100, 102, 108.
3. Ibid.

schaft, for him the true community.⁴

A Dooyeweerdian Pluralistic International Legal Order

The continuing conceptual question raised by such a community underscores both the lack and need for a plausible and fruitful framework for understanding the international legal order. There is, as the reformational political philosopher Jonathan Chaplin remarks, a missing dimension of "sociality" in much of the prevailing liberal theorizing on institutional rights, which has been decidedly individualistic in orientation. "Because contemporary liberalism lacks an adequate notion of sociality," says Chaplin, "liberal legal, constitutional, and political [theories] have proved unable to generate a convincing account of the reality and character of the legal rights of institutions."⁵ Liberal theorists tend to construe the phenomenon of institutional rights as merely derived from the rights of associating individuals rather than as having some independent foundation and status not finally reducible to individual rights. The traditional opposition between individual rights and community rights simply fails to grasp the idea of various societal spheres with their respective competencies. Individualism absolutizes the inter-individual relations while universalism (or collectivism) absolutizes the communal bond. Yet in his pluralistic social ontology, founded on the principle of societal sphere sovereignty, communities and inter-linkages presuppose each other; indeed, wherever such communal wholes exist, there also exist relationships between such communities (inter-communal relations) and between members of such communities (inter-individual relationships).⁶ Sphere sovereignty posits that beyond it being a *sociological* principle designed to guarantee the independence of various spheres of life, it expresses an ontological, or as Dooyeweerd preferred to say, a *cosmological* principle, which

---

4. Dooyeweerd, *Essays in Legal, Social and Political Philosophy*.
5. Jonathan Chaplin, "Towards a Social Pluralist Theory of Institutional Rights," *Ave Maria Law Review* 3 (2005): 147–149.
6. Dooyeweerd, *A Christian Theory of Social Institutions*.

guarantees the irreducibility of the various aspects of reality. There is no single communal whole that absorbs everything else; the state is but one of many societal spheres with their respective areas of material competence. The same can be said of inter-individual relationships – these are coordinational relationships, not communal wholes. In the case of the state, *contra* those who accord to it unrestrained power, in Dooyeweerd's normative theory, while power is foundational to its establishment, it is balanced by its indissoluble tie to justice, which is its leading function, or its intrinsic purpose qualifying its internal structure.[7]

This intrinsic purpose is expressed through norms of public justice, which is shorthand for those norms that pertain to the common good, and the various multiple collective, communal and coordinational interests that the state is to balance.[8] The limits to state power are found in the structural principles that govern its functioning: "[t]he state is led by norms of justice, not ethics; the accomplishment of public justice is the structural principle of the state, not the enforcement of non-public morals."[9] Dooyeweerd's theory of the state, while agreeing that the state's duty is toward the whole society, restricts state power not by some supposedly external limits set by another institution (the church, or business, for example) and enforced by the competing power of the other, but by the very nature of the state itself. "It is the state's own internal structure which sets its proper limits."[10]

Dooyeweerd assiduously argues against theories that conceive of

---

7. Cf. René van Woudenberg, "Theories of Thing-Structures," in *Philosophical Foundations I: Reader for the Master's Program in Christian Studies of Science and Society* (Amsterdam: Free University Press). p. 3.
8. D. F. M. Strauss, *Philosophy: Disciplines of the Disciplines* (Grand Rapids: Paideia, 2009), 552–553.
9. Dooyeweerd, *Essays in Legal, Social and Political Philosophy*, p. 385.
10. Roy A. Clouser, *The Myth of Religious Neutrality*, rev. ed. (Notre Dame UP, 2005), p. 218.

society from its supposed basic elements, the allegedly elementary interrelations between human individuals, so that communities they form are merely legal fictions. Dooyeweerd argues that "the civil legal personality is only a specific component of the full legal subjectivity. This latter is equally constituted by various internal legal relationships implied in the membership of various communities." Moreover, for him, the "human I-ness" transcends every temporal societal relationship so that it is totally wrong to think of human beings as an organic member or part of any temporal social whole.[11] The radical implications of his social ontology (and by extension, his legal ontology) for international law may be glimpsed in the following description by Skillen: "[d]ifferent social relationships have different characters, different kinds of law-making requirements, different foundations."[12] Societal sphere sovereignty in this context means that each societal sphere has an intrinsic jural competence as an entity, community, or institution. Because for the most part, international law has been dominated by the Westphalian model, it has been difficult for many international legal scholars to conceive of a type of international law where the state is not the only entity that matters.

From 'International Community' to 'Inter-Communal Legal Order'

Dooyeweerd rejects the idea of an all-embracing "civitas maxima" – "a world-State embracing all nations without exemption" – as an historically supported proposition; in fact, he says it is a matter that has not gone beyond the sphere of the speculative, and we might add, the existence of the United Nations notwithstanding.[13]

---

11. Dooyeweerd, *Essays in Legal, Social and Political Philosophy*, p. 280.
12. James W. Skillen, *The Development of Calvinistic Political Theory in the Netherlands, With Special Reference to the Thought of Herman Dooyeweerd* (unpub. PhD diss., Duke Univ. 1973), p. 388.
13. Dooyeweerd, *A New Critique*, III, 661.

THE THEORY OF AN INTERNATIONAL LEGAL ORDER

This is a conclusion that needs elaboration. Indeed, when he speaks of international (public) law, Dooyeweerd refers to it as an "inter-communal legal order." Hence, Dooyeweerd rejects the idea that international law could arise from a single state or "the single body politic."[14] A corollary to this is that according to Dooyeweerd, international law could not be the basis of constitutional law and its validity, and neither is constitutional law the basis of international law and its validity. To subscribe to the idea that constitutional law and its validity are based on international law, according to him, is "tantamount to the fundamental denial of international law as an inter-communal legal order."[15] Meanwhile, to subscribe to the idea that international law and its validity is based on constitutional law is "the denial of the inner communal character of the Constitutional State-law, which is the very presupposition of international public law as an inter-communal legal order."[16] Thus, the following inter-related propositions can then be reconstructed: *First*, the inner communal character of the "Constitutional State-law" is the very presupposition of international law as an inter-communal legal order. *Second*, such an inner communal character of the state finds full realization in a plurality of States, so that the rise of the latter implied their international political relations and vice versa. This means that without a plurality of states, there can be no international law. *Third and fourth*, the relations obtaining in this inter-communal legal order (that is, international law) illustrate a "correlative type of enkapsis", which in the end – our *fourth* proposition – runs counter to the idea of a *civitas maxima* – an all-embracing World-State. Dooyeweerd differentiates between communal relations and social relations as transcendental categories. On the one hand, there are communal relations, which bind people together as members of a whole. On the other hand, there are social relations – they

---

14. Ibid.
15. Ibid.
16. Ibid.

be of cooperation, complementation, indifference, or hostility – that make it possible for people to coexist in society.[17] These relations are only possible in correlative enkapsis.[18] Social relationships are interlinkages between individuals, communities, or communities and individuals. Dooyeweerd identifies two types of social relationships: the inter-individual and inter-communal, which have identical functions. By inter-individual or inter-communal relationships, he means "such in which individual persons or communities function in coordination without being united into a solidary whole. Such relationships may show the character of mutual neutrality, of rapprochement, free cooperation or antagonism, competition, or contest."[19]

States, though communities in their own right, also engage in relations with one another, becoming intertwined in enkaptic inter-communal relations, in which communities interact in friendly cooperation, mutual competition or enmity. Yet they do not bind their peoples into a social whole or part-whole relations as these relations are by mutual consent. Moreover, there are no relations of authority and subordination in these relations, although certain groups and classes can exert a powerful influence through these interlinkages. Dooyeweerd also holds that generally, it is only in inter-structural intertwinements with other individuality-structures that any single structure of individuality is realized. According to him, both the sphere sovereignty of modal aspect as well as the sphere sovereignty of structural types of individuality only reveal themselves in an inter-structural enkaptic coherence, barring any attempt to absolutize them.[20] But "[a] lack of insight into the principal difference between social relations of enkapsis and the social whole-part relation," he warns, "leads to a universalistic view

---

17. Dooyeweerd, *A Christian Theory of Social Institutions*.
18. Ibid.
19. Dooyeweerd, *Essays in Legal, Social and Political Philosophy*, 117.
20. Ibid.

THE THEORY OF AN INTERNATIONAL LEGAL ORDER

of society."[21] In the case of the inter-communal legal order of states, Dooyeweerd specifically identifies what kind of enkapsis is involved: correlative enkapsis. Correlative enkapsis as a structural relation is one where the interlacement has a reciprocal character. It is a definition that echoes the nature of inter-communal relations. "Correlative enkapsis assumes greater significance with the increasing differentiation and division of labor in society," says Dooyeweerd. "This in turn leads to an increasing mutual dependence of communities."[22]

Correlative Enkapsis as Reciprocity and the Possibility of International Law

Dooyeweerd critiques the popular view of Hegelian thought, which grants that a nation proves its right to exist in war. Such Hegelian view, in "dangerously" confusing might with right and arguing that the comity of nations is nothing but a contest won by the "law of the strongest", also wrongfully denied the validity of international law.[23] Hence, if correlative enkapsis is to work as it should, might and right must also go together in the inter-communal relations between and among states. The states forming the international legal order have a common duty to observe and uphold the norm of public justice in their individual and collective acts. What they must not violate as individual states within their own spheres, they must not violate as well as a collectivity. The protection given to the differentiation of spheres on the national level must also be observed in the international level as they integrate themselves into an international legal order through correlative enkapsis, which is characterized by mutual interdependence and reciprocity.

Reciprocity and interdependence in the international legal order also means that no state ought to absolutize its own interests at the expense of its relations with the other states, as any state's external rela-

---

21. Ibid., 627.
22. Dooyeweerd, *A Christian Theory of Social Institutions*.
23. Dooyeweerd, *Encyclopedia of the Science of Law*, 89.

tions are qualitatively different from its internal relations. "The rules of private inter-individual legal intercourse do not suffice here," he says.[24] In the first place, there is the reality of unequal positions of power among states. In the second place, the primary interests involved in international relations are "of a characteristically public societal nature". But national interest, all too often, is used as an excuse for national selfishness, of "sacred egotism" of states as a kind of natural justification in international relations. However, "[t]he internal vital law of the body politic is not a law of nature but bears a normative character". "For in this case the different states have external inter-communal societal relations to each other of a very different kind, which implies neither the internal communal structure of the state, nor that of private inter-individual relations". Thus, he criticizes Kant for reducing inter-state relations to the level of the individual (that is, treating states as individuals. An individualistic natural law view such as that which Kant propounds cannot adequately account for the fact that "the vital interests of the nations are in a great many ways mutually interwoven."[25]

In a globally integrated world of various state and non-state networks is a world where governments need to fight transnational and international crimes, protect the environment, regulate financial markets against predatory practices, guarantee civil rights and liberties, regulate financial markets, and provide social security, ensure the safety of consumer products, and represent the interests of their citizens fairly and accurately. Yet this does not mean the states are outright losing their sovereignty, "although they would certainly recognize that with respect to some specific problems, only genuinely powerful supranational institutions could overcome the collective action problems inherent in formulating and implementing global solutions."[26]

---

24. Dooyeweerd, *A New Critique*, III, 474.
25. Ibid., III, 474–476.
26. Ann-Marie Slaughter, *A New World Order* (Princeton UP, 2004), p. 270.

43

Are Norms and Principles Ethical or Moral in Nature?

by Danie F. M. Strauss

NORMS OR PRINCIPLES are supposed to guide human conduct and therefore they immediately call forth the idea of norm-conformity and antinormativity (*obedience* and *disobedience*). This distinction, in turn, presupposes the (human) capacity to *identify* and *distinguish* the possible avenues of action and to freely choose between the available options. There are not many *choices* at any specific moment – just one choice amongst multiple *options*. Therefore, a *freedom of choice* presupposes an *accountable agent* to which the choice made and its consequences can be *attributed*.

Traditionally the awareness of what *ought to be* done was placed within the category of the *ethos* of life (the *ethical*), also designated as the domain of *morality* or what is considered to be *moral*. Sometimes ethics and morality are distinguished in the sense that the former designates the *academic discipline* reflecting upon what is moral, the "ought (to be)." Prominent thinkers, however, exceeded this limitation. Habermas, for instance, speaks of "ethical" and "moral" aspects ["ethischen und moralischen Aspekten"],[1] of the *juridical aspect* and of the fact that the "ought" remains non-specific as long as the

---

1. J. Habermas, *Faktizität und Geltung. Beiträge zur Diskurstheorie des Rechts und des demokratischen Rechtsstaats* (Frankfurt am Main: Suhrkamp, 1998), 202.

relevant problem is not determined and the *aspect*[2] within which it must be solved has not been identified.[3] This suggests that we have to distinguish between *moral* normativity and *a-moral* or *non-moral* normativity – which of course is different from the *immoral*.

> In other words, the freedom of choice we have to act in norm-conforming or antinormative ways also calls forth (and presupposes) the *responsibility* and *accountability* which we have to assume for those consequences attributed to our actions.

Acknowledging that the domain of normativity encompasses more than *moral* normativity liberates us from a "basket" understanding of normativity according to which all instances of norm-guided behavior must be located within the category of the "ethical" or "morality." This legacy denies other normative aspects their proper right of existence. Distinguishing what is logically sound from what is illogical, for example, presupposes the existence of logical norms or principles and the latter do not coincide with *ethical normativity*. Similarly, avoiding excesses and acting in frugal ways exemplifies the normativity underlying the distinction between proper and improper economic activities and also this normative domain does not coincide with the moral.

Causal Determination versus Freedom

Whereas these initial remarks are guided by an understanding of normativity within the context of norms or principles and human actions subjected to them, modern philosophy actually opted for a dialectical understanding of freedom and normativity, one in which freedom and causal determination are juxtaposed.

Since the Renaissance this development revealed a tension between the natural science ideal and the personality ideal of human freedom and autonomy. An abbreviated characterization speaks of

---

2. Habermas, *Faktizität und Geltung*, 207.
3. Habermas, *Faktizität und Geltung*, 197.

the dialectic between *nature* and *freedom*.

The term *dialectical* should be understood in the sense of two opposing motives mutually threatening and presupposing each other. In such a tension the only option is to give *primacy* to one of the opposing motives, while at the same time depreciating the other motive. Initially modern philosophy advanced under the primacy of the science ideal which aimed at reconstructing the universe from its simplest elements, *atoms* in the case of nature and *individuals* in the case of human society (individuals are the atoms of human society). This view lies at the foundation of the well-known *social contract theories* of modernity. However, as long as the science ideal maintained its supremacy, its *deterministic universe* constantly threatened to eliminate *human freedom*.

Within the initial dominance of the science ideal all of reality was reduced to natural functional categories, such as *spatial extension* (Descartes and Spinoza), the *discrete* and *continuous* (Leibniz with his discrete monads and his law of continuity [*lex continui*]), and *perception* (Locke, Berkeley and Hume – the British empiricists). The deterministic consequences of this humanistic natural science ideal continued to endanger the personality ideal. But within the on-going dialectical development of modern thought, Rousseau forms a transitional figure in the sense that he attempted to liberate himself from the grip of the natural science ideal.[4] Rousseau was indeed the first philosopher who called Humanism back to a radical reflection on its truly deepest motivation, namely the Renaissance ideal of a free and autonomous humanity. However, his transitional position is underscored by the fact that his social contract theory still proceeded from the "atoms" of society, the "individuals," which means that in this regard he still adhered to the attempts of the science ideal to provide a *rational explanation* of an ordered society by reconstructing it from its supposedly

---

4. See D. F. M. Strauss, "Normativity I – The Dialectical Legacy," *South African Journal of Philosophy* 30, no. 2 (2011): 209.

simplest elements, the *individuals*.

The Primacy Given by Kant to the Freedom Motive

Kant gave primacy to the personality ideal and he did that in terms of the classical distinction between *essence* (*thing-in-itself*) and *appearance* – to the latter (the world of appearances) he assigned the science ideal and to the former to the personality ideal. This division is amply captured in his well-known exclamation that he was always intrigued by the starry sky above, governed by the universal law of causality (cause and effect), and the moral law within. ["Der bestirnte Himmel über mir, und das moralische Gesetz in mir"].[5] Implicit in his wonder and awe is an awareness of the difference between *laws of nature* and a *domain of normativity*, of ought to be, but unfortunately, he turned this difference into a *dualism*, into a *separation* of what he called the domains of *Sein* and *Sollen*, of *is* and *ought*. In his third *Critique* Kant wanted to bridge the gap between *nature* and *freedom*, that is, between the causally determining and the teleologically reflecting view of nature. The reconciliation is sought in the unity of a supra-sensory principle which is supposed to be valid for the totality of nature as a system.[6] However, this "solution" did not really reconcile the opposing poles of *nature* and *freedom*, since it simply reinforced the basic dualism between *natural necessity* and *super-sensory freedom* – each with its *own* law-giver.[7]

Already since early Greek philosophy the idea of a world-order acquired prominence (Heraclitus called it the *logos* of the universe).[8] Subsequently we had to distinguish between conditions and whatever meets these conditions. The latter were understood

---

5. I. Kant, *Kritik der Urteilskraft* (Darmstadt: Wissenschaftliche Buchgesellschaft, [1790] 1968), A:289.
6. Kant, *Kritik der Urteilskraft*, B:304.
7. Cf. Kant, *Kritik der Urteilskraft*, B:LIII-LIV.
8. H. Diels and W. Kranz, *W. Die Fragmente der Vorsokratiker*, Vols. I-III (Berlin: Weidmannsche Verlagsbuchhandlung, 1959-60), B Fr. 30 ff.

in an ontic sense and eventually such conditions were largely absorbed within the perspective of classical *realism*. Through the so-called *Copernican turn* in epistemology these ontic conditions were transferred to the human subject.

The ultimate issue is the opposition between the human subject as its own (individual and social) law-giver and the acceptance of given (ontic) principles enabling and making possible typically normed human activities. In the chapters on nominalism it was noted that in Kant's mature philosophy human understanding, through its thought categories, was promoted to become the *a priori* (formal) law-giver of nature: "Understanding creates its laws (*a priori*) not out of nature, but prescribes them to nature."[9]

While Kant maintained universality, historicism and its after-effect within postmodernism sized it down to the level of the individual and social *construction* of reality and society.[10]

Apart from the question where the (universal a priori) laws of nature are located (within the human subject or as ontically given), the modern idea of law in respect of natural reality still maintained the distinction between *law* and what is *subjected* to it. Yet, when nature, governed by the law of causality, is distinguished from the domain of *ought* (*Sollen*), it effectively was identified with the domain of *factuality* in its *separation* from normativity.

Facts and Values

The form in which this separation emerged at the beginning of the 20th century is found in the opposition of *facts* and *values*. Particularly the Baden school of neo-Kantian thought distinguished between the realm of factual statements and the realm

---

9. I. Kant, *Prolegomena zu einer jeden künftigen Metaphysik die als Wissenschaft wird auftreten können* (Hamburg: Felix Meiner, [1783] 1969), II:320; § 36.
10. See D. F. M. Strauss, "The (social) Construction of the World – at the Crossroads of Christianity and Humanism," *South African Journal of Philosophy* 28, no. 2 (2009): 222-233.

of value-judgements. This is an example of a philosophical school introducing a distinction that soon was absorbed within the everyday parlance of ordinary people. This reception was enhanced by two views. The one is found within the Baden school and became known as the *value-freedom of science*, particularly advocated by Max Weber. The other is associated with *positivism* and *neo-positivism* in their claim that "science" (physics and perhaps mathematics) is *objective* and *neutral*, bound only to sensory perception (sense-data).

Description and Evaluation

Neo-Kantian value-philosophy merely introduced their value-idea *within* the sphere of ought-to-be. It resulted in the opposition of facts and values, identified with (scientific) *description* and (non-scientific) *evaluation*. However, this split cannot account for the nature of logical-analytical normativity. We merely have to consider the question whether or not it is possible to obey or disobey logical-analytical principles. Whenever proper identification and distinguishing took place these principles are obeyed. Therefore, being subject to the modal logical norms of identity and contradiction causes every analytical act – as an act of identification and distinction – to conform to these (and other logical) norms. Hence it should be seen as just a different form of evaluation, viz. *analytical evaluation*.

Acknowledging this at once cancels the ideal of *objectivity* and its denunciation of human subjectivity. The generally accepted view is that subjectivity should be seen as something *disturbing* scientific endeavours. For this reason, it is assumed that it should be replaced by the ideal of *objectivity*. Yet, to see subjectivity as a *disturbing factor or* as a form of arbitrariness in scientific activities, presupposes the existence of one or another *normative standard*. If the input of subjectivity in the course of scientific research is evaluated as something *arbitrary*, this very evaluation already applies a *normative standard* by judging subjectivity (in its arbitrariness) as not conforming to the norm. However, the opposite of *arbitrary subjectivity* is not *objectivity*, but *norm-conforming subjectivity*! Arbitrariness is an *anti-normative configuration* which presupposes the existence of a norm, which leaves open the possibility for norm-conforming subjective human actions. And suddenly the bifurcation between "values" and "facts" is unveiled in its untenability.

At this point we have to consider the fact that logical-analytical principles are *making possible* human logical thinking and therefore cannot be generated by means of thought activities, for then the conditioned will coincide with what it conditions. Since Kant investigations directed towards what makes our *experience possible* are designated as being *transcendental* in nature. What we have in mind is to proceed by following a *transcendental-empirical* method. This method is closely related to the foundational coherence between *constancy* and *change* – where constancy relates to what is *transcendental* and change to what is *variable*.

Different trends within the social sciences embody elements of this approach. For example, the methodology developed by Parsons did see something concerning the relationship between a constant universal ontic order on the one hand and the dynamically changing experiential phenomena made possible by this order on the other. Johnson *et al.* explains his view as follows: He suggests instead that while the scientific concepts do represent universal, constant features of human action, the particular values or contents they have vary historically, and are problems of empirical research.[11]

What Parsons calls the "universal, constant features of human action" relates to an ontic order and what he reserves for historically variant problems of empirical research represent the second element of the transcendental-empirical method.

---

11. T. Johnson, C. Dandeker, and C. Ashworth, *The Structure of Social Theory* (London: Macmillan, 1984), 72.

The problem with the theoretical stance of Parsons is that his position still, in a subtle way, continues the neo-Kantian opposition of *facts* and *values*. He understands society in a purely factual sense and opposes it to "culture" which turns out to be a *basket term* for all forms of normativity, encompassing norms, values, meanings and symbols (in a similar way also present in the thought of Sorokin and MacIver). The implication is that society turns into something *a-normative* which is purely *factual* in nature.

Yet ontic normativity only makes sense if there is a strict correlation between normativity and what is determined by it (in the sense of being subjected to it). Our reference to the two most basic logical principles already illustrates this claim, for without these underlying logical principles no logical or illogical thinking is possible. While physics, for example, may distinguish between physical laws ("laws of nature") and what is subjected to such laws, within the domain of normativity we may likewise distinguish between principles or norms to which human beings (and societal collectivities) are subjected. Every normative aspect of human experience therefore will display this correlation between norm side and factual side.

This strict correlation belongs to the intrinsic nature of these normative aspects, *in casu those initially mentioned in the Introduction* to this work: the logical-analytical, cultural-historical, lingual, social, economic, aesthetic, jural, moral and certitudinal. These aspects are designated as *normative* aspects, because within each of the post-logical aspects we find contraries analogous to the contrary *logical/illogical*. This contrary is dependent upon the logical principle of non-contradiction and this contrary serves as the *foundation* of those contraries discernible within the post-logical aspects (such as historical/unhistorical, polite/impolite, frugal/wasteful, legal/illegal, and moral/immoral).

44

What is Inherent in Normativity?

by Danie F. M. Strauss

IT IS QUITE NORMAL that methodological considerations would not pay attention to the fact that our scientific knowledge merely *deepens* and *discloses* our non-scientific experience of reality in its diversity. Prior to developing a method serving the investigation of reality from the vantage point of any specific aspect, every special scientist already must have a non-scientific insight into the nature of her field of inquiry. The method eventually designed to investigate its field of inquiry could never provide or substitute this *presupposed knowledge*. The unique nature of whatever is investigated, ultimately determines every method aimed at acquiring knowledge of it.

This means that the rich diversity of different kinds and forms of normative practices may vary across cultures and at once undeniably shows that humankind partakes in shaping its world without avoiding its *basic functional contours*. Therefore, when we observe the peculiarities of different kinds of *logical* thinking, *cultural* habits, *lingual* discourses, *economic* systems, *social* organizations, *aesthetic* expressions, *legal* arrangements, *moral* preferences and *cultic* activities, however diverse they may be, none of them succeeds in bypassing the constant and underlying multiplicity of functional modes italicized in the previous sentence. The mere fact that amidst such a variety of practices one can still refer to *logical, cultural, lingual, social, economic, aesthetic, jural, moral* and *certitudinal* states of affairs underscores the presence of overarching *ways of existence* or *modes of being*, each displaying its own functional or modal universality. However, the claim that each one of these underlying modes displays a unique *universality* needs an explanation. What is meant is that every aspect co-conditions all possible kinds of entities functioning within it. Different instances and forms of *economic* or *jural* relations presuppose their shared functioning within these aspects, for otherwise it would be meaningless to use the same functional characterization to refer to them. Let us briefly look at an attempt to relativize the universality of modal aspects in terms of cultural differences.

Cultural-Historical Relativism

Oswald Spengler, pursues such a relativistic approach in which *cultural relativity* is over-emphasized. He argues that *number as such* does not exist, for there are *different worlds* of number, owing to the existence of *multiple cultures*. According to him we therefore find Indian, Arabic, Antique, and Western types of number, each with its own distinctive uniqueness and each bringing to expression a different tone of the world and as an ordering principle each with a limited symbolical validity. There are therefore more than one instances of mathematics.[1] Ironically enough he does not realize that the possibility to speak of different types of number presupposes that each culture still has a number concept! That is to say, every culture (a universal claim!) has a specific (culturally shaded) awareness of the multiplicity (quantitative) *mode of reality*.

The normativity inherent in the various normative aspects of reality is therefore not only *universal* but also *constant*, underscoring the fact that change can only be detected on the basis of persistence or constancy.

---

1. O. Spengler, *Der Untergang des Abendlandes. Umrisse einer Morphologie der Weltgeschichte*, vol. 1 (Munich: Beck, 1923), 78ff.

The Normativity of Entities and Functions

Similar modes of being or aspects of reality are also found within nature, because material things, plants and animals (as well as human beings) function in the aspects of *number, space, movement, energy-operation, life* (the biotic) and the *sensory* facet. Every material thing, plant, animal or human being therefore displays numerical properties, spatial properties, kinematic features, and physical traits. In fact, the same applies to human artefacts. These remarks actually refer to a very basic ontological distinction, namely that between the *how* and the concrete *what* of our experience. After the "what-question," when something concrete is identified (like a chair), one can only proceed with "how-questions," such as: how *many* are there (number)? how *large* is it (space)? how *strong* is it (physical)? how *expensive* is it (economic)? and so on – see the *Introduction*.

The next question to explain is of course what the "how-dimension" of reality entails and how it relates to the normativity of life? First of all, these aspects, with the modal universality displayed by each of them, are functional ontic conditions, co-determining whatever concretely exists in subjection to them. They are therefore not merely *modes of thought* (as Descartes already claimed): they have an *ontic* status. A prominent mathematician, Paul Bernays, and a famous logician, Kurt Gödel, both argue for the *ontic* nature of quantitative properties, without identifying this "ontic existence" with concrete material "objects."[2]

Uniqueness and Coherence

The idea of universal modal aspects encompasses the awareness of the above-mentioned *normative contraries* within all the post-sensitive aspects. The theory of modal aspects is a response to the

---

2. Their views are analyzed in more detail in D. F. M. Strauss, "Bernays, Dooyeweerd and Gödel – the Remarkable Convergence in their Reflections on the Foundations of Mathematics," *South African Journal of Philosophy* 30, no. 1 (2011): 70-94.

perennial philosophical problem of *unity and diversity*. Instead of attempting to use a particular aspect as mode of explanation in terms of which one can understand all the others, the uniqueness and irreducibility of each mode is acknowledged. This uniqueness entails an element of *indefinability*, which accounts for the *irreducible core meaning* of each aspect. It is also designated as the *meaning-kernel* of each aspect.

The reverse side of uniqueness is found in *coherence*. The meaning of every unique aspect comes to expression in its *coherence* with other aspects. In the *Introduction* it is explained that these aspects are fitted in an order of before and after and the connections between them are called backward-pointing and forward-pointing analogies, also known as *retrocipations* and *anticipations*.

The underlying *rationale* of this perspective is given in the acknowledgement of a *non-reductionist ontology*. Such an ontology, in turn, depends on a more-than-logical principle, namely the *principium exclusae antinomiae* (the principle of the *excluded antinomy*). This principle forms the foundation of the logical principle of non-contradiction, as explained in the chapter on *Contradiction and Antinomy*.

It should be noted that natural and social entities as well as human beings are not mere "bundles" of functions (aspects or properties), just as little as aspects are merely aspects of individual entities. Entities exceed the boundaries of every aspect and every aspect has a scope transcending the existence of individual entities, as explained in more detail in the chapter on *Modal Universality*.

Against this background *ontic normativity* requires a further explanation. The important point in this context is the insight that the *conditions for being something* do not coincide with whatever *meets* these conditions, not even if these conditions are an instance of *ontic normativity*. The implication is that although human beings undoubtedly *give shape* or *form* to all kinds of *principles*, this reality cannot escape from an *ontic element*. The expression "an ontic element" refers to something *given*, something not *created* by a human being. With reference to Spengler, we have seen that the ontic universality of the quantitative aspect of reality lies at the foundation of all the other modal aspects, including the normative (norming) modes.

Imagine a given *multiplicity* of entities ("objects") in their "pre-counted" condition. The human act of *counting* them normally requires the creation of *number words* or *numerals*. The well-known phrase from the German mathematician, Leopold Kronecker, namely that the integers were made by God and that everything else is the work of humans, is therefore misguided, because humans are not responsible for a given *ontic multiplicity*, they are merely capable to respond to such a given multiplicity by discerning it and by naming the numerals corresponding to the natural numbers and integers as pointed out in the chapter on Dooyeweerd's understanding of infinity.

Discovering or Construing Norms?

Habermas wrestles with the same problem when he remarks that those moral norms which govern the social life of lingual and action-competent subjects as such in a reason-conformative way, are not only "discovered," since they are also at once "construed." He does leave room for something "ontic" (which is "discovered") and for the response of the human subject ("construing" something). In his discussion of the peculiarities of normativity Turner says something similar: "The thingness of normativity is the source of its normative force – it is in some sense outside and inside us at the same time."[3] What is "outside us" corresponds to what Habermas designated as being "discovered" and what is "inside us" is the equivalent of what Habermas designated as "construed." Korsgaard mentions the stance of realism which aims to escape from an infinite regress

---

3. S.B. Turner, *The New Blackwell Companion to the Sociology of Religion* (Oxford: Wiley-Blackwell, 2010), 16.

where the question "why?" is repeatedly asked.

Realism holds that its "move is to bring this regress to an end by fiat: he declares that some things are intrinsically normative."[4]

Distinguishing between (normative) ontic conditions (discovered outside us) and the human response to them boils down to the well-known distinction found in everyday life, namely that between a *principle* and its *application*. Another way in which this state of affairs is captured is by speaking of *giving shape* or *form* to underlying principles. Yet, when humans engage in form-giving activities an *ontic point of departure* is presupposed. Its scope cannot be restricted to a specific place and time since it must have a *universal* appeal. In addition, it must be *constant*, for only applications or acts of form-giving are *varying*. Another important feature of a principle is that it is not *valid* by and of itself: it always requires *human intervention* in order to hold, that is, to be *made valid* or to *be enforced*.

Keep in mind that *natural law* is traditionally appreciated as a *moral* issue that should not be confused with the so-called "laws of nature." Physical laws are therefore not *natural laws* but *laws of nature*.

Modern theories of *natural law* recognized something of the underlying (universal, constant) structure of legal principles but it distorted its meaning by assuming that those underlying principles *are already valid (enforced)* for all times and all places. Nonetheless only human beings can give a positive form or shape to *ontic* principles. The activity of giving form to such underlying principles is sometimes designated as acts of *positivizing* – and the result of such acts is accordingly known as *positivizations*. Habermas explicitly uses this term, for example when he speaks of "the positivization of law."[5]

---

4. C.M. Korsgaard, *The Sources of Normativity* (Cambridge: Cambridge University Press, 1998), 33.
5. J. Habermas, *Between Facts and Norms: Contributions to a Discourse Theory of Law and Democracy*, trans. William Rehg (Cambridge, MA: MIT Press, 1996), 71, and J. Habermas, *Faktizität und Geltung. Beiträge zur Diskurs-*

Already in 1930 the word "Positivierung" was used by Smend.[6] Hartmann also employs the idea of *positivizing* ('Positivierung'). A French legal scholar, François Gény, also draws a sharp distinction between what is *given* (*donné*) and what is *constructed* (*construit*).[7] This distinction runs parallel with that between a given (constant) principle and the multiple ways in which it can be positivized (constructed) in unique historical circumstances ("construit").

The Complexity Entailed in the Concept of a Norm or Principle

The basic distinction between aspects and entities does not provide us with the intellectual tools needed to characterize the complex nature of a principle. We may focus on any particular aspect but we are then at most confronted with its analogical interlinkages with other aspects (retrocipations and anticipations). We may also direct our attention to concrete societal entities (normed social collectivities such as the family, the state or a business enterprise). In both cases we have to account for modal and typical principles. In addition, and distinct from the modal concept of function and type concepts, we have to acknowledge *modal total concepts* that are constituted by the *simultaneous* incorporation of terms derived from multiple, uniquely differing, aspects. The concept of a principle or a norm is an instance of such a *modal totality concept*.

Surely there is much more involved in the concept of a norm or principle than merely acknowledging the *freedom of choice* and *accountability* it presupposes. It is also completely insufficient to characterize a norm merely in terms of what is *desirable* — a characterization often used in the description of *values*. What is at

---

    theorie des Rechts und des demokratischen Rechtsstaats (Frankfurt am Main: Suhrkamp, 1998), 71, 101, 173, 180.
6. R. Smend, *Der Staat als Integration* (Berlin und Leipzig: W. de Gruyter & Co., 1930), 98.
7. F. Gény, *Science et Technique en Droit Privé Positif*, 4 vols., 2nd ed. (Paris: Recueil Sirey, 1922-1930), III:16 ff.

stake is to proceed with an analysis of the meaning of normativity in such a way that the *constitutive contribution* of various aspects is explicitly highlighted.

Since the ontic order of modal aspects commences with the numerical which is then followed by the spatial, kinematic, physical, and so on, an analysis of the nature of principles should start with these foundational aspects — keeping in mind that the normative status of principles entails the possibility of norm-conforming as well as antinormative human (individual and collective) actions.

Without an awareness of the meaning of number it would be impossible to identify a multiplicity of principles. Every one of them serves as a starting-point for *normed* actions. However, such a norming *unitary* point of departure has its own universal domain which cannot be limited to one or a few places — it has to be *universal* in its scope. The notion of *universality* clearly explores our spatial intuition, because it claims that wherever we are (at whatever *place*) the appeal of the principle under consideration is present (an instance of *simultaneity*). Furthermore, such a universal starting-point cannot itself be variable for then it lacks *constancy*. Our insight into the nature of principles is varying, but this does not apply to the nature of principles themselves.

When we start with the numerical aspect the switch to every subsequent aspect adds something more. A principle (*one*), serving as the starting-point of human actions, obtains a closer determination when its *universality* is additionally affirmed (with an appeal to the aspect of space). Another closer determination is introduced when the kinematic intuition is added in the specification that a universal point of departure is *constant*.

The contribution of the first three modal aspects therefore "authorizes" us to state that the following three features are indispensable for an understanding of a principle: a principle is a (i) *universal*, (ii) *constant* (iii) *starting-point* for human action. These hall-marks are not pulled together at random, for they are derived from the three most basic ontic (functional) traits of reality, namely the modes of *number*, *space* and the *kinematic* aspect of uniform, rectilinear movement.

Remark: *Constancy, being static and having validity*

The dynamic process of disclosure, taking place on what we shall designate below as the *norm side* of the normative aspects, shows that we should not identify *constancy* with something *static*. Derrida does comprehend the constitutive meaning of physical force for an understanding of the jural aspect (law):

> Applicability, "enforceability", is not an exterior or secondary possibility that may or may not be added as a supplement to law. It is the force essentially implied in the very concept of justice as law, of justice as it becomes law, of the law as law [*de la loi en tant que droit*].[8]

Hartmann adds:

> By contrast it is here important that these values inherently display the tendency to be realized.[9] If a value is to be realized, and an aim to be achieved, then this goal must first be acknowledged and as such be posited. That is to say, that the value must first be positivized.[10]

To summarize: Every principle is *distinct*, *one* amongst *many others* (number). It is *universal* (derived from our spatial awareness of *everywhere*). And finally, the term *constancy* makes an appeal to the kinematic meaning of uniformity (persistence or constancy).

To appreciate what is here at stake, we have to highlight the difference between the *elementary basic concepts* of the scholarly disciplines and their *compound* or *complex basic concepts*. The former captures the coherence between those aspects delimiting the

---

8. J. Derrida, "Force of Law," in *Acts of Religion*, J. Derrida (London: Routledge, 2002), 233.
9. N. Hartmann, *Ethik* (Berlin und Leipzig: Walter de Gruyter, 1926), 154 ff.
10. Hartmann, *Ethik*, 160 ff.; see R. Horneffer, *Die Entstehung des Staates. Beiträge zum öffentlichen Recht der Gegenwart* (Tübingen: Mohr, 1933), 105.

fields of investigation of the various special sciences and the other aspects of reality (retrocipatory and anticipatory analogies). For example, cause and effect reflect the core meaning of the physical aspect while the science of law employs the (backward-pointing) analogical basic concept of *jural causality*. Alternatively, *aesthetic integrity* is an ethical forward-pointing analogy.

In the case of an *elementary* or *analogical basic concept* only *two* aspects are observed in their inter-modal coherence, although an analysis of the meaning of any elementary basic concept is dependent upon a complex analysis, using terms from more than one aspect.

Does Normativity Exclude Causality?
Since Kant we have become familiar with the dualistic opposition of *causality* and *normativity*.

When Turner pays attention to the normativity of law as a paradigm case[11] he pays attention to neo-Kantianism, without distinguishing between the two schools of thought — the Marburg school (Cohen, Natorp, Cassirer, Kelsen) and the Baden school (Windelband, Rickert, Weber). It is important to take into account that the former mainly returned to the primacy of the science ideal, whereas the latter amended the primacy of the personality ideal. The former school of thought gave rise to the idea of a *pure theory of law* (Kelsen's *reine Rechtslehre*) — as if concept formation within the discipline of law can proceed in *isolation* from the non-jural aspects.

Turner correctly explains that Kelsen advanced a pure theory of law which is stripped of all *causal* elements. He writes that the challenge of a sociological account of the law "pushed Kelsen to formulate a conception of the pure normativity of the law, by which he meant a science of law purified of causal consider-

---

11. S.P. Turner, *Explaining the Normative* (Malden, MA: Polity, 2010), 66 ff.

ations."[12] The physical *law of causality* applies to whatever happens factually. Yet, according to Kelsen, the decisive question is not whether our actions are caused by our will, but rather whether or not the will is *causally determined*.[13] And in line with the modern science ideal Kelsen indeed considers it undeniable that the human will is objectively determined by the law of causality.

For Kelsen the law of causality belongs to the domain of *factuality* (*Sein / is*). By contrast, to the domain of the *Sollen* (ought / normativity) he ascribes the feature of *Geltung* (*validity*). He mentions as an equivalent to this term the expression "*in Kraft*" ("in force") and he holds that all statements of the discipline of law are not assertions belonging to the "is" (*Seinsaussagen*), since they have to be assertions of what "ought to be" (*Sollaussagen*). He also holds that the statement: a particular legal norm is *in force* means the same as: "a particular jural norm is valid." The key terms here are those of *validity* and *being in force*. But they are clearly derived from the *physical aspect* where *causes* and *effects* have their original modal meaning. Validity points at having an effect (being valid), and an effect is intimately connected to the *cause* of such an effect.

The irony of this approach is therefore immediately evident, for in order to escape from the determinism entailed in *physical causality* (the causal law), recourse is taken to the idea that the domain of "Sollen," being totally separate from the domain of "Sein," is characterized merely by "Geltung." Yet the term *Geltung* is *synonymous* with the terms *Kraft* (German) and *force* (English) – and both have no other *source domain* than the *physical* function of reality! Once energy operates it *causes* particular *effects* (causality) in the exercise of physical forces. *Validity* as being-in-force therefore belongs to the same aspectual domain as what became known

---

12. Turner, *Explaining the Normative*, 68.
13. H. Kelsen, *Reine Rechtslehre, Mit einem Anhang: Das Problem der Gerechtigkeit* (Vienna: Verlag Franz Deuticke, 1960), 100.

as the physical and therefore it is just as antinomous as the (neo-) vitalisic claim that living entities are characterized by an *immaterial*, vital *force* (!), since the term *force* is derived from a "material" (i.e., *physical*) context.

The aim is to arrive at an understanding of the "norm" that, in its *validity*, is separated from physical operations, without realizing that the term *validity* is indeed itself derived from the physical function of reality. On the one hand, Kelsen emphatically argues that, since the *validity* of the norm is a "Sollen," which is not a "Sein," its *validity* must be distinguished from its operation (*Wirksamkeit*). On the other hand, he promotes the operation of the legal order to be the condition (*Bedingung*) of *Geltung*.[14]

The neo-Kantian dualism between *is* and *ought* moved Kelsen to a position in which he wanted to say something "purely" in legal or jural terms, separated from the inherent causality of the realm of *Sein*. But since also the jural aspect of reality can only reveal its meaning through its coherence with other aspects, it turned out to be impossible to avoid the causal physical analogy within the structure of the jural aspect, as it is present in the way in which Kelsen unwittingly coined the analogical concepts *jural validity* and *jural being-in-force*.

Furthermore, as a serious legal positivist, Kelsen distances himself from natural law theories. But once again, his conception of the *Grundnorm* (basic norm) had to surrender to the enemy by accepting a (pre-positive) starting point serving as the "ultimate reason for the *validity* (!) of all the legal norms forming the legal order":

A *Grundnorm* is a "basic norm" because nothing further can be asked about the reason for its validity, since it is not a posited norm but a presupposed norm. It is not a positive norm, posited by a real act of will, but a norm presupposed in juridical thinking, i.e., a fictitious norm — as was indicated previously. It represents

---

14. Kelsen, *Reine Rechtslehre*, 82.

the ultimate reason for the validity of all the legal norms forming the legal order. Only a norm can be the reason for the validity of another norm.[15]

Unless the antinomic dualism between *Sein* and *Sollen* is rejected, on Kelsen's standpoint no single *jural fact* could be established. For example, stealing something has no *jural* meaning apart from the application of *jural norms*. A burglary as (factual) material delict causes loss and this specific jural effect also cannot be established apart from the application of jural norms. This means that jural normativity inherently contains a physical analogy and therefore cannot ever be divorced from the inter-modal coherence between the jural aspect and (one of) its foundational aspects, namely the physical mode.[16]

Moreover, as Dooyeweerd observes, the domain of civil private law (common law) is presupposed in recognizing this legal fact, for such an infringement of a property right enables one to speak of *unlawfully laying claim to what rightfully belongs to the legitimate owner*. In this account, the nature of jural causality once again is inherently normatively structured — suggesting that we should not try to avoid speaking of causality within the domain of law, but rather that we should account for the difference between *physical causality* and *jural causality* in order to avoid all kinds of antinomies. When the science of law naturalistically defines a human action as *a willed muscle movement*, no *omission* will be possible. Not switching a train signal to unsafe when one had the *obligation* to do it, and therefore not moving a single muscle, may cause a train accident in a *jural* sense, which explains why legal practice speaks of an action both as a *commission* and as an *omission*.

---

15. H. Kelsen, *General Theory of Norms*, trans. Michael Hartney (Oxford: Clarendon Press, 1991), 255.
16. An extensive analysis of *Jural Causality* is found in H. Dooyeweerd, *Essays in Legal, Social and Political Philosophy*, Collected Works of Herman Dooyeweerd, Series B, vol. 2, General Editor D.F.M. Strauss (Lewiston, NY: Edwin Mellen, 1997).

Moreover, every discipline which find its field of investigation delimited by one of the normative modes employs its own distinct concept of causality. Just contemplate the relationship between premise and conclusion (*logical causality*), or *historical causes* and *effects*, or *social causality*, and so on.

45

Compound Basic Concepts

by Danie F. M. Strauss

IN THE CHAPTER on *Ontic Normativity* we explained that *jural causality* represents an elementary (analogical) basic concept of the discipline of law. Yet the concept of a jural principle or norm, or a norm in general, is more complex, because any meaningful definition of a norm is constituted by terms derived from multiple modal aspects.

Terms derived from the first three aspects provide us with a foundational perspective: every principle is a constant, universal starting-point for human action. This formulation highlights the *pre-positive* meaning of a principle, because their ontic universality and constancy principles do not display any *validity* since they are not yet *in force*. The Dutch and Afrikaans term "beginsel" literally indicates a *point of departure* or a *starting-point*. If one only has the starting-point of a line, the line itself should be envisaged as an *extension*, moving ahead from the point of departure. And it is only by virtue of this "moving ahead" that the starting-point given in a principle can be embodied within concrete reality. Since describing such a starting-point had to use terms derived from the first three modal aspects, captured in their reverse order by the statement that a principle is a constant, universal point of departure for human action, the next modal aspect which has to be taken into account is the *physical aspect*.

We know that this aspect concerns physical inter-actions having certain effects and therefore embodies the relation between cause and effect (causality). It is noteworthy to mention that Heisenberg describes *determinism* as follows: "If one interprets the word causality in such a strict sense, one also speaks of determinism and means by it that there exist laws of nature determining univocally from the present the future condition of a system."[1] Indeterminism believes that the entire concept of causality must be discarded. In order to avoid both these extremes one can say: *nothing happens without a cause – but what the effect of a specific cause may be need not be fixed in advance*. This formulation grants determinism that the concept of a *cause* is meaningful and should not be discarded, as claimed by indeterminism and it grants indeterminism that the *effect* need not be fixed in advance (just think of the half-value of radio-active elements), thus highlighting the untenability of determinism in this regard.

Only when the explanatory power of terms derived from the physical aspect are added to our analysis of the compound basic concept "principle" is it possible to account for *making* principles *valid* or of the *enforcement* of principles. Once a universal, constant starting-point has been made valid, it obtained a positive shape, a concrete form. Therefore, prior to its *being made valid* it displays its *pre-positive* form. Yet it is only human beings who can give a positive form to pre-positive principles. Therefore, human intervention is required if pre-positive principles are made valid. The *validity* of a positivized principle shows that it *holds*, that it is *in force*.

Once the involvement of human beings is recognized, we can proceed by exploring modal terms derived from the post-physical aspects as well. What we have in mind are terms derived from the biotic, sensitive, logical-analytical, historical and sign modes. To account for the *positive form* of a principle we need to employ terms coming from these other aspects. Consider human desires and feelings (what someone wills – the sensitive mode), accountability (manifest in the normative contrary of norm-conforming or antinormative actions), a competent organ (terms derived from the biotic and the cultural-historical aspects) and interpretation (the lingual). From the cultural-historical aspect of formative control

---

1. W. Heisenberg, *Das Naturbild der heutigen Physik* (Hamburg: Rowohlt, 1956), 25.

(power/competence) we actually derive the general idea of a principle and its application, its *positivization*.

We are in a position to attempt a nuanced articulation of the way in which a principle can be described in the light of the foregoing considerations:

> A principle is a universal, constant starting-point, that can only be made valid (enforced) by a competent organ with an accountable free will enabling a norm-conforming or antinormative positivization of the (ontically) given point-of-departure in the light of an adequate (or inadequate) interpretation of the unique historical circumstances in which the principle concerned is applied.

Surely human beings, in their individual and collective societal actions, are always guided by norms and humans constantly give shape to basic principles. This at once also explains why humans, functioning in diverse societal relations, do not cease to be norm-oriented – for in these instances they have to observe *collective societal norms*. When a just state acts in the pursuit of public justice, it has to observe collective norms that are embedded in the ontically given type law for being a state. Moreover, when a just state strives to secure and protect basic rights, it assumes a task that could be performed in a better or worse manner.

Modal and Typical Norms
At this point we have to introduce another distinction already alluded to in other chapters, namely that between *modal* and *typical* norms. Modal norms (similar to *modal laws* within the natural aspects of reality) are universal in scope without any restriction or specification. Individuals as well as societal collectivities all function alike within all the normative modal aspects, including the logical-analytical, the cultural-historical, the sign mode, the economic aspect, the aesthetic function, the jural, moral and certitudinal. When one proceeds further up the order of normative aspects, each next one adds another modal term to its specific compound concept of modal normativity.

For example, individuals as well as families, states and business enterprises have to observe economic considerations of frugality. From a universal modal economic perspective this entails that the contrary *economic-uneconomic* applies across board. It means that the scope of economic norms is applicable to whatever functions within the economic aspect (all classes of entities). Type-laws, by contrast, are specified and therefore they apply to a *limited class* of entities only. They display a *specified universality*. The normative principle (structural principle or type-law) for being a state is universal in that it applies to *all* states, but it is *specified* because it applies to states *only* and not to all possible classes of entities. What Korsgaard designates as *practical identities* refers to the multiple social roles anyone can assume.[2] The normativity involved in these multiple identities are instantiations of normative societal type-laws which specify the modal universality of the various norming modal aspects.

Perhaps the most important feature of modal norms is that they can be discerned through an analysis of the analogical links between the various aspects of reality, because, as we have noted, within all modal aspects we find a strict correlation between their law sides (norm sides) and their factual sides. In order to identify modal norms, one therefore has to analyze the inter-modal coherence on the law side of the normative aspects of reality and the other aspects.

Discerning Modal Norms

We argued that the possibility of discerning modal norms or principles is given in the inter-modal coherence between any normative aspect as it comes to expression in the retrocipations and anticipations on its norm side. The well-known contrary *legal-illegal* presupposes the normativity of the jural aspect and analogically reflects the meaning of the logical principle of non-contradiction.

Let us begin our discussion of modal norms by looking at the analogy of the economic aspect within the jural aspect as it is explained by Dooyeweerd in an article on the *modal structure of jural causality*.

---

2. C. M. Korsgaard, *The Sources of Normativity* (Cambridge: University Press, 1998), 17-18, 117-118, 128, 174-178.

The economic analogy in the legal relation of balance concerns the economical handling of legal means and interests of others within the context of alternative possible choices a person is free to pursue. Every excessive, every unrestrained exploration of one's own legal interest, within legal life, is an interrupting causal intervention in the legal balance of interests against which the legal order reacts with restorative legal consequences. The driver of a car, who, when another car approaches from a side-street, continues driving on a road that gives the first-mentioned motorist the right of way, does not cause the subsequent accident when the same driver had no reason to expect that the other motorist would not yield. However, if the first motorist still continues to drive on, while having had the opportunity to stop in time after realizing that the other driver had disobeyed the traffic rules, then the loss-causing effect should also be imputed to the former's act since it is in conflict with the *principle of jural economy* and constitutes as such an excessive pursuit of one's own legal interest.[3]

The picture may be reversed when we focus on an anticipation within the economic aspect of which we are well aware in our everyday experience. Modern money economies are guided by the principle of *economic trust* – and when this trust fades an entire economic system may suffer, as was amply demonstrated by the international economic crisis of 2008 (compare the position of ENRON). Although he does not operate with a theory of modal aspects, Jacques Derrida places *credit* against the background of economic trust (faith). He acknowledges the universality of "faith" by stressing that "faith is absolutely universal,"[4] and then, with reference to credit [as economic trust] he states:

> There is no society without faith, without trust in the other. Even if I abuse this, if I lie or if I commit perjury, if I am violent because of this faith, even on the economic level, there is no society without this

---

3. H. Dooyeweerd, *Essays in Legal, Social and Political Philosophy*, Collected Works of Herman Dooyeweerd, Series B, vol. 2, General Editor D.F.M. Strauss (Lewiston, NY: Edwin Mellen, 1997), 65.
4. J. Derrida, *Deconstruction in a Nutshell, A Conversation with Derrida*, ed. John D. Caputo (New York: Fordham University Press, 1997), 22.

faith, this minimal act of faith. What one calls credit in capitalism, in economics, has to do with faith, and the economists know that. But this faith is not and should not be reduced or defined by religion as such.[5]

In societies where the meaning of economic life is not yet opened up through anticipatory analogies, *economic trust* in the sense of *credit* is absent. Within such societies, an *exchange economy* is found.

Another example will explore a few elements of the retrocipatory and anticipatory analogies within the cultural-historical aspect. The kinematic analogy within the cultural-historical aspect, which at once reveals its own foundational coherence with the spatial aspect, is found in the norm of historical continuity. The struggle between *progressive* and *reactionary* tendencies in history may result in the antinormative options of *revolution* or *reaction*. But when the norm of *historical continuity* prevails, these extremes are turned into norm-conformative *reformation*.

Likewise, when the meaning of the cultural-historical aspect is deepened and disclosed through its anticipatory analogies, the first element of deepening the meaning of the historical aspect is found when the awareness of what is *historically significant* materializes in *inscriptions, monuments, written historical accounts*, and so on. The latter serve as *sources* for the historian. The difference between what is historically significant and what is insignificant is made possible by the anticipatory coherence between the cultural-historical aspect and the sign mode. Cultures in which this anticipatory moment is not yet disclosed do not, strictly speaking, participate in world history, as Hegel already realized.

Similarly, the meaning of the jural aspect is not yet disclosed in the practice of a tooth for a tooth and an eye for an eye (the *lex talionis*).

In pursuing a more encompassing analysis of modal norms we commence with the example of *logical principles*.

---

5. Derrida, *Deconstruction in a Nutshell*, 23.

COMPOUND BASIC CONCEPTS

The numerical aspect is foundational to the logical aspect. For this reason, we find *numerical analogies* within the logical-analytical aspect. The failure to appreciate this foundational position of the numerical aspect (in an *ontic* sense), tempted Frege, Peano, Whitehead and Russell to reduce the meaning of number to the logical mode, which at once meant that they believed that mathematics ought to be reduced to logic. Quine mentions Frege, who "claimed in 1884 to have proved in this way, contrary to Kant, that the truths of arithmetic are analytic. But logic capable of encompassing this reduction was logic inclusive of set theory."[6] Weyl goes one step further when he states that mathematics is totally – also according to the logical form in which it operates – dependent upon the essence of the natural numbers and induction.[7]

Phrased from the perspective of the analytical mode, the nature of analysis, owing to its quantitative foundation, differentiates into *identification* and *distinguishing*. When a mathematician says that x is different from y ($x * y$), then both the original meaning of number and its analogical recurrence within the logical analytical mode is present. The contribution of the primitive spatial meaning of continuous extension (which is synonymous with the whole-parts relation), is found in the specification acquired by analysis because identification and distinguishing rest upon subdivisions from a given *field*, *domain* or *totality*.

The numerical analogy on the norm side of the analytical aspect presents itself in the configuration of a *logical unity and multiplicity*. The positive side of this analogy provides the ultimate (modal-analogical) foundation for the *logical principle of identity* (whatever is distinctly identified is identical to itself). Based upon what is distinct the logical principle of contradiction demands that whatever is *distinct* ought not to be considered as being *identical*.

In other words, the numerical analogy on the norm side of the analytical aspect explores the two sides of *unity* and *multiplicity*,

---

6. W.V.O. Quine, *Philosophy of Logic* (Englewood Cliffs: Prentice Hall, 1970), 66.
7. H. Weyl, *Philosophie der Mathematik und Naturwissenschaft*, 3rd rev. ed. (Vienna: R. Oldenburg, 1966), 52 ff., 71 ff., 86 ff.

and thus serves as the basis of the two most basic logical principles underlying every analytical act of identification and distinguishing. The freedom of choice in the human ability to identify and distinguish can pursue the option to identify and distinguish properly (correctly) or improperly (incorrectly). The former is achieved when acts of identification and distinguishing conform to the logical principles of identity and non-contradiction, while the latter prevails whenever the normative appeal of these principles is violated. The unity and diversity within reality thus make possible all instances of identification and distinguishing – guided by the normative demand to identify A with A and to distinguish A from non-A. Therefore, taking into account their direct ontic foundation, the primary formulation of these two principles may be phrased as follows:

1) Identity: Within what is analyzable, A will always be identical to A.
2) Non-contradiction: Within what is analyzable, A will never be identical to non-A.

The act of identification entails an affirmation, and the act of distinguishing entails a denial — affirming that A is A is at once denying that A is non-A. This brings *truth* and *falsehood* into the picture, and therefore makes possible an alternative formulation of these principles in terms of truth and falsity — as done by Copi in his standard *Introduction to Logic*:

> The principle of identity asserts that if any statement is true, then it is true.
>
> The principle of contradiction asserts that no statement can be both true and false.
>
> The principle of the excluded middle asserts that any statement is either true or false.[8]

---

8. I.M. Copi, *Introduction to Logic,* 9th ed. (New York: Macmillan, 1994), 372.

COMPOUND BASIC CONCEPTS

In axiomatic set theory, two classes v and w are said to be identical if and only if they have exactly the same members.[9] One can also take the equality symbol ("=") to denote *identity*. Lemmon's choice is "to take identity as a primitive notion... and regard it as part of our underlying logical framework."[10] Where equality is understood to denote identity, it is also regarded as belonging to the underlying logic.[11] Weyl speaks of logical identity ('x = y') as a two-valued (*zweistellige*) relation,[12] and later on, in the context of his discussion of automorphisms, he characterizes identity as a one-to-one mapping.

When a mathematician does not accept *infinite totalities* (such as is the case with intuitionism), the logical principle of the *excluded middle* is not applicable. Of course, in the finite case the bifurcation of A and non-A excludes any third possibility. However, in order to ensure the *universal* applicability of this logical principle, the anticipatory idea of infinite totalities must be acknowledged. This idea explores a spatial anticipation within the meaning of the numerical aspect. Therefore, via the (retrocipatory) analogy of number within the structure of logical analysis, this principle finds its ultimate foundation in the numerical anticipation to the meaning of space. This justifies the claim that the ontic status of the principle of the excluded middle is found in the fact that it is a *retrocipation to an anticipation*! In other words, the meaning of the principle of the excluded middle is in a retrocipation from the logical-analytical mode to the arithmetical mode, which in turn anticipates towards the factual spatial whole-parts relation in subjection to and determined by the spatial time order of simultaneity.[13]

The logical *movement* from premise to conclusion analogical-

---

9. E. J. Lemmon, *Introduction to Axiomatic Set Theory* (London: Routledge & Kegan Paul, 1968), 10.
10. Lemmon, *Introduction*, 11.
11. A. Fraenkel, Y. Bar-Hillel, A. Levy, and D. Van Dalen, *Foundations of Set Theory*, 2nd rev. ed. (Amsterdam: North-Holland, 1973), 25.
12. Weyl, *Philosophie der Mathematik*, 19.
13. See D.F.M. Strauss, "The Ontological Status of the Principle of the Excluded Middle," *Philosophia Mathematica* II, 6 no. 1 (1991): 73-90.

ly reflects the meaning of the kinematic and physical aspects. The principle of sufficient ground, providing another specification of the physical analogy on the norm side of the logical-analytical aspect, exceeds the confines of the logical aspect, for whereas the principle of non-contradiction cannot tell which one of two contradictory statements is true, the principle of sufficient reason points beyond logic to the *grounds* helping us to decide which one actually is true.

The modal norms of logical differentiation and integration on the norm side of the logical aspect serve as a foundation for the *logical sensitivity* required from *discerning* logical subjects. When, through modal abstraction, a particular modal aspect is identified and distinguished from others, special scientific thought acquires a *logically* integrating *control* or *mastery* over a given knowledge domain – highlighting the cultural-historical anticipation within the logical-analytical aspect and explaining the nature of *systematic* thought. Particularly scientific terminology strives towards a consistent, univocal and therefore unambiguous use of its symbols and terms. Deepened logical thinking flourishes in the logical interaction between argument and counter-argument (social anticipation). The principle of thought-economy (Occam's razor) is well-known because it favours thought-economy above tedious and cumbersome arguments. The latter creates logical harmony and is embedded in the required logical justification (the aesthetic and jural anticipations). The logical integrity with which scholars have to proceed leads to logical trust or logical confidence – which is an indispensable element of argumentative competence, apart from the fact that an axiom is an instance of logical certainty.

Human Intervention Required

If human beings can only give shape to pre-positive universal and constant principles, then, as we noted, principles cannot obtain *validity* apart from human intervention. Only human beings can positivize principles in concrete historical circumstances. This view accounts both for the ontic conditions and the active involvement of human agents in the positivization of principles. But there is more at stake.

COMPOUND BASIC CONCEPTS

A distinction ought to be drawn between the principles norming human activities, and the norm-conformative (or: antinormative) ways in which human beings can respond to underlying principles. In the case of societal entities and processes, there is always a difference between "structures for" and "structures of." For example, the scope of the structural principle for being a state encompasses all past, present and future states, wherever they may be found – whereas any concretely existing state, in being a state, exhibits the reality that it *is* a state. *Being a state* is the universal way in which any particular state shows that it is subject to the structure for being a state, that is, the structural principle, norming every state. The modern idea of autonomy, as well as the idea of the *social construction of the world*, reify the human freedom to positivize. At the same time, it denies the existence of universal and constant principles underlying every human act of shaping and form-giving (positivization).

Anthony Giddens wrestled with these issues in his own way in introducing his theory of structuration in order to emphasize the actuality of temporal societal processes through which such societal structures are produced and reproduced. According to him, a "double hermeneutic" is implied in all forms of sociological theorizing, because the scholar is simultaneously participant and analyst.[14] The acknowledgement of the "subject-dependency" of societal structures explains why Giddens prefers to speak of "structuration" instead merely of "structure." Structuration embodies the typical human activities of positivizing the type-laws (structural principles) of societal collectivities.

Concluding Remark

Because human beings cannot at one and the same time be the conditions for being human and the subjects conforming to these conditions, it is necessary to acknowledge *ontic normativity*. This makes it possible to discern different kinds of (modal) norms and also provides a way in which we can analyze universal modal norms. Once this is done one can proceed by analyzing the typical way in

---

14. C. Calhoun, J. Gerteis, J. Moody, S. Pfaff, and I. Virk, eds., *Contemporary Sociological Theory* (Oxford: Blackwell, 2002), 222.

which the various societal type-laws specify (not: individualize) the universal meaning of modal principles.[15]

The integral account of modal and typical principles transcends the inherent dilemma of all dialectical approaches to normativity. Within the order of modal aspects those belonging to nature (from the numerical up to the sensory) are not *handicaps, impediments* or *obstacles* in the way of human freedom. Rather they form unavoidable, enabling, foundational conditions, necessary for the existence of accountable human freedom. Both norm-conformative and antinormative actions operate on *the basis of* foundational conditions and therefore can never (dialectically) be appreciated as a threat to freedom. Just consider the acknowledgment phrased by Jaspers: "Since freedom is only through and against nature, as freedom it must fail. Freedom is only when nature is."[16]

---

15. See H. Dooyeweerd, *A New Critique of Theoretical Thought*, vol. 3, Collected Works of Herman Dooyeweerd, Series A, General Editor D.F.M. Strauss (Lewiston, NY: Edwin Mellen, 1997), 157-693.
16. K. Jaspers, *Philosophie* (Berlin: Springer Verlag, 1948), 871.

46

Traditional Societies

by Danie F. M. Strauss

IT IS CUSTOMARY to refer to *traditional societies* when *undifferentiated* societies are investigated. Lowie, for example, who is known for his work on *Culture and Ethnology*, published one of the classical works in the field of ethnology under the title *Primitive Society* (1921). At the time he was the Associate Curator, *Anthropology*, at the *American Museum of Natural History*.

Normally the *extended family* ("*Grossfamilie*") is identified as the smallest *undifferentiated society*. It is striking that societies such as these are bound together on the basis of an *undifferentiated form of organization*.

The cultural anthropologist Kammler identifies the following characteristics of undifferentiated societies. First of all, technology is undeveloped in such societies. In the second place, they lack a large degree of societal differentiation, which entails that most of what we are familiar with in a differentiated society are at most present in undifferentiated societies in a *rudimentary* form. Kammler therefore distinguishes between *differentiated societies* and *undifferentiated societies*.[1] It should be noted that even at the lowest level of technological and economic development, undifferentiated societies display elements of *social ordering* which in particular include a politi-

---

1. H. Kammler, *Der Ursprung des Staates, Eine Kritik der Ueberlagerungslehre* (Köln: Westdeutscher Verlag, 1966), 17-18.

cal element, evinced in relations of super- and subordination.[2] We shall return to this point below in connection with the distinction between subject-object relations and subject-subject relations.

An Undifferentiated Form of Organization

Within differentiated societies, each distinct social form of life has its own form of organization. The administration of the state differs from that of a business enterprise, a university, an ecclesiastical denomination, and so on. These distinct forms of organization are dependent upon some or other unique aspect of reality serving as its *characteristic* or *qualifying function* (*guiding function*). This means that the actions of a state, embracing government and subjects, are directed by jural considerations, focused on the integration of a multiplicity of legal interests into one public legal order. Similarly, a business enterprise finds its guiding principle in the economic aspect, a sport club in the social aspect, a church denomination in the aspect of faith, and so on.

Yet within undifferentiated societies such a distinct qualifying function is absent, because within them the leading role is assigned to one of the intertwined *societal entities*. This means that what Groen van Prinsterer approximated and what Abraham Kuyper and Herman Dooyeweerd designated as the principle of *sphere sovereignty*, has not yet been realized in undifferentiated societies. It was Jean Bodin who introduced, as a distinctive feature of political authority, the term "sovereignty." Since one of the interlaced societal entities fulfill the leading role in an undifferentiated society, such a society in its totality will act in *different societal capacities*. As a whole it will act as an *economic entity* which is equivalent to what we discern within a differentiated society as a business enterprise. The same applies to the whole of society acting as a *political unit*, which within differentiated societies will assume the form of a state. Because undifferentiated societies

---

2. Kammler, *Der Ursprung des Staates*, 30.

share in an undifferentiated organizational form, the possibility of any of the above-mentioned differentiated qualifying functions is absent here. Instead, the various social forms of life—which will eventually and inescapably surface in the course of a gradual process of cultural-historical differentiation, disclosure and integration—are bound together in an undifferentiated manner. From this angle we can state that an undifferentiated society does not merely exhibit an economic aspect, because as a whole it acts as something which is recognized on a differentiated cultural level as economically qualified (regardless whether it be an economy of hunting-gathering, agriculture, or animal husbandry). An undifferentiated society also does not merely exhibit a juridical aspect, for it acts as a whole as something similar to what much later came to be identified as a *state* within a differentiated society. The same applies to the faith aspect—the undifferentiated society acts as a whole in cultic-religious capacity, similar to a differentiated collective faith community. Within the undifferentiated total organizational form, a variety of typical structural branches are therefore found, such that each one of them, alternatively, can bring into action the entire undifferentiated society. Within differentiated societies distinct and independent societal forms of life perform these activities.

From the *Grossfamilie* to the Sib and Clan

In addition to the *Grossfamilie* (extended family) the sib also represents an undifferentiated society. The *sib* (as the Americans designate it) or the *clan* (as British anthropologists prefer to denote it)[3] is more encompassing, while the *tribe* displays a stronger (political) organization. This state of affairs implies that the correlate of an undifferentiated foundation (namely, one all-encompassing form of organization) is given in what may be called an *undifferentiated qualification*, because instead of a qualifying aspect of reality,

---

3. See R. H. Lowie, *Primitive Society* (London: George Routledge & Sons, 1921), 105.

one of the "not-yet-differentiated" societal structures, intertwined within the encompassing whole, assumes the leading or guiding role. In the case of the extended family, which binds parents, children and grandchildren together in a patriarchal unit, the patriarch and the oldest son are positioned in such a way that it reflects a specific kind of historical power organization which cannot be explained exclusively on the basis of the blood relationship existing between them.

The extended family does not merely display the structure of a family, because in its undifferentiated total structure, other social forms of life are also intertwined. In particular, the intertwined political structure is observed in the (political) force with which internal order and peace is maintained. Similarly, the economic enterprise is recognized by the way in which the subsistence economy operates. However, the decisive question is: Can we establish which one of the interwoven social forms of life present in such a society actually plays a leading role in its undifferentiated total structure? It appears that within the *Grossfamilie* the interwoven extended family structure is truly of a central leading nature, even though as such it does not inherently possess an enduring structure of super- and sub-ordination.[4]

The *sib* (clan or *gentes*), which apparently only appears when agriculture and livestock farming partly or completely replaces hunting as the basis of economic life, is constituted by a larger group of organized relations (where either only the father's or the mother's line of descent is taken into account). Although membership in the extended family is normally dependent upon blood relationship (natural birth), the sib is so large that it is no longer possible to assume direct descent from a communal father—although such descent may function as a fictitious presupposition or

---

4. See the extensive analysis of H. Dooyeweerd, *A New Critique of Theoretical Thought*, vol. 3, Collected Works of Herman Dooyeweerd, Series A, General Editor D.F.M. Strauss (Lewiston, NY: Edwin Mellen, 1997), 346–376.

mythological conception. Besides activities like the ancestor cult (typical of an eventually differentiated cultic institution), taking revenge (which at a higher level of development is executed by an independent state), and the presence of forms of division of labor, also the family structure is present in the sib. In reality this interwoven family structure takes on the undifferentiated leading role within the sib—a leading role which, as noted above, rests on a particular historical form of power organization (just as in the case of the extended family). This feature anticipates the stronger political organization of the tribe.

The Stronger Political Organization of the Tribe

Vinogradoff mainly employs features of the sib to define a tribe when he states that when human society "has assumed the form of a tribe" it is "an association based mainly on real or supposed kinship."[5]

Only within the much stronger organized tribe does the political organization assume the leading role. But this role does not yet entail an enduring monopolistic organization of the sword power. This is clear from the fact that fights between members do not provoke any tribal punishment, because only a relative of someone killed in such a fight could consider revenge (in the context of the *lex talionis*). It is also necessary to keep in mind that our current acquaintance with the correlation between legal rights and legal remedies was absent in undifferentiated societies where there was not yet an integrated monopoly of power on a limited territory capable of enforcing the resolution of legal conflicts. Regarding the absence of this correlation Vinogradoff remarks: "And yet it is with such states of society that we have to deal in early Germanic as well as early Greek and Roman Law. When self-help was the principal mode of enforcing right, when juridical conflicts commonly resolved themselves into feuds, or had to be managed

---

5. P. Vinogradoff, *Essays in Legal History* (New York: WM. W. Gaunt & Sons, 1993), 10.

by arbitration, when even legal proceedings were initiated by ceremonial agreements, the practical enforcement of liability naturally took the shape of an appeal, not to public force, but to private execution."[6]

Noteworthy is that although tribal law ensured the presence of particular kinds of legal order, there was no uniform integration of legal rules, apart from the fact that every tribe had its own law. According to Berman this situation applied to the "Franks, Alemanns, Frisians, Visigoths, Ostrogoths, Burgundians, Lombards, East Saxons, Vandals, Suevi, and other peoples that were eventually combined in the Frankish Empire, embracing much of what later became Germany, France, and northern Italy; the Angles, West Saxons, Jutes, Celts, Britons, and other peoples of what later became England; the Danes, Norwegians, and other Norsemen of Scandinavia and later of Normandy, Sicily, and elsewhere; and many others, from Picts and Scots to Magyars and Slavs."[7]

The subsequent developments during the Middle Ages are addressed in other chapters.

---

6. Vinogradoff, *Essays in Legal History*, 8.
7. H. J. Berman, *Law and Revolution. The Formation of the Western Legal Tradition* (London: Harvard University Press, 1983), 52.

47

Differentiation and Integration

by Danie F. M. Strauss

Increasing Differentiation and Integration – A Perspective on Societal Development

IN A CERTAIN SENSE one may see in *integration* a task running parallel with differentiation. Prior to the late eleventh and early twelfth centuries, diverse legal rules and procedures prevailed within the distinct legal orders of the West. Berman points out that these legal orders were "largely *undifferentiated* from social custom and from political and religious institutions." No attempt was made to integrate the prevailing laws and legal institutions into a unified legal order. This situation was understandable if we consider that very little of the law existed in writing and that there was not yet a professional judiciary (no professional class of lawyers and an absence of professional legal literature). No conscious effort was made to systematize law because it "had not yet been 'disembedded' from the whole social matrix of which it was a part. There was no independent, integrated, developing body of legal principles and procedures clearly differentiated from other processes of social organization and consciously articulated by a corps of persons specially trained for that task."[1]

What is striking in some of the typical undifferentiated societal entities, which lasted up to the French Revolution, is that they embraced different types of communities—just think of the above-mentioned *guilds*—and the same applies to medieval *towns*, which were

---

1. H. J. Berman, *Law and Revolution: The Formation of the Western Legal Tradition* (Cambridge, MA: Harvard University Press, 1983), 50.

dependent upon the customs and privileges granted to them by the feudal lords. Their relative autonomy therefore included much more than what eventually was captured by the acknowledgment of different societal spheres with their own *inner laws*. Although he still adheres to the universalistic (holistic) implications of sociological *system theory* (with its emphasis on systems and subsystems, i.e., *wholes and parts*), some of the formulations articulated by the sociologist Münch, who analyzed processes of differentiation, do reveal a sound view of a differentiated society. In line with his system theoretic approach, he explains that "[D]ifferentiation means the growing autonomy of subsystems of interaction which have their own rules."[2] Yet on the previous page he correctly refers to the theory of the rationalization of modern society developed by Max Weber, who holds that this resulted into spheres of society "that are guided to an increasing extent by their own inner laws." Within the legacy of the Anti-Revolutionary Party in the Netherlands, Groen van Prinsterer already in the 19th century captured the same idea by introducing the phrase sphere sovereignty. He influenced Abraham Kuyper who erected the Free University of Amsterdam in 1880 and whose opening address in that year was entitled *Sphere Sovereignty*.[3]

His plea was that an academic institution (such as the Free University), owing to its sphere sovereignty, ought to be free from interference both by the Church and the State. He influenced Herman Dooyeweerd who further explored the implications of the principle

---

2. R. Münch, "Differentiation, Rationalization, Interpenetration: The Emergence of Modern Society," in *Differentiation Theory and Social Change*, ed. J. C. Alexander and Paul Colomy (New York: Columbia University Press, 1990), 443.

3. In passing we may note that Kuyper, in spite of his adherence to the idea of sphere sovereignty, at the same time was still influenced by an organic view of human society, revealing ideas advanced in the romantic movement and intellectual schemes going back to the thought of Aristotle. This explains why he designated the state as an "ethical organism" (*zedelijk organisme*) and why he advocated an organic idea of the right to vote, which he reserved for the (male) head of households, similar to what Rawls holds in his *Theory of Justice* (see J. Rawls, *A Theory of Justice*, rev. ed. [Cambridge, MA: Harvard University Press, 1999], 111.)

of sphere sovereignty in a non-reductionist ontology (including his theory of modal aspects) and who in particular made it fruitful in his analysis of the structure of human society.

John Rawls clearly stumbled upon the implications entailed in the principle of sphere sovereignty when he writes: "Thus, although the principles of justice do not apply directly to the internal life of churches, they do protect the rights and liberties of their members by the constraints to which all churches and associations are subject."[4]

Rawls is just one of many prominent contemporary social thinkers who, in spite of exploring a systems-theoretical approach, do reveal an insight into the uniqueness of different societal entities. For example, in spite of the fact that Rawls's thought is torn apart by atomistic and holistic affinities, he does acknowledge different societal principles holding for distinct kinds of subjects: "But it is the distinct purposes and roles of the parts of the social structure, and how they fit together, that explains there being different principles for distinct kinds of subjects."[5]

On the same page he alludes to the distinctive autonomy of elements in society, where principles within their own sphere fit their peculiar nature. This way of addressing the issues undoubtedly approximates the idea of sphere sovereignty. Just consider these words: "Indeed, it seems natural to suppose that the distinctive character and autonomy of the various elements of society requires that, within some sphere, they act from their own principles designed to fit their peculiar nature"! These formulations support our pledge for a limited positioning of the state within a differentiated society.

Surely one cannot argue in terms of a whole-parts relation (systems and subsystems) *and* at the same time attempt to advocate an acknowledgment of the "own inner laws" of societal entities. Yet the mere fact that leading sociological theorists adhere (at least partially) to a perspective of "own inner laws" shows that they can contribute

---

4. J. Rawls, *Collected Papers*, ed. Samuel Freeman (Cambridge, MA: Harvard University Press, 2001), 597.
5. J. Rawls, *Political Liberalism*, rev. ed. (Cambridge, MA: Harvard University Press, 1996), 262.

to a better understanding of the issue under discussion.

Parting Ways: Church and State

Because the guild system obstructed the realization of a genuine state-organization it was imperative for the differentiation of society to break down the artificial hold of power of the Roman Catholic Church. This increasingly occurred during the period subsequent to the Renaissance, which witnessed a process of societal differentiation that took shape. This process was decisive for the emergence of the modern state because it generated the *distinct legal interests* which eventually had to be bound together within the public legal order of the state. The first major step in this process of differentiation is therefore given in dissolving the unified ecclesiastical culture of the Roman Catholic Church. This process initiated the differentiation of church and what eventually became known as the *state*. Later on, in a similar process of differentiation, the nuclear family and the business enterprise each came into their own during the Industrial Revolution.

In part at least, one can see the disintegration of the unified ecclesiastical culture of the late medieval period as the outcome of the untenable synthesis between ancient Greek views and those of biblical Christianity. According to Berman, this attempted synthesis resulted in splitting life into "two realms, the eternal and the temporal," with the result that "the temporal was thereby depreciated in value."[6] During the transition from the medieval era to the modern dispensation, the speculative metaphysics of *universalia* (universals) was questioned by the new nominalistic movement.[7]

---

6. Berman, *Law and Revolution*, 82.
7. More detail about this movement with its historical significance for the rise of the modern idea of the state is found in the work of Waldecker, *Allgemeine Staatslehre* (Berlin: Rotschild, 1927), and Von Hippel, *Geschichte der Staatsphilosophie in Hauptkapiteln*, vol. 1 (Meisenheim am Glan: Verlag Anton Hain, 1955), especially chapter 8: "Nominalism and the Origination of the Idea of the State," 37–351. For an exposition of the more general philosophical nuances of nominalism see Von Hippel, *Geschichte der Staatsphilosophie in Hauptkapiteln*, vol. 1 (Meisenheim am Glan: Verlag Anton Hain, 1955), 352-365, Strauss, *Philosophy* (Grand Rapids, MI: Paideia Press, 2009), 370–379, and the chapter in this work on realism and nominalism.

48

Dooyeweerd on Romanticism[1]

> Read in Dooyeweerd's own words how he characterizes the transition from the *Enlightenment* (18th century) to the *Romantic* reaction (transition from 18th to the 19th century).

THE FRENCH REVOLUTION finally translated the individualistic notions in the humanistic theory of natural law into political reality. However, the Revolution was soon followed by the great reaction of the Restoration period. The Restoration period initiated a new spiritual upheaval within the humanistic worldview. It was a time of ferment and spiritual confusion in which many again dreamt of a synthesis between Christianity and humanism, as in our own postwar period. But in actual reality humanism maintained the absolute spiritual leadership in western culture.

The New Personality Ideal

The religious turn within humanism's worldview occurred from out of its deepest dynamic; namely, the freedom motive of the personality ideal. During the Restoration period the personality ideal began to emancipate itself from the influences of the classical nature motive and its mechanistic world picture. The personality ideal acquired a new and irrational form which assimilated and reinterpreted many familiar Christian motives in a humanistic fashion. Even prominent Christian thinkers and statesmen, Roman Catholic as well as Protestant, were misled by this and mistook the

---

1. Extracts taken from *Roots of Western Culture*, 175-180.

new spiritual movement as a dependable ally in their fundamental battle against the revolutionary principles. We shall attempt to sketch this new spiritual movement within humanism in terms of the inner dialectic of humanism's own ground-motive.

. . .

Conversely, this rationalistic and individualistic view of the personality ideal did not grant the true idea of community its rightful place. Kant shared with the entire Enlightenment the individualistic view of society produced by the overextension of the natural-scientific way of thinking. For him the state is an aggregate of individuals joined together under general legal rules of conduct by means of a social contract. For him even marriage is not a true community. He viewed it merely as a contract between two individuals of different sex for the mutual and lasting possession of each other's bodies.

Romanticism and the "Storm and Stress" [Sturm und Drang] movement bitterly opposed this rationalistic and individualistic view of the personality ideal. For Romanticism the motive of freedom demanded a different understanding of personality. Kant's "bourgeois morality" was ridiculed already in the early years of the Romantic era. The Romantics did not wish to interpret the autonomy of the person in such a way that the human *autos*, the true self, would lose itself in the *nomos*, the universal moral law. On the contrary, for them the nomos, the rule for human conduct, must find its origin in the full individuality of the autos, in one's individual disposition. Human personality must indeed be a law unto itself! But if this is taken seriously, then the law must be wholly individual, in harmony with each person's disposition and special calling.

Early Romanticism placed this "ethics of genius" over against "bourgeois ethics." The thesis that general laws are completely opposed to true morality typified the change from a rationalistic to an irrationalistic conception of the autonomous personality.

...

For instance, the sexual surrender of a woman to a man out of spontaneous love – quite apart from the civil bond of marriage – was glorified as aesthetic harmony between "sensuous nature" and "spiritual freedom." Friedrich Schlegel's romance Lucinde glorified this kind of "free love" which is guided only by the harmony of the sensual and spiritual inclinations of the individual man and woman.

...

In order to escape the anarchistic implications of its new personality ideal, irrationalistic Romanticism needed to discover limits for the individual freedom of the autonomous personality. But such limits could of course not be sought in a universally valid moral law. They could only be found by viewing the individual person as a member of an all-embracing community which itself possesses a uniquely individual disposition and personality.

...

It seemed that with this change Romanticism had given the old, abstract, and rationalistic idea of world citizenship a much richer content, filled with individuality. Autonomous and free personality could now express its individual inclination fully. But this individuality of any particular person is co-determined by that person's family, people, and the national community of which she is a member. Romanticism no longer acknowledged the existence of "a universal human being" as a nondescript individual with human rights; it viewed the individual personality only as a member of this individual national whole.

The humanistic personality ideal thus deepened and broadened itself as a community ideal. In its irrationalistic turn it simultaneously acquired a universalistic character. Freedom and autonomy were conceived of as the freedom and autonomy of the individual community of persons. This universalism is the ideology of community.

Ideology of Community

Thus the "autonomous individual," in terms of whom complex societal phenomena were constructed, was the rational component of all social relations, stripped of all authentic individuality and endowed only with the universal faculties of reason and will which were viewed as autonomous and free in accordance with the humanistic freedom motive. This was the background of the proclamation of the French Revolution: freedom and equality for all human individuals.

In opposition to this individualistic and rationalistic view of the humanistic personality ideal, Romanticism posited its universalistic and irrationalistic conception. For Romanticism the autonomous freedom of the human personality cannot be understood in terms of a universal colorless individual constituted by rational lawful relationships, but rather in terms of the fully individual disposition of a person. In accordance with the humanistic ground-motive, a person's individual and irrational disposition is a law unto itself. The individual and ultimately irrational disposition of a person cannot be grasped in terms of any universal concept of understanding. Yet, in accordance with the humanistic ground-motive, it must be a law unto itself. A genius like Napoleon, for example, cannot be judged in terms of universal standards. The autonomous freedom of humankind requires that genius be understood in a strictly individual sense.

In order to avoid the anarchistic implications of this break with universal laws and norms for judgment, Romanticism needed new ties to restrict the individual personality in some fashion. The limits to the expression of personality were found not in a general law judging all human beings but only in the individual's membership in a higher human community which had a completely individual disposition itself. Romanticism enthroned the national community and its utterly individual, national spirit [*volksgeest*]. This community replaced the indistinct individual of humanistic natural law and of the French Revolution. Abstract individuals, instances of the general concept of "a human being," do not exist. Individual Germans, Frenchmen, Englishmen, Dutchmen do exist; and their individuality is determined by the individual character of the volk to which they belong. They share in that character because they have organically [*naturwüchsig*] come forth out of a specific people. The wholly individual character or spirit of a people is also the free and autonomous source of its culture, state, legal system, art, social customs, and moral standards. In other words, moral rules and positive laws valid for societal relationships are the autonomous products of the spirit of an individual people and therefore cannot serve as the normative standards for other peoples which possess a different individual character or disposition. This is thus the irrationalistic and universalistic change in the humanistic freedom motive.

A new ideology of community was the immediate result of this change. Romanticism replaced the gospel of the autonomous and nondescript individual with the gospel of the autonomous and individual community. Both Romanticism and all of post-Kantian "freedom idealism" clung to the idea of a "community of humankind" of which all other communities are individual parts. This idea constituted Romanticism's "idea of humanity" or, in Goethe's words, respect for whatever "bears the human countenance" [*was Menschenantlitz trägt*]. But the community of humankind remained an eternal, supratemporal ideal which manifests itself in temporal society only in individual, national communities.

I trust that by now the intrinsically humanistic origin of this new community ideology is evident. This is a crucial matter since this ideology again poses a dangerous threat in our own day, as it is irreconcilably engaged in a battle against the scriptural ground-motive of creation, fall, and redemption in Jesus Christ.

49

Classifying Social Forms of Life

by Danie F. M. Strauss

THE REFORMATIONAL TRADITION is best known by its adherence to the principle of sphere sovereignty, a term used by Abraham Kuyper and anticipated by Groen van Prinsterer. However, in order to classify social forms of life it is necessary first of all to analyze the elementary (analogical) basic concepts of the discipline of sociology.

It is indeed significant that leading sociologists throughout the 19th and 20th centuries did not realize that they oftentimes overemphasized one (or a select few) elementary basic concepts, and in doing so they not only failed to appreciate the unavoidable role of other basic concepts but also distorted the meaning of the social dimension of reality itself. The guiding supposition of the analysis of elementary basic concepts—namely, that the meaning of the social aspect only comes to expression in its coherence with all the other aspects of reality—has found more than enough examples in the diverging trends and sociological schools of thought to confirm its claim.

No single orientation in modern sociology managed to develop its distinctive theoretical stance without inevitably employing (implicitly or explicitly) basic concepts referring to the field of study of other disciplines distinct from sociology. This appeared to be the case with some of the best-known terms, such as "system," "causality," "order," "constancy," "dynamics" and many more. Terms such as these find their "seat" not just in non-social aspects of reality since they also call for an account of the specific meaning attached to them when they are employed in sociological theorizing. Elementary basic concepts such as "social system," "social causality," "social order," "social constancy" and "social dynamics" reveal the fact that they are multivocal and are capable of assuming, analogous to their original meaning, other meanings as well. Many sociological theorists thought they could side-step the problem of analogical concepts simply by employing them in their original sense, but in doing so they actually reduced social phenomena to the aspect in which the analogical term resides. For example, when "social life" is understood in its original biotic sense, social phenomena are reduced to the biotical level (normally accompanied by claims that society itself is an "organism").

By contrast, on the basis of an analysis of the elementary (analogical) basic concepts of sociology, the complex concepts and typical concepts acquire a well-articulated account that demonstrate the intimate connection between these different kinds of basic concepts entailed in sociological theorizing, and at the same time they highlight the fact that an integrated practice of sociological theorizing ought to do justice to every conceptual element of its scholarly endeavors.

Complex basic concepts are built up by the simultaneous employment of the different elementary basic concepts of sociology. Discussing the classification of *forms of social interaction* prevalent in sociological literature will provide an example of applying what is known as the transcendental-empirical method to this domain of concept formation. This method investigates those conditions that make possible what we can experience.

From Elementary Basic Concepts to Complex Concepts

The elementary basic concepts of sociology immediately open up several avenues to us. For example, we can commence by using the perspective of the *biotical analogy*. It entails that the social intercourse between people living in a *differentiated* society always occurs within *integrated* spheres of life, with their "own inner laws."[1] Does this mean that there is no room left at all for the *personal freedom* of *social subjects*? Do we have to accept the contrast between "action" and "order" as a strict either/or?[2] What about the numerous less fixed and less durable relationships where people interact on an equal footing—be it in cooperation or in competition—with and over against each other? These kinds of interaction are often *purely incidental*.

A consistent individualism, that wants to explore the perspective of "individuals-in-interaction," proceeds from a notion of *action* that denies the inherent *social function* of any human action. The only option left on the basis of this assumption is then to *add* the *social* dimension afterwards as something different. As soon as we acknowledge the embracing *transcendental* nature of every modal aspect of reality, we have to start from a notion of the social function of reality which is *co-constitutive* for whatever *actions* of any *individual* human being. All the less durable relationships already entail the mere fact that individuals *function* in the social aspect as well. As a structural element that co-conditions by the *manner* in which human beings function within reality, inter-individual interactions are, in a truly transcendental sense, just as "social" as are the existence of any super-individual societal wholes.

Any *genetic* distinction between these two kinds of social functioning, such as intended by Tönnies with his distinction between *Gemeinschaft* and *Gesellschaft*, should therefore be questioned. Initially he understood this distinction in historical-genetic terms—a

---

1. Cf. R. Münch, "Differentiation, Rationalization, Interpenetration: The Emergence of Modern Society," in *Differentiation Theory and Social Change*, ed. J.C. Alexander and Paul Colomy (New York: Columbia University Press, 1990), 443.
2. Thus J.C. Alexander and Paul Colomy, eds., *Differentiation Theory and Social Change* (New York: Columbia University Press, 1990).

period of *Gesellschaft* (community) follows a period of *Gemeinschaft* (society).[3] However, in his *Introduction to Sociology* it turns out that he wants to relativize these oppositions. He remarks that in addition to *social relations* and *social connections* he distinguishes a third category, *Samtschaften* (collectives). Social entities are classified as *Samtschaften*, social relationships as *Verhältnisse*, and social "bodies" or organizations as *Körperschaften*.[4]

However, only a few analogical concepts are used in this classification of Tönnies. He starts with the numerical analogy by first looking at a *social multiplicity* combined into a *social unity*—designated as a *corporation* or *organization* (*Körperschaft*). These two terms, *corporation* and *organization*, remind us of the original meaning of the biotical aspect. On the basis of a subdivision of the human will into an artificial rational part and an organic-psychic bodily part, Tönnies then uses the physical and biotical analogies to characterize the difference between *Gemeinschaft* and *Gesellschaft*.

The principal category used to designate the nature of *Gemeinschaft* comes from the biotical aspect: *organic*. *Gesellschaft* is described in kinematical-physical terms: it is seen as a *mechanical aggregate*. The logical analogy implicitly surfaces inasmuch as Tönnies wants to classify *mutually affirmative* relationships. More recent sociological thinkers subsumed these relationships under the notion of *social consensus* (concord). Tönnies did not want to incorporate *social conflict* in his perspective. Sociology has the task to "point the way to the establishment of peaceful human relationships among groups, classes, and nations."[5]

Sorokin is convinced that the classification proposed by Tönnies is inadequate, since it does not consider the role of *social con-*

---

3. F. Tönnies, *Einführung in die Soziologie* (Stuttgart: Enke, [1931] 1965), 251.
4. Tönnies, *Einführung in die Soziologie*, xlv and ff.
5. C.P. Loomis and J.C. McKinney, "Introduction," in *Community and Society*, F. Tönnies (New York: Harper & Row, 1957), 10-11.

flict. Without discussing the inherent antinormativity incorporated in social conflict, Sorokin wants to use it in a *positive way* in his classification of forms of social interaction.[6] He uses the opposition between *solidarity* and *antagonism*—both sensitive-psychic phenomena in their original modal meaning—to serve as a basis for his classification of *social interaction*. Forms of social interaction in which *solidarity* dominates are called *familistic*; forms of social interaction in which both *solidarity* and *antagonism* appear are called *mixed* or *contractual*; whereas predominantly antagonistic forms are classified as *compulsory*.[7] That the *familistic type* closely resembles the *Gemeinschaft*-form of Tönnies is clear from this statement by Sorokin:

> The familistic relationship *eliminates or reduces to a minimum the feeling of being a stranger or outsider among its members*. It is the relationship in which the whole life of each member in all its important aspects and values tends to be merged into a warm and hearty collective "we."[8]

The particular emphasis which Sorokin places on the sensitive-psychic analogies of *solidarity* and *antagonism* in social interaction—sometimes combined with *love* and *hate*—distorts the equally important contribution provided by other analogical structural moments. For example, the spatial and historical analogies are completely relativized in his "familistic type." He even wants to deprive intimate relationships within the (nuclear) family from every possible structure of authority and subordination. This is partly due to the negative contents given by him to the distinction between office-bearers and those subjected to their authority:

---

6. P.A. Sorokin, *Society, Culture and Personality* (New York: Cooper Square Publishers, 1962), 106 ff., 113.
7. Sorokin, *Society, Culture and Personality*, 99ff, 102ff, and 106ff. respectively.
8. Sorokin, *Society, Culture and Personality*, 101.

... in a truly familistic interaction or group ... there is no formal *domination and subordination*, no master and servant, no arbitrary government and suppressed subjects.[9]

Instead of extending our list of examples of sociologists who tried to classify forms of social interaction indefinitely, we shall now briefly look at the comprehensive outcome of an integrated approach.

Classifying Forms of Social Interaction

The coherence between the kinematical and the physical analogies in the structure of the social aspect helps us to identify a property that could be denoted as a *solidary unitary character* of certain social forms of life. This feature intends to capture the phenomenon that in spite of the constant flow (coming and going/entering and leaving) of individual members of a societal collectivity, the durability and identity of the life-form concerned are not destroyed. Ryan fittingly captures this trait:

> There are regularities and constancies in the behavior of groups of people which allow us to talk about groups having a stable structure in spite of fluctuating membership, and about the existence of social roles which can be filled by different people at different points in time.[10]

We want to argue that *every one* of the constitutive modal analogies within the structure of the social aspect is required to fully explain the meaning of the *solidary unitary character* of certain social forms—and not only the kinematical and physical analogies. We can only identify a *solidary unitary character* if an *integrated* social *order* is given positive *shape* within the *sphere* of a particular social *totality* in spite of the presence of possible or

---

9. Sorokin, *Society, Culture and Personality*, 100-101.
10. A. Ryan, *The Philosophy of the Social Sciences* (London: Macmillan, 1970), 174.

actual social conflict (the numerical, spatial, biotical, analytical, and cultural-historical analogies are captured in this formulation).

Let us now differentiate, within the context of the *spatial* analogy, between social relations of *next-to-each-other* and social relations of *super- and subordination*, and then choose for a relation of *super- and subordination*. In this case we have to combine our perspective on the *solidary unitary character* with the presence of durable relations of authority and subordination (compare the cultural-historical analogy of *social competence*). This choice provides us with a second basic *attribute* pertaining to the different forms of social interaction in a differentiated society: a *permanent authority structure*. The full meaning of this feature is also co-constituted by the other analogical moments.

The durable organization of any social life-form receives its *maximum specification* when it shares in *both* these mentioned characteristics: (i) a *solidary unitary character*, and (ii) a *permanent authority structure*. The Dutch term denoting this form of social interaction is "*verband.*" Unfortunately, the English language has no suitable *translational equivalent* for this word. I have attempted to capture its connotation by introducing the term *consociation*, but perhaps the simplest option is to speak about *social collectivities* when "*verbanden*" are intended. Social collectivities then refer to all those forms of social interaction which exhibit both features (i) and (ii). Examples of *social collectivities* are the *state*, the *church*, the *firm*, the *school*, the *university*, the (nuclear) *family*, the *art society*, the *sports club*, the *cultural society* and the *language association*. The state possesses a durable sub- and superordination of authority and subjects (i.e., a permanent authority structure), while the unity and identity of a state is not abolished by the exchange of its citizens (either office-bearers or subjects). The same applies for all the other societal collectivities that we have named in the list of examples.

When societal life forms possess only one of these characteristics, the term *communities* may serve as an appropriate designation. A *nation* ("volk"/"people") and the *extended family* possess a *solidary unitary character* (that is why there may be continuity between the nation of a hundred years ago and that of today in the midst of changes), but *no permanent authority structure* can be indicated. The *marriage community* does possess a permanent authority structure, although a solidary unitary character is absent. In terms of these distinctions neither a state, nor a province, nor a rural town is a *community*. With reference to the state-side of the given facts, we are working with (higher or lower) forms of governmental authority—and therefore with subordinate and superordinate relations which are absent from the community as we have described it. In reality a city and a town exhibit an enkaptic interweaving of diverse societal collectivities, communities and *coordinational* relationships. The expression *coordinational relationships* intends to reflect what is meant by the Dutch term "*maatschap*". The term "*maatschap*" does not have a suitable English equivalent. The intended kind of relationship surely does not have a *permanent authority structure*, nor does it possess a *solidary unitary character*. It concerns social interaction normally related to phenomena of friendship, partnership, fellowship, mate, pal, peer, and the freedom we have to *associate* with an accountable freedom of choice. For the lack of a better alternative, we want to apply the proposed designation *coordinational* with the intention to include those connotations shared by the phenomena referred to in the previous sentence—which are all instances of coordinational relationships.

However, the concept "coordinational relationship" concerns not only the inter-relations between individuals, since it also wants to reflect those relations on an equal footing that obtain between different *communities* and *social collectivities*.

Specified in this way, the distinction between forms of social interaction that are *coordinational*, *communal* or *collective* remains confined to the modal structure of the social aspect as such. These three forms of social interaction are therefore *modal totality concepts*, i.e., complex basic concepts built up out of the foundational (constitutive) modal analogies of the social aspect. Unfortunately, Dooyeweerd did not approach the intended classification from the vantage point of the complex basic concepts of sociology as a special science. As a consequence, he links the criteria used by him with a reference to the *founding function* of certain social life-forms. He starts with a comprehensive understanding of communities—which are all supposed to be "natural" in the sense of having their *founding function* in the biotical aspect.

The approach which we have followed in distinguishing coordinational, communal and collective social relationships explicitly disregards the *more-than-social* totality structure of societal wholes. It means that the typical totality structure of life-forms is ignored in such a way that account is taken of neither their founding nor their qualifying function.

Having linked the nature of communities directly to their (natural-biotic) foundational function, Dooyeweerd proceeds by claiming that historically founded (i.e., *organized*) communities can be referred to as "*verbanden*" (in our proposed term: societal collectivities). *Natural communities*, on the other hand, are unorganized.[11] The result of this approach is that Dooyeweerd cannot meaningfully distinguish between a *marriage* and the *nuclear family*. According to him they are both natural (i.e., *biotically* founded) and *ethically* qualified "communities." In terms of our distinctions: a nuclear marriage is a *community*, whereas the nuclear family represents a *collective social bond*.

---

11. Cf. H. Dooyeweerd, *A New Critique of Theoretical Thought*, vol. 3, Collected Works of Herman Dooyeweerd, Series A, General Editor D.F.M. Strauss (Lewiston, NY: Edwin Mellen, 1997), 178ff.

The Correlation between Social Collectivities and Communal Relationships on the One Hand and Coordinational Relationships on the Other

In differentiated societies there are various life-forms which bind their members together for the greater part of their lives in a way which is independent of their will. The state, for example, does not originate in a hypothetical "social contract," which explains why it can organize the collective life of its citizens independent of their will (think for example about their tax obligations). Participation in the political process—co-determination and co-responsibility—does not entail opting out of this life-form altogether. Even if a person decides to emigrate, such a person simply enters into a different state, for nowhere on this planet is there a "stateless" society. All those life-forms which embrace the lives of their members partially or fully for the greater part of their life-span could be called *institutional*.[12]

Marriage exhibits an institutional nature because it is meant to constitute the spouses' marriage relationship for the duration of their lives. A person is born within a family and a circle of relatives and grows up in it without any choice. Like this life-form, the church is also institutional because baptizing (as a sign and seal of the covenant) is done independently of the child's will.

Not all social collectivities possess an *institutional* character. Think only of a business enterprise, a university college, or a sports club—all examples of social collectivities which rest totally on *voluntary* membership.

Yet it is impossible for any person to let his life be absorbed completely by any of the various societal collectivities and communities in which one functions—simply because he also takes part in various other interrelations. Social collectivities such as two families, for example, stand in an (inter-collective) *coordinational* relationship; and two married couples in an (inter-communal)

---

12. Cf. Dooyeweerd, *A New Critique*, III, 187.

coordinational relationship. Furthermore, every individual is, in a differentiated society, taken up in countless inter-individual co-ordinational relationships where he or she relates informally with fellow humans in co-ordinate relations. Conversely, no one's life is completely involved in coordinational relationships, because the opposite of them is found in the institutional and non-institutional collectivities and communities in which they are involved.

Individualism and Universalism: A More Precise Characterization

Our first characterization of individualism (atomism) and universalism (holism) latched on to the original meaning of the numerical and spatial aspects, or to analogies of these two aspects in cosmic later aspects. (In both instances, basic denominators for the entire diversity within reality are formulated as part of what could be denoted as the *modal skeleton* of a theoretical view of reality.) Given the articulation of the modal totality, (complex) basic concepts involved in classifying coordinational, communal, and collective societal relationships, we can now introduce a more precise understanding of these two *isms*.

Sociological *individualism* separates coordinational relationships and uses them as the exclusive explanatory device in its analysis of societal relationships. Sociological universalism, on the other hand, exclusively orients itself to one or another communal or collective social relationship at the expense of the remaining communal and collective relationships as well as all coordinational relations in society. The fascism of Mussolini absolutized the *State* and the national socialism of Hitler absolutized the *Volk* as cultural community.

The humanistic science-ideal attempted to "construct" human society out of its supposed simplest "elements," the "autonomous individuals." In reaction to this, the holistic ideology of a supra-individual community emerged, advanced by the freedom-idealism of post-Kantian thought. In pursuing this line of thought further, Othmar Spann placed all emphasis on the primary reality of a societal totality. According to him the individual comes to full development only through other people. This process is "a genuine whole, which is more than the sum of its individual parts, and therefore logically precedes the parts."[13] Spann merely characterizes the form of individualism which proceeds from isolated and self-contained autonomous individuals, and he then contrasts it with his own understanding of universalism—which is also different from other forms of universalism.

---

13. O. Spann, *Gesellschaftslehre*, 3rd rev. ed. (Leipzig: Verlag Quelle & Meyer, 1930), 131.

50

Context Is Everything. Or Is It?

by Albert Weideman

Not the Whole Story

To UNDERSTAND, we are often told, requires attention to context. Without context, we are unable to make sense of morality, law, economics, culture and all things human. So too, the claim is, with language. Consider all the contextual conditions that must be known to understand the remark in exhibit [1]:

[1] This is cute! "Bosal wants to lift the world"![1]

It will not make sense if the person who is being addressed cannot see, or does not know, that the speaker is reading a newspaper at the time of the utterance. He must know, too, that she is commenting on the caption of a report in the newspaper she is reading. The observation in question can be more fully interpreted and understood only if we know that "Bosal wants to lift the world" is the caption heading a report in the business section of the newspaper, and, furthermore, that the report dealt with the success a motor vehicle component manufacturing company called Bosal had had in increasing its profits, achieving that chiefly through the production of car jacks during the financial year that was under scrutiny in the report.

---

1. Discussed, along with the following exhibits, in Weideman, *A Framework for the Study of Linguistics*, 60; see also Weideman, *Beyond Expression*, 39ff.

So the example provides a simple illustration of the phenomenon that an utterance, when taken out of its context, or out of the situation in which it is used, will not make any sense. Moreover, this illustrates a well-known premise of reformational philosophy: that language *an sich*, pure language, does not exist. In whatever form, written or spoken, language is always used in context.

Yet this is not the whole story. Language indeed does not exist in a void, but in concrete situations. Nonetheless, in those "situations," there are various spheres in which language operates, and the concrete language used in these zones differs from one lingual sphere to the next. Consider some further examples, exhibits [2] to [5]:

[2] My aspens dear, whose airy cages quelled,
Quelled or quenched in leaves the leaping sun,
Are felled, felled, are all felled...
(G. M. Hopkins)

[3] When Kant comes to the transcendental exposition of time, we would expect that he would attempt to prove that time as an a priori intuition is a necessary and sufficient condition for making synthetic a priori judgements in arithmetic.[2]

[4] It is hereby declared and agreed that should a tenant of the Insured in the within insured building do or omit to do, without the knowledge or consent of the Insured, anything which would vitiate the within policy conditions and/or warranties, section 7 of this policy will not be held to be void on that account provided that the Insured shall notify to the Company the happening ...

[5] BT UNCLASS INF/161 JUL 75

---

2. J. Harnack, *Kant's Theory of Knowledge*, 25.

CONTEXT IS EVERYTHING. OR IS IT?

1. G/TRG 6/37 INF 7526 OVER G/TRG/6/37 441R

2. YOUR TRG/269 JUL 75 REFERS

3. ITO THE AMNEDED ATI A COMDS TO INFORM UNITS CONCERNED OF PARA 6 OF 2 ABOVE

If one compares the language of poetry in exhibit [2] to that of academic discourse (exhibit [3]), or the long-winded legal language of an insurance policy (exhibit [4]) to the terseness of an army telex message (exhibit [5]), one soon discovers that there are distinct differences among the many varieties of language used in these typically different contexts. Formally, one may try to come to an understanding of these differences by pointing out, for example, that they exist on both the lexical and syntactic levels. Thus, one would find words like "Russellian," "transcendental" and "ontological" in academic discourse, but not the suggestive alliteration of "wilful-wavier," "wanwood," "wind-wandering" and "weed-winding" we find in the Hopkins poem. Likewise, the formulaic "declared and agreed", and "shall notify to the Company" that are so typical of the contractual legal language of the insurance policy, will be absent in the rather cryptic syntax of the army telex message (exhibit [5]), where indexical combinations like "G/TRG/6/37 INF 7526" may occur side by side with highly specific abbreviations like "ITO" and "ATI" (meaning respectively "in terms of" and "Army Training Instructions"). All these differences are formal ones.

Not Merely Formal or Informal

The difference in content between these various types of language soon leads one to discover, however, that there are not only objective, formal differences, but also various *typical* norms, principles that give a different content to the factual language used within each typical sphere.

We call the various lingual spheres typical if we wish to refer to the typically different social relationships (such as that of the academic community, the army, club, home, school, business, church and so forth) that each requires typically different uses of language. On the other hand, these typically different spheres of language may be called material if we acknowledge, with Halliday, that the "field of discourse" (as one of the features of the lingual sphere or context) to a large extent determines the *content* or subject matter of the concrete language used in such a sphere.[3]

The various material lingual spheres are integrated with many typically different concrete situations that we encounter every day, and these different situations all have their own particular language register. In their subjective lingual role as speakers, writers, hearers or readers, humans build up a whole repertoire of such lingual registers, a repertoire that enables them to make the delicate choices of how to communicate in a given context without crashing their lingual gears.

Material Lingual Spheres, and Lingual Subjects and Objects

The linguistic idea of typically or materially distinct lingual spheres consists of a differentiated classification of language types that is inextricably bound up with the *subjective* human lingual capacity for producing *objective*, factual language in various social spheres. But the idea of differentiated lingual ranges is linked not only with this correlation of lingual subject and lingual object, but also with the complex linguistic idea of lingual norm and lingual fact.

This becomes clear as soon as one attempts to ascribe the typical differences between one material lingual sphere and another only to the different factual situations in which language may be used. The factual context can never fully determine the type of language used, because the situation is itself regulated by normative principles of a logical, technico-formative, social, econom-

---

3. Halliday, *Language as Social Semiotic*, 223.

ic, aesthetic, legal, ethical or confessional nature. Each different situation has different language requirements that act as lingual conditions or norms. One has to distinguish between the lingual requirements and conditions *for* the situation and the situation itself.

Applications

The distinctions referred to above derive from Dooyeweerd's insights into the associations, communities and institutions operative within differentiated societies.[4] Their applications to the design of language teaching and the assessment of language ability are obvious. There is, for example, a range of language assessments[5] that are built upon the idea that the mastery of academic discourse depends on its being characterized by distinction making,[6] that is, by the nuclear meaning of the logical modality.[7] There are language courses that proceed from the same premise.[8] When we acknowledge that the material differences among the various lingual spheres are related to typical differences among social structures such as the school, the university, the club, the business firm, the art studio, the family, the media, marriage, the state, the church and so forth, we begin to do full justice to our experience of language and "context".

So is context everything? In the case of human language and communication, only if we fully appreciate its typical nature, the layers of interaction it exhibits between lingual subjects and ob-

---

4. See esp. vol. III of *A New Critique*.
5. Weideman, Read & Du Plessis, eds., *Assessing Literacy in a Multilingual Society* (2021).
6. Weideman, "Definition and Design: Aligning Language Interventions in Education," 33-48.
7. Patterson and Weideman, "The Typicality of Academic Discourse," 107-123.
8. Weideman, *Academic Literacy: Prepare to Learn* (2007).

jects, as well as between lingual norms and lingual facts. This is one of the main debts that linguistics (together with some of its applications) owes to reformational philosophy.

51

The Meaning of Technology

by Egbert Schuurman

MOST PEOPLE, when I write or speak critically about "technicism," think that I am a "culture pessimist" who has a negative attitude toward technology itself. That is and cannot be the case. Therefore, we need to deal with the meaning of technology.

In Reformational philosophy, the idea of the meaning-character of reality occupies a central place. All created things are from, through and unto God. Through the Fall into sin the relation to God was affected. In Jesus Christ as the God-man and mediator between God and humanity, the original relation is restored. The purpose and destiny of the entire creation is at bottom the honour and service of God through Jesus Christ. In this way all things, technology included, are related to God as the *Origin of all meaning*.

Two directions are to be distinguished in connection with the meaning-character of reality. First, there is the "vertical" direction, the dependence of everything upon the Origin. Next, we also speak of a "horizontal" direction—the history of the creation from beginning to end. Submitting to the *given* meaning of everything signifies that humanity allows itself to be guided by the meaning-*dunamis* as the law, the regulator, the norm for all being-as-meaning.

What the foregoing means with respect to the scientific-technological development is that the direction of this development ought to be subjected to the meaning-*dunamis*. Human responsibility can help to disclose meaning, and scientific-technological thought can render its meaningful service. When humanity fails to submit radically and integrally to the Origin of all meaning and to the meaning-*dunamis* of the creation, then the original dynamic *of* the creation turns into an original dialectic *within* creation. The dialectic resists the disclosure of meaning; it dislocates and stifles development. Now then, *technicism* — i.e., absolutizing technology on the one hand and promoting technological imperialism on the other—entails disruption or perversion of the meaning of technology. Meanwhile, this dialectic process is a parasite on the meaning-*dunamis*.

In developing technology we ought to honor the *dunamis* of creation. What this means concretely for technology is that humanity submits to the given normative principles which obtain for the cultural and supra-cultural modalities, and that people positivize—i.e., give shape to and thus realize—these principles. These principles motivate people and acquaint them with the perspective of the fullness of the meaning-disclosure that all structures of creation point to.

The meaning of technology is in the first place founded in and related to the cultural/historical aspect of reality in the sense of free and responsible formation of technological objects and processes and obeying the cultural norms of effectiveness, and of continuity and discontinuity, and of differentiation and integration.

Technological meaning-disclosure implies a deepening of meaning or enrichment of meaning whenever the post-cultural aspects lead technological meaning.[1]

Technological meaning, when disclosed, is first of all meaning that is expressed *symbolically*. A design is indicated in formulas and drawings which serve as guidelines for technological formation. Everyone who is involved in the technological process

---

1. See H. Dooyeweerd, *A New Critique of Theoretical Thought*, vol. 2, Collected Works of Herman Dooyeweerd, Series A, General Editor D.F.M. Strauss (Lewiston, NY: Edwin Mellen, 1997), 285–305; E. Schuurman, *The Technological World Picture and an Ethics of Responsibility* (Sioux Center, IA: Dordt Press, 2005), 45–48; E. Schuurman, *Technology and the Future – A Philosophical Challenge*, 2nd ed. (Grand Rapids: Paideia Press, 2009), 382–433.

must participate in it with his or her specific responsibility, thus entailing disclosure of the *social* aspect. In the *economic* disclosure of the technological process man is a steward: waste of materials and harm to the environment have to be prevented; making profits should be incorporated into the enterprise and disclosed in connection with service to God and service to one's neighbor. An *aesthetic* meaning disclosure of technology should become evident in a harmonious development among all persons, while harmony should also exist between nature and technology; technology must not be permitted to make a wasteland of nature. Technological meaning disclosure should in addition be led by the *juridical* aspect. This has many dimensions—too many to mention them all.[2] But in any case, this disclosure should prevent the destruction of the environment.

After juridical disclosure, a further deepening of technological meaning ought to advance toward *ethical* or *moral* disclosure. Again, the protection of neighbor and nature is at stake here, calling for care and love. Finally, technological meaning disclosure ought to be led by the *belief* that humanity is called to the task of technology and that people are obliged to accept this mission in *faith* and *trust* as a responsibility before God. Faith is always the boundary-function and horizon of meaning-disclosure. To tie one's faith to something absolutized will inevitably result in meaning shut-down rather than disclosure.

In its analysis of meaning-disclosure at the point where it involves faith, philosophical-scientific thought approaches a fundamental boundary, demonstrating that it is not self-sufficient. Theoretical thought can serve only to point to this *transcending in faith*; it can only approach its substance *by describing an idea,* as it were—an *idea* that ought to lead and guide people when working in technology.[3]

We have seen so far that in an analysis of the meaning-disclo-

---

2. Cf. Schuurman, *The Technological World Picture.*
3. Dooyeweerd, *New Critique,* 2:304f; Schuurman, *Technology and the Future,* 421.

sure of technological development, philosophical-scientific thought ultimately arrives at *faith* as the boundary-function of the process of meaning-disclosure. Humanity should believingly, in faith and trust, transcend technological development in the direction of the fullness of meaning and thus the Origin of all meaning. Humanity does not freely dispose over the fullness of meaning as the basis for the disclosure of the meaning of technology. Rather, this foundation ought to be presupposed in all technological activity as well as reflection on it. Its meaning can only be approached in the *idea* which ought to lead and inspire people in their work in technology, the *idea* through which people are filled with hope.

In approaching this technological development idea, we have come back again to the question of the ground for a liberating perspective for technological development. This ground appears to be religious in nature. We reject as unsuitable for such a ground both an absolutized idea of control or power and an absolutized idea of freedom, since such ideas represent a closed view of the world and humankind. These ideas, furthermore, do not offer a meaningful perspective for the dynamic development of modern technology. On the contrary, they are the very source of the tremendous problems called forth by this technology and the real dislocations that are currently making themselves felt in our culture on a global scale.

To get at the substance of the technological development idea, we shall have to *listen,* believingly, in a position of childlike faith, to the fullness of meaning that is revealed in Jesus Christ. The Bible speaks of it. When people listen, they understand more and more about God's purpose with the creation. As related to the present subject, it is important to perceive to what extent God's Word reveals the meaning of technology to us.

As God's image-bearers, people received at their creation the command to be stewards of God's completed work of creation and to disclose or open up that work. Contained in this calling is the task of technology as the disclosure of the nature side of creation and as the realization of its technological side. The final purpose of all this activity is the service and honor of God: this is the path along which humanity must unfold and fulfill its life.

The Fall into sin broke humanity's power, and nature was cursed. Now people no longer live in harmony with God's law, which obtains for the whole creation. Thus they have to live in a creation that is broken and dislocated by sin. Humanity is no longer in fit condition to administer and disclose nature. On the contrary, people are constantly threatened by nature and forced to contend with floods, drought, forest fires, and hurricanes of unprecedented violence.

Restoration is given in Jesus Christ. He heals the brokenness of the entire creation and turns it again, in fullness, toward God, the Origin. Jesus Christ came into a world broken by sin to undergo the chastisement of death for sin. He also fulfills humanity's task of having custody over creation and opening it up. Jesus Christ *saves* and *fulfills* creation in the Kingdom of God.

It is especially difficult, if not impossible, to discern to what extent the pristine creation is present in nature as it now exists. Certainly the original elements are dominant. Sin did not and does not have the power to lay creation waste in an integral way, to destroy it as a whole. In any case, it is clear in biblical perspective that Jesus Christ saves creation from the curse and turns it again toward its original destination. This is all the more astonishing when we consider that the creation still abundantly bears the effects of sin. In history, Jesus Christ has laid the foundation for the salvation and fulfillment of the creation. In Christ the meaning-disturbance resulting from the Fall into sin is itself destroyed, and the meaning of all that is created is disclosed.

Through faith, humanity participates in the work of Jesus Christ. People have to acknowledge His leading in history and are to work with Him. It is given to humankind to know that in the groaning of the creation, amid thorns and thistles, a new perspective has opened up: the world is being propelled toward complete salvation and fulfillment, toward the consummation of the Kingdom of God. That Kingdom is forging a path right through the disturbances and dislocations of meaning occasioned by the technological development led by secularized motives and fraught, today, with far-reaching consequences.

When people live rooted in this conviction, they are able to accept their task in technology, freely and responsibly. A liberated technology—from technicism for instance—will then be able to ease the difficult circumstances in which people live "by nature." All norms are concentrated in the paradigm of the garden model; all technology has to serve life. It can enlarge life's opportunities, relieve the aches and pains, the difficulties and hardships of work. It can help withstand natural disasters, conquer disease, protect wealthy ecological conditions, and improve social security. It can expand communication, multiply information, augment responsibility, vastly increase material prosperity in harmony with spiritual well-being, and abolish alienation from self, nature, and culture. Technology frees man's time and fosters the developments of new possibilities. Given these possibilities, culture will advance to new disclosures. Such technology, disclosed and redeemed, will also create room for multifaceted work—for careful, creative, love-filled work. And not to forget, caring for and loving all kinds of plants, trees, animals, and humanity and the great variety of community associations corresponding to the garden model.

In all of this, humanity finds its share and portion of the *meaning of technology* in the disclosure of the meaning of the creation as a whole—a disclosure that must attain its final destination in the Kingdom of God, the re-created universe, and so come to rest in that Kingdom.[4]

---

4. E. Schuurman, *Faith and Hope in Technology* (Toronto: Clements Publishing, 2003), 64–70, 160–168, 201–205; Schuurman, *The Technological World Picture*, 41–59; Schuurman, *Technology and the Future*, 416–433.

52

Human Freedom and Political Order

by James W Skillen

CRIES FOR FREEDOM heard around the world today grow louder and louder. But what is the freedom that millions of people are crying for? Those who suffer under intense oppression, whether from unjust governments or from armed bands of revolutionaries, want *freedom from* oppression. Such freedom, however, cannot exist in a vacuum. Freedom from oppression depends on a non-oppressive government that will guard against unlawful, unjust oppression.

Moreover, *freedom from* oppression takes us only halfway toward understanding human freedom. If one is *free from* oppression, what is one *free for*? Presumably, free persons are those who make decisions, exercise responsibilities, speak their minds, and engage in relationships with others. Yet to be free *for* something depends on capabilities and training that enable people to exercise that freedom. To exercise the responsibility of a doctor or lawyer, a teacher or mechanic, an artist or broadcaster presupposes that one has submitted to, and is mastering, the disciplines and institutional requirements required to do the job. The exercise of such responsibilities requires keen insight and sound judgment to distinguish between constructive actions and errant ones, between good decisions and bad ones, between sound practices and destructive ones.

Dooyeweerd emphasizes, however, that "freedom" is not understood in the same way by everyone. It is not a neutral, univocal term. The way people understand freedom depends on the deepest convictions—religious basic motives—of their understanding of the meaning of life and of being human.[1] From a Christian point of view, true freedom for humans, created in the image of God, to exercise responsibilities means heeding and responding in obedience to God's love commandments. The apostle Paul says that human freedom is found in becoming a slave of Christ Jesus. By contrast, modern humanism, which emerged with the European Renaissance and the Enlightenment, was driven by a very different quest for freedom. That quest aimed to displace Christianity as the dominant religion of the age. They urged people to *free themselves from* ecclesiastical and governmental oppression and become autonomous—a law unto themselves. The modernist freedom ideal is liberation from any outside authority. The cry of the French Revolutionaries was "Neither God nor Master."

At first the modern freedom ideal was locked arm in arm with faith in science. Liberation would be won through human reason, working scientifically to gain control of nature for the progress and perfection of human life. Explains Dooyeweerd: "the control motive of autonomous humanity aims at subjecting 'nature' and all of its unlimited possibilities to humankind by means of the new method of mathematical science. Nowhere in reality does it tolerate the validity of *limits* to the operation of the natural-scientific method." Before long, however, a fundamental problem became apparent: If science were to determine that all of reality is "an uninterrupted chain of cause and effect, there would no longer be room anywhere in that reality for human freedom. Human willing, thinking, and acting required the same mechanical explanation as did the motions of a machine. . . . 'Nature' and 'freedom'—science ideal and personality ideal—turn out to oppose each other as declared enemies."[2]

---

1. On the four religious basic motives shaping Western life and thought, see Dooyeweerd, *In the Twilight of Western Thought*, 27-61.
2. Dooyeweerd, *Roots of Western Culture*, 153.

HUMAN FREEDOM AND POLITICAL ORDER

The internal dialectic of modernism's belief in, and aspiration for, freedom became apparent not only in theoretical thought but also in social, institutional practices. If autonomous reason is to take control of nature, it would also need to organize education, politics, and economic life to advance human autonomy and prosperity. But many social efforts to control human behavior led, and continue to lead, to all kinds of restrictions, on workers, students, and citizens, robbing them of their experience of freedom.

Dooyeweerd makes clear from the start that his philosophical explorations are grounded in the Christian basic motive of creation, fall, and redemption in Christ Jesus. He challenges the modern religious basic motive of nature/freedom just as he does the earlier medieval religious basic motive of nature/grace, and the ancient Greek religious basic motive of form/matter. What we find in Dooyeweerd then are insights into the meaning of freedom from a Christian point of view. Our particular focus will be on what he understands to be necessary for political freedom. Let's consider three of Dooyeweerd's important insights.[3]

First, political life needs to be recognized as an institutional community.

Second, in the course of historical development, political communities have been differentiated from a wide variety of non-political institutions and organizations. Freedom means something specific in each case.

Third, citizens will not be free to exercise their civic and other responsibilities if governments act as omnicompetent sovereigns.

1. Until late in the nineteenth century, the study of political life focused on governments and the governing process. Two developments changed that. One was an academic decision, under the

---

3. My summary of these insights has been drawn from several of Dooyeweerd's books and essays. For a compact presentation of his philosophy, see his *Roots of Western Culture* (2003), translated from a 1959 Dutch volume, see especially pp. 41–61; 74–82; 89–110; 156–70; 189–217.

influence of the science-ideal, to try to separate the study of facts from the study of values (mere opinions). Normative judgments about what constitutes a good government would no longer be included in a scientific (factual) study of political behavior because such judgments express subjective opinions of no help to scientific search for the truth. The second development in political science circles was to focus less on government institutions and more on the behavior patterns of citizens, lobby groups, businesspeople, the media, and public officials. Political science needed to become more like sociology, psychology, and economics that appeared to yield exact measurement of facts.

Dooyeweerd shows, however, that the behavior of citizens, lobby groups, public officials, and others takes place within the inescapable bounds of a public-legal institution. To ignore the normative obligation that demands of governments and citizens to act to uphold public justice is to ignore a crucial dimension of political reality. Political scientists may describe a wide range of practices that characterize slavery, taxation, sex-trafficking, GDP, crime rates, or car sales, for example, as facts without making any judgment about their legitimacy or moral quality. But heated political debates and conflicts over the legitimacy of such practices show that citizens and governments are inescapably making normative judgments about what they believe is right or best. Norms inescapably press upon us to act in response to them; they are part of political reality. Norms of justice, love, mercy, and so forth, come with the very order of our creatureliness even when selfishness and unjust acts go against those norms.

2. For citizens to be free requires that they are not hindered in exercising various political responsibilities, such as voting, appealing to the courts, and organizing to influence lawmaking. Freedom is not a generality but the ability to exercise diverse responsibilities without illegitimate interference. Civic freedom is something dif-

ferent from the freedom to exercise familial, or economic, or academic responsibilities. The same persons exercise different kinds of responsibility. To recognize this means two things for a political community. First, it helps to clarify the kind of limits that should be recognized by different institutions and organizations, including the political community. And second, it means that a political community can be just and well-ordered only if the government is constitutionally obligated to protect the freedom of citizens to engage responsibly both in political life and in the exercise of their non-political responsibilities.

3. The third insight of Dooyeweerd I want to highlight here concerns the last point just made about the obligation of a political community to protect the freedom of people to exercise both their civic and their non-political, non-government responsibilities. A government that acts as if it has omnicompetent authority may try to interfere in, or override the freedom of parents, business and labor leaders, professors, scientists, or religious clerics to exercise their responsibilities. A judgment has to be made at the constitutional level, therefore, about whether government may or may not act omnicompetently. And if it may not, then how is its unique public-legal authority to be defined and restricted?

The judgment Dooyeweerd makes and explains in detail in his writings is that government's responsibility must be specified in a particular public-legal way that disallows omnicompetence. The integrating and umbrella-like reach of public law over the entire territory of a political community does not entail omnicompetent authority over every human responsibility. To the contrary, public law must, if it is to uphold public justice, recognize and protect what is not political and governmental. It is not enough to say that individuals should be free *from* an oppressive or repressive government. We must insist that government is obligated to act strictly in keeping with its own jurisdictional competence to deal justly with all citizens so they may freely exercise both their civic responsibilities and their non-government, non-civic responsibilities.

53

The Good of Politics: Dooyeweerd's Contribution

by James W Skillen

ONE OF THE MOST influential convictions about government and political life in the history of Christianity was articulated by Augustine in the fourth century A.D. Government, he believed, has been given by God because of sin. Political life is not natural; it is not an inherent potential of our creatureliness. Rather, government has been given by God to restrain public disorder and violence and to punish evildoers. That is how Romans 13:1–7 has been read by many if not most Christians for nearly two millennia: government is a servant of God that "does not bear the sword in vain." It exists to punish those who do wrong. The emphasis is on *retributive* justice.

However, reading Romans 13 in that way does not do justice to other verses in that passage or in other parts of the Bible. Romans 13 also says that government's duty is to approve good conduct. Government is God's servant for your good, writes Paul; it is not a terror to good conduct. In fact, for governments to make and enforce laws to restrain and punish evildoers, they need an understanding of what is good and just that is violated by unjust conduct. The proper aim in punishing evildoers should be to recover, restore, and uphold what is good. This brief passage in Paul's letter to the Romans does not provide details about how government should uphold the good and punish evil. Romans 13 does not outline the limits of government in relation to other authorities, such as parents, teachers, and church leaders, who bear non-governmental responsibilities, and who must also encourage good behavior and punish bad behavior in families, schools, and churches. Yet it seems clear that the appropriate punishment of evildoers by governments depends on standards of the public good—public justice—which expose every violation of that good.

In Dooyeweerd's philosophical exposition of the nature of a good political order he affirms that the core meaning of justice is retribution.[1] However, most of his exposition takes for granted that the norms for a just political community are given with creation. And his expansive discussion explains how a good and just political order is crucial for upholding the normative good of persons, other institutions and organizations, and other creatures. Consequently, although "retributive justice" does not seem to be sufficient as a term for the normative standard of a political community, Dooyeweerd's broader exposition of the meaning of "public justice" provides great insight into the good of politics.

Dooyeweerd affirms the high calling of those who hold public office. Government officials are God's servants to encourage the good and to restrain and punish evildoing that arises from human sinfulness. Dooyeweerd's inquiry into the nature of the state—the political community of government and citizens—also seeks to

---

[1]. Dooyeweerd explains, however, that the term "retribution" "has been often wrongly restricted to criminal law.... Retribution is not only exercised in *malam* but also in *bonam partem*" (*A New Critique of Theoretical Thought* II, 130). For a thorough discussion of Dooyeweerd's use of the term "retribution" in regard to law and justice, see Jonathan Chaplin, *Herman Dooyeweerd: Christian Philosopher of State and Civil Society* (Notre Dame: University of Notre Dame Press, 2011), 176–93. Dooyeweerd's thinking on law, society, and politics is presented in a collection of his writings, *Essays in Legal, Social, and Political Philosophy* (1997), edited by D.F.M. Strauss. Most comprehensively Dooyeweerd develops his philosophy of the state, or political community, in *A New Critique*, III, 379–508.

clarify the difference between a political community and other institutions and organizations such as the family and the church. A good political order, qualified by the norm of justice, manifests in all its functions—moral, jural, aesthetic, economic, social, psychological, physical, and more—a distinctive political character.

A political community exists to uphold public justice for all within a particular territorial jurisdiction. And the power of such an institution comes from its monopoly of the use of lethal force. No other institution or organization is structured in that way. In a family, parents have an obligation to do justice to their children, but that is not a responsibility to uphold public justice, nor may parents use lethal force in disciplining their children. A business is not a political organization or a family, yet it, too, must do justice to its employees, customers, the environment and more. The limits of government, therefore, are not determined first of all from outside the political community by the responsibilities that belong to individuals, families, and businesses. Government's limits come first of all from within its own identity and responsibility as a public-legal community, and government is the public lawmaking, enforcing and adjudicating body of that community with responsibility to promote the *common* public good.

It is important at this juncture to remark on Dooyeweerd's distinction between *things* (including institutions) and their *functions* if we are to acquire a more precise account of the differences between types of institutions. We just noted that a family is not a political community or a business enterprise. A family is a community qualified by the kind of love that nurtures familial bonds and promotes maturation and cooperative responsibility in members of the family. A political community, on the other hand, has as its guiding or qualifying function the norm of public justice. A political community will also need to function economically, socially, ethically, and in other ways, but it is a public-legal institution, not an extended family, or a business enterprise.

Dooyeweerd argues that WHAT exists are *things* such as animals, plants, stones, persons, institutions, and so forth. All things *function* in ways that account for HOW things exist. Many political scientists, in their theoretical work, try to reduce the political community to its power function, or its social, economic, or jural function. While those are important functions of a political community, the latter cannot be reduced to one or more of those functions. All things—the WHATs—including institutions, function simultaneously in all the ways—the HOWs—that everything functions. We can see, consequently, that the scientific study of the functions of a thing necessarily presuppose the thing, the whole WHAT, that exists and functions in many ways.

A good political community, therefore, is one that upholds the common public good through its lawmaking and execution of those laws that serve all citizens and residents who live within the territory of its jurisdiction. Political freedom is realized by means of the equitable and impartial treatment of citizens and residents under law, which affirms and protects civic participation through various means, including free and open election of representatives to government. At the same time, human life entails more than political life. A just political order, consequently, is one that recognizes and protects in law the responsibilities, associations, and institutions that originate outside the bonds and obligation of the political community. And public-legal recognition of non-political responsibilities highlights the external limits of government's responsibility. Public law touches everything, but government and its laws should not have omnicompetent authority over human life.

Here we should emphasize another, closely related insight of Dooyeweerd. He distinguishes the *part/whole relation* within an institution from the *interdependent relations* between different kinds of institutions. We recognize, for example, that a legislature, military organizations, and a court system are parts of the political whole of a political community. Similarly, we recognize that parts of a business enterprise are its managers and employees, an accounting system, and manufacturing plants or other kinds of buildings. The parts don't exist apart from the whole political community or the whole business enterprise. By contrast, families, churches, art galleries, sports clubs, and media organizations are not parts of a political community. Each has an independent identity that has developed on its own terms and does not serve as a department of government. Confusion arises when the distinct identities of different kinds of institutions and organizations are ignored. This can happen when the government of a political community legislates on matters that are the internal responsibility of families, schools, or business enterprises.

A healthy and just political community is one that works to strengthen and properly balance its parts for the good of all citizens and other residents of the political order while making sure that institutions and associations of a different kind are not treated as subordinate parts of the political community. People enjoy constructive and creative freedom when they can exercise different kinds of responsibility belonging to different types of institutions. This is especially important when we recognize that most independent institutions have interdependent relations with one another. Think for example of families and schools where teachers in a school serve *in loco parentis* (in the place of the parents) for young children when the children are students in the school. A family and a school are separate institutions, yet their interdependence during certain hours of the day means a distinct kind of relationship between the parents and the teachers. There are many kinds of interdependence among institutions and organizations, but we must recognize the difference between whole/part relations within an institution and the relations between different kinds of organizations where each of them maintains its own identity in relation to others. Good government and the free exercise of all human responsibilities depend in a major way on the public-legal recognition of those kinds of differences and interrelationships.

54

Political Idolatry: Assessing the Ideologies of Our Day

by David T. Koyzis

A CHRISTIAN WORLD and life view, as articulated by the tradition extending from Abraham Kuyper to Herman Dooyeweerd and his spiritual heirs, is in principle nonreductionist, meaning that those indwelling this worldview recognize the full complexity of God's creation. If we think of the natural world, we can easily distinguish amongst the myriad different things that make it up. Traditionally we differentiate among broad categories of things, grouping them into animal, vegetable, and mineral. The ancient Greeks thought everything could be classified into the four basic elements of earth, air, fire, and water. Other ancient peoples similarly acknowledged the diversity of the world they inhabited but attached to these phenomena godlike properties, which amounts to what students of religion call animism, namely, the attribution of consciousness to sun, moon, stars, wind, thunder, volcanoes, trees, and so forth, along with power to affect the human world. Among such primitive, undifferentiated peoples, society was, by contrast, simple, with the tribe constituting the center of their lives, their leaders combining several functions in their persons, including political, economic, cultic, and familial.

Beginning in the modern age, particularly the seventeenth century, the scientific community made a concerted effort to understand a variety of phenomena by breaking them down into their component parts. Physicists began to search for the smallest particle of matter, whose discovery would ostensibly give them the key to reality. Following their lead, political philosophers, beginning most notably with Thomas Hobbes (1588–1679), took a similar approach to society, asserting that community can be grasped only by reference to the individuals it comprises. This produced something of a paradox: at the very moment when western societies were becoming more differentiated, with primitive sibs unfolding into a complex pattern of families, guilds, schools, universities, occupational groupings, towns, church congregations, and political communities or states, the early modern political philosophers were taking their readers in the opposite direction by arguing that the increasingly wide variety of communities of which they were part could be reduced to the component individuals.

The new emphasis on the individual was in one sense a progressive development in that it liberated people from traditional constraints imposed by, among other things, the class structure, mercantilist economic policies, and centralized royal courts. However, the long-term effect was to level out these communities by defining them, not by a structure intrinsic to their makeup, but as mere aggregations of consenting individuals. Under this new reduced understanding of society, the only two salient components left to account for are the state and the individual. This has provided fertile soil for the proliferation of political visions that distort reality for those attempting to grasp society and the ills plaguing it.

Although the political ideologies with which we are familiar in the modern and postmodern worlds have roots in the early modern era, the French Revolution of 1789 gave them a huge boost as they worked their way into the hearts of Europeans and those elsewhere affected by European trends. These political visions and illusions could be grouped around one of the two poles thought to characterize any social order, namely, the individual and the community. Liberalism, which arguably began with Hobbes and had even older roots in epicurean philosophy, places the individual at the centre of the world. Nationalism, socialism, democratism, and some varieties of conservatism exalt the community over the individual, disagreeing only on the identity of this community. For nationalists it is obviously the nation, while for socialists it is the economic class. For democratism it is the democratic people, while conservatives champion a larger community shaped by tradition and subject to an unconscious growth characteristic of a biological organism. Other conservatives, by contrast, embrace an earlier form of liberalism with its emphasis on the individual and the voluntary assumption of social obligations. This is especially true of English-speaking conservatives and less so of their continental European counterparts.

Although different collectivists claim to exalt different communities, in practice their doing so empowers the state, that is, the community of citizens and their government. Thus it is scarcely surprising that, although Karl Marx (1818–1883) and Friedrich Engels (1820–1895) envisioned a future classless society in which the bourgeois state would have no place, efforts to implement their ideas led to a totalitarian state recognizing no intrinsic limits to its competence. The result was a rigid social order in which ordinary human activities, including the formation of horizontal loyalties and attachments, were suppressed in favour of an all-encompassing "solidarity" that amounted to the top-down rule of a single party organization.

Against this totalitarian trend, many people took refuge in the individualism of historic liberalism, including Austrian economic philosopher Friedrich Hayek (1899–1992), whose *Road to Serfdom*[1] would become the manifesto of a postwar libertar-

---

1. F. A. von Hayek, *The Road to Serfdom* (Chicago: University of Chicago Press, 1944).

ian revival. Indeed, the early liberals believed in a strictly limited state, often labelled the night watchman state, which largely restricts itself to keeping internal order and defending against external attack. However, as liberalism developed over the centuries, a process I describe in my *Political Visions and Illusions*,[2] followers increasingly called on the state to enhance people's right to choose, requiring a more extensive government apparatus than what was envisioned by their spiritual forebears. If the state is nothing more than a voluntary association of sovereign individuals, then those individuals are entitled to make of the state what they will and call upon it to perform a potentially limitless variety of functions within the larger social order.

Ironically, then, liberalism turns out to empower the state as effectively as its collectivist opponents. Patrick Deneen argues that liberalism has failed precisely because of tensions within this ideology—tensions due to its sharing many of the same assumptions as collectivism.[3] Thus the two major political ideologies in most of our parliamentary bodies, namely, liberalism and socialism, might better be seen, not as true opposites, but as quarrelling siblings, bound together by shared assumptions about the nature of the world and of our place within it.

As with other reductionisms, the tacit decision to ascribe ultimacy to a particular element of reality possesses a basic religious character. It is something that cannot be reasoned to but only reasoned from. In this respect, it is a manifestation of an ancient phenomenon which we can hardly be said to have outgrown as human beings created in God's image, namely, idolatry. Idolatry takes something out of the total panorama of God's creation and effectively ascribes to it divine status. Doing so inevitably imports distortions into our understanding of God's world and the way we

---

2. D. Koyzis, *Political Visions and Illusions* (Downers Grove, IL: InterVarsity Press, 2019), 40-56.
3. P. Deneen, *Why Liberalism Failed* (New Haven, CT: Yale University Press, 2018).

live within it. The Canaanites of the Bronze Age worshipped false deities who demanded human sacrifice—something that God expressly prohibited (Leviticus 18:21; Deuteronomy 18:10). This horrific practice set the tone for their society, thereby incurring God's wrath and ultimate judgement upon them.

Our own idols are more subtle, but they too demand a form of human sacrifice. If we so idolize the individual, subordinating to her subjective will all other considerations, including the overall health of our communities, we will find ourselves inadvertently fomenting social fragmentation and encouraging the proliferation of conflicts that the state will be required to adjudicate. If we persist in viewing the various communities of which we are part as ultimately derivative from a larger entity such as the nation, the democratic people, the economic class, or the state itself, we run the risk of failing to recognize their unique characters and tasks, thereby facilitating a society marred by stifling conformity and lack of vitality. Such a society will be poor in several respects, not only economically, but politically, socially, artistically, and culturally. A civic culture, crucial to democratic governance, will fail to develop and may even be eroded where it once existed and thrived.

Can we speak of a more biblical alternative to the ideologies that have so affected our polities in the western world? Yes, although we will not expect to find a blueprint in the pages of the Scriptures themselves. Instead, we must immerse ourselves in the biblical redemptive narrative, finding our own place within it, and taking seriously its implications for our common life in between the times. As created, fallen, and redeemed human beings, awaiting God's final consummation of the new heaven and the new earth (Isaiah 66; Revelation 21), we do well to recognize that, because we are liberated from sin, we are freed from all efforts to find a point of ultimacy within God's creation. As Oliver O'Donovan correctly puts it, "unity is proper to the creator, complexity to the created world."[4] In one way or another the modern political ideologies deny this reality, which I have labelled *societal pluriformity*, or the *pluriformity of authorities*.[5] This corresponds to what Abraham Kuyper called, rather inelegantly, sphere sovereignty.

To be sure, we will not go to the Bible to learn directly about this pluriformity. Indeed, if our powers of perception are not too adversely affected by the ideological illusions undertaking to account for the world, we will readily intuit that families are families, marriages are marriages, business enterprises are business enterprises, and so forth. We will easily comprehend at a pretheoretical level that families are different from classrooms, that classrooms are different from gathered church congregations, and that church congregations are different from financial institutions. The Bible's role is nicely summarized in Psalm 119:105: "Your word is a lamp to my feet and a light to my path." We are already in motion, walking along the path of life from birth to the present moment. We pick up the Scriptures to give us clarity in the midst of a sinful world. They illumine our way to prevent us stumbling or straying from the path, thereby enabling us to reach our ultimate destination on God's seventh day.

Dooyeweerd's nonreductionist ontology focuses specifically on the modal aspects of created reality, which he deems irreducible. But his philosophy is also applicable to the concrete things of life, which he calls individuality structures. As such, it constitutes a formidable challenge to the distorting illusions of the dominant political ideologies.

---

4. O. O'Donovan, *The Desire of the Nations: Rediscovering the Roots of Political Theology* (Cambridge: Cambridge University Press, 1996), 177.
5. D. Koyzis, *We Answer to Another: Authority, Office, and the Image of God* (Eugene, OR: Pickwick, 2014).

55

Dooyeweerd and Vollenhoven: What They Share, How They Differ, and How They Complement One Another

by Jeremy Ive

Background

HERMAN DOOYEWEERD (1894–1977) and Dirk H. Th. Vollenhoven (1892–1974) took the stage against the background of Reformational thought as seen in the work of Abraham Kuyper.

Dooyeweerd and Vollenhoven shared Kuyper's vision of the Lordship of Christ over every area of life. Together they were to develop a systematic elaboration of Kuyper's notion of sphere sovereignty. However, whereas Kuyper had largely developed his insights in a social context, Vollenhoven and Dooyeweerd carried this basic insight through with far greater rigor and comprehensiveness than had their pioneering predecessor. They built on the foundations laid by Kuyper and elaborated his social vision to develop a global philosophy of the created order as a whole and not merely human society.

The two men were students together at the Free University of Amsterdam founded by Kuyper, and Vollenhoven came to marry Dooyeweerd's sister, Hermina. After graduating with his doctorate, Vollenhoven served as pastor of the Gereformeerde Kerken, first in a congregation in Oostkapelle, Zeeland, and then, from May 1921, in the church of The Hague. In December 1920, Dooyeweerd, who was then working as a civil servant in The Hague, had written to him expressing his interest in deepening his own philosophical understanding with Vollenhoven's help. He mentioned his interest especially in the way in which Vollenhoven was starting to identify the diversity of forms of knowledge, reflecting the diversity of reality. With both brothers-in-law living in The Hague, the opportunity for close and intensive conversations was greatly enhanced.

The conversations between the two brothers-in-law rapidly bore fruit. As noted in the previous section, in mid–1922 (as the evidence seems to indicate), there was the "discovery" of the modalities during, it seems, a walk in the dunes near The Hague. The task that they now undertook together involved working out Kuyper's principle of *sphere sovereignty* ("souvereiniteit in eigen kring") in a systematic way. Whereas for Kuyper this was primarily a social vision, for Dooyeweerd and Vollenhoven it extended to a philosophical account of the whole of created reality which they, together and individually, worked out in a philosophically rigorous way.

The Basic Philosophical Questions for Dooyeweerd and Vollenhoven

Dooyeweerd and Vollenhoven together worked to develop a Christian philosophy that would take full account of the totality of human experience. From a Reformational perspective, the systematic philosophical task involves two basic questions which together give rise to a third.

The first basic question is the issue of *structure:* In what way is our experience of the world structured? This is itself a composite of two further questions: the question of what there is (the ontology of the world), and the question of how we know it (the epistemology of the world).

The second basic question is the issue of *direction:* What is the "religious" orientation of those engaged in the philosophical task? This second basic question is not one which secular philosophy asks, or even recognizes as valid, committed as it is to the ideal of religious neutrality. From a Reformational perspective, however, the ideal of religious neutrality conceals a religious commitment of its own, so that the question of religious orientation can be suppressed but cannot be evaded.

Linking these two questions is the third question: What are the presuppositions (or basic assumptions) that Dooyeweerd (explicitly) and Vollenhoven (implicitly) argue are the necessary foundations for any systematic philosophical thinking?

The Problem of Reductionism

Attempts to reduce all other features of reality to thought, and, more specifically to analytical thought (which takes its character from considerations of logic) result in antinomies (internal contradictions). Before embarking on logical analysis, it is necessary to experience that which is analyzed; logic cannot itself provide the content for logical analysis. Moreover, logic cannot itself account for aspects of the world such as beauty and justice. These latter involve non-logical—though not illogical—considerations.

As Vollenhoven and Dooyeweerd both point out, a similar result awaits any project seeking to understand the world which takes as its point of departure one aspect or a selection of aspects. Such projects include attempts to describe the world purely in physico-chemical terms, or it attempts to understand human relationships purely in biological terms. Any attempt to reduce the description of the world to one form of explanation cannot do justice to the many-sided diversity of everyday experience; any attempt to construct society based on any one form of explanation risks undermining that society. As in the story of Midas, if all things are turned to gold, they become lifeless. Dooyeweerd mentions the dominance of "isms" each of which absolutize one or other aspect of concrete experience.

Vollenhoven and Dooyeweerd argue that while the more extreme forms of reductionism achieve their consistency at the cost of distortion, the less extreme forms collapse into incoherence. For example, one's understanding of the world cannot fully be based on physical relations, that is, on relations concerning the exchange and conversion of physical energy. Physical relations alone (or biological, psychological, "historical"/cultural-formative relations, etc.) cannot adequately exemplify for us relations of justice, beauty, love, or faith, to mention just a few. Any attempt to exclude these latter from the picture gives one an impoverished and distorted worldview. However, even taking any of the latter on its own cannot provide one with a full and balanced picture either.

Dooyeweerd's and Vollenhoven's Common Alternative to Reductionism

As an alternative approach, both philosophers start with experience in its rich and irreducible diversity in this respect; Vollenhoven speaks of "non-scientific" experience while Dooyeweerd speaks of "naïve" experience. Non-scientific or naïve experience involves encounters with whole persons or things, engagement in specific relationships, and participation in actual events.

Naïve experience involves the encounter with all reality at once in its irreducible diversity yet indissoluble "coherence." It is "pre-theoretical" in that it seeks no explicit analysis of reality's norms and laws. Naïve experience does not exclude analysis; but this must be distinguished from "scientific" or "theoretical" analysis.

"Scientific" (Vollenhoven) or "theoretical" (Dooyeweerd) thought, by contrast, seeks the explicit differentiation of the different aspects of the world through *epochè*, the process of modal abstraction or theoretical analysis.

"Discovery" of the Modalities or Modal Aspects by Dooyeweerd and Vollenhoven

Dooyeweerd and Vollenhoven came eventually to identify fifteen functions or modalities, the mutually irreducible ways or modes of being and knowing. The name for each of them tended to vary between the two philosophers, and there were subsequent refinements as well. Vollenhoven tends to see the functions arranged "vertically," so that he speaks of them being "lower" or "higher," while Dooyeweerd, as we shall see, tends to speak of the functions as "earlier" and "later" in what he (problematically, as I shall argue) calls "cosmic time."

Each modality has what Dooyeweerd calls a "cosmonomic" side, which comprises the laws or norms specific to each of the modalities, and a "factual" side which differentiates into the factual subject-side and the factual-object side (also designated as the [factual] subject-object relation [see Diagram 1 of the Introduction]) which is governed by these laws or norms. "Cosmonomic" indicates both laws proper and norms—i.e., pertaining to what applies or ought to apply. How these distinctions function in the two thinkers' respective philosophical positions is far less clear and somewhat controversial. Vollenhoven explicitly rejects the distinction between the cosmonomic and factual side and instead he sees the law as mediating between God and cosmos.

D. F. M. Strauss argues that the differences between the accounts presented by the two philosophers are more terminological than substantive, since while Vollenhoven speaks of the law as "above" the temporal order and Dooyeweerd of the cosmonomic "side," both share the notion of being "subject," i.e., "under" the law (note that this sense of "subject" needs to be distinguished from the sense of "subject" as in the "subject-object" relation where it refers to the active pole of that relationship).

Dooyeweerd's distinction between the cosmonomic and the factual sides of created reality should not be confused with that between naïve experience and theoretical thought. Naïve experience is equally subject to laws or norms, even if these are not explicitly differentiated according to the modalities; while theoretical thought investigates both the laws and norms according to those different modalities—for example, quantitative theoretical concepts are governed by quantitative "logic," spatial concepts by spatial "logic" and so on.

There is much less agreement between the two philosophers about the other crucial feature of their philosophical systematics, which Vollenhoven calls the "determinations," and which Dooyeweerd calls the "transcendental dimensions in the experiential horizon" (or "transcendental dimensions" for short).

The Structure of Dooyeweerd's Philosophy

For Dooyeweerd there are three "transcendental dimensions" in what he calls the "experiential horizon." Each of these "transcendental dimensions" provides a different point of entry for our experience of and reflection upon the world. Unlike Vollenhoven, Dooyeweerd does not start with concrete individuals and their functions; instead, he starts with modal relations which constitute and define the different modalities or modal aspects, and then second, sees these as being "individualized" in what he calls "individuality structures."

There is also the third transcendental dimension, what he calls "cosmic time." "Cosmic time" indicates a "supra-temporal" view of the ordering of the world. This involves, on the one hand, identifying and placing in sequence the laws and norms which govern the different kinds of relation, and, on the other, providing a characterization in modally structured terms of the individuals which perdure. For Dooyeweerd, "cosmic time" is, on the one hand, a systematic opening up of the modalities (the "cosmic temporal order of the modal aspects" which, as we have seen, he traces out primarily in terms of the different kind of relations—the "cosmonomic side" of "cosmic time"), and, on the other, the perdurance of individuality structures (the "factual" side of "cosmic time"). Thus, for him there is something of an *a priori* necessity of cosmic time, unfolding according to the order of the modalities from number or quantity onward.

In what he calls the "opening process," Dooyeweerd describes how the different modalities are successively revealed and distinguished from one another, as society becomes more complex. This can take different forms. First, there is a process of "differentiation" *across* the modalities, with the different sorts of relations being distinguished from one another over time. He calls this "the external opening process." This is complemented by the internal opening process or "individualization": an individual, whether human or non-human, endures *through* time; its individuality-structure—the structured diversity of diverse functions with which that individual operates—is opened up over the course of the duration of time.

The Structure of Vollenhoven's Philosophy

For his part, Vollenhoven starts with individuals. In his syllabus *Isagôgè* or *Introduction*, his basic philosophical instruction manual, Vollenhoven calls the first two "determinations" the "thus-so" and the "this-that." The thus-so determination refers to the functions of individuals, while the this-that deals with individuals in relationship with one another.

Vollenhoven complements Dooyeweerd's account of individuals as individuality structures, whether seen as complexes of functional laws and norms ("structures for"), or as complexes of individuals' factual functions ("structures of"). Vollenhoven deals with individuals both from the standpoint of the diversity of functions (the "thus-so" determination), and from that of relationships between linking concrete individuals to one another (the "this-that" determination).

There are, however, problems in Vollenhoven's account of the externality and universality of relations. For him, relations do not have their own status of being, but are derived from the linking together of the constituent individuals over time—they apply only to a specific context or chain of events. Relations cannot therefore be seen as having universal status beyond a specific relationship and the individuals concerned. Dooyeweerd, by contrast, opens the way for a much stronger conception of relations in "external" terms i.e., in terms independent of the individuals concerned, which is important because otherwise values are reduced merely to tendencies specific to the individuals concerned, or the product of purely local arrangements—in short, they are reduced to historical relativism.

With respect to time, Vollenhoven later explicitly rejected what he calls the "modalization" (*modaliseering*) of time that Dooyeweerd's notion of "cosmic time" represents, i.e., the conflation of narrative, or a sequence of events, with (or, one might say, the reduction of narrative to) the order of the modalities. However, there is also implicitly a third determination. Vollenhoven calls this the "genetic connection." This is about the flow of time.

The genetic connection concerns the unfolding of individual character in actual time, the inter-relations between them ("inter-individual connections"), and the inter-relations within them ("intra-individual connections"). New individuals, and new inter-relations between or among them, come into being, develop their individual character over time, and cease to exist. Vollenhoven speaks of "lifelines" which express the change and development of each individual over time.

Perhaps we can think of a doctor–patient situation, where the doctor can better understand and so treat their patient by considering their patient's medical history, or alternatively, a merchant can build up a picture of a customer's credit history and so build up trust, and discern how better to serve them given their previous preferences, or even changes in these, over time.

A new individual can evolve out of one or more previously existing things, so that whereas the constituents were previously interrelated in an inter-individual manner, now they take on an intra-individual interrelation. This can involve two individuals joining to become a new individual, for example two businesses can merge to become one; or when an individual takes on a constituent of another, for example a plank of wood can be taken from a tree to become part of a fence; or when two or more individuals each contribute constituents of what then becomes a new individual, as in the case of biological reproduction.

With his conception of the genetic determination Vollenhoven provides a way to account for time in a narrative way, detailing the coming into being and development of new individuals. This allows for the insights of Dooyeweerd's account of the "opening process" to be appreciated without falling into a form of modal determinism, where the process of history "must" or "ought" to proceed purely in a pre-ordained modal order.

So, for Vollenhoven, both in terms of the individuality functions (the "thus-so" determination, which for him is the "modal" determination), and individual factuality (the "this-that" determination which concerns inter-individual relationships), he provides an account of how relations between and among individuals are constructed over time as well as how individuals themselves change and develop over time. So, while he starts with individuality, it is the implicit third determination (the "genetic" connection) that is systematically central to his ontology and epistemology, since it both gives actuality to individuals and provides a basis on which relations are constructed.

Conclusion

Overall, then, as Dooyeweerd and Vollenhoven shared the vision of the Lordship of Christ over every area of life, so, in response to the problem of reductionism, they came to a similar picture of the many different modalities or aspects which constitute the rich tapestry of God's created order.

They differ in how this is approached, with Vollenhoven providing a stronger account of individuality and time, while Dooyeweerd is stronger on the modalities as different kinds of relation ordered in what he calls "cosmic time" (a notion which Vollenhoven rejected). Each has different problems in the manner in which their account of the diversity of the created order is worked out.

But in the end, it is better to see their different approaches as complementary rather than contradictory. And indeed, by drawing on both of their philosophical systems, a fuller and better account of the richness of God's created order can be arrived at.[1]

Diagram Comparing the Two Approaches

This diagram links the emphases of Dooyeweerd and Vollenhoven: For Dooyeweerd, "cosmic time" links relationality and individuality. Vollenhoven starts with individuality over time and sees relations constructed on that basis. Dooyeweerd is italicized while Vollenhoven is underlined; what they have in common is in bold.

---

1. Greater detail, further background, and more references can be found in Jeremy Ive, *A Critically Comparative Kuyperian Analysis and a Trinitarian, "Perichoretic" Reconstruction of the Reformational Philosophies of Dirk H. Th. Vollenhoven and Herman Dooyeweerd* (PhD Thesis, King's College London, 2012), or in the updated version, *The Roots of Reformational Philosophy: The Thought of Dirk H. Th. Vollenhoven and Herman Dooyeweerd in the Light of the Trinitarian Vision of Abraham Kuyper* (unpub. ms., 2014), with an Index of Persons.

DOOYEWEERD AND VOLLENHOVEN

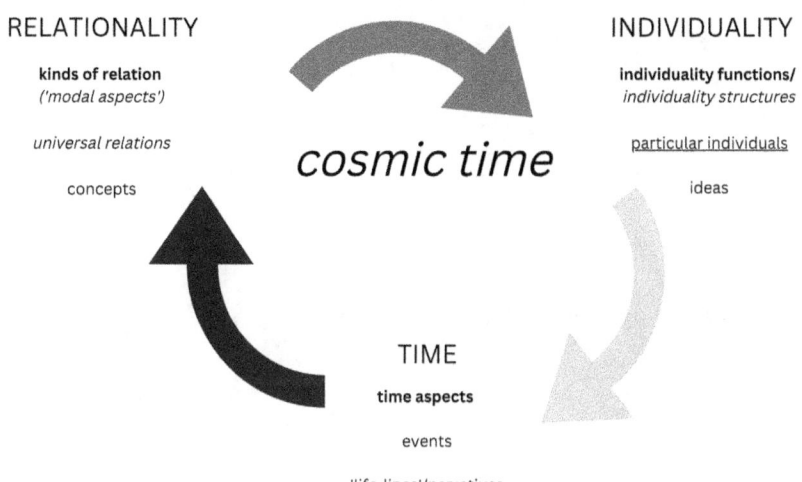

RELATIONALITY

kinds of relation
('modal aspects')

universal relations

concepts

cosmic time

INDIVIDUALITY

individuality functions/
individuality structures

particular individuals

ideas

TIME

time aspects

events

*'life-lines'/*narratives

56

Everyday Life with Dooyeweerd

by Andrew Basden

Introduction

WE LIVE IN AN ocean of meaningfulness.[1] According to Dooyeweerd, not only is everything around us meaningful, but meaningfulness is what enables us, and everything around us, to exist and function at all. This meaningfulness is diverse, and he identified and studied fifteen ways in which it is possible to be meaningful—to be spheres of meaningfulness. Dooyeweerd called them *aspects*. Aspects are also modes of being and modes of functioning and give answers to "Why?"

Nearly everything in our everyday lives exhibits nearly every aspect. Take *having breakfast*, for example. (Refer to the list of aspects in Table 1 below and in the next chapter.) The main reason for having breakfast is *biotic*—sustenance—but very important also is the sense of taste, which is meaningful in the *psychical* aspect, and enjoyment of food, which is meaningful in the *aesthetic* aspect. I might make up my muesli or cook my food, which is a *formative* aspect of breakfast. I think about which food to have: an *analytical* aspect. Chewing food is a *physical* aspect. There is the social aspect of sharing the meal together, along with another *aesthetic* aspect of enjoying the company (or not!). Conversation occurs, which is a *lingual* aspect, and so is listening to the radio (which is what I do at breakfast). I limit what I eat, because I have

---

1. This chapter is written in a less philosophical style, to reflect its topic.

limited time or money, which are *economic* aspects of breakfast. I try to do justice to my food and to others present, and also to my day ahead by eating sufficient; doing justice is a *juridical* aspect. I might offer others the last piece of toast, which is a minor example of the *ethical* aspect of self-giving love. This is because I believe courtesy is important; believing is pistic—the faith aspect. The three mathematical aspects, *quantitative*, *spatial* and *kinematic*, occur several ways for food, people or other things—for example, number of cups of tea, their placement, and movement of cup to mouth.

This is shown in Figure 1, where the lines from the aspects point to where they are mentioned above.

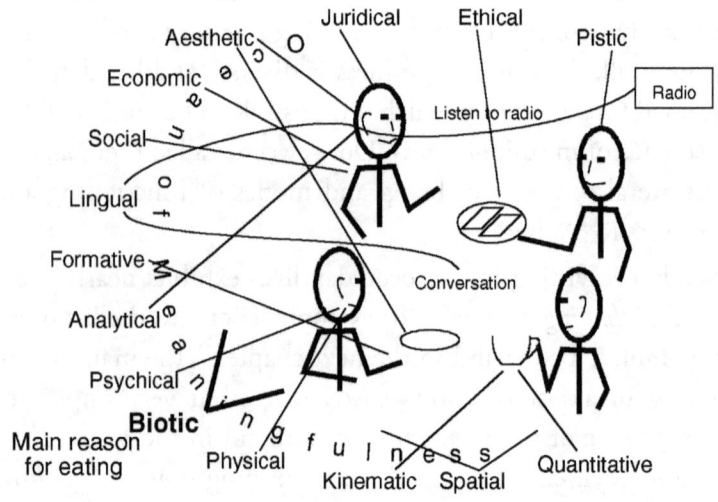

Figure 1. Aspects of eating breakfast

It might surprise us to find so many aspects of such a mundane activity as having breakfast. Breakfast is never "just" eating; it is all these aspects simultaneously; all Dooyeweerd's fifteen aspects are there, and in myriad other ways not mentioned above. We can find these aspects in almost every situation, from mundane ones to situations of national and global importance. Suppose you are in a group that is deciding strategy to tackle climate change: even there most of the aspects mentioned above can be found, though appearing in different ways. All we do and all we are is meaningful in all aspects together, simultaneously, and in coherence—a state that Dooyeweerd called "coherence of meaning."[2]

Dooyeweerd emphasized meaningfulness as a foundation of all temporal reality ("Creation"), which sets him apart from most philosophers and makes his philosophical ideas useful in practical ways.[3]

Knowing something of Dooyeweerd's aspects can help us in our lives, in at least four ways. Knowing aspects can:

- Help us separate things out - as I did with breakfast.
- Help us understand things more deeply and "listen" more attentively.
- Help us see what might be missing: hidden issues.
- Offer guidance, because each aspect comes with norms to guide us.

Let us look at each of these in turn.

Aspects Help Us Separate Things Out

Every aspect contributes to our everyday experience, our day-to-day living, when we are just getting on with things rather than thinking abstractly. This is what Dooyeweerd called the "pre-theoretical attitude of thought" as distinct from the "theoretical atti-

---

2. Dooyeweerd, A New Critique, I, 4.
3. For a philosophical account of Dooyeweerd's understanding of meaning, see Basden, "Dooyeweerd's Understanding of Meaning (1): Some Main Themes," and Basden and Joneidy, "Dooyeweerd's Understanding of Meaning (2): Some Implications"; see also Chapters 3 and 4 of Basden, *Foundations and Practice of Research*.

tude", in which we abstract and isolate aspects. Abstraction is what happens in research, which is the topic of the next chapter.

In between pre-theoretical and full theoretical attitudes lies what Clouser calls low-level abstraction, in which we are aware of the different aspects of things, without isolating them.[4] This is what we did above, in separating out the different aspects of having breakfast.

Each of Dooyeweerd's fifteen aspects gives a different class of issues that we can separate out conceptually and think about. For example, we noticed the difference between taste of food and enjoying the taste—food's *psychical* and *aesthetic* aspects. We also noticed two aesthetic aspects of breakfast: enjoying food and conversation. In fact, each aspect is manifested in several ways in our lives, which, for the *aesthetic* aspect, include enjoyment, harmony (as in music), poetic allusion, fun, humor, leisure, art, sport, and so on.[5] The *aesthetic* aspect is what differentiates both sport and art from "mere" technical achievement or skill, which are meaningful in the *formative* aspect, along with such things as plans, aims, goals, making, constructing, techniques, technology and history.[6] Sport and art depend on such things, but cannot be reduced to them; this is known as "inter-aspect dependency." Likewise, things like love, goodness, generosity, mercy, forgiveness, which are meaningful in the *ethical* aspect, cannot be reduced to, but depend on, law, rights, responsibility, and other things meaningful in the *juridical* aspect.[7]

Being aware of such aspectual differences can help us describe things—especially complex things—more meaningfully to others, so that different issues need not be confused and communications can become clearer. Dooyeweerd believed that the aspects are

---

4. Clouser, *The Myth of Religious Neutrality*.
5. Basden, *Foundations and Practice of Research*, 201.
6. Ibid., 194.
7. Ibid., 203, 205.

common to all people, cultures and eras of history, at least in their most fundamental meanings, which Dooyeweerd called "meaning kernels." So they make basic understanding and communication between people possible in the first place. (Note: No kernel meaning can be fully expressed in words, so Dooyeweerd often used several names for each.)

It is when we recognize this variety of meaning in things that we begin to understand them more clearly and fully—our second point.

Aspects Help Us Understand and Assess Things More Deeply
By clearly understanding the meaning kernel of each aspect and the ways it can be manifested in life, we can gain deeper insights. Each aspect offers different kinds of laws that enable things to operate in multiple ways. Insight comes from understanding these and how each depends on others.

For example, when I hear something I disagree with, such as on breakfast radio, maybe even violently because of culture-war boundaries, I can see the workings of the pistic/faith aspect in my and their strong responses, and can see how that impacted our thinking and language (analytical, lingual functioning). So I can give myself different language and judge more dispassionately—and even acknowledge some validity in what they say. So I can offer the "soft answer" that "turns away wrath."

I find that understanding aspect kernel meanings helps me more truly listen to people and situations. A friend was telling me about his financial and social problems and physical disabilities, and the unfairness of local government response to his needs. I could see these as separate aspects (economic, social, physical and juridical aspects), and so could listen meaningfully as he spoke about each. We tried to rectify some of these in ways meaningful in these aspects. However, I could also feel undertones of unforgiving attitude and lack of dignity. Some might assume these are caused by his various problems, but, recognizing them as of different aspects, the *ethical* and *pistic* aspects, I could see that these might exacerbate his problems, rather than only being caused by them. This is why our rectification attempts had not worked well. He needed love and dignity, and to love and to believe in return, not just have us solve economic, social, physical and legal problems.

Understanding of aspects provides a basis for making wider and wiser judgments and making them more clearly understood.

Aspects Reveal Hidden Things

Understanding aspects makes one more sensitive to hidden issues and those that are overlooked or taken for granted.

Have you been in conversations or discussions where you felt something was being missed, but you could not quite make out what? Almost all situations function in all aspects, but most conversations, discussions and analyses cover issues that are meaningful in only a few of the aspects. Awareness of aspects can help reveal what is missing, overlooked, or taken for granted—also hidden agendas or "elephants in the room." How often, in conversations about feelings or mental states, are juridical, ethical, and pistic issues not mentioned except in passing?

In the past, most economists ignored all but the economic aspect. In recent years, some economists have been considering social and environmental "capital" as partners with economic capital. That is, they want to bring the social and the biotic-physical aspects alongside the economic aspect. The social, biotic and physical aspects have come out of hiding, because problems that are meaningful in them became apparent (e.g., climate crisis). But what about the others? What about attitude (ethical aspect), religion (pistic), or technology (formative)? An awareness of aspects makes us sensitive to aspects that are being overlooked, and it can do so in any field.

Ethical and pistic issues are often overlooked because they lie deep and affect all else, unseen. They constitute what the Bible calls the human heart: our deeper attitudes, aspirations, assumptions, expectations and what we treat as divine.

When we notice an aspect being overlooked in conversation or in public policy, we can gently guide towards the issues meaningful in it.

Aspects Can Guide Us in Life

To Dooyeweerd, most aspects provide norms that, if fulfilled, will contribute to the "health" of any situation or success of any venture. Going against such norms undermines this and causes harm. For example, the lingual aspect allows us to record, communicate, and understand each other, but deceit (lingual dysfunction) undermines these. Depending on how we function in the lingual aspect, good or bad decisions are made, friendships are strengthened or weakened, investments are sound or unsound, and so on (repercussions in the formative, social, and economic aspects respectively). You can think of other examples of good and bad functioning and possible repercussions. In the later aspects, the health and harm take longer to emerge, sometimes decades for the pistic aspect.[8]

Awareness of aspectual normativity can help guide our decisions in life. Table 1 gives examples of good and bad functioning and repercussions in each aspect. (The quantitative to physical aspects offer good but no possibility of dysfunction.)

---

8. Basden, *Philosophical Frameworks for Understanding Information Systems*, 77.

Table 1. Aspects and their norms, in functioning and repercussions (examples)

Aspect	Functioning	Dysfunction	Repercussions Good	Repercussions Harmful
Quantitative	Amount as given		Reliable sequence	
Spatial	Simultaneity Continuity		Continuous extension	
Kinematic	Movement		Change (non-stasis)	
Physical	Force, causality		Persistence	
Biotic	Feeding, symbiosis	Starvation, parasitism	Vitality, survival	Disease, extinction
Psychical	Interaction	Insensitivity	Emotional and sensory vitality	Insensitivity
Analytic	Distinction	Conflation	Conceptual clarity	Confusion
Formative	Working, planning, constructing	Laziness, destroying	Achievement, construction	Lost opportunities, destruction
Lingual	Expressing, signification	Deceiving, obfuscating	Information	Misinformation
Social	Relating, befriending	Disdaining, hating	Friendship, achieve more together	Working against each other
Economic	Frugality	Squandering	Prosperity	Waste, poverty
Aesthetic	Harmonizing	Fragmentation, narrowing	Integrality, interest, fun	Conflict, boredom
Juridical	Giving due, responsibility	Irresponsibility	Justice	Injustice
Ethical / Attitudinal	Self-giving love, vulnerability, trust	Selfishness, self-protection	Culture of goodwill	Competitive, harsh culture
Pistic / Faith	Belief, courage, commitment	Idolatry, disloyalty	Hope	Hopelessness Loss of identity

Important note: Dooyeweerd warned that no suite of aspects is ever final. So we must use aspects with due caution. We should not be dogmatic about what aspects there are, what their kernel meanings are, nor how they are manifested above.

As an exercise, try working out how each of the aspects could contribute to making breakfast successful or unsuccessful.

Conclusion

There is much more that can be said about how Dooyeweerd can help us in daily life, but this shows how awareness of aspects can help us in four ways. Hopefully, this offers you a starting point to begin to understand the breadth and validity of Dooyeweerd's aspects in all you do, and perhaps begin to see life through the lens of aspects.

One wonderful feature of these aspects, if Dooyeweerd is correct, is that they are better grasped by intuition than by theoretical thought, so they are relatively easy to understand and use in daily life.[9] We found so when interviewing people.[10]

Theoretical thought (research) does have its place, though. This is discussed in the next chapter of this book.

---

9. [For Dooyeweerd's view of meaning in terms of concept-transcending knowledge, see Strauss, "Understanding the Linguistic Turn and the Quest for Meaning," *South African Journal of Philosophy* 32 (2013): 90–108.]
10. Basden, *Foundations and Practice of Research*, 267–270.

57

Understanding and Practicing Research with Dooyeweerd's Help

by Andrew Basden

THIS CHAPTER is for researchers, to briefly show how they may employ Dooyeweerd in their research, outlining the discussion in my book of 2020, *Foundations and Practice of Research: Adventures with Dooyeweerd's Philosophy*. It contains research-style argument and referencing.

Introduction: What Is Research?
Research is for finding things out. Suppose we wanted to research people having breakfast, as depicted in the previous chapter. The very first question we face is: What do we research (want to find out) about breakfast—the social relationships around breakfast; the taste of breakfast food; its nutritional value; expectations people have about breakfast; generosity at breakfast; economy of breakfast? Similarly, several questions arise when we study physics, though perhaps fewer in number, concerning for example quantities, spatial arrangements, movement, and forces. Research usually focuses on one kind of issue—one aspect of the complicated reality that faces us when we study it.

Figure 1 shows a researcher studying people having breakfast, using a diagram similar to the one in the previous chapter on Everyday Life. Both researcher and those researched function in the same set of aspects—within an "ocean" of diverse meaningfulness. The significance of this, and the lines and various labels, are explained below.

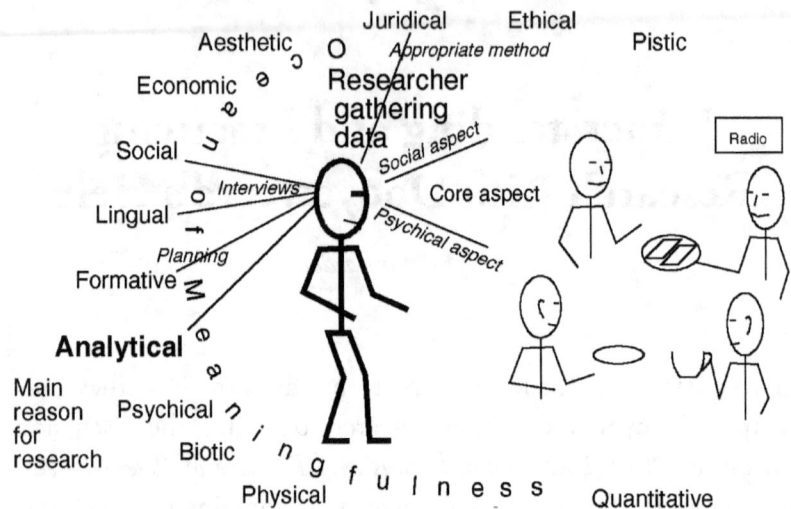

Figure 1: Researching people eating breakfast.
See Figure 1 in previous chapter

Contrary to popular assumptions, research does not yield certain *truths* so much as *beliefs* about reality on which it is reasonable to rely. These reasonable beliefs are what we call theories. For example, it is reasonable to rely on Newton's theories of (beliefs about) physics, except when going to extremes, when Einsteinian or Quantum theories are more reasonable. Different fields—physics, psychology, sociology, theology, and so on—yield different kinds of theory, with different criteria for reasonableness.

Oversimplifying perhaps, there are two main types of research. What we might call *professional research* tries to understand individual situations: "Why did our profits fall last year?" *Academic research* seeks understanding of the way the world works in general: "Why do profits fall?" Some research mixes the two. Notice the question "Why?" in both types: most research seeks to understand "laws" according to which reality operates.

This chapter is mainly about academic research, though most of it applies also to professional research. The *mandate of academic research* (main reason for doing it) is to build up humanity's bodies of knowledge by offering generalized understanding of how reality works—whether physically, socially, or whatever. Contributing to humanity's bodies of knowledge places an onerous responsibility on research, so the findings of our research are submitted for critical (usually peer) review, so that they can be made robust and understandable before being published. They are then refined further by means of subsequent public debate of the published work.

To ensure reasonableness of reliance on theories, research involves systematic methods of study. These are different for each field—experiment in physics, surveys in sociology, etc.—and below we will see why that is so.

Dooyeweerd's extensive philosophical discussion of theoretical thought in his 4-volume work *A New Critique* is surprisingly useful in guiding research practice. What we call research is included in what Dooyeweerd called "theoretical thought."

The Many Aspects of Doing Research

Despite pretensions otherwise, real research ("theoretical thought") exhibits an everyday complexity. Just as eating breakfast involves many aspects, so does doing research. The main aspect of research is, of course, the analytical, because it is that aspect which makes theoretical thinking meaningful and possible. In quantitative research, the quantitative aspect is also very important. Research involves method, planning and technology, and hence has an important formative aspect. It involves reading, communication and dissemination (lingual), other people (social), resources (economic), truthfulness and accuracy (juridical), willingness to share (ethical), and commitment, courage and belief (pistic). Less visible, until a breakdown occurs, are the biotic and psychical aspects (bodily and mental health) and physical aspect (e.g., power outages, climate change).

Taking account of all aspects in such a way helps us understand the full reality of research and guides us in planning and executing it.[1] Whereas some see this multi-aspectual reality as a departure from an ideal, Dooyeweerd argued that it is fundamental to what makes all research possible. However, Dooyeweerd wanted to understand the nature of research more clearly than this.

Dooyeweerd's Understanding of the Nature of Research

Since ancient Greece, thinkers have presupposed the superiority of theoretical thought over pre-theoretical, as a way to knowledge. They presupposed its neutrality and authority in which, in particular, emotion and religious commitment have no place.

Dooyeweerd disagreed. By extensive immanent critique, he demonstrated that religious commitment in particular always has played a part in theoretical thought (including research). By deep transcendental critique, he argued that it always will do so, as fundamental and universally necessary to theoretical thought.[2] We can see this, for example, in commitment to paradigms, and there are also deeper commitments. Dooyeweerd's view is variously supported by several twentieth-century thinkers, including Husserl, Heidegger, Habermas, Kuhn, Polanyi, Foucault, and others. Arguably, Dooyeweerd's account of theoretical thought is deeper and more comprehensive than theirs.

The starting-point for Dooyeweerd's transcendental exploration of the nature of theoretical thought was to accept its embeddedness within everyday experience and the full humanness of

---

1. For a fuller discussion, see Chapter 10 of Basden, *Foundations and Practice of Research*.
2. Dooyeweerd, *A New Critique*, I, 37.

the thinker. This led Dooyeweerd to pose a seldom-asked question, "What is the difference between theoretical and pre-theoretical (everyday) attitudes of thought?" His answer: While pre-theoretical (everyday) thought adopts an "integral vision of the whole" in which all aspects play their part, theoretical thought abstracts aspects from the whole, thus narrowing its focus.[3] Dooyeweerd called this an "antithetical attitude" to the situation we are researching or a "Gegenstand relation," in which the thinker "stands over against" what is being thought about in order to observe it clearly.[4]

By asking fundamental questions about the very nature of theoretical thought itself, he identified three "transcendental problems," in each of which faith plays a fundamental role, manifested in several ways.

- TP1.[5] In theoretical thinking we select an aspect that we believe to be important. By focusing on it (the "*Gegenstand*"), isolating (abstracting) it from the others, we can study its laws without confusing them with laws of other aspects. Each field has its own different aspect; see Table 1. (Dooyeweerd aligns this with Kant's *theoretical analysis*.)
- TP2.[6] Such isolation "sets asunder" the selected aspect, obscuring its coherence with the others, hence preventing the thinker from gaining a full understanding. But to properly build humanity's bodies of knowledge necessarily involves reuniting aspects. On what grounds may this reuniting be done and then subjected to critique?

---

3. Ibid., I, 84.
4. For fuller views, see Basden, *Foundations and Practice of Research*, § 6-3.2, and Clouser, *The Myth of Religious Neutrality*.
5. Dooyeweerd, *A New Critique*, I, 38–35.
6. Ibid., I, 45–52.

Many answer, "By analytical logic," but Dooyeweerd argued that each aspect has a distinct rationality, as Winch[7] and Habermas[8] also argued, and that logical rationality has no privileged place among them, and no authority to judge between them. Instead, Dooyeweerd's answer: We must harmonize the rationalities in ways that do not yield antinomies (such as Zeno's Paradox: Achilles racing a tortoise). Ultimately, doing this involves responsibility, a self-critical attitude, and belief.

- TP3.[9] What makes proper self-critique possible? Dooyeweerd argued that it can only be done, ultimately, by reference to a presupposed Origin of Meaning, which is self-dependent and on which all else depends—what Clouser calls the "Divine."[10] This necessarily involves faith of a religious kind. Dooyeweerd discusses four ground-motives that operate as origins of meaning, the Greek motives of form versus matter, the biblical motives of creation, fall, redemption, the Scholastic motives of nature versus grace (or supernature), and the humanist motives of nature versus freedom.[11]

Dooyeweerd developed these arguments painstakingly for philosophy,[12] but he believed they apply to scientific thought too, and later[13] he briefly applied them to sociology. Further development, it seems, was left to us, as for example in Basden.[14]

---

7. P. Winch, *The Idea of a Social Science and Its Relation to Philosophy* (1958).
8. J. Habermas, *The Theory of Communicative Action*, vol. I (1986).
9. Dooyeweerd, *A New Critique*, I, 52-68.
10. See Chapter 1 in this book.
11. See the discussion in Chapters 2 to 5 of this book and the explanation in Chapter 5 of my *Foundations and Practice of Research*.
12. Dooyeweerd, *A New Critique*, I, 38–68.
13. Ibid., III, 168–171
14. Cf. my *Foundations and Practice of Research*.

Applying Dooyeweerd's Ideas to Research

I have found that Dooyeweerd's starting-point and his three transcendental problems closely match what occurs in the realities of research, and can help us understand research in all fields. Let us go through each in turn.

1. Dooyeweerd's idea of a *Gegenstand* relationship is about clearly identifying a *research aim*. To Dooyeweerd, *Gegenstand* is one aspect, though interdisciplinary research has more than one. Identifying which aspect(s) makes our aim meaningful, and untangling it from others is a good route to clarity. This is the *core aspect* of the research. Each field of research has a different core aspect (see Table 1 below), which defines its boundaries. It is useful to express the aim as a question that the research seeks to answer, as in column 3 of Table 1.

2. In research, TP1, of abstracting aspects, is about *collecting data*. From the multi-aspectual reality being studied, researchers gather data that is meaningful to the core aspect and exclude data meaningful in other aspects. Examples: economists study costs, markets, etc. which are meaningful in the economic aspect; physicists study forces, meaningful in the physical aspect. For each aspect, different data collection methods are appropriate, such as experiment for the physical aspect, and interviews for the social (see column 4 of Table 1). Sometimes we collect data that is meaningful in other aspects, on which the laws of our core aspect most directly depend, especially in interdisciplinary research. For this, open interviews are useful because what interviewees say often ranges over several aspects, which can be identified when analysing interview text.

3. TP2, of reuniting the abstracted aspect with others, emerges in research when *analyzing data to generate findings*. Inappropriate application of the rationality of one aspect to things meaningful in another can result in distorted, misleading research findings. For example, in economics a purely *quantitative*

measure like GDP (Gross Domestic Product) is wrongly treated as a measure of *economic* health.[15] So, in good research, we take account of the distinct rationalities of different aspects. (This is why research papers should clearly describe analysis in full.)

I have found other, non-core aspects present themselves in four ways during analysis. Dooyeweerd's warning to avoid antinomies applies mainly to the first. 1. When studying how the core aspect depends on others, for example social aspect on lingual or pistic, or biotic on physical or psychical. 2. When thinking about future application of the findings of the research in the wider world—in which every aspect is potentially relevant. 3. When preparing data for analysis, especially the judgement about which data are to be removed as outliers, for example, once physical data has been abstracted from measuring equipment, we must take into account the possibility of equipment malfunction (formative aspect) or even malicious sabotage (juridical-pistic). 4. From methods chosen for analysis. In quantitative methods, the quantitative aspect is obviously important, but in two ways, counting or modelling. Counting items can give useful statistical overviews, but quantitative modelling often distorts, because it assumes the laws that govern the core aspect may be reduced to quantitative laws. Though sometimes valid in physics, it is less valid in economics,[16] such as the value of a rainforest. In qualitative analysis, the analytical aspect is important, enabling us to distinguish and identify factors. Often this involves analysis of texts, such as interview transcripts, when the lingual aspect becomes important, and using aspects to identify what the source means has proven very useful.[17] In prototype development, used in the design sciences, the formative aspect is

---

15. M. Carney, *Value(s)* (2021).
16. Ibid.
17. See extensive discussion of this in my *Foundations and Practice of Research*, §11.7.

important. Awareness of aspects can help the researcher remain aware and responsible in employing the multiple rationalities involved. We must be careful because, often, the influence of some aspects is hidden.

4. TP3, of origin of meaning, arises when setting the research *in the wider context*, where the multiple spheres of meaning that impinge on the entire field are debated. This is self-critique by the community and can operate at several levels.

At an overview level, Dooyeweerd's idea of ground-motives as origin of meaning may be used to bring some harmony in a field riven with conflicts between supposedly mutually exclusive and antagonistic paradigmatic approaches. Paradigms / approaches express what a community finds fundamentally meaningful[18] and this shifts from time to time.[19] In the information systems field, for example, positivist approaches were first adopted, which are driven by the nature pole of the humanist ground-motive. An interpretivist reaction towards the freedom pole grew during the 1990s. Later, a socio-critical reaction set in against both. Supporters of the three approaches tended to talk past each other. During the 2000s, some sought integration and eventually Dooyeweerd was called upon to assist. The operation of the dualistic nature-freedom ground-motive was unveiled[20] and a suggestion made that the three mutually opposed approaches could all be understood as emphasizing different aspects, which makes their integration possible.[21]

---

18. Basden and Joneidy 2019, "Dooyeweerd's Understanding of Meaning (2): Some Implications."
19. See my article on "Engines of Dialectic."
20. D. Eriksson, "Identification of Normative Sources for Systems Thinking: An Inquiry into Religious Ground-motives for Systems Thinking Paradigms" (2003).
21. Basden, "Enabling a Kleinian Integration of Interpretivist and Critical-social IS Research: The Contribution of Dooyeweerd's Philosophy" (2011).

At the level of the research project, the incorporation of other aspects needs to be discussed and justified, not just unquestioningly accepted. Such discussion is carried out by reference, usually implicit, to a ground-motive. This is seen in the following example.

Example

We may see the roles TP1, TP2 and TP3 play in the following example.[22]

In the field of information systems, Davis published a landmark paper which began to answer the question of how to predict the actual usage of information technology.[23] He suggested a Technology Acceptance Model, TAM, in which actual usage (U) is viewed as behavior determined by Intention to Use (IU), which is in turn influenced by Perceived Usefulness (PU) of the technology and Perceived Ease of Use (PEoU). In turn, PU and PEoU are derived from External Variables such as "Quality of Work," the choice of which depends on the context. See Figure 2.

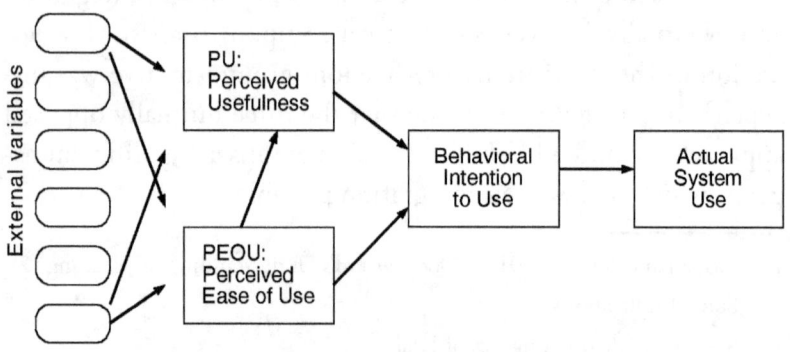

Figure 2. The Technology Acceptance Model

---

22. For a fuller account, see my *Foundations and Practice of Research*.
23. F. D. Davis, "Perceived Usefulness, Perceived Ease of Use, and User Acceptance of Information Technology" (1989).

We may first notice that TAM is based solely on psychology, in fact on the Theory of Reasoned Action and Theory of Planned Behavior. All its variables are meaningful in the psychical aspect, so its TP1 is about abstracting the psychical aspect from the diversity of reality. Its rationality (TP2), expressed for example by the links between variables, is also purely psychical. This aspectual homogeneity lends the model both a harmony and a parsimony that partly explains its great popularity and success.

The genius of Davis, however, was that other aspects are not entirely excluded, but are allowed to be represented in the anonymous External Variables. In employing TAM, appliers of the theory would select a set of variables that they believe are meaningful in situations they will research and by which PU and PEoU can be measured, and use these as questions to IT users. Davis demonstrates how.

Once TAM was published, use, critiques and refinements over 20 years generated three major new versions. Bagozzi's account of this development is useful because it shows the roles played by TP1, TP2, TP3, even though he knew nothing of Dooyeweerd.[24]

TP1. In the earliest critiques, researchers began adding variables to TAM, for example age and gender, thus widening the range of aspects to abstract during data collection, adding the biotic aspect alongside the psychical. One of the later models has 41 variables and, over time, more than 80 external variables were proposed. Yet, "Even here, arguments can be made that important independent variables have been left out."[25] This is "because few of the included predictors are fundamental, generic, or universal, and future research is likely to uncover new predictors not subsumable under the existing predictors." By contrast, Dooye-

---

24. R. P. Bagozzi, "The Legacy of the Technology Acceptance Model and a Proposal for a Paradigm Shift" (2007).
25. Ibid., p. 244.

weerd's aspects are "fundamental, generic, or universal", and this is why they are good at uncovering what is hidden (see the previous chapter) and can be used to classify the variables added.[26]

TP2. Bagozzi discusses each of the links in TAM. For example, when he remarks that "the intention-behavior linkage is probably the most uncritically accepted assumption" in TAM,[27] he is questioning whether other aspectual rationalities should be recognized. Yet,

> little theoretical insight is provided into the mechanism, or "the why", behind proposed interaction effects, and a potentially infinite list of such moderators exists, making such broadenings of TAM both unwieldy and conceptually impoverished. The consideration of moderating variables is one way of deepening any model, but introductions of these should be grounded in theory and with an aim toward including policy variables whenever possible.[28]

Light can be shone on such "interaction effects" and "moderators" by Dooyeweerd's penetrating exploration of inter-aspect dependency and analogy, of anticipations and retrocipations. For example, does the link involve social, economic, aesthetic, juridical, ethical and pistic impacts on the psychical?

TP3. Critiques related to TP3 tend to emerge more slowly, as the community opens itself to the question of why other aspects (kinds of meaningfulness) are to be considered, by (usually implicit) reference to an origin of meaning. This reference may be detected in Bagozzi, and that of two kinds. On the one hand, in opposing a "control"[29] presupposition Bagozzi is almost explicit in appealing to the humanistic nature-freedom ground-motive.

---

26. See Table 7.1 in my *Foundations and Practice of Research*, where nearly all aspects are represented.
27. Bagozzi, "The Legacy of the Technology Acceptance Model," p. 245.
28. Ibid., 244.
29. Ibid., 251.

Table 1. Fields meaningful in each aspect, with typical main research questions and appropriate research method

Aspect	Science / Discipline	Typical research questions	Typical research methods
Quant'ive	Arithmetic, Algebra, Statistics	Is every even integer the sum of two primes (Goldbach Conjecture)?	Reductio ad absurdum Computation
Spatial	Geometry, Topology	How to fill a rectangle with different-sized squares?	Geometric proofs
Kinematic	Kinematics, Mechanics, Dynamics	How can we get linear motion from rotary motion?	Differential calculus
Physical	Physics, Chemistry (Quantum, Material, Fluid, Geo-, Astro-, ...)	What is the electric charge radius of the proton?	Laboratory experiment
Organic / Biotic	Life sciences, Biology, Ecology, Taxonomy, Surgery (Physiology)	How do cells determine when to divide? Why do trees need fungi?	Experiments, Dissection, Field studies
Psychic / Sensitive	Psychology, Behavioural sciences	How does experience alter behaviour? How do young cuckoos know migration routes?	Stimulus-response trials Experiments with control grpups
Analytic	Logic, Analysis Some cognitive science	What are the limits of understanding thinking as a form of computing?	Thought experi ments, Logic, Cognitive methods
Formative	'Sciences of the Artificial' Design science, Engineering, History	How to optimally cut cake so that each recipient receives a fair piece?	Game playing, Puzzle-solving, Build + test Forensic analysis History analysis
Lingual	Linguistics, Semiotics, Hermeneutics, Literature Language studies, Information Systems (Sociolinguistics)	Grammaticalization: how does it function?	Text analysis, Discourse analysis
Social	Sociology, Organisational science	Does social media make us lonely?	Opinion surveys Interviews Focus groups
Economic	Economics, Management science	Why is it that many institutions hold only modest amounts of foreign equity?	Input-output analysis Statistical analysis
Aesthetic	Aesthetics, Art, Music, Sport science, (Systems thinking?)	What is the line between art and non-art?	Observing, analysing creative practice
Juridical	Jurisprudence, Political Science	How may we compare Indian and Iranian laws?	Review of cases and histories,
Ethical / Attitudinal	Ethical theory	Why do people pursue hedonistic lifestyles?	Anthropological studies of attitude
Pistic / Faith	Theology, Some anthropology	What is the relationship between belief, commitment, courage and motivation?	Studies of beliefs, Exegesis of 'sacred' writings, Apologetics, Hermeneutics

Important note: Dooyeweerd warned that no suite of aspects is ever final. So we must use aspects with due caution. We should not be dogmatic about what aspects there are, what their kernel meanings are, nor how they are manifested above.

But, on the other, in arguing for various aspects, what he actually does is to implicitly presuppose a pluralistic origin of meaning. Dooyeweerd names the biblical ground-motive as a pluralistic ground-motive, perhaps the only one possible.

In this way, Dooyeweerd's analysis of ground-motives with aspects could contribute significantly to such post-publication debates. He urged that presuppositions should be openly declared when publishing research—which, interestingly, prefigured many subsequent socio-critical and feminist thinkers.

Research in Different Fields

The above discussion applies, as far as I know, to all fields. Different fields center on different core aspects, as shown in Table 1. Each aspect makes a different kind of aim or research question meaningful (column 3), and type of research method appropriate (column 4).[30]

Conclusion

This chapter has briefly outlined how Dooyeweerd's ideas can help research in many fields from the mathematical and natural sciences, through the psychological ones, to social sciences and humanities. We showed how awareness of aspects can help us find our way amidst the complexity of real-life experience of doing research, looked at how Dooyeweerd's transcendental critique of theoretical thought can help us understand what is going on in research, and looked at the range of fields by aspect.

Much more can be said, but these could make our research more systematic and productive, especially for interdisciplinary

---

30. For a fuller discussion of this, see A. Basden, "Understanding the Relationships between Fields of Research," *The Electronic Journal of Business Research Methods*, 19, no. 1 (2021): 27-41, Chapter 8 in Basden, *Foundations and Practice of Research*, or http://dooy.info/science.html.

research. A fuller discussion may be found in Basden,[31] with Chapter 11 giving examples of actual research using Dooyeweerd. To date, however, experience of doing so is patchy, so the challenge lies before us of expanding it.

---

31. Basden, *Foundations and Practice of Research*.

58

Adam and Biology

by Willem J. Ouweneel

DOOYEWEERD'S THEORY of the modal aspects of cosmic reality is one of the best known elements of his philosophy. This is fine, but it is also one-sided: his theory of entities ("thing"-like matters) and of enkapsis (the way entities can be intertwined) should also be recognized. In my book, *Adam, Where Are You?* I have tried to map out what these theories could mean for philosophical anthropology. I have described five levels in the *immanent* structure of the human corporeal mode of existence. The anthropology that I present is a theory, a model—but one, I trust, that is in the spirit of Scripture (cf. my chapter on psychology).

In the spirit of the work of Dooyeweerd and Vollenhoven I distinguish five *structural layers* in humans, five levels of organization, one on top of the other, so to speak; they are the following:

(1) The *physical* structural layer. This organizational level includes the chemical elements, physical processes and chemical reactions that, on the one hand, guarantee the unity of the material structure of humans and by which, on the other hand, the material components are yet able to undergo constant change. All living as well as lifeless material things share this structural layer.

(2) The *biotic* structural layer. This organizational level includes the cell structure, the tissue structure, the organic structure, and the physiological life processes of a living organism (breathing, digestion, metabolism, reproduction, hormonal processes, and the

like). All living organisms share both the physical and the biotic structural layer in such a way that all living organisms presuppose the physical structural layer, but the biotic structural layer, which comes "on top of it," *cannot be derived from it or reduced to it*. This is the same as saying that, on the biblical standpoint, the biotic structural layer demanded a new, separate creative act of God. In other words, abiogenesis (the *unsteered* origin of life from non-life) is impossible.

(3) The *perceptive* structural layer. This organizational level includes the sensory phenomena, which are "supported" or "carried" by physico-chemical structures and processes, and also by biotic processes, but they themselves, as such, are subject to perceptive laws (such as the laws of stimulus and response). All animals share the physical, the biotic, and the perceptive structural layers. In my view, the origin of such creatures that possess a certain form of "awareness" (which plants do not have) demanded again a separate creative act of God because the perceptive structural layer cannot be reduced to the lower structural layers. That is to say, awareness cannot develop from unawareness.

(4) The *sensitive* structural layer (sometimes taken together with [3]). This organizational level includes feeling-life: affections, emotions, drives. There are no feelings without physiological and perceptive processes, but feelings cannot be reduced to the latter. Sensitive life is a level of functioning that presupposes (is "carried" by) the previous structural layers, which form the foundation for it, and at the same time the sensitive structural layer is entirely new. All higher animals share the physical, the biotic, the perceptive, and the sensitive structural layers. Again, in my view, the origin of this sensitive structural layer demanded a separate creative act of God. That is to say, feelings cannot develop from non-feelings.

(5) The *mental* structural layer ("mental" in the immanent, not to be confused with the transcendence of the human heart).

In addition to the structural layers already mentioned, humans also have a *mental* structural layer, which includes thoughts, deliberations, decisions, imagination, and so on. We must note carefully what this means. We cannot construe here some evolutionary process in which higher forms of life gradually acquire a new structural layer, *which allegedly sprouts from the previous structural layers*. There is no sprouting here; each structural layer represents an essentially new and different mode of existence, a new level of organization, *irreducible* to previous structural layers. There is no developmental process involved; I have stressed that this is the same as saying that each new level demanded a new, special creation of God.

There is one more point that is vital for our discussion. It is that plants, animals and humans share, say, the physical structural layer but this does not at all mean that this physical structural layer is the same in each of these categories of life forms. What I mean is that the physico-chemical matter in humans must be capable of "carrying" (enabling, conditioning, rendering possible) not only the physiological ("life") processes, as well as the perceptive and the sensitive processes, but must also be capable of "carrying" the mental life of humans (thoughts, deliberations, decisions, imagination, etc.). This makes the physical structural layer in humans absolutely unique: it is capable of doing things that the physical structural layer in gorillas and chimpanzees cannot do.

Human mental functioning is proper to this new, fifth organizational level, which I have called the mental structural layer. This structural layer means that humans can think, deliberate, make decisions, speak, invent, create, trade, do art, love, believe, and so on. However, I repeat: on the one hand, this thinking, deliberating, etcetera, cannot be reduced to the physical, the biotic, the perceptive or the sensitive, but on the other hand, these mental processes would not be possible without the lower structural layers, which "carry" (form the indispensable substratum for) them.

Especially moral and religious norms are characteristic of human beings. Morality and religion cannot be reduced to animal features, although people have tried it; to put it bluntly, the "primeval soup" did not contain any morals. Morals come from the Creator, who laid them in the human heart (see below).

Five Human-Structures

The five structural layers that together make up immanent-human existence may be called "human-structures" (German: *Humanstrukturen*; Dutch: *humaanstructuren*), in order to make it clear that humans differ from plants and animals not only in possessing a mental structure, but also in the fact that the four lower human structural layers differ fundamentally from the corresponding structural layers found in plants and animals. For instance, the physical structural layer in plants and animals can "carry" biotic processes, but no mental processes. The important conclusion from this is that the creation of humans *not only demanded the special creation of the mental structural layer but also the special creation of the previous (physical, biotic, perceptive, and sensitive) structural layers.* In other words, humans differ from plants and animals not only in the fact that the former have a mental structural layer, and the others have not, but also in the fact that they have different physical, biotic, perceptive and sensitive structural layers than the others.

I repeat, the mental structural layer includes the so-called mental functioning, or, if you like, the functioning of the human mind (as long as you do not make the mind some "thing" [substance] independent of the body). It is within this structural layer that human deliberations, imaginings, and decisions occur. Such operations of the human mind are sometimes called *acts*. Acts are inner operations of the mind that are directed toward resulting actions, to external behaviors. An animal also performs certain *actions,* but they do not arise out of "acts," for animals do not have a mental life or act-life. The actions of an animal follow instead from its perceptively determined instincts and/or sensitively determined urges or drives, not from mental deliberations and free decisions of the will.

Such instincts and drives are not absent in humans but, if humans truly behave like humans, their deeds are determined primarily by human act-life or mental life, that is, the free, deliberate functioning of his mind. This is why humans must take responsibility for their deeds, whereas an animal does not have to. Responsibility is "response-ability": a human being has the ability, and the duty, to give a response to the question as to why he or she did this or that, in other words, from which (mental) *acts* his/her *actions* arose. In our mode of existence, we cannot account for those phenomena that are entirely governed by natural laws. But we *can* and *must* account for our actions insofar as they are governed by *norms*.

Mental Acts

In each aspect of mental life there is an *essential* difference between animals and humans:

(1) The *logical* aspect: I have argued before that higher animals have feelings. But logical thinking—thinking that is ruled by the laws of logic, and that can be judged according to these laws—is a very different matter. Something that resembles this type of thinking is found among animals only at the most elementary level, namely, that of conceptualizing (e.g., recognition of pictures).

(2) The *formative* aspect: no one wishes to deny that certain animal species know elementary forms of creativity, be it that we are far more struck by the fact that beavers have been constructing the same type of dams over the centuries, and birds the same type of nests (only sometimes changing the building materials when newer materials become available). What a difference with the formative potentials of even a three-years old child.

(3) The *lingual* aspect: it is generally known by now how poor the results are of so many attempts to teach certain animals con-

ceptual languages that go beyond the instinctive communication means they already possess. No animal can be taught to talk—but a child born into a community is *ready* to talk: it will master the language of its surroundings in one or two years. Human kids have a LAD ("Language Acquisition Device"), which even the "highest" animals apparently have not.

(4) The *social* aspect: of course, animals know certain forms of social life; some are even very "social" animals (think of beehives, anthills, and herds). Yet, such anthropomorphisms can easily obscure the fact that such "social" animal behavior is strictly bound to the animals' innate instincts. Humans, however, have built families, marriages, villages and cities, nation-states, schools, companies, associations, clubs, you name it—and their creativity in doing so is inexhaustible.

(5) The *economic* aspect: many animals know about saving and exchanging; but what are these instinctive behavioral patterns in comparison to the production and consumption of goods and services, the buying and selling, the markets and stock exchanges, as we know them in the human world?

(6) The *aesthetic* aspect: what animal species have any demonstrable sense of beautiful and ugly, of harmony and disharmony, that is, of music, of literature, of the visual arts, or of something remotely similar?

(7) The *juridical* aspect: Animals may have a sense of what is advantageous and disadvantageous to them—but even young children have a clear idea of what is "fair" and "unfair," which is a very different notion.

(8) The *moral* aspect: Many scholars have attempted to minimalize the uniqueness of humans. Yet, the question remains: how can a natural world produce features that are characteristic of what we call a "personality": intellect, moral awareness, and the like?

(9) The *pistical* aspect: this is the modal aspect of faith, trust, confidence, not as a basically sensitive notion, but especially as an

awareness of the transcendent, of the Last Grounds of life and of the world, and the inner desire to surrender to them. This is what we call "religion" in the widest sense. Who would wish to suggest that anything of such an awareness of the transcendent is present in even the highest animals?

Humans differ essentially from animals, not only in mental, but also even in sensitive, perceptive, biotic and physical respects. The human condition cannot be explained from the animal world. This would be true even if we would only consider the five structural layers that we have distinguished in the human immanent mode of existence. Already here the differences are unbridgeable. However, this is even far more strongly the case if we now come to the *transcendent* dimension of human existence. This is the subject of the next sections.

The Person's Religious Center

The heart is the deepest node in the inner person, his most genuine and essential concentration point. Often, the heart is the authentic inner person, standing in opposition to the, often insincere, outer person (Deut. 8:2; 1 Sam. 16:7; Ps. 28:3; 55:21; Prov. 23:7; 26:23, 25; Eccl. 7:3; Isa. 29:13; Jer. 3:10; 17:9; Hos. 10:2). In the heart, all aspects and all structural layers of the human mode of existence come together as in a node or in a focal point. At the same time, this heart lifts the person in his deepest being above the entire temporal-immanent reality. This brings us to the most important point: the heart in its *transcendent-religious* meaning, that is, as the reference to the deepest creaturely orientation of the human being toward his Creator. In fact, already many of the passages mentioned had a clearly transcendent-religious meaning. In the heart, it comes out whether a person is directed toward God, or is turned away from him (toward the idols).

Many times, the heart is referred to as the place where sin is planned, as the source of false prophecy (where it is not God revealing but the person himself making up things), of the *hybris* (anti-divine over-confidence), of self-deification, of wicked arrogance, and so on (Isa. 14:13; 47:10; Ezek. 28:2, 6; Ob. 1:3; Zeph. 2:15). However, it is also the focal point of the awareness of guilt (2 Chron. 6:37; Lam. 1:20, 22), of divine operation and conversion (e.g., Jer. 24:7; 31:33), the "organ" for seeking God (e.g., 2 Chron. 11:16; 12:14), and for fellowship with God (1 Kings 8:61; 14:8; 15:14), and so further: for the fear of the Lord, the service to God, the walk with God, the grief toward God, the joy in God, the worship of God, the study and keeping of God's commandments, praying to God, trusting in God.

In the New Testament, the use of Greek *kardia* ("heart") is different from that in the Hellenist world, but it comes close to the meaning of "heart" in the Old Testament. Besides expressions such as the "heart" (most inner part) of the earth (Matt. 10:40), and the biotic meaning (Acts 14:17; James 5:5), the heart is the node of the psychical (affections, impulses, emotions) and the mental life, with its thinking and knowing, its imagination and creativity, and its volitional life. Here again, the heart stands in opposition to the "outer" person (2 Cor. 5:12; 1 Thess. 2:17), to mouth and lips (Matt. 15:18; Mark 7:6; Rom. 10:8–10), and to the outer flesh (Rom. 2:28–29; 1 Pet. 3:3–4). The heart is the most inner life of the person, that which represents the Ego, the personality (Col. 2:2; 1 John 3:19–20). It is the source of sin (Matt. 15:19), but also the point on which God can work (Acts 15:9; Rom. 2:15; Eph. 3:17).

Here, in "the hidden person of the heart" (1 Pet. 3:4), we find the root of human transcendent-moral-religious life, of the human relationship with God *or*, since the Fall, with the idols. Here, in the heart, the person finds his unbreakable unity; here, all the lines of his existence come together. Here lies what is most proper to the person: basically inaccessible to the sciences, basically only known through the divine revelation concerning nature and being of humans. It is that which is spiritually grasped, not by feeling or intellect, but only by the heart itself.

We call everything transcendent that, in some way or another, surpasses our immanent, cosmic, empirical, created reality. One might think that transcendence is a unique characteristic of God, but this would be a mistake. In my view, the very fact that humans have been created in the image and after the likeness of God means that they are not only immanent but also transcendent beings. As far as their corporeal existence is concerned, humans belong to the cosmic, empirical reality. However, in their Ego, their heart, their personality center, of whatever one wishes to call it, humans transcend this corporeal mode of existence, and all immanent, cosmic, empirical, created reality.

This polar duality of the transcendent and the immanent is of the greatest importance. Thus, the pole of the one, transcendent, imperishable *heart* stands over against the variety of immanent, perishable (biotic, psychical, and mental) *functions*.

Please note that the expression "over against" here has nothing to do with a dual*ism*; what we have here is the dual*ity* of the heart and the functions. The fact that this is not a dual*ism* (in the ancient, substantialist sense of the term) is evident from the fact that the heart is nothing but the transcendent focal point *of the functions themselves*, and that the immanent functions are nothing but the diversity going out *from the heart itself*. The heart *is* the functions in their transcendent unity, the functions *are* the heart in its immanent diversity. We have to do here with the one self-awareness of the human person, which on the one hand transcends the immanent reality in its religious orientation toward God (*or* the idols), and on the other hand functions within the entire diversity of the immanent human existence.

In my view, the human heart *must* be transcendent because, on the one hand, within the immanent cosmic reality we find only a diversity of functions, structural layers and acts, no deeper unity and fullness. On the other hand, it must be transcendent because it turns out to be ontically and essentially oriented toward God, and to be designed for religious fellowship with him. In the whole Bible, humanity is viewed *sub specie Dei*, "under God's sight," and *coram Deo*, "before God." There is no Man-as-such, no Man-in-himself; there is only the "eccentric" Man-in-relationship-with-the-transcendent, being transcendent himself.

59

Dooyeweerd's Approach to Philosophical Anthropology

by Gerrit Glas

DOOYEWEERD INITIALLY intended to devote the third part of *Reformatie en Scholastiek in de Wijsbegeerte* to philosophical anthropology, but never finished this project. The 32 *Theses on Man* offer, however, a succinct and important contribution to the reformational philosophical view of man.[1]

---

1. H. Dooyeweerd, "De leer van de mens in de wijsbegeerte der wetsidee," *Correspondentiebladen van de Vereniging voor Calvinistische Wijsbegeerte 7* (1942): 134-44. The earliest version of the Theses dates from 1942. This text was later published in the students' periodical *Sola Fide*, 1954, pp. 8-18. I use a translation by John Vander Stelt of the *Sola Fide* publication. References in the text are to the theses. Other relevant texts are H. Dooyeweerd, "The Problem of Time in the Philosophy of the Cosmonomic Idea," in *Time, Law, and History: Selected Essays*, Collected Works of Herman Dooyeweerd, Series B, vol. 14, General Editor D. F. M. Strauss (Grand Rapids, MI: Paideia Press: 2017); H. Dooyeweerd, *A New Critique of Theoretical Thought*, vol. 3, Collected Works of Herman Dooyeweerd, Series A, General Editor D. F. M. Strauss (Lewiston, NY: Edwin Mellen, 1997), pp. 694ff, 765ff, pp. 781ff; H. Dooyeweerd, "Van Peursen's critische vragen bij 'A New Critique of Theoretical Thought,'" *Philosophia Reformata* 25 (1960): 97-150; H. Dooyeweerd, *In the Twilight of Western Thought* (Philadelphia: Presbyterian and Reformed Publishing Company, 1960); H. Dooyeweerd, "De taak ener

Two of the key characteristics of Dooyeweerd's philosophy can easily be recognized in the Theses: the fine-grained analysis of structures, and the emphasis on the religious dynamic that pervades human existence.

With respect to structures, Dooyeweerd focuses on the human body as an interlacement of different substructures. Dooyeweerd shows how our existence as humans is based on the fine-tuned collaboration and attuning of these substructures. This idea crystallizes in the idea of man as "enkaptic structural whole."

With respect to the religious dynamic, Dooyeweerd attaches much importance to the fact that human existence is driven (or: directed) by ground-motives that operate in what he calls the "supra-temporal heart." Ground-motives are fundamental, existential driving forces that ultimately find their roots in what Dooyeweerd calls people's ideas about the "true or a presumed Origin of meaning." The true Origin is God, for Dooyeweerd, but in his systematic philosophy he avoids the term God and speaks, instead, of the Origin, or Origin of meaning. It is in our heart that we open ourselves toward a true or presumed Origin, says Dooyeweerd, in the footsteps of Abraham Kuyper. What we do, think, and experience ultimately flows from and is directed by fundamental convictions about this Origin. These convictions are philosophically indicated with the term ground-motive. These convictions are not arbitrary

---

wijsgerige anthropologie en de doodlopende wegen tot wijsgerige zelfkennis," *Philosophia Reformata*, 26 (1961): 35-58; Summaries of the discussion about Dooyeweerd's anthropology can be found in W.J. Ouweneel, *De leer van de mens. Proeve van een christelijk-wijsgerige antropologie* (Amsterdam: Buijten & Schipperheijn, 1986), and G. Glas, "Ego, Self, and the Body. An Assessment of Dooyeweerd's Philosophical Anthropology" in *Christian Philosophy at the Close of the Twentieth Century. Assessment and Perspective*, eds. S. Griffioen & B.M. Balk (Kok: Kampen, 1995): 67-78; G. Glas, "Christian Philosophical Anthropology. A Reformation Perspective," *Philosophia Reformata*, 75 (2010): 141-189.

opinions, but fundamental ideas and driving forces that guide our actions. Ground-motives are the inescapable soil in which our existence is rooted. They provide the motivation which helps us in our search for meaning and purpose.

Readers should understand that these two strands of thought — the analysis of structures and the emphasis on ground-motives that operate in our heart — do not stand apart but, in fact, presuppose one another. Structure and directedness (or: direction) go together, there is no structure without directedness and no directedness without structure. This is because of the creational nature of everything that exists. Creation means that there is no part in the cosmos that can be seen as existing by itself and on its own. Dooyeweerd radicalizes this idea by saying that everything exists "as meaning," i.e., as referring to and as an expression of the Origin. This referring and expressing has both a structural and a dynamic aspect; and these aspects are interwoven. Later reformational philosophers would speak of created reality as a "responding" reality.[2] Responding is then the common denominator of everything that exists. The structural and the directional aspects are completely interwoven in the responding.

Let us now focus on the two key ideas.

Man as (Enkaptic) Structural Whole

Our existence as humans is structured. We function as organisms (biotic), we experience (psychic), we think (logical), we relate to others (social), and so on. We do all these things synchronically: when we think (logical), our heart is beating (biotic); and while interacting with others (social), we feel (psychic) and make gestures (symbolic expression). The question is how to make philosophical sense of the complex, highly dynamic and relational nature of our existence as humans.

---

2. H.G. Geertsema, *Homo Respondens. Essays in Christian Philosophy* (Ancaster: Paideia Press, 2021).

Dooyeweerd makes, as has been spelled out in previous chapters, a fundamental distinction between modes and entities. Modes (or: aspects; modal aspects) are ways of functioning. Entities are things, i.e., all kinds of things, including events and processes (events with a duration). Things possess modes and these modes function in a coordinated way because they are the expression of — what Dooyeweerd calls — an individuality structure. The individuality structure can be described with the help of modal terms. Things, in fact, function in all modes, either as subject (actively) or as object (passively). Modes may, furthermore, adopt different roles: they may for instance acquire a qualifying or a foundational function in a particular thing.

Given this set of concepts and distinctions it would have been easiest for Dooyeweerd to say that human beings are things and have a thing-like individuality structure, just like trees, chairs, and companies. Remarkably enough, Dooyeweerd does not say this and suggests something different. There are two reasons for this, I think. The first is that there are aspects in our functioning as humans that are not, so to say, absorbed into the whole of our existence. These aspects have a relatively independent existence and can be studied as if they function as things. Dooyeweerd suggests that there are four such relatively independent substructures: a physical, a biotic, a psychical, and an act (sub)structure. More about this in a moment. The second reason is that human beings relate differently to the Origin of meaning than things like trees, chairs, and companies. This is because their "hearts" are a window to the transcendent – the Origin of meaning by and through which everything exists. They relate to the Origin differently, not only by referring and expressing, but also by responsibly answering God's call, by listening to his revelations, by acting as his servants and by obeying commands. Unlike other entities, man is the *imago Dei*, which means that she/he has special tasks as representative of God.

To indicate how the substructures relate to one another,

Dooyeweerd introduces the terms enkapsis and enkaptic structural whole. Enkapsis means, literally, enclosure, interweavement, intertwinement, interlacement. Dooyeweerd distinguishes enkaptic relationships from relations between a whole and its parts; and, also, from what he calls "aggregates." In part-whole relations the parts give up their independence and are absorbed by the whole. The sum of the parts displays characteristics that none of the separate parts possesses. Aggregates, on the other hand, are just interacting parts, they do not form a whole. Dooyeweerd mentions as example the mud at the bottom of a river that is mingled with a random collection of other materials (stones, waste from industry, organic material).

Enkaptic structural wholes differ from both. These wholes represent an (enkaptic) interlacement of parts, in which the properties of the parts are retained and in which the parts are caught up together in a whole, with new properties. These properties are ordered by a new (embracing) structural principle. This whole is known by its form and represents a form-totality. In other words, we can discern these wholes because we perceive them or because we have made them.

To be precise, Dooyeweerd also discerns enkaptic relations that do not form new wholes. An example is eco-systems in which there exists a mutual dependence between animals and plants. These kinds of dependence (or interlacement) are structured unlike the dependencies within aggregates.

Examples of enkaptic structural wholes are molecules (in the relation with their atoms), birds (in relation to their nests), sculptures (in the relation to the physical material they are made of). Atoms, nests and physical material like marble continue to function according to their internal structural principle. These parts acquire a new function because of their enkaptic interwovenness within the new structural whole. Enkaptically bound thing structures are, therefore, qualified by the nature of these entwinements.

The goal of nests is qualified by the fact that they serve birds as biotic object, i.e., as repository of their eggs and as shelter for their offspring. Apart from the bird they lose their goal and are just physically qualified compilations of physical material. In the case of sculptures — Dooyeweerd's paradigm case is the famous Hermes of Praxiteles — the situation is even more complex. Here it is not only the physical structure of the marble that should be included in the analysis, but also the design of the work as intentional object in the mind of its maker. The work of art is an objectification of this design within the physical structure of the marble — a structure that is now deepened and disclosed. As structural whole the sculpture is aesthetically qualified, whereas it is founded in the (historical) formative labour of the artist. The structural potential of physical material is deepened and disclosed in the artist's actualization of the marble's object functions. The design in the mind of the maker discloses possibilities in the physical material that are realized in the artistic labor, by opening up of the aesthetic object function of the physical material.

How about man? Dooyeweerd, as indicated, considers humans as enkaptic structural wholes, however, again, with some qualifications. First, Dooyeweerd remarkably enough, considers not the person, or the I, as representing the enkaptic structural whole, but the human body. This is because of the important role he assigns to what he calls the "form-totality." The term form-totality applies to all enkaptic structural wholes. Form-totalities help us identify entities as either perceivable (visible, audible) objects or as products of our hands, i.e., as cultural objects. In case of humans, it is the body that serves as the identifiable locus of interlacement of the different part-structures. Dooyeweerd speaks of the human body as the outer corporeal form that functions as nodus of interlacement.

Next, and secondly, Dooyeweerd understands the human body in the broadest possible sense, i.e., as "temporal, existential form of human life" (Thesis VII). The body is much more than a compilation of physico-chemical material. It is also a living organism, a sentient person and an active agent. All four part-structures belong to the human body as enkaptic structural whole. Even the organs in the body function in all four substructures (Thesis XII).

Third, there is a difference between the human body and non-human enkaptic structural wholes such as nests and sculptures. The difference is that the body is not itself qualified by one normative modal aspect (Thesis XXI). This, in turn, is a result of specific features of the so-called act-structure, as 'highest' substructure in the enkaptic framework. Dooyeweerd describes the act-structure as non-differentiated and "plastic." The latter term refers to the flexible and expressive nature of the human spirit.

Fourth, the physico-chemical, biotic, sensitive (psychic) substructures and the act-structure are hierarchically interlaced, such that the lower substructures are "morphologically bound" to the higher substructures (Thesis X). This means that none of these substructures functions on its own, even the physical substructure. It is only after death, in the process of decomposition of the body, that this substructure follows the physical laws only. The biotic substructure has a so-called "vegetative" qualification. The term vegetative refers to the autonomous nervous system, which is responsible for the homeostatic regulation of breathing, heart-rate, and perspiration. With regard to the sensitive substructure, Dooyeweerd is thinking of the role of sensory awareness, temperament, emotion and affective expression. Elsewhere he speaks of an "animal" structure whose operations fall largely outside the control by the human will (Thesis XIII). It is only because of its being bound within the act-structure that the psychical sphere acquires its human destination. The same holds for the other substructures (Thesis XI). The act-structure, finally, serves as the norm-responsive structure that helps us act and orient ourselves in the world. Acts are not visible deeds, but inner intentional performances that proceed from the human soul (or: spirit). These performances function with the enkaptic structural whole of the human body. As a result, they are by definition norm-responsive. Or, to use a more Dooyeweerdian terminology, human beings, led by normative points of view, direct themselves intentionally to states of affairs in the real or the imagined world, and appropriate these intended states of affairs by relating them to their selfhood. The act life of human beings manifests itself in three basic directions: knowing, imagining, and willing (Thesis XIV). With this Dooyeweerd joins the tradition of faculty psychology, which made a division between the faculties of thinking, imagining, and willing (volition). Human act life functions as a kind of intermediary between the human soul (or selfhood) and states of affairs in the outer or the imagined world.

The Heart as Spiritual Centre of the Human Being

The question of who we are as human persons remains first and for always a religious question for Dooyeweerd. Dooyeweerd speaks about the soul (or spirit) as the heart of our temporal existence from which all issues of temporal life proceed. The heart is the "religious root" of the body and the concentration point of our entire temporal existence. The notion of concentration suggests an inward orientation and a movement toward the most inner spheres of our existence. This is however not the way Dooyeweerd speaks about concentration. Dooyeweerd speaks of an "innate impulse," an inborn, fundamentally religious response that expresses how we relate to the Creator. The heart is the integral center and concentration point of our bodily existence, the sphere in which we orient ourselves toward the Origin of everything that exists.

Unlike the body, the soul, or heart, is not subjected to death, because it transcends all temporal things. The heart, conceived in its Scriptural sense, is not a thing nor an immaterial substance. As integral centre of the whole of corporeality, it is at the same time entirely correlate with God's self-revelation as Creator of heaven and earth.

Many themes come together in the idea of the heart as center of our existence: the idea that religion involves human existence as a whole and not just one of its aspects; the radical non-self-sufficiency of all creatures; the fundamental restlessness of human existence in its longing for unity and wholeness (with references to Augustine); and the relation between self-knowledge and knowledge of God. This latter idea is inspired by the opening sentences of Calvin's *Institutes* which state that there is no self-knowledge apart from knowledge of God.

Dooyeweerd usually speaks of the heart as supra-temporal. With this he does not mean that the heart is eternal or simply beyond time. That would bring him dangerously close to dualist conceptions of body and soul. The soul is present in everything we do and experience. It is a dynamic that guides our intuitions, feelings, and actions. It brings life to and shapes our existence. The soul is, indeed, not subjected to temporal death, but it is subjected to eternal death. With this Dooyeweerd aims at the Scriptural idea of eternal death, conceived as the soul's impossibility to exist outside Christ. In this Scriptural sense people can already be spiritually dead before they die.

The biblical notion of the soul has many meanings and is difficult to grasp. Core elements are the association with breathing, being alive, procreation, responsiveness to God, and faithfulness. Despite this broadness and plurality, Dooyeweerd tries to integrate elements of the biblical idea of the soul (heart) within his systematic framework. One thing to account for is that the soul belongs to our everyday existence in its temporality and diversity. But the soul also directs us to what goes beyond the temporal sphere. We saw that it even persists after the cessation of our temporal existence. The solution for the puzzle lies, for Dooyeweerd, in the idea of the supra-temporal heart. In everyday language this idea expresses that the core of our existence is to be found in the longing for and directedness at what lies beyond our existence in time. The soul is supra-temporal because it belongs to its nature to dynamically connect us to the transcendent sphere. More technically: The soul, as inescapable religious dynamic that originates in the heart as concentration point, aims at the fulfilment and wholeness of our existence, which can only be found when we direct our doings and experiences to the only source of meaning, God, as the Origin of meaning.

To add to the understanding of the term supra-temporal, it should be mentioned that in Dooyeweerd's systematic philosophy temporality is intrinsically connected with temporal modal diversity, i.e., the "refraction in time" of the so-called cosmic time order. Modal aspects are temporal phenomena, they express not just order, but the time-order of the cosmos. The terms retrocipation and anticipation also testify of the association between temporality and modal diversity. Further information about this position can be found in other chapters in this book. Dooyeweerd himself uses the metaphor of the prism. Imagine a prism that refracts a bundle of white light in a multitude of colours. The totality (of the cosmic time-order) and the unity (of the Origin of meaning) are, philosophically speaking, ideas that should be presupposed to make sense of a world that we only experience and know in a temporally refracted way. It is the soul (or heart) that orients and directs us out of the diversity to the supratemporal sphere of wholeness (totality) and unity. Based on the above we now understand what Dooyeweerd sees as the fundamental problem of anthropology. It is the problem of how our temporal human existence with its theoretically separated aspects and individuality structures can be understood as a deeper whole and a unity (Thesis VII).

The idea of the supra-temporal heart is fundamental. It is nothing less than an anthropological a priori. It is not a mental act, or experience. It is even not just a theoretical idea. It is transcendentally presupposed, in a religious way. The term transcendental idea refers to the philosophy of Immanuel Kant and his followers. Transcendental ideas are fundamental assumptions that cannot be grasped conceptually but should nevertheless be presupposed to know what we know. They have a regulative significance. They lack empirical content but have, nevertheless, a formative effect on the process of acquiring knowledge, by directing our faculty of thinking to that which lies beyond our epistemic capacities. Dooyeweerd gives this Kantian notion of (transcendental) ideas a religious twist by viewing them as necessarily religious, instead of as logical-transcendental presuppositions. The other difference with Kant is that, for Dooyeweerd, the ideas are not only relevant for our knowing but also for the way we understand reality as a whole. Philosophy can approach the ideas only tentatively, though in close harmony with Scriptural revelation. Dooyeweerd's religious transcendental ideas are therefore fallible attempts to philosophically indicate what should be presupposed from a religious point of view to understand reality and, in the case of anthropology, our existence as humans. It is not via the ideas that we know what we know (as in traditional Kantian and neo-Kantian forms of transcendental philosophy). The ideas are meant to philosophically account for that which precedes and is presupposed in our attempts to know ourselves as humans. In other words, philosophical anthropology is based on a pre-given religious understanding of the human condition. It does not itself provide the theoretical foundation for our self-understanding, even not our religious self-understanding.

Closing Remarks

How is the heart related to the act-structure, the highest of the substructures? The act-structure itself functions as "plastic field of expression" of the human spirit. The soul is interwoven with all different aspects of the act life and thus with the body. It is the human body itself that has the faculty of spiritual expression. Being-human is, so to say, spiritually breathing in and breathing out, it is concentration and divergence. It is the whole human being in the unity of soul and body who performs the acts. Outside of the body no acts in their temporal structure are possible. The acts are, in other words, neither purely spiritual nor purely corporeal (Thesis XX). Note that Dooyeweerd does not say that the act-structure should be understood both spiritually and corporeally. The act-structure is and remains a body structure. It is a philosophical-scientific term which refers to a structure of temporal reality. The acts of the actual body, however, are characterized by the mutual permeation of the spiritual and the corporeal. The other substructures (physical, biotic, psychic) have a more rigid delimitation. The human spirit should in its religious freedom be in command of its bodily field of expression. That is why the act-structure has the greatest possible plasticity. It is because of the operations of the act-structure that activities in the other substructure take on a typically human character (Thesis XXII). Animals lack an acts-structure and are, therefore, bound by the relative rigidity of their un-disclosed psychic functioning.

Denial of the tendency of the heart to point-beyond-itself is fruitless and will only lead to a situation in which the religious dynamic is directed at something within temporal reality itself. This "something" is then taken as the ultimate and absolute. Historical examples are the absolutization of reason (scientific thinking) or the deification of individual freedom (autonomy). Such absolutizations will always lead to unsolvable tensions and lack of coherence in one's conception of the world; and therefore, to dualism and monism. In the "Theses" Dooyeweerd focuses mostly on the traditional dualism between *anima rationalis* (rational soul) and material body. This dualism rests on the absolutization of rationality from the full, temporal (hence corporeal) existence of humans. In our time, he would also criticize naturalistic (evolutionary, reductionistic, materialist) conceptions of man. He would point to the fact that nothing in the world exists by and of itself.

He would attempt to raise awareness for man's religious nature. And he would offer a (religiously) transcendental critique of the inconsistencies that inevitably emerge when parts of reality (our evolutionary history; the concept of matter; the scientific reconstruction of reality) are deified.

As has been said earlier, Dooyeweerd's notion of the "supra-temporal" heart is not uncontroversial. Is this notion not too theoretical or a kind of mystification? Once again, it must be said that the heart is not a "thing" nor a "thing in itself," and even not just a theoretical construct. The heart is the dynamical source from which all human activity originates. It can only be understood in a religious sense. Terms like "religious" and "heart" do not refer to something "before us," an activity or process we can think about and that can be objectified in a theoretical sense. We have the heart, as religious center, always in our back. We cannot go behind it. It is the most essential characteristic of our existence as humans.

60

What Could Dooyeweerd Teach Us About the Study of the Brain

by Gerrit Glas

DOOYEWEERD HAS NEVER written about neuroscience. This science was still in its infancy during his lifetime. Dooyeweerd's systematic philosophy, nevertheless, may offer important contributions to the philosophy of neuroscience. This chapter gives a sketch of how Dooyeweerd's philosophy could be applied to the sciences of the brain.

The Brain: A Blind Spot in Our Experience
Most people will identify the brain with the mass of tissue, blood vessels and meninges that is located within the confines of the skull. They will describe it as the organ that in a rather mysterious way is involved in the production of movements, perceptions, other experiences, thoughts, memories, and plans. Our brain is invisible to us. We cannot touch, see, or smell it. We know of its existence from what we have heard about it at school or via popular media. The most important vehicle for the understanding of ourselves and the world, manifests itself, paradoxically, as a kind of blind spot. We are unable to perceive and know it and, therefore, use metaphors when we speak about it. We base our brain-talk on pictures and schemes in books, newspapers, and social media. Based on these pictures and schemes, we are inclined to see the

brain as an organ, just like the liver or the heart, with only this difference, that the output of the brain consists of material and immaterial things. Livers produce bile; and hearts beat and pump blood in our vessels. The brain produces material things like hormones, brings about reflexes and movements, but also, mysteriously, thoughts, emotions, memories, and the like.

Metaphors are based on analogies that offer an imaginary perspective on the object they refer to.[1] In science, they are useful tools that add meaning and draw attention to a particular aspect of the object under study. Metaphors may crystallize into models. This has occurred with the organ metaphor, which is a popular, usually implicit, way of thinking about the brain that has shaped our conception of the brain and its functions. Other popular metaphors are based on analogies with the computer and the camera. The analogy between the computer and the brain concerns the distinction between software and hardware. Hardware, as the "machinery" of the brain, can be broken; software, the collection of "programs" that run on the hardware, can be changed and repaired. Learning processes are conceived as a form of re-programming. The analogy with the camera highlights that perception is seen as a form of inner representation, i.e., the projection of impressions generated by the outside world on an inner screen. One step further and these analogies/models are taken to depict the "essence" or the "core" of the object (process, function). This has, in fact, occurred with the computer metaphor and, also, more implicitly, with the camera metaphor. Instead of saying that one should view

---

1. C. Borck, "Toys are Us – Models and Metaphors in Brain Research," in *Critical Neuroscience: A Handbook of the Social and Cultural Contexts of Neuroscience*, S. Choudhury and J. Slaby (Chichester: Wiley – Blackwell, 2012), 113-133; M. E. Botha, *Metaphor and its moorings* (Bern: Peter Lang, 2007); K. L. Slaney and M. D. Maraun, "Analogy and Metaphor Running Amok: an Examination of the Use of Explanatory Devices in Neuroscience," *Journal of Theoretical and Philosophical Psychology* 25, no. 2 (2005): 153-172.

the brain "as if" it behaves like a computer, neuroscientists have said that brains "are" computers. And instead of saying that we may compare perceptual processes with a camera-like form of representing, psychologists and philosophers began to identify knowing with the construction of inner images, or copies, of the outside world. The transition from the "as-if" to the "is," from metaphor to identification, is called "reification." Reification means literally to make a thing of something more abstract. Reification is more or less similar to what Dooyeweerd would call absolutization.

Neuroscience

The science of the brain and of its many functions is called neuroscience. Today, it is better to speak about neurosciences (plural). Neuroscience has grown so fast, and its topics vary so much that there are at least five subdisciplines, focusing on molecules, cells, circuits, behaviour, and cognition, respectively. There are several philosophical issues inherent to the neurosciences.[2] One of them is what neuroscientific knowledge does explain. A related issue is how neuroscientific findings "translate" to (what they have to say to and mean for) other scientific disciplines and to practices like neurology, psychiatry, education, and psychology.[3] In the background there is the age-old problem of how the relation between body (brain) and mind should be conceived. Still another issue is how neuroscience may affect our image of man (and of society). All these issues can be addressed from a Dooyeweerdian perspective, and we will do so with some of them in the next sections. We will build our case step by step, bottom-up and starting within neuroscience itself. We focus first on the image of the brain as an

---

2. See also L. C. de Bruin, M. Slors, and D. Strijbos, *Philosophy of mind, brain and behaviour* (Amsterdam: Boom, 2015).
3. J. C. Francken, M. Slors, "Neuroscience and everyday life: Facing the translation problem," *Brain and Cognition* (2017), http://dx.doi.org/10.1016/j.bandc.2017.09.004

"organ" that "produces" mental phenomena.

The Brain-as-organ View

What would Dooyeweerd make of the description of the brain as an "organ" or organ-like material entity, that produces something immaterial? Let us first acknowledge that the question is somewhat simplistic. It overlooks that in the dominant view brains also produce material things, like hormones, and bring about physical events, like reflexes and movements. For our purposes, however, it is sufficient to say that the organ-metaphor implies that the brain does something, more or less on its own, by producing things other, and of a different order, than itself. The brain as organ is biotic (biotically qualified) and its productions are distinct from it (reflexes, motor movements) and often higher than biotic (feelings, thoughts, inclinations, acts).

The topic is tricky, because, as such, there is nothing wrong with metaphors about the brain and their functioning in everyday life. A problem arises when these metaphors are transposed to science and, in the scientific context, are identified with reality. This occurs when the brain — in other than everyday contexts — is seen as an organ and as functioning on its own, given its organ-like existence. As I said, the use of this metaphor is somewhat implicit. But it is still a dominant image that neuroscientists are inclined to concur with and see as a paradigm case. The brain-as-organ model has, in other words, become reified.

What is problematic with this reification? I will discuss several problems. Keep in mind that we are talking about a reified conception of the brain. What we are going to discuss are the philosophical problems that arise when this conception forms the basis of one's scientific and clinical work.

Three Problems

The first problem is, obviously, how to explain that a biotic "entity" may produce something "higher" than biotic. How can the brain produce mental processes? For livers that produce bile and for hearts that pump blood into our vessels the answer is clear: it is possible to describe how processes in the liver or heart step by step, from event to event, lead to the desired outcome. In these cases, it is possible to describe a causal history of processes that start with and within the liver/heart to the final result, i.e., the bile that is produced or the blood that is pumped into the arteries. But how would this work for mental processes? Are there causal paths from molecular and cellular processes to mental processes? How would these causal paths look? The answer to this question depends on one's philosophical position in the mind/brain discussion. Most of these answers are unsatisfactory and don't solve the problem of how to conceive the relationship between the brain and its products. Dooyeweerd's philosophy helps to see why these answers don't work.

One, currently very unpopular, philosophical position is mind-body (brain) *dualism*. Dualism presupposes that there are two realities: matter and mind; and that these two may interact (dualistic interactionism) or run parallel to one another in some mysterious way (parallelism; occasionalism). For the dualist the mental world stands on its own, like the material world. It can therefore not be "produced by" matter. Matter may at best "exert influence on" or "interfere with" already existing mental content. Since there is no causal path from matter to mind, dualism is not compatible with viewing the brain as an organ that produces mental states. That is why dualism cannot count as a possible solution to the question about how mental states are produced.

Another approach is known as *epiphenomenalism*. Epiphenomenalists hold the view that what we consider to be mental is in fact nothing else than a by-product of material processes. The production of mental phenomena by material processes should not be understood as the emergence of something new, apart from the material processes, but as a concomitant by-product of these processes. The by-product itself is, ontologically speaking, not of a different order; it is another way of appearing of the initial material process. This approach also fails as a solution to the "production" question. What is produced is not something new but a by-product. This by-product is perceived and interpreted as something new, but this newness is not based on ontic differences. The epiphenomenon is another manifestation of the same entity.

A third answer is *emergence*.[4] Mental phenomena arise out of material interactions. They are real and new. And there exists continuity between matter and mind. The production metaphor is, therefore, insufficient. It presupposes that there exists a distinction between "producer" and product. But proponents of the emergence view argue that there exists continuity between matter and mind. It is the producing process itself that undergoes a transformation into a higher order phenomenon. This occurs while producing the "product." Brains change, so to say, from organs into self-organizing subjects.

In the chapter on anthropology, we have seen why Dooyeweerd would reject these three answers.[5] Dooyeweerd rejects dualism because it is based on the absolutization of substances, in this case the biotic and the mental (psychic). There is no organic (biotic) entity that produces things on its own. Nothing exists on its own, the brain is part of the body, and the body involves all substructures, including the actstructure. Similar for the mental. There are all kinds of mental acts and events and none of them operates on

---

4. E. Thompson, *Mind in Life. Biology, Phenomenology, and the Sciences of Mind* (Cambridge, MA: The Belknap Press of Harvard University Press, 2007).
5. See also G. Glas, "Christian Philosophical Anthropology. A Reformation Perspective," *Philosophia Reformata*, 75 (2010): 141-189; G. Glas, "Creation Order and the Sciences of the Person," in *The Future of Creation Order. Philosophical, Scientific, and Religious Perspectives on Order and Emergence Volume I: Philosophy, Sciences, and Theology*, eds. G. Glas & J. de Ridder (Dordrecht/New York/Berlin: Springer, 2018), 203-229.

its own or should be conceived as the product of something just material. It is in the interwovenness of the different substructures (physical, biotic, actstructure) that mental processes and acts develop and acquire their focus and meaning.

Dooyeweerd would also reject epiphenomenalism, because of its denial of mental phenomena as real, ontic processes and acts.

And he would resist emergence because it would erase the distinction (or boundary) between types of entities (biotic and mental types of things, in this case) and, ultimately, between modal aspects (i.e., between the biotic and the psychic modal aspect). There is no such thing that exists as a biotic entity at t1 and that – based on some form of "self-organization" – evolves into a psychic entity at t2 (t = point in time, t1 occurring earlier than t2). Such transitions may in fact take place, but always in interaction with other things than the initial one and, above all, under the umbrella of higher order structural principles that already hold for the original thing at t1.

Actorship

There is still another problem with the organ metaphor which is related to the notion of actorship (or: identity/personhood). How to account for actorship given that brains are conceived as organs that can do things on their own. To what extent is the brain doing things on its own? Is doing-on-its-own a specimen of actorship? Or is there an actor (agent) behind the brain as organ and should we consider the brain as an instrument in the hands of the actor. The brain's "acting on its own" suggests at least a relative independence. The question is, How relative? Complete or almost complete independence suggests that agency resides in the brain and that we are in a way our brains. Limited independence would leave room for a form of agency apart from the brain and would allow the existence of an "I" or actor apart from the brain. Both options are unattractive, however. The "we-are-our-brains" option is unattractive because of its reductionism and the apparent difficulty of making agency, free will, and volition compatible with a materialistic framework. The other option leads easily to a disembodied and abstract notion of agency that lacks embodiment and is conceptually dissociated from the body and the brain; and, therefore, also from the sciences of the brain.

A Positive Account

How would a positive account of the brain look like when we adopt a Dooyeweerdian point of view?[6] First, Dooyeweerd would start by emphasizing the fundamental difference between everyday and scientific knowledge. In everyday life the brain is the malleable substance we would see after the opening of the skull during a neurosurgical procedure. Neuroscientists, on the other hand, talk about gene expression, neural signals, circuits, structural and functional connectivity, and the like. These are concepts that refer to processes within or parts of the brain; processes and parts that are viewed from a certain theoretical perspective. Genes don't express themselves literally. Gene expression is a metaphorical technical term that refers to the process of replication of (parts of the) DNA that is studied by a science called genomics. Neural signals are not traffic lights. They are registered and made visible with technical devices like CT and MRI scanners. Connectivity does not literally refer to connecting things like ties or ropes. Connectivity is a highly abstract measure for the co-occurrence of neural events. Images of the brain produced by neuro-imaging techniques look concrete but are in fact abstract and difficult to interpret because of their dependence on sophisticated techniques that deliver data that need extensive mathematical elaboration and repeated calibration. Looking at the different colorings of the MRI-pictures of a patient

---

6. See also G. Glas, "Churchland, Kandel, and Dooyeweerd on the Reducibility of Mind States," *Philosophia Reformata*, 67 (2002): 148-172; Glas, "Creation Order and the Sciences of the Person," 203-229.

with dementia, the clinician is tempted to say: "Look here, this is your dementia." In fact, the clinician and patient would be looking at a highly artificial product of intricate technology. Dooyeweerd would say that the image is produced by technical procedures and should be interpreted by the science that applies to these technical procedures. The image is, in other words, an artefact that can only be understood in the light of the theories behind its construction. This artefact can never be identified with the "fullness" of reality itself, i.e., with the brain – or parts of it – as it exists in daily life. Most neuroscientists would agree with this, when challenged to give their opinion. It is in the translation of scientific findings to practices like medicine, psychology, education, that the risk of identifying abstractions with reality proves to be largest.

Next, Dooyeweerd would argue for a view in which the brain, as a concrete, visible part of the human body is conceived as responding to, and operating within several part-structures and, ultimately, in the body as structural whole. In the chapter on anthropology four of such structures were discussed: a physical-chemical part-structure, a biotic part-structure, a psychical part-structure and the act-structure. Each "lower" part-structure is encompassed by a "higher" part-structure; with the act-structure encompassing them all. Each encompassed part-structure functions in a foundational sense within the next "higher" part-structure, the physical-chemical within the biotic, the biotic within the psychic, and the psychic within the act-structure. Part-structures are qualified by the function (modal aspect; mode) that is used to denote them. The physical part-structure is qualified by the physical aspect, the biotic by the biotic aspect, the psychic by the psychic, whereas the act-structure should be seen as an open structure that has no fixed qualifying function. The act-structure, in other words, can function in all so-called "normative" spheres (modes), from the logical to the pistical sphere. Which mode prevails depends on the activity of the person and the context in which this takes place.

Part-structures have an "entitary" structure, which means that they obey their own internal structural principles. These structural principles indicate which modal aspect (or: function) qualifies a given part-structure and which aspect should be conceived as the foundation of that part-structure. All part-structures are encompassed by the body conceived as structural whole. "Body" denotes here the human person in a full sense, including the functioning of the person in logical, social, economic, legal, aesthetic, moral and religious relations. These relations and ways of functioning are all corporeal, according to Dooyeweerd. They, in other words, don't exist apart from human corporeality. They are "embodied."

Importance of These Ideas

Agreeing upon the above is no small thing. It would imply that all parts of the human body, the brain included, function in all four part-structures at the same time. This means that the brain not only functions within the physical and biotic part-structure, but also in the psychical part-structure and in the act-structure. Brains are, in a way, active in all these spheres. Instead of being a biological entity that is used as an instrument or vehicle to realize the purposes of its owner, the brain becomes an indispensable contributor to the functioning of other (higher, post-biotic) part-structures.

This idea gains plausibility when the role of the context is considered. As a biotic structure the brain is embedded in the structure of the body and in relations with the body's biophysical environment. As an entity that functions in the psychic structure, it anticipates what occurs in one's immediate environment, for instance by attuning to the perceptual and sensitive aspects of the environment. As an entity that functions in the act-structure, the brain is interacting with still wider contexts, not only existing ones but also imaginary contexts. The brain is involved in reflection on what occurs, it helps us to imagine what could happen, and to change our plans when needed.

Does this mean that the brain itself feels, reflects, imagines and makes plans? The answer is: No, it does not. Ascribing agential qualities to the brain would imply that our account has fallen prey to what is known as the "mereological fallacy" (from "meros," the Greek word for part).[7] This fallacy describes the situation where a feature that belongs to the whole is attributed to one of the constituting parts. It is in other words based on a category mistake. Activities like feeling, thinking, and making plans can conceptually ("logically," grammatically) only be attributed to persons, not to brains. Persons think and feel, not brains.

Does the above mean that the brain itself, as part of the human body, functions in an active sense within modal aspects higher than the biotic modality? Or are these higher-than-biotic functions only opened in a passive sense? Here, I think the notion of enkapsis in a foundational sense may prove to be helpful. Enkapsis is Dooyeweerd's term for intertwinement, encapsulation. Enkapsis in a foundational sense means that the interlacements between the part-structures occurs as in Matrioshka dolls, i.e., the Russian tea dolls that from small to big can be placed inside one another. The physical part-structure becomes the foundation of and is placed within the biotic part-structure, which in turn becomes the foundation of and is placed in the psychic part-structure, and so on. The "placing within" is what Dooyeweerd calls 'enkapsis' (encapsulation).

This kind of interwovenness enables the brain, as an entity that functions within the biotic part-structure, to be opened-up toward psychical and higher functions. While functioning in the biotic part-structure, the brain does not lose its internal biotic destination. The encapsulation with the higher part-structures implies that so-called object-functions are opened-up. These new functions enable further specialization and lead to an increasing

---

7. M. R. Bennett and P.M.S. Hacker, *Philosophical Foundations of Neuroscience* (Malden/Oxford: Blackwell, 2003).

potential for variation at the biological level.

When the brain functions within the psychical part-structure, we view it from the perspective of the psychical structure, in which the brain is engaged in all kinds of psychological processes. At this level we expand our view beyond the body and focus on the brain's embedding in a world that can be perceived and felt and that responds to our drives and inclinations. This broadening of perspective is reflected by the fact that psychologists must take this broader context into consideration to explain phenomena like temperament, emotion, and sensory perception. These phenomena are not productions of the brain but specify the relationship between persons and their immediate environments. There exists an irreversible order in these relationships which means that without the biotic (and physical) part-structure the psychical part-structure cannot function, whereas the biotic part-structure can exist and function without presuming the higher part-structure(s). From this account it might be predicted that the "higher" the part-structures that are involved in a particular human activity, the wider the context neuroscientists should consider when attempting to make sense of their findings.

Conclusion

Translation, explanation, mind/brain relationship and the image of man—these were the topics that were identified as central issues in the philosophy of neuroscience. We have tried to indicate why Dooyeweerd's distinction between everyday and scientific understanding makes sense for the topics of translation and explanation. Concepts like the brain-as-organ may be innocent in practical contexts, but in the context of science there is the risk of reification and absolutization. Concepts in neuroscience are often based on analogies and have, strictly speaking, a metaphorical character. Metaphors are indispensable but should be treated with caution. When reified they lead to restricted and even reductionistic images of who we are.

Dooyeweerd would strongly distinguish causal history from nomological explanation (nomos = law). He would emphasize that the explanatory power of causal histories depends on the holding of laws and structural principles. He would also argue that there are no causal paths from matter to mind. There exists a variety of material and immaterial ways of functioning and these different ways of functioning are intricately intertwined within our functioning-as-a-whole. More precisely, the many ways of functioning are assembled in (lawful or law-abiding) (part-)structures that are closely intertwined within the overall (lawful) structure of the body as an enkaptic structural whole.

The key-term here is "coherence," not causation. Brains do not cause mental phenomena: they cohere, given the structure of the body. Biotic and psychic structures show relationships of dependency because of their coherence within the structure of the body. This coherence is guaranteed by the holding of structural principles, including their enkaptic interlacement within the structural whole of the human body, based on his view concerning the coherence between part-structures.

61

Health Care from a Dooyeweerdian Perspective: A Normative Practices Approach

by Gerrit Glas

Medicine as a Science and a Practice

AT THE HEART OF MEDICINE are relationships: the relationship between physicians and patients, between nurses and patients, and so on. Patients ask doctors for help for difficulties with their body and/or mind. They tell them what they experience and share their worries. Doctors listen, perform physical examinations, request lab tests, and so on. While doing so they "apply" scientific knowledge. This knowledge helps them to interpret what they observe and to form their opinion about what is going on. Medicine is, in other word, a practice as well as a science. As science it finds its roots in many disciplines: anatomy, histology, embryology, physiology, pathology, pharmacy, statistics, epidemiology, psychology, and sociology. As a practice it is not only based on knowledge and technical skills, but also on competencies like communicating, collaborating, organizing, and patient advocacy.

Scientism in Medicine

In the past medicine has shown a tendency to scientism. Scientism is the idea, or even conviction, that science, and science alone, offers the most reliable and trustworthy route to knowledge and truth. This scientism implies, for instance, that only illness manifestations that are amenable to scientific explanation, are medically relevant. These manifestations are objective and reflect the reality, the hard core, of the disease. Illness manifestations that resist scientific explanation are subjective and, therefore, medically irrelevant. They belong, so to say, to medicine's soft margin. Medicine-as-a-practice should enlarge its objective, scientific core. Soft aspects of the patient's condition should only be addressed in so far as this contributes to patient compliance, i.e., the willingness of the patient to accept the doctor's diagnosis and the proposed treatment.

This scientism has led to much dissatisfaction in patients. It feeds paternalistic tendencies among doctors and instills the idea that they know what is best for the patient. It also leads to difficulties with respect to the legitimacy of the profession in cases in which there exists insufficient scientific evidence for the proposed diagnosis or treatment strategy. Scientistic tendencies have finally contributed to the almost complete disregard of the role of the so-called "social contract" in the establishment of the medical profession in general.

The Social Contract

The idea of social contract entails that professionalism is seen as being based on mutual agreement between parties about the goals and conditions for certain services. Among the parties that are relevant for healthcare are: citizens, health care professionals, the government, insurance companies and other payers, authorities responsible for public health and safety, and the like. Services that professionals provide cannot be left to the market, because the market provides no safeguards with respect to the interests of the weakest people. Nor should these services be relegated to the government. Governments typically do not possess the required level of specialist knowledge. The expansion of government's responsibilities could moreover threaten other interests of citizens, for instance, their privacy and autonomy. The social contract itself is a specific form of giving-and-taking that allows professionals certain privileges, such as regulation and control of their professional practices, on the condition that they bind themselves to norms and codes of conduct that guarantee that they behave in the interest of those in need of their services.

The idea of social contract undergirds the notion of medicine as a practice that responds to norms. These norms involve a much broader spectrum than the norms that hold for the sciences and their application to medical practice. This is important, because it implies that to legitimize their behavior, doctors cannot solely base themselves upon their expert role, i.e., the fact that they possess the necessary scientific knowledge and technical skills for medicine as a practice. This knowledge and these skills form the basis (foundation), but the relationship between physicians and patients is responsive to a much broader spectrum of norms than those for the appropriate use of scientific insights and skills. This idea is the starting point for a Dooyeweerdian reflection on medicine as a normative (or: norm-responsive) practice.

Medicine as a Normative Practice

The idea of normative practices starts with the assumption that human relationships are intrinsically norm-responsive and, ideally, may be seen as representations or embodiments of this norm-responsiveness. Essential for medical professionalism is that the physician-patient relationship is understood as an intrinsically moral relationship, i.e., as a relationship that is fundamentally characterized by benevolence, the striving to do well to the patient. This striving is not the manifestation of an accidental subjective intention, it, instead, "qualifies" the physician-patient relationship. All the other aspects of the physician-patient relationship (emotional, cognitive, economic, social, jural) are subservient to this qualifying moment. Without it the relationship between the professional and the patient would not be a physician patient relationship, but, for instance, a supplier-consumer relationship (economic) or a merely contractual relationship (jural).

So far, we have distinguished knowledge and skills that function as the *foundation* of medical practice and the intrinsically moral nature of the patient-physician relationship as a *qualifying* characteristic. The normative practices approach (NPA) addresses them as foundational, respectively qualifying dimensions of medical practice. There is still another type of norms that applies to medical practice. This type refers to so-called *conditioning* norms; norms, in other words, that need to be recognized to sustain the economic, jural, and institutional (social) aspects of medicine. So, we have qualifying norms that qualify (characterize, mark, define) medicine as a fundamentally moral practice. There are foundational norms that safeguard the scientific basis and the role of technology in medicine. And there are conditioning (or: condition-enabling) norms that need to be respected to maintain and support the social, economic, jural, and institutional aspect of medicine, i.e., the norm-responsiveness of the many stakeholder relationships that help to maintain health care in its current, highly developed form.

Background in the Dooyeweerdian Tradition

The normative practice approach (NPA) makes a distinction between structure and direction. Structure refers to what is called the "constitutive" side and direction to the so-called "regulative" side of medical practice, i.e., to the moral, spiritual, and religious values and spirit that guide health care as a practice. The terms *structure* and *direction* became commonplace through the work of Wolters[1] and Mouw and Griffioen.[2] They build forth on

---

1. A. Wolters, *Creation Regained* (Grand Rapids: Eerdmans, 1984).
2. R. J. Mouw and S. Griffioen, *Pluralisms and Horizons: An Essay in Christian Public Philosophy* (Grand Rapids: W.B. Eerdmans, 1993).

Dooyeweerd's distinction between structural types and the religious dynamic that helps to bring a certain structural type (or individuality structure) to its destination. Structural types refer to the structure, the constitutive side, of medicine as a professional practice. The religious dynamic refers to the regulative side, i.e., the spiritual (and historical) dynamic of a certain practice, i.e., the way it evolves over time under the guidance of fundamental intuitions and ideas. Dooyeweerd used the term ground-motive for this spirit. The term direction is a somewhat shallow version of what Dooyeweerd meant with the term ground-motive.

The additional distinctions with respect to the constitutive side of medical practice, i.e., the distinctions between qualifying, conditioning and foundational norms, were proposed by Hoogland et al.,[3] Jochemsen and Glas,[4] and Hoogland & Jochemsen.[5] Like Dooyeweerd, these authors discerned *qualifying* as well as *foundational* principles (or: structures). But they also introduced the term *conditioning* (or: conditions-enabling) principles (or: structures) to indicate the relevance and complexity of current healthcare practices; especially, its dependence on non-foundational, non-qualifying, but nevertheless crucially enabling conditions (agreements, codes, social circumstances, economic conditions, and juridical prerequisites). Jochemsen and Glas[6] associated the

---

3. J. Hoogland, J. J. Polder, S. Strijbos, and H. Jochemsen, *Professioneel beheerst. Professionele autonomie van de arts in relatie tot instrumenten voor beheersing van kosten en kwaliteit van de gezondheidszorg*, rapport no. 12 (Ede: Lindeboom Instituut, 1995).

4. H. Jochemsen and G. Glas, *Verantwoord medisch handelen. Proeve van een Christelijke medische ethiek* (Amsterdam: Buijten & Schipperheijn, 1997).

5. J. Hoogland and H. Jochemsen, "Professional Autonomy and the Normative Structure of Medical Practice," *Theoretical Medicine and Bioethics*, 21, no. 5 (2000): 457–475.

6. H. Jochemsen and G. Glas, *Verantwoord medisch handelen. Proeve van een Christelijke medische ethiek* (Amsterdam: Buijten & Schipperheijn, 1997).

regulative dimension of medical practice with the *ethos* of the profession, i.e., the ensemble of core values and ultimate concerns of medicine as professional practice. And they began to write about the existential core of professionalism[7] and applied the normative practices approach to curriculum development.[8] Diagram 1 gives a schematic picture of medicine as normative practice.

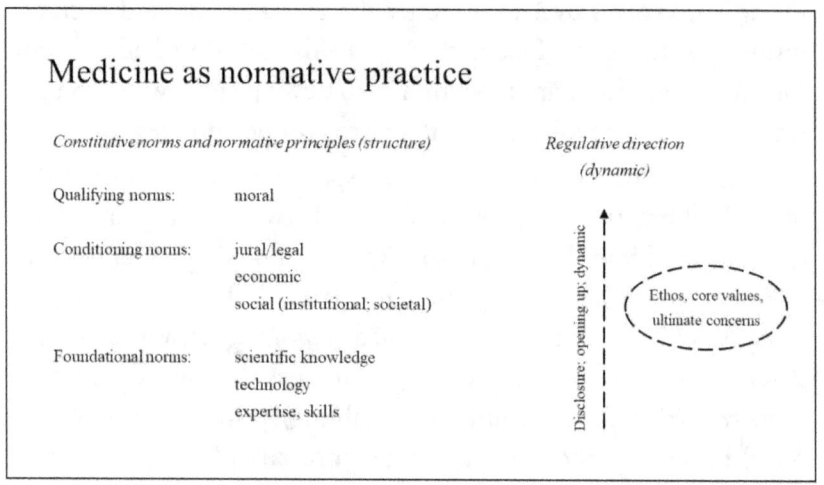

Diagram 1

Mouw and Griffioen[9] were the first to pay attention to the context of practices, especially family life and societal institutions. They worked with the triad of structure, context, and direction. Verkerk et al.[10] used this triad in their analysis of the role of tech-

---

7. G. Glas, "On the existential core of professionalism in mental health care," *Mental Health, Religion & Culture* 20, no. 6 (2017), DOI: 10.1080/13674676.2017.1380122

8. G. Glas, "Competence development as normative practice—Educational reform in medicine as heuristic model to relate worldview and education," *Koers—Bulletin for Christian Scholarship* 77, no. 1 (2012): 70–75, http://dx.doi.org/10.4102/koers.v77i1.411

9. Mouw and Griffioen, *Pluralisms and Horizons*.

10. M. Verkerk, J. Hoogland, J. van der Stoep and J. de Vries, *Philosophy of Tech-*

nology in organizations. Glas[11] gave contexts their due weight in his analysis of health care practices. In most of its initial formulations,[12] the NPA aimed at the individual professional–client relation. Glas[13] broadened the perspective by discussing the role of other actors at meso- and macrolevels of institutional practices, e.g., the representatives of other institutions, policy making bodies, advisory committees, patient representatives, and the government.

The distinction between a constitutive and a regulative side might be interpreted as suggesting a separation between the two sides of medical practice. The two are completely interwoven, however. The constitutive side is opened-up under the guidance of regulative intuitions and ideas, whereas the regulative side can only be brought to life by the constitutive role of norms and principles in the formation of a practice.

---

nology: An Introduction for Technology and Business Students (London: Routledge, 2015).

11. G. Glas, "Public and Institutional Aspects of Professional Responsibility in Medicine and Psychiatry," *Philosophia Reformata* 82, no. 2 (2017): 146-166; G. Glas, *Person-centered Care in Psychiatry. Self-relational, Normative, and Contextual Perspectives* (Abingdon/New York: Routledge, 2019).

12. J. Hoogland, J.J. Polder, S. Strijbos, and H. Jochemsen, *Professioneel beheerst. Professionele autonomie van de arts in relatie tot instrumenten voor beheersing van kosten en kwaliteit van de gezondheidszorg*, rapport no. 12 (Ede: Prof. Dr. G.A. Lindeboom Instituut, 1995) is an exception, especially section 4.4 and chapter 10.

13. G. Glas, "On the Existential Core of Professionalism in Mental Health Care," *Mental Health, Religion & Culture* 20, no. 6 (2017), DOI: 10.1080/13674676.2017.1380122; G. Glas, *Person-centered Care in Psychiatry*; G. Glas, "A Normative Practice Approach to Healthcare," in *The Normative Nature of Social Practices and Ethics in Professional Environments*, eds. M.J. de Vries & H. Jochemsen (Hershey, PA: IGI Global, 2019), 164-184, DOI: 10.4018/978-1-5225-8006-5.ch008.

To clarify the relevance and possible use of the NPA to medicine, I will discuss two developments in medicine that have evoked much discussion: the role of medical knowledge viewed in the light of previous paternalism and current tendencies to decontextualize knowledge; and the role of managerial control in health care in current Western societies. The NPA is helpful for the analysis of both developments. Both are about role reversal between qualifying, conditioning and foundational norms.

Medical Knowledge, Paternalism, and the Decontextualization of Knowing

Let us begin with paternalism and the role of medical expert knowledge. There is still a strong tendency among doctors to define their professionalism as being competent as (and fulfilling the role of) medical expert. With expert role I mean the application of (scientific) expert knowledge and skills in the medical context. "I am, who I am, as a doctor, because of my medical knowledge and skills." In a way this is true, but it is only half the story. Doctors are doctors because of their knowledge and skills. These two form the foundation, the sine qua non. The question is, however, what authority can be based on the competence of being a medical expert. This was a key question during the heydays of paternalism (sixties and seventies of the previous century). Medical experts tended at that time to legitimize their authoritarian attitude by referring to their expert knowledge and skills. It is because of their knowledge and technical skills that doctors assumed they know what is best for their patients; also in matters that do not fall under their jurisdiction, such as life style.

From a normative practices perspective these developments are not only interesting, but also obvious and predictable. Authoritarianism in medicine is wrong in two ways: the fulfilment of the expert role as such is not the essence but a precondition for medical care. Expert knowledge is foundational for medical practice but does not qualify it. The authority of the doctor is, ultimately, determined and guided by the moral aims of medicine, not by knowledge and skills as such. Knowledge and skills fulfil a crucial role in this, but contextualized, i.e., in practices that involve more than mere application of knowledge and skills. What they do and say should always be guided by a wider, ultimately moral perspective. Doctors who claim to possess authority solely on the basis of their knowledge and skills have fallen prey to the temptation to reverse the role of medical knowledge (and skills) by viewing it as qualifying instead of as foundational. They are also mistaken by erasing the important distinction between scientific and non-scientific contexts, such as the context of the patient. Validity in a scientific context legitimizes certain statements in scientific contexts. But these statements need "translation," i.e., adaptation, refinement, precision, specification of their relevance when they are transferred to other, non-scientific contexts; contexts in which other truths need to be balanced with the truths of science.

The question about the kind of authority that comes along with the expert role is also highly relevant today, in times of fake-news and of people who think that science offers just another opinion. How to balance the scientific knowledge of physicians with knowledge by experience of patients? How should expert knowledge with its validity in a scientific context, be translated to the life world of patients, in which other "truths" have equal validity. Answering this question requires high sensitivity with respect to the diversity of norms that are intrinsic to the practices in which doctors operate. Doctors may recommend the use of medication on solid scientific grounds, but patients may refuse to take it because of the impact of certain side-effects. Patients are not bad because they don't obey the doctor's medical advice. They may have good reasons to do so. There are things in life that are more valuable than the treatment of disease or the prevention of future harm. Shared decision-making, the new mantra for medical professionalism, recognizes this. It indicates that doctors need to step into the shoes of the patient and try to understand from their perspective why a certain treatment would or would not make sense. Shared decision-making requires a dialogue about the pros and cons of the suggested treatment.

Today, with the erosion of professionalism and scepticism about science, the frontlines are different. There exists a need to emphasize that scientific understanding legitimizes certain judgments and that doctor's advices are not just random opinions. These judgments and advices have legitimacy within a certain sphere. But in the context of the patient's life, this legitimacy is relative and needs to be balanced with the legitimacy of other perspectives. This balancing is a sensitive matter. Many factors need to be considered. The weighing of different perspectives is not a distanced activity. It requires wisdom, i.e., moral engagement with the patient, keen awareness of the relevance and relative contribution of the different normative perspectives for a given situation; and, maybe most of all, a proper understanding of the context in which the balancing itself takes place. With this, the NPA resists modern tendencies to uncouple knower and known, knowledge and the producers/users of knowledge.

This uncoupling involves a reduction of complexity. It reduces and decontextualizes competence by transforming it into a transferrable skill. The uncoupling suggests that knowledge is "generic," i.e., that it consists of neutral bits of information, that deliberately can be used by anyone. This radical decontextualization is just as scientific and instrumentalist as the earlier authoritarian, technicist and paternalistic conceptions of medicine and medical knowledge. The NPA emphasizes that knowledge and skills are intrinsically intertwined with the normative contexts in which they play their proper role. These contexts follow a variety of norms and principles. These norms and principles remain often implicit, but in times of uncertainty or conflict they need to be spelled out. In short, to understand what a certain piece of knowledge means and implies for a particular situation requires that the implicit is made explicit, i.e., that the variety of relevant normative intuitions about a certain condition or situation are made explicit in order to understand what a given scientific insight would imply. With respect to the execution of skills something similar holds. To know the focus, aim, and extent of an intervention we need a deeper understanding of the particularities of the patient's condition.

Managerialism in Health Care

Another example of role reversal between different constitutive norms (principles) can be found in today's tendencies to bureaucratic control. Doctors and nurses are burdened by managerialism, i.e., the urge to bring their practices under control, not only economically, but also in terms of efficiency, accountability, and transparency. Managerialism is the societal response to the suspicion that medical professionals do not really put all their efforts into the service of others but instead are mainly interested in their own interests. Whereas this suspicion may have had solid grounds, the measures that were taken to diminish it did not lead to restoration of trust. This can be understood from a normative practice's perspective. The problem was lack of trust, it was related to the core of medicine, the patient-physician relationship as moral relationship. The measure however focused on control of the conditions under which medical professionals do their jobs. The massive increase of control—administrative, economic, and in terms of accountability, safety, and access—paradoxically led to an increase in discomfort and distrust, both in (service) users, who were confronted with an increasingly complex system of care, and in professionals, who felt alienated from their proper role. The overemphasis on bureaucratic control ultimately led to a diminishment of control.

With the help of the NPA we can understand the course of events as the product of a role reversal between conditioning and qualifying norms. The conditioning, economic norm of efficiency was dealt with as if it had to become a qualifying norm. This role reversal leads to a different definition of professionalism. In healthcare systems in which efficiency norms prevail above other values, a good doctor is an efficient doctor, not primarily a caring doctor. Efficiency, instead of beneficence, becomes the overarching and qualifying norm for sound and sustainable practice. Advocates of efficiency in medicine claim that there need be no contradiction between efficiency and caring for suffering people. They argue that these aims are complementary. But that is not the issue. The issue is the lack of understanding of the diverse roles (qualifying, condition, foundational) of the relevant norms. In the hierarchy of values of medical practice., efficiency was no longer an auxiliary quality, together with the other necessary conditions. It became the most defining (i.e., qualifying) characteristic of good practice. This distorted view of the structure of medical practice eroded subsequently the ethos of medical professionalism.[14]

The Relation Between Regulative Principles and Constitutive Norms

We can approach these two examples also in terms the of interaction between regulative principles and constitutive norms. Distortions at the structural side of medical practice ultimately lead to antinomies at the regulative side, i.e., in the "direction" of that practice. The opposite may occur too: tensions at the regulative side may lead to antinomies at the structural side. The unbounded urge for technocratic control (regulative side; direction; ethos; ground-motive) may lead to one-sided emphasis on science, technology, and professional specialization as prerequisites for professionalism (constitutive side, structure). This urge may subsequently jeopardize norms that qualify medical practice, especially the norm of beneficence. What is possible in a technological sense

---

14. R. Tallis, *Hippocratic Oaths: Medicine and Its Discontents* (London: Atlantic Books, 2004).

does not always coincide with what is good for users or groups of people that are the target of professional efforts. On the other hand, the spirit of managerial control (dynamic, regulative side) that pervades contemporary medicine has an alienating effect on service users and professionals. The system, medicine as an entrepreneurial edifice is put central, instead of the caring relationship between a professional and a patient. The effects if this are well-known: service users feel not understood; professionals complain about being alienated from their core concerns; departments and institutions focus on competitiveness and market share instead of patient value.[15]

---

15. More on this in G. Glas, *Person-centered Care in Psychiatry*, chapters 6, 7, 9; and G. Glas, "A Normative Practice Approach to Healthcare," 164-184, DOI: 10.4018/978-1-5225-8006-5.ch008.

Bibliography

Alchian A. A. and H. Demsetz. "Production, Information Costs, and Economic Organization." *American Economic Review* 62, no. 5 (Dec. 1972): 777–795.

Alexander, J. C. 1990. *Differentiation Theory and Social Change*. Co-edited by Paul Colomy. New York: Columbia University Press.

Althusius, J. *The Politics of Johannes Althusius*. Translated by Frederick S. Carney. London: Eyre & Spottiswoode, 1965.

Altman, A. *Critical Legal Studies: A Liberal Critique*. Princeton: Princeton University Press, 1990.

Apolin, A. "Die Geschichte des Ersten und Zweiten Hauptsatzes der Wärmetheorie und ihre Bedeutung für die Biologie." *Philosophia Naturalis* 4 (1964).

Aristotle. *The Politics of Aristotle: A Revised Text, with Introduction, Analysis and Commentary*, by F. Susemihl and R. D. Hicks. New York: MacMillan, 1894.

Aristotle. *The Basic Works of Aristotle*. Edited by Richard McKeon. New York: The Modern Library, 2001.

Augustine. *The Confessions of Saint Augustine*. Translated by E. M. Blaiklock. London: Hodder and Stoughton, 1983.

Augustine. *The City of God*. Translated by Wm. Babcock. Notes by B. Ramsey. Hyde Park, NY: New City Press, 2012.

Bagozzi, R. P. "The Legacy of the Technology Acceptance Model and a Proposal for a Paradigm Shift." *Journal of the Association for Information Systems* 8 (2007): 244–54.

Barth, K. *Credo*. London: Hodder & Stoughton, 1936.

Basden, A., and S. Joneidy. "Dooyeweerd's Understanding of Meaning (2): Some Implications." *Philosophia Reformata* 84

(2019): 1–28.

Basen, A. "Engines of Dialectic." *Philosophia Reformata* 64 (1999): 15–36.

———. *Philosophical Frameworks for Understanding Information Systems*. Hershey, PA: IGI Global, 2008.

———. "Enabling a Kleinian Integration of Interpretivist and Critical-Social IS Research: The Contribution of Dooyeweerd's Philosophy." *European Journal of Information Systems* 20 (2011): 477–89.

———. "Dooyeweerd's Understanding of Meaning (1): Some Main Themes." *Philosophia Reformata* 84 (2019): 102–129.

———. "Understanding the Relationships between Fields of Research." *The Electronic Journal of Business Research Methods* 19 (2021): 27–41.

———. *Foundations and Practice of Research: Adventures with Dooyeweerd's Philosophy*. New York: Routledge, 2021.

Baumgartner, H. M. "Von der Möglichkeit, das Agathon als Prinzip zu denken. Versuch einer transzendentalen Interpretation zu Politeia 509 b." *Flasch* (1965): 95–96.

Beck, H. "Metaphysische Implikationen im Konstruktiven Realismus." In *Konstruktion und Verfremdung*, ed. F. G. Wallner and B. Agnese. Vienna: Universitäts-Verlagsbuchhandlung, 1999.

Becker, O., ed. *Zur Geschichte der griechischen Mathematik*. Wege der Forschung 43. Darmstadt: Wissenschaftliche Buchgesellschaft, 1965.

Bennett, M. R., and P. M. S. Hacker. *Philosophical Foundations of Neuroscience*. Malden/Oxford: Blackwell, 2003.

Berger, P. L. *Invitation to Sociology: A Humanistic Perspective*. Harmondsworth: Penguin Books, 1982.

Berlinski, D. "The Deniable Darwin." Discovery Institute, June 1, 1994, https://www.discovery.org/a/130/.

Berman, H. J. *Law and Revolution: The Formation of the Western Legal Tradition*. London: Harvard University Press, 1983.

Bernays, P. *Abhandlungen zur Philosophie der Mathematik*. Darmstadt: Wissenschaftliche Buchgesellschaft, 1976.

Bernstein, R. J. *Beyond Objectivism and Relativism: Science, Hermeneutics and Praxis*. Philadelphia: University of Pennsylvania Press, 1983.

Beth, E. W. *Mathematical Thought*. New York: Reidel, 1965.

Bigwood, R. *Exploitative Contracts*. Oxford: Oxford University Press, 2003.

Bodin, J. *Sechs Bücher über den Staat*. Buch I–III. Translated by Bernd Wimmer. Edited by P. C. Meyer-Tasch. Munich: C. H. Beck, 1981.

Borck, C. "Toys are Us – Models and Metaphors in Brain Research." In *Critical Neuroscience: A Handbook of the Social and Cultural Contexts of Neuroscience*, edited by S. Choudhury and J. Slaby, 113–133. Chichester: Wiley – Blackwell, 2012.

Bos, A. P. *The Soul and Its Instrumental Body: A Reinterpretation of Aristotle's Philosophy of Living Nature*. Leiden-Boston: Brill, 2003.

Botha, M. E. *Metaphor and Its Moorings*. Bern: Peter Lang, 2007.

Bowell, T. and G. Kemp. *Critical Thinking: A Concise Guide*. London: Routledge & Kegan Paul, 2005.

Boyer, C. B. *A History of Mathematics*. London: John Wiley & Sons, 1968.

Breuer, T. "Universell und unvollständig: Theorien über alles?" *Philosophia Naturalis* 34 (1997).

Bril, K. A. *Westerse denkstructuren*. Amsterdam: VU Uitgeverij, 1986.

Brouwer, L. E. J. "De Onbetrouwbaarheid der Logische Principes." In L. E. J. Brouwer, *Wiskunde, waarheid, werkelijkheid*. Groningen: Noordhoff, 1919.

———. *Wiskunde, waarheid, werkelijkheid*. Groningen: Noordhoff, 1919.

———. "Consciousness, Philosophy, and Mathematics." In *Philosophy of Mathematics, Selected Readings*, ed. P. Benacerraf and H. Putnam, 78–84. Oxford: Basil Blackwell, 1964.

Butts, R. E. and J. R. Brown, eds. *Constructivism and Science*. Dordrecht: Kluwer, 1989.

Calhoun, C., J. Gerteis, J. Moody, S. Pfaff, and I. Virk, eds. *Contemporary Sociological Theory*. Oxford: Blackwell, 2002.

Calvin, J. *Institutes of the Christian Religion*. Translated by Henry Beveridge. Peabody, MA: Hendrickson Publishers, 2008.

Cameron, A. "Legal Ideology and Ideology Critique." *Bulletin of the Australasian Society of Social and Legal Philosophy* 16 (1991): 80–90.

———. "Dooyeweerd on Law and Morality: Legal Ethics - A Test Case." Victoria University of Wellington *Law Review* 28 (1998): 263–81.

———. "Dooyeweerd's Jurisprudential Method: Legal Causality as a Case Study." ALTA Conference Proceedings (1998), 595–634.

———. "Liberal Foundations of a liberal Conception of Exploitative Contracts – A Challenge." *Australian Journal of Legal Philosophy* 32 (2007): 127–39.

———. 2020. "The Jural Aspect in Dooyeweerd's Philosophy of Law." In C. Benge, ed., *In a Reformational Key: Papers presented in thankfulness for the life, work and vision of Duncan L. Roper*, 279–308. Wellington: Reformational Studies Trust, 2020..

Carnap, R. *The Logical Structure of the World: Pseudoproblems in Philosophy*. London: Routledge & Kegan Paul, 1967.

Carney, M. *Value(s)*. London: William Collins, 2021.

Cassirer, E. *Substance and Function*. New York: Dover, [1923] 1953.

———. *Das Erkenntnisproblem in der Philosophie und Wissenschaft der neueren Zeit*. 3 vols. 1922–23. Stuttgart: Kohl-hammer Verlag, 1957. Reprinted by Wissenschaftliche Buchgesellschaft, Darmstadt, 1973.

———. *Substanzbegriff und Funktionsbegriff*. Darmstadt: Wissenschaftliche Buchgesellschaft, [1910] 1969.

Cathrein, V. *Recht, Naturrecht und positives Recht. Eine kritische Untersuchung der Grundbegriffe der Rechtsordnung*. 2nd ed. Freiburg im Breisgau: Herder, 1909.

Caudill, D. *Disclosing Tilt, Law, Belief and Criticism*. Amsterdam: Free University Press, 1989.

Chandler, A. D. *The Visible Hand*. Cambridge, MA: Harvard University Press, 1978.

Chaplin, J. *Herman Dooyeweerd: Christian Philosopher of State and Civil Society*. Notre Dame, IN: University of Notre Dame Press, 2011.

———. "Towards a Social Pluralist Theory of Institutional Rights." *Ave Maria Law Review* (2005): 147–49.

Chartier, G. *Anarchy and Legal Order: Law and Politics for a Stateless Society*. Cambridge: Cambridge University Press, 2012.

Clouser, R. "A Critique of Historicism." *Acta Academica Supplementum* 2 (2005): 1–19.

———. *The Myth of Religious Neutrality: An Essay on the Hidden Role of Religious Belief in Theories*. 1991. 2nd rev. ed. Notre Dame, IN: University of Notre Dame Press, 2005.

Coase, R. H. "The Nature of the Firm." *Economica* 4 (Nov. 1937): 386–405.

Coleto, R. "Science and Nonscience: The Search for a Demarcation Criterion in the 20th Century." *Journal for*

Christian Scholarship 47 (2011): 63–79.

Collingwood, R. G. *The Idea of History*. Oxford University Press, 1963.

Comperz, T. *A History of Ancient Philosophy*. London: William Clowes & Sons, 1964.

Copi, I. M. *Introduction to Logic*. 9th ed. New York: Macmillan, 1994.

Copleston, F. *A History of Philosophy*. New York: Doubleday, 1985.

Coyne, J. A. *Why Evolution Is True*. Oxford: Oxford University Press, 2009.

Danzig, T. *Number: The Language of Science*. Garden City, NY: Doubleday-Anchor, 1954.

Darwin, C. *On the Origin of Species by Means of Natural Selection or the Preservation of Favoured Races in the Struggle for Life*. Ed. with an Introduction by J. W. Burrow. Hardmondsworth: Penguin Books, [1859] 1968.

———. *On the Origin of Species by Means of Natural Selection or the Preservation of Favoured Races in the Struggle for Life*. Accessed Oct. 29, 2005. http://www.infidels.org/library/historical/charles darwin/origin of species/Intro.html

Davis, F. D. "Perceived Usefulness, Perceived Ease of Use, and User Acceptance of Information Technology." *MIS Quarterly* 13 (1989): 319–40.

De Bruin, L. C., M. Slors, and D. Strijbos. *Philosophy of Mind, Brain and Behaviour*. Amsterdam: Boom, 2015.

De Saussure, F. *Course in General Linguistics*. Edited by C. Bally and A. Sechehaye. London: McGrawHill, 1966.

De Vleeschauwer, H. J. *Handleiding by die Studie van die Logika en Kennisleer*. Pretoria: Uitg. J. J. Moerau & Kie, 1952.

Deneen, P. *Why Liberalism Failed*. New Haven, CT: Yale University Press, 2018.

Dengerink-Chaplin, A. and H. Brand. *Art and Soul: Signposts for Christians in the Arts.* 2nd ed. Downers Grove, IL: IVP Academic, 2001.

Derrida, J. *Deconstruction in a Nutshell, A Conversation with Derrida.* Edited with a commentary by J. D. Caputo. New York: Fordham University Press, 1997.

———. "Force of Law." In J. Derrida, *Acts of Religion.* 230–98. London: Routledge, 2002.

Descartes, R. *A Discourse on Method, Meditations and Principles.* Translated by John Veitch. London: Everyman's Library, 1965.

Diels, H. And W. Kranz, *Die Fragmente der Vorsokratiker.* Vols. I–III. Berlin: Weidmannsche Verlags-buchhandlung, 1959–60.

Dillenberger, J. *Martin Luther.* Garden City, NY: Anchor Books, 1961.

Dilthey, W. *Der Aufbau der geschichtliche Welt in den Geisteswissenschaften.* Göttingen: VandenHoeck & Ruprecht, 1927.

Diwald, H. *Wilhelm Dilthey, Erkenntnistheorie und Philosophie der Geschichte.* Göttingen: Musterschmidt-Verlag, 1963.

Dobzhansky, T. *The Biology of Ultimate Concern.* New York: New American Library, 1967.

Dooyeweerd, H.. *De Ministerraad in het Nederlandsche staatsrecht.* Amsterdam: Wed. G. van Soest, 1917.

———. "The Problem of Time and Its Antinomies on the Immanence Standpoint II." *Philosophia Reformata* 4 (1939): 1–28.

———. "De leer van de mens in de Wijsbegeerte der Wetsidee." *Correspondentiebladen van de Vereniging voor Calvinistische Wijsbegeerte* 7 (1942): 134–44.

———. "Van Peursen's critische vragen bij 'A New Critique of Theoretical Thought.'" *Philosophia Reformata* 25 (1960):

97–150.

———. *In the Twilight of Western Thought*. Philadelphia: Presbyterian and Reformed Publishing Company, 1960.

———. "De taak ener wijsgerige anthropologie en de doodlopende wegen tot wijsgerige zelfkennis." *Philosophia Reformata* 26 (1961): 35–58.

———. *Roots of Western Culture: Pagan, Secular, and Christian Options*. Toronto: Wedge Publishing Foundation, 1979.

———. *A Christian Theory of Social Institutions*. Grand Rapids, MI: Paideia Press, 1986.

———. *Christian Philosophy and the Meaning of History*. Lewison, NY: Edwin Mellen, 1996.

———. *A New Critique of Theoretical Thought*. Collected Works of Herman Dooyeweerd, Series A, 4 vols. General Editor D. F. M. Strauss. Lewiston, NY: Edwin Mellen, 1997.

———. *Essays in Legal, Social and Political Philosophy*. Collected Works of Herman Dooyeweerd, Series B, Vol. 2. General Editor D. F. M. Strauss. Lewiston, NY: Edwin Mellen, 1997.

———. *Encyclopedia of the Science of Law: Introduction*. Edited by A. C. Cameron. Collected Works of Herman Dooyeweerd, Series A, Vol. 8. General Editor D. F. M. Strauss. Grand Rapids, MI: Paideia Press, 2002.

———. *The Crisis in Humanist Political Theory: As seen from a Calvinist cosmology and epistemology*. Translated by Harry Van Dyke. Collected Works of Herman Dooyeweerd, Series B, Vol. 7. General Editor D. F. M. Strauss. Grand Rapids, MI: Paideia Press, 2010.

———. *In the Twilight of Western Thought. Studies in the Pretended Autonomy of Philosophical Thought*. Collected Works of Herman Dooyeweerd, Series B, Vol. 4. General Editor D. F. M. Strauss. Grand Rapids, MI: Paideia Press, 2012.

BIBLIOGRAPHY

———. *Reformation and Scholasticism in Philosophy*, I. Collected Works of Herman Dooyeweerd, Series A, Vol. 5. General Editor D. F. M. Strauss. Grand Rapids, MI: Paideia Press, 2012.

———. *Roots of Western Culture, Pagan, Secular and Christian Options*. Translated by John Kraay. Edited by Mark Vander Vennen and Bernard Zylstra. Collected Works of Herman Dooyeweerd, Series B, Vol. 15. General Editor D. F. M. Strauss. Grand Rapids, MI: Paideia Press, 2012.

———. *The Struggle for a Christian Politics*. Translated by Phil Brouwer et al. Collected Works of Herman Dooyeweerd, Series B, Vol. 17. General Editor D. F. M. Strauss. Grand Rapids, MI: Paideia Press 2012.

———. *Reformation and Scholasticism in Philosophy*, Vol. 2, Collected Works of Herman Dooyeweerd, Series A, Vol. 6, General Editor D. F. M. Strauss. Grand Rapids, MI: Paideia Press, 2013.

———. *Christian Philosophy and the Meaning of History*. Collected Works of Herman Dooyeweerd. Series B, Vol. 13. General Editor, D. F. M.Strauss. Grand Rapids, MI: Paideia Press, 2013.

———. *Essays in Legal, Social, and Political Philosophy*, Series B, Vol. 14, Collected Works of Herman Dooyeweerd, General Editor, D. F. M.Strauss. Grand Rapids, MI: Paideia Press, 2013.

———. *A New Critique of Theoretical Thought*. 4 vols. Collected Works of Herman Dooyeweerd. Series A. 4 vols. General Editor D. F. M. Strauss. Grand Rapids, MI: Paideia Press, 2015.

———. "The Problem of Time in the Philosophy of the Cosmonomic Idea." In *Time, Law, and History: Selected Essays*, Collected Works of Herman Dooyeweerd, Series B, Vol. 14. General Editor D. F. M. Strauss. Grand Rapids, MI:

Paideia Press: 2017.

———. *Time, Law, and History: Selected Essays*, Collected Works of Herman Dooyeweerd, Series B, Vol. 14, General Editor D. F. M. Strauss. Grand Rapids, MI: Paideia Press: 2017.

———. *The Secularization of Science*. Jordan Station, ON: Paideia Press, 2020.

———. *Encyclopedia of the Science of Law: History of the Concept of Encyclopedia and Law*. Edited by Harry van Dyke. Collected Works of Herman Dooyeweerd, Series A, Vol 9/II. Grand Rapids, MI: Paideia Press, 2021.

Donoghue v Stevenson. [1932] UKHL 100. 1932 All ER Rep 1.

Drake, S. *Essays on Galileo and the History of Philosophy of Science*. Vol. I. Toronto: University of Toronto Press, 1999.

Driesch, H. *Philosophie des Organischen*. Leipzig: Engelmann, 1921.

Dummett, M. A. E. *Elements of Intuitionism*. Oxford: Clarendon Press, 1978.

Dummett, M. A. E. *Frege, Philosophy of Mathematics*. Cambridge, MA: Harvard University Press, 1995.

Dworkin, R. *Law's Empire*. London: Fontana, 1986.

Eibl-Eibesfeldt, I. *Grundriß der vergleichenden Verhaltensforschung, Ethologie*. 8th rev. ed. Vierkirchen-Pasenbach: Buch Vertrieb Blank, 2004.

Einstein, A. "Autobiographical Notes." In *Albert Einstein, Philosopher-Scientist*, edited by P. A. Schilpp. New York: Harper Torchbooks, 1959.

Einstein, A. *Grundzüge der Relativitätstheorie*. Wiesbaden: Friedrich Fieweg & Sohn, [1922] 1982.

Einstein, A. *Relativity: The Special and General Theory*. Bristol: Arrowsmith, [1920] 1985.

Eriksson, D. "Identification of Normative Sources for Systems Thinking: Inquiry into Religious Ground-Motives for Systems

Thinking Paradigms." *Systems Research and Behavioral Science* 20 (2003): 475–87.

Esmain, A. "La Maxime Princeps Legibus Solutus Est dans l'ancien Droit Public Français." In *Essays in Legal History,* edited by P. Vinogradoff. New York: Wm. W. Gaunt & Sons, 1993.

Fara, P. *An Entertainment for Angels: Electricity in the Enlightenment.* Duxford: Icon Books, 2002.

Finnis, John. *Natural Law and Natural Rights.* New York: University Press, 1980.

Flasch, K. *Parusia; Studien zur Philosophie Platons und zur Problemgeschichte des Platonismus.* Festgabe fur Johannes Hirschberg. Frankfurt: Minerva, 1965.

Fourie, F. C. v. N. "A Structural Theory of the Nature of the Firm." PhD diss., Harvard University, 1981.

———. "The Nature of Firms and Markets – Do Transactions Approaches Help?" *South African Journal of Economics* 57 (1989):142–60.

———. "The Nature of the Market: A Structural Analysis." In *Rethinking Economics: Markets, technology and economic evolution,* edited by G. Hodgson and E. Screpanti. Aldershot: Edward Elgar, 1991.

———. "In the Beginning There Were Markets?" In *Transaction Costs, Markets and Hierarchies,* edited by C. Pitelis. Oxford: Basil Blackwell, 1993.

———. "Shareholder Associations, Control Contracts and the Organisation of the Firm." Paper presented at the 22nd Conference of the European Association for Research in Industrial Economics, Juan les Pins, France, September, 1995.

———. "Separation of Ownership and Control: What is the Problem?" *South African Journal for Economic and Management Sciences* (1996).

———. "Informal-sector Employment in South Africa: An

Enterprise Analysis Using the SESE Survey." In *The South African Informal Sector: Creating Jobs, Reducing Poverty*, edited by F. C. v. N. Fourie. Cape Town: HSRC Press, 2018.

Fourie, F. C. v. N. and E. P. Beukes. "Government in the Economy: A Reformational Rethink." *Philosophia Reformata* 57 (1992): 57–77.

Fraenkel, A., Y. Bar-Hillel, A. Levy, and D. Van Dalen. *Foundations of Set Theory*. 2nd rev. ed. Amsterdam: North Holland, 1973.

Francken, J. C., and M. Slors. "Neuroscience and everyday life: Facing the translation problem." *Brain and Cognition* (2017). http://dx.doi.org/10.1016/j.bandc.2017.09.004.

Fränkel, H. "Zeno von Elea im Kampf gegen die Idee der Vielheit." In *Um die Begriffswelt der Vorsokratiker*, Wege der Forschung 9, edited by H. G. Gadamer, 425ff. Darmstadt: Wissenschaftliche Buchgesellschaft, 1968.

Freeman, K. *Ancilla to the pre-Socratic Philosophers. A Complete Translation of the Fragments of Diels, Fragmente der Vorsokratiker*. Oxford: Basil Blackwell, 1956.

Freeman, S., ed. *The Cambridge Companion to Rawls*. Cambridge: Cambridge University Press, 2003.

Frege, G. *Schriften zur Logik und Sprachphilosophie: Aus dem Nachlaß*. Hamburg: Felix Meiner, 2001.

Fuller, L. L. *The Morality of Law*. Revised edition. New Haven: Yale University Press, 1969. Internet Encyclopedia of Philosophy. https://iep.utm.edu/legalpos/ (accessed 4/03/2022).

Gadamer, H. G., ed. *Um die Begriffswelt der Vorsokratiker*. Wege der Forschung 9. Darmstadt: Wissenschaftliche Buchgesellschaft, 1968.

Gadamer, H. G., and P. Vogler. *Neue Anthropologie*. Vol. II. Stuttgart: Georg Thieme, 1972.

Gadamer, H. G. *Truth and Method*. 2nd rev. ed. New York: The Continuum Publishing Company, 1989.

Gadamer, H. G. "Die Hermeneutik und der Diltheyschule." *Philosophische Rundschau* 38 (1991): 161–177.

Geehan, E. R., ed., *Jerusalem & Athens: Critical Discussions on the Philosophy and Apologetics of Cornelius Van Til*. Phillipsburg, NJ: Presbyterian and Reformed Publishing Co., 1971.

Geertsema, H. G., J. Zwart, J. de Bruijn, J. van der Hoeven, and A. Soeteman, eds. *Herman Dooyeweerd 1894–1977. Breedte en Actualiteit van zijn filosofie*. Kok: Kampen, 1994.

Geertsema, H. G. *Homo respondens. Essays in Christian Philosophy*. Jordan Station, ON: Paideia Press, 2021.

Gehlen, A. *Theorie der Willensfreiheit und frühe Philosophische Schriften*. Berlin: Luchterhand, 1965.

Gellner, E. *Relativism and the Social Sciences*. Cambridge: Cambridge University Press, 1985.

Gény, F. *Science et Technique en Droit Privé Positif*. 4 vols. 2nd ed. Paris: Recueil Sirey, 1922–1930.

Glas, G. "Ego, Self, and the Body. An Assessment of Dooyeweerd's Philosophical Anthropology." In *Christian Philosophy at the Close of the Twentieth Century. Assessment and Perspective*, edited by S. Griffioen and B. M. Balk, 67–78. Kampen: Kok, 1995.

———. "Churchland, Kandel, and Dooyeweerd on the Reducibility of Mind States." *Philosophia Reformata* 67 (2002): 148–72.

———. "Christian Philosophical Anthropology. A Reformation Perspective." *Philosophia Reformata* 75 (2010): 141–89.

———. "Competence Development as Normative Practice – Educational Reform in Medicine as Heuristic Model to Relate Worldview and Education." *Koers – Bulletin for Christian Scholarship* 77 (2012): 70–75. http://dx.doi.org/10.4102/koers.v77i1.411.

———. "On the Existential Core of Professionalism in Mental Health Care." *Mental Health, Religion & Culture* 20, no. 6

(2017). DOI: 10.1080/13674676.2017.1380122.

———. "Public and Institutional Aspects of Professional Responsibility in Medicine and Psychiatry." *Philosophia Reformata* 82 (2017): 146–66.

———. "Creation Order and the Sciences of the Person." In *The Future of Creation Order. Philosophical, Scientific, and Religious Perspectives on Order and Emergence. Volume I: Philosophy, Sciences, and Theology*, edited by G. Glas and J. de Ridder, 203–29. Dordrecht/New York/Berlin: Springer, 2018.

———. *Person-centered Care in Psychiatry. Self-relational, Normative, and Contextual Perspectives.* Abingdon/New York: Routledge, 2019.

———. "A Normative Practice Approach to Health Care." In *The Normative Nature of Social Practices and Ethics in Professional Environments*, edited by M. J. de Vries and H. Jochemsen (Hershey, PA: IGI Global, 2019), 164–184, DOI: 10.4018/978-1-5225-8006-5.ch008.

Goerttler, K. "Morphologische Sonderstellung des Menschen im Reich der Lebensformen auf der Erde." In *Neue Anthropologie*. Vol. 2, edited by H. G. Gadamer and P. Vogler, 215–57. Stuttgart: Georg Thieme, 1972.

Goethe, J. W. *Goethe's Faust.* Translated by Walter Kaufmann. Garden City, NY: Doubleday & Company, 1961.

Gosztonyi, A. *Der Raum; Geschichte seiner Probleme in Philosophie und Wissenschaften*, Vol. 1. Freiburg: Alber, 1976.

Goudzwaard, B. *Capitalism and Progress: A Diagnosis of Western Society.* Toronto: Wedge and Grand Rapids, MI: Eerdmans, 1997.

Gould, S. J. *Full House: The Spread of Excellence from Plato to Darwin.* New York: Harmony, 1996.

———. *Life's Grandeur: The Spread of Excellence from Plato to Darwin.* London: Jonathan Cape, 1996.

———. *The Structure of Evolutionary Theory*. London: The Belknap Press of Harvard University Press, 2002.

Gould, S. J. and Niles Eldredge. "Punctuated Equilibria: The Tempo and Mode of Evolution Reconsidered." *Paleobiology* 3, no. 2 (Spring 1977): 15–151.

Greene, B. *The Elegant Universe*. New York: W. W. Norton & Company, 2003.

Griffioen, S. "De Betekenis van Dooyeweerd's ontwikkelingsidee." *Philosophia Reformata* 51 (1986): 83–109.

Grünbaum, A. *Philosophical Problems of Space and Time*. 2nd ed. Dordrecht: Reidel, 1974.

Gunton, R. M. and F. Gilbert. "Laws in Ecology: Diverse Modes of Explanation for a Holistic Science." *Zygon* 52 (2017): 538–60. doi: 10.1111/zygo.12334.

———, M. D. Stafleu and M. J. Reiss. "A General Theory of Objectivity: Contributions from the Reformational Philosophy Tradition." *Foundations of Science* (2021). doi: 10.1007/s10699-021-09809-x.

Guthrie, W. K. C. *A History of Greek Philosophy*. Vol. 1. Cambridge: Cambridge University Press, 1962.

Guthrie, W. K. C. *A History of Greek Philosophy*. Vol. 2. Cambridge: Cambridge University Press, 1980.

Haas, J. *Sein und Leben, Ontologie des organischen Lebens*. Karlsruhe: Badenia Verlag, 1968.

Habermas, Jürgen. *Moralbewußtsein und kommunikatives Handeln*. Frankfurt am Main: Suhrkamp Verlag, 1983.

———. *The Theory of Communicative Action*. Volume I: *Reason and the Rationalization of Society*. Translated by T. McCarthy. Cambridge, UK: Polity Press, 1986.

———. *Between Facts and Norms: Contributions to a Discourse Theory of Law and Democracy*. Translated by William Rehg. Cambridge, MA: MIT Press, 1996.

———. *Faktizität und Geltung. Beiträge zur Diskurstheorie des Rechts und des demokratischen Rechtsstaats*. Frankfurt am Main: Suhrkamp, 1998.

Halliday, M. A. K. *Language as Social Semiotic: The Social Interpretation of Language and Meaning*. London: Edward Arnold, 1979.

Happ, H. *Hylè: Studien zum Aristotelischen Materie-Begriff*. Berlin: De Gruyter, 1971.

Harmsen, J., and M. J. Verkerk. *Process Intensification. Breakthrough in Design, Industrial Innovation Practices, and Education*. Berlin: De Gruyter, 2020.

Hart, H. L. A. and T. Honore. *Causation in the Law*. 2nd ed. Oxford: Oxford University Press, 1985.

Hart, H. L. A. *The Concept of Law*. 2nd ed. Oxford: Clarendon Press, 1994.

Hartley, A. M. *Christian and Humanist Foundations for Statistical Inference: Religious Control of Statistical Paradigms*. Eugene, OR: Resource Publications, 2007.

Hartmann, N. *Ethik*. Berlin und Leipzig: Walter de Gruyter, 1926.

Hartnack, J. *Kant's Theory of Knowledge*. Translated by M. Holmes Hartshorne. London: MacMillan, 1968.

Hayek, F. A. *The Road to Serfdom*. Chicago: University of Chicago Press, 1944.

Heidegger, M. *The Concept of Time*. Oxford: Blackwell, 1992.

Heisenberg, W. *Das Naturbild der heutigen Physik*. Hamburg: Rowohlt, 1956.

Heisenberg, W. *Physics and Philosophy. The Revolution in Modern Science*. New York: Harper Torchbooks, 1958.

Heitler, W. *Ueber die Komplementarität von Lebloser und lebender Materie*. Abhandlungen der mathematisch-naturwissenschaftlichen Klasse, Nr. 1. Mainz, 1976.

Henderson, R. D. "Dooyeweerd's esthetica." In *Kunst D.V. (Neo)calvinistische perspectieven op estetica, kunstgeschiedenis en kunsttheologie* edited by M. Hengelaar-Rookmaaker and R. D. Henderson. 75–89. Amsterdam: Buijten & Schipperheijn, 2020.

Henderson, R. *Illuminating Law: The Construction of Herman Dooyeweerd's Philosophy, 1918-1928*. Amsterdam: Free University Press, 1994.

Herder, J. G. *Abhandlung über den Ursprung der Sprache*. Edited by Wolfgang Proß. Munich: Carl Hanser Verlag, 1978.

Hersh, R. *What Is Mathematics Really?* Oxford: Oxford University Press, 1997.

Heyting, A. *Intuitionism. An Introduction*. Amsterdam: North Holland Pub. Co., 1971.

Hilbert, D. "Über das Unendliche." *Mathematische Annalen* 95 (1925): 161–190.

———. *Gesammelte Abhandlungen*. Vol. 3, 2nd ed. Berlin: Verlag Springer, 1970.

Hobbes, T. *Leviathan*. Cambridge: Cambridge University Press, [1651] 1996.

Holtkamp, F. C., E. J. M. Wouters, J. van Hoof, Y. van Zaalen and M. J. Verkerk. "Use of and Satisfaction with Ankle Foot Orthoses." *Clinical Research on Foot & Ankle* 2, no. 2 (2015): 1–8. DOI: 10.4172/2329-910X.1000167.

Holtkamp, F. C., M. J. Verkerk, J. van Hoof and E. J. M. Wouters. "Mapping User Activities and User Environments During the Client Intake and Examination Phase: An Exploratory Study from the Perspective of Ankle Foot Orthosis Users." *Technology and Disability* 28, no. 4 (2016): 145–57. DOI: 10.3233/TAD-160452.

Homer. *The Odyssey of Homer*. Translated by Richmond Lattimore. New York and London: Harper and Row, 1965.

Hommes, H. J. *Major Trends in the History of Legal Philosophy.* Amsterdam: North Holland Pub. Co., 1979.

Hoogland, J., J. J. Polder, S. Strijbos, and H. Jochemsen. *Professioneel beheerst. Professionele autonomie van de arts in relatie tot instrumenten voor beheersing van kosten en kwaliteit van de gezondheidszorg.* Rapport no. 12. Ede: Prof. Dr. G. A. Lindeboom Instituut, 1995.

Hoogland, J., and H. Jochemsen. "Professional Autonomy and the Normative Structure of Medical Practice." *Theoretical Medicine and Bioethics* 21 (2000): 457–75.

Horneffer, R. *Die Entstehung des Staates. Beiträge zum öffentlichen Recht der Gegenwart.* Tübingen: Mohr, 1933.

Hunt, A. and G. Wickham. *Towards a Sociology of Law as Governance.* London: Pluto Press, 1994.

Ive, Jeremy. "A Critically Comparative Kuyperian Analysis and a Trinitarian, 'Perichoretic' Reconstruction of the Reformational Philosophies of Dirk H. Th. Vollenhoven and Herman Dooyeweerd." PhD diss., King's College London, 2012.

———. (2015). "The Contribution and Philosophical Development of the Reformational Philosopher, Dirk H. Th. Vollenhoven," *Philosophia Reformata* 80 (2015): 159-77. doi: https://doi.org/10.1163/ 23528230-08002001

———. (2022). "The Contribution and Philosophical Development of the Reformational Philosopher Herman Dooyeweerd and His Conversation with Dirk Vollenhoven." *Philosophia Reformata* doi: https://doi.org/10.1163/23528230-bja10056

———. "The Roots of Reformational Philosophy: The Thought of Dirk H. Th. Vollenhoven and Herman Dooyeweerd in the Light of the Trinitarian Vision of Abraham Kuyper." Unpublished manuscript, 2014.

Jaeger, W. *The Theology of the Early Greek Philosophers*. Oxford: Clarendon Press, 1947.

Janich, P. "Tragheitsgesetz und Inertialsystem." In *Frege und die moderne Grundlagenforschung*, red. Chr. Thiel. Meisenheim am Glan: Hain, 1975.

Jaspers, K. *Philosophie*. Berlin: Springer Verlag, 1948.

Jochemsen, H., and G. Glas. *Verantwoord medisch handelen. Proeve van een Christelijke medische ethiek*. Amsterdam: Buijten & Schipperheijn, 1997.

Johnson, T., C. Dandeker, and C. Ashworth. *The Structure of Social Theory*. London: Macmillan, 1984.

Jones, A., ed. *Science in Faith: A Christian Perspective on Teaching Science*. Essex: Romford, 1998.

Jones, S. *Almost Like a Whale: The Origin of Species Updated*. London: Doubleday, 1999.

Kammler, H. *Der Ursprung des Staates, Eine Kritik der Ueberlagerungslehre*. Köln: Westdeutscher Verlag, 1966.

Kant, I. *Kritik der reinen Vernunft*. 2nd ed. Hamburg: Felix Meiner, [1787] 1956.

———. *Critique of Pure Reason*, trans. Norman Kemp Smith. New York: St. Martin's Press, 1965.

———. *Kritik der Urteilskraft*. Darmstadt: Wissenschaftliche Buchgesellschaft, [1790] 1968.

———. *Prolegomena zu einer jeden künftigen Metaphysik die als Wissenschaft wird auftreten können*. Hamburg: Felix Meiner, [1783] 1969.

Kelsen, H. *Reine Rechtslehre, Mit einem Anhang: Das Problem der Gerechtigkeit*. Vienna: Verlag Franz Deuticke, 1960.

———. *General Theory of Norms*. Translated by Michael Hartney. Oxford: Clarendon Press, 1991.

Kiontke, S. *Physik biologischer Systeme. Die erstaunliche Vernachlässigung der Biophysik in der Medizin*. Munich:

Mintzel, 2006.

Klapwijk, J. *Purpose in the Living World? Creation and Emergent Evolution*. Edited by H. T. Cook. Cambridge: Cambridge University Press, 2008.

Korsgaard, C. M. *The Sources of Normativity*. Cambridge: Cambridge University Press, 1998.

Koyzis, D. *Political Visions and Illusions*. Downers Grove, IL: InterVarsity Press, 2019.

———. *We Answer to Another: Authority, Office, and the Image of God*. Eugene, OR: Pickwick, 2014.

Krämer, H. J. *Arete bei Platon und Aristoteles, Zum Wesen und Geschichte der platonischen Ontologie*. Heidelberg: Winter, 1959.

Kugler, R. *Philosophische Aspekte der Biologie Adolf Portmanns*. Editio Academica: Zürich, 1967.

Kuitert, H. M. *Filosofie van de theologie*. Leiden: Martinus Nijhof, 1988.

Kuyper, A. *Encyclopedia of Sacred Theology*. Translated by J. H. de Vries. New York: Charles Scribner's Sons, 1898.

Kuyper, A. *Lectures on Calvinism*. Grand Rapids, MI: Eerdmans, 1931.

Kuyper, A. "Sphere Sovereignty." In *Abraham Kuyper: A Centennial Reader*, edited by James D. Bratt, 461–90. Grand Rapids, MI and Carlisle, UK: Eerdmans and Paternoster Press, 1998.

Kuyper, A. 2022. "Sphere Sovereignty." *On Charity and Justice*, pp. 111–49. Bellingham, WA: Lexham Press.

Laitman, J. T. "Evolution of the Upper Respiratory Tract: The Fossil Evidence." In *Hominid Evolution*, edited by P. V. Tobias. New York: Liss, 1985.

Leftow, B. "Eternity and Immutability." In *The Blackwell Guide to the Philosophy of Religion*, edited by W. E. Mann, 48–77.

Oxford: Blackwell Publishing, 2005.

Leibniz, G. W. L. "Correspondence with Clarke, Third Paper." In *Leibniz, Philosophical Writings*. Translated by M. Morris. London: Everyman's Library, 1965.

———. *Philosophical Papers*. Edited by Leroy E. Loemker. Synthese Historical Library 2. Dordrecht, Neth.: Reidel, 1976.

Lemmon, E. J. *Introduction to Axiomatic Set Theory*. London: Routledge & Kegan Paul, 1968.

Lloyd, D. *Introduction to Jurisprudence*. 4th ed. London: Stevens, 1979.

Loomis C. P. and J. C. McKinney. "Introduction." In F. Tönnies, *Community and Society*. New York: Harper & Row, 1957.

Lorenzen, P. *Die Entstehung der exakten Wissenschaften*. Berlin: Springer-Verlag, 1960.

———. "Das Aktual-Unendliche in der Mathematik." In *Methodisches Denken*. Suhrkamp Taschenbücher Wissenschaft 73. Pp. 94–119. Frankfurt: Suhrkamp, 1968.

———. "Zur Definition der vier fundamentalen Meßgrößen." *Philosophia Naturalis* 16 (1976): 1–9.

———. "Geometry as the Measure-Theoretic A Priori of Physics." In *Constructivism and Science*, edited by R. E. Butts and J. R. Brown. 127–44. Dordrecht, Neth.: Kluwer, 1989.

Lowe, E. J. *The Possibility of Metaphysics, Substance, Identity and Time*. Oxford: Clarendon, 1998.

Lowie, R. H. *Primitive Society*. London: George Routledge & Sons, 1921.

MacCormick, N. *H. L. A. Hart*. London: Edward Arnold, 1981.

MacCormick, N. and Weiberger, O. *An Institutional Theory of Law: New Approaches to Legal Positivism*. Dordrecht, Neth.: Reidel, 1986.

MacIntyre, A. *After Virtue. A Study in Moral Theory*. 2nd ed. Notre

Dame, IN: University of Notre Dame Press, 1984.

Mackenzie, L. *Studies in Roman Law with Comparative Views of the Laws of France, England, and Scotland*, 7th ed., edited by J. Kirkpatrick. Edinburgh: William Blackwood & Sons, 1898.

Maddy, P. "Three forms of naturalism." In *The Oxford Handbook of Philosophy of Mathematics and Logic*, edited by S. Shapiro, 437–59. Oxford: Oxford University Press, 2005.

Maier, A. 1949. *Die Vorläufer Galileis im 14. Jahrhundert*, Roma: Edizioni di Storia e letteratura.

———. "Diskussion über das Aktuell Unendlichen in der ersten Hälfte des 14. Jahrhunderts." In *Ausgehendes Mittelalter*, Vol. I. Rome: Edizioni di storia e letteratura, 1964.

Mann, W. E., ed. *The Blackwell Guide to the Philosophy of Religion*. Oxford: Blackwell Publishing, 2005.

Mannheim, K. *Structures of Thinking*. Edited and introduced by David Kettler, Volker Meja, and Nico Stehr, and translated by Jeremy J. Shapiro and Shierry Weber Nicholson. London and Boston: Routledge & Kegan Paul, 1982.

Marrou, H.-I. *De la connaissance historique*. Paris: Éditions du Seuil, 1954.

Marsden, G. and F. Roberts, eds. *A Christian View of History?* Grand Rapids, MI: Eerdmans, 1977.

Mayr, E. *One Long Argument: Charles Darwin and the Genesis of Modern Evolutionary Thought*. Cambridge: Harvard University Press, 1991.

McGarr P., and S. Rose. *The Richness of Life, The Essential Stephen Jay Gould*. London: Jonathan Cape, 2006.

Medley, J. D. *A Student's Manual of English Constitutional History*. Oxford: Blackwell, 1925.

Menzel, A. *Beiträge zur Geschichte der Staatslehre*. Vienna-Leipzig: Hölder-Pichler-Tempsky, 1929.

———. "Griechische Staatssoziologie." *Zeitschrift für öffentliches*

Recht 16 (1936).

Meyendorff, J. *A Study of Gregory Palamas*. London: Faith Press, 1964.

Meyer, S. *Darwin's Doubt*. New York: Harper Collins, 2013.

Meyer-Tasch, P. C. "Einführung in Jean Bodins Leben und Werk." In Jean Bodin, *Sechs Bücher über den Staat*, Buch I–III. Translated by Bernd Wimmer, edited by P. C. Meyer-Tasch. Munich: Verlag C. H. Beck, 1981.

Milbank, J. *Being Reconciled, Ontology and Pardon (Radical Orthodoxy)*. London: Routledge, 2003.

———. "Foreword." In *Introducing radical orthodoxy, mapping a postsecular theology*, J. K. A. Smith, 11–20. Grand Rapids, MI: Baker Academic, 2004.

———. *Theology and Social Theory. Beyond Secular Reason*. Oxford: Blackwell, 2006.

———. "The theological critique of philosophy in Hamann and Jacobi." In *Radical Orthodoxy*, edited by J. Milbank, C. Pickstock and G. Ward, 21–37. New York: Routledge, 2006.

Morgan, J. "Feminist Theory as Legal Theory." *Melbourne University Law Review* 39 (1997): 127–48.

Mouw, R. J., and S. Griffioen. *Pluralisms and Horizons: An Essay in Christian Public Philosophy*. Grand Rapids, MI: Eerdmans, 1993.

Münch, R. "Differentiation, Rationalization, Interpenetration: The Emergence of Modern Society." In *Differentiation Theory and Social Change*, edited by J. C. Alexander and Paul Colomy. New York: Columbia University Press, 1990.

Naylor, S. and S. Schaffer. "Nineteenth-century Survey Sciences: Enterprises, Expeditions and Exhibitions." *Notes and Records* 73 (March 2019): 135–47. doi: 10.1098/rsnr.2019.0005.

New Oxford Dictionary of English. Oxford: Oxford University Press, 2001.

Nicolini, D. *Practice Theory, Work, & Organisation, An Introduction.* Oxford: Oxford University Press, 2012.

Nilsson, M. P. *A History of Greek Religion.* 2nd ed. Translated by F. J. Fielden. New York: W. W. Norton & Company, 1964.

O'Donovan, O. *The Desire of the Nations: Rediscovering the Roots of Political Theology.* Cambridge: Cambridge University Press, 1996.

O'Neill, O. "Constructivism in Rawls and Kant." In *The Cambridge Companion to Rawls,* edited by S. Freeman, 347–67. Cambridge: Cambridge University Press, 2003.

Ouweneel, W. J. *De leer van de mens. Proeve van een christelijk-wijsgerige antropologie.* Amsterdam: Buijten & Schipperheijn, 1986.

———. *What Then Is Theology?* Grand Rapids, MI: Paideia Press, 2014.

Overhage, P. *Der Affe in dir.* Frankfurt am Main: Josef Knecht, 1972.

———. *Die biologische Zukunft der Menschheit.* Frankfurt am Main: Joseph Knecht, 1977.

Patterson, R. and A. Weideman. "The Typicality of Academic Discourse and Its Relevance for Constructs of Academic Literacy." *Journal for Language Teaching* 47 (2013): 107–23. http://dx.doi.org/_10.4314/jlt.v47i1.5

Paulus, Andreas. "US Influence on the Concept of 'International Community," In *United States Hegemony and Foundations of International Law,* edited by Michael Byers and Georg Nolte, 57–58. Cambridge: Cambridge University Press, 2003.

———. "From Territoriality to Functionality? Towards a Legal Methodology of Globalization." In Ige F. Dekker and Wouter G. Werner, editors, *Governance and International Legal Theory,* 42–60. Leiden: Brill, 2004.

Pegis, A. C., ed. *Basic Writings of Saint Thomas Aquinas.* 2 vols.

New York: Random House, 1945.

Pelican, J., editor. *Luther's Works*. St. Louis: Concordia Publishing House, 1958.

Penrose, R. *The Road to Reality. A Complete Guide to the Laws of the Universe*. London: Vintage Books, 2004.

Plamenac, M. "Bio-physical Analysis of Vital Force of Living Matter." *Philosophia Naturalis* 12 (1970).

Planck. M. "Die Stellung der neueren Physik zur mechanischen Naturanschauung." In *Vorträge und Erinnerungen*, M. Planck, 52–68. 5th ed. Darmstadt: Wissenschaftliche Buchgesellschaft, 1973.

———. "Neue Bahnen der physikalischen Erkenntnis (Rede, gehalten beim Antritt des Rektorats der Friedrich-Wilhelms-Universität)." In *Vorträge und Erinnerungen*, M. Planck, 69–80. 5th ed. Darmstadt: Wissenschaftliche Buchgesellschaft, 1973.

———. *Vorträge und Erinnerungen*. 5th ed. Darmstadt: Wissenschaftliche Buchgesellschaft, 1973.

Plantinga, A. *God, Freedom, and Evil*. New York: Harper & Row, 1967.

Plato. *The Collected Dialogues of Plato, including the Letters*. Edited by E. Hamilton and C. Huntington. Princeton, NJ: Princeton University Press, 1973.

Plotinus. *The Enneads*. Translated by Stephen MacKenna. London: Faber & Faber, 1956.

Popma, K. J. *De Plaats der Theologie*. Franeker: T. Wever, 1946.

———. *Scriptural Reflections on History*. Translated by Harry van Dyke. Aalten, Neth.: Wordbridge, 2020.

———. *Gospel and History*. Translated by Harry van Dyke. Aalten, Neth.: Wordbridge, 2021.

Popper, K. *The Open Society and its Enemies*. 2 vols. London: Routledge & Kegan Paul, 1966.

Portmann, A. *A Zoologist Looks at Humankind*. Translated by

Judith Schaefer. New York: Columbia University Press, 1990.

Prinsloo, E. D. "Logic and culture." *South African Journal for Philosophy* 8 (1989): 94–99.

Quine, W. V. O. *Philosophy of Logic*. Englewood Cliffs, NJ: Prentice Hall, 1970.

Rawidowicz, S. *Ludwig Feuerbachs Philosophie; Ursprung und Schicksal*. 2nd ed. Berlin: De Gruyter, 1964.

Rawls, J. *A Theory of Justice*. Revised Edition, Cambridge: Harvard University Press, 1999.

———. *Collected Papers*. S. Freeman, editor. Cambridge Massachusetts: Harvard University Press, 2001.

———. *Political Liberalism*. Revised edition. Cambridge: Harvard University Press, 1996.

Reid, C. *Hilbert*. With an appreciation of Hilbert's mathematical work by Hermann Weyl. New York: George Allen & Unwin, 1970.

Rensch, B. *Biophilosophy*. New York: Columbia University Press, 1971.

———. *Gedächtnis, Begriffsbildung und Planhandlungen bei Tieren*. Hamburg: Parey, 1973.

Risse, W. "Die Geschichte der Dialektik im Überblick bis Kant." In *Historisches Wörterbuch der Philosophie*, edited by J. Ritter, K. Gründer and G. Gabriel, II, 163–67. Basel-Stuttgart: Schwabe & Co, 1972.

Rookmaaker, Hans. *The Complete Works of Hans Rookmaaker*. Edited by M. Hengelaar-Rookmaaker. 6 vols. Carlisle, UK: Piquant, 2003.

Rorty, R. *Contingency, Irony and Solidarity*. New York: Cambridge University Press, 1989.

Ross, James F. "Analogy as a Rule of Meaning in Religious Language." *International Philosophical Quarterly* I (September 1971): 468–504.

Russell, B. *The Principles of Mathematics*. Cambridge: Cambridge University Press, 1903.

Ryan, A. *The Philosophy of the Social Sciences*. London: Macmillan, 1970.

Scheler, Max. *Die Stellung des Menschen im Kosmos* [1928]. 6th ed. Bern-Munich: Francke, 1962.

Schilpp, P. A., ed. *Albert Einstein, Philosopher-Scientist*. New York: Tudor, 1951.

Schnatz, H., ed. *Päpstliche Verlautbarungen zu Staat und Gesellschaft, Original Dokumente mit deutscher Uebersetzung*. Darmstadt: Wissenschaftliche Buchgesellschaft, 1973.

Schopenhauer, A. *On the Fourfold Root of the Principle of Sufficient Reason*. Translated by E. F. J. Payne. La Salle, IL: Open Court, 1974.

Schrödinger, E. *What is Life? The Physical Aspect of the Cell*. New York: Macmillan, 1955.

Schulte, J. "Nachwort." In G. Frege, *Die Grundlagen der Arithmetik: Ein logisch mathematische Untersuchung über den Begriff Zahl*. Stuttgart: Reclam, 1987.

Schuurman, E. *Faith and Hope in Technology*. Toronto: Clements Publishing, 2003.

———. *Technology and the Future – A Philosophical Challenge*. 2nd ed. Grand Rapids, MI: Paideia Press, 2009.

———. *The Technological World Picture and an Ethics of Responsibility*. Sioux Center, IA: Dordt Press, 2005.

Schuurman, E. *Transformation of the Technological Society*. Sioux Center, IA: Dordt Press, 2021.

Seerveld, C. *Normative Aesthetics*. Edited by John Kok. Sioux Center, IA: Dordt College Press, 2014.

Shapin, S. *The Scientific Revolution*. Chicago: University of Chicago Press, 1996.

Shapiro, S. *Philosophy of Mathematics, Structure and Ontology*.

Oxford University Press, 1997.

———, ed. *The Oxford Handbook of Philosophy of Mathematics and Logic.* Oxford: Oxford University Press, 2005.

Shields, C. *Aristotle.* New York: Routledge, 2007.

Sinnige, T. G. 1968. *Matter and Infinity in the Presocratic Schools and Plato.* Assen: Van Gorcum, 1968.

Sinnott, E. W. *The Problem of Organic Form.* London: New Haven, 1963.

———. *Matter, Mind and Man, The Biology of Human Nature.* New York: Atheneum, 1972.

Skillen, J. W. *Development of Calvinistic Political Theory in the Netherlands, With Special Reference to the Thought of Herman Dooyeweerd.* Unpublished Ph.D. Dissertation, Duke University, 1974.

Slaney, K. L. and M. D. Maraun. "Analogy and Metaphor Running Amok: An Examination of the Use of Explanatory Devices in Neuroscience." *Journal of Theoretical and Philosophical Psychology* 25 (2005): 153–72.

Slaughter, A. M. *A New World Order.* New Jersey: Princeton University Press, 2004.

Smend, R. *Der Staat als Integration.* Berlin und Leipzig: W. de Gruyter & Co., 1930.

Smit, M. C. *Writings on God and History.* [1987] Sioux Center, IA: Dordt College Press, 2021.

Smith, J. K. A., and J. H. Olthuis, eds. *Radical Orthodoxy and the Reformed Tradition.* Grand Rapids, MI: Baker Academic, 2005.

Sokal, S. and J. Bricmont. *Fashionable Nonsense: Postmodern Intellectuals' Abuse of Science* New York: Picador, 1998.

Sokal, S. and J. Bricmont. *Eleganter Unsinn: Wie die Denker der Postmoderne die Wissenschaften missbrauchen.* Munich: C. H. Beck, 1999.

Sorokin, P. *Crisis of our Age*. New York: E. P. Dutton & Co., 1946.

Sorokin, P. A. *Society, Culture and Personality*. New York: Cooper Square Publishers.

Spengler, O. *Der Untergang des Abendlandes. Umrisse einer Morphologie der Weltgeschichte*. 2 Volumes. Munich: Beck, 1923.

Spykman, G. J. *Reformational Theology: A New Paradigm for Doing Dogmatics*. Grand Rapids, MI: Eerdmans, 1992.

Stafleu, M. D. *Time and Again, A Systematic Analysis of the Foundations of Physics*. Toronto: Wedge, 1980.

———. *Theories at Work: On the Structure and Functioning of Theories in Science, in Particular during the Copernican Revolution*. Lanham: University Press of America, 1987.

———. *De Verborgen Structuur*. Amsterdam: Buijten & Schipperheijn, 1989.

———. *Time and Again: A Systematic Analysis of the Foundations of Physics: Philosophy of Dynamic Development*. 2019. http://www.mdstafleu.nl/421197815.

Steffens, H. J. *James Prescott Joule and the Concept of Energy*. Folkstone, UK: Dawson and New York: Science History Publications, 1979.

Stegmüller, W. *Metaphysik, Skepsis, Wissenschaft*. Berlin: Springer, 1969.

———. *Main Currents in Contemporary German, British and American Philosophy*. Dordrecht: D. Reidel Publishing Company, 1969.

Stokes, M. C. *One and Many in pre-Socratic Philosophy*. Washington DC: Center for Hellenic Studies, 1971.

Strauss, D. F. M. *Philosophy: Discipline of the Disciplines*. Grand Rapids: Paideia Press, 2010.

———. "The antinomies entailed in Dooyeweerd's epistemological view of a Gegenstand." *Journal for Christian*

Scholarship 55 (2019): 169–85.

———. "Scholasticism and Reformed Scholasticism at Odds with Genuine Reformational-Christian Thinking." *Ned. Geref. Teologiese Tydskrif* 5 (March 1969): 97–114.

———. "Scholasticism and Reformed Scholasticism at Odds with Genuine Reformational-Christian Thinking," accessed June 23, 2022, https://vcho.co.za/wp-content/uploads/2018/05/Scholasticism-and-Reformed.pdf.

———. "The Ontological Status of the principle of the excluded middle." *Philosophia Mathematica II* 6 (1991): 73–90.

———. "Kant and Modern Physics. The Synthetic a priori and the Distinction Between Modal Function and Entity." *South African Journal of Philosophy* 19 (2000): 26–40.

———. "The Scope and Limitations of Von Bertalanffy's Systems Theory." *South African Journal of Philosophy* 21 (2002): 163–179.

———. "Popper and the Achilles heel of Positivism." *Koers* 68 (2003): 255–78.

———. "The Concept of Number: Multiplicity and Succession between Cardinality and Ordinality." *South African Journal for Philosophy* 25 (2006): 27–47.

———. "The Bestknown but Least Understood Part of Dooyeweerd's Philosophy." *Journal for Christian Scholarship* 42 (2006): 61–80.

———. "Die Grenzen der Logik übersteigen: Zum Unterschied zwischen Widerspruch und Antinomie." *Die Suid-Afrikaanse Tydskrif vir Natuurwetenskap en Tegnologie* 26 (2007): 37–61.

———. *Philosophy: Discipline of the Disciplines.* Grand Rapids, MI: Paideia Press, 2009.

———. "The Significance of a Non-Reductionist Ontology for the Discipline of Mathematics: A Historical and Systematic

Analysis." *Axiomathes* 20 (2009): 19–52. doi: 10.1007/s10516-009-9080-5.

———. "Bernays, Dooyeweerd and Gödel – the Remarkable Convergence in their Reflections on the Foundations of Mathematics." *South African Journal of Philosophy* 30 (2011): 70–94.

———. "Normativity I – The Dialectical Legacy." *South African Journal of Philosophy* 30 (2011): 207–18.

———. "Is Infinity Purely Arithmetical in Nature?" *PONTE, International Journal of Sciences and Research* 74, no. 5/1 (2018): 1–19.

———. "The Philosophy of the Cosmonomic Idea and the Philosophical Foundations of Mathematics." *Philosophia Reformata* (2020): 1–19.

Tallis, R. *Hippocratic Oaths: Medicine and Its Discontents*. London: Atlantic Books, 2004.

Ter Horst, G. *De Ontbinding van de substantie, Een deconstructie van de beginselen van vorm en materie in de ontologie en de kenleer van Thomas Aquinas*. Delft: Uitgeverij Eburon, 2008.

Thompson, E. *Mind in Life. Biology, Phenomenology, and the Sciences of Mind*. Cambridge, MA: The Belknap Press of Harvard University Press, 2007.

Tobias, P. V., editor. *Hominid Evolution*. New York: Liss, 1985.

Tönnies, F. *Community and Society*. Translated and edited by Charles P. Loomis. East Lansing: Michigan State University Press, 1957. Translation of Tönnies, *Gemeinschaft und Gesellschaft*. 1887.

———. *Einführung in die Soziologie* (1931). Third reprint. Stuttgart: Enke, 1965.

Troeltsch, E. *Aufsätze zur Geistesgeschichte und Regiossoziologie*. Edited by Hans Baron. Tübingen: J. C. B. Mohr [Paul Siebeck], 1925.

Troost, A. *Vakfilosofie van de geloofswetenschap, Prolegomena van de theologie*. Budel: Damon, 2004.

———. *What is Reformational Philosophy? An Introduction to the Cosmonomic Philosophy of Herman Dooyeweerd*. Translated by Anthony Runia. Jordan Station, ON: Paideia Press, 2012.

Tsagorias, N. "The Will of the Community as a Normative Source of International Law." In *Governance and International Legal Theory*. Edited by Ige F. Dekker and Wouter G. Werner. Leiden: Brill, 2004.

Turner, B. S. *The Blackwell Companion to Social Theory*. Malden, MA: Blackwell Publishers, 2000.

Turner, S. P. *Explaining the Normative*. Malden, MA: Polity, 2010.

Unger, R. *Knowledge and Politics*. New York: Free Press, 1975.

———. *Law in Modern Society*. New York: Free Press, 1976.

University of Cambridge. "Department A - Z." Accessed October 27, 2021. https://www.cam.ac.uk/colleges-and-departments/department-a-z.

Van Belle, H. *On Being a Christian Academic Psychologist*. 1997. https://www.allofliferedeemed.co.uk/1014.doc.

Van den Berg, Dirk. "Coping with Art Historical Diversity in Methodological Terms." *Acta Academica* 22 (1989): 35–52.

Van den Beukel, A. "Darwinisme: wetenschap en/of ideologie?" In *Schitterend ongeluk of sporen van ontwerp?* Edited by C. Dekker, R. Meester and R. van Woudenberg. Kampen: Ten Have, 2005.

Van Deursen, A. Th. *De Eeuw in ons hart*. Franeker: Van Wijnen, 1991.

Van Deursen, A. Th. *De Geest is meer dan het lichaam*. Amsterdam: Bert Bakker, 2010.

Van Dyke, H. "Professing God in History," Inaugural Address. Ancaster, ON: Redeemer University College, 2002.

Van Kley, Dale K. "Dooyeweerd as Historian." In *A Christian View *of History?* edited by George Marsden and Frank Roberts. 139–79. Grand Rapids, MI: Eerdmans, 1977.

Van Woudenberg, R. *Het Mysterie van de Identiteit, Een Analytisch-Wijsgerige Studie*. Nijmegen: SUN, 2005.

———. "Theories of Thing-Structures." In *Philosophical Foundations I*. Reader, International Masters in Christian Studies of Science and Society Program (3). Amsterdam: VU University Amsterdam Press, 2006.

Verburg, M. E. *Herman Dooyeweerd: The Life and Work of a Christian Philosopher*. Grand Rapids: Paideia Press, 2015.

Verkerk, M. J. "A philosophy-based 'toolbox' for designing technology: The conceptual power of Dooyeweerdian philosophy." *Koers – Bulletin for Christian Scholarship* 79, no. 3 (2014): 1-7, DOI: 10.4102/koers.v79i3.2164.

Verkerk, M. J., J. Hoogland, J. van der Stoep, and M. J. de Vries. *Philosophy of Technology. An Introduction for Technology and Business Students*. New York: Routledge, 2016.

Verkerk, M. J., F. C. Holtkamp, E. J. M. Wouters, and J. van Hoof. "Professional Practices and User Practices: An Explorative Study in Health Care." *Philosophia Reformata* 82 (2017): 167–91.

Verkerk, M. J., P. F. Ribeiro, A. Basden, and J. Hoogland. "An Explorative Philosophical Study of Envisaging the Electrical Energy Infrastructure of the Future." *Philosophia Reformata* 83 (2018): 90–110. https://doi.org/10.1163/23528230-08301006.

Vinogradoff, P., editor. *Essays in Legal History*. New York: Wm. W. Gaunt & Sons, 1993.

Vogel, H. *Zum Philosophischen Wirken Max Plancks. Seine Kritik am Positivismus*. Berlin: Akademie-Verlag, 1961.

Vollenhoven, D. Th. *Geschiedenis der Wijsbegeerte*. Volume I: *Inleiding en Geschiedenis der Grieksche Wijsbegeerte vóór*

Platoon en Aristoteles. Franeker: T. Wever, 1950.

Von Bertalanffy, L. *General System Theory*. Penguin University Books, 1973.

Von Hippel, E. *Geschichte der Staatsphilosophie, Vol. I*. Meisenheim am Glan: Verlag Anton Hain, 1955.

Von Weizsäcker, C. F. *Der Mensch in seiner Geschichte*. München: Deutscher Taschenbuch Verlag, 1993.

———. *Große Physiker, Von Aristoteles bis Werner Heisenberg*. Munich: Deutscher Taschenbuch Verlag, 2002.

Vorster, N. "A Critical Assessment of John Milbank's Christology." *Acta Theologica* 32 (2012): 277–98.

Vries, M. J. and H. J. Jochemsen. *The Normative Nature of Social Practices and Ethics in Professional Environments*. Hershey, PA: IGI Global, 2019.

Wallner, F. G. *Konstruktion und Verfremdung*. Edited by F. G. Wallner and B. Agnese. Vienna: Universitäts-Verlagsbuchhandlung, 1999.

Weideman, A. *Academic Literacy: Prepare to Learn*. Pretoria: Van Schaik, 2007.

———. *Beyond Expression: A Systematic Study of the Foundations of Linguistics*. Grand Rapids, MI: Paideia Press, 2009.

———. *A Framework for the Study of Linguistics*. Pretoria/Grand Rapids, MI: Van Schaik/Paideia Press, 2011.

———. "Definition and Design: Aligning Language Interventions in Education." *Stellenbosch Papers in Linguistics Plus* 56, (2019): 33-48, DOI: 10.5842/56-0-782.

———, J. Read and T. Du Plessis, eds. *Assessing Academic Literacy in a Multilingual Society: Transition and Transformation*. New Perspectives on Language and Education 84. Bristol: Multilingual Matters, 2021, https://doi.org/10.21832/WEIDEM6201.

Weinert, F. "Fundamental Physical Constants, Null Experiments and the Duhem-Quine Thesis." *Philosophia Naturalis* 35 (1998): 225–51.

Weyl, H. *Philosophie der Mathematik und Naturwissenschaft*. 3rd ed. Vienna: R. Oldenburg, 1966.

Williamson, O. E. *Markets and Hierarchies: Analysis and Antitrust Implications*. New York: The Free Press, 1975.

Winch, P. *The Idea of a Social Science and Its Relation to Philosophy*. London: Routledge and Kegan Paul, 1958.

Wittgenstein, L. *Tractatus Logico-Philosophicus*. 3rd ed. London: Routledge & Kegan Paul, [1921] 1966.

———. *Philosophical Investigations*. 3rd ed. Oxford: Basil Blackwell, 1968.

Woldring, H. E. S. "The Constitutional State in the Political Philosophy of Johannes Althusius." *European Journal of Law and Economics* 5 (1998): 123–32.

Wolters, A. *Creation Regained*. Grand Rapids, MI: Eerdmans, 1984.

Zeller, E. *Outlines of the History of Greek Philosophy*. London: Longmans, Green & Co., 1909.

Zippelius, R. *Geschicte der Staatsideen*. Vierte, verbesserte Auflage. München: Beck, 1980.

Zuidema, S. U. *De Mensch als Historie*. Inaugural Oration, Free University of Amsterdam. Franeker: T. Wever, 1948.

Zuidervaart, L. Systematic Philosophy Paper, Institute for Christian Studies, March 19, 1973.

———. *Explorations into a Philosophical Aesthetics*. Stenciled Paper. Toronto: Institute for Christian Studies.

———. *Artistic Truth. Aesthetics, Discourse, and Imaginative Disclosure*. Cambridge: Cambridge University Press, 2004.

Index of Subjects

act-structure, 555, 559–61, 568, 571, 572
aesthetics, 335–43
analogical concepts, 8f, 286, 423, 426, 460–62
animals, 543–45, 560
animism, 495
anthropology (philosophical), 211–14, 539–61
anticipation analogies, 7f, 9, 92, 286, 302, 420, 423, 426, 434, 436, 439, 440
antinomic, 3, 145, 152, 238, 248, 429
antinomy, xii, 91, 235–42, 248f, 253, 420
apologetics, 30
asceticism, 109
aspects (modal), 5, 6, 11, 13, 44, 89f, 92f, 151, 262f, 265, 308–313, 382, 424, 502, 513–21, 523–37, 552
   – core of, 6, 7
   – kernel of, 388, 517
   – laws for, 13
   – normative, 416
   – nucleus of, 6, 7, 11

aspects (modal law-spheres), 4–6, 311–13; *et passim*
– numerical (quantitative), 5, 90, 136, 191–97, 221, 424, 437
– spatial, 5, 8, 158, 180, 182, 191–97
– kinematic, 21, 179, 215–19, 224
– physical, 5, 15, 22, 168, 179–90, 217–19, 426
– biotic (organic), 22, 36, 56, 168, 551, 554, 566, 569
– psychic (sensitive), 5, 211, 513, 532, 551
– analytical (logical), 12f, 437, 439f, 525, 543
– historical (formative), 23, 283–91, 478
– lingual (symbolical), 23, 339, 342, 474, 475, 478
– social, 6, 23f, 314, 467, 513, 544

– economic, 6, 12, 14
– aesthetic, 6, 7, 204–05, 308, 335–43
– jural (juridical), 6, 7, 24, 388
– moral (ethical), 514, 525
– certitudinal (pistical), 6, 101–04, 544

Augustinian, 80, 174, 288

Big Bang, 173
biology, 539–48
body/soul, 114
body (human), 539, 542, 550–61, 568, 571f
brain (human), 563–75
business (enterprise), 14, 118, 199–201, 321, 400, 471, 491, 493, 500; *see also* firms

capitalism, 353
causality
– jural, 429, 434
– logical, 430
– physical, 216, 427, 429, 431
change and continuity, 286, 299, 466
chemistry, 31, 92, 180, 225, 231, 263, 265
– biochemistry, 92, 180, 225, 265
– organic, 92, 225

church, 121–29, 468
civil law, 25, 391, 394, 395, 397–400
clans, 445f; *see also* sibs
climate change, 285, 356, 515, 526
communities
– natural, 467
– organized, 467
– institutional, 468
community, ideology of, 456, 469, 497
collectivism, 497, 498
concept-transcending, 20, 159, 160, 161, 221, 222, 223, 270
continuity, xii, 91, 117, *et passim*
conservatism, 497
constancy and change, 18, 90, 91, 167, 169, 219, 223, 299, 363n, 415, 418
constitutional law, 405, 483–94
construction (theoretical), 91, 134f, 246, 385, 413, 441, 561

INDEX OF SUBJECTS

coordinational relationships, 397f, 403, 466, 468
cosmic time, 506, 508
creation-fall-redemption ground-motive, 75, 95, 118, 288, 381, 458, 485
criticism, kinds of, 243–57

Darwinism, 273–82; *see also* evolution(ism)
democratism, 497
differentiation, 301, 303, 358, 443–48, 449–52, 468, 475, 496, 507
disclosure, 303f, 478–82; *see also* opening process
discourse, fields of, 474
doctor-patient relationship, 579, 589

economism, 353
encyclopedia, concept of, 82f, 335, 381, 393
enkapsis, enkaptic, 151, 229–34, 309, 315, 320, 551, 573
Enlightenment, 74, 139, 454, 484
entities, 4, 44, 101, 125, 179–90, 221–34, 283, 293, 294, 420, 552; *see also* individuality structures

epiphenomenalism, 567, 569
epistemology, 28, 29, 31, 135
ethical, 6, 24, 101, 409–16, 479, 514, 516, 519, 525
ethics, 6, 31, 100, 211, 318f, 403, 409–16, 454
evolutionism, 165–70, 273–82, 348, 540
    see also Darwinism

facts and values, 413f, 416
faith, 85–87, 93f, 100, 148, 251, 290, 304, 391, 480, 514
family
   – extended, 443, 446, 466
   – nuclear, 358, 367, 452, 463, 465, 467, 491
firms, 201, 358, 361, 363–72, 423, 433, 444, 452, 475; *see also* business enterprise
form-matter ground-motive, 49–54, 106, 254, 485
fossil record, 275–80
founding function, 366, 467
freedom (civic), 483–88
free love, 455
French Revolution, 449, 453, 456, 457, 484, 496

frugality, 9, 14, 86, 199, 338, 390, 410, 416, 434

Gegenstand relation, xi note, 382, 527, 529
genius (according to Romanticism), 454, 456
global warming, 317
Gross Domestic Product, 530
ground-motive, xii, 253, 261, 286f, 340, 381, 456, 528, 531, 532, 550, 581
guiding function, 444, 491
guilds, 374–76, 452

health care, 325–34, 577–89
heart, 104, 116, 212, 213, 383, 519, 545–48, 550–61
   – supra-temporal, 558–61
hermeneutics, 141, 263, 291
historicism, 91, 141, 246f, 289, 303, 383
   see also relativism
historical laws, see principles: historical
history, science of, 283–91
   – laws for, 209–305
   – patterns in, 285
humanism, 2, 61–65, 67–72, 137, 413n, 453

   – "biblical," 62
   – secular, 74f, 146, 484
ideologies, 495–500
idolatry, idols, 545, 546, 547, 560f
individuality structures, 3, 16, 44n, 229, 283, 394, 500, 506, 507; see also entities
individualism, 18, 139, 368, 402, 461, 470, 496, 497
institutions, communal and natural, 364
intelligent design, 161
international law, 401–08
intuition, intuitive, 6, 45, 103, 142, 160, 172, 180, 184, 193, 195f, 206, 221f, 223, 239, 363, 365, 388, 424, 500, 521, 557, 581, 583, 587
irrationalism, 20, 136, 139, 142–45, 148, 246, 383, 453, 455–57
irrational numbers, 158, 181f, 194
"isms" xii, xiii, 16–21, 127–29, 383, 504

kingdom of God, 123–27
knowledge
   – everyday, 570; see also

naive experience
– scientific, 570

language, 345–49, 473–76
law science of, 377–96
   – basic concepts in, 380, 387–94, 425
   – bias in, 319
   – encyclopedia of, 1, 7, 381–85
laws of nature, 10, 137, 201, 203, 245, 267, 412, 416, 422, 430
legal pluralism, 393–96, 491
liberalism, 497, 498
logical norms, 410, 414f
logical principles, 436–40

manors, 374, 376
market, 367–70
marriage, 398, 466–68
Marxism, 251, 253
mathematical, 5, 32f, 44n, 71, 194f
mathematics, 6, 18, 27, 68, 86, 158, 182, 192, 194f, 239–41, 264, 266, 418, 421, 437, 439, 484
   – intuitionist school of, 164, 192, 195, 241

matter, 17, 33f, 37f, 49, 55–65, 106–110, 136, 175, 179, 182, 186, 189, 222, 496, 541, 561, 567, 568
medicine, medical arts, 577–89
   –doctor-patient relationship, 578–80, 585
   –scientism in, 577f, 586
   – social contract in, 578
meta-narratives, 145
modal
   – laws, 13, 14, 199–204, 433
   – norms, 10, 238, 301, 433f, 436, 440, 441
   – universality, 14, 199–206, 301, 418–20, 434
modalities, 505; *see also* aspects
monasticism, 109

naive experience, 205, 339, 382, 504
nationalism, 497
natural law, 247, 378
natural science, 133, 142, 203, 205, 253n, 254, 259–71,

354

natural science ideal, 2, 133, 167, 254f, 351, 410f

nature-freedom ground-motive, 61–72, 287, 351, 411, 484, 485, 531, 534

nature-grace ground-motive, 55–59, 83, 110, 485

nature, laws of, *see* laws of nature

neo-Calvinism, 74, 288, 291

neo-positivism, 144, 200, 202, 414

neo-vitalism, 161, 250

neuroscience, 563, 565

nominalism, 133–36, 143–46, 246, 254

non-scientific, 504

normativity, 417–29

object function, 200, 345, 554

omnicompetence (of the state), 485, 487, 492, 497

ontology, 28, 31, 42, 43

opening process, xii, 92, 268, 286, 290, 302, 391f, 436, 480, 481, 506f, 509, 554, 573, 583

    see also disclosure

paradigms, 102, 149, 209, 253, 286, 354, 526, 531

part-whole relation, 230, 233f, 406, 492, 553

    see also whole-parts relation

personality ideal, 133, 351, 410f, 426, 453f

philosophy, 28, 30; *et passim*

– Christian, 27–45, 73, 98f, 100, 210f, 214

– early Greek, 31, 153–64

– pagan, 31, 57, 110, 111

– Vollenhovian, 501–511

physicalism, 225, 273

physics, 215–19

pistical aspect, 101f, 126, 210; *see also* faith

popular sovereignty, 357–61

positivism, positivistic, 175f, 202, 207f, 414

– legal positivism, 377

positivization, 288, 422, 432, 433, 440, 441, 478

post-modernity, 138, 144f, 245f

pre-theoretical, 103, 214, 342, 500, 504, 515, 527

see also naive
principles, 12, 431–42, 583, 586
— historical, 299–305
—logical, 10, 235–42, 253
— normative, 409–16, 474, 588f
prior commitments, 275, 290
see also ground-motives; paradigms
prism, image of, 558
private law, 373, 394–400
property, 359, 367, 371, 376, 394, 400, 429, 464
psychology, 207–14, 270
— faculty school of, 556
public good, 490–92

qualifying function, 444, 491

Radical Orthodoxy, 79–95
rationalism, 136, 143, 144
realism (philosophical), 131–33, 141–43
reduction (theoretical), 17, 46, 237, 368, 498, 503f
Reformed Scholasticism, 84, 105–119
relativism, 246f, 383, 418, 508

see also historicism
religion, 16, 210, 545, 557
religious basic motive, 484
see also ground-motive
Renaissance, 2, 61–63, 133, 254, 411, 484
repristination, 286
research, 523–37
Restoration period, 453
retributive justice, 489, 490n
retrocipations, 190, 269, 286, 390, 420, 423, 426, 434, 436, 439
Roman law, 373–76, 447
Romanticism, 139, 453–58

science-ideal, 3, 133, 279, 410f, 426
scientific method, 268
scientism, 352
Sein / Sollen, 427, 428, 429
sex, 454f
sibs, 445f, 496; *see also* clans
shareholders, 370
sociology, 211, 262, 421n, 459–62, 467
speech organs, 347
sphere sovereignty, 6, 85, 86, 151, 165–70, 303, 402, 404, 406, 444, 450f, 459, 493,

500, 502
socialism, 497, 498
soul, 556f
— and body, 249
state (political community), 21–24, 357–62, 364, 433, 452, 465, 468, 490–94
structure and direction, 147–52, 502f
subject functions, 10, 167, 200, 345, 346
subject-object relations, 284, 392, 442, 505
subject-subject relations, 284, 444
    see also doctor-patient relationship
supra-temporal, 506, 558–61
synthesis, 2, 33–48, 107, 112, 132, 452, 453

technicism, 351–56, 477, 478
technology, 307–23
— disclosure of, 479–82
— meaning of, 477–82
— and nature, 481
theology, science of, 27, 30, 82, 87, 97–104
theories, 28, 30
thermodynamics, laws of, 216, 217, 218, 226, 250

time, 14f, 171-77, 215–19
    see also cosmic time
time and eternity, 171f, 176
tradition, 300
tribes, 447, 495
type laws, 13f, 44, 200, 201, 202, 203, 434
typical norms, 473

undifferentiated, 301, 359, 373, 374–76, 495
vitalism, 244

whole-parts relation, xii, 90, 91, 163f, 182f, 193, 359, 361f, 406, 437, 439, 451, 493
    see also part-whole relation
wholes, 313f, 320; *see also* entities
world citizenship, 455
World-State, 404, 405
worldviews, 73–78, 209, 214, 260, 268

Glossary

[The following glossary of Dooyeweerd's technical terms and neologisms is reproduced and edited by Daniël F. M. Strauss, with the permission of its author, Albert M. Wolters, from C. T. McIntire, ed., *The Legacy of Herman Dooyeweerd: Reflections on Critical Philosophy in the Christian Tradition* (Lanham MD, 1985), pp. 167-171.]

THIS GLOSSARY OF HERMAN DOOYEWEERD'S terms is an adapted version of the one published in L. Kalsbeek, *Contours of a Christian Philosophy* (Toronto: Wedge, 1975). It does not provide exhaustive technical definitions but gives hints and pointers for a better understanding. Entries marked with an asterisk are those terms which are used by Dooyeweerd in a way which is unusual in English-speaking philosophical contexts and are, therefore, a potential source of misunderstanding. Words or phrases in small caps and beginning with a capital letter refer to other entries in this glossary.

* **Analogy** (see LAW-SPHERE)

    Collective name for a RETROCIPATION or an ANTICIPATION.

* **Anticipation**

    An ANALOGY within one MODALITY referring to a later modality. An example is "efficiency," a meaning-moment which is found within the historical modality, but which points forward to the later economic modality. Contrast with RETROCIPATION.

* **Antinomy**

    Literally "conflict of laws" (from Greek *anti*, "against," and *nomos*, "law"). A logical contradiction arising out of a failure to distinguish the different kinds of law valid in different MODALITIES. Since ontic laws do not conflict (Principium Exclusae Antinomiae), an antinomy is always a logical sign of ontological reductionism.

* Antithesis

Used by Dooyeweerd (following Abraham Kuyper) in a specifically religious sense to refer to the fundamental spiritual opposition between the kingdom of God and the kingdom of darkness. See Galatians 5:17. Since this is an opposition between regimes, not realms, it runs through every department of human life and culture, including philosophy and the academic enterprise as a whole, and through the heart of every believer as he or she struggles to live a life of undivided allegiance to God.

Aspect

A synonym for MODALITY.

Cosmonomic idea

Dooyeweerd's own English rendering of the Dutch term *wetsidee*. Occasionally equivalents are "transcendental ground idea" or "transcendental basic idea". The intention of this new term is to bring to expression that there exists an unbreakable coherence between God's *law* (nomos) and created reality (*cosmos*) factually subjected to God's law.

Dialectic

In Dooyeweerd's usage: an unresolvable tension, within a system or line of thought, between two logically irreconcilable polar positions. Such a dialectical tension is characteristic of each of the three non-Christian GROUND-MOTIVES which Dooyeweerd sees as having dominated Western thought.

*Enkapsis (enkaptic)

A neologism borrowed by Dooyeweerd from the Swiss biol-

GLOSSARY

ogist Heidenhain, and derived from the Greek *enkaptein*, "to swallow up." The term refers to the structural interlacements which can exist between things, plants, animals, and societal structures which have their own internal structural principle and independent qualifying function. As such, enkapsis is to be clearly distinguished from the part-whole relation, in which there is a common internal structure and qualifying function.

Factual Side

General designation of whatever is *subjected* to the LAW-SIDE of creation (see SUBJECT-SIDE).

Founding function

The earliest of the two modalities which characterize certain types of structural wholes. The other is called the GUIDING FUNCTION. For example, the founding function of the family is the biotic modality.

* Gegenstand

A German word for "object," used by Dooyeweerd as a technical term for a modality when abstracted from the coherence of time and opposed to the analytical function in the theoretical attitude of thought, thereby establishing the Gegenstand relation. Gegenstand is therefore the technically precise word for the object of SCIENCE, while "object" itself is reserved for the objects of NAIVE EXPERIENCE.

Ground-motive

The Dutch term *grondmotief*, used by Dooyeweerd in the sense of fundamental motivation, driving force. He distinguished four basic ground-motives in the history of Western civilization: (1) form and matter, which dominated pagan Greek philosophy; (2) nature and grace, which underlay medieval Christian synthesis thought (3) nature and freedom, which has shaped the philosophies of modern times; and (4) creation, fall, and redemption, which lies at the root of a radical and integrally scriptural philosophy.

Guiding function

The highest subject function of a structural whole (e.g. stone, animal, business enterprise, or state). Except in the case of humans, this function is also said to QUALIFY the structural whole. It is called the guiding function because it "guides" or "leads" its earlier functions. For example, the guiding function of a plant is the biotic. The physical function of a plant (as studied, e.g. by biochemistry) is different from physical functioning elsewhere because of its being "guided" by the biotic. Also called "leading function".

* **Heart**

The concentration point of human existence; the supratemporal focus of all human temporal functions; the religious root unity of humans. Dooyeweerd says that it was his rediscovery of the biblical idea of the heart as the central religious depth dimension of human multifaceted life which enabled him to wrestle free from neo-Kantianism and phenomenology. The Scriptures speak of this focal point also as "soul," "spirit," and "inner man." Philiosophical equivalents are Ego, I, I-ness, and Selfhood. It is the heart in this sense which survives death, and it is by the religious redirection of the heart in regeneration that all human temporal functions are renewed.

* **Immanence Philosophy**

A name for all non-Christian philosophy, which tries to find the ground and integration of reality *within* the created order. Unlike Christianity, which acknowledges a transcendent Creator above all things, immanence philosophy of necessity absolutizes some feature or aspect of creation itself.

* **Individuality-structure**

This term represents arguably one of the most difficult concepts in Dooyeweerd's philosophy. Coined in both Dutch

GLOSSARY

and English by Dooyeweerd himself it has led sometimes to serious misunderstandings amongst scholars. Over the years there have been various attempts to come up with an alternate term, some of which are described below, but in the absence of a consensus it was decided to leave the term the way it is.

It is the general name or the characteristic law (order) of concrete things, as given by virtue of creation. Individuality-structures belong to the law-side of reality. Dooyeweerd uses the term individuality-structure to indicate the applicability of a structural order *for* the existence of *individual* entities. Thus the *structural laws* for the state, for marriage, for works of art, for mosquitoes, for sodium chloride, and so forth are called individuality-structures. The idea of an individual whole is determined by an individuality-structure which precedes the theoretical analysis of its modal functions. The identity of an individual whole is a relative unity in a multiplicity of functions. (See MODALITY.) Van Riessen prefers to call this law for entities an *identity-structure*, since as such it guarantees the persistent **identity** of all **entities** (*Wijsbegeerte*, Kampen 1970, p.158). In his work (*Alive, An Enquiry into the Origin and Meaning of Life*, 1984, Ross House Books, Vallecito, California), M. Verbrugge introduces his own distinct systematic account concerning the nature of (what he calls) *functors*, a word first introduced by Hendrik Hart for the dimension of individuality-structures (cf. Hart: *Understanding Our World, Towards an Integral Ontology*, New York 1984, cf.pp.445-446). As a substitute for the notion of an individuality-structure, Verbrugge advances the term: *idionomy* (cf. *Alive*, pp.42, 81ff., 91ff.). Of course this term may also cause misunderstanding if it is taken to mean that each individual creature (subject) has its *own unique* law. What is intended is that every *type of law* (*nomos*) is meant to delimit and determine unique subjects. In other words, however *specified* the universality of the law may be, it can never, in its bearing upon unique individual creatures, itself become something *uniquely individual*. Another way of grasping the meaning of Dooyeweerd's notion of an *individuality-structure* is, in following an oral suggestion by Roy Clouser (Zeist, August 1986), to call it a *type-law* (from Greek: *typonomy*). This simply means that all entities of a certain *type* conform to this law. The following perspective given by M.D. Stafleu elucidates this terminology in a *systematic way* (*Time and Again, A Systematic Analysis of the Foundations of Physics*, Wedge Publishing Foundation, Toronto 1980, p.6, 11): *typical laws* (type-laws/typonomies, such as the Coulomb law – applicable only to charged entities and the Pauli principle – applicable only to fermions) are special laws which apply to a limited class of entities only, whereas *modal laws* hold universally for all possible entities. D.F.M. Strauss ('*Inleiding tot die Kosmologie*,' SACUM, Bloemfontein 1980) introduces the expression *entity structures*. The term **entity** comprises both the *individuality* and the *identity* of the thing concerned – therefore it accounts for the respective emphases found in Dooyeweerd's notion of *individuality-structures* and in Van Riessen's notion of *identity structures*. The following words of Dooyeweerd show that both the **individuality** and **identity** of an entity is determined by its 'individuality-structure': "In general we can establish that the factual temporal duration of a thing as an individual and identical whole is dependent on the preservation of its structure of individuality" (*A New Critique of Theoretical Thought*, Vol.III:79).

Irreducibility (irreducible)

Incapability of theoretical reduction. This is the negative way of referring to the unique distinctiveness of things and aspects which we find everywhere in creation and which theoretical thought must respect. Insofar as everything has its own peculiar created nature and character, it cannot be understood in terms of categories foreign to itself.

* **Law**

The notion of creational law is central to Dooyeweerd's philosophy. Everything in creation is subject to God's law for it, and accordingly law is the boundary between God and creation. Scriptural synonyms for law are "ordinance," "decree," "commandment," "word," and so on. Dooyeweerd stresses that law is not in opposition to but the condition for true freedom. See also NORM and LAW-SIDE.

Law-Side

The created cosmos, for Dooyeweerd, has two correlative "sides": a law-side and a factual side (initially called: SUBJECT-SIDE). The former is simply the coherence of God's laws or ordinances for creation; the latter is the totality of created reality which is subject to those laws. It is important to note that the law-side always holds universally.

Law-Sphere (see MODAL STRUCTURE and MODALITY)

The circle of laws qualified by a unique, irreducible and indefinable meaning-nucleus is known as a law-sphere. Within every law-sphere temporal reality has a modal function and in this function is subjected (French: *sujet*) to the laws of the modal spheres. Therefore every law-sphere has a law-side and a subject-side that are given only in unbreakable correlation with each other. (See DIAGRAM on p.151.)

* **Meaning**

Dooyeweerd uses the word "meaning" in an unusual sense. By it he means the referential, non-self-sufficient character of created reality in that it points beyond itself to God as Origin. Dooyeweerd stresses that reality *is* meaning in this sense and that, therefore, it does not *have* meaning. "Meaning" is the Christian alternative to the metaphysical substance of immanence philosphy. "Meaning" becomes almost a synonym for "reality." Note the many compounds formed from it: meaning-nucleus, meaning-side, meaning-moment, meaning-fullness.

* **Meaning-nucleus**

The indefinable core meaning of a MODALITY.

Modality (See MODAL STRUCTURE and LAW-SPHERE)

One of the fifteen fundamental ways of being distinguished by Dooyeweerd. As modes of being, they are sharply distinguished from the concrete things which function within them. Initially Dooyeweerd distinguished fourteen aspects only, but since 1950 he introduced the kinematical aspect of *uniform movement* between the spatial and the physical aspects. Modalities are also known as "modal functions," "modal aspects," or as "facets" of created reality. (See DIAGRAM on p.151.)

Modal Structure (see MODALITY and LAW-SPHERE)

The peculiar constellation, in any given modality, of its meaning-moments (anticipatory, retrocipatory, nuclear). Contrast INDIVIDUALITY-STRUCTURE.

* **Naive experience**

Human experience insofar as it is not "theoretical" in Dooyeweerd's precise sense. "Naive" does not mean unsophisticated. Sometimes called "ordinary" or "everyday" experience. Dooyeweerd takes pains to emphasize that theory is embedded in this everyday experience and must not violate it.

Norm (normative)

Postpsychical laws, that is, modal laws for the analytical through pistical law-spheres (see LAW-SPHERE and DIAGRAM on p.151). These laws are norms because they need to be positivized (see POSITIVIZE) and can be violated, in distinction from the "natural laws" of the pre-analytical spheres which are obeyed involuntarily (e.g., in a digestive process).

GLOSSARY

* **Nuclear-moment**

A synonym for MEANING-NUCLEUS and LAW-SPHERE, used to designate the indefinable core meaning of a MODALITY or aspect of created reality.

* **Object**

Something qualified by an object function and thus correlated to a subject function. A work of art, for instance, is qualified by its correlation to the human subjective function of aesthetic appreciation. Similarly, the elements of a sacrament are pistical objects.

Opening process

The process by which latent modal anticipations are "opened" or actualized. The modal meaning is then said to be "deepened." It is this process which makes possible the cultural development (differentiation) of society from a primitive ("closed," undifferentiated) stage. For example, by the opening or disclosure of the ethical anticipation in the juridical aspect, the modal meaning of the legal aspect is deepened and society can move from the principle of "an eye for an eye" to the consideration of extenuating circumstances in the administration of justice.

* **Philosophy**

In Dooyeweerd's precise systematic terminology, philosophy is the encyclopedic science, that is, its proper task is the theoretical investigation of the overall systematic integration of the various scientific disciplines and their fields of inquiry. Dooyeweerd also uses the term in a more inclusive sense, especially when he points out that all philosophy is rooted in a pretheoretical religious commitment and that some philosophical conception, in turn, lies at the root of all scientific scholarship.

Positivize

A word coined to translate the Dutch word *positiveren*, which means to make positive in the sense of being actually valid in a given time or place. For example, positive law is the legislation which is in force in a given country at a particular time; it is contrasted with the *legal principles* which lawmakers must positivize as legislation. In a general sense, it refers to the responsible implementation of all normative principles in human life as embodied, for example, in state legislation, economic policy, ethical guidelines, and so on.

Qualify

The GUIDING FUNCTION of a thing is said to qualify it in the sense of characterizing it. In this sense a plant is said to be qualified by the biotic and a state by the juridical [aspects].

* Radical

Dooyeweerd frequently uses this term with an implicit reference to the Greek meaning of *radix* = *root*. This usage must not be confused with the political connotation of the term *radical* in English. In other works Dooyeweerd sometimes paraphrases his use of the term radical with the phrase: *penetrating to the root of created reality*.

* Religion (religious)

For Dooyeweerd, religion is not an area or sphere of life but the all-encompassing and direction-giving root of it. It is service of God (or a substitute no-god) in every domain of human endeavor. As such, it is to be sharply distinguished from religious faith, which is but one of the many acts and attitudes of human existence. Religion is an affair of the HEART and so directs all human functions. Dooyeweerd says religion is "the innate impulse of the human selfhood to direct itself toward the *true* or toward a *pretended* absolute Origin of all temporal diversity of meaning" (*A New Critique of Theoretical Thought*,

Vol.I, 1953, p.57).

* Retrocipation

A feature in one MODALITY which refers to, is reminiscent of, an earlier one, yet retaining the modal qualification of the aspect in which it is found. The "extension" of a concept, for example, is a kind of logical space: it is a strictly logical affair, and yet it harks back to the spatial modality in its original sense. See ANTICIPATION.

* Science

Two things are noted about Dooyeweerd's use of the term "science". In the first place, as a translation of the Dutch word *wetenschap* (analogous to the German word Wissenschaft), it embraces all scholarly study – not only the natural sciences but also the social sciences and the humanities, including theology and philosophy. In the second place, science is always, strictly speaking, a matter of modal abstraction, that is, of analytically lifting an aspect out of the temporal coherence in which it is found and examining it in the Gegenstand relation. But in this investigation it does not focus its theoretical attention upon the modal structure of such an aspect itself; rather, it focuses on the coherence of the actual phenomena which function within that structure. Modal abstraction as such must be distinguished from NAIVE EXPERIENCE. In the first sense, therefore, "science" has a wider application in Dooyeweerd than is usual in English-speaking countries, but in the second sense it has a more restricted, technical meaning.

Sphere Sovereignty

A translation of Kuyper's phrase *souvereiniteit in eigen kring*, by which he meant that the various distinct spheres of human authority (such as family, church, school, and business enterprise) each have their own responsibility and decision-making power which may not be usurped by those in authority in another sphere, for example, the state. Dooyeweerd retains this usage but also extends it to mean the IRREDUCIBILITY of the modal aspects. This is the ontical principle on which the societal principle is based since each of the societal "spheres" mentioned is qualified by a different irreducible modality.

* Subject

Used in two senses by Dooyeweerd: (1) "subject" as distinguished from LAW, (2) "subject" as distinguished from OBJECT. The latter sense is roughly equivalent to common usage; the former is unusual and ambiguous. Since all things are "subject" to LAW, objects are also subjects in the first sense. Dooyeweerd's matured conception, however, does not show this ambiguity. By distinguishing between the *law-side* and the *factual side* of creation, both subject and object (sense (2)) are part of the factual side.

Subject-Side

The correlate of LAW-SIDE, preferably called the factual side. Another feature of the factual subject-side is that it is only here that individuality is found.

Substratum

The aggregate of modalities *preceding* a given aspect in the modal order. The arithmetic, spatial, kinematic, and physical, for example, together form the substratum for the biotic. They are also the necessary foundation upon which the biotic rests, and without which it cannot exist. See SUPERSTRATUM (and the DIAGRAM on p.151).

Superstratum

The aggregate of modalities *following* a given aspect in the modal order. For example, the pistical, ethical, juridical and aesthetic together constitute the superstratum of the economic. See SUBSTRATUM.

GLOSSARY

* **Synthesis**

The combination, in a single philosophical conception, of characteristic themes from both pagan philosophy and biblical religion. It is this feature of the Christian intellectual tradition, present since patristic times, with which Dooyeweerd wants to make a radical break. Epistemologically seen the term *synthesis* is used to designate the way in which a multiplicity of features is integrated within the unity of a concept. The re-union of the logical aspect of the theoretical act of thought with its non-logical 'Gegenstand' is called an inter-modal meaning-synthesis.

* **Time**

In Dooyeweerd, a general ontological principle of intermodal continuity, with far wider application than our common notion of time, which is equated by him with the physical manifestation of this general cosmic time. It is, therefore, not coordinate with space. All created things, except the human HEART, are in time. At the law-side time expresses itself as time-order and at the factual side (including subject-subject and subject-object relations) as time duration.

Transcendental

A technical term from the philosophy of Kant denoting the *a priori* structural conditions which make human experience (specifically human knowledge and theoretical thought) possible. As such it is to be sharply distinguished from the term "transcendent." Furthermore, the basic (transcendental) Idea of a philosophy pre-supposes the transcendent and central sphere of consciousness (the human HEART). This constitutes the *second* meaning in which Dooyeweerd uses the term transcendental: through its transcendental ground-Idea philosophy points beyond itself to its ultimate religious foundation transcending the realm of thought.

Affiliations

Alan Cameron
Independent Legal Scholar

Albert Weideman
Professor of Applied Language Studies & Research Fellow
Department of English
University of the Free State
South Africa

Dr. Andrew Basden
Professor Emeritus of Human
Factors and Philosophy in Information Systems,
ex. University of Salford, U.K.

Calvin Seerveld
Senior Member in Philosophical Aesthetics, emeritus
Institute for Christian Studies
Toronto, Ontario
Canada

David T Koyzis
Global Scholar
Politics and International Affairs
Global Scholars Canada

Prof. D.F.M. Strauss
First Director of the Dooyeweerd Centre

AFFILIATIONS

Former Dean of the Faculty of Humanities
University of the Free State
Currently Research Fellow at North-West University
Potchefstroom, South Africa

Egbert Schuurman
Philosopher and Politician:
Prof. Emeritus Technologial University, Delft, The Netherlands
Prof. Emeritus Technological University Eindhoven, The Netherlands
Prof. Emeritus Wageningen University, The Netherlands
Senior Senator of the Dutch Parliament

Frederick C.v.N. Fourie
Research Fellow
Department of Economics and Finance
University of the Free State, Bloemfontein, South Africa

Professor Gerrit Glas
Vrije Universiteit Amsterdam
and GGzE, Eindhoven.
In the latter institution Gerrit works as psychiatrist, director of residency training

James W. Skillen
President (retired), Center for Public Justice, Washington D.C. (1981–2009)
Independent Scholar (2009–   )
Birmingham, Alabama, USA

DISCOVERING DOOYEWEERD

Jeremy Ive
Vicar of Tudeley and Capel
with Five Oak Green, Kent, England

Joseph J. Boot
Founder and President
Ezra Institute
Tennessee, USA; Ontario, Canada; Hertfordshire, UK

Maarten J. Verkerk
Emeritus Professor
Maastricht University /
Technical University Eindhoven, The Netherlands

Martin A. Rice, Jr.
Associate Professor of Philosophy
Department of Philosophy/Division of Humanities
The University of Pittsburgh--Johnstown
Johnstown, Pennsylvania, USA

Dr Michael Goheen
Senior Professor of Missional Theology
 and Academic Director of Theological Education
Missional Training Center
Phoenix, AZ, USA

Dr Richard M. Gunton
Senior Lecturer
Faculty of Business and Digital Technologies

AFFILIATIONS

University of Winchester
United Kingdom

Romel Regalado Bagares
Professorial Lecturer I
Department of International Law
and Maritime Law
Philippine Judicial Academy

Roy Clouser, PhD
Prof Emeritus
Dept. of Philosophy & Religion
The College of New Jersey
Ewing, NJ 08628, USA

Willem J. Ouweneel, PhD
Professor of the Philosophy of the Natural Sciences,
Potchefstroom, South Africa
Retired Professor of Philosophy and Systematic Theology,
Evangelical Theology Faculty, Leuven, The Netherlands

www.ingramcontent.com/pod-product-compliance
Lightning Source LLC
Chambersburg PA
CBHW052306300426
44110CB00035B/1940